Human Milk in the Modern World

Psychosocial, Nutritional, and Economic Significance

DERRICK B. JELLIFFE

M.D., F.R.C.P., F.A.A.P.
*Professor of Public Health and of Pediatrics,
and Head, Division of Population, Family and
International Health,
University of California at Los Angeles*

*Formerly Director, Caribbean Food and
Nutrition Institute, Jamaica*

E. F. PATRICE JELLIFFE

M.P.H., F.R.S.H.
*Lecturer and Associate Researcher
Division of Population, Family and
International Health,
University of California at Los Angeles*

*Formerly Research Fellow/Nutritionist,
Caribbean Food and Nutrition Institute,
Jamaica*

OXFORD UNIVERSITY PRESS

OXFORD   NEW YORK   TORONTO

Oxford University Press, Walton Street, Oxford OX2 6DP

OXFORD LONDON GLASGOW NEW YORK
TORONTO MELBOURNE WELLINGTON CAPE TOWN
IBADAN NAIROBI DAR ES SALAAM LUSAKA
KUALA LUMPUR SINGAPORE JAKARTA HONG KONG TOKYO
DELHI BOMBAY CALCUTTA MADRAS KARACHI

CASEBOUND ISBN 0 19 264921 3
PAPERBACK ISBN 0 19 264919 1

First published 1978
Reprinted (with corrections) 1979

*Set, printed and bound in Great Britain
by Cox & Wyman Ltd, London, Fakenham and Reading*

Preface

How can cogent arguments be marshalled for balance, for cooperation, for that awareness of reality which all the great sages of mankind, without exception, have held to be the root of human wisdom and hence of human survival?

Barbara Ward and René Dubos (1972), *Only One Earth*

Ours is an age of a multitude of socially undirected technical advances, divorced from any other end than the advancement of science and techno-logy. We live, in fact, in an exploding universe of mechanical and electronic inventions, whose parts are moving at a rapid pace ever further and further away from their human centre, and from any rational, autonomous purpose. . . . There are two ways of development for human culture . . . in biological terms, the symbiotic and the predatory.

Lewis Mumford (1961), *The City in History*

Considerable information has existed for years concerning lactation in man and other mammals, but in the last decade there has been a very large outpouring of important newer research into the unique properties of human milk, and the psychophysiology and significance of breast-feeding. In the past three years or so, this stream of relevant publications has become a flood, as indicated by the large bibliography in the present volume.

This book is intended to draw this fresh data together analytically, not, it is hoped, with a narrow monovalent perspective, but rather with a wide-ranging view of human milk and breast-feeding considered as a low-cost, readily available 'biological system', operating dyadically between mother and baby and with a wide range of interacting metabolic, hormonal, and emotional factors related to precise species-specific nutrition, to natural chemoprophylaxis, to endocrinological spacing of offspring, and to assisting mother–infant emotional *rapport*.

Adaptation and interdependence: one world's dilemma

Recent years have dramatically highlighted the fact that ecological prob-lems, including health and nutrition, are interconnected on a global basis. This is plainly so with environmental pollution and with population pres-sure. Also, as the events to date in the 1970s emphasize, the use of limited food resources, the impact of competitive nationalistic trade patterns, and the shock-waves of oscillating economics affect all the world's inhabitants — from slum dwellers in tropical shanty towns to the affluent minority, mainly located in North America and Western Europe.

Likewise, problems of infant feeding and patterns of malnutrition in early childhood have much more in common throughout the world than is often appreciated. There are different proportions of young children with 'malnutrition-minus', such as protein–calorie malnutrition and iron-deficiency anaemia, and with 'malnutrition-plus', particularly infantile obesity and dental caries, in all countries. There appear to be more similarities than are frequently recognized in the ultimate causes of these apparently very different syndromes, especially changes in patterns of infant feeding.

For hundreds of millennia, human milk was the only food for the young baby. Plainly, without successful breast-feeding, the species could not have survived. By contrast, in the last few decades great changes have occurred in methods of infant feeding, especially from the universal use of human milk and breast-feeding to bottle-feeding with formulas based on cow's milk. This has become so prevalent that the majority of health professionals and nutritionists have been taught little about human milk and breast-feeding in their training.

Many recent changes and developments suggest that there is a need to reappraise the role of human milk and breast-feeding in both the developed and the developing countries of the world. Concerns with global food supplies, with the need for the regulation of child spacing, with the prevention of infectious diseases, with the economics of infant feeding, with newer knowledge of mother–neonate interaction, and with continually emerging information on the specific nutritional needs of young infants all overlap into the question of breast-feeding, as does recent awareness of the need to try to achieve a balance between technology, biology, and tradition.

In the past ten years, an abundance of new information has accumulated, based on modern scientific research into all aspects of the subject, including, for example, biochemistry, immunology, nutrition, endocrinology, and psychophysiology. Much comparative information has become available from all over the world, including a wealth of new knowledge concerning factors that make for failure or success in human lactation both in individuals and in communities.

Such recent work covers a wide range, but is usually presented in a monovalent fashion. For example, nutritional aspects are looked at without concern for immunological considerations, or for the effects on mother–baby interaction, and so on. Plainly, that is absurd. It is more logical to consider breast-feeding as a biological and ecological system, principally involving the mother–infant dyad, but also including the rest of the family and indeed the community.

The purpose of this book is to review and evaluate the modern scientific information concerning a wide range of different aspects of human milk and breast-feeding, which have not been brought together before. To accommodate brief mention of the most up-to-date references practicable, an addendum has been included just prior to publication (p. 389).

This book is written particularly for health professionals (including physicians, paediatricians, obstetricians, nurses, and midwives), for nutritionists, for community workers, and for national planners. It is hoped that it will also be useful for others concerned with trying to achieve optimal child nutrition, particularly mothers' groups.

The core of the book is concerned with the examination of several questions. Firstly, are there unique properties and functions of human milk and the process of breast-feeding? Secondly, is there evidence of a decline in lactation performance in the world as a whole, including the developing countries? Thirdly, if that is so, what are the reasons? Fourthly, what are the consequences? And, lastly, what steps, if any, is it necessary or feasible for the health worker, the nutritionist, and the development planner to take in different parts of the world?

DERRICK B. JELLIFFE
E. F. PATRICE JELLIFFE

Los Angeles 1977

Acknowledgements

The authors would like to thank the many colleagues for much constructive advice and assistance, especially the following:
Dr. J. Arena, Dr. Justin Call, Dr. L. Hambraeus, Dr. J. Glaser, Dr. J.W. Gerrard, Dr. A.S. Goldman, Mrs. D. Haire, Ms. Elisabet Helsing, Dr. R. Jackson, Dr. Marshal Klaus, Drs. Niles and Michael Newton, Dr. Franz Rosa, Mrs. Marian Tompson, Dr. Bo Vahlquist, Dr. Cicely Williams and Dr. Joe Wray.

Material in Chapter 4 is based on a paper published in the *American Journal of Clinical Nutrition*.

Contents

1 Mammalian antecedents and adaptive suckling

The essential characteristic of a mammal is not the capacity for gestation, but the further manifestation of maternal care, the possession of mammae to secrete milk for the young.
Alan Parkes (1966)

Out of the book of Nature's learned breast.
Du Bartas (1544–90)

Lactation in its simplest form is an extremely ancient physiological function, probably dating back some 200 million years, certainly antedating the evolution of placental gestation. The many thousands of species that have evolved over the centuries in the mammalian class, and the estimated 4237 existing mammals (Mepham 1976), indicate clearly the functional value and adaptability of lactation. Different stages in the evolution of lactation are mirrored in various living species, including the egg-laying monotremes, such as the duck-billed platypus, and marsupials, such as the kangaroo, whose simple placentas are of relatively limited effectiveness.

The class Mammalia comprises three subclasses: (1) Prototheria — a single order of egg-laying Monotremata; (2) Metatheria — a single order of pouched Marsupiala; and (3) Eutheria — 17 orders of placental mammals, making up 95 per cent of the class. All are characterized by the secretion of milk to nourish their young. Other features, such as viviparity and the presence of hair, are variable (Mepham 1976). The German word for mammal is very apt: *Säugetier* or 'sucking animal'.

The offspring of the most evolved of the class — placental mammals — are entirely dependent in early life on nourishment in the form of milk secreted by exocrine glands — the mammae. It has been suggested that primitive mammary glands may have developed originally from modified apocrine sweat glands in brooding sites in reptiles. Such highly developed mammals have certain universal characteristics. They are warm-blooded, and carry the early stages of their young *in utero* nourished by placental nutrient exchange. Their offspring are all immature in varying degrees, so that they are usually unable to search for food and all are in need of warmth, contact, and maternal protection. Lastly, and in contrast with all other classes, including birds, who also care for their post-embryonic young, the mammal mother is the sole supplier of food in the form of milk produced directly by her body. Infant survival depends on the mother's presence, her ability to secrete milk, and on the partly reflex, partly learnt interaction by the mother-neonate dyad that leads to the initiation and successful continuation of lactation.

Adaptive suckling

Over the millennia, 'adaptive suckling' has developed in mammals in which the process of nursing, the composition of the milk, and the 'lactatory apparatus' have all become modified to suit the needs, circumstances, and way of life of the particular species.

Suckling is a dyadic process — that is, a two-way interaction between mother and offspring with effects on both. In most mammals, it is largely the result of instinct and reflexes. In higher mammals, notably primates and man, the process is not entirely instinctive, but is partly based on learned behaviour, on information obtained from experienced females, mainly by observation and example (p. 175). The first two chimpanzees born in a zoo to a non-wild mother were reported in 1920 to have died of starvation from failure of nursing (Gunther 1955). In 1974 a non-wild female gorilla in a California game park was successfully assisted to nurse by the use of films of lactating gorillas shown to her during her pregnancy.

Also, as Raphael (1966, 1973 *a*) has noted, higher social mammals, including such differing species as the elephant, the dolphin, and the baboon, have developed group behaviour patterns to protect the female and conceptus during late pregnancy, labour, and the subsequent post-delivery period, when mother and newborn are weak and vulnerable to predators, and when lactation is becoming established. This need for supportive help seems to be universal in social mammals, and female assistants — termed *doulas* by Raphael — assist during the birth process and the newborn period. In most such species, this aid is physical and protective. In the human, *doulas* also supply information and emotional support (p. 175).

In other words, in primates, including chimpanzees, gorillas, and man, successful lactation is a practical art and depends on instinctive reflex behaviour on the part of the young, combined with maternal behaviour initiated by instinct, encouraged by social support, and guided by knowledge and information.

Suckling is most obviously concerned with nourishing the young and with supplying warmth, stimulation, and protection. It is also a major mechanism in the psychological process of emotional 'bonding' between mother and newborn (p. 142). It is less appreciated that suckling also produces endocrinological effects mediated largely by pituitary secretions on the mother's uterus (p. 114) and, in the human and some other species, on ovulation (p. 118) and on the conservation of water (p. 19).

Suckling has become adapted to the needs and way of life of different mammalian species, particularly to the maturity of the newborn, their special nutritional requirements (including the age at which other foods are

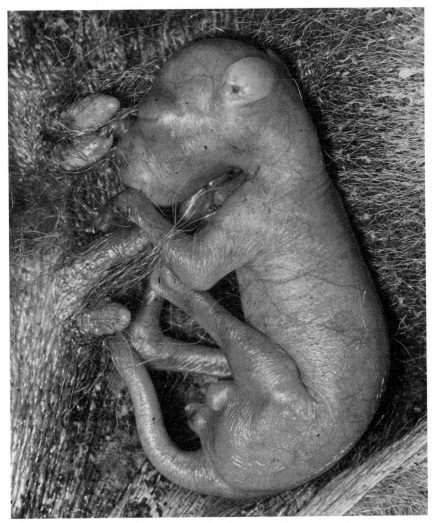

Fig. 1.1. Fifty-day-old red kangaroo ('pouch foetus') photographed in mother's pouch (courtesy of Dr. E. Slater, Division of Wildlife Research, C.S.I.R.O., Canberra, Australia)

taken), the usual number of offspring, the need for sensory stimulation, and various other biological considerations.

Maturity of newborn

Mammals vary greatly in their maturity at birth, from the eggs of the spiny ant-eater, to the pouch embryos of marsupials, to the more mature neonates of most species.

Among placental mammals, those who have to be able to run almost immediately after birth, such as grazing animals, have a relatively long gestation period and are born mature, as are those who have to swim at once, such as dolphins and whales, or very soon, such as seals.

Predators have shorter gestation periods and are relatively immature at birth, as are the newborn of species with well-hidden burrows or nests, such as the rabbit and mouse.

Man is unique in this respect, as there is both a long gestation period and an immature newborn, incapable of unaided locomotion and completely dependent on the mother. The newborn is unable even to reach the breast unaided. This contrasts with other mammals, as emphasized by Gunther (1955):

> In the animal kingdom the initiative is often taken by the neonate, who may have the mobility and the instinctive compulsion which enable it to find the nipple, and the mother's part is to be completely inert. For instance, the piglet at birth is compelled, presumably by smell, to scramble round, or over, its mother's hind legs until it reaches an unseen nipple, while the mother lies still. The human mother must take the active part which brings the two together.

Immaturity can be best understood by the hypothesis of Bostock (1962), which suggests that the human foetal period should be considered as of 18 months duration. Labour occurs after only about 9 months to permit the large head to pass through the relatively narrow birth-canal. In other words, the termination of uterine gestation takes place when the limit of brain (and head) size has been reached, compatible with birth, and long before the offspring is mature.

The human newborn can be considered to be an 'extero-gestate' or external foetus for about the first 9 months after birth. During this time, he is completely dependent on the mother for protection and warmth, and her breasts function nutritionally as an external placenta. Following this, in traditional circumstances, the baby passes slowly through the 'weaning period',* when he is gradually accustomed to new foods and moves from breast milk to the full adult diet. During this phase, the human infant has been termed a 'transitional'.

Nutritional requirements

The composition of the milk and the length of lactation of different species appear to have been modified and adapted to the needs of the particular creature.

---

* The word 'weaning' is derived from Anglo-Saxon *wenian*, 'to accustom'. However, in modern English (and in other Germanic languages, such as Dutch) the word is used ambiguously, both to cover the process of adjusting to a mixed diet and for total cessation of breast-feeding — that is the separation from the breast (or even sometimes from the bottle). By contrast, Romance languages are more specific: the French *sevrage* and the Spanish *destetar* clearly refer to the separation from the breast.

In general terms, the protein content of milk varies with the rate of growth of the offspring. This approximate relationship was first recorded in Bunge's Rule in 1898, when the protein content of different mammalian milks was correlated with growth rate, as indicated by the time taken to double the birth-weight. For example, the horse with 2 per cent protein in the milk takes 60 days, whereas the rabbit (10–13 per cent protein) doubles the birth-weight in only six days. Interestingly, inverse associations can also be seen between the protein content of many mammalian milks and both length of gestation and longevity. For example, human milk has protein content of 1·2 per cent; and he has a gestation period of 280 days and a life span of about 70 years; while the rabbit (10–13 per cent protein) has a gestation of only 28 days and lives about 5–7 years (Cowie and Tindal 1971, Jenness 1974, Blaxter 1961).

In some species, low-solute milk, particularly with lower concentrations of protein, is related to a pattern of frequent feedings — these are the so-called 'continuous-contact species'. This may be exemplified by the human species, whose milk has one of the lowest solute and protein concentrations of all mammals. By contrast, high-solute, high-protein milks are found in mammals giving large infrequent feeds to their young. For example, the rabbit, whose milk contains over 10 per cent protein, usually feeds her offspring once daily; while the mouse, with relatively low-solute milk, spends some 80 per cent of the time suckling.

High calorific density, principally due to the fat concentration of the milk, is usually related both to animal size and to low environmental temperatures, when the young have to develop and maintain a thick layer of insulating subcutaneous fat. For example, elephant milk contains only about 20 per cent fat (McCullagh and Widdowson 1970), while seal milk has 43 per cent. The most 'calorie-dense' milk is that of the blue whale (50 per cent fat), whose huge newborn (7 m in length) lives in the cold waters of the arctic seas (Slijper 1962). The resulting rate of growth in the young of marine mammals is prodigious. For example, a sea-elephant pup in California recently showed a weight increase from 40 to 400 lb in the first month of life.

In addition, and on a much more subtle level, scientific investigation increasingly demonstrates that the milk of each species is a uniquely complex secretion with very large numbers of different ingredients with almost certainly interrelated special metabolic and nutritional functions.

Conversely, metabolic difficulties in hand-rearing some baby mammals on milk of another species are well-known at zoos and aquaria. For example, walrus milk contains very little lactose, so that cow's milk (4 per cent lactose) causes severe diarrhoea in a newborn walrus, who is therefore often reared on a formula of blended raw fish and whipping cream.

Young pet kangaroos brought up on cow's milk develop cataracts of the lenses of both eyes, as they lack the enzymes to metabolize galactose, derived from milk sugar, lactose (Stephens *et al*. 1974*a*,*b*). Their condition parallels the human genetic disorder galactosaemia.

Number of offspring

The lactatory apparatus of mammals has also become adapted to the needs of the species. The mammae of the Pinnipedia (seals, walruses) are flattened beneath the animal's blubber, so that the efficient streamlining is not affected. The teats in the whale are recessed with overlying sphincter-like skin folds (mammary slit).

Of more general application, the number and siting of the usually paired breasts and nipples are related to the average numbers of the litter, to the relative anatomy and sizes of mother and offspring, and the mode of life of the species, especially its need for rapid post-partum mobility. In the human, singletons or twins comprise almost all births, which can in most cases be catered for nutritionally by the mother's two breasts (p. 64).

Sensory stimulation

The intimate contact of suckling and the many sensory stimuli involved (touch, smell, sound) play major roles in mother–neonate interaction in mammals, which can also include grooming, licking, and touching. Such patterns of behaviour are species-specific and with much consequence as regards 'bonding' and subsequent mother–infant relationships. Current views on mother–infant interaction in the human are given later (p. 142).

Other biological considerations

A variety of endocrinological consequences of biological importance occur in the mother as a result of suckling. Apart from being an imperative stimulus to milk secretion (p. 17), suckling also leads in different species to hormonally-induced conservation of body water (p. 19), uterine contraction (p. 114), alteration of maternal temperament (p. 19) and, in man and some marsupials, spacing of pregnancies (p. 118).

Examples
To illustrate the variety of protective mechanisms involved, some aspects of adaptive suckling will be summarized for certain contrasting species.

Echidna (Spiny ant-eater). This ancient mammal species lays a single egg, which is then lodged in a deep depression in the mother's abdominal wall over which the loose skin can close (*incubatorium*) (Griffiths 1965). The young (1·3 cm long) hatches from the egg and remains in the primitive pouch, in which there are teats from two mammary glands. Contrary to previous views, the female has a 'let-down reflex' (p. 19). This is perhaps particularly needed as the milk is thick (14–20 per cent fat, 12 per cent protein) and probably difficult for the small, immature offspring to express.

Kangaroo. The bean-sized (50 mg), blind neonate ('joey') is born at an early foetal stage, after only 3–4 weeks gestation, and migrates up the mother's abdominal wall to her pouch, where it becomes permanently firmly attached to a nipple (at this stage it is termed a 'mammary foetus') until mature.

The uneven maturity of the kangaroo newborn has been emphasized: 'The marsupial at birth is a marvellous composite of embryonic structures and precociously developed functional organs, which enable it to reach the pouch, respire and gain nourishment from the mammary gland.'

The milk is pink in colour, from a reddish pigment of unknown function produced in the pouch. It is very concentrated, with 8 per cent protein. There is no lactose and one-fifth of the total solids present are of undetermined origin. Growth is very rapid; the weight increases from 50 mg to 50 g in 50 days. The milk changes as the embryo grows, becoming less concentrated (Bollinger and Gross 1960, Bollinger and Pascoe 1953).

The pouch joey is securely fixed to the teat, which runs through the mouth in a ridge on the hard palate and an indentation on the tongue. The joey's lips are fused and the swollen tip of the teat is in the embryo's pharynx, thus ensuring an oral umbilical cord-like continuity of feeding, and physical attachment during the mother's hopping locomotion. The concentrated milk is squeezed into the very small joey by a particularly powerful let-down reflex (p. 19), probably assisted by a special maternal muscle (*compressor mammae*).

The adaptation of suckling in the kangaroo and some similar marsupials is remarkable. In addition to the neonatal joey at one nipple, the preceding offspring — now known as a 'young-at-foot' — spends most of the time out of the mother's pouch. However, if alarmed, it can return temporarily, and can suckle occasionally from a different nipple from the joey, obtaining milk of lesser concentration appropriate for its maturity. Samples from the two teats show milks of quite different compositions.

Finally, oestrus occurs shortly after the joey becomes fastened to the teat in the pouch (Menhaut and Sharman 1966). However, the female kangaroo's fertilized ovum remains dormant until the joey ceases to be permanently attached, that is at about 4 months. In other words, the intense stimulus of continuous lactation delays implantation of the fertilized ovum (Marshall 1967).

Blue whale. Suckling in the huge blue whale has to be adapted to the high calorie needs of the large newborn and to the cold environment (Slijper 1962). In addition, the mother needs to conserve water, and the calf can only nurse relatively briefly, as it can remain underwater for a much shorter period than the mother, who can 'sound' for up to 30 minutes. All these circumstances are dealt with by the very concentrated milk (50 per cent fat) and by the powerful let-down reflex (p. 19). In other words, the whale calf has cream pumped into it rapidly, while the mother loses little water.

Seals. In general, seals have a very short period of lactation, lasting only a few weeks, and the young can eat fish early on. They are born very mature, as judged by their early ability to swim with extreme agility. Their milk is very low in lactose and the California sea-lion's milk contains none (Pilson and Kelly 1962). In view of the role that lactose may play in the biochemical development of the brain (p. 40), it may be that the 'transitional' newborn seal needs little lactose as the brain has already undergone most of its development prior to birth. As with all marine mammals, they have very considerable calorific needs, catered for by milk with high fat (45 per cent) and protein (10 per cent) contents. The pregnant female becomes extremely obese and the newborn then receives an 'oral fat transfusion'.

Hokkaido or Japanese monkey. As noted by Helsing (1976): 'This mammal has a breast-feeding pattern of great interest in this connection: the infant monkeys are born in the spring-time, and they are suckled at the breast until autumn approaches. At that time the mother leaves the young infant to nourish itself, with roots, wild berries, and nuts, while she herself eagerly eats in order to fill up her physiological winter stores. When some months later heavy snow covers most edible items, and only hard sprouts and bark requiring strong teeth and jaws are available, the infant again seeks the mother's breasts. At that time, the mother has not been lactating at all for some months. The infant monkey is then fed at the breast throughout the winter-time'.

This adaptation to seasonal food shortage in this cold northern island is a 'double-cycle' lactation.

Relevance to man. Since the emergence of true man about 1–2 million years ago, his young offspring has been reared almost exclusively on human milk in the early months of life during the exterogestate foetal period (p. 4), until the past two generations. During this vast period of time, it seems reasonable to assume that selection and modification occurred to ensure that adaptive suckling developed to suit the needs of the human infant and to promote the survival of the species. That this is so can be easily observed in more traditional communities of mankind (p. 179), not only in relation to the composition of breast milk, but also in the psychological and endocrinological interchanges between mother and baby, and in relation to child spacing (p. 117) and the prevention of infections (p. 84). More difficult to appreciate is the fact that the process of adaptive suckling developed in the course of earlier millennia of human evolution has significance and importance for modern urbanized technological man. Recent evidence suggests increasingly that this is the case and this will be discussed later (p. 179).

2 Psychophysiology of lactation

The secretion of milk proceeds best in a tranquil state of mind and with a cheerful temper; then the milk is regularly abundant and agrees well with the child. On the contrary, a fretful temper lessens the quantity of milk.

Ashley Cooper (1840)

Cushy cow, bonny, let down thy milk,
And I will give thee a gown of silk,
A gown of silk and a silver tee,
If thou will let down thy milk for me.

Eighteenth-century charm used by milk maids in England to assist the milk-ejection reflex.

Successful lactation in higher mammals is the end-result of numerous interacting factors, including the vigour, maturity, and intact oro-facial anatomy of the newborn, and the health, nutrition, and nipple structure of the mother. Physiologically, lactation is under the control of numerous endocrine glands, particularly the pituitary hormones, prolactin and oxytocin, influenced by the sucking process and by maternal emotions. (For detailed information see Wolstenholme and Knight 1972, Reynolds and Folley 1969, Sulman 1970, Falconer 1971, Cowie and Tindal 1971, Josimovitch *et al*. 1974, Larson and Smith 1974, Vorherr 1975, and Findlay 1974*a*.)

That emotional responses play a key role in the failure or success of lactation, both in dairy animals and in nursing mothers, has been recognized in practice for centuries. For example, the traditional peasant farmer of India and elsewhere recognizes the decreased yield if the cow or buffalo is upset or apprehensive, as when milked by a stranger, and sometimes tries to induce a tranquil state in the animal and a good 'draught reflex' or let-down reflex (p. 19) by showing her a model calf made of a stuffed skin. Likewise, the fact that the milk could rapidly dry up in women following the shock of unpleasant news has long been recognized in world-wide folk experience.

Considerable work has recently been undertaken on the psychophysiology of lactation, principally, as one might expect, by the modern scientific dairy farmer who values his product since it is sold. Also, in the last few decades the physiology of milk secretion has been studied practically in man, particularly the mechanism of milk ejection through the let-down reflex (p. 19). Only in very recent years has human lactation been investigated in modern endocrinological laboratories, using newly developed techniques for measuring circulating hormones.

Stages of breast development

The human breast is technically a large exocrine gland (Salazar and Tobon 1974), which, uniquely, is largely quiescent, and in childless women may never become active.* It is composed of about 18 segments (lobules or lactiferous duct systems) embedded in fat and connective tissue and lavishly supplied with blood vessels, lymphatics, and nerves. Each segment is made up of thousands of sac-like milk-secreting alveoli, surrounded by myoepithelial cells, draining into ductules, ducts, lactiferous sinuses, and a single ampulla (nipple pore) opening into the nipple, at the centre of the areola (Fig. 2.1). In contrast with milch animals such as cows and goats, women have no cisterns (or dilated containers) in the terminal ducts. Only a small volume of milk can be found in the lactiferous sinuses, so that an adequate let-down reflex (p. 19) is needed if the baby is to obtain a sufficient

---

* Recent investigation by Petrakis and associates (Petrakis *et al*. 1975) has shown that small quantities of breast-fluid secretion occur in non-lactating women, and can be obtained by aspiration suction.

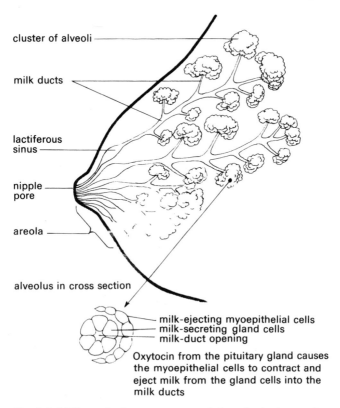

cluster of alveoli

milk ducts

lactiferous sinus

nipple pore

areola

alveolus in cross section

milk-ejecting myoepithelial cells
milk-secreting gland cells
milk-duct opening

Oxytocin from the pituitary gland causes the myoepithelial cells to contract and eject milk from the gland cells into the milk ducts

Fig. 2.1. Milk-producing structures and ducts in the human breast (simplified cross section) (courtesy of Mrs. Jimmie Avery)

quantity for its needs.

The areola contain numbers of modified apocrine sweat glands (Montgomery's tubercles or glands). Their physiological function is uncertain, but their secretion may act as a skin protection and lubricant during breast-feeding. An anti-bacterial effect has also been suggested; while analogy with the sexual attractant function of the secretion of other apocrine glands suggests that Montgomery's tubercles may function as a scent organ to guide the nursing baby's 'rooting reflex' (p. 13).

The size of the breast is largely related to the amount of fat present and gives no indication of functional capacity. Interestingly, the aboriginal Juangs of India consider small flat breasts ('tiger breasts') to be the most effective lactators (Elwin 1948). The size and pendulousness of the breasts also vary with age (pre-puberty; fertile adult; post menopause), with the pregnancy-lactation history, and with the support given to the breast (brassière, etc.). Morphological variations (and possibly ability as lactators) have been suggested between different ethnic groups, but no such investigations seem to have been undertaken. They would be important research studies, although difficult to undertake for practical reasons (p. 60).

Newborn. Hypertrophy of the primary ducts and secretion of colostrum-like 'witch's milk' can be caused in the newborn by the maternal hormones of pregnancy. The phenomenon is self-limiting, lasting for a few days.

Puberty. Hormonal changes just prior to and during puberty markedly increase breast and nipple size. The main changes are in the development of stroma, made up of fat and connective tissues, with some development of alveoli and branching of ducts to form lobules.

Pregnancy. The principal feature of mammary growth in pregnancy is a great increase in ducts and alveoli, under the influence of many hormones, including oestrogens, progesterone, corticosteroids, and hypophyseal and placental lactogens. Nipple length and proctractility also increase.

Late in pregnancy, there is a maximal development of the lobulo-alveolar system and presumably a sensitization of glandular tissue for action by prolactin. Colostrum (p. 30) is secreted in small amounts during the last 3 months of pregnancy.

Puerperium. Following the delivery of the placenta, oestrogen levels drop precipitously. Prolactin levels rise and are further increased by the prolactin reflex (p. 14), resulting from the infant taking the breast. For about 10 days after birth, the breast secretes colostrum, and in societies where birth takes place in hospital and breast-feeding is subjected to 'feeding schedules', a short period of transitional milk is succeeded by the 'coming-in' of the mature milk at about 10 days. In other cultures, when the neonate is put to the breast immediately after birth, this whole process is shorter (D.B. Jelliffe 1956).

In addition to breast changes in pregnancy and lactation, numerous other physiological adjustments are occurring, geared to the nutrition of mother and offspring. Maternal iron absorption is increased in pregnancy, and calcium excretion is decreased in lactation (Hytten and Leitch 1971). In societies where food is abundant, the pregnant woman gains 10–12 kg (20–25 lb) in body weight in pregnancy. About $4 \cdot 5$ kg (9 lb) of this is subcutaneous fat, designed as a store of calories and fat for subsequent lactation (Hytten and Leitch 1971, Naismith 1971, Naismith and Ritchie 1975). Conversely, breast-feeding can be considered as a part of maternal weight homoeostasis — in Western cultural body imagery, it has a 'slimming' function.

Stages of lactation

Lactation — or more properly the process of breast-feeding — results from the interplay of the hormones and of instinctive, reflex, and learned behaviour by mother and newborn (Kon 1972, Larson and Smith 1974, World Health Organization 1975). Four overlapping stages may be recognized:

(i) *Milk initiation (lactogenesis)*. This process commences during the latter part of pregnancy when colostrum (pp. 30 and 90) secretion occurs as a result of stimulation of the breast alveolar cells by placental lactogen, a prolactin-like substance, and is continued after birth as an automatic process in all women.

Full lactogenesis — the initiation of a copious flow — consists of the synthesis of milk by the alveolar cells (as evidenced by changes in intracellular enzyme content and the appearance of milk constituents), secretion into the alveolar lumen, and alteration in the composition of milk while stored in the alveoli and lacteal ducts, as a result of osmotic transfers between milk and blood (Findlay 1974a,b). This process is under the control of complex interacting hormones, but is closely related to rising levels of the anterior pituitary hormone prolactin, which has been shown to enhance specific enzymes concerned with the synthesis of milk protein and lactose. This hormone is stimulated by the post-delivery rapid fall in inhibitory ovarian and placental steroids, especially progesterone, which follows expulsion of the placenta, and by the sucking of the newborn (p. 13).

(ii) *Milk secretion (galactopoiesis or maintenance of established lactation)*. Although also under complex hormonal control, for practical purposes the continuing secretion of milk is mainly related to sufficient production of the anterior pituitary hormone prolactin* — and to maternal nutrition (p. 59).

___

* Large numbers of recent publications have appeared recently on human prolactin (Bowers *et al*. 1971, Davies and Hartree 1973, Dixon and Li 1964, Forsyth 1969, Forsyth 1973, Forsyth and Edwards 1972, Grosvenor *et al*. 1967, Jacobs and Daughaday 1974, L'Hermite *et al*. 1973, McNeilly 1973, Pasteels *et al*. 1973, Redman *et al*. 1975, and Turkington 1974).

The major role of the pituitary in the initiation and continuing secretion of breast milk is emphasized clinically by the absence of milk production in Sheehan's syndrome, an uncommon, severe disease in which the pituitary is markedly damaged at or just before delivery (Sheehan and Davis 1968).

The mechanisms of secretion of milk are highly complex and under intense investigation, especially by the dairy farmer. Details of both physiology and ultrastructure may be found in several recent scientific publications (Mepham 1976). Findlay (1974*a,b*) has summarized the situation by noting that the secretory cells of the alveoli display marked features of nutrient synthesis, including free ribosomes, rough endoplasmic reticulum, mitochondria, obvious Golgi apparatus, fat globules, and protein granules. Milk secretion occurs by a process of extrusion from the cells by: '(a) an *epocrine-like* process involving the pinching-off of fat globules, sometimes with cell organelles, leaving the apical cell membrane intact; (b) an *eccrine* process involving no loss of protoplasm' (Findlay 1974*a*). The glandular cells in the alveoli vary in size, therefore, from cylindrical or conical to flat, depending upon the state of milk extrusion.

(iii) *Milk ejection*. In man, as in other higher mammals, movements of milk from the alveoli, where it is secreted, to the mouth of the infant is an active process within the breast, brought about by the let-down or milk-ejection reflex (draught reflex) (p. 19).

(iv) *Milk ingestion*. The last stage of human lactation is the ingestion of breast-milk by the sucking baby. This is dependent on interaction between mother and newborn, and especially on the functioning of the let-down reflex on the maternal side, and on the existence of the neonatal feeding reflexes.

Breast-feeding reflexes

Successful breast-feeding depends in large measure on the meshing and mutual reinforcement of interacting neonatal and maternal reflexes.

1. *Neonatal reflexes*

The full-term healthy newborn baby possesses three instinctive reflexes needed for successful breast-feeding: (i) *the rooting reflex*, in which tactile pressure on the cheek or circumoral area (and possibly the smell of the mother's breast) leads to turning of the head and opening and closing the mouth as the baby seeks for the nipple; (ii) *the sucking (or suckling)* reflex*,

---

* The verb 'to suck' is not really correct as it refers to the effect of negative intra-buccal pressure, and not to the milking process produced by squeezing of the terminal lacteals by the tongue against the hard palate. 'To suckle' refers to the mother's action to the baby — 'to give suck'. In Latin, the verb *emulgere* was used exclusively for milking by young mammals or milkmen. Pirie (1976) has suggested a similar word in English, 'to mulge'. However, for the time being, 'to suck' remains the process by which the baby gets milk from the breast. This was the original meaning, 'various analogical, engineering, and metaphysical meanings are later accretions'.

in which the tactile 'sign stimulus' of the nipple and areolar area of the breast filling the mouth sufficiently and adequately leads to a milking action by the tongue against the hard palate, and (iii) *the swallowing reflex*.

The suckling reflex begins to develop by the seventeenth week of foetal life and matures by the thirty-second to thirty-sixth week of pregnancy. In healthy full-term babies, the rooting and sucking reflexes are strongest shortly (20–30 minutes) after birth, so that the vigorous nipple stimulation at that time can assist in initiating a let-down reflex (p. 19). Also, early nursing after birth avoids mammary congestion which can interfere with breast-feeding mechanically, as the swollen oedematous breast may make it difficult for the baby to grasp the nipple.

These neonatal feeding reflexes are feeble or absent in smaller premature or low-birth-weight babies, or in a variety of general illnesses of the new-born, including generalized infection (septicaemia), severe jaundice, or cerebral birth damage. The sucking reflex may be impaired by various congenital anatomical abnormalities in the newborn, in particular severe cleft palate. The sucking reflex response to the breast can be interfered with and superseded by the 'super-sign stimulus' of the larger, more easily flowing teat of the feeding bottle (Gunther 1955). The detailed oro-dynamics are quite different in bottle-feeding and breast-feeding, as will be discussed later (p. 109).

2. *Maternal reflexes*

There are three main maternal reflexes involved in breast-feeding:

(i) *Prolactin reflex (milk-secretion reflex)*. A prolactin hormone occurs in almost all vertebrates. In man, until very recently, there was uncertainty as to whether human prolactin was the same as human growth hormone or not. In 1971, Hwang and colleagues (Hwang, Guyda, and Friesen 1971) demonstrated with new immunological methods that human prolactin was a separate hormone. They also developed a more rapid and sensitive bio-immunoassay procedure for estimation of prolactin levels in the human, which has led to an increasing output of research in this field of great practical significance (Hwang, Hardy, Friesen, and Wilansky 1971).

Recent work has shown that prolactin secretion shows regular daily changes (circadian rhythm) with high levels found between 1 and 5 a.m., which may be of significance in relation to nocturnal feeds (p. 17). Its secretion from the anterior pituitary is under the control of the hypothalamus where two 'balancing' centres are found, one producing prolactin-inhibiting factor and the other prolactin-release factor. The pharmacological effects of ergot and 'l-dopa' in inhibiting lactation, and of the 'hypothalamic tranquillizers' such as reserpine, chlorpromazine, and various phenothiazine compounds, in inducing lactation are currently believed to be through action on these control centres (Sulman 1970).

The endocrine control of lactation is a complex matter (Bryant and

Greenwood 1972, Cobo 1974, Count 1967, Cowie 1973, Cowie and Tindal 1971, Cross 1955, Cross and Findlay 1969, Cross and Silver 1956, Meites 1966, Riddle *et al.* 1932). However, for practical purposes, prolactin can be considered the key lactogenic hormone in initiating and maintaining milk secretion. Its production by the anterior pituitary is mainly the result of the prolactin reflex, resulting from the infant sucking the breast (Fig. 2.2), although it may be diminished by severe maternal malnutrition or by the hormonal responses to environmental psychosocial stress (Geissler *et al.* 1975). It is a quantitative phenomenon in that the prolactin secreted, and hence the milk produced, is related to the amount of sucking stimulus (Egli and Newton 1961), that is the frequency, intensity, and duration with which the baby nurses. This has been demonstrated by clear responses in experimental animals and in lactating women using hormone assay. For example, the earlier and more frequently the newborn is allowed to suck the breast, the more rapid is the return to birth-weight, partly because of speedier milk production (Archavsky 1952, D.B. Jelliffe 1956) (Fig. 2.3). General obstetrical sedation diminishes neonatal sucking and hence milk intake (Kronn *et al.* 1966) (Fig. 2.4); regional anaesthesia causes little interference (Tronick *et al.* 1976).

Investigation of the role of human prolactin has been assisted by research into the following different forms of abnormal non-puerperal lactation and galactorrhoea (Besser and Edwards 1972, Thorner *et al.* 1974):

(1) *Endocrinological disease* pituitary-hypothalamic pathology; milk secretion in the newborn of either sex ('witch's milk').

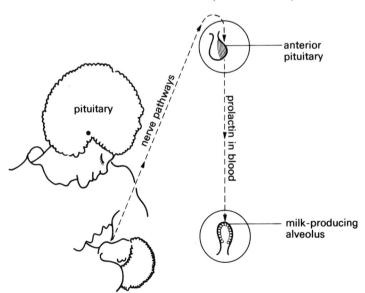

Fig. 2.2. The prolactin reflex (simplified)

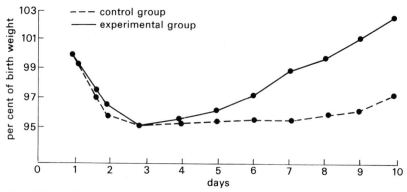

Fig. 2.3. Weight gain in per cent of birth weight in experimental (early breast-feeding) and control group (routine hospital regimen) (from Chao, Y. M. (1971). *Int. Nurs. Rev.* **18**, 15)

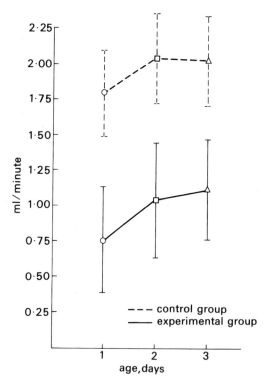

Fig. 2.4. Effect of obstetric sedation (sodium secobarbitone administered by slow intravenous drip) on neonatal sucking and milk intake (Kron, R. E., Stein, M., and Goddard, K. E. (1966). *Pediatrics* **37**, 1012)

(2) *Anatomical* (involvement of sensory nerve supply of chest): thoracic *Herpes zoster*, chest operations, benign cystic fibrosis.

(3) *Pharmacological* ('hypothalamic tranquillizers'): Reserpine, chlorpromazine, various phenothiazines; cessation of the use of oral contraceptives.

(4) *Induced* (stimulation of prolactin reflex by repeated prolonged sucking): 'survival lactation' (p. 163), 'adoptive lactation', and 'relactation', after initial cessation of breast-feeding (p. 368).

The practical effectiveness of the sucking stimulus in initiating prolactin production is recognized in domestic animals and is indicated by the practice of induced lactation as a 'survival technique' in some traditional cultures (p. 163). The recent practice of 'adoptive lactation' or 'relactation' (p. 368) by some women in the Western world who wish to breast-feed their adopted babies has the same physiology (Waletzky 1976). Likewise, there are occasional recorded instances of babies being breast-fed by mothers who are chronically comatose following severe head injury, in whom continuing sucking stimulus by the infant lead to the necessary prolactin secretion.

The significance of the additional sucking stimulus of night feedings can be seen in the studies of Omolulu in traditional families in West Nigeria, when about one-third of total feedings were given in the night, locally defined as from 8 p.m. to 6 a.m. (Table 2.1).

TABLE 2.1 *Night feeds: analysis of percentage of total feeds and total volume of breast-milk in mothers in traditional families in West Nigeria* (from Omolulu 1975)

Age	Percentage of feeds taken at night	Percentage of breast-milk obtained at night feeds	Range of percentage of breast-milk obtained at night
1 month	37	37	0–70
4 months	37	35	0–75
7 months	31	31	0–53
10 months	38	36	25–52

TABLE 2.2 *Serum prolactin levels in non-lactating women before and after manual mammary stimulation* (from Kolodny *et al.* 1972)

Stimulus site		Baseline	Immediately after stimulation	15 minutes after stimulation
Breast + nipple	($n = 8$)	$5 \cdot 1 \pm 2 \cdot 0$*	$108 \cdot 1 \pm 14 \cdot 3$	$37 \cdot 4 \pm 3 \cdot 9$
Breast alone	($n = 8$)	$5 \cdot 8 \pm 0 \cdot 8$	$60 \cdot 8 \pm 4 \cdot 3$	$22 \cdot 6 \pm 2 \cdot 7$
Sternum	($n = 4$)	$7 \cdot 9 \pm 1 \cdot 8$	$7 \cdot 1 \pm 2 \cdot 3$	$9 \cdot 3 \pm 1 \cdot 4$
Forearm	($n = 4$)	$9 \cdot 5 \pm 2 \cdot 0$	$5 \cdot 5 \pm 0 \cdot 3$	$5 \cdot 8 \pm 1 \cdot 5$

* Mean ± S.E., expressed as mg/ml of serum.

Experimentally, radio-immunoassay studies show that manual mammary stimulation even in non-lactating women leads to raised serum prolactin levels (Table 2.2). The mechanism of the prolactin reflex also explains both the 'prolonged' lactation in cultures where breast stimulation is continued both night and day for several years by a sucking child, and the decline in milk secretion if bottle-feedings are introduced (or a 'pacifier' is used) which diminish the sucking vigour of the baby, and when non-milk foods are given early on to breast-feeding babies, as these obviously diminish the infant's appetite.

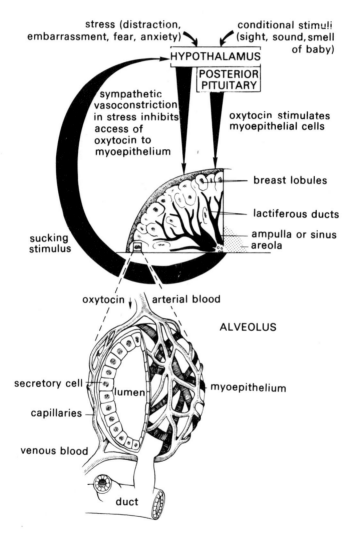

Fig. 2.5. 'Let-down reflex' — detailed diagrammatic representation of afferent and efferent areas, and of alveolus structure with special reference to myoepithelium (courtesy of Dr. A. L. R. Findlay, International Planned Parenthood Federation, London)

The prolactin reflex enables the human breast to become refilled after about 2–3 hours and to operate on an approximate supply-and-demand basis, with output adjusted automatically as regards the infant's needs of both food and water. In catering terms, it is a 'self-service' system. Provided it is sufficiently vigorous, the sucking response of twins leads to adequate additional production of milk sufficient for their needs in the early months of life (p. 64). Likewise, in most warmer climates, the baby's additional fluid needs are also taken care of by the increased secretion of low-solute human milk as a result of extra sucking at the breast as a response to thirst.

Recent work has also shown that prolactin is a 'broad-spectrum' hormone, with other functions of great importance including child spacing (p. 118), water conservation (Horrobin *et al.* 1971) and alteration of maternal behaviour through its actions on other target organs, including the ovaries (Friesen 1976), the kidneys, and possibly the brain.

(ii) *Nipple-erection reflex.* Stimulation of the mother's nipple by the baby's mouth leads to nipple erection — which is pleasurable for the mother and also makes the nipple more protractile (Gunther 1955), thereby assisting in the milking of the breast by the sucking reflex.

(iii) *Let-down reflex. (draught or milk-ejection reflex)* (Figs. 2.5 and 6).

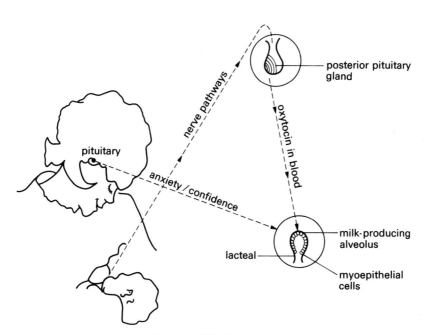

Fig. 2.6. The 'let-down' reflex, simplified

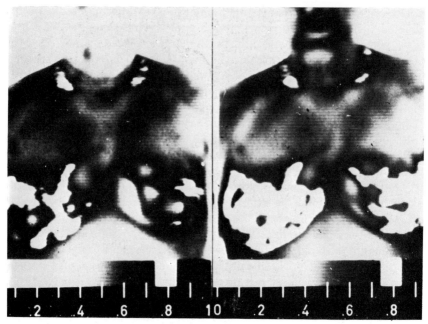

Fig. 2.7. Thermogram of anterior chest wall of primiparous woman before (left) and after (right) hearing her baby cry, showing raised temperature due to increased blood flow (from Lind, J., Vuorenkoski, V., and Wasz-Hockert, O. (1971). In *Psychosomatic medicine in obstetrics and gynaecology. Third International Congress,* London, p.293. S. Karger A. G., Basel.

This key neuroendocrine reflex differs from other breast-feeding reflexes in that it is psychosomatic (Bisset 1968, Caldeyro-Barcia 1969, Ely and Peterson 1941, Grosvenor and Mena 1974, M. Newton and N. Newton 1968, N. Newton and M. Newton 1967). It makes the difference between milk production in the alveoli and milk availability in the terminal lacteals — between making milk and giving milk.

The somatic component of the reflex consists of stimulation of mechanoreceptors in the nipple and areolar area by the sucking infant, leading to the passage of nerve impulses to the hypothalamus (especially the paraventricular nucleus) and thence to the posterior pituitary, which secretes oxytocin. This hormone is carried in the bloodstream both to the uterus causing contractions and promoting involution and back to the breast, where it is associated with increased blood flow and raised skin temperature (Fig. 2.7). Its most important effect, however, is on the myoepithelial 'basket' cells surrounding the alveoli (Fig. 2.8). The contraction of these cells squeezes the milk out of the alveoli and 'lets it down', or ejects it, into the terminal lacteals (Cowie and Tindal 1971, Findlay 1971). With a successful let-down reflex, 90 per cent of the available milk can be obtained by the baby in seven minutes or less (Boette 1974).

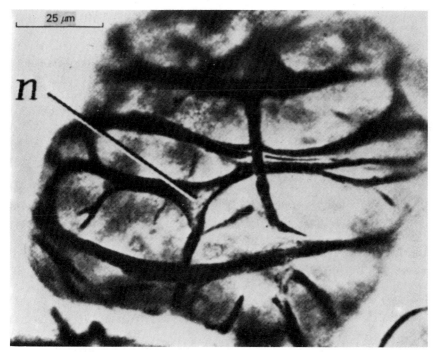

Fig. 2.8. Photograph of a myoepithelial cell nucleus and branching processes on an alveolus in the mammary gland of a lactating goat (from Richardson, K. C. (1949). *Proc. roy. Soc. Biol. B.* **136**, *30*).

The production of oxytocin in the mother's blood can be assayed by modern endocrinological techniques and the effect on milk ejection demonstrated as a rise in pressure in the mammary ducts. Likewise, let-down of milk can be induced artificially by the injection of oxytocin, when it occurs about one minute after intravenous administration (Table 2.3) or after the use of 2–4 international units of synthetic oxytocin ('Syntocin'), absorbed from the nose after intra-nasal spray (Newton 1968).

TABLE 2.3 *Let-down reflex impaired by maternal distraction restarted by oxytocin injection* (from Newton 1968)

Maternal disturbance	Mean amount of milk obtained by baby, ml
No distractions — no injection	168
Distraction — saline injection	99
Distraction — oxytocin injection	153

The human let-down reflex can be markedly facilitated or initiated by psychological factors. In some women, it may be triggered partly as a conditioned reflex responding to such stimuli as the sight or sound of her baby, or even the thought of nursing (Fig. 2.9). The let-down reflex can be facilitated or inhibited by the mother's emotions. Stress due to anxiety or uncertainty can inhibit or block the let-down reflex. This is because adrenaline (epinephrine) is released causing constriction of blood vessels around the alveoli, with decreased opportunity for circulating oxytocin to reach their target organ, the basket-like myoepithelial cells surrounding the alveoli.

Lactation has been termed a 'confidence trick', and failure in healthy well-nourished women with normal full-term babies is most frequently due to the 'anxiety–nursing-failure cycle', based on emotional interference with the let-down reflex (Fig. 2.10). In westernized communities, the basic anxiety is related to lack of knowledge and social support, to the realization that alternatives are feasible and available, and to competing professional and social pursuits for women during which breast-feeding may be culturally unusual or logistically impossible.

The attitudes of mothers towards breast-feeding, whether positive, doubt-

Fig. 2.9. Psychological triggering of let-down reflex in mother by thought of breast-feeding her baby ('conditioned stimulus') (courtesy Prof. T. Matsumura, Department of Paediatrics, Gunma Medical School, Maebashi, Japan)

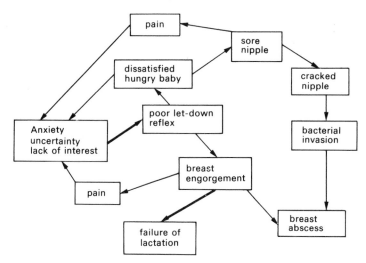

Fig. 2.10. Factors responsible for inhibition of the let-down reflex and lactation failure (from Findlay, A. L. R. (1974). *Res. Reprod.* **6**, 6)

ful, or negative, are powerful factors in achieving successful lactation and in influencing milk production. Again, the major result is probably inhibition of the let-down reflex. In other cultures, fear of bewitchment and of ultra-human forces can be responsible. In Ethiopia, 15 per cent of the relatively small number of failures of lactation were attributed by rural mothers to the effect of the 'evil eye' (Chang 1974).

If the let-down reflex is inhibited, the result is a hungry dissatisfied baby, who has received small amounts of relatively low-fat milk from the terminal lacteals only. The already anxious mother is made more so by her failure, by the baby's crying, and by the discomfort of her own engorged breasts. She approaches subsequent feedings with even greater apprehension and doubt, and with mammary engorgement (which interferes with nipple protractility and the baby's ability to suckle), and with sore nipples. Engorgement of the breast due to stasis of milk in the alveoli leads to decreased secretion, as a result of pressure on the secretory cells and on surrounding blood vessels. This lessens prolactin circulation. The swollen breast may make the nipple less easy for the infant's mouth to grasp, so that emptying of the milk stasis becomes more difficult. The combination of traumatized, even cracked nipples and breast engorgement due to poor milk drainage produce ideal circumstances for ascending infection, which can lead to infective mastitis, and if neglected, to breast abscess.

More usually, failure of the let-down reflex is interpreted by the mother as 'insufficient milk' or as milk that 'didn't suit the baby'. In fact, milk was sufficient, or could have been, but remained in the alveoli out of reach of the baby. Likewise, the milk suited the baby, but the breast-feeding experience did not, again because he received only the small quantity in the terminal lacteals.

Milk is moved from the breast to the baby's throat by three processes: (1) suction produced by negative pressure in the mouth, (2) the tongue milking the terminal lacteals, and (3) actual ejection through the let-down reflex. The significance of the last as an active maternal process is not sufficiently appreciated. Its importance is very great in other mammals, for example in dolphins and whales (p. 7), which feed their offspring underwater while swimming.

The let-down reflex was appreciated by illiterate cattle-keeping peoples and by the artists of ancient civilizations (Folley 1969). Artefacts from the ancient city of Ur depicted milkmen trying to induce the draught reflex in their animals. Rubens' painting 'The Milky Way' shows Hera, wife of Zeus, with an exuberant and premature let-down reflex intended for her son but giving rise to the starry phenomenon known as the Milky Way (Fig. 2.11). In the Renaissance, relaxation for a successful let-down reflex was sought by music played to nursing mothers. In recent times, the reputation in parts of Europe of stout (strong porter-like beer) as a stimulator of milk production (galactogogue) can be related to the reassuring 'sympathetic magic' effect of administering fluid to produce a fluid secretion, milk, and to the tranquillizing effect of small amounts of alcohol. Elsewhere in the world, a large number of galactogogues have been employed in other cultures (p. 164). Most seem to work through the effect of reassurance on the let-down reflex, although some may have pharmacological effects, possibly via the hypothalamus.

Conversely, the common Western practice of giving complementary feeds to young babies interferes with both major reflexes. By decreasing appetite, it can lead to diminished sucking at the breast by the infant; by suggesting the mother's inadequacy, it can lead to anxiety and interference with her let-down reflex. It may also habituate to bottle-feeding because milk can be obtained with less effort. 'Mixed milk feeding' can also confuse the baby, as the sucking mechanisms are different for breast and bottle.

Conclusions

Present-day knowledge of the psychophysiology and endocrinology of lactation clearly endorses certain practices, often already used in many traditional cultures (p. 161), as being most likely to lead to success in breast-feeding. These include the early sucking of the breast following delivery in relation to maximally developed rooting and sucking reflexes and to the initiation of lactation; the frequent sucking of the breast, and increased prolactin production; and the minimizing of anxiety by socially supportive behaviour that helps to ensure an uninhibited let-down reflex.

Likewise, recent scientific research also indicates some aspects of practical

Fig. 2.11. 'The Milky Way' by Rubens. Hera, wife of Zeus, about to nurse her son demonstrating an unphysiologically exuberant let-down reflex, which should be bilateral.

regimens for mother and newborn which can assist, rather than hinder, the initiation and maintenance of lactation and which can be incorporated without much difficulty into modern methods of maternity care (p. 304).

3   Biochemical considerations

The very success of commercial preparations has lured us into believing that we need to know very little about nutrition, as all infants thrive on any number of formulas readily available at the pharmacy and, in some instances, the supermarket. Is our sense of confidence well-founded? I am not certain.

Charles V. Lowe (1972)

Biologically, man has remained unspecialized — put all his organic capital, so to say, into one feature of animal development that could invent substitutes for such specialized organs — the central nervous system.

Lewis Mumford (1970)

It's a bit late in the day to introduce the idea now, but almost any mammal's milk would be easier to modify than cow's milk. Pig's milk is actually nearest to human milk. Camel milk and mare's milk have a better balance for humans. Sheep's milk is OK and so is goat's. Reindeer milk would be a bit fat, dog's milk a bit thin. Now, otter's could be just right. Perhaps we should look into it.

M. Bateman (1975)

Biologically, human milk is a highly complex and unique secretion with many marked differences from the milks of other species, including the cow, buffalo, goat, reindeer, yak, camel and horse (Table 3.1). All these have been used successfully to rear human children in different cultures. However, in the Western world, cow's milk has been the basis of bottle-feeding, originally using domestically modified fresh cow's milk, followed by processed cow's milk, followed by a continually changing succession of cow's-milk based formulas. For practical reasons, therefore, it is more useful to consider biochemical differences between cow's milk and human milk, and to ask whether these have nutritional significance.

Major differences in the gross composition of human milk and cow's milk have been well known for many years (Table 3.2). However, even at this level, closer examination shows considerable variation of data reported by different workers in relation to both human and cow's milk (see p. 34). Nevertheless, for over a hundred years, since the days of Liebig (1867), general knowledge of these differences has enabled the 'proximate principles' of cow's milk — protein, fat, and lactose — to be modified domestically and commercially for greater digestibility and to supply more accurately the infant's needs of these major nutrients.

However, closer scrutiny of the levels of the nutrients given in textbooks shows that they are often based on analyses of small amounts of breast-milk from limited numbers of women, with little understanding of the normal variation between women and in individual mothers, cyclically and at differ-

TABLE 3.1 *Percentage composition of milks used for human consumption* (from Falconer, 1971)

Species	Total solids	Fat	Protein		Lactose	Ash	Reference*
			Casein	Whey protein			
Homo sapiens (man)	12·4	3·8	0·4	0·6	7·0	0·2	Macy et al. (1953)
Equus asinus (donkey)	8·5	0·6	0·7	0·7	6·1	0·4	Anantakrishnan (1941)
Equus caballus (horse)	11·2	1·9	1·3	1·2	6·2	0·5	Neseni et al. (1958)
Lama glama (llama)	16·2	2·4	6·2	1·1	6·0		Jenness (unpublished observations)
Camelus dromedarius (camel)	13·6	4·5	2·7	0·9	5·0	0·7	Kheraskov (1961)
Rangifer tarandus (reindeer)	33·1	16·9	11·5		2·8		Aschaffenberg et al. (1962)
Alces alces (moose)	21·5	10·0	8·4		3·0	1·5	Ivanova (1964)
Bos taurus (cow)	12·7	3·7	2·8	0·6	4·8	0·7	Macy et al. (1953)
Bos grunniens (yak)	17·3	6·5	5·8		4·6	0·9	Vsyakikh (1943)
Bubalus bubalis (buffalo)	17·2	7·4	3·6		5·5	0·8	Dastur (1956)
Capra hircus (goat)	13·2	4·5	2·5	0·4	4·1	0·8	Knowles and Watkin (1938)
Ovis aries (sheep)	19·3	7·4	4·6	0·9	4·8	1·0	Godden and Puddy (1935)

* References are given in the original paper

ent stages of lactation (p. 55). There is a clear need for detailed investigation of sufficient numbers of women at various times throughout lactation.

Moreover, recent research has shown increasingly the complex nature of all mammalian milks. For example, human milk contains over 100 constituents, which are present in different proportions and in different chemical forms than are found in the equally complex milks of other species. In the last decade, over 300 scientific papers have been published on the biochemical properties of human milk, and yet the incompleteness of knowledge in this field is indicated, for example, by the recognition as recently as 1966 of six new polysaccharides in breast milk (Grimmonprez 1966).

TABLE 3.2 *Approximate composition of mature human milk and cow's milk* (from Fomon 1974)

Composition	Human milk	Cow's milk
Water (ml/100 ml)	87·1	87·2
Energy (kcal/100 ml)	75	66
Total solids (g/100 ml)	12·9	12·8
Protein (g/100 ml)	1·1	3·5
Fat (g/100 ml)	4·5	3·7
Lactose (g/100 ml)	6·8	4·9
Ash (g/100 ml)	0·2	0·7
Proteins (% of total protein)		
Casein	40	82
Whey proteins	60	18
Non-protein nitrogen (mg/100 ml)		
(% of total nitrogen)	15	6
Amino acids (mg/100 ml)		
Essential		
Histidine	22	95
Isoleucine	68	228
Leucine	100	350
Lysine	73	277
Methionine	25	88
Phenylalanine	48	172
Threonine	50	164
Tryptophan	18	49
Valine	70	245
Non-essential		
Arginine	45	129
Alanine	35	75
Aspartic acid	116	166
Cystine	22	32

Glutamic acid	230	680
Glycine	0	11
Proline	80	250
Serine	69	160
Tyrosine	61	179
Major minerals per litre		
Calcium (mg)	340	1170
Phosphorus (mg)	140	920
Sodium (mEq)	7	22
Potassium (mEq)	13	35
Chloride (mEq)	11	29
Magnesium (mg)	40	120
Sulphur (mg)	140	300
Trace minerals per litre		
Chromium (μg)	—	8–13
Manganese (μg)	7–15	20–40
Copper (μg)	400	300
Zinc (mg)	3–5	3–5
Iodine (μg)	30	47*
Selenium (μg)	13–50	5–50
Iron (mg)	0·5	0·5
Vitamins per litre		
Vitamin A (I.U.)	1898	1025†
Thiamin (μg)	160	440
Riboflavin (μg)	360	1750
Niacin (μg)	1470	940
Pyridoxine (μg)	100	640
Pantothenate (mg)	1·84	3·46
Folacin (μg)	52	55
B_{12} (μg)	0·3	4
Vitamin C (mg)	43	11‡
Vitamin D (I.U.)	22	14§
Vitamin E (mg)	1·8	0·4
Vitamin K (μg)	15	60

* Range 10–200 g/l.
† Average value for winter milk; value for summer milk, 1690 I.U./l.
‡ As marketed; value for fresh cow's milk 21 mg/l.
§ Average value for winter milk; value for summer milk, 33 I.U./l.

Until now, the preparation, analysis, and testing of cow's milk formulas have had, by necessity, to be made in a very blinkered, monovalent, and simplistic way — for example, focusing exclusively on fat absorption (p. 33) or bifidogenic effects (p. 86) without taking into account the side-effects, nutritional and otherwise, that may be precipitated in the 'biological systems' that comprise all milks.

Rather than old-style comparison dealing only with proximate principles such as the casein: whey-protein ratios, and percentages of lactose and milk 'fat', or of major minerals, such as calcium, newer investigations are becoming more concerned with the detailed biochemical and physiochemical properties of these major ingredients and with the large number of newly recognized constituents, including what György (1976) has termed 'unexpected differences'.

General

The composition and output of human milk varies with many factors, including the stage of lactation, maternal nutrition, and individual variation. The normal variation between the visual appearance of the milks of different species is often not realized. For example, kangaroo's milk is pink (p. 7) while the buffalo's is completely white. Human milk is not usually seen, but mothers making an inspection can become worried as the normal thin, bluish appearance does not conform to their expectation based on cow's milk.

Colostrum, in particular, has a bright lemony-yellow viscous appearance. It is high in antibody-rich protein, especially secretory IgA and lactoferrin (p. 89), and in cells, including 'colostrum corpuscles' (p. 90). There is less fat and lactose than in mature milk, but more sodium chloride, and zinc is present. Its function is primarily anti-infective (p. 84), but its biochemical composition may have a laxative, even proteolytic effect to help clear out meconium, and perhaps to supply a concentrated 'dose' of certain nutrients, such as zinc (p. 51).

The composition and volume of mature human milk varies between mothers, and perhaps between different ethnic groups. Diurnal variations in breast-milk are well documented, especially as to the fat content and volume secreted (Hytten 1954). The volume and composition of human milk in relation to maternal nutrition and the two lactation reflexes is discussed later (p. 59), as are recent concepts concerning the possible significance of the variation and uniformity of breast milk (p. 55).

Fat

Fat has been given rather little attention in infant feeding, and 'protein has dominated the science of nutrition' (Hall 1976). In fact, it is the main source of calories in human milk and the supply of fat-soluble vitamins and essential fatty acids.

The fat content varies with the time of sucking; there is a three-fold increase in fat content with the last milk of the feed ('hind-milk'). Diurnally, the fat rises from early morning to a plateau at about midday; the mean rise is about 2·5-fold (Hall 1976). Fat content is lower in the later months of lactation.

Although the approximate overall fat contents of human and cow's milk appear to be similar, detailed analysis (Moore *et al.* 1968) shows marked differences in composition and in the serum-lipid portions and fatty-acid patterns (Hatsuno 1975). In particular, levels of essential polyunsaturated fatty acids are greater in breast milk, notably linoleic acid, which is often 7–8 times as high. However, this will vary somewhat with the mother's diet and bodily reserves (Cuthbertson 1976), although major changes in a downwards direction only occur in cases of maternal malnutrition (Crawford *et al.* 1974), and in an upwards direction with very artificial diets (Hall 1976). For example, extremely high concentrations of linoleic acid were found in the milk of a woman who was taking large amounts of sunflower-seed oil to try to treat the multiple sclerosis from which she was suffering (Hall 1976). On the whole, there is a 'remarkable similarity of milk lipids' in women with different dietary backgrounds, as noted in a recent study undertaken in five widely different places in Europe, Africa, and Asia (Crawford, Laurance, Hall, Berg-Hansen, and Munhambo 1976).

Also, as noted by Sinclair and Crawford (1972), the long-chain polyenoic acids (arachidonic and docadexaenoic) are present in lower concentrations in cow's milk (Table 3.3). This may be important as these substances may play a significant role in the biochemical development of the brain (Sinclair and Crawford 1973), since they are found particularly in the human central nervous system.

TABLE 3.3 *Fatty acids in human and bovine colostrum* (from Crawford *et al.* 1973)

Fatty acid	Ethanolamine phosphoglyceride		Triglyceride	
	Human	Cow	Human	Cow
12:0	2·0	1·4	1·5	2·7
14:0	3·0	3·1	5·2	11·0
16:0	12·1	9·4	25·6	29·9
16:1	2·2	0·8	2·7	3·1
18:0	18·0	13·1	8·4	12·9
18:1	19·0	31·1	35·6	29·1
18:2, n–6 (linoleic)	10·0	11·0	8·7	2·1
18:3, n–3 (linolineic)	1·3	3·9	3·4	1·9
20:2, n–6	0·9	0·2	0·8	0·02
20:3, n–3	2·8	1·3	0·5	0·1
20:4, n–6 (arachidonic)	12·4	5·9	2·2	0·2
20:5, n–3	0·3	3·8	0·1	0·3
22:4, n–6	2·1	0·1	1·3	0·03
22:5, n–3	3·2	4·9	0·6	0·45
22:6, n–3 (docadexaenoic)	7·0	0·6	1·1	0·1

Recent investigations on blood levels of long-chain polyenoic acids in breast-fed or formula-fed neonates showed similar levels up to the seventh day, but a rapid decline in the latter after that time. It has been suggested that the newborn is unable to convert linoleic to arachidonic acid, so that this 'structural lipid' is a specific dietary requirement (Crawford, Laurance, Hall, Berg-Hansen, and Munhambo 1976).

The level of fat in human milk decreases somewhat with malnourished mothers (p. 80), and the pattern of fatty acids present varies with maternal diet and stores (p. 72). In turn the depot fat of babies is influenced by their diet (Fig. 3.1). The influence of the fat in the infant's diet on the composition of adipose tissue has been emphasized by findings that at 4 months of age 33–37 per cent of subcutaneous fat was linoleic acid in Dutch babies, compared with 3 per cent in British infants of the same age (Widdowson *et al*. 1975). These extreme differences were due to the use of relatively unchanged cow's milk formulas by the British and the replacement of the cow's milk fat by maize oil in the Dutch. The ultimate effects on health and nutrition are unknown.

Investigations of the young of a variety of mammals, including calves, lambs, and piglets, have shown a low cholesterol at birth, rising while on mother's milk ('suckling hypercholesterolaemia') and falling when weaned (Carroll and Hamilton 1973). Similar findings may occur in humans. A comparative study among Australian and New Guinean villages showed both to have similar low neonatal levels and high levels in the first year of life. Later the levels diverged, with a gradual rise in the Australians and a gradual fall in the New Guineans, on a largely vegetable, non-western diet (Whyte and Yee 1958).

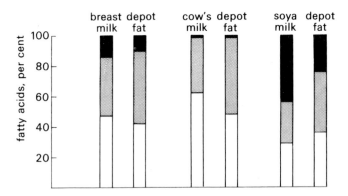

Fig. 3.1. Fatty-acid composition of triglycerides of depot fat of infants aged 6 weeks compared with that of their milk feed. Polyunsaturated fatty acid, ■; monounsaturated, ▨; saturated, □. Results from Sweeney, Etteldorf, Throop, Timma, and Wren (1963) and Ballabriga, Martinez, and Gallart-Catala (1972) (from Gairdner, D. (1974). *Proc. nutr. Soc.* **33**, 119)

The cholesterol levels in human milk are higher than in cow's milk and even more so than in adapted formulas using vegetable oil. Animal experiments (Reiser and Sidelman 1972) suggest that critical levels of cholesterol may be needed in the early weeks of life to ensure the development of appropriate enzyme systems, but long-term follow-up is needed to test this hypothesis (Friedman and Goldberg 1975). In addition, although cholesterol can be synthesized by the infant, it is possible that abundant and easily available supplies of cholesterol may facilitate myelinization of the central nervous system. In view of the rapid growth of the brain in the human neonate and its high lipid content (60 per cent), it is apparent that further research is required into the effects of different lipid intakes in the development of the central nervous system and of dietary variations in the fatty acids in mother's milk. Current confusion concerning perinatal cholesterol metabolism is apparent in a recent review of the subject (Tsang and Glueck 1975).

Triglycerides, the main constituents of milk fat, are broken down to diglycerides and then to monoglycerides. The splitting of fatty acids from triglycerides is an enzymatic reaction under the influence of lipase present in intestinal secretion. However, in contrast with cow's milk preparations, human milk is itself rich in lipase, which at a temperature of 4° C or lower liberates free fatty acids from triglycerides. It has been shown that free fatty acids are the most important source of energy for the young infant. The lipase in human milk makes free fatty acids available, even before the digestive phase in the intestine, thus improving the supply of necessary energy for the infant (Freudenberg 1953). Consequently, the fat of human milk is more efficiently digested and absorbed (92 per cent) than cow's-milk fat (György 1971, Milner *et al.* 1975, Southgate *et al.* 1969).

The fat of human milk contains a high proportion of palmitic acid in the 2-position, which will be absorbed as 2-monoglycerides from the intestine. By contrast, lipase liberates palmitic acid in the 1- or 3-position from cow's-milk fat. This free palmitic acid is precipitated by calcium in the intestinal lumen and excreted as calcium-palmitate soap. This leads to loss of fat, and, as important, of calcium, so that hypocalcaemia of the newborn (p. 45) is much more likely in babies fed on cow's-milk formulas (György 1971).

In addition to the probable species-specificity of the lipid content of human milk, the nutritional significance of a successful let-down reflex (p. 19) includes the additional lipid (and hence calories) found in the fat-rich hind-milk.

Protein

It has been known for decades that cow's milk contains about three times more protein than human milk (György 1971, Wickes 1953), largely in the form of casein (cow 82 per cent, human 18 per cent). Curd formation in the stomach, due to precipitation of casein, occurs in all mammals and appears to have the biological function of supplying the intestine with a continuous flow of nutrients, initially as soluble lactose and whey proteins, and later from digested curd.

The curds formed by the two milks have quite different densities, sizes, and forms of lamination and tensions, largely related to the casein and calcium precipitated in the stomach (Platt 1961). Cow's-milk curd is tough and rubbery, while the curd of human milk is soft and flocculent. The effect of this considerable variation in curd formation in relation to stomach emptying and to ultimate digestion is difficult to assess. However, it is known that the gastrointestinal passage time is much faster with cow's-milk feedings (Fomon 1974). Experimental difficulties obviously exist with the breast-fed baby, as the human milk cannot be 'marked' at all radiologically nor easily in other ways. It is of interest that an early concern of infant feeding with fresh cow's milk was to decrease the protein content and to successfully produce a softer curd, as by boiling the milk and diluting with water.

Modern formulas produce less dense gastric curds than unprocessed cow's milk. Danger can occur, however, if over-concentrated feedings are inadvertently prepared from powdered milks. Inability to absorb the solid content of the high-fat, high-calcium curd can lead to 'milk-bolus obstruction' (p. 268)

Very recent work by Hambraeus and colleagues suggest that the protein content of human milk may be much lower than previously believed (Hambraeus *et al.* 1977). In a series of well-nourished Swedish women, the protein content was only $0 \cdot 88$ per cent. These workers note that older data available were obtained long before the development of modern techniques, such as immunoelectrophoresis, and used methods originally developed for the analysis of cow's milk. They are not completely relevant for analysis of human breast milk due to the differences in the composition of the nitrogen-containing components of human milk, as well as the physicochemical properties of the individual proteins. Thus, the protein content is usually based on the determination of total nitrogen by means of the Kjeldahl method and the conversion factor $6 \cdot 25$ or $6 \cdot 38$, despite the fact that a much larger amount of nitrogen in human breast milk (25 per cent) is derived from non-protein nitrogen than in cow's milk (5 per cent). Another example of the lack of relevance of the methods used is the fact that casein is determined by precipitation at pH $4 \cdot 6$. However, human casein is not as easy to precipitate at this pH as bovine casein. This difference might also have its physiological importance (Hambraeus *et al.* 1977).

This important work shows much greater differences between the usual rough groupings of nitrogen-containing components in cow's milk and human milk (Table 3.4) than is usually appreciated.

TABLE 3.4 *Major nitrogen (N)-containing components of cow's milk and human milk* (from Hambraeus *et al.*1977)

	Human breast-milk*		Cow's milk†	
	mg N/ml	%	mg N/ml	%
Protein nitrogen	1·3	77	5·3	95
Non-protein nitrogen	0·4	23	0·3	5
Casein nitrogen	0·41	35	4·3	81
Whey protein nitrogen	0·76	65	1·0	19

* Lönnerdal *et al.* (1975)
† Webb *et al.* (1974)

These investigators have also demonstrated that the biochemical and physicochemical properties of cow's milk and human milk are very far apart. For example, the main whey proteins found in the two milks show great, often almost opposite, differences in composition (Table 3.5).

Breast-milk is much richer in lactoferrin, lysozyme, and Ig A with no β -lactoglobulin; cow's milk contains much more Ig G and β -lactoglobulin (Fig. 3.2). Longitudinal investigation of 50 Swedish women over 170 days showed the high protein of the colostrum was due in large measure to secretory Ig A and lactoferrin, and fell rapidly to mature milk levels after a few days.

TABLE 3.5 *Main components of whey proteins in human and cow's milk* (from Hambraeus *et al.* 1977)

	Human breast-milk*	Cow's milk†
Lactoferrin	1·5	Traces
α -lactalbumin	1·5	0·9
β -lactoglobulin	–	3·0
Serum albumin	0·5	0·3
Lysozyme	0·5	0·0001
Ig A	1·0‡	0·03
Ig G	0·01	0·6
Ig M	0·01	0·03

* Lönnerdal *et al.* (1975)
† Gordon and Kalan (1974)
‡ Hanson and Winberg (1972)

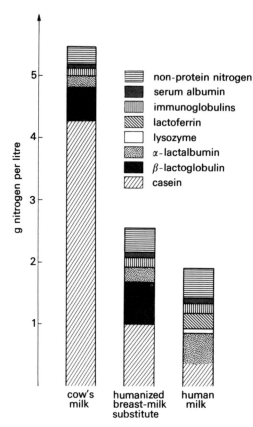

Fig. 3.2. Main components of the protein of human milk, cow's milk, and humanized breast-milk substitutes (from Hambraeus, L., Forsum, E., and Lönnerdal, B. (1977). In *Food and Immunology Symposium* No. 12 (eds. L. Hambraeus and L. A. Hanson), Swedish Nutrition Foundation, Uppsala, Sweden)

The various proteins present in human milk can be classified in different ways, for example as milk-specific proteins and serum proteins. Alternatively, they may be considered as 'nutritional' or 'active', such as lactoferrin, with its antibacterial effect, and α-lactalbumin, which has a key role in the synthesis of lactose.

The published data on the amino-acid content of human breast milk also show discrepancies (Food and Agricultural Organization 1970, Schwerdtfeger 1965, Soupart *et al*. 1954). These seem, in part, to be due to the difference in analytical and collecting methods used, which makes it difficult to draw final conclusions about variations and their causes. However, as judged by present data, the amino-acid composition of the two milks differs considerably in a variety of ways (Fig. 3.3). The cystine content of human milk (24 mg per 100 ml) is higher than that of cow's milk (13 mg per 100 ml); while levels of tyrosine and phenylalanine are greater in cow's milk (Table 3.6). These differences have recently been recognized as being important or even critical, in feeding the newborn, especially premature babies (p. 251), when 'transient tyrosinaemia' has been noted frequently (Wong *et al*. 1967), with potential late sequelae (Mamunes *et al*. 1976).

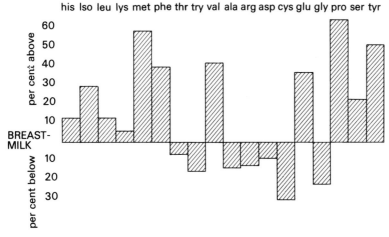

Fig. 3.3. The amino-acid profile of cow's milk compared with breast-milk (from Food and Agriculture Organization (1970). *Nutritional studies: amino-acid content of foods*, p.134. Rome, Italy)

TABLE 3.6 *Comparison of sulphur amino acids and aromatic amino acids in breast-milk and cow's milk, including methionine/cystine (met/cys) and phenylalanine/tyrosine (phe/tyr) ratios* (from Hambraeus *et al.* 1975)

	Sulphur amino acids		Aromatic amino acids	
	Total amount	Ratio met/cys	Total amount	Ratio phe/tyr
Breast-milk	190	0·69	384	1·30
Cow's milk	220	2·72	614	0·98

These recent findings are of considerable practical importance. For example, the 'Recommended Dietary Allowance' for infants will need to be reconsidered (National Academy of Sciences 1975). Also, the nutrition values of protein components differ, so that the nutritional significance of milks and formulas will vary. For example, 'casein' has a lower nutritive value than the proteins of whey ('lactoserum', as it is aptly termed in French), in which α-lactoglobulin rates highly.

The methionine:cystine ratio of cow's milk is seven times that of breast milk, which is uniquely low compared with other mammals, being close to or below 1·0. This conforms with the work of Sturman and his collaborators who examined the transsulphuration of methionine to cystine and found that cystine seems to be an essential amino acid in neonates and premature infants (Pohlandt 1974), as the enzyme cystothianase is low or absent in their livers and brains (Sturman *et al*. 1970)

The same workers have shown that the amino acid taurine is present in large amounts in rat milk for the first few days after birth, and accumulates rapidly in the brain of the newborn rat. The human infant cannot synthesize taurine and is totally dependent on dietary intake. Human milk is rich in taurine, while synthetic formulas contain virtually none. These workers suggest that taurine may be an essential nutrient for the newborn (Sturman *et al*. 1976).

At a physicochemical level, newer investigations show greater complexity and divergence (Bell and McKenzie 1964, Findlay and Brew 1972, Nagasawa, Kiyosawa, and Takase 1973, Nagasawa, Kiyosawa, Fukuwatan, Kitayama, Uechi, and Hyodo 1973, Ribadean-Dumas 1971). The term 'casein' covers mixtures of at least three main components of what are 'species-specific casein systems': α_{s1}-, β-, and κ-caseins. Human milk contains $0 \cdot 4$ per cent 'casein, mostly β-casein, with some κ-casein and with α_{s1}-casein not present in appreciable quantities; whereas bovine 'casein' is 45 per cent α_{s1}-casein. The situation is further complicated by the fact that these caseins can have various forms; in the case of β-casein, six different forms have been identified, with different amino-acid alignments (Ribadeau-Dumas, Grosclande, and Mercier 1975).

In relation to differences in 'casein systems', Ribadeau-Dumas (Ribadeau Dumas, Mercier, Addeo, Gainot, and Pelissier 1975) comments:

> Milk obviously has a nutritional role. In the species where it constitutes at birth the only food for the young mammal, it contains all the essential elements including proteins, lipids, carbohydrates, minerals and vitamins. If it is assumed, rightly or wrongly, that dietary proteins play a role in the receptor organism identical with that of a corresponding amino acid mixture, one wonders why the mother organism 'wastes' so much energy making several well-defined polypeptide chains from amino acids. One must admit that milk proteins have, or have had during their evolution, roles differing from that of simple 'amino-acid carriers'. The role of κ-lactalbumin, one of the whey proteins, in the biosynthesis globular proteins that occur in milk, such a β-lactoglobulin, must also have definite roles, irrespective of their ability to carry amino acids. On the other hand, the caseins seem to have evolved towards types of molecules especially suitable for nutritional purposes, since their loose structures allow for easy degradation by the enzymes of the digestive tract. It seems obvious, however, that the 'messages' written in their primary structure are, or have been, meaningful.

In other words, knowledge of the 'primary structure' of caseins may assist in understanding their physiological and nutritive roles. For example, κ-casein in cow's milk has been shown to have a specific effect in the calf's digestive tract physiology, stimulating the secretion of chymosin, the dominant protease of the ruminant fourth stomach (Grosclande *et al*. 1973).

Hambraeus and colleagues (1977) understate the situation when they note:

The protein composition of human milk and breast milk substitutes based on cow's milk is profoundly different. This is true even in the case of so called 'humanized' infant formulas where the ratio between casein and whey protein is adjusted to simulate that of human milk. In fact, we think that the differences in the protein and nitrogen composition between breast milk and breast milk substitute are so great that its physiological implication has to be elucidated and the composition of breast milk substitutes possibly should be reevaluated.

Present lack of certainty, indeed, confusion, with regard to the ingredients needed or effects of cow's milk-based formulas are also indicated by the same Swedish workers who pose the following questions:

1. Will a premature infant or a neonate do as well on a low-protein intake with a high quality protein as in human breast milk, as on a high-protein intake using a nutritionally inferior protein source?

2. Which is the real optimal protein quality and quantity?

3. What is the nutritional significance of the relatively high non-protein nitrogen content of human breast milk? It is in this connection of interest to refer to the positive effect of urea on the nitrogen balance which has been reported on low-protein diet.

4. How does the protein and nitrogen intake influence the intestinal micro-flora and the immunological response?

5. Will the difference in the protein composition have any nutritional or immunological implications?

6. The iron-binding milk-protein lactoferrin which makes iron less available for microorganisms has been suggested to be one essential factor in the defence against gastrointestinal infections in the newborn. How does this fit with the use of iron-enriched infant formulas based on cow's milk where lactoferrin is lacking?

7. Does the beta-lactoglobulin content or the effect of processing on the cow's milk proteins in humanized breast-milk substitutes include any increased risk of allergic reactions in the neonates?

8. What are the variations in the composition of breast milk between individuals and within individuals and are they related to internal or external factors?

9. What is the significance of a malnutrition in the mother for the qualitative and quantitative composition of breast milk?

Another distinctive biochemical difference between human and cow's milk concerns the important group of nucleotides. Although both human and cow's colostrum are rich in a variety of nucleotides, mature cow's milk contains only a small amount represented chiefly by orotic acid. By contrast, mature human milk still contains a great variety of nucleotides, but no orotic acid. Nucleotides are required indirectly for protein synthesis, with the high molecular-weight ribonucleic acid as intermediary (György 1971).

Additionally, numerous other substances, such as glycoproteins, are present in human milk and cow's milk in different forms and proportions. For example, the polyamine content of breast milk is much higher, particularly the levels of spermidine and spermine. As with the nucleotides, it has been suggested that the polyamine pattern facilitates protein sythesis, although further proof is required (Sanguansensri *et al.* 1974).

Lactose

Almost all the carbohydrate in human milk is lactose, but small quantities of other substances are present, including galactose, fucose, and numerous nitrogen-containing carbohydrates, such as *N*-acetylglucosamine, *N*-acetylneuraminic acid (sialic acid), and 'bifidus factor' (György 1953) (p. 86). *N*-containing carbohydrates make up about $0 \cdot 7$ per cent of milk solids (Grimmonprez 1971, Montreuil and Mullet 1959).

Lactose itself is a curious nutrient (Flatz and Rotthauwe 1973, D.B. Jelliffe 1972 *a*, King 1972). Although described as a constituent of milks by Bartoletus in 1633, it was only synthesized in 1927 (Haworth and Long 1927). It is only found in mammal milks, in contrast to the varied sources of other sugars in the plant and animal world, such as sucrose, fructose, and glucose. Conversely, the intestinal enzyme lactase is not found in most mammals, including the majority of mankind, after infancy. The exclusiveness of lactose in mammal milk strongly suggests a specific function in the metabolism of the exterogestate foetus.

Lactose has four known functions. It enhances calcium absorption (Lengemann 1959), and may play a part in the prevention of rickets. Its high solubility conserves maternal water. It is metabolized in the infant's body to galactose, a constituent of the galactolipids, such as cerebroside, needed for the development of the central nervous system. Together with the 'bifidus factor' (p. 86), the relatively high lactose in the intestine promotes the growth of lactobacilli in the intestine, and fermentation of the lactose in the large intestine and stools is partly responsible for relative faecal acidity.

Lactose in mammal milk varies from nil in the California sea lion (p. 8) to the highest level ($7 \cdot 0$ per cent) in man (Fig. 3.4). Human milk contains much more than does cow's milk (about 4 per cent) (Table 3.2). Although galactose can be synthesized by the baby (Varma *et al.* 1962), the high lactose in breast milk ensures a readily available source of galactose for the large and rapidly growing human brain.

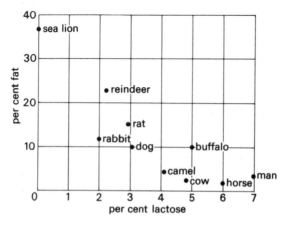

Fig. 3.4. Lactose and fat contents of mammal milks (from Hambraeus, L., Forsum, E., and Lönnerdal, B. (1977). *Food and Immunology Symposium* No. 12, Swedish Nutrition Foundation, Uppsala, Sweden)

Vitamins

The level of vitamins in human milk is affected by inadequate maternal nutritional status (p. 73), especially the water-soluble vitamins (such as ascorbic acid), and vitamin A. Human milk has higher levels of vitamin A, ascorbic acid, and vitamin E than does cow's milk (Kuratani 1966). In addition, the vitamin E is present in the appropriate ratio with the polyunsaturated fatty acids present. The heat treatment used in preparing processed cow's milk-based formulas will reduce or destroy heat-labile vitamins, such as ascorbic acid and folate. The vitamin B_{12} present in cow's milk (mainly deoxyadenosyl cobalmin) is in a different form from that of human milk (Craft *et al*. 1971).

Vitamin K is present in somewhat lower concentration in human milk than in cow's milk. The risk of haemorrhagic disease of the newborn has been stated to be greater in the breast-fed, but this appears to be based only on poorer 'medically indigent patients (Sutherland *et al*. 1967). Absorption of vitamin K may be facilitated in human milk, as with other nutrients, such as calcium; while the differences resulting from the dissimilar bowel flora need consideration. Moreover, vitamin K is obtained in the newborn from foetal hepatic stores as well as ingested milk, until the newly established intestinal flora commence synthesizing sufficient vitamin K (Iyengar and Apte 1972). It is therefore important that a mother should have a diet rich in vitamin K in pregnancy and lactation, with special emphasis on dark-green leafy vegetables. Vitamin K should be administered parenterally to the mother during, or to the neonate after, any prolonged or otherwise difficult labour. Further research is needed with careful differentiation of bleeding syndromes in the newborn of well-fed mothers in Western and other cultures (Glade and Buchanan 1976).

In mothers who have been well-nourished in pregnancy and in lactation, there is no evidence that additional vitamins are needed for their solely breast-fed offspring in the first six months of life. A possible exception is relatively cloudy, cold countries where the lack of maternal exposure to the ultraviolet radiation of sunlight could make additional vitamin D necessary for the body. However, under the circumstances prevailing in most Western communities, mothers can be expected to obtain sufficient vitamin D from a variety of enriched foods, particularly cow's milk, combined with a limited amount of exposure to ultraviolet light (see also p. 389). The situation in poorly nourished communities is discussed later (p. 69).

A quite new consideration has emerged recently with the identification of 'vitamin-binders' in mammal milks. It has been suggested that they act in the mammary gland to accumulate the vitamins from blood plasma into milk, and in the intestine to facilitate their absorption both directly and indirectly by preventing their uptake by intestinal microorganisms. Their significance in human milk and cow's milk needs further research (Ford 1974). Recent work suggests that folate-binding and vitamin B_{12}-binding proteins in pig's milk facilitate the absorption of these vitamins during the neonatal period (Ford *et al*. 1975). Unsaturated vitamin B_{12}-binding protein is present in much higher concentrations in human milk than cow's milk, and an anti-*Escherichia coli* effect has been suggested (Gullberg 1974).

Minerals and Water

The concentration of minerals is over three times greater in cow's milk than in human milk. The cow's milk:human milk ratio of concentrations varies for different minerals. It is most striking for phosphorus (5·9:1), calcium (3·7:1), and sodium (3·6:1).

Infants fed with cow's milk formulas or human milk are dissimilar metabolically, especially low birth-weight babies (Kagan *et al*. 1972). In other words, they are biochemically different and have a different body composition, as shown by serum-electrolyte estimations. For example, a recent study in Britain showed the average blood urea of 75–88 per cent of a group of healthy artificially-fed 1–3-month-old infants to be above the accepted 'normal' of 40 mg per 100 ml (Davies and Saunders 1973) (Table 3.7 Fig. 3.5). Apart from anything else, this can pose problems in diagnosing early renal failure.

The renal solute load of cow's milk is much greater than that of breast milk (Shaw *et al*. 1973, Ziegler and Fomon 1971), especially as an additional load has to be added because of the metabolic breakdown of products of high protein content, notably urea (Rossier and Denavit 1976).

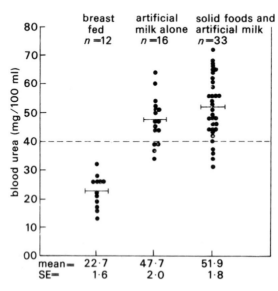

Fig. 3.5. Blood urea levels in 61 healthy infants aged 1–3 months (from Davies, D. P. and Saunders, R. (1973). *Arch. Dis. Childh.* **48**, 563)

It has been long the clinical opinion of some experienced paediatricians that the muscle tone and turgor differs in breast-fed and bottle-fed babies. This is, of course, difficult to prove, but, if such is the case, an electrolytic explanation cannot be ruled out. Certainly, sodium retention occurs more easily in infants fed on cow's milk (Fig. 3.6) with coincident subclinical water retention facilitating the development of oedema. Some of the increased weight-gain in the bottle-fed may be, in some measure, related to retention of sodium and of water.

Differences in body electrolytes can become emphasized if dehydration occurs. For example, in Liberia, breast-fed infants with gastroenteritis showed much lower levels of blood urea and of serum sodium and potassium than did babies similarly affected who had been fed on cow's milk (Kingston 1973) (Table 3.8).

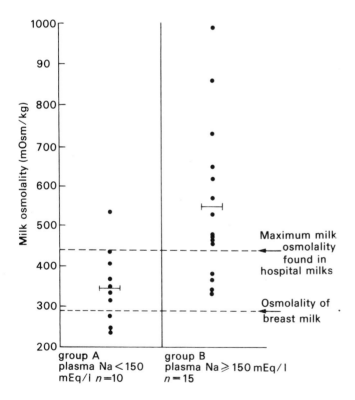

Fig. 3.6. Plasma sodium concentration and osmolality of milks that were usually fed to dehydrated infants, with or without hypernatraemia. Significance of difference of means, $P < 0.0025$ (from Dale, G., Goldfinch, M. E., Sibert, J. R., and Webb, J. K. G. (1975). *Arch. Dis. Childh.* **50**, 731)

TABLE 3.7   *Blood urea levels in 1–3-month-old infants on different feeding regimens* (from Davies and Saunders 1973)

Infant group	Blood urea (mg/100 ml)			Individual values>40 mg/100 ml as % of total observations
	n	mean±s.e.	n	
Breast-fed	12	22·7±1·6	0	0
Artificial milk alone	16	47·4±2·0	12	75
Artificial milk + solid foods	33	51·9±1·8	29	88

These basic dissimilarities make a different routine approach to rehydration necessary. Uraemia and hypernatraemia are essentially serious ill-effects of dehydration in infants fed on cow's milk. This has special significance, as it is well recognized that hypernatraemia has a toxic effect ('sodium poisoning'), which can lead to irreversible brain damage, and has an inherent mortality rate (28 per cent in a recent study) (Rosenbloom 1975).

TABLE 3.8   *Electrolyte levels in breast-fed and bottle-fed infants with dehydration from gastroenteritis in Liberia* (from Kingston 1973)

Values	Method of feeding		P
	Breast $n=66$	Bottle $n=14$	
Blood/serum			
K (mEq/1)	2·2	3·7	0·001
Na (mEq/1)	119	134	0·001
pH	7·30	7·07	0·001
Urea (mg/100ml)	27	52	0·001
Urine			
Specific gravity	1·005	1·016	0·001

The risks of hypernatraemia and uraemia have been much accentuated in several recorded instances of over-concentrated formulas prepared accidentally (by adding extra or over-full scoops of powder or by failing to dilute concentrated liquid feeds) or purposely, by overanxious, solicitous mothers.* A metabolic vicious circle leading both to increasing hypernatraemia and to infantile obesity (p. 242) can be initiated, especially in hot weather, when both climate and high serum-electrolyte levels lead to thirst,

* Inaccuracies, difficulties, and potentiality for 'over-dosage' are greatest with powdered milk. The water added may be significant; for example, the use of softened water can increase the sodium by 50 per cent (Philpott 1975).

which, in turn, may be interpreted as hunger by the mother, who responds by giving additional concentrated feeds. In Britain, it has been said that the commonest deficiency in infancy may be water. In fact, the other face of over-feeding and hypernatraemia is under-watering (Hughes-Davies 1975).

By contrast, human milk is a low-solute fluid (Table 3.9), which appears to be designed as a 'supply-and-demand' source of nutrients and water, in response to both hunger and thirst. This aspect of lactation is endorsed biologically by the recently demonstrated renal antidiuretic, water-conserving effect of prolactin.

Two recent autopsy studies on infants dying unexpectedly show that the vitreous fluid in the eye showed high electrolyte levels in some instances (Emery *et al*. 1974). Further study is plainly indicated in children succumbing with sudden infant-death syndrome (p. 257).

The higher calcium in cow's milk is, paradoxically, associated with a much greater incidence of neonatal hypocalcaemia (Oppé and Redstone 1968, Roberts *et al*. 1973), with characteristic tetany and convulsions. Metabolically, neonatal hypocalcaemia develops because calcium absorption is diminished by the digestion of bovine triglycerides into palmitic acid in the 1- or 3-positions, which is precipitated by calcium in the intestinal lumen, and excreted as calcium-palmitate soap. In addition, the higher concentration of phosphorus in cow's milk leads to its increased absorption and to a diminished uptake of calcium, so that serum-electrolyte estimations in neonatal hypocalcaemia show both low calcium and high phosphorus levels.

TABLE 3.9   *Estimated renal-solute load and minimum urinary osmolarity of a hypothetical 6 kg infant from various feedings* (from Reynolds 1974)

Feeding	Estimated renal-solute load	Osmolarity of 730 ml urine
Whole cow's milk	221 mOsm	303 mOsm/l
Human milk	79 mOsm	108 mOsm/l
Boiled skim milk	308 mOsm	422 mOsm/l

Assumptions:
1. 6 kg infant consuming 1000 ml milk feedings per day.
2. Minimal insensible water losses of 270 ml.
3. 730 ml water (1000 ml − 270 ml) available for renal excretion.

The effect of the type of milk used in infant feeding on acid-base metabolism is under-appreciated. A recent study in the U.K. showed the following pH levels: breast-milk 7·29, cow's milk 6·57, and various formulas 6·4–6·97 (Barrie *et al*. 1975). Breast-fed babies have more acid stools (pH 5·0–5·5) and bottle-fed more alkaline (pH 6·8–7·0). This difference is initially due to the higher buffering action of cow's milk (Fig. 3.7) and to the added effect of the *Lactobacillus bifidus* intestinal flora which predominates in the breast-fed. The effect of overconcentrated feeds has been noted recently (Smith 1974, Wilkinson *et al.* 1973): using dried formula, it was found that each extra 'scoop' lowered the pH by 0·05 (Barrie *et al.* 1975).

Because of the chemical and microbiological characteristics (p. 84) of the two stools, they have different physical appearances. Cow's milk stools are pale, chalky, bulky, firm, and, in old-style terminology, 'putrefactive'. Breast-milk stools are characteristically mustard-yellow, soft, 'fermentative', and often more frequent.

Iron

Needs for this nutrient are high in the first years of life (*British Medical Journal* 1973*a*), as there is a rapid increase in haemoglobin in the expanding red-cell mass and in the myoglobin of the musculature. Attention is often focused too much on the low iron content of both human and cow's milk, and on the high incidence of iron deficiency anaemia in pre-school age children in numerous parts of the world. It is true that the levels of iron in milks are so low that care must be taken in the collection of samples to avoid contamination in iron-containing vessels. However, this really avoids the main issue, which is that iron metabolism during infancy can only be considered in relation to all biological sources of iron drawn upon during this period, including foetal stores and the placental transfusion, as well as the diet (Sanchez-Mendal 1975). Iron may be lost in intestinal microhaemorrhages in some infants fed on cow's milk (Wilson *et al.* 1964).

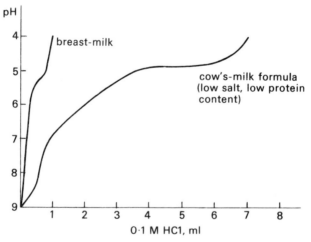

Fig. 3.7. Buffering capacity in faeces from infants fed on breast-milk and on cow's-milk formula (from Winberg, J. and Gothefors, L. (1976). *J. trop. Pediat. env. Chld Hlth* (In press))

Chang has recently reviewed the literature from Africa, Israel, Singapore, and elsewhere on hepatic iron stores in the newborn (Chang 1973). Liver iron, mostly in the form of ferritin, is at a higher concentration in the full-term neonate than in the adult. It rises steeply in the last weeks of pregnancy to a total of about 50–70 mg of iron. Before the 36th week of pregnancy, the liver iron is half that found in the mature newborn. Storage iron (ferritin) is low in babies of poor Indian mothers among whom iron deficiency anaemia is common, endorsing the need for an adequate iron intake in pregnancy (Iyengar and Apte 1972). Daily supplementation of the diet with 60 mg of ferrous iron has been recommended for all pregnant women for at least the last six weeks of pregnancy and the World Health Organization (1972) also recommends a supplement of 120–240 mg/day in areas where maternal iron stores are likely to be low.

The last 1–3 months of pregnancy seems the most significant period. The role of the 'placental transfusion' as a source of iron is under-appreciated (Yao and Lind 1969, Yao *et al.* 1969). In most traditional cultures, the umbilical cord is not tied and cut at once; by contrast, it has become customary in Western institutional practice for the cord to be clamped and cut as soon as the baby is born. There seems no particular scientific reason for this; it is more related to the speedy removal of the neonate from the delivery room. Numerous investigations have shown that so-called 'late' clamping of the cord — that is after three minutes or more preferably with the newborn at a lower level than the placenta — can ensure a 40–60 per cent increase in neonatal blood volume, with a parallel increase in iron stores. From the opposite point of view, early clamping has the same effect as a haemorrhage from the umbilical stump.

TABLE 3.10   *Iron metabolism: comparison between human milk and cow's milk*

	Human milk	Cow's milk
Iron content	Low ($\pm 1 \cdot 5$ mg/l)	Low ($\pm 1 \cdot 0$ mg/l)
Iron Absorption	More	Less
Iron Loss	Nil	Sometimes (Intestinal microhaemorrhages)
Iron facilitators	More vitamin C	Less vitamin C
Placental transfusion	? More common in breast-fed	? Less common in bottle-fed
Iron-deficiency anaemia (6–12 months)	Uncommon	More common

Plainly, at the same time, the haemolysis of the additional blood will increase physiological jaundice. However, this has been shown to be of no significance in full-term babies. In premature neonates, there is a dilemma. On one hand, iron stores are particularly low, while at the same time hepatic immaturity, reflected by deficiency of the enzyme glucuronyl transferase, facilitates the development of dangerous levels of unconjugated bilirubin (Saigal *et al*. 1972). On balance, it seems best to clamp the cord early in small prematures, and still more so in haemolytic disease of the newborn due to Rhesus incompatibility.

As Hipsley (1975) notes, the newborn baby has considerable iron stores in his body, while the daily intake of the breast-fed baby can be estimated to be as low as 1 mg per day. The raising of the Recommended Daily Allowance for dietary iron to 10 mg per day for the first 6 months of life is unnecessary, certainly for the breast-fed. Recent evidence suggests that extra iron in infancy may even be detrimental because it can saturate the 'transport protein' lactoferrin (p. 89) in human milk, interfering with its anti-infective properties, while iron appears to be needed for the metabolism of some intestinal pathogens, notably *Shigella* spp. (Masawe *et al*. 1974). Added iron also increases the incidence of vitamin-E deficiency haemolytic anaemia in premature babies (Williams *et al*. 1975).

Milk — human or bovine — is the usual food for the exterogestate foetus. Both are low in iron: breast milk $1 \cdot 5$ mg/l and cow's milk $1 \cdot 0$ mg/l. Recent analyses of 350 samples from 50 women taken at different times have shown much variation, from $<0 \cdot 1 - 1 \cdot 6$ mg/l; there was considerable difference for individual women from one sample to another (Picciano and Guthrie 1976). However, recent work in Japan by Tsuchiya (1972) suggests that iron is better absorbed from human milk than from cow's milk (Table 3.11). This has been confirmed in adults in the U.S.A. recently who were given human milk tagged with the isotope ^{59}Fe (McMillan *et al*. 1976).

In addition, in relation to the prevention of nutritional anaemia in general,

TABLE 3.11   *Comparison of iron metabolism between infants fed on human and whole cow's milk* (from Tsuchiya, 1972)

	Amount of iron taken per day (µg)	Iron in faeces (µg)	Amount of iron excreted per day (µg)	Amount of iron absorbed (µg)	Ratio of iron absorbed (per cent)
Human-milk group	1148	$12 \cdot 68$	$293 \cdot 3$	$854 \cdot 3$	$74 \cdot 15$
Whole cow's milk group	1160	$12 \cdot 56$	399	760	$65 \cdot 4$

human milk is a richer source of other haematinic nutrients, such as ascorbic acid, copper, and vitamin E.

Fluoride

Human milk contains fluoride in varying levels (Bercovici *et al*. 1960, *British Medical Journal* 1968, Dale 1964, Feltman and Kosel 1961, Grossman 1975) depending to a certain extent on the content of the drinking water. In one community in Switzerland in an area where the water supply contains 9·55 p.p.m., a study showed fluoride to be a small but constant constituent of breast milk varying from 0·13 to 0·17 p.p.m. In Alberta, Canada, human milk was found to have 0·20 p.p.m. when the drinking water contained 0·26 p.p.m. After fluoridation of the water supply to 1 p.p.m., the level in milk rose, but only to 0·49 p.p.m. (Simpson and Tuba 1968). However, caution is needed in interpretation of such results, as methods of analysis have changed.

Cow's milk contains more fluoride than human milk (Fomon 1974). The fluoride ingested by the infant fed on dried powdered milk diluted with water containing 1 p.p.m. of fluoride can lead to an intake of this mineral up to 50 times greater than in breast-fed infants in the same community. However, studies in Sweden have shown no ill-effects in the form of dental mottling (Ericsson 1969, Ericsson and Ribelius 1971).

Reduced solubility of the enamel and consequent resistance to caries can be developed if optimal fluoride is available during tooth calcification and especially during the last stages of enamel formation, when fluorapatite can be laid down instead of hydroxyapatite. With both deciduous and permanent teeth, the final phases of enamel development are largely post-natal.

In areas where the fluoride level in the water is low, fluoride tablets have been given to pregnant women. Results are not uniform (Lilienthal and Lang 1971). Evidence suggests that the placenta has a barrier effect on the transfer of fluoride to the foetus; moreover, the most susceptible teeth do not complete their enamel formation until after birth. Also, the effects on foetal stores are difficult to verify. The consensus seems to be that primary teeth receive little benefit from prenatal fluoride supplementation for pregnant women.

After birth, protection from caries in the deciduous eruption would seem in large measure to depend on the characteristics of the diet and method of feeding (p. 110), and on the fluoride available possibly from foetal stores and from milk, whether human or bovine.

The question of fluoride supplementation in early infancy is fundamentally complicated by difficulties of assessing optimal needs in relation to foetal stores and to dietary intake. In communities with optimal levels of fluoride (1 p.p.m.) in the drinking water, no addition is needed. With breast-fed or bottle-fed babies in populations with lesser levels in the water, increased fluoride intakes have been suggested either via the mother or directly to the baby. The dose and regimen suggested need to be adjusted to the fluoride level in the local water supply and environment, and the climate (and hence intake of fluid). However, in Stockholm, Sweden, with a water supply containing $0 \cdot 2$ p.p.m., Hamberg (1971) has shown that the use of fluoride drops ($0 \cdot 5$ mg/day) for infants from the age of 2 to 3 weeks was non-toxic and reduced cavities in 3–6-year-olds by 50 per cent, in both breast-fed and bottle-fed children. Some workers have noted that occasional allergic reactions to fluoride can occur (Shea *et al.* 1967). More recently, Fomon and Wei (1976) have noted that difficulties in assessing fluoride sources in the baby suggest that supplementary fluoride drops are not needed in the first four months of life. Finally, the possible role of bottle or breast-feeding in dental caries need to be considered in relation to factors other than fluoride intake (p. 110).

Trace elements

There is an obvious need for investigation into the relative content of trace elements in cow's milk and breast-milk in relation to diet and to the possible effects of environmental pollution. Manganese has been studied in New Zealand (McLeod and Robinson 1972). An investigation in Russia (Grebbenikov and Soroka 1963) showed considerable differences (Table 3.12).

TABLE 3.12   *Ratios of trace elements in breast-milk seven days after delivery and in the milk of Red Steppe cows* (from Grebbenikov and Soroka 1963)

	Human milk ($n = 50$)		Cow's milk ($n = 40$)
Manganese	1	:	$2 \cdot 1$
Silicon	1	:	$1 \cdot 9$
Aluminium	1	:	$1 \cdot 9$
Titanium	$1 \cdot 9$	:	1
Copper	$5 \cdot 4$	:	1

Copper. A higher concentration of copper is present in human milk than in cow's milk. Recent analyses of multiple samples of breast milk from fifty women in the U.S.A. showed much variation, from $0 \cdot 09 – 0 \cdot 63$ mg/l. As with iron (p. 46), samples from individual women varied considerably from time to time (Picciano and Guthrie 1976).

It has also been suggested that the ratio of zinc to copper may be important. For example a study by Klevay (1974) in 47 cities in the U.S.A. has noted that mortality rates from coronary heart disease are correlated with diets with high zinc-to-copper ratios (Zn:Cu), as reflected by levels in market milk. The zinc-to-copper ratio in human milk is much lower than in cow's milk and may perhaps play a role in the early aetiology of coronary heart disease.

Zinc. The significance of zinc in paediatric nutrition has been emphasized (Moynahan 1974) by the dramatic curative effects of zinc preparations (35 mg/day) in the serious inherited metabolic abnormality acrodermatitis enteropathica (p. 252). Recent work suggests the possibility of some degree of zinc deficiency being common, including severe forms (zinc-deficient dwarfing), in Iran and Egypt, but also less obvious manifestations in the U.S.A. (Hambridge 1977). It has been suggested that cow's-milk-based formulas should be supplemented with 4 mg/l of zinc, and that this improves growth performance (Walravens and Hambridge 1975).

Zinc is present in high concentrations (20 mg/l) in human colostrum, and similar levels have been stated to be present in both human milk and cow's milk (3–3·5 mg/l). However, recent analyses of 350 samples from 50 American women showed considerable variation, from 0·14–3·95 mg/l. The variation was mostly between one woman and another; samples from an individual did not vary much (Picciano and Guthrie 1976).

Zinc metabolism appears to be facilitated by the high dosage in the colostrum, and newborn mice denied colostrum but fed with later milk develop the clinical features of zinc deficiency (Nishimura 1953). If levels are similar in bovine and human milks, absorption from breast-milk must be much superior, as acrodermatitis never occurs in the breast-fed, and human milk was curative in most cases, prior to the recently discovered effectiveness of zinc.

Recent work indicates that the efficacy of human milk probably results from the presence of low molecular weight zinc-binding factor (Evans and Johnson 1976), (Fig. 3.8).

Enzymes

Fresh mammal milks, including human, are living fluids with enzymes (e.g. lipase) (p. 33), hormones, such as corticosteroids, and cells present (p. 90). In breast-milk, fat-splitting lipase (p. 33) has already been mentioned. However, a comparative profile carried out by Heyndrickx (1962) showed marked differences between bovine and human milk, with the latter containing less alkaline phosphatase and more phosphohexase isomerase. Much further work is needed on the enzymes of breast-milk and their functions, which, apart from the fat-splitting lipase, do not seem to have been investigated (Montreuil 1971) (see p. 389).

Not strictly in this category is thromboplastin which was noticed to be high in breast-milk as long ago as 1935 (Solé 1935). This substance usually forms part of the sequence of events leading to blood-clotting and haemostasis. However, Quick (1974) has suggested that it seems more logical to regard the thromboplastin in breast-milk as belonging in the list of nutrients needed for the rapid development of the central nervous system, since it is established that the brain is so rich in tissue thromboplastin that it serves as the

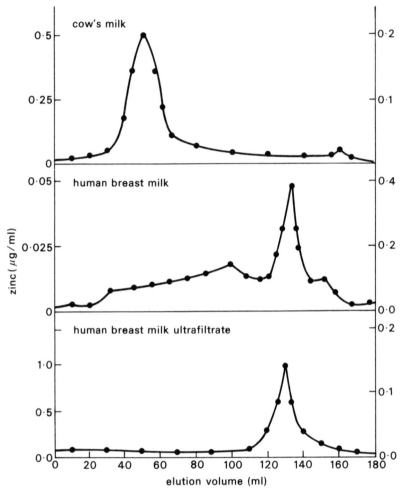

Fig. 3.8. Distribution of zinc from human and cow's milk after gel filtration chromatography. The top two frames show contrasting patterns, indicating that the zinc in human milk is bound to a ligand with a much lower molecular weight than it is in cow's milk (Evans and Johnson, 1976, Lanar)

source of the thromboplastin reagent in the routine one-stage prothrombin-time method used in the laboratory.

Discussion

Biochemical uniqueness

In all species, the activities of the mammary gland are extremely complex and have been summarized by Hall (1976) as follows: 'The mammary gland is an open, essentially one-way system, in which the nutrients taken up from the blood are completely or partly broken down, resynthesized, rearranged, repackaged, and exported. It differs from other secretory glands in the body in the amount of secretion produced, in its perpetual availability, and in that it is directed outside the body itself to sustain the growth and development of another being.'

The mammary gland has one of the highest metabolic rates in the body, comparable to that of the liver (Mepham 1976). Physiological details of the process of milk synthesis are very difficult to obtain in the human, but considerable experimental work has been carried out in animals, including analysis of arterial and venous blood differences, the use of isotopes, and perfusion of isolated organs (Mepham 1976).

From this review, it is apparent that cow's milk is very different from human milk in every way. Both are highly complex, unique biological systems, so that comparisons have to consider not only differences in amount, concentration, and specific composition of ingredients, but also their subtle interactions and interrelationships. For example, the calcium content of breast-milk is considerably less than that of bovine milk and yet, for reasons mentioned earlier (p. 42) and summarized in Table 3.13, it has a higher absorption and causes a much lower incidence of hypocalcaemia of the newborn.

TABLE 3.13   *Calcium metabolism: comparison between human milk and cow's milk*

	Human milk	Cow's milk
Calcium content	+	++
Calcium absorption	+++	+
Calcium loss	−	++
Neonatal hypocalcaemia	Rare	Common

Also, direct nutritional considerations cannot be viewed in isolation from other related aspects — for example, host resistance to infections (p. 84) and the consequences of mother–child development (p.142). Breast-feeding is much more than the mathematical supplying of nutrients to the baby. It is a biological interaction with very wide ramifications.

Mann ist was mann isst is an often misused cliché. However, even the clinically well, bottle-fed baby is biochemically dissimilar to the breast-fed — with subcutaneous fat of different composition, with greater water retention, and with a characteristic pattern of serum electrolytes and urea, as well as quite distinct intestinal bacterial flora. Currently, these are regarded as metabolic variations of no concern, but so were the convulsion-producing pyridoxine-deficient formulas of 1953 (Coursin 1954).

Even the alimentary physiological differences in response by the human infants to biochemical and physical characteristics of the two milks are distinct, in addition to the differing oropharyngeal mechanisms in breast-feeding and bottle-feeding (p. 109). The intragastric curd of human milk appears to permit a more constant flow of food to the intestine (p. 34), which, together with the relatively low concentration of the solution, is adapted to the needs of the infant human, as a 'constant-contact, continuously feeding' species (p. 5).

Sucking and breathing rates differ in babies fed the two milks, even when both are administered by bottle (Johnson and Salisbury 1975). The normally increasing fat content in breast-milk obviously cannot occur with cow's-milk formula, which is of uniform composition. This may have an appetite-controlling (or fluid-seeking) effect, the baby ceasing to take later hind-milk, possibly in response to changes in flavour or viscosity but restarting feeding when moved to the second breast.

Presently it is assumed that these biochemical and physiological differences have no immediate or long-term consequences. This is an assumption without proof, and possible relationships with pathological conditions in infancy or later in life need critical investigation. Indeed, the possible biochemical stress of chronic electrolytaemia is appreciated by infant food manufacturers, who are continuously striving to modify metabolic loads in formulas, although probably precipitating other imbalances by so doing.

Teleonomy
It is often said that the superiority of human milk is probable on teleological grounds — that is, that 'the phenomena of organic life and development can be fully explained by the action of design or purpose and not by mechanical causes'. In other words, the individuality of mammal milks, including that of the human, must have evolutionary survival value.

Some years ago, the question was posed by Barness and György as to whether the main goal of infant feeding was to produce 'dwarfs or giants, idiots or savants' (D.B. Jelliffe 1973). Certainly a major aim must be to furnish abundant supplies of key nutrients to facilitate brain development during the rapidly growing period in early life. For this, it seems increasingly clear that the composition of human milk is particularly suited, in relation to the high levels of lactose, cystine, taurine, and cholesterol, and long-chain fatty acids.

With the regard to the special significance of breast-milk lipids, Crawford and Sinclair (1972) put the situation well:

> In the qualitative sense, the human species is usually thought of as superior to other mammals, yet there are many biological attributes of other species which could well be considered superior to those of man; for example, the development of musculature in the antelopes and bovids, the night vision of the cats, and the remarkable agility of the tree-living primates.
>
> The feature which is outstanding in man is unquestionably the brain and the peripheral nervous system. It is clear that whereas protein is quantitatively the most important structural factor in muscle, lipid is the most important in the brain and peripheral nervous system.

Bearing the chemistry of the brain in mind, the apparent paradox of 6% protein in pig's milk, 4% in cow's milk, and only 1% in human milk can be resolved if one discards the equation between maximum growth and excellence and substitutes brain growth, or what Widdowson describes as the "harmony of growth". Since the brain is predominantly a lipid-rich structure, a harmony of growth implies at least a proper balance between lipid and protein nutrients and indeed, for man, the lipids may be just as important as protein.

Such an alteration from the conventional view of nutrition introduces elements of interrelated nutrients rather than isolated "protein", and qualitative factors rather than quantitative measures of body growth that omit brain growth.

Measurements of brain growth using DNA have shown that most of the cells have accumulated in the human brain by birth, leaving about 20–30% of the total cell division to be completed in the first postnatal months. The significant increase in brain-weight which occurs subsequently is due to some extent to an increase in the cellular content of RNA, protein, and lipid, but mainly to the development of myelin, although extrapyramidal cells in the brain and nervous system must continue to appear until very much later. The grey matter, which is mainly cellular material, is about 50%, and the white matter, which is mainly myelin, is about 70% structural lipid on a dry-weight basis. Consequently, lipid factors will be important to post-natal development.

Even among primates, this specialization has been marked: 'The gibbon has specialized in long arms and the ability to swing gracefully through the trees; the gorilla in great size and ability to digest stems and roots; the baboon in quadrupedalism, and high speed; man in bipedalism, the striding walk, and the enlarged brain', especially the size and complexity of the frontal lobes, the centres for learning, intelligence, foresight, and processing of complex data (Tiger and Fox 1972).

Difficulties with using cow's milk for human infants is emphasized zoologically, when it is realized that it is 'intended for the young of a different species which is hoofed, horned, and herbivorous' (Smibert 1975).

Variation and uniformity
An underappreciated fact of considerable significance is the variation in composition of human milk 'from mother to mother, from day to day, from feed to feed, and even from the beginning to end of any feed' (Barrie *et al*. 1975), or possible patterns of variation 'throughout the day, from day to day, and from week to week' (Picciano and Guthrie 1976).

Well-known examples include the fluctuations of fat content diurnally and between fore- and hind-milk (p. 30), the drop in protein after the first days of lactation (p. 34), and increased levels of linoleic acid with marked dietary changed (p. 31). Recent work has shown varying levels of zinc, copper, and iron in samples of milk from healthy women at different times (Picciano and Guthrie 1976).

Some differences in reported levels of various constituents by different investigators have been due to technique of assessment. A striking example has been the recent Swedish analyses of milk protein (p. 34) (Hambraeus *et al*. 1977). Real variation in levels can be classified into physiological and non-physiological.

Physiological variations in the constituents of milk from well-nourished healthy mothers with babies who are being successfully breast-fed can be between individuals and/or in the same individual at different times. Similar differences are to be found with other aspects of body physiology, for example serum biochemistry.

Genetic variations in the composition of cow's milk have been recognized for decades — for example, the high fat content of Jerseys. Also, in the last 10 years or so, genetic variations in the milk of different breeds of cattle has been demonstrated in their 'milk-protein systems', notably in the forms of α_{S1} casein and β -lactoglobulin (Thompson and Farrell 1974). Despite the very large amount of new scientific information that has become available recently, these authorities maintain that 'we have barely scratched the surface of the complex behaviour and properties of the (cow's) milk system' and other 'fundamentals of dairy chemistry'. However, by comparison there are very few analyses of the detailed structure of the protein systems in human milk (Hambraeus *et al*. 1977; Ribadeau-Dumas *et al*. 1975a). No information is available concerning possible genetic difference in milk composition or lactational ability in varying ethnic groups. Known variations in composition, for example, β -carotene (Gebre-Mehdin *et al*. 1976) and linoleic acid (Cuthbertson 1976), appear more related to marked dietary differences.

The level of some nutrients varies with breast-feeding itself or possibly in relation to the stage of maternal digestion. The fat content increases with an uninhibited let-down reflex (with a possible appetite-controlling significance), and the prolactin produced as a result of sucking appear to have a controlling effect on mammary fat synthesis (Hall 1976). Periprandial variation in constituents secreted may also occur. Blood levels of sugar, fat, amino acids, and other nutrients will rise at different times after the mother's meals according to their speed of digestion and absorption, and this may make supplies to the breast's secretory cells fluctuate also.

Cyclical chronobiological changes are continually occurring in all living organisms, from plankton to flowers to vertebrates. In man, well-recognized cycles include those that occur each 24 hours (circadian rhythms), each month (menstruation), and each life-time, as manifest by ageing. Circadian changes in humans involve many aspects of body physiology, including for example, the secretion of steroids, body temperature, the rate of cell division, and levels of brain electrical activity.

Some chronobiological variations in the constituents of breast-milk are well known, particularly the diurnal fluctuation in fat content (p. 30). It also seems that, as with pregnancy, lactation can be considered as a 'free-running biological cycle', although open-ended and without a clear-cut end-point. During this cycle, marked changes in composition of human milk occur between the colostrum, with its high protein (protective immunoglobulins, etc) (p. 84), high zinc (p. 51), and probably changing pattern of fatty acids (Hall 1976), and subsequent mature milk. Later, chronobiological changes in the lactation cycle are unclear, but it seems likely that such changes are gradual rather than sudden (Rolles 1976).

Lastly, the needs of individuals for all nutrients varies, and this is certainly the case for infants (Beal 1970). This individuality can be partly taken care of by the 'demand and supply' nature of the volume of milk produced in breast-feeding, with greater sucking stimulus leading to greater secretion (p. 17). In addition, the composition may vary with the individual need of the exterogestate foetus, possibly on a genetic basis or as a result of feedback mechanisms acquired transplacentally by the mother while the foetus was *in utero*. Also, it is possible that stimuli from the nursing baby may affect the milk composition, by as yet unappreciated mechanisms, such as alteration in the details of suckling or even the weight of the baby. These suggestions are speculative and seem fanciful. However, the ability of the female kangaroo to secrete two milks of quite different compositions in response to differing stimulation of the young of varying stages of development (p. 7) may be indicative.

Non-physiological variations in the constituents of human milk seem to occur primarily in women with marked dietary and/or nutritional abnormalities. For example, maternal dietary overload with β -carotene (Honda *et al.* 1975) or linoleic acid (Cuthbertson 1976) can lead to substantially raised levels of these substances in breast-milk. Similarly, the very high dietary iron intake in Ethiopia has been considered to be responsible for the raised lactoferrin levels found in breast-milk in that country in women of all socio-economic levels (Gebre-Mehdin *et al.* 1976).

Conversely, as noted elsewhere (p. 59), different planes and forms of severe maternal malnutrition can lead to lower levels of nutrients in milk secreted. This does not occur until the nutritional status of the mother is considerably affected. Nutrients affected may be considered on a 'sliding scale', with water-soluble vitamins, such as ascorbic acid, thiamine, and vitamin B_{12}, appearing to be most easily affected, with fat, protein, and calcium uncommonly affected and to a minor degree, and with lactose apparently least affected.

The physiological variation in composition of human milk is unsurprising. Genetic variations and cyclical changes occur in other mammals and, as noted, in other body tissues and fluids. The expectation that breast-milk will be a 'standardized entity' (Stewart 1976) reflects a common fallacy based on 'medical education, thought, and practice, for the past 100 years [which] has placed emphasis on the constancy of physiological systems, and [has stated] *inter alia* that constancy is a characteristic of life' (Simpson 1973). Rather the normal healthy human being is an 'oscillating system' that is fluctuating chronobiologically (Simpson 1973).

In solely breast-fed infants of well-nourished mothers with established lactation and unimpaired let-down reflexes, growth is excellent in the first 4–6 months of life and nutritional deficiency is non-existent, despite variation in milk composition between individuals and in any one individual. Breast-feeding does not consist of ingesting milk obtained at a single time, but over a continuing period of time. Human milk can, therefore, be considered as physiologically variable in composition, responding to various factors suggested earlier and doubtless to others, but uniformly adapted to supply the nutrients required for the infant, both as an individual and at the particular stage of growth and development.

Conclusion

Earlier domestic modifications of cow's milk — by boiling, diluting, adding sugar — were widely used in infant feeding with success as judged by survival and weight-gain. Since then, infant-food companies have continually tried to utilize the newer knowledge on the composition and properties of human milk by modifying their formulas. This is ultimately a hopeless task even biochemically, in view of the detailed and unique complexity of all milks, including human, as being endorsed increasingly by new research.

Recent appreciation of the physiological variation of the levels of nutrients in normal breast-milk indicate that the Recommended Dietary Allowances on which the composition of infant formulas is based need reassessment and possibly revision, based on estimates of milk samples from numbers of women taken over prolonged periods. Together with the recent reappraisal of the protein content of human milk, this adds further uncertainty to the composition of processed mixtures for babies. This is made even more problematical as, partly for economic reasons, recent 'cow's milk-based formulas' have moved away from their cow's milk base towards novel 'formulas' of various ingredients, showing great variation in, for example, solute load, acid-base, vitamin E, and fatty acids (Stern *et al.* 1972, Taitz and Byers 1972, Ansell 1975, Healy 1972, Kildeberg and Winters 1972, LeMarquand *et al.* 1974, Widdowson *et al.* 1975) (see p. 205).

Finally, the question of possible disadvantages of rigidly constant formula composition needs consideration. Such is the case with regard to absence of a colostrum-surrogate, but whether inability to match the flexible variability of breast milk is significant or not will only become more apparent when more detailed investigations are undertaken into the mechanisms and purpose of physiological chronobiological changes in human milk.

4   Maternal nutrition

How is it that poor men's wives, who have no cold fowl or port wine on which to be coshered up, nurse their children without difficulty, whereas the wives of rich men, who eat and drink everything that is good, cannot do so, we will for the present leave to the doctors and mothers to settle between them.
Anthony Trollope (1847)

The question of the composition and volume of breast-milk produced by mothers on different planes of nutrition at different phases of lactation is a major issue in paediatric public health (E.F.P. Jelliffe 1976c). The fundamental issues are the nutritional adequacy of such milks for young infants in terms of calories, proteins, vitamins, and minerals, and the physiological and practical efficacy of supplementing the maternal or infant diets, when and if necessary.

However, it must be re-stressed that infant feeding cannot be considered in relation to the dietary supply of nutrients alone, but rather in an ecological context. For example, with regard to breast-feeding in less-developed countries, the nutritional and health consequences of the prevention of diarrhoeal disease (p. 285), the lactation contraceptive phenomenon (p. 118), and economic and agronomic considerations (p. 132) have to be borne in mind at the same time.

Conversely, for the majority of the world, breast-feeding cannot only be compared with adequate feeding with cow's milk — that is with sufficient formula available and with reasonable home hygiene. From a practical point of view, it is more usually a comparison of breast-feeding and formula-feeding as they exist in the nutritional, hygienic, and economic circumstances usually found in villages and urban shanty towns in resource-poor, less-developed countries, mainly in the sub-tropics and tropics.

Considerations of the volume and composition of breast milk in poorly nourished communities can only be made in relation to other ecological circumstances affecting both mother and baby (Hytten 1954a–h). However, the present chapter attempts to draw together the main relevant information from different parts of the world, in which widely varying cultural, genetic, economic, and nutritional circumstances prevail (Gunther 1952, Jelliffe and Jelliffe 1976b, Kamal et al. 1969, Karmarkar et al. 1963). Differences, when they exist, may be related mainly to nutrition, to physical overwork, or to environmental psychosocial stress. Also, other variables such as maternal parasitic diseases and genetic physiological differences may be more relevant than presently appreciated. Also, variations in results in different studies are difficult to interpret, especially those of minor degree, because of dissimilarities in times and methods of sampling and analysis, in types and levels of maternal undernutrition, and in degrees of environmental psychosocial stress (Jelliffe & Jelliffe, 1977).

(i) *Methods*

Recent work has re-emphasized the possibility of very considerable variations in findings as a result of using different biochemical methods. This is particularly so with regard to protein (p. 34).

It is difficult to obtain a truly representative sample of human milk, because the normal destination is the baby's stomach and not a test-tube or laboratory container. The ejection of breast milk is mediated by the psychosomatic let-down reflex (p. 19), and milk production is proportional to the secretion of the anterior pituitary hormone prolactin, resulting from nipple stimulation ('prolactin reflex' p. 17), and to the degree of intra-alveolar tension, related to emptying. Methods employed must, therefore avoid interfering with normal mechanisms as much as possible, but in fact, all do so considerably. As Hytten (1954) noted, 'the suckling of a baby has, for the mother, psychological overtones beyond the mere local stimulation of the areola and nipple; and the mechanical replacement of this local stimulus cannot hope to be an entirely effective substitute for the baby'.

Diurnal variations in milk volume and composition have been noted (Benedek 1956, Nims, Macy, Brown, and Hunscher 1932, Nims, Macy, Hunscher, and Brown 1932). The invariable and considerable difference in fat content between fore- and hind-milk (1–2 g/100 ml) means that the time of sampling during a feeding can be highly significant.

In addition, in some areas of the world, seasonal variation has been noted, for example lower levels of ascorbic acid in parts of Africa during the rainy season when crops have not ripened and fresh food is in short supply (Squires 1952). In Egypt, 'milk solids' are higher in winter, notably fat (Zawahry *et al*. 1974). Such seasonal changes in cattle have long been recognized by dairy farmers. The stage of lactation is another variable, as is frequency, intensity, and duration of nipple stimulation (and reflex prolactin secretion). Important reducers of such stimulation are complementary bottle feeds (*allaitement mixte*) and the early introduction of semi-solid foods (p. 201).

Likewise, data on total output are often based on day-time estimations. However, in traditional cultures, the baby sleeps by the mother's side and must obtain considerable quantities as 'night feedings' (Omolulu 1975).

Two methods can be employed to try to measure the volume produced: test-feeding and expression (Hytten 1954*b*).

Test-feeding. In this venerable technique, the baby is weighed before and after each feeding. Difficulties are numerous and obvious. Results depend on the vigour of the infant and the success of the mother–baby interaction. To ensure larger, more measurable samples, it may be considered preferable for mothers to nurse their babies at prescribed intervals rather than on demand — as under non-experimental conditions at home. Expensive, accurate scales are required to measure relatively small weight increases in an uncooperative infant. There is considerable likelihood of interference with the emotionally sensitive let-down reflex (p. 19) in the unnatural, anxiety-producing circumstances and embarrassment inevitably created by the investigations, which often have been carried out in hospitals. Practically, there may be a need for continuous surveillance to ensure that no feeding takes place between weighings, and, as noted earlier, ideally this should be on a 24 hour-basis, which is almost never possible.

Expression. Milk may be expressed from the breast manually or by some form of mechanical or electrical pump. These methods can be used to estimate total output, and, of course, are required if samples are to be obtained for analysis.

The same difficulties exist as with test-feeding. Indeed, anxiety can be greater with expression, especially with an unfamiliar, uncomfortable apparatus, possibly combined with concern over feeding the baby later with the expressed milk. Also, the influence of expression on prolactin secretion, compared with suckling by the baby, is unknown.

Comparative results have varied in different studies. In some, expression has given greater volumes; in others, test-feeding. With either, it is apparent that results are only approximations.

(ii) *Maternal nutrition*

Comparisons are also made more difficult by variables in the nutritional status of mothers, both between mothers in a particular group and between various communities, and by the possibility of different degrees of adaptation. The nutrients involved, the degree and duration of deprivation, methods of nutritional assessment, and the previous nutritional situation and stores can have many and varying combinations. There may, for example, be considerable difference between the nutritional past and present histories in poorer women in São Paulo, Brazil (Sousa 1975 *b*), in Ibadan, Nigeria (Bassir 1956, 1958, 1959, 1975), and in southern India (Gopalan and Belavady 1961).

An aspect of the situation about which nothing is known is the effect of the nutritional status of the pregnant mother towards the end of gestation on the sensitive, developing mammary glands of the female foetus (Lindblad *et al*. 1975). More directly, the physiological weight-gain in pregnancy, about one-third due to deposition of subcutaneous fat ('lactation stores'), can vary considerably from the 12·5 kg suggested for Western women to 5 kg (or even weight loss) reported in poorly-fed communities An estimated average increase in body fat of 4 kg (9 lb) represents an energy store of some 35 000 kcal, enough to subsidize lactation by nearly 300 kcal daily for 3–4 months (Hytten and Leitch 1971). Dietary inadequacy in pregnancy may be sometimes complicated by associated hard physical work and by restrictive food customs (p. 162).

Likewise, in all communities, lactation itself leads to weight loss (Table 4.1). In very ill-fed mothers this can sometimes be as much as 7 kg after a year, even leading to the development of nutritional oedema in very poorly nourished women (Bailey 1962).

Many accounts from different parts of the world suggest that malnourished women often lactate with unexpectedly little clinically obvious deterioration of their nutritional status. However, in recent years there has been increasing evidence of shorter periods of satisfactory lactation than previously (p. 190), at least in some parts of the world. The effect of maternal malnutrition may be partly hormonal, with decreased secretion of cortisol and possibly prolactin (Geissler *et al*. 1975). Certainly the cumulative effects of sequential reproductive cycles, including prolonged lactation, can lead to general 'maternal depletion', as shown by progressive weight loss and a prematurely aged appearance (Jelliffe and Maddocks 1964). More specific nutrient deficiencies may occur with repeated reproductive cycles — for example, an increasingly large goitre, anaemia, osteomalacia, or nutritional oedema (Jelliffe and Maddocks 1964).

(iii) *Environmental psychosocial stress*
It has not been sufficiently appreciated in the past that environmental psychosocial stress can have an effect on lactation performance. Such stress is occasioned by poverty and unemployment, by poor housing and crime, by illegitimacy and family instability, and by cultural confusion and uncertainty, and is probably manifested through the effect of anxiety on the let-down reflex — and possibly on the secretion of various hormones, such as cortisol (Geissler *et al*. 1975). This is mainly of concern in urban slums and shanty towns.

Despite these differences, certain general findings seem to be usual and they enable principles to be suggested on which practical action can be based. These can be considered under three headings: volume, composition, and adequacy of breast-milk in poorly nourished communities.

Volume
Well-nourished mothers
To interpret the adequacy of yields of breast-milk in mothers in communities with defective nutrition, it is plainly important to compare results with those from well-nourished communities. Unfortunately, such data are scanty, out-of-date, and difficult to compare because of differences in technique and sampling and because of recent lack of interest in the whole subject of lactation.

TABLE 4.1   *Progressive weight loss during 12 months' lactation in women of lower socio-economic status in Hyderabad, India* (from Ebrahim 1976)

	Initial	Before delivery	Immediately after delivery	Period of lactation in months 3	6	9	12
Number	82	82	82	72	59	60	56
Mean weight (kg)	41·91	48·52	42·59	41·27	40·57	40·41	40·36
Change from initial weight (kg)		+6·62	+0·68	−0·18	−1·33	−1·39	−1·61

Typical outputs of mature breast-milk in well-nourished women in the first six months of lactation may be between 600 and 700 ml/day, according to a recent interpretation by Thomson and Black (1973) of the data collected by Morrison (1952). However, much variation occurred between the results of different investigations, depending on the methods employed and the type of subjects. For example, a series of studies from Detroit contained professional wet-nurses (Macy 1949, Macy *et al*. 1953).

Carefully conducted investigation of 363 babies of normal Swedish mothers was undertaken five years ago by Wallgren (1945), using test-weighing at home for two consecutive days (Table 4.2). Recently, Lönnerdal *et al*. (1975) estimated the yield of 53 mothers in the same country by test-weighing (Table 4.3). Despite different detailed techniques and the intervening time between the studies, the results are quite similar.

TABLE 4.2   *Mean intake of breast-milk in 363 Swedish babies* (from Wallgren 1944)

Age, months	Mean intake, ml Girls	Boys
1	576	645
2	704	750
3	733	798
6	740	817

TABLE 4.3   *Daily volume of breast-milk in Swedish women* (from Lönnerdal *et al*. 1975)

Month post-partum	Number of mothers	Breast-milk volume, ml mean± s.d.
0 – ½	15	558± 83
½–1½	11	724±117
1½–3½	12	752±177
3½–6½	12	756±140

Various studies have been undertaken which have sometimes shown minor variations between the volume produced by each breast, and on different days or times of nursing. Diurnal variation in the amount secreted has also been noted, often with maximal yields in the early morning and lowest yields towards evening.

Results concerning variation with age or parity of mother have been rightly termed 'confused and inconclusive', but probably of no significance. Variation in volume of milk secreted between individual women is recognized as being considerable, although difficulties in making comparisons are great, including variation in the weight and sucking vigour of the baby. Breast size does not appear to be related to yield. However, the influence of emotional factors on milk yield has recently been re-endorsed by Lindblad *et al.* (1975) who found that hospitalization of healthy Swedish mothers merely to collect samples of milk, blood, and faeces caused a significant drop of 210 ml/24 hours.

Variation in yield with 'later' lactation is difficult to judge in well-nourished communities as, until the resurgence of interest in breast-feeding in recent years, nursing into the second semester of life or longer has not been usual in western industrialized countries. Also, there seems little doubt that the main stimulus responsible for the volume of milk produced, and hence of prolactin secreted, is the amount of sucking at the breast (p. 17). This is shown by 'induced lactation' in some traditional societies (p. 163) and by recently introduced 'adoptive lactation' or relactation in non-lactating American women, who wish to breast-feed their adopted babies. In both, frequent sucking at the breast is the main factor in initiating and continuing milk secretion. Likewise, 24 per cent of a series of twins have been shown to be solely breast-fed adequately for 3–6 months (H.L. Addy 1976). Similarly the 'perpetual', or at least very prolonged, high output by traditional wet-nurses is in part a reflection of continuing vigorous sucking stimulus by successive hungry infants. In fact, the volume of milk secreted has to be viewed against the pattern of infant feeding in the particular family (or culture) and the consequent degree of sucking stimulus and its effect on the prolactin secretion.

The common concept of the normal pattern in Western-type cultures is of rise in output in the first month or so, followed by a decline thereafter to a plateau lasting until the baby is about six months of age, followed by a slow decline thereafter. Consideration of lactation patterns elsewhere and the previously mentioned results in twins, in wet-nurses, in induced lactation, and in relactation, suggest that the Western pattern may not be a biologically inevitable fact, but rather a response to a particular pattern of sucking stimulation.

Very few studies have been undertaken on dietary effects on the volume of milk produced in well-nourished women. By contrast, numerous investigations have shown that variation in water intake between wide limits by the mother has no physiological effect on the volume of milk secreted. This seems endocrinologically explicable in light of the renal anti-diuretic, water-sparing effect of prolactin (Horrobin *et al*. 1971). The common belief that fluid intake affects milk yield probably operates more through a 'sympathetic magic' effect on confidence ('fluid in = fluid out'), and hence on the psychosomatic let-down reflex (p. 19).

Poorly nourished mothers
Estimations of the volume of breast-milk produced have also been undertaken in a variety of countries in Asia and Africa, and in New Guinea. The results have been extracted from published information and these approximations are presented in Table 4.4. Despite differences in methods of collection, sampling, and analysis, and levels and forms of maternal undernutrition (Janz *et al*. 1957), it seems that the volumes produced were usually somewhat below those reported from well-nourished countries in Europe and north America.

Volumes reported varied greatly and seem to be lowest in communities with poor levels of nutrition and with inadequate living conditions, whether urban (Colombo, Sri Lanka (De Silva 1964)) or rural (New Guinea highlands (Bailey 1965)). However, working approximations in round figures can be suggested: 500–700 ml/day in the first six months of life, 400–600 ml/day in the second six months, and 300–500 ml/day in the second year. The few studies undertaken in the third year of lactation show very considerable differences, varying from 230 to 488 ml/day.

Also, it is well recognized in practice that the milk output of extremely malnourished mothers in famines declines and ultimately ceases, with fatal consequences for the nursing baby (Jelliffe and Jelliffe 1971 *b*). The nutritional point at which human lactation becomes seriously inhibited or ceases in famine circumstances is not known, but early marasmus (in the first six months of life) in solely breast-fed babies may be occurring increasingly in the babies of very poorly nourished women, for example in Karachi, Pakistan (Lindblad and Rahimtoola 1974). Sometimes this may be partly 'contraceptive marasmus', from further interference with breast-milk secretions by oestrogen-containing contraceptive pills (p. 121). In parts of the world with seasonal food shortages ('hungry seasons'), as in central Africa, the daily output may drop by 100–200 ml (Vis 1976).

Supplementation
Limited studies have been carried out on the effect on output of supplementation of the mother's diet. Gopalan (1958) showed an increase in volume secreted from 420 to 540 ml, in poorly nourished Indian women following protein supplementation (from 61 g/day to 99 g/day). Similar results were obtained in Western Nigeria by Bassir (1975) using a vegetable-protein supplement (30 g of soya flour daily). Another study in India, where inadequately nourished mothers were fed with milk biscuits, showed a rise in

TABLE 4.4 *Approximate quantities of milk produced daily at different periods of lactation in some poorly nourished communities**

Country and reference	1–6 months, ml	6–12 months, ml	12–24 months, ml	24 months and over, ml
India (Belavady 1963, 1969)	600	500	350	—
India (Baroda) (Rajalakshmi and Ramakrishnan 1969)	660 (3 months) (range 350–1100)	735 (6 months) (range 540–1100)		
New Guinea, Chimbu (Venkatachalam 1962)	525	525	343	142–343
Biak Island (Jansen et al. 1960)	427	390–430	127–338	243
New Guinea (Becroft 1967)	720	660	705	448
New Guinea, Chimbu and Maprik (Bailey 1965)	400	400	400	—
New Guinea, Baiyer River (Bailey 1965)	600	600	600	—
New Guinea, Ajamaru (Oomen 1961)	—	350–480	270–360 (12–18 months) 230–310 (18–24 months)	230–300
New Guinea, Nubuai (Oomen 1961)	—	310–410	250–340 (12–18 months) 150–210 (18–24 months)	—
Egypt: healthy	922	—	—	—
malnourished (Hanafy et al. 1972)	733	—	—	—
Sri Lanka (De Silva 1964)	475	495	506	—
Nigeria, Benin (Johnson et al. 1975)	555 (2–3 months)	590 (6–9 months)		
Mexico (Chavez et al. 1975, 1976)	650	400–500	350	—

TABLE 4.5 *Effect of maternal dietary supplementation with protein on the volume and protein content of breast-milk and weight gained by baby (Nigeria) (from Edozien et al 1976)*

	Daily protein intake					
	50 g Initially, mean±s.d.	100 g mean±s.d.	P	25 g Initially mean±s.d.	100 g mean±s.d.	P
No. of subjects	7	7		3	3	
Total milk solids, g100 ml	13·8 ±1·3	13·4 ±0·9		12·0 ±0·6	11·9 ±0·5	
Milk protein, g/100 ml	1·61±0·15	1·57±0·19		1·20±0·21	1·25±0·23	
Milk lactose, g/100 ml	8·1 ±0·9	7·9 ±1·0		7·3 ±1·4	8·0 ±1·8	
Milk produced, ml/day	742±16	872±32	<0·05	817±59	1059±63	<0·05
Milk consumed, ml/day	617±15	719±10	<0·05	777±38	996±74	<0·05
Weight gained by baby, g/day	30·4 ±3·6	45·7 ±2·0	<0·05	10·5 ±3·6	32·2 ±10·1	<0·05

Subjects were fed the initial diets for the first 14 days and then a diet providing 100 g protein/day for the next 14 days. Results for each subject represent the mean values for milk samples collected during days 8–14 (for initial diet) and days 21–28 (for diet providing 100 g protein/day). Duration of lactation for all subjects was between 30 and 90 days.

serum albumen paralleled by increase in albumen in the breast-milk, presumably by 'spill-over' (Deb and Cama 1962). An early investigation in
1931 showed that an increase in output of breast-milk could be achieved in
New Zealand women by increasing the calorie and/or the protein intake.
Recently, a study in England seemed to suggest that poor lactation could be
related to inadequate energy reserves, in the form of subcutaneous fat laid
down in pregnancy, and calorie intakes in lactation. In the U.K., slimming
diets in lactating mothers lead to 'an immediate reduction in milk supply'
(Whichelow 1975, 1976).

A recent detailed investigation by Edozien *et al.* (1976) from Nigeria
showed that protein supplementation of the lactating mother's diet
increased the milk produced and the weight-gain in the baby, but not the
protein content of the milk (Table 4.5). Similarly, Sosa *et al.* (1976) demonstrated a rapid increase in milk production in a malnourished Guatemalan
woman following a diet, improved particularly in calories and protein
(Fig. 4.1).

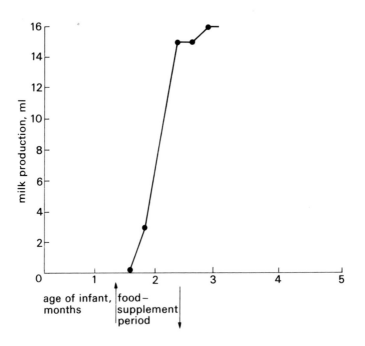

Fig. 4.1. Increase in milk production per feed in severely malnourished Guatemalan
woman following a food supplementation of her diet, particularly with calories and
protein. Milk production was estimated by measuring the amount of milk obtained
from each breast by a hand pump, one hour after feeding the baby (from Sosa, R.,
Klaus, M., and Urrutia, J. J. (1976). *J. Pediat.* **88**, 668)

As usual, those concerned with the production of cow's milk as a business, the dairy farmers, have infinitely more practical knowledge than those concerned with human milk and breast-feeding. Thus, Lindblad and colleagues (1975) quoted the following aphorism from Morrison's 1948 *Handbook of Stockmen*, which may not be completely correct for the human, but is certainly generally so: 'Any inadequacy in the ration or fault in the methods of care or management will generally manifest itself in the yield of milk, rather than by a change in its chemical composition.'

However, the effect of increasing the maternal diet on human milk output may be less than in dairy cows, since it should be remembered that such farm animals have been bred to produce much greater yields than are required by the offspring (Thomson and Black 1973).

Composition

The biochemical composition of human milk has been examined in different parts of the world. Comparison can be made between various communities, and with well-nourished mothers, for protein, fat, lactose, vitamins, and calcium, keeping in mind previously-mentioned variations with sampling (period in lactation cycle; single, repeated or 24-hour samples; season; one subject or pooled specimens; etc.), with laboratory techniques, and with levels of maternal nutrition (Table 4.6).

(i) *Protein*

The protein content of human milk has been described as varying between $1 \cdot 0$ and $1 \cdot 6$ g/100 ml in well-nourished women. Morrison (1952) reported the mean of European analyses to be $1 \cdot 6$ g/100 ml and American $1 \cdot 2$ g/100 ml. He suggested that differences in methods of estimation may be mainly responsible, and that $1 \cdot 2$ g/100 ml probably represented an overall mean. There seems little evidence for significant diurnal variation or fluctuation with age or parity.

However, very recent Swedish studies (Hambraeus *et al.* 1977) have shown the protein content to be only $0 \cdot 8$–$0 \cdot 9$ g/100 ml in apparently-well nourished women in that country, when determined by amino-acid analysis. These investigators pointed out that earlier analyses of breast-milk were made with the same methods as used for cow's milk.

Retrospective examination of analyses undertaken with similar methods in Brussels (Soupart *et al.* 1954) and in Tokyo (Saito *et al.* 1965) shows similar 'low' levels for 'true protein content' as with recent Swedish figures.

In poorer, technically developing countries, the average protein content of the milk of inadequately nourished mothers, based on previously used methods of total nitrogen assessment, is usually surprisingly high ($1 \cdot 0$–$1 \cdot 1$ g/100 ml), although the range may be quite wide (Table 4.6).

In some places with probably poorer nutrition, analyses with older methods have sometimes shown the protein content to be lower

TABLE 4.6 *Fat, lactose, protein, and calcium content of mature human milk from some well nourished and poorly nourished communities*[*]

	Fat, g/100 ml	Lactose, g/100 ml	Protein, g/100 ml	Calcium, mg/100 ml
Well-nourished				
America (Macy 1949)	4·5	6·8	1·1	34·0
Britain (Kon and Mawson 1960)	4·78	6·95	1·16	29·9
Australia (Winikoff 1944)	—	—	—	28·6-30·7
America and Europe (combined means) (Morrison 1952)	3·33±s.d. 0·57	7·2±s.d. 0·67	1·32±s.d. 0·32	—
Egypt, Alexandria (healthy women) (Hanafy et al. 1972)	4·43	6·65	1·09	—
Brazil (high economic status) (Carneiro and Dutra 1973)	3·9	6·8	1·3	20·8
Poorly-nourished				
India (Belavady and Gopalan 1959)	3·42	7·51	1·06	34·2
S. Africa, Bantu (Walker, Arvidsson, and Draper 1952)	3·90	7·10	1·35	28·7
Egypt, Alexandria (Hanafy et al. 1972)	4·01	6·48	0·93	—
New Guinea (Becroft 1967)	2·3	6·48	0·93	—
Sri Lanka (De Silva 1964)	2·8	6·8	1·5	—

Brazil (low economic status) (Carneiro and Dutra 1973)	4·2	6·5	1·3	25·7
Pakistan (Underwood et al. 1970)	1·3–2·9	—	1·2	—
Tanzania (Crawford et al. 1974)	often below 2·00	—	—	—
Nigeria, Ibadan (Naismith 1973)	4·05	7·67	1·22	—
Pakistan (Lindblad and Rahimtoola 1974)	2·73	6·20	0·8–0·9	28·4
New Guinea Highlands, Chimbu (Venkatachalam 1962)	2·36	7·34	1·01	—
New Hebrides (Peters 1953)	3·8	5·0	1·40	25·8
Germany, Wuppertal (Immediately after World War II) (Gunther and Stanier 1951)	3·59	—	1·20	—
Nauru (Bray 1928)	—	—	1·06	—
Nigeria, Ibadan (E.F.P. Jelliffe 1974)	—	—	1·1	—
New Guinea, Biak (Jansen et al. 1960)	—	—	0·83–0·9	—

* Modified from Gopalan and Belavady (1961) with added data.

(0·8–0·9 g/100 ml). However, in a careful study of poorly nourished women in Karachi, Pakistan (Lindblad and Rahimtoola 1974), the 'true protein content', determined by an exchange chromatography after acid hydrolysis and addition of the calculated amino-acid residues, was 0·8±0·1 g/100 ml. These results are comparable to those obtained by similar techniques in Sweden, Belgium, and Japan, although the lysine and methionine levels were lower.

Varying results have been obtained with estimations of the protein content in what is termed by modern Western cultural definition 'prolonged lactation' — that is breast-feeding into the second year of life and later. Some have found a decline, some a rise, and others no material change. Likewise, one study demonstrated that breast-feeding continued into the following pregnancy was associated with milk of an unchanged protein content (Gopalan and Naidu 1972).

The effect of maternal dietary supplementation on protein content does not appear to have been investigated adequately. However, in the protein-supplementation study carried out by Gopalan (1958), the increased output of milk was associated with a corresponding fall in protein concentration, with the result that the total protein output in 24 hours was not significantly altered. Modern laboratory methods such as immunoelectrophoresis, which enables accurate quantities and measurement of the individual proteins of milk to be made, were not available at the time of earlier studies.

Recent investigations by Lönnerdal *et al.* (1975 *a*, 3b) have shown many unexplained variations in healthy, well-fed women, for example in milk-specific proteins (those synthesized by the mammary gland), notably α -lactalbumin and lactoferrin. The decrease in total nitrogen in the first period of lactation, for example in the first month, was mainly due to a dramatic drop in the level of secretory IgA.

(ii) *Fat*

The significance of the fat content of milk has been under-emphasized. It is the main source of calories; it contains fat soluble vitamins, especially vitamin A; it is also the source of fatty acids needed for the growth and development of the central nervous system. Lastly, the higher fat in the after-milk may act as an appetite control for the sucking baby (p. 56).

The fatty-acid pattern of breast-milk can be altered to some extent without affecting milk volume or milk fat output by variation in the types of dietary fat or by changes in the calorie intake (Insull *et al.* 1959, Wellby *et al.* 1973). During energy equilibrium, milk fat resembles the fatty-acid pattern of dietary fat, but when inadequate calories are eaten, the fat in human milk follows the composition of human subcutaneous depot fat. The major factor influencing the fatty-acid composition of milk is the carbohydrate supply in the diet. High lauric and myristic content was found in milk in Tanzania by Read *et al.* (1965) in comparison with milk from women in Jordan, Saudi

Arabia, and Lebanon. Seventy-five per cent of calories in the diet of the Tanzanian mothers was derived from carbohydrate and only 7 per cent from fat. Linoleic acid was high in the Lebanese diet and low in the Bedouin diet, and led to significantly increased and decreased levels respectively in the mother's milk. Ultimately, the fatty-acid composition of the breast-milk (or cow's-milk-based formula) appears to be reflected in the fatty acids in the infant's subcutaneous fat (p. 32).

The relevance of the fatty-acid (and cholesterol) contents of human milk is currently under consideration in relation to the development of the central nervous system (p. 32) and atheroma in adults in industrialized countries (p. 255). In developing regions, the polyenoic fatty acids may be diminished in the breast-milk of malnourished mothers, with possible ill-consequences in relation to brain growth (Crawford *et al.* 1974).

(iii) *Lactose*
The third 'proximate principle', lactose, is generally recognized as being most constant in concentration and shows no diurnal variation. Morrison's (1952) figure based on 1010 samples examined in various American and European studies showed a mean of $7 \cdot 2$ g/100 ml, while Kon and Mawson (1950) found $6 \cdot 9$ g/100 ml in 586 samples of mature milk. In poorly nourished mothers, lactose does not seem to vary very much (Table 4.6) (range $6 \cdot 20$–$7 \cdot 67$ g/100 ml), except in one study in the New Hebrides where $5 \cdot 0$ per cent was reported (Peters 1953).

(iv) *Calories*
The calorie intake from breast-milk is a product of the volume produced (or taken by the baby) and its caloric content, which is primarily derived from fat, together with lactose and possibly protein. In well-fed communities, the caloric content varies greatly. Macy, Kelly, and Sloan give a mean figure of 75 calories per 100 ml (range 45–119).

In poorly nourished communities, both the volume secreted and the fat, the main calorie containing constituent, (and other nutrients) may be less than in well-fed mothers.

(v) *Vitamins*
Vitamin A. The concentration is influenced by the adequacy of the diet of the mother in pregnancy and lactation (Belavady 1969, Belavady and Gopalan 1959, Gebre-Mehdin *et al.* 1976). The vitamin-A content of breast-milk is often much lower in poorer populations of some developing countries (India, Ceylon, Indonesia, Jordan), where this nutrient is marginal, than in Europe and North America. Maternal serum levels are also low. The intake is generally higher in the spring and summer months due to greater supplies of dark-green leafy and yellow vegetables. Particularly high levels of retinol (vitamin A) and linoleic acid have been noted in Western Nigeria, presuma-

bly because of the widespread use of palm oil in cooking (Naismith 1973).

In a recent comparative investigation, the vitamin-A content of breast-milk was significantly higher in normal Swedish mothers than in non-privileged Ethiopian mothers, whose milk showed greater concentrations of β -carotene (Gebre-Mehdin *et al*. 1976).

Kon and Mawson (1950) found that supplementation with vitamin A, before and after parturition or later during lactation, led to the secretion of milk richer in vitamin A than normally produced. In central America, Arroyave *et al*. (1974) observed that a rise in the level of vitamin A in breast-milk followed the introduction of vitamin-A fortified sugar in the diet.

Thiamine. The thiamine content of breast-milk in areas with a high incidence of infantile beriberi has been found to be low, due to insufficient maternal stores and intake in communities with diets largely based on polished rice (Simpson and Chow 1956). Under these circumstances, this specific form of malnutrition — infantile beriberi — occurs exclusively in apparently normal breast-fed babies, and is due to a thiamine-deficient diet in the mother during pregnancy and lactation. It is so characteristic in time of onset that the 2–5-month mortality has been suggested as an age-specific rate for this condition in the regions at risk (D.B. Jelliffe 1966*a*).

Riboflavin. Human milk is a good source of riboflavin, provided the maternal diet is adequate. However, in south India, Gopalan and Belavady (1961) found an average of only $17 \cdot 2\,\mu g/100$ ml of riboflavin in breast-milk, as compared with a value of about 25 μg/100 ml found by Kon and Mawson (1950) in Britain.

Vitamin B12. Low levels of vitamin B_{12} have been found in the milk of poorer vegetarian women in Bombay (Jathar *et al*. 1970), and in various parts of India the 'syndrome of tremors', described in solely breast-fed babies, has been ascribed to a deficiency of vitamin B_{12} in the mother's milk (Jadhar *et al*. 1962).

Vitamin C. The level of ascorbic acid (vitamin C) in breast-milk is subject to variations in dietary intake, particularly with the seasonal availability of fresh fruits and vegetables (Ingalls *et al*. 1938, Rajalakshmi *et al*. 1974, Stransky *et al*. 1950, Stuart and Connelhan 1973). In well-nourished mothers, human milk contains an average of 4 mg/100 ml of vitamin C. In Botswana (formerly Bechuanaland), Squires (1952) found the content to be $1 \cdot 7$ mg/100 ml in the dry season and $2 \cdot 7$ mg/100 ml in the wet seasons. The subjects were poorly nourished Tswana women.

Since the ascorbic-acid content of breast-milk (Rajalakshmi*et al*. 1974) is greater than that of blood plasma, which is generally below $2 \cdot 5$ mg/100 ml, secretory activity in the mammary glands must play a part in determining the level of vitamin C in milk. Apparent adaptation to low maternal intakes of vitamin C have been noted in Baroda, India (Rajalakshmi *et al*. 1974) and the Philippines (Stransky *et al*. 1950). The possibility of placental synthesis in pregnancy has been suggested. Certainly both the placenta and the breasts appear to be able to actively secrete ascorbic acid for the offspring.

Levels of folic acid and vitamin B_6 seem to reflect maternal nutritional status (Nogueira *et al*. 1966, Kirksey and West 1975).

Vitamin supplementation. Deodhar and Ramakrishnan (1960) carried out a dietary survey among women in south India with special reference to pantothenic acid, riboflavin, nicotinic acid, ascorbic acid, and thiamin. Subsequently, the breast-milk was analysed for the concentrations of the same vitamins. A positive and significant correlation was found between dietary intake and vitamin content of the milk for the vitamins investigated, which underlines the need for an adequate diet for the lactating women.

In a more recent investigation (Deodhar *et al*. 1964), supplementation with ascorbic acid, nicotinic acid, riboflavin, thiamin, pantothenic acid, cyanocobalamin, biotin, pyridoxine, and folic acid was undertaken. As a result, the vitamin content of the milk increased steadily with the dose used in supplementation.

(iv) *Calcium*

Levels of calcium reported in the milk of well-fed mothers vary considerably. The calcium content in poorly nourished mothers has been reported to range from 'normal' levels to somewhat low concentrations (Table 4.6). Again, differences in sampling and technique may be in part responsible.

Levels of other minerals will not be considered here. Analyses are given elsewhere by Morrison (1952). The question of the content of trace minerals will be much under investigation in coming years, in relation both to nutritional need (p. 50) and to possible effects of environmental pollution (p. 105).

Adequacy

The nutritional adequacy of breast-milk for the infant can be roughly assessed by measuring 24-hour output and chemical composition, or by recording of satisfactory growth, 'good health', and absence of clinical malnutrition.

Adequacy of nutrients

The nutrient needs of the baby during the exterogestate-foetal stage are not derived only from the diet, but also from foetal stores acquired *in utero*, from the placental transfusion (iron), and to a limited and variable extent from ultraviolet irradiation of the skin (vitamin D). The Recommended Dietary Allowances for babies are estimated mainly by analogy with breast-fed infants (National Academy of Sciences 1974), and yet it is agreed increasingly that presently available data on the composition of human milk are incomplete and out of date. Fomon (1974) rightly notes the need for more modern studies, and remarks that 'until such data are available, many of our calculations relating to nutrients in human milk will be likely to be misleading'.

In this regard, it is often insufficiently appreciated that the Recommended Dietary Allowances given for infants are themselves derived from estimated intakes of breast-fed babies, with an additional safety factor added for the less certain situation of infants fed on cow's-milk formulas (Jelliffe, Ifekwunigwe, and Jelliffe 1975). This is the case, for example, with the very high Recommended Dietary Allowance of iron (10 mg/day) for the first six months of life, which can not be attained with human milk (National Academy of Sciences 1974).

The derivations of Recommended Dietary Allowances (RDAs) for infants are often not understood by paediatricians or nutritionists, so that the advertisers of commercial baby foods for physicians can issue the following appeal to 'logic':

A stimulating exercise for professionals would be sorting one's beliefs about breast feeding into those based on scientific fact and those stemming from hearsay and emotion. One could thus more objectively counsel that growing membership in lay organizations dedicated to breast feeding. Many sincerely believe that breast milk is all sufficient without any supplementation for at least six months if not the full duration of breast feeding. The fallacy of this concept is obvious if one compares the nutrient content of breast milk with recommended RDA for infants.

The inanity of this comment is apparent especially in view of the biological adaptation that has occurred over hundreds of millennia. Carried to extremes, this argument would mean that breast-milk was unfit for consumption by human babies, without additional iron or vitamins. Barrie (1976), in supporting the scientific advances of 'modified milks', pursues this bizarre argument: 'Its (breast-milk) poor vitamin C, D and iron content necessitates supplementing these substances by other means. Its borderline protein content is probably inadequate for the greater demand of the premature and low-birth-weight infant'.

The Recommended Daily Allowances of protein and calories suggested for infants have been very considerably derived from the important, but special, studies by Fomon and May (1958) on babies bottle-fed *ad libitum* with pasteurized breast-milk. Based on their findings, it has been suggested that infants need:

1st month: 836 ml/day (protein 2·6 g/kg body-weight; cals. 143/kg body-weight)

6th month: 990 ml/day (protein 1·7 g/kg body-weight; cals. 90/kg body-weight)

However, as noted earlier, outputs in well-nourished groups are usually lower than this, a common range being 600–700 ml/day for the first six months. Among poorly nourished tropical communities estimated volumes often seem to range from 500 to 700 ml/day during the first six months (Table 4.4).

As noted earlier (p. 70), many of the constituents of breast-milk can be affected by inadequate maternal nutrition, depending upon its severity, length, and the mothers's previous nutritional status. Water-soluble vitamins are particularly affected, including ascorbic acid and riboflavin. Likewise, levels of vitamin A and the pattern of fatty acids reflect maternal diet and stores. The protein content of human milk in poorly nourished women is usually within 'normal' limits $(1 \cdot 0 – 1 \cdot 1\,g/100\,ml)$ or sometimes somewhat below this $(0 \cdot 7 – 0 \cdot 9\,g/100\,ml)$ (Table 4.6).

By comparison with estimates of volume and composition in well-fed mothers, information derived from poorly nourished women suggests that their babies may sometimes receive lesser intakes of nutrients. However, five factors need to be taken into account before making too sweeping conclusions:

(i) The figures on volume gained in general studies are often those obtained by expression or following test-feeding with the errors implicit, and often having a risk of underestimations because of interference with the psychosomatic let-down reflex and inadequate stimulation of prolactin production.

(ii) Such investigations are usually based on day-time output, when, in most traditional cultures, babies sleep by the mothers side with frequent night-feedings the normal practice.

(iii) There is a possibility of lower calorie intakes being needed by infants in truly tropical areas, such as India.

(iv) Smaller babies have a lesser need of nutrients, but also may have less sucking potential.

(v) The data on which the Recommended Dietary Allowances are based are inadequate and approximate for infants. The babies in the Fomon and May investigation were receiving *pasteurized* breast-milk from a feeding bottle, with an easier rate of flow and without the possibly appetite-controlling function of high fat found in the hind-milk (Hall 1975), and possibly other 'powerful self-regulatory controls within the infant' (Ounsted and Sleighs 1975). In other words, the intake of milk noted, and hence of calories and protein recommended, are probably high. As noted earlier (p. 60), the reported consumption of milk in direct breast-feeding studies are lower — for example in the two Swedish studies (Tables 4.2 and 3).

The difficulties with understanding the meaning of results obtained by analysis of single samples are increased by recent increased awareness of the physiological variation in human milk composition (p. 59), and by the need to recognize breast-milk as a biological system with interacting nutrients, which modify absorption and utilization, rather than as a solution of independent chemicals.

Adequacy by growth
It is apparent that the ultimate test of the adequacy of human milk output in breast-feeding is not reflected by estimates of volume produced or by the composition, but rather by assessment of physical growth, metabolic

equilibrium, and 'good health and nutrition'. From an immediate and rough point of view, adequate growth is normally assessed anthropometrically, usually judged approximately by serial weight gain, and by the absence of recognizable nutritional deficiency, as the main practical yard-sticks. Laboratory tests for specific nutrients may rarely be possible, but in any case, are often difficult to evaluate. Clinical impressions concerning 'good health', vigour, and well-being are helpful, but impossible to measure objectively.

There is sufficient evidence from widely scattered areas, including such diverse sources as the U.S.A. (Jackson *et al*. 1964), and the People's Republic of China (Shanghai Child Health Co-ordination Group 1976), that *solely* breast-fed infants do well and show satisfactory gains in weight during the first six months or so of life when the lactating mothers are well nourished. From about six months, flattening of the weight curve usually indicates that the intake of calories and protein are no longer adequate; in other words, that the baby has outgrown the breast as a *sole* source of food.

The adequacy of unsupplemented human milk (and the prolactin-mediated 'supply and demand' nature of breast-feeding) is indicated by a recent investigation of 173 pairs of twins in southern California (H.L. Addy 1976); $23 \cdot 7$ per cent of the pairs were breast-fed, and, of these, $59 \cdot 5$ per cent received no food other than human milk for three months or more, and $21 \cdot 9$ per cent for 6 months or more. Growth is being investigated in detail, but in general seemed comparable to those bottle-fed.

With the babies of poorly nourished mothers in resource-poor, technically developing countries, difficulties in interpreting growth curves exist in relation to the prevalence and significance of low birth-weights in the particular community, in the selection of reference standards thought to be the most appropriate for the particular group, the significance of infections (including diarrhoea with fluid loss), and the usual problem of sorting out weight gain in relation to increases in fat, muscle, or water-electrolyte retention.

Earlier evidence from various parts of Africa and India in the 1950s indicated that breast-feeding, with little or no supplementation, resulted in excellent growth for about the first 5–6 months of life (Gopalan 1958, D.B. Jelliffe 1968 *b*, Welbourn 1955).

However, as a generalization, more recent studies from such varied, but all poorly nourished, parts of the world as New Guinea (Bailey 1965), Ethiopia (Eksmyr 1969), and Tanzania (Poeplau and Schlage 1969), often show comparable weight curves to those of Western standards of reference only up to about 4 months of age. However, in some studies growth has continued to be similar up to 5 months of age, as in Malaysia (Dugdale 1961), while in other investigations in Jordan (Kimmance 1972), in north eastern Tanzania (Poeplau and Schlage 1969), and in Mexico (Martinez and Chavez 1971, Chavez *et al*. 1975, 1976) the weight gain in some babies was reported to have become inadequate after only 3 months. It seems possible, then, that decreasing lengths of satisfactory lactation are becoming evident in poorer communities in some less developed countries, perhaps especially in slum areas.

Conclusions

The investigations summarized in the present account of knowledge concerning the quantity and quality of human milk in both well and poorly nourished communities in different ecological circumstances are very far from satisfactory. Understandably, studies have on the whole been piecemeal with different emphases and techniques employed by various investigators.

It is not usually appreciated that until the 1975 studies in Sweden (Hambraeus *et al*. 1977) and New Zealand (Mickelson *et al*. 1975), the most recent investigations in well-nourished communities were made about a quarter of a century ago.

Likewise, the technical difficulties of obtaining representative samples, especially on a 24-hour basis, can be almost insuperable, especially in the field. The degrees of severity, chronicity, and specificity of maternal malnutrition (and of maternal depletion from numerous previous reproductive cycles) are rarely indicated, and indeed, with many of these variables are difficult to classify. Lastly, the questions of genetic differences in lactation ability in different human groups has never been explored adequately (Lutz and Platt 1958, Prinsloo *et al*. 1970), and would be difficult to undertake, because of variations in diet and forms of environmental psychosocial stress.

At another level altogether is the fact that most research undertaken has been concerned with gross analyses of occasional samples, with no recognition of the degree of variation seen normally or of the more newly recognized considerations mentioned elsewhere, such as the pattern of amino acids, the different protein components, polyenoic fatty acids, polyamines, and nucleotides, and the presence of anti-infective substances.

There is a need for co-ordinated comparative modern studies into all aspects of human lactation in well-fed and in poorly-nourished communities, using similar sampling methods and analytic techniques. These would include investigations covering the volume and major nutrients, preferably in more than one 24-hour sample, as well as more recently recognized biochemical components and physio-chemical elements (such as the forms of casein present) in different communities with various levels of maternal over- and under-nutrition, including women using oral contraceptives (p. 121).

Generalizations

Nevertheless, present-day incomplete knowledge appears to warrant the following generalizations for practical action:

(i) Unsupplemented human milk is all that is required to sustain growth and good nutrition for the first six months of life in the babies of well-nourished mothers, who have produced foetuses with optimal stores, who

have themselves laid down adequate nutritional reserves, including subcutaneous fat, in pregnancy, and who are well-fed during lactation (Jelliffe,
Gurney, and Jelliffe 1975).

(ii) The volume and composition of human milk in poorly nourished
women is surprisingly good, possibly due to some metabolic adaptations, but
probably usually to their cumulative nutritional detriment ('maternal depletion'). However, it is often suboptimal in quantity and in quality with lower
values of fat (calories), water-soluble vitamins, vitamin A, calcium, and
protein, than in well-nourished women.

(iii) Limited studies with supplementary feeding of poorly-nourished
lactating women (and common sense) have suggested improvement in volume of output and in nutritional quality of breast-milk to be feasible.

(iv) The adequacy of breast-milk as the sole food for the baby is related to
the mother's diet in pregnancy; to maternal puerperal calorie reserves in the
form of subcutaneous fat; to foetal stores (Iyengar and Apte 1972), mainly
hepatic; to birth-weight (Lechtig *et al*. 1975); and to the iron obtained from
the placental transfusion.

(v) Breast-milk produced in so-called 'late lactation' (i.e. 7 months to 2
years or more) is insufficient by itself for the rising nutrient needs (and
declining stores) of the rapidly growing infant, and forms a decreasing, but
valuable supplementary source of 'complete' protein, and of fat, calcium,
and vitamins.*

Practical approaches
If growth, as evidenced by the weight curve, becomes inadequate in solely
breast-fed babies at four months or earlier in poor communities in less-
developed countries, it is necessary to consider why this should be the case.
Maternal nutrition is often considered as though it was occurring in isolation, with the mother as a temperament-less, disease-free 'breast-machine'.
As Lindblad *et al*. note: 'The most important variable behind lactation
failure in poor women, namely milk volume, does not seem to be primarily
dependent on food intake, but the combined stress of maternal disease,
undernutrition, and the increasingly difficult living conditions in rapidly
developing city slum areas' (Lindblad *et al*. 1975).

It follows, therefore, that diagnosis of an individual and a community in
relation to lactation failure must be concerned with factors considered to be
responsiole in some measure, including maternal infections and environmental psychosocial stress. Nevertheless, the two main forms of interference
with lactation performance appear to be through the maternal reflexes and

* Rohde (1975*b*) in Indonesia comments that, in domestic terms, the output in the second year
means that the child is receiving at least one 8-oz glass of milk daily, with 3–5 g protein
(supplementary to the usual vegetable-protein weaning diet), essential fatty acids, and
200–500 I.U. of vitamin A. In well-fed mothers, Findlay (1974*a*) notes that approximately ¾
of major nutrient needs are met by breast-milk from 6–12 months.

through nutrition, so that the relative significance of these two requires consideration in any individual woman or community.

Interference with reflexes. Present-day infant feeding practices in the particular area should be scrutinized to identify possible practices which may be affecting the two main maternal reflexes responsible for the production and ejection of milk: the prolactin and the let-down reflexes.

Various factors may be found in the traditional culture or, more often, in the stressful nature of urban life or imported Westernized practices in maternity units which reduce sucking stimulus and, hence, diminish the prolactin secretion (such as the separation of mother and baby in the maternity unit or the taboo in breast-feeding in public) and/or create uncertainty and anxiety and thus inhibit the let-down reflex, such as the impact of poverty, advertising of formula milks, or breakdown of family ties.

There is little doubt that disturbed reflex behaviour is often more important in the causation of lactation failure than maternal subnutrition, unless severe. In devising an appropriate programme to improve breast-feeding, both aspects need consideration.

Inadequate maternal nutrition. If the infant is judged to be receiving breast-milk which is insufficient in volume and/or composition because of poor maternal nutrition, three approaches need to be considered:

(1) Cow's-milk supplementation. A 'logical' possible solution may seem to be the introduction of bottle-feeds with cow's-milk-based formulas from just prior to the usual age of flattening of the weight curve.

In the circumstances of most resource-poor, less developed countries, this approach (*allaitement mixte*) should usually be avoided. It introduces the danger of weaning diarrhoea (p. 285) at an early and vulnerable age. It decreases the secretion of breast-milk, as it interferes with sucking stimulation and proportional secretion of pituitary prolactin. It is an additional endorsement by the paediatric nutritionist of the unfortunate trend away from breast-feeding. Lastly, if viewed on a family or on a large-scale community basis, it has economic and agronomic consequences of very considerable dimensions (p. 132).

(2) Early introduction of semi-solids. Again, in the circumstances found in most parts of the world, the risks of weaning diarrhoea are great if unavoidably unclean semi-solid foods are introduced before needed nutritionally. Also, in average kitchen circumstances in tropical countries and with the foods most usually available, it is very difficult to prepare digestible, well-tolerated, and nutritionally adequate supplementary semi-solid foods for an infant in the first months of life. However, the introduction of semi-solids by cup or by spoon would have less effect on lactation performance than cow's milk by bottle and can be based on the use of mixtures of locally available foods, nutritionally blended as 'multi-mixes', particularly cereal-legume blends.

(3) Supplementation of maternal diet. Current knowledge suggests that the most economical, safe, physiologically sound, and practicable method of approaching the situation is by laying maximum emphasis on feeding the mother during *both* pregnancy and lactation.* Some nutrient stores may be replenished rapidly (e.g. vitamin C); some will take months, particularly calories (subcutaneous fat) and protein (muscle). An optimal diet in pregnancy leads to improved foetal stores and a higher birth-weight and more vigorous baby.

Adequate feeding, again based on 'multi-mixes' of locally available foods or sometimes on maternal dietary supplements, *during pregnancy* (as well as lactation) can assist in ensuring adequate maternal weight-gain and sufficient nutrient stores. Similarly, an appropriate maternal diet, again based on locally available food mixtures, should be the emphasis during lactation, with semi-solids slowly introduced to the baby, probably from about the age of 4–6 months onwards, depending on local circumstances, particularly the usual weight curve in infancy in the community concerned. Recent studies have shown that the main additional nutrients needed during lactation are less than previously thought, and that they can usually be obtained from economical, everyday foods. In the still relatively affluent Western world, with food increasing greatly in cost but still abundant, probably most mothers obtain their extra calories (and probably most other nutrients also) with little extra expense by taking somewhat larger portions of the dishes in their everyday diet. However, guidance may be needed in widening that diet, and one wonders whether the Nutrition Section, Ministry of Agriculture, or other appropriate body, could suggest economical and culturally acceptable additions to the diet during lactation (and pregnancy). In other words, a mother could be advised not only that she needs more calories and protein but also that these can be obtained by eating more mashed potato (with milk) or bread-and-cheese, rather than by consuming large volumes of milk or other animal products (Jelliffe and Jelliffe 1976*b*).

Evidence for the adequacy of human milk as the sole food for young infants up to 6 months is available, at least in well-nourished communities. There is evidence of improvement in lactation performance, especially the volume of milk produced, with dietary supplementation in less well-fed circumstances (Table 4.4, Fig. 4.1).

The message seems clear. As with so much else concerning the health and nutrition of young children, the emphasis should be in large measure on the mother. The title of a recent paper by Sosa *et al*. (1976) encapsulates this approach: 'Feed the mother: thereby the infant'. By feeding the mother with locally available foods during pregnancy and lactation, it will be possible to

---

*The *additional* Recommended Dietary Allowances in lactation have been stated to be: 500 kcals, 20 g. protein, 400 IU vitamin A, 35 mg. ascorbic acid, 10 mg. zinc, etc. (National Academy of Sciences, 1974).

optimize the volume and composition of breast-milk, to avoid the economic, infective, and distributive complexities of introducing cow's milk and bottle-feeding unnecessarily, and also to avoid assisting still further a decline in breast-feeding in the community.

At risk of over-repetition, it must be emphasized again that those concerned with infant feeding often do not give adequate appreciation to the associated effects of great nutritional significance of the anti-infective, child-spacing, and economic significance of human milk and breast-feeding.

Almost a quarter of a century ago in 1952, Morrison concluded his painstakingly detailed analysis of available evidence concerning the 'yield, proximate principles, and inorganic constituents' of human milk by commenting: 'It is clear that there is plenty of room for work on every constituent. This review may serve to show where special care is needed in sampling technique and the spacing of samples.'

The need for further investigations is greater at the present day in view of the increasing realization of the significance of human milk on a world basis, but especially in resource-poor, less developed countries. Such studies need to take into account modern knowledge of the psychophysiology and endocrinology of lactation, and, if feasible, should be undertaken on a collaborative and comparative basis in various representative ecologies in different parts of the world. Priority should be given to practical issues of immediate application, particularly the effect of improved maternal diet on lactation and, conversely, the breast's ability to biosynthesize nutrients and to supply these to cover the infant's needs on a continuing basis.

At the same time, within the labyrinth of available data, sufficient knowledge already exists to permit a rational practical approach to be suggested (p. 346), based on the important information available, on probability, and on an understanding of the biological background of man's mammalian needs. As Ounsted and Sleigh (1975) comment in a recent paper on the infant's self-regulation of food intake and weight gain in the offspring of presumably well-nourished women: 'The range of optimum intake and growth-rate varies widely, and the individual infants needs would best be met, if he is allowed to take what he wishes, preferably from his mother only'.

5 Protection and Hazards

What are all these germs doing there? The answer is that they are almost certainly minding their own business as quietly as possible, or they (or the host) would not be there. But things might be very different without them.

Editorial, *British Medical Journal* (1969) **3**, 249, 'Bacteria of the gut'

Apart from nutritional and metabolic considerations, mammalian milks appear to provide species-specific protective effects during the time when the newborn are becoming adjusted to the risks (particularly infections) of their new extra-uterine environment, as part of the process of 'adaptive suckling' (p. 2). In man, recent evidence suggests that such defence is not only anti-infective, but also helps to protect against the early development of some forms of infantile allergy.

Conversely, both cow's milk and human milk can develop special toxic hazards from substances secreted by lactating females. The risk of this usually becomes greater in modern urbanized life and in mechanized agriculture and dairy farming.

Lastly, a very diverse group of oral conditions (e.g. malocclusion, p. 109) has been considered to be related to whether the infant is breast or bottle fed. In some of these, the relationship is clear, for example in 'nursing-bottle syndrome' (p. 112). In others, evidence appears to be suggestive enough to warrant further up-to-date investigation.

1. Anti-infective properties

The protective effect of breast-feeding against infections has been recognized clinically for decades, particularly in relation to diarrhoeal disease in conditions of poor hygiene and in hot weather (Goldman and Smith 1973, Hannson and Johansson 1970, Hannson *et al.* 1975, Jelliffe and Jelliffe 1973*c*). This has usually been attributed solely to the cleanliness and lack of opportunity for contamination of human milk, and to the physical closeness and the relatively restricted micro-environment between the mother and baby. In fact, human milk, including colostrum, is never strictly sterile microbiologically when it reaches the neonate (Wyatt and Mata 1969). In Swedish studies, several hundred staphylococci per mm^2 have been isolated from the areola of normal women — a lesser count than obtained from other body skin, perhaps partially related to secretions from Montgomery's glands (Gothefors 1975) (p. 11). In Guatemalan Indian women in poor hygienic circumstances, human milk contains an average of 300 000 'skin organisms' and enterobacteria per μl, presumably derived mainly from the mother's nipple (Wyatt and Mata 1969). Nevertheless, the bacterial level is low, and there is no opportunity for growth and multiplication of micro-organisms, as occurs easily with cow's milk, if a prolonged period elapses between milking and consumption without pasteurization or refrigeration.

However, viraemia in the mother may lead to virus excretion in breast-milk (virolactia) and this has been demonstrated with hepatitis B (HBsAg) (Linneman and Goldberg 1974), cytomegalic virus (Hayes *et al*. 1972), and type-B virions (Fraumeni and Miller 1971). Probably, this is not usually of significance in the newborn as invasion will already have taken place transplacentally or during the birth process (Beasley *et al*. 1975). However, virolactia, real or potential, poses new practical and legal problems in the establishment of 'banks' of unprocessed fresh breast-milk (p. 362).

The active anti-infective properties of human milk are both humoral and cellular (Gerrard 1974*b*, Winberg and Gothefors 1976, Hannson 1961, Hannson and Winberg 1972, Gothefors 1975). Until recently, it was believed that the baby received antibodies only transplacentally, in contrast to the calf and piglet, where the main protection has been known for years to be derived from immune substances in the dam's colostrum, without which *E. coli* diarrhoea ('scours') and septicaemia were likely to occur (Bourne 1973). The antibodies received by the human foetus *in utero* are largely against certain systemic infections; while 'host resistance factors' from breast-milk appear to act mainly within the intestine.

Humoral effects
Various protective factors are present in human milk, including immuno-globulins, lysozyme, the bifidus factor, and nutrient-carrier proteins which bind vitamin B_{12}, folate, and iron (lactoferrin) and limit their availability for intestinal bacteria, especially *E. coli* (Gullberg 1974, Rolles 1976, Bullen 1976). The immunoglobulins include IgC, IgM, and IgD. The most important of these in man appears to be secretory IgA (sIgA) (Gindrat *et al*. 1972, Cheron 1971), which differs antigenically from serum IgA. Secretory IgA is synthesized even in the non-lactating 'resting' breast, as has been shown in healthy tissue removed at operation for benign breast disease (Drife *et al*. 1976). It is especially high in colostrum (2–4 mg/ml) supplying an 'initial bolus' of immunoglobulin (Mata *et al*. 1969, 1971) (Fig. 5.1). After 2–4 days, this falls to lower levels (1–2 mg/ml), which continue for several months, although substantial amounts are still ingested with the larger volume of breast-milk taken. sIgA is a compact molecule, and is resistant to proteolytic enzymes of the gastro-intestinal secretions and low stomach pH, so that still active 'copro-antibodies' can be found in the stools of the breast-fed (Kenny *et al*. 1967). Secretory IgA in human milk is in 10–100 times greater concentration than in maternal serum (Carlsson *et al*. 1976). It originates in part by intense local secretion by the mammary gland, and in part from cellular lymphocytes in breast-milk. sIgA is only present in small amounts in cow's milk (p. 35).

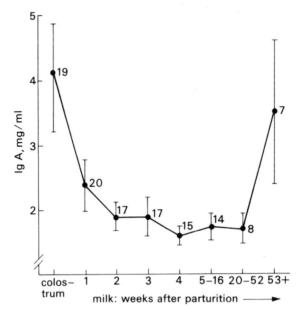

Fig. 5.1. Concentrations (mean ± ISD) of 11-S IgA in colostrum and milk of Mayan Indian women, Santa Maria Cauqué, Guatemala, 1968. Numbers of women studied are indicated on curve (from Mata, L. J., Urrutia, J. J., and Lechtig, A. (1971). *Amer. J. clin Nutr.* **24,** 249)

In older individuals, sIgA is normally produced by subepithelial plasma cells in the intestinal tract. However, during the early weeks of life, the neonate does not secrete this antibody, so that sIgA in colostrum and milk act as an 'antiseptic intestinal paint', protecting intestinal epithelial surfaces until the infant's own immune mechanisms mature (Walker and Kong 1973).

While there is some recent evidence that small amounts of antibodies, particularly IgC are absorbed (Iyengar and Selvaraj 1972), the proven effect of sIgA appears to be enteral, including as a mucosal protection, particularly against the dominant pathological bacteria in the newborn, (especially pathogenic *E. coli*, and enteroviruses (such as polio virus and probably such newly recognized pathogens as rotaviruses (p. 266)), and, to a lesser extent, against other microbacteria, including streptococci, staphylococci, and pneumococci. This is extremely important as not only is infective diarrhoea a serious neonatal disease, but in addition many systemic generalized infections, such as some cases of septicaemia of the newborn and poliomyelitis,* commonly enter via the intestinal tract.

The 'bifidus factor' is an N-containing carbohydrate first identified by György (1953). It is present in very high concentrations in colostrum, and human milk contains forty times as much as cow's milk. It is lost if breast-milk is boiled.

*Oral polio vaccine can be used after the first days of life (Deforest *et al.* 1973, Katz and Plotkin 1968). The dosage of virus administered is sufficient to overcome the declining concentration of milk antibody.

TABLE 5.1 *Composition of the intestinal flora of breast-fed and bottle-fed infants and adults* (from Gothefors 1975)

Group	Breast-fed infants	Bottle-fed infants	Adults*
Bifidobacteria	Dominant, some types prevailing	Constantly present but in smaller numbers than in breast-fed infants; gradual change in type distribution	Constant, numerous, sometimes prevailing; other types than those in breast-fed infants
Aerobic lactobacilli	Appear later and in smaller numbers than Bifidus; mainly *L. acidophilus*	Almost constantly present in small numbers; mainly *L. acidophilus*	Commonly found in small numbers; various types
Enterococci	Constantly present in small numbers	Constantly present in large numbers	Constantly present in varying amounts
E. coli and other Enterobacteriaceae	Fairly constantly present in small numbers	Constantly present in varying amounts, sometimes dominant	Constantly present in small numbers
Bacteroides and other obligate gram-negative anaerobes	Mostly absent, occasionally present in small numbers	Present in increasing amounts, sometimes in large numbers	Constantly present, numerous, sometimes predominant

* Western-type diet

The bifidus factor in human milk (combined with the low pH of the intestinal contents) facilitates the growth of *Lactobacillus bifidus* (Bifidobacteria), which appears to have an 'intestinal guardian' function, in particular checking the growth of undesirable, possibly harmful organisms, such as pathogenic *E. coli*. Colonization of the alimentary canal differs in infants fed on cow's milk or human milk. The bacterial population is predominantly *L. bifidus* in the breast-fed (acquired during birth from the mother's vagina (Haenel 1970)), whereas the intestinal flora of babies fed on cow's milk is principally made of gram-negative bacteria, especially coliforms and bacterioides. The effect on microbial populations is both qualitative and quantitative (Table 5.1).

In addition to the type of feed received, the neonate's immediate environment is also important, and Klaus (1975) has made the following comments.

The removal of an infant from his mother immediately after birth may have other consequences. It is known that the infant is effectively colonized with indigenous bacteria shortly after birth. Colonization of the intestinal tract begins with the first aspiration of amniotic fluid containing genital and fecal bacteria. INCAP [Institute of Nutrition of Central America and Panama] studies by Mata revealed that infants may excrete fecal bacteria in significant amounts 12 hours after birth and that by the end of the first week, when exclusive breastfeeding has been effected, more than $99 \cdot 8\%$ of the total fecal flora consists of bifido-bacteria. These indigenous organisms are responsible for the synthesis of significant amounts of acetic and lactic acids (and to a lesser extent of succinic and formic acid) responsible for the low pH of stools and for the remarkable resistance to infection and colonization with enterobacteriaceae. Artificially-fed infants also are colonized rapidly but the predominant flora consists of bacterioides and coliforms. The artificially-fed infant is more susceptible to enteric pathogenic infection because he lacks the protective mechanisms derived from human milk. If the child lives in a highly polluted environment (like the poor in cities and rural areas), this observation acquires greater relevance. Likewise, it has been known for some time that the human skin is effectively colonized by staphylococci as early as 8 hours after birth, at the level of the ducts of the sebaceous glands and hair follicles. This colonization is responsible for the phenomenon of bacterial interference, which explains the greater protection against staphylococcal infections of babies born outside hospitals. The isolation and characterization of an "avirulent" strain of staphylococcus (502A) enabled American workers to colonize infants at birth iatrogenically during the occurrence of epidemics of staphylococcal disease in four U.S. hospitals. The long-term INCAP studies in Indian villages have pointed out the almost total absence of neonatal staphylococcal disease, a feature contrasting vividly with the very poor hygienic situation in the village environment.

The evidence suggests that early maternal–infant interactions are beneficial to the child not only in terms of emotional adjustment (p. 142) and the initiation of breast-feeding, but also in relation to optimal colonization of intestinal tract and skin.

In addition, the superior resistance of breast-fed babies to intestinal infections (Winberg and Gothefors 1976), including gastroenteritis, may be due to human milk's lower buffering effect, together with the production of volatile acids (acetic, butyric) by lactobacilli (Table 5.2), and consequent higher stool acidity (p. 46) (Table 5.3), and possibly even to the different intestinal motility with cow's milk and human milk (Fomon 1974).

TABLE 5.2 *Volatile fatty acids present in faeces from newborn infants* (from Winberg and Gothefors 1976)

	Breast-fed	Bottle-fed
Acetic acid	+ +	+ + +
Propionic acid	(+)	+ +
Isobutyric acid	(+)	(+)
Butyric acid	+	+ +
Isovaleric acid		+
Valeric acid		+
Lactic acid	+	+
Total amount 50–300 mM		

Human milk contains large amounts (about 2 mg/100 ml) of lactoferrin, a powerful bacteriostatic, which may also be effective against *Candida albicans*. It has been suggested (Bullen *et al*. 1976) that lactoferrin acts synergistically with sIgA, perhaps especially against pathogenic strains of *E. coli* (Bullen and Willis 1971, Bullen *et al*. 1972, Spik 1971). Lactoferrin is an unsaturated iron-binding compound, which competes for iron with enteral organisms. For this reason, the use of supplemental oral iron in the breast-fed may be contra-indicated, as interfering with the protection afforded by lactoferrin (Bullen *et al*. 1972). The high level of proteins that bind vitamin B_{12} and folate in human milk may also act by denying these nutrients to intestinal bacteria (Gullberg 1974).

Lysozyme (muramidase) (Chandan *et al*. 1964, Dubois-Prevost 1967, Haneberg and Finne 1974), the well-recognized anti-infective substance in lachrymal secretion, is also found in breast-milk (up to 2 mg/100 ml) — that is concentrations up to 5000 times as great as in cow's milk (Hambraeus *et al*. 1975). It is not destroyed in the intestines and is found in the faeces. Its role may be related to the fall in serum lysozyme that occurs between the seventh and thirtieth day in the newborn (Xanthou *et al*. 1975). This enzyme is bacteriolytic against enterobacteriacae and gram-positive bacteria, and may play a role in protecting against various viruses, including *Herpes hominis* virus. Fresh breast-milk has been used in some traditional cultures as eye-drops in the treatment of conjunctivitis.

Other substances also occur, which may have protective functions, such as interferon, derived from lymphocytes, which may have anti-viral properties against neonatal infections with, for example, herpes virus. Also, György (1971) has identified an 'anti-staphylococcus factor' in human milk. This substance is non-dialysable, thermostable, and found in the free fatty-acid fraction of milk. Injection of human milk into mice enhanced their resistance to challenge by lethal doses of *Staphylococcus aureus*. Likewise, Gothefors (1975) has demonstrated that lactoperoxidase found in breast-milk is a host resistance factor, and Downham *et al.* (1976) have shown that human colostrum contains effective amounts of respiratory syncytial virus antibody.

Recently, Stoliar and colleagues (1976) have demonstrated that fresh colostrum and breast-milk from both Guatemalan and U.S. mothers neutralizes the enterotoxins of both *Vibrio cholera* and *E. coli*, when tested *in vivo* in rabbit ileal loops. The effect occurs while the responsible organisms are still present in the stools.

Need for research into the mechanisms involved is indicated by reports (Allardyce *et al.* 1974, Goldblum *et al.* 1976) that prior intestinal infection in mothers with non-pathogenic *E. coli* or *Salmonella typhimurium* leads to raised levels of milk antibodies, via the so-called 'gut–mammary axis' (Beer 1975) which has suggested the possibility of immunizing mother and baby by intestinal colonization (Hannson 1961). Studies in calves have shown that immunity can be diathelic — that is acquired through the teat (Campbell *et al.* 1957). Studies showed that salmonella organisms introduced into the mouth of the suckling calf lead to raised antibodies against these bacteria in the cow's milk. As noted by Klaus (1975), the work of Campbell and colleagues demonstrates that:

> The lactating breast of the cow is itself an immunological organ capable of producing specific antibodies in response to pathogens reaching the breast tissue from the lacteal ducts. Such specific antibodies elaborated by the reticular endothelial tissues of the breast are discharged into the milk within eight hours of immunologic stimulation. They are absorbed by the gastrointestinal tract and become available as a protection against gastrointestinal and/or respiratory infection. Such a mechanism of diathelic immunization may operate in the human situation. Thus, an important mechanism of immunological protection is suggested which can become specific for each mother–infant pair. It is not only the breast milk which is important, but it is the process of breast feeding itself which provides the immunological protection.
>
> The mother does not serve merely as a passive transmitter of immunity. Instead the mammary gland is able to react to the microbes brought to it by the infant and respond with a fast production of specific antibody. . . . The mammary gland is an exocrine reticuloendothelial gland which is 'lend-leased' functionally to the infant at a time when his own reticuloendothelial system is inadequate.

Cellular effects

In the Koran, breast-milk is called 'white blood' and this is a very good comparison. Recent work by Smith, Goldman, and Murillo clearly shows

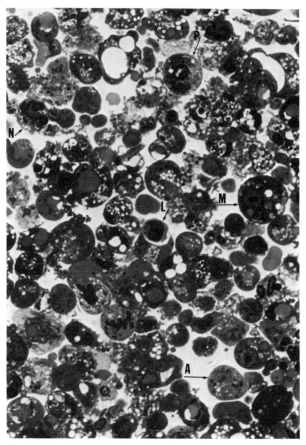

Fig. 5.2. A thin (0·5 μm) section through a concentrated suspension of cells obtained from rat's milk, stained with toluidine blue, pH 9; ×1100. Note the macrophages or milk corpuscles with numerous lipid vacuoles in their cytoplasm. A few polymorphonuclear leukocytes, plasma cells, and lymphocytes can also be identified. Sections of human milk have a similar appearance. (Courtesy Dr. Judith R. Head, Department of Cell Biology, University of Texas Health Science Center at Dallas, Dallas, Texas.) N = polymorphonuclear neutrophil, M = macrophage, L = lymphocyte, P = plasma cell, A = anucleate cell body (courtesy of Judith R. Head, Department of Cell Biology, University of Texas Health Science Center at Dallas, Texas).

that human milk is a 'live fluid', as is blood, with active enzymes (lysozyme, lipase), hormones (corticosteroids), and cells (Murillo and Goldman 1970, Smith and Goldman 1968, Smith *et al.* 1971) (Fig. 5.2). Breast-milk contains up to 4000 leucocyte-like cells per μl during the first two weeks of life. The cellular content is particularly high in colostrum, when it is not greatly inferior to the concentration in blood (Fig. 5.2), but declines to lower levels after the early weeks of life.

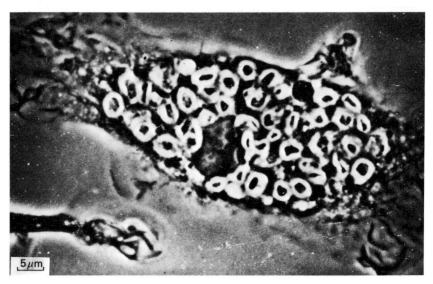

Fig. 5.3. Macrophage from human colostrum *in vitro* showing phagocytosed particles of zymosan (courtesy of Dr. C. Waynes Smith, Department of Anatomy, Michigan State University)

The primary cell in human milk appears to be the macrophage (at least 2000 per μl), with lymphocytes, neutrophils, and ephithelial cells. The key macrophages secrete lysozyme and lactoferrin. They are motile, amoeboid, and phagocytic, as can be demonstrated by cytoplasmic uptake of added vital dyes, such as neutral red (Fig. 5.3). The colostral corpuscles noted microscopically in human milk by Dieudonné in 1846 were macrophages that had ingested fat globules. Lymphocytes are also abundant (2700 per μl) and produce sIgA and inteferon. The responsiveness of such cellular mechanisms has been indicated recently by Goldblum *et al.* (1976). Three pregnant women's intestinal canals were colonized with an unusual non-pathogenic strain of *E. coli* (083) given orally. On delivery one week later, high levels of specific sIgA were found in the cells of the colostrum. Such studies endorse the particular resistance developed in human milk against maternal micro-organisms.

The function of live 'milk cells' appears to be to assist repelling infection both in the mammary lacteals and in the baby's intestinal tract, by phagocytic action and by liberation of humoral factors (sIgA, lysozyme, lactoferrin, and interferon). Such cells represent 'a highly ordered cytological system of functional importance' (Murillo and Goldman 1970).

Discussion
The protective effects of breast-feeding against infections, especially diarrhoeal disease was clear in industrialized countries early this century. Some effects are also apparent to a lesser extent in, for example, the U.K. and

Sweden. However, the consequences are dramatically obvious in communities with poor environmental hygiene, overcrowding, and poverty (p. 211). Thus, in Kingston, Jamaica, attacks of gastroenteritis were $3 \cdot 4$ times commoner in the bottle-fed (McGregor and Black 1970). However, as will be discussed later (p. 284), diarrhoeal disease in infants is still more important in many industrialized societies than often believed, and, indeed, may be increasing in prevalence. Certainly, new infective aetiologies appear to have been isolated recently, including the orbiviruses, the reoviruses, etc.

Also, the condition known as 'epidemic infectious diarrhoea of the newborn' seems to be a relatively 'new' disease. It was initially described in 1940, in an outbreak with an 82 per cent mortality rate. The authors also noted that 'only formula-fed babies died. Breast-fed infants either did not contract the disease or if they did were able to conquer the infection. Treatment was unavailing, except for the feeding of mother's milk' (Cron *et al.* 1940).

Subsequent to this, it has become clear that most outbreaks are due to infections with pathogenic *E. coli* in maternity-unit nurseries, where neonates are separated from their mothers and bottle-fed (American Academy of Pediatrics 1974*a*, Brenneman and Fortuine 1966, Frant and Abramson 1937, Staley *et al.* 1972). The practical significance at the present day is considered later (p. 265).

The first comprehensive account of 'acute necrotizing enterocolitis' was made in 1974 (Santulli 1974). It is uncertain whether it is a new condition or recently recognized to be of significance. It appears to be related not only to prematurity, but to perinatal hypoxia and to lack of breast-milk in babies fed with formulas or intravenously. The basic aetiology appears to be an infection of an intestinal wall damaged by oxygen lack by Klebsiella (or other) gram-negative organisms (Fig. 5.4), or possibly Clostridia (*Pédiatrie* 1976). It can be produced experimentally in newborn rats and prevented by fresh maternal rat milk (but not when frozen or boiled) (Table 5.4). In the human, breast-milk also suppresses the growth of gram-negative bacteria in the intestine, including Klebsiella.

In the U.S.A. (and elsewhere) there is currently a resurgence of interest in breast-milk banks, capable of supplying fresh milk for use in special care premature units (p. 362).

Another condition which appears to be common in bottle-fed infants in the first 6 months of life, especially in some areas of the world, is otitis media (p. 291). It is of uncertain aetiology, but may be infective, related to low antibodies. Also, recent investigations in Sweden suggest that the volume of milk taken by the neonate is a key factor in protecting against infection in the newborn, especially septicaemia due to gram-negative organisms appears to be increasingly common in all age-groups, including the newborn, in Western countries (p. 262).

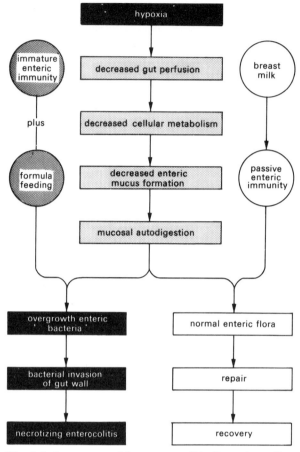

Fig. 5.4. Acute necrotizing enterocolitis (from Santulli, T. V. (1974). *Hosp. Pract.* Nov., 129)

It seems clear that, in addition to the provision of the most appropriate blend of nutrients, human milk (particularly colostrum) also makes available to the young infant a subtle, complex, effective, and specially tailored system of no-cost oral immunization and chemoprophylaxis — which is in no way available in cow's-milk-based formulas. Breast-milk has rightly been termed a 'potent medicine' (Behar 1976); 5 ml breast-milk per kg body-weight per day has been shown to reduce the incidence of neonatal *E. coli* diarrhoea in a maternity unit from 8 per cent in 1972 (with a mortality rate of 29 per cent) to 1 per cent from 1973 onwards (with no deaths) (Larguia *et al.* 1977).

The practical public health consequences of the mode of infant feeding on neonatal and infantile infections, both in industrialized and less developed countries (Behar 1976, *British Medical Journal* 1975*b*), will be reviewed later (p. 260, 284).

The recent 'explosion of information' of immune mechanisms has already had a considerable effect on understanding of the host resistance effects of breast-milk. However, research opportunities are numerous in relation to the actions and interactions of known and as yet unrecognized factors. The need is endorsed, for example, by a recent authoritative review on neonatal immunity in which the subject was dealt with as though the newborn could realistically be considered biologically as an immunologically independent 'free-living' individual, rather than as part of the mother–infant dyad (Gotoff 1975).

TABLE 5.3 *Differences in bacterial flora, pH, and physical characteristics of intestinal contents of infants fed human milk and cow's milk* (from Reisinger 1974)

	Human milk	Cow's milk
E. coli	10^6–10^7/g	10^9–10^{10}/g
pH, Faeces	4·5–5·6	7·0–8·0
Curds	Soft and fine	Hard and coarse
Bowel movements	Frequent	Infrequent

TABLE 5.4 *Mortality from experimentally-induced enterocolitis in Sprague-Dawley rats as a function of diet* (from Pitt et al. 1976)

Feeding	Mortality
Fresh breast-milk*	0/10
Frozen breast-milk	9/10
Frozen breast-milk + milk leucocytes	0/5
Frozen breast-milk + peritoneal leucocytes	1/5
Formula	30/30
Formula + milk leucocytes	1/5
Formula + peritoneal leucocytes	1/5
Formula + blood leucocytes	2/10

* Rat maternal milk.

The complexity of the interrelated aspects of what is a delicate and complex defence system has been hypothesized recently by Gothefors (1975):

In the process of normal bacterial colonization of the gut a great number of factors are involved. It can sometimes be relatively easy to study the effect of single factors in clearcut *in vitro* experiments, but transferred to *in vivo* reality, it is often extremely difficult to evaluate the relative importance of different factors, alone or in combination.

There seems to be no doubt as to the effect of human milk on the intestinal flora. The beneficial role of milk in prevention of different types of *Esch. coli* infections is well established. The mechanisms are not fully understood, but the secretory immune system is presumably of great importance in this connection. Although these antibodies — according to this study and to animal experiments — have no major effect on the selection and total number of organisms, they may prevent adherence to the intestinal mucosa and select mutant strains with reduced pathogenicity and thus contribute to the first line of defence against pathogenic organisms.

However, this local immunity appears to function only when the population of gram-negative organisms is kept small. This might be of certain importance when pathogenic bacteria are present in the gut. Here, perhaps, is the meaning of all other factors in milk, which partly have been discussed in this paper. The number of pathogens may be reduced by direct action of lysozyme or lactoperoxidase or indirectly by competition for space and nutrition with the indigenous flora of bifidobacteria and lactobacilli, which is favoured by the physico-chemical properties in milk. When the number of invaders is kept low the immune system is able to handle the remaining few pathogens.

2. Anti-allergic properties

Allergic diseases in early childhood due to food seem to be particularly common in Westernized communities, where they appear to be increasing in incidence. At least the more easily identified, severe syndromes, especially infantile eczema (atopic dermatitis), would be recognizable in developing countries even in the flood of children with protein-calorie malnutrition, diarrhoea, etc (Dean 1967). In fact, their clinical uncommonness in largely breast-fed communities is suggested by health service statistics. For example, in a one-year admission (1959) to a very busy 100-bed paediatric ward in the university teaching hospital at Kampala, Uganda, no severe disease due to allergy to food was reported (Musoke 1961). However, less clear-cut manifestations are almost certainly missed or misdiagnosed, as infectious diarrhoea, respiratory infection, etc.

Without a doubt, many factors are responsible for food allergy in young children, but, as cow's-milk protein is the commonest allergen, and three-quarters of such cases commence in the first 1–2 months of life (Fig. 5.5), an association with the newer practice of bottle-feeding seems likely (Gopalan

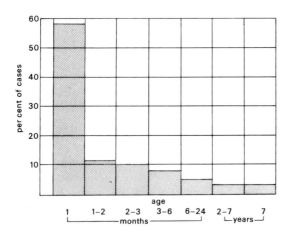

Fig. 5.5. Age of onset of cow's-milk allergy in young children (from Goldman, A. S. (1975). *Proceedings of Swedish Nutrition Foundation Symposium on Food and Immunology*)

and Belavady 1961). The high incidence of allergic disease with bottle-feeding was recognized in the U.S.A. several decades ago, when it was found that infantile eczema and other conditions were seven times as common in bottle-fed infants consuming undenatured cow's milk, compared with children who had been breast-fed (Grulee *et al*. 1934).

The 'dose' of allergen involved in cow's-milk feeding is large: a fully bottle-fed infant of three months is consuming his body-weight in cow's milk weekly or about 6 g/kg body-weight of cow's-milk protein daily. This is the equivalent of about 7 litres of liquid milk per day for an adult. The situation is complicated by possible allergy to one or more of the components of milk protein, such as α-lactalbumin or β-lactoglobulin. In Goldman's series of children allergic to cow's milk, reactions with multiple symptoms to one or more components were considerable (casein 60 per cent, α-lactalbumin 53 per cent, β-lactoglobulin 62 per cent, and bovine serum albumin 52 per cent) (Goldman 1975). The high rate of involvement of α-lactoglobulin and bovine serum albumin is significant, as these are not present in human milk. Also, recent work on the differing physicochemical properties and constituents of milk proteins, including the 'casein systems', indicates widely different allergenic potential (Ribadeau Dumas *et al*. 1975). Likewise, modern studies have shown intolerance to heat-stable proteins in commercial evaporated and powdered milks. Modern processing of cow's milk (denaturing) has reduced but not eliminated allergenicity.

Proteins are antigenically species-specific, so that human milk protein is non-allergenic and no antibody response occurs following its ingestion. Usually it is not possible to develop cow's milk allergy unless cow's milk is being taken, and it has been known for years that macromolecules of breast-milk proteins are not absorbed from the baby's gut to the circulation (Gugler and Muralt 1959). However, recent work (Glaser 1975, Matsumura *et al*. 1972, Oguri *et al*. 1971) has shown that sensitization can occasionally occur in the foetus *in utero* or in the breast-fed as a result of very small amounts of bovine protein or other food allergens in human milk. Such instances appear to be extremely uncommon. They are also mild and easily treatable by modification of the *mother's* diet (Giobbi *et al*. 1976).

The range of syndromes in early childhood which can be associated with milk protein intolerance is considerable (Goldman 1975) (Fig. 5.6), including atopic dermatitis (infantile eczema), rhinitis, possibly some cases of otitis media, Heiner's syndrome (Heiner *et al*. 1962, Upadhyay and Gerard 1969) (severe recurrent non-infectious bronchopneumonia-like disease, with fever and pulmonary infiltrates and with poor weight-gain and spells of diarrhoea, pulmonary haemosiderosis, anaemia, and failure to thrive), various forms of allergic gastroenteropathy (which can be characterized by diarrhoea, vomiting, and weight-loss, by malabsorption (Linneman and Goldberg 1974), by colitis or by hypersensitivity microhaemorrhages (Goldman 1975) (p. 46), or possibly some cases of 'colic' and even intussus-

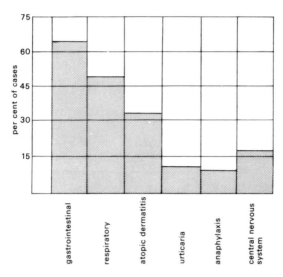

Fig. 5.6. Syndromes in cow's milk allergy in young children (from Goldman, A. S. (1975). *Proceedings of Swedish Nutrition Foundation Symposium Food and Immunology*)

ception (Freed 1976, Trulove and Jewell 1975).

In addition, it has been suggested that systemic anaphylaxis may be responsible for some cases of 'sudden infant death syndrome' (or 'cot deaths') (Parish, Barrett, Coombs, Gunther, and Camps 1960, Parish, Barrett, and Coombs 1960). More recently, similar sudden 'apparently allergic and often fatal reactions' have been described in rabbit pups hand-reared on cow's-milk formulas. It is correctly suggested that this re-emphasizes the need for 'further investigation into milk hypersensitivity in man, particularly in relation to its possible connection with sudden unexplained death in infancy' (Henschel and Coates 1974).

Similarly, the possibility of some cases of cot death being due to hypersensitivity is suggested by the finding of significantly higher levels of serum IgE antibodies to both housedust-mite and to β-lactoglobulin in cot deaths in W. Australia (Turner *et al.* 1975). Various chronic diseases in later life, including ulcerative colitis (Acheson and Truelove 1961), coronary artery disease (Scott *et al.* 1976), and multiple sclerosis (Agranoff and Goldberg 1974), have been suggested as being related to cow's milk allergy commencing in early childhood, but proof is needed.

The recent situation concerning the incidence of infantile allergy is complicated by changing forms of cow's-milk formulas (particularly the use of formulas with denatured protein), by the earlier introduction of semi-solids, and by different techniques of diagnosis. However, evidence suggests that infantile allergy to various foods, including cow's milk, is common and probably increasing (Gunther *et al.* 1962) (p.96). Coeliac disease (gluten enteropathy) has also increased considerably in recent decades, possibly mainly because of the very early introduction of wheat-containing foods in the first weeks or months of life (Department of Health and Social Security, U.K. 1974).

As noted earlier (p. 85), secretory IgA in colostrum and breast-milk has a highly significant protective function against intestinal infections. In addition, it has a blocking effect preventing the ingress and absorption of foreign macromolecules, while the infant's own immune system is still immature. This stage of developmental lack has been recognized in piglets and lambs for some years (Lecce and Morgan 1962). It has long been suggested that a major factor in the aetiology of allergy in childhood is an increased permeability of the neonatal intestinal to foreign proteins, both from cow's milk and other foods (Walker and Isselbacher 1974). In fact, cow's-milk protein antigen can be detected in the serum of the formula-fed baby.

Recent investigations indicate that for the first six weeks or so of life the intestinal tract is immature, anatomically and immunologically. The early absorption of protein macromolecules in young farm animals is well recognized, followed by what is termed 'closure', that is cessation of transport of macromolecules across the gut epithelium (Lecce and Morgan 1962). The subepithelial plasma cells of the lamina propria and the lymphoid nodes of the mucosa do not produce secretory IgA in the first few weeks, though after that time production increases and reaches adult levels by 2 years. It has been shown that the children of parents with a general history of allergy appear to have a more prolonged, but transient, period of IgA deficiency, lasting for three months or so, thereby increasing their susceptibility to ingested food proteins (Walker and Hong 1973).

The introduction of foods other than breast-milk in the early weeks of life, including cow's milk, leads to rapidly detectable rise in corresponding blood antibodies (Truelove and Jewell 1975), and the presence of a higher percentage of subjects with nasal-secretion eosinophilia (Table 5.5).

TABLE 5.5 *Nasal-secretion eosinophilia and feeding in the first month of life* (from Murray 1971)

| | Nasal-secretion eosinophilia | |
	Present	Absent
Foreign foods in first month	22 (32%)	46 (68%)
Only breast-milk in first month	2 (11%)	16 (89%)

Plainly, allergic disease in childhood and in adult life is of highly complex origin, related to constitutional factors and non-dietary environmental allergens. As noted, even in the newborn, the question of contact with antibodies *in utero* and the excretion of very small quantities of food protein macromolecules in breast-milk is recognized. Breast-feeding will not eliminate food allergies, not even completely to cow's milk. It will, however, reduce their incidence very greatly and/or delay their onset. Conversely, because 'many of the major proteins in cow's milk are potentially allergenic, it is not possible to produce a processed cow's milk which is hypo-allergenic. Furthermore, the processing of cow's milk may possibly lead to the formation of new allergens' (Goldman 1975).

In a recent review of the literature, Woodruff (1976) concludes that:

> Clinical milk intolerance of the first two years of life is a fairly common event in infants who are not breast fed. Present thinking would relate this phenomenon to immunologic maturation. However, the finding of similar syndromes in older children and adults would suggest that recovery, although it might occur in the majority of infants, does not always take place and that continued or recurrent sensitivity to cow's milk protein may occur.

Gerrard (1974a) emphasizes five considerations which suggest the role of breast-feeding in the prevention of infantile allergy:

> First, pediatric allergists such as Glaser, who practised when breastfeeding was common, noted a greater prevalence of allergies in infants brought up on formula than in those brought up on the breast. Second, breast fed babies, after developing allergies when given supplemental foods, recover from their allergies when these foods are avoided. Third, babies on the breast alone may develop allergies that subside as soon as the food to which the baby is sensitive is eliminated from the mother's diet. Fourth, some babies — approximately 20 per cent in our experience — grow out of their cow's milk allergy by the age of 12 months. (Such babies, if brought up on breast-milk and not given cow's milk until the age of 12 months, would not be expected to develop cow's milk allergy.) Finally, it has been our experience that babies with gastroenteritis due to cow's milk allergy often develop normal gastrointestinal function when given breast milk alone.

The investigation of intolerance and allergy to foods in infancy, including cow's milk, has recently entered a new phase with modern immunological methods, and much remains to be learned. Nevertheless, current scientific knowledge concerning the natural development of allergic 'immunity' indicates clearly how a considerable amount of allergic disease related to foods, especially cow's milk, can be reduced in childhood, especially in the offspring of allergic parents.

First, the secretory IgA lacking in the intestinal canal of the normal newborn for 6 weeks (and three months in the infant of allergic families) can be made good by secretory IgA found in human milk, especially colostrum. Breast-feeding is the single most important approach to the prophylaxis of allergy in infancy (Walker and Hong 1973).

Secondly, potential food allergens should not be introduced into the diet unnecessarily during this vulnerable period, including cow's milk and semi-solids, especially those particularly known to be hyperallergenic, such as wheat and eggs. This endorses, from a totally different point of view, the optimal pattern of feeding in early infancy — that is human milk without early supplementation with milk or other foods for 4–6 months.

In allergic families, Mellon and co-workers (1976) reduced infantile allergy from 41 per cent to 7 per cent by a preventive programme of (a) exclusive breast-feeding for 6 months (or more), (b) screening to exclude dust and mites, and (c) delaying immunization with triple vaccine (against whooping cough, tetanus, and diphtheria). Soothill (1976) advocates a similar programme which 'avoids possibly damaging antigens' by exclusive breast-feeding and reduced contact with house-dust and pets.

As Goldman (1975) writes in an authoritative review: 'It is therefore evident that breast-feeding and avoidance of cow's milk is the most practical method of preventing the occurrence of cow's-milk sensitivity in infancy.'

3. Chemical toxicants

Potentially toxic chemical substances can be taken by mouth (or other route) and excreted in both human and bovine milks. The risks of such being present in either depend on their availability in the different environments, diets, and forms of medication that may be in use in each species.

(i) *Medications* (see p. 389)

Probably most drugs taken therapeutically are excreted in the breast-milk, but to very varying degrees. Scientific information is inadequate, and excretion of different medicaments appears to be related to various factors, including the dose given to the mother and the duration of therapy. Two main mechanisms occur for drug secretion into milk: diffusion of some substances directly ('preformed ingredients') or synthesis within the breast ('milk-specific ingredients', such as the nutrient lactose). Pharmacologically, the amount of a drug present will be related to its lipid-solubility, its binding capacity with protein, and its degree of ionization, which varies in the pH of breast-milk ($6 \cdot 6$–$6 \cdot 8$) compared with that of plasma ($7 \cdot 4$–$7 \cdot 8$) (Rasmussen 1973). Rarely, the baby may ingest toxic material (for example, boracic acid) from the areolar surface of the breast.

The paucity of knowledge concerning the excretion of drugs in human milk and their potential immediate and long-term effects on the nursling is related to the lack of scientific interest in breast-feeding in recent decades and the parallel flood of new drugs during the same period, especially in industrialized countries. At the same time, the subject is made difficult by the obvious ethical impossibility of planned experimentation with nursing mothers, by problems of interpretation of results in light of variations (related to the age and weight of the baby, time after dosage, amount given to mother, time of milk sample, etc.), by the practical technical problems of carrying out studies on non-human primates, and by the uncertainty of extrapolating results obtained from milking animals, such as goats and cows.

The basic question is not 'Which drugs are passed on to the infant through milk?', but 'Do they affect him in any way?'. In other words, are they absorbed and do they cause any ill-effects? (Catz and Giacoia 1973). Another basic consideration is whether the benefit of the drug for the mother outweighs any possible dangers to the infant.

The excretion of certain drugs in breast-milk has even been suggested for chemoprophylaxis in the nursling. Some years ago, protection against malaria in the baby was sought by the administration of the anti-malarial drug atabrine to the nursing mother, as this yellow compound is visibly present in breast-milk. The attempt does not appear to have been successful.

In view of the present incomplete information on drug excretion in breast-milk and the effect on the nursing baby, it is best to avoid medication during lactation, unless clearly and specifically indicated. Similarly unforeseen tragedies to those produced by the 'harmless' symptomatic drug thalidomide in pregnancy obviously must be avoided. Conversely, nursing mothers should inform their physicians that they are breast-feeding, if drug therapy is contemplated.

Drugs given to lactating women need to be considered in relation to the dosage used, the duration administered, and the known toxicity in breast-fed babies, and in newborns and adults given the substance therapeutically. As a possible guide and tentative working rule, Arena (1970) suggests the basic 'rule of thumb' question should be asked — whether $\frac{1}{20}$th of the dose given to the mother could be administered directly to a newborn with safety.

Plainly, there is a great deal of difference between prolonged drug dosage for a chronic or permanent ailment, such as epilepsy or diabetes, and for an acute, severe, usually short illness, such as pneumonia, when brief exposure may be needed to a very active drug. For example, the issue with regard to aspirin is quite different with women taking large continuing amounts for months for rheumatoid arthritis, or occasional tablets for headache (Thaller 1976).

Catz and Giacoia (1973) suggest that toxicants in human milk may have pharmacological effects through various mechanisms, including a cumulative effect (mercury, chlorinated insecticides), altered genetically determined response (glucose 6-phosphate-dehydrogenase-dependent haemolytic effect of vicine from broad beans in favism), changes in homeostatis (anticoagulants with danger of haemorrhage following trauma), interference with normal physiological functions (the anti-thyroxine effect of thiouracil), and hypersensitivity (penicillin).

Various practical classifications have been suggested including one by Catz and Giacoia (1973): 'substances excreted into breast-milk with undesirable effects (for the baby)' or those without. The La Leche League, information sheet *Breast-feeding and drugs in human milk* giving pertinent medical references for physicians, gives three categories — section A: 'Drugs for which published references in the medical literature indicate no demonstrable harmful effect on the nursing baby when taken by his mother';

section B: 'Drugs for which there are in some cases no specific references in the literature, but which have been frequently prescribed for nursing mothers by their doctors and which have not been found to present any detectable complications for the baby'; section C: 'Drugs which are contraindicated for the nursing mother except as indicated'.

Various tentative lists have been drawn up, for example, by Arena (1970), by Catz and Giacoia (1973), by Knowles (1965), by the La Leche League, by Rothermel and Faber (1975), by T.E. O'Brien (1974), and by Vorherr (1974). Based on these and on examination of the presently available, very incomplete evidence, it is suggested that the following drugs should not be given to lactating women even in usual doses: anti-thyroid compounds (thiouracil), steroids, oral contraceptives, bromides, anthraquinone laxatives (cascara), ergot, anticoagulants, reserpine, morphine (and derivatives), methadone, radioactive preparations, dihydrotachysterol, metronidazole, novobiocin, chloramphenicol, diphenylhydantoinate ('Dilantin'), lead, mercury, radioactive iodine, flagyl, and antimetabolites. The drug nitrofurantoin is secreted in breast milk and, as it can cause haemolysis of red blood cells in individuals lacking the enzyme glucose 6-phosphate dehydrogenase, its use should be avoided in communities where this genetic condition is common, as in the Eastern Mediterranean region (Tarj-Eldrin 1971).

Numerically and in public-health importance, the oral contraceptives head the list. Those containing oestrogen diminish the volume of milk produced and alter the composition, (p. 121). Reported ill-effects on the nursling are few; for example, one case of feminization of a male child (Miller and Hughes 1970). Oral contraceptives should, if possible, be avoided during lactation. Further research is needed into the excretion of progestogens and their effects (p. 121).

While no proven ill-effect has been described as a side-effect of such tranquillizing psychopharmacological drugs as 'Valium', it has been commented that these can 'invoke langour which makes the bare necessities of housework, child care, and mothering an overwhelming task' (Fowler 1974, 1976).

Short courses of antibiotics for the mother are not contraindicated *when really needed*. Conversely, as a practical approach, it may be possible to substitute a drug of less potential toxicity. However, any drug given to the mother in a larger than usual therapeutic dose should be considered as a possible contraindication to breast-feeding, either temporarily or completely, especially if medication is prolonged.

A cautious approach is indicated with newly introduced drugs, especially if likely to be toxic or with an unusual pharmacological action. These should be avoided, if possible. If a particular toxic drug is positively indicated therapeutically, breast-milk can be expressed, manually or by electrical pump, and discarded during a short course of treatment.

Basically, the use of drugs in the treatment of lactating women has to be based on a balance of risks, but with extra caution because of uncertainties in relation to excretion into breast-milk and of consequent effects on the baby. Further research is badly needed into the excretion of drugs (especially those commonly used) in human milk (using, for example, gas chromatography–mass spectrometry with small milk samples (Homing *et al*. 1973)) and their effects, if any, on the nursling. Limited but useful data can sometimes be acquired even on expressed samples, as in a recent investigation in a woman treated with cyclophosphamide for lymphosarcoma (Wiernik and Duncan 1971), or by means of blood-testing of breast-fed infants, as with a recent investigation carried out on the neonates of nursing mothers receiving therapy with diazepam (Cole and Hailey 1975), carbamazepine (Pynnonen and Sillanpaa 1975), and lithium (Schou and Amdisen 1973). Occasionally, investigation may be possible immediately after the baby has been weaned from the breast. For example, McKenzie *et al*. (1975) measured the secretion of prednisolone into the milk of healthy mothers whose infants had just ceased breast-feeding, by giving the women concerned a single small dose of isotope-tagged prednisolone.

With this type of information, the option of adjusting the amount and dosage schedule may be feasible for some drugs that cannot be changed and are needed for the mother's health.

(ii) *Nutrients*

In previous times, long lists of foods, such as spicy items, were prohibited during breast-feeding. Consideration of this matter has gone out of fashion. Thus, 16th-century European advice to wet nurses '. . . warned against bad air, bad smells, salty or spiced foods, garlic, mustard, stale cheese, and also roast meat if the infant's complexion is moist or phlegmatic. She should spurn all raw fruit, and drink only ale, beer, barley water or wine, rest whenever she can, keep her bowels open and shun all disquietness of mind.' (Wickes 1953).

Currently it is considered unlikely that compounds in foods usually cause significant ill-consequences for the nursling, except in cases of favism (p. 107) and uncommon cases of allergy related to small amounts of protein macromolecules from foods excreted in the breast-milk. Nevertheless it seems wiser to keep an open mind, as alimentary upsets, including vomiting and colic, are reported to be associated with certain items in the lactating mother's diet, as for example chocolate.

Little information exists concerning possible secretion of very high levels of nutrients in breast-milk in mothers taking unphysiologically high doses, as, for example, with the recent vogue for very large daily amounts of certain vitamins, such as A and C. In parts of Japan in summer, tangerines are cheap, popular, prestigious (as historically associated with the Emperor), and believed to be particularly health-promoting. In adults eating 10–20 tangerines daily, 'orange-colour disease' (aurantiasis) occurs, without symptoms but with β-carotene staining of the skin and mucosa. In lactating women, the milk also becomes orange in colour due to higher levels of β-carotene ($200\,\mu g/100\,ml$) than in maternal serum. No ill-effects have been noted in the nursing baby, except for striking orange staining of the skin and mucous membranes (Honda *et al*. 1975).

(iii) *Social toxicants*

In the human, social, mood-changing toxicants are used in most cultures. They include tobacco (nicotine), coffee, tea, and '*mate*' (caffein), alcohol (ethanol), marijuana (tetrahydrocannabinol), and heroin. Their active principles are excreted in human milk to varying extents.

The case of heroin is a special one. Babies born to addicts suffer withdrawal symptoms, and the neonatal abstinence syndrome resulting from this 'chemical separation' is characterized particularly by an uncoordinated and ineffective sucking reflex (Kronn *et al*. 1966). The social and psychological condition of the mother may in any case preclude breast-feeding. These factors make this a contraindication to nursing.

With the toxicants from more widespread and socially acceptable drugs in the western world, such as ethanol, caffein, and nicotine, occasional usage seems unlikely to be harmful. High intakes should be avoided, especially as known ill-effects have been observed in foetuses of mothers addicted to alcohol or cigarette-smoking. Indeed, 20 cigarettes daily can lead to relatively high levels of fat-soluble nicotine in the breast-milk, which could be harmful to the baby. According to Vorherr (1974), nicotine can also diminish milk secretion, but this seems to need more investigation.

Larger doses of ethanol have been shown to inhibit the let-down reflex (Cobo 1973) (p. 19), but small amounts appear to facilitate it (p. 24). The possibility of as yet unrecognized ill-effects from larger doses of social toxicants needs consideration. This is emphasized by the fact that the 'foetal alcohol syndrome' has been recognized in the offspring of alcoholic mothers only in recent years, although it must have occurred for many years.

(iv) *Environmental toxicants* (see p. 389)

A variety of different environmental toxicants have been introduced in the course of recent technological developments, both accidentally (e.g. industrial wastes) and by design (e.g. pesticides, herbicides), which have contaminated both human milk and cow's milk. For example, a circumscribed outbreak of poisoning occurred in Turkey in 1956, as a result of the population eating grain containing the fungistatic hexachlorobenzene, which was secreted in breast-milk. The clinical picture was of severe porphyria. In Iraq, an outbreak of poisoning occurred due to methyl mercuric fungicide in wheat (Amin-Zaki *et al*. 1974).

The levels of different man-made environmental chemical pollutants differ in cow's milk and human milk depending on the relative contamination of the environments of the two species. Human milk has been shown to contain only one-fifth as much radioactive strontium-90 as cow's milk (Jarvis *et al.* 1963). However, fat-soluble DDT has been demonstrated to be present in considerable levels in human fat (8 p.p.m.) all over the world with concentrations in breast-milk greater than in cow's milk (Quinby *et al.* 1965). There have been, as yet, no known ill-effects of DDT in the human adult (Hayes *et al.* 1971) or infant, compared with the recognized serious consequences on the calcification of eggs of some species of birds ('thin-shell syndrome') or growth rate in newborn rats (Fahim *et al.* 1971). The new-born's DDT levels will probably have already reached a 'steady-state' during foetal life, although this does not take into account further accumulation of DDT in the new tissue acquired during postnatal growth, especially increases in subcutaneous fat. However, in one study in the U.K., the DDT content in adipose tissue at birth was found to be about one-third of the content in adult adipose tissue, and it did not increase during the first year of life (Abbott *et al.* 1968).

DDT is more likely to be ingested in meat-eating communities because man is higher in the food chain than domestic animals; and in urbanized industrialized countries until recently, DDT-containing insecticides were widely used domestically. However, the DDT problem is by no means confined to Western countries, where levels in human milk have ranged from $0 \cdot 05$ to $0 \cdot 37$ p.p.m. (Hayes 1971). This insecticide has also been exported in very large quantities. In Guatemala, levels of $1 \cdot 2$–$4 \cdot 9$ p.p.m. in breast-milk have been reported due to the widespread and ill-controlled use of DDT in anti-malaria campaigns and as an insecticide in crop dusting, when it can be inhaled as well as swallowed (Olszyna-Marzys 1975).

Also, in the U.S.A., persistently very high levels of DDT have been found in breast-milk of poor, rural black women in Mississippi and Arkansas one year after the ban on its use in January 1973. DDT had been used extensively in spraying and dusting cotton crops from the air. Results suggest that DDT is present in the fat stores of adults and continues in the environment. The effects of the health of newborn babies and young infants needs further investigation (Woodard *et al.* 1976).

Fortunately, recent restrictions on the use of DDT in the U.S.A. and other similar countries have resulted in falls in levels in breast-milk from $0 \cdot 13$ p.p.m. in 1950 to $0 \cdot 03$–$0 \cdot 04$ in 1968. In the Stockholm area of Sweden, DDT levels in breast-milk were $0 \cdot 04$ p.p.m. in 1967, but had fallen to $0 \cdot 02$ p.p.m. in 1971–2 (Westöö and Noren 1972). However, levels in Norway in 1976 were similar to those found prior to the ban on DDT six years previously (Bakken and Seip 1976). Largely due to insect resistance, DDT is everywhere being less used than previously, including in anti-malaria campaigns, although other potent residual insecticides are taking its place (e.g. dieldrin). However, in general the effect of pesticides (Szokolay *et al*. 1975, Kroger 1972) and other agricultural chemicals, especially those which are fat soluble, on the foetus and breast-fed baby need continuing research, as to prevalence, possible consequences, and alternatives. In the meantime, the balance of risks in less developed countries clearly endorses the urgency of minimizing the contact of lactating women with DDT, but also the need for human milk for infant survival compared with the hypothetical, unproven danger of DDT ingestion. At the same time, world-wide investigations are needed to determine the geographical variation of DDT levels in breast-milk (and other pesticides), together with information on tolerance and health implications to nursing babies.

Parallel problems of contamination of human milk have occurred in several parts of the world with benzene hexachloride, polychlorinated biphenyls, and mercury compounds, particularly in Japan, where mercury poisoning (Minamata disease) occurred, also involving some breast-fed babies (Catz and Giacoia 1973). High levels were noted in human milk in that fish-eating country, but have also declined with more stringent control and with widespread and effective health education that fish from the industrially contaminated 'inland sea' should not be eaten, especially their viscera (Szokolay *et al*. 1975).

Two particular toxins have been associated with cow's milk: aflatoxin and lead. The former can be present in low levels in the milk of cows fed with cattle-cake prepared from ground-nut, soy, or cereal-grains contaminated with the fungus *Aspergillus flavum*. No ill-effects have been recorded, but, in view of well-known carcinogenic effects of aflatoxin in animals, care should be taken by dairy farmers to avoid using contaminated cattle-cake.

High lead levels were reported in 1973 in samples of canned milk. Concentrations as consumed were evaporated milk $0·18$ p.p.m., infant formula $0·25$ p.p.m., and evaporated skimmed milk $0·52$ p.p.m., compared with homogenized cow's milk $0·04$ p.p.m. and human milk $0·02$ p.p.m. (Lamm *et al*. 1973). In 1974, the same workers recorded marked reduction in lead levels (Lamm and Rosen 1974). The significance of these findings is uncertain, and a committee of the American Academy of Pediatrics (1974*c*) was of the opinion that differences in techniques of analysis could explain differences in level. Again, further work on levels of lead and possibly of other metals and their consequences is needed on processed canned milks.

In the human, certain foods eaten by the mother may lead to toxic effects in the nursing baby. In particular, favism can occur in susceptible breast-fed babies, whose mothers are consuming broad beans (*Vicia faba*). This can be a practical problem in some parts of the world, such as the Eastern Mediterranean, where favism essentially due to glucose 6-phosphate-dehydrogenase deficiency is common and broad beans a major item of the diet (Belsey 1973).

In some circumstances, breast-feeding may minimize intakes of possibly harmful poisons. For example, in areas where high nitrate levels occur in the soil, often due to added chemical fertilizer, methaemoglobinaemia is a risk for infants drinking the water. Under these circumstances, human milk protects, as the nitrates are metabolized by the mother, while preparations of cow's milk which require water added locally (e.g. powdered forms) may be hazardous (Shuval and Gruener 1972).

Very recently (1970), a newly recognized, uncommon form of neonatal jaundice has been described associated with the excretion of 3- α, 2- β-pregnanediol in the breast-milk, which competes for glucuronyl transferase in the infant's liver (Hargreaves and Piper 1971). The management of babies with pregnanediol jaundice consists of observation, with serial measurements of bilirubin levels. If these reach 15 mg of indirect bilirubin per 100 ml, discontinuance of breast-feeding for 48 hours is indicated, followed by return to the breast thereafter. This condition has never been associated with *kernikterus* or other type of brain damage. In view of the intense study of icterus in the newborn in recent decades, it would seem possible that *pregnanediol jaundice* is a new entity (Cole and Hargreaves 1972, Hargreaves and Piper 1971). Its aetiology is unknown, but if it is of recent occurrence then a toxic-environmental causation seems more likely than an inherent metabolic anomaly. An unproven suggestion has been made that there may be a relationship with the taking of oral contraceptives (Wong and Wood 1971), either at the time or previously, or the use of oxytocin (Chalmers *et al.* 1975) or prostaglandin in the induction of labour somewhat prematurely, with hepatic neonatal enzyme immaturity (Sims and Neligan 1976). Further investigation is needed, including comparative prevalence studies in non-Western communities. Recent studies suggest that it is uncommon (Garng *et al.* 1976).

In severe classical haemolytic disease of the newborn, including Rhesus incompatibility, small amounts of antibody are detectable in breast-milk (Moulinier 1953). This is partly destroyed in the infant's stomach and falls rapidly. From a practical point of view, it is of no significance, and there is no contraindication to breast-feeding.

The overall question of the excretion of potentially dangerous chemical toxicants in milk, both human and bovine, is largely related to the widespread distribution of chemicals in agriculture and the increased use of potent drugs in therapy. Some are necessary, therapeutically or as part of the modern mass-production of food. At the same time, their potential or actual hazards and ill-effects need to be appreciated in general, and, in particular, consideration needs to be given to minimizing the intakes of pregnant and lactating women, in view of the possible susceptibility of both the foetus *in utero* and the baby at the breast (American Academy of Pediatrics 1974*b*). As with other aspects of the 'chemicalization' of modern living, these are important areas for general caution and further research.

Specially designed, controlled studies in mothers and their nursing babies will usually be impossible to devise, technically and ethically. Further studies are certainly needed on the excretion of chemical toxicants in human colostrum and milk in both industrialized and less technically developed countries in potentially hazardous situations, such as in areas where particular forms of environmental pollution are known to occur, as rural Mississippi and Arkansas (Woodard *et al.* 1976) (compared with those where they do not), or with lactating mothers receiving medication.

4. Oral conditions

In addition to the effects of fluoride ingested on the prevention of caries in the deciduous teeth (p. 49), oral effects may perhaps result from the very different mechanics of feeding from the bottle in general and from the practice of giving a 'night bottle' in particular.

(i) *Malocclusion*

Mechanical differences in bottle-feeding and breast-feeding are very considerable (Brambleton 1956, Hanna 1967). In bottle-feeding, the main action is sucking, by use of negative intrabuccal pressure, with consequent increased likelihood of 'air-swallowing', especially with the vacuum created in old-style feeding bottles. (It is little appreciated that 'burping' or 'bringing up the wind' is a Western cultural practice, not usually found in other communities, and undoubtedly in large measure related to the almost obligatory aerophagy in artificially-fed babies, especially using older models of bottles.) From the infant's side, breast-feeding is a process of 'suckling' or 'mulging', in which negative pressure suction plays a minor role, and 'expression' from the terminal lacteals by the 'milking action' of the tongue moving posteriorly and squeezing the end of the breast, including the nipple and areola, against the hard palate is the main element, aided by actual milk expulsion by the let-down reflex (p. 19) from the maternal side of the nursing dyad.

In bottle-feeding, much less work is involved in obtaining milk, especially jaw motions, than occurs in breast-feeding. The tongue is thrust anteriorly to control the inflow of formula, rather than moved backwards rhythmically as in breast-feeding, and the pattern of breathing has been shown to differ, even when both milks are offered by bottle (Johnson and Salisbury 1975).

A pattern of abnormal 'tongue-thrusting' and swallowing occurs more in bottle-fed babies (Stanley 1972) and, according to some authorities, may be one aetiological factor in malocclusion, with open bite, premaxillary protrusion, and apparent retrusion of the mandible. Thumb sucking (or, more generally, 'prolonged non-nutritive sucking habits') also play a part in the causation of malocclusion. Differences of opinion exist regarding the aetiology of this condition and its relationship, if any, with mode of infant feeding (Anke 1971).

In a parallel fashion to the attempts to 'humanize' cow's-milk formulas, recent bottles and other devices have been 'mammarized' to try to make the feeding process more similar to that of breast-feeding. For example, a valve has been introduced to prevent the development of a vacuum, and, in recent years, even a breast-like plastic feeding device has been invented.

Perhaps one of the more curious devices in this regard is the 'Nuk exerciser'. This is a specially designed rubber pacifier intended for use between feeds in order to counteract the effects of 'improperly designed rubber nipples and harmful bottle-nursing techniques' (Graber 1966, Schwartz and Gratzinger 1966). Its purpose is mostly to exercise the baby's mouth in the same way as in breast-feeding.

(ii) *Dental caries*

The question of optimal fluoride intake in early infancy is of importance in the prevention of caries of the deciduous teeth (James 1975, James *et al* 1957, Winter *et al*. 1971), and is related to method of infant feeding in rather complicated ways. Earlier work suggested that a high selenium content in human milk might be protective (Hadjimarkos 1963).

Also, very probably, the sugar content of early feeding may habituate to over-sweetness ('sweet tooth') with cariogenic potential and an increased tendency to obesity — the two major nutritional–dietary public-health problems in Westernized communities. In addition, malocclusion itself is associated with an increased rate of caries (Brucker 1953).

Several studies in the U.S.A. and U.K. have shown a lower incidence of caries in the deciduous eruption in breast-fed babies compared with those bottle-fed. Apparently quite unrelated to the question of fluoride intake, one study on the effect of fluoridation on dental caries undertaken in the U.S.A. noted differences in the prevalence of caries in the breast-fed compared with those bottle-fed (Tank and Storvick 1965). Results were markedly in favour of the breast-fed (Table 5.6). In England, an investigation of children under 5 years of age with and without caries of the upper incisors showed less affected in the breast-fed than in those infants fed entirely on bottle-feeds or with supplementary feeds (Robinson and Naylor 1963) (Table 5.7).

Reasons for these differences are not clear, especially in view of many other variables, such as the type of formula, age of introduction of semi-solids, use of 'night bottles', etc. This subject deserves much further epidemiological investigation.

On a more clear-cut level is the condition usually known as 'nursing-bottle syndrome' (Golnick and Mathewson 1967, Kroll and Stone 1967, Kullberg and Hansen 1963, Rosenstein 1966). This occurs in children under the age of three years, who sleep throughout the night with the feeding bottle continually in the mouth. The child lies with the nipple against the palate, with stagnation of formula or other liquid around the upper incisors, aided by the decrease in both salivary flow and swallowing during sleep. The lower incisors are not affected as the tongue covers them. In advanced cases,

TABLE 5.6 *Decayed, missing, and filled primary teeth of Albany and Corvallis children in the U.S.A., aged one to six years of age, as related to the extent of breast-feeding in infancy* (from Tank and Storvick 1965)

Breast-feeding	Number of children examined		Number of decayed, missing, and filled primary teeth per child		Percentage difference from non-breast-fed children	
	Albany	Corvallis	Albany	Corvallis	Albany	Corvallis
Less than 3 months	82	110	4·00	1·75	−10	−20
More than 3 months	38	80	2·4*	0·91*	−46*	−59*
None	109	132	4·43	2·20	–	–

* Difference significant at the 5 per cent level.

TABLE 5.7 *Caries incidence in breast-fed and bottle-fed English children under 5 years of age* (from Robinson and Naylor 1963)

	With caries	Without caries	Total
Breast-fed only	1	4	5
Supplementary bottle-fed	12	29	41
Bottle-fed only	46	18	64
	—	—	—
	59	51	110

however, the back teeth also may be involved (Fass 1962, Goose 1967).

Milk or formula can produce this picture, because of the lactose present. However, it is more marked when sucrose-rich fluids are used, such as sweetened fruit juice or vitamin syrups. The use of sugar-coated comforters or pacifiers can have similar results.

The condition appears to be common and its public-health significance will be considered later (Nizel 1975). It is certainly a major cause of rampant caries in the deciduous teeth. Its aetiology is appreciated by a variety of picturesque descriptive labels, such as 'apple-juice mouth' or 'nap-bottle mouth' (Powell 1973).

Preventive emphasis is almost always only geared to the need for health education of parents, for the use of water only if night bottles are felt to be unavoidable, and for early dental surveillance. In breast-fed babies weaned without use of feeding bottles, the condition does not occur.

6 Maternal effects

The effects of lactation on the mother will depend on many factors, including her nutritional condition. Psychological and emotional outcomes are discussed later (p. 142). The present chapter is concerned with the effect of breast-feeding on maternal nutrition, on breast condition, and on contraception.

1. Maternal nutrition

As noted earlier (p. 59), the effect of lactation on maternal nutrition depends on the woman's diet before and during pregnancy, as well as during breast-feeding. In well-fed females about 4 kg (9 lb) of subcutaneous fat is laid down physiologically in pregnancy as calorie stores for subsequent lactation. In Westernized societies with adequate food, breast-feeding can even be considered to have a postnatal slimming effect. For example, a prolonged follow-up study by Dennis (1971) showed that breast-feeding mothers had lost about 2 lb (1 kg) more weight than bottle-feeding mothers by three months after delivery (Fig. 6.1). Hytten and Leitch calculated that the contribution of pregnancy stores to breast-milk production is about 300 kcal/day for four months — equivalent to the loss of 33 g (about

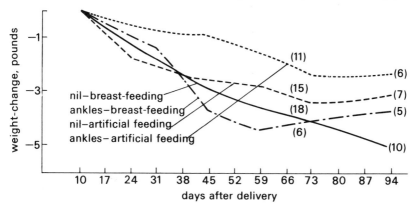

Fig. 6.1. Body-weight changes in the puerperium between the 10th and 94th days (the numbers in brackets are the total number of cases represented by each line) (from Dennis, J. K. (1965). *J. Obstet, Gynec.* **72**, 94, Changes in body weight after delivery).

1 oz) of fat daily, or almost half a pound weekly (Hytten and Leitch 1971).

There is inadequate evidence that the range of diets expected in Western countries can affect the yield or composition of breast-milk significantly (except for the fatty acids), although few studies have been undertaken, and mostly some decades ago. However, in poorly nourished communities in developing countries the nutrition of the mother in pregnancy and lactation can affect that of her offspring through inadequate foetal stores and low birth-weight, through inadequate weight-gain in pregnancy, and through usually slight–moderate, but significant, decreases in the composition and volume of the breast-milk produced (p. 62). Conversely, although the poor nutrition of the chronically ill-fed mother often appears to be surprisingly little affected, eventually it can be worsened by the cumulative drain of repeated pregnancy–lactation cycles. Forms of 'maternal-depletion syndromes can ensue ultimately (Jelliffe and Maddocks 1964), either with specific nutritional deficiencies, such as osteomalacia, goitre, iron-deficiency anaemia, or oedema (Bailey 1962), with general protein–calorie malnutrition, or with a decreasing body-weight and premature ageing with increasing numbers of reproductive cycles (Venkatachalam 1962). In recent studies in New Guinea, it has shown that the relative uncommonness of extreme progressive weight-loss in 'prolonged' lactation (up to two years) may be due to natural adaptive, calorie-sparing mechanisms, particularly decreased activity. Loss of weight in older women may be related more to ageing than to the drainage of reproductive cycles (Greenfield 1975).

Conversely, the prolonged amenorrhoea and spacing of childbirths characteristic of uninterrupted lactation conserve the iron normally lost in the menses and the nutrients that would be used in another pregnancy. Also, the initiation of lactation leads to reflex secretion of oxytocin by the posterior pituitary, causing uterine contraction, and the speeding-up of involution. The effect on reducing blood-loss is slight in well nourished women, but the significance in repeatedly pregnant, anaemic iron-deficient mothers whose babies suckle the breast from shortly after birth may be expected to be important.

The significance of ensuring adequate maternal nutrition has already been emphasized, but cannot be overstressed. This applies to all parts of the world (Filer 1975). A biologically rational approach to infant feeding has to be dyadic — dealing with the interaction between mother and offspring as uterine foetus, as extero-gestate foetus, and as transitional.

2. Breast conditions

Postnatal complications
Successful lactation with an unimpaired let-down reflex leads to adequate emptying of the breasts without milk engorgement and less chance of nipple trauma and, hence, a decreased probability of cracked nipples, infective

mastitis, or breast abscess (*British Medical Journal* 1976*a*, Fulton 1945, Newton and Newton 1950). Conversely, both unsuccessful or even 'token' breast-feeding (limited number of often scheduled feedings during the day-time), sometimes with poor function of the let-down reflex, can increase these mammary complications. Contrasting incidences have, for example, been noted between urbanized élite bottle-feeding Bengali mothers and traditional village women of the same genetic stock in West Bengal for whom breast-feeding was the norm (D.B. Jelliffe 1956).

Breast size

In Westernized societies, the mammae have become predominantly associated with their sexual–aesthetic functions, so that in these cultures the size and shape of the female breasts are of predominantly psychosexual significance, in relation to attractiveness to men and to youthfulness (Weiss 1975). For these reasons, the controversy concerning breast-feeding 'ruining the figure' is important. As discussed earlier (p. 11), the pre-pregnancy size of the breasts is due largely to the amount of fat present, which presumably is mainly genetic, but also influenced by overall calorie intake. The main enlargement in reproduction is during pregnancy, quite independent of lactation. During pregnancy and during breast-feeding, the avoidance of additional, culturally objectionable 'droop' can be assisted by minimizing the effect of gravity with a brassière. Also, as noted earlier (p. 113), breast-feeding itself causes a physiological *decrease* in body fat, including mammary fat.

However, suitable objective studies have not been undertaken. Assessment of volume is possible by water displacement techniques, but methods of measurement of shape and contour would be difficult to define objectively. This is culture-bound to a considerable extent. Viewing of 1940s films indicates the jutting pointed, uplift of the time compared with the more natural shape and lack of concealment in the 1970s. End-results vary from, say, traditional rural African women for whom the matter is irrelevant and who have a larger number of offspring, prolong lactation (often two years or more), wear no brassière or breast support and are poorly nourished, to, at the other extreme, the affluent well-fed woman in Europe or America or Africa, with one or two widely spaced children, using a brassière in late pregnancy and lactation. Probably and usually, breast size is more affected by pregnancy, diet (including obesity), ageing, and the degree of mammary support than by lactation, especially relatively short, and 'occasional' (with, say, two children).

Cancer (see p. 389)

Lower incidences of breast cancer have been observed clinically in communities in less technically developed countries where breast-feeding is widespread and prolonged (*British Medical Journal* 1974*c*, Lee and Weatherall 1975, Miller and Fraumeni 1972). Difficulties in interpretation include a common lack of unbiased, representative statistics. Also, recent international epidemiological studies have shown that the lesser frequency of mammary carcinoma is rather in communities where the reproductive pattern of early and frequent pregnancies, large families, and prolonged lactation are usual. The apparent protective effect, however, could not be ascribed to any one aspect, but to the whole cluster of factors or their interaction. Indeed, recent work (Chan and Cohen 1974) suggests that other possible aetiological factors, also need to be considered, including the effects of the lipid content of the woman's diet, with unsaturated, fatty-acid peroxidases in breast tissue suggested as possibly leading to the irreversible formation of tissue-damaging free radicals (Horwitt 1974), her prolactin production (*The Lancet* 1972*a*), and certain newly-recognized possibly genetic associations, particularly the presence of breast-fluid secretions obtained by aspiration from non-parous, non-lactating women, and seemingly present more commonly in groups with genetically-determined 'wet-type' ear cerumen (Petrakis *et al.* 1975).

In the last few years, considerable furore has occurred following the finding of type-B virus particles (virions) in breast-milk, which resemble the viral agent responsible for mouse breast cancer (Le Page 1971, McCabe and Chang 1971, Moore *et al.* 1971, Schlom *et al.* 1971). Despite lack of proof and despite the well-known fact that man normally carries several other viruses which can produce cancer in animals — for example, herpes simplex virus — it was immediately suggested that breast-milk of mothers with a family history of mammary cancer should be examined for virus particles (a practical impossibility for technical, logistic, and financial reasons) and that the babies, especially girls, of mothers with a family history should not be breast-fed (Macklin 1959, McMahon *et al.* 1970, Morgan *et al.* 1974, Tokuhata 1969).

The controversial matter was recently analysed epidemiologically by Fraumeni and Miller (1971) of the U.S. National Cancer Institute, Bethesda:

Virus particles detected in human milk have lately been under intensive investigation as possible etiological agents in breast cancer. These particles: (a) are structurally similar to the milk-transmitted virus which caused mammary adenocarcinoma in mice; (b) show reverse transcriptase activity, which is characteristic of certain oncogenic viruses; and (c) have been observed in a high proportion of milk samples obtained from women whose near relatives had breast cancer. Women with a positive family history of breast cancer have an increased risk of the neoplasm. It has been suggested that such women, though healthy, should not breast-feed their children because of the possible transmission of a cancer-causing virus.

This recommendation should be weighed against the evidence concerning possible viral spread from mother to daughter; (a) in countries where breastfeeding is common and prolonged, rates for breast cancer are low (this finding is not due, as previously thought, to a protective influence of lactation on the mother); (b) familial aggregations of breast cancer are low and breast cancer occurs equally in the maternal and paternal lines (aunts and grandmothers); if the disease was maternally transmitted, as in *kuru*, one would expect an excess of familial cases on the maternal side; (c) mother/daughter occurrences of breast cancer are not associated with a history of breastfeeding; (d) in the United States, as breastfeeding has declined in frequency, the incidence of breast cancer has climbed — a finding that runs counter to the hypothesis that human milk contributes to the occurrence of breast cancer in the off-spring; (e) data for other variables also run opposite to the hypothesis; the risk of breast cancer is low among groups that favor breastfeeding (e.g., rural dwellers, lower economic classes, and the foreign-born).

Thus, the available human data do not support the claim that breast cancer is related to breastfeeding.

Nevertheless, present-day intense research into cancer, including that involving the breast, needs to cover further investigations into the effects of lactation on both benign and malignant mammary tumours in different ecologies, as well as the influences of genetics, diet, age, family size, chemicals, including drugs, oral contraceptives, and environmental pollutants.

3. Contraception*

In numerous parts of the world, such as in communities in India, the Middle East, and Africa, there is commonly a traditional belief that breast-feeding delays the onset of the next pregnancy. For example, Mayer (1966) notes that lactation is recognized for its contraceptive effect in rural Tanzania. Indeed, a major cultural motivation for breast-feeding can be its anti-fertility effect, as was the case in Europe in the past.

In some societies, this belief was made much more effective and prolonged by culturally-defined periods of abstinence from sexual intercourse after childbirth, as in parts of Java (Singaringbun and Manning 1976). In some cultures this may last as long as the child was being breast-fed. In a survey of 51 traditional African societies, Murdock (1934) found such restrictions on sexual intercourse in 29. Conversely, but uncommonly, some communities breast-fed for a short time in an attempt to *increase* the birth rate. Such is the case among the Arsi Galla in the Rift Valley in Ethiopia, whose population is declining (Knutsson and Mellbin 1969).

The concept of lactation contraception has been difficult for modern health workers to accept, because their training leads them towards technological rather than biological solutions, and because the relationship of the hormonal effectiveness of breast-feeding has only recently become scientifically recognized (Buchanan 1975, Giosia 1955, Hartfield 1972, Jelliffe and Jelliffe 1975 c). Indeed in recent years, scientific evidence has shown that breast-feeding suppresses ovulation, as can be demonstrated by

*Recent reviews are available by Solien de Gonzalez (1964), Jelliffe and Jelliffe (1972b), Chopra (1972), Latham (1972), Simpson-Herbert (1975), Rosa (1976b), and *Population Reports* (1975).

serial post-partum basal body-temperature recordings (Cronin 1968) and by histological examination of endometrial biopsies (Udesky 1950), associated with a period of lactation amenorrhoea.

Mechanisms

The closed interval between successive conceptions is illustrated schematically in Fig. 6.2. The pregnancy-spacing effect of lactation occurs by extending the length of post-partum amenorrhoea. The principal mechanism appears to be hormonal, probably mainly due to the anovulatory effects of pituitary prolactin.

Post-partum plasma prolactin levels differ greatly in the breast-fed and non-breast-fed (Bonnar *et al.* 1975). The secretion of prolactin has been shown to vary quantitatively with the sucking stimulus to the breast (p. 17)

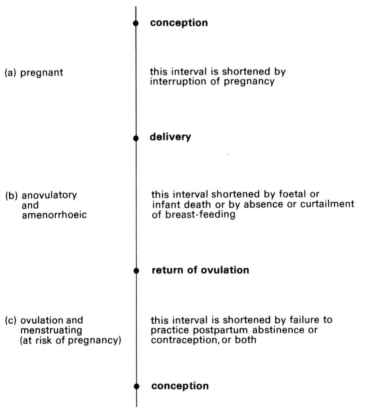

Fig. 6.2. The closed interval between successive conceptions (reproduced with the permission of the National Academy of Sciences (1974). *Nutrition and fertility interrelationships*, National Research Council, Washington, D.C.)

(Kolodny *et al.* 1972). In practical terms, this varies with the number of feedings in the 24 hours (and their duration) and the vigour of the baby. Conversely, limitation of number of feedings or practices which blunt the infant's sucking drive, such complementary bottles or the use of a 'pacifier', diminish prolactin secretion.

This helps in explaining the success of lactation contraception in communities with biological or natural breast-feeding — that is in traditional communities where the baby takes the breast soon after delivery, and thereafter frequently and at short intervals (both day and night), without supplementary feedings of cow's milk or semi-solids. It also partly explains the decline in effectiveness in prolonged lactation when the sucking stimulus of breast-feeding decreases with increase in the infant's age and widening of the diet.

By contrast, the contraceptive effect of lactation is greatly reduced if breast-feeding is partial, token, or non-natural (or 'dosed') (Van Balen and Ntabomvura 1976), and supplemented early with other feeds of cow's-milk formula or semi-solids, or if the baby is left 'to cry itself out', or if a pacifier (dummy) is used — all of which reduce sucking stimulus and prolactin secretion.

In addition to the prolactin effect, evidence suggests that maternal malnutrition may play a role in extending the length of post-partum amenorrhoea (Delgado *et al.* 1975, May 1963, Salber *et al.* 1965). In famines and very severe food shortages (e.g. concentration camps, anorexia nervosa), starvation amenorrhoea is well recognized (Jelliffe and Jelliffe 1971 *b*). Temporary cessation of menstruation has been reported during over-rigorous slimming in teenage girls (Nakamura *et al.* 1975), with a return to normal with re-feeding (McArthur *et al.* 1976).

In poorly fed communities, the prolonged amenorrhoea seen may be a cumulative result from the prolactin effect, together with maternal malnutrition, due to an inadequate diet made worse by too frequent, too closely spaced reproductive cycles. Suggestive evidence comes from Bangladesh where it was observed that lactating women resume menstruation more commonly between November and March, coinciding with the major rice harvests (Chen *et al.* 1974). However, the possible relative significance of the prolactin effect and of maternal malnutrition is at present uncertain and needs further study. For example, one of the longest average lengths of post-partum amenorrhoea (14·6 months) was noted in the U.S.A. in well-fed women practising 'natural' (or biological) breast-feeding (Kippley 1974, Kippley and Kippley 1972, 1974). Also, in the Hutterite community in the U.S.A., breast-feeding for an average of over one year is the norm, but the strict routine makes relaxed nursing difficult, while semi-solids are introduced in the early weeks and the comforter is widely used (Huntington and Hostetler 1970). Presumably because of limited sucking stimulus, the birth-spacing effect of lactation is lessened.

Community evidence

Recent analyses of the birth records have been made in some parts of the world where prolonged breast-feeding was usual and where such information has been available as from nineteenth-century Bavaria (Knodel 1968, Knodel and Van de Walle 1967), nineteenth-century French Canada (Henripin 1960), and eighteenth-century Florence (Corsini 1974). In these, the birth spacing in the absence of known family planning suggests the role of lactation amenorrhoea.

Also, numerous investigations have been carried out in present-day communities. For example, in a study in the central African country of Rwanda, Bonté and Van Balen (1969) showed that prolonged lactation produced amenorrhoea in 50 per cent of women for over one year and also was responsible for an overall delay in pregnancy of 15 months, as compared with a group of women of the same genetic and cultural group whose babies had died at birth and hence were not protected from conception by lactation. It may be noted that amongst this community sexual intercourse was culturally permitted from about eight days after delivery.

Similarly, a study undertaken by Del Mundo and Adiao (1970) in the Catholic Philippines demonstrated that a 24–35 months birth-spacing interval was achieved in $51 \cdot 2$ per cent of mothers who breast-fed their children for 7–12 months, as opposed to only 30 per cent in mothers whose infants were artificially fed.

In distant Arctic communities, the influence of changing breast-feeding practices has been dramatically documented in the Eskimos and Indians of Canada and Alaska (Schaefer 1971 a). Romaniuk's data (1973) on the James Bay Indians shows that the increase in bottle-feeding and the decrease in the average duration of breast-feeding from 15 to 5 months between 1940 and 1960 appeared to be an important factor in the reduced birth interval.

The considerable amount of information correlating length of lactation with amenorrhoea and birth interval in numerous parts of the world has been collected recently by Van Ginneken (1974), and extended by Rosa (1974, 1976a,d) (Table 6.1). Also, Van Balen and Ntabomvura (1976) have shown the progressive differences in both length of amenorrhoea and of intervals between birth in communities (a) without the protective effects of either breast-feeding or technological contraceptives, (b) 'natural' (biological) breast-feeding, and (c) with 'natural' breast-feeding and culturally defined abstinence (Figs. 6.3 and 6.4).

The effect of lactation on post-partum amenorrhoea varies with customs in relation to suckling practices and to the use of other foods, and probably with maternal malnutrition and degree of motivation. In general, non-breast-feeding mothers have post-partum amenorrhoea for about 4 months; in lactating women, amenorrhoea extends up to about 10 months (Rosa 1976d). However, pre-menstrual ovulation can occur, and was noted in

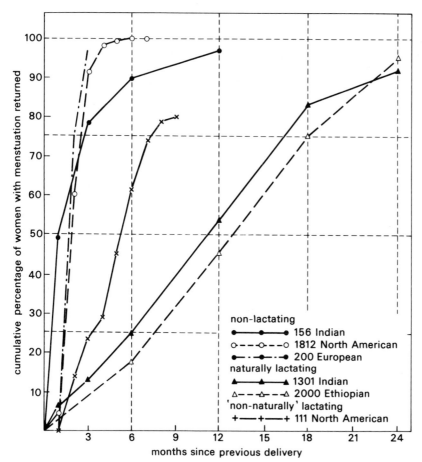

Fig. 6.3. Postpartum amenorrhoea and lactation (from Van Balen, J. and Ntabom-vura, A. (1976). *J. trop. Pediat. env. Chld Hlth*, **22**, 50)

30–60 per cent of a group of women in Chile (Perez *et al.* 1971). Conversely, anovulatory menstruation can occur sometimes for the first cycle or so.

In other words, lactation amenorrhoea does not represent complete anovulatory protection, and in various studies from 3 to 15 per cent of pregnancies have been found to occur without menstruation since the previous birth. Fertility protection from lactation beyond the amenorrhoea period is totally unreliable. In typical developing areas where prolonged breast-feeding is practised, half the women become pregnant in late lactation (often with disastrous effects for the weanling) and most will become pregnant if they continue lactation indefinitely (Rosa 1976*d*).

Oral contraceptives and lactation
While the contraceptive role of breast-feeding has become increasingly

TABLE 6.1   *Lactation, postpartum amenorrhoea, and conception interval* (from Rosa 1975)

Area	Source*	Sample†	Lactation Percentage of women starting	Duration, months	Amenorrhoea, months Lactating women	Non-lactating women	Conception interval, months‡ Lactating women	Non-lactating women
Africa								
Algeria	Aardes (1971)	8000 UR		17·6	6·0			
Egypt, Cairo	Kamal (1968)	300 U		15·1	5·3			
Cairo	Malkani (1960)	282 U				2·0		
Ethiopia, Tigre	Knuttson (1964)	162 R		20·0				
Sidamo	Knuttson (1964)	154 R		15·0				
Arussi	Knuttson (1964)	214 R		9·0				
Gondar	Obrian (1970)	200 R	100					
Gambia	Thompson (1967)	44 R		22·0				
Nigeria, Ibadan	Orwell (1974)	480 U	100	16·0				
Imassi	Martin (1964)	291 R	100	23·0			26·5	8·0
Rwanda	Bonté (1974)	235 U		9·0	9·0		11·7	5·6
Rwanda	Bonté (1974)	601 R		24·0			28·8	8·9
Senegal	Cantrelle (1971)	8500 R		24·0	11·0		23·9	10·7
Tanzania	Mayer (1966)	RL			9·0			
Tanzania	Mayer (1966)	RH			10·8			
Zaire	Jespers (1960)			16·4		18·0		
Asia								
Bangladesh, Matlab	Chen (1974, 1972)	200 R	100	25·0	18·9	2·0		
India, Baroda	Rajalakshmi (1971)	H			6·0			
Baroda	Rajalakshmi (1971)	L			18·0			
Bombay	Peters (1958)	272 U			12·0			
Bombay	Baxi (1957)	523 U		16·5	11·9			
Bombay	Jain (1967)				6·0			
Calcutta	Sen (1971)	2225 U	93	16·6	9·0	3·0		
Tamal Nadu	Gandhigram (1973)	3000 R		22·2	14·4	1·9		
Maharashtra	Dandekar (1957)	488 R			13·5			
Punjab	Potter (1959)	1400 R	98	21·0	10·8			
Ramanagram	Blacker (1954)				11·0			
Singur	Rao (1960, 1963)	936 R		28·0	13·0			
U.P.	Seghal (1966)	2500 R			13·0			
Jordan	Pharaon (1965)		95	16·0				
Lebanon	Harfouche (1965)	379 UL	97	10·0				

Location	Reference	n						
Philippines, Manila	Osteria (1974)	501	77	10·2	6·8	3·4	20·1	15·8
4 Towns	Rosa (1974)	309 U	79		8·5	3·5	20·3	16·9
Manila	Guthrie (1965)	100 U	83	11·0				
Luzon	Guthrie (1965)	150 R	89	19·0				
Luzon§	Osteria (1973)	165 R	90	12·3	9·8	1·9		
Indonesia, Mojolama	Masri (1974)	2195 R	99	25·6	22·1	5·1	28·7	
South Korea	Koh (1968)	1900 UR	96	24·0	15·0			
Seoul	Kwon (1972)	335 U	80		6·0	3·9		
Sungdong Go	Kwon (1972)	139 R	92		12·0	4·4		
South Korea,	Kang (1972)	600 U	95	20·0	12·5			
South Korea,	Kang (1972)	375 R	97	27·7	15·3			
Taiwan	Jain (1970, 1972)	1175 U	88	14·0	9·7	3·5		
Taiwan	Jain (1970, 1972)	1516 R	96	17·7	11·4			
Thailand§	Sivin (1969)	1600 U	84	12·0	6·6	2·9		
Thailand	Knodel (1972)	600 R	98	24·0				
Thailand	Knodel (1972)	700 R	85	16·0				
Ankara§	Sivin (1968, 1969)	400 U	95	13·0				
West Irian	Becroft (1967)	100	100	54·0	6·2	4·4	53·0	6·0
Americas								
Chile, Santiago	Perez (1971)	154 U	75	3·7	3·8	1·6		
Chile	Plank (1969, 1970)	1900 R	68	6·0				
Columbia, Medallin	Oberndorfer (1968)	2000	79	5·5				
Guatemala	Gonzalez (1963)	Ladino U		13·0				
Guatemala	Gonzalez (1963)	Ladino R		15·0				
Guatemala	Gonzalez (1963)	Indian R		30·0				
Jamaica	Grantham (1970)	300 U	95	6·0				
Martinique	Leridon (1970)	900 R		10·3				
St. Vincent	Antrobus (1971)	300		9·6				
Venezuela, Colombia§	Sivin (1968, 1969)	1100 U	82	7·6	2·3			
Canada, Eskimos	Hildes (1971)			30·0			25·0	3·0
James Bay Indians	Romaniuk (1940)	116 R	31	15·0				
James Bay Indians	Romaniuk (1960)	29	5	5·0				
Alaska, Eskimos	Berman (1971)		'Natural' lactation		10·0			
U.S.A.	Kippley (1972, 1974)				14·6	3·2		
Guatemala, Catarinecos, Highland Indian	Hinshaw (1971)	75 R		24·0	12·0		13·8	5·1

* References given in original paper
† R = Rural   U = Urban   H = High Economic   L = Low Economic
‡ Interval from delivery to next conception
§ I.U.D. follow-up study

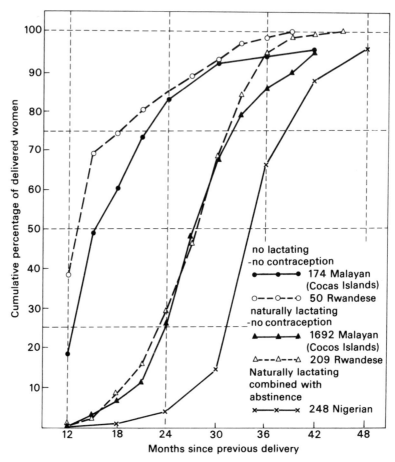

Fig. 6.4. Birth interval, natural lactation, and abstinence (from Van Balen, J. and Ntabomvura, A. (1976). *J. trop. Pediat. env. Chld Hlth*, **22**, 50)

clear, recent concern has developed regarding the possible effects of oral contraceptives on lactation (Ibrahim and El Tawil 1968, Kora 1969, Pomerance 1974).

Mixed pills. There is clear evidence that the earlier ovulation-suppressing contraceptive pills given by mouth — that is, relatively 'large-dose' mixed tablets, containing both estrogens and progestogens — have a deleterious effect on the production of human milk, especially if introduced soon after delivery, and often made it impossible to continue breast-feeding. In a review of a large series of reports, Rosa noted that suppression of milk production occurred in all, varying from 'probable' to 'mild' to 'moderate', or, in those where measurements were made, with decreases of from 15 to 80 per cent of volume (Rosa 1976b).

Oral contraceptives have an effect on maternal nutrition, interacting with some essential nutrients (Wynn 1975). For example, increased iron absorption may occur, and there can be higher needs than usual for folic acid, vitamin B_{12}, pyridoxine, and tryptophan (Chopra 1972). These can be especially manifest in communities where deficiencies of some of these nutrients are already common, as in parts of India. The effect of oral contraceptives on the composition of breast-milk has not been studied sufficiently, and, although the pattern of change is not clear, studies have shown somewhat diminished levels of protein, fat, lactose, calcium, and phosphorus.

Such effects on volume and composition have lead in some countries to severe growth failure in the nursling (Cobo 1974*b*), even leading to what has been termed 'contraceptive marasmus'. This effect has been recognized by mothers in some countries, such as Egypt and Tunisia.

Progestogen pills. In some less developed countries, recent contraceptive experience has been with progestogen compounds alone, which appear to act by inhibiting sperm penetration into the cervical mucosa, and do not affect ovulation. Such pills, for example, chlormadinone, have been used orally in Egypt and in East and central Africa. Also noteworthy is the successful contraceptive use of repository intramuscular progestogen ('Depo-Provera') at prolonged intervals in Uganda, in Egypt, and elsewhere, although psychological difficulties in accepting the resulting prolonged amenorrhoea may pose difficulties (Jelliffe and Jelliffe 1972*b*).

Rosa (1976*b*) has analysed the effects on lactation in 20 studies in the literature. In all of them, progestogens used alone did not interfere with milk secretion and possibly even increased the volume produced. Evidence concerning the effect of progestogens on the composition of milk varies. In Cairo, Egypt, a significant decrease in protein, fat, and calcium was noted (Kader and Kamal 1969, Sammour *et al.* 1973). By contrast, in Bombay, India, no such change was found (Barsivala and Virkar 1973).

Excretion of progestogens occurs in human milk and, although no evidence of toxicity to the neonate was found in a small study by Miller and Hughes (1970), much further investigation is needed. Only one case of possibly associated feminization has been described in a breast-fed boy. Also, recent reports indicate possible risks of congenital limb-reduction defects when progestogens are inadvertently continued into early pregnancy (Nora and Nora 1973).

Discussion. Biological breast-feeding has a definite contraceptive effect during lactation amenorrhoea. It is less effective if the sucking stimulus is reduced, as when early supplementary feeds are given. This contraceptive effect declines with time, and ultimately menstruation, ovulation, and conception are resumed during prolonged breast-feeding.

It is evident that breast-feeding is an important, ill-appreciated mode of child spacing. It is valuable in any women using biological breast-feeding in any part of the world, with theoretical maxima of 10 babies in 30 years of fertility, compared with 30 babies in a non-breast-feeding woman. Lactation amenorrhoea is not appreciated by religious groups concerned with natural methods of contraception (Martin 1975). Moreover, there is no cost, no problem of availability, and no logistical or cultural problems of acceptability of new technological devices.

With regard to hormonal contraceptives, the low-dose progestogen drugs, both those given by mouth (*The Lancet* 1971) and by intramuscular injection (Rinehart and Winter 1975), do not appear to have ill-effects as far as milk production is concerned, and may even increase the yield. However, further investigation is needed into the effect of various types and doses of contraceptives on the composition and yield of milk in various nutritional circumstances, into possible effects on the nursing baby (and early foetus), and into nutritional and other consequences in the women concerned (Jelliffe and Jelliffe 1972 *b*).

The most appropriate regimen will vary with local circumstances, and with careful assessment of the balance of risks and advantages in the particular ecology. In more technically developed countries, 'token' or 'partial' breast-feeding is more usual, and this has unreliable contraceptive effects. However, it is neither wise nor advisable to prescribe oral contraceptives as these not only interfere with lactation but also may be secreted in breast-milk, so another technological form of birth control is indicated.

If biological breast-feeding is practised, as in many traditional communities and in a small number of women in industrialized countries, then lactation amenorrhoea has a satisfactory contraceptive effect. However, this effect declines and reinforcement may be suggested with another technological or other biological mode of contraception. The method and time of such a reinforcement are currently uncertain, and will be discussed later.

The use of a progestogen oral (or intramuscular) contraceptive may be suggested if the unproven disadvantages of the hormone are outweighed by the clear and well recognized risks to infant, mother, and subsequent children of too closely spaced pregnancies (Pan American Health Organization 1970*a*). Ideally, cheap, simple, culturally acceptable methods are needed which are not only a contraceptive, but also have no nutritional or hormonal ill-consequences for the mother or baby and complement, reinforce, or even enhance lactation.

In some circumstances, long-established methods may be feasible and suffice, including the I.U.D. (intra-uterine device), and various 'natural' systems, which are currently being reappraised (Martin 1975). In addition, work is needed (and already under way) on the so-called 'milk-pill', probably a progestogen which may have both contraceptive and galactopoietic properties (p. 12). However, care will be needed to ensure the absence of ill-effects, immediate and long-term, of such preparations on the nursing baby, as well as the mother.

Conclusion

The birth-spacing effect of lactation is really unsurprising. The 'common-sense' adverse consequences of too many children, too closely spaced can be shown statistically, as judged by morbidity and mortality (foetal, neonatal, infant and young child, maternal (*Population Reports* 1975 *b*)), by malnutrition of mother and offspring (both immediate and long-term, as measured by subsequent growth in the child, and by eventual nutritional 'maternal depletion'), and by intellectual development, as shown in the offspring by I.Q. tests. Similarly, the effects of limited family income in expenditure on food and medical care can have increased, measurable ill-effects. These apply in very different degrees to all socio-economic levels, but plainly the effects are made worse by poverty, or ignorance, or more usually both (*Population Reports* 1975 *b*, Wray 1971). The high maternal morbidity or mortality seen in developing countries is the result of frequent births at too close intervals, and, in turn, leads to increased numbers of infants with health problems and to death. Smaller families with more widely spaced births is a universal denominator of all the major health problems of mothers and children in developing countries, and of social and economic progress.

Other mammals have mating or oestrus seasons, which serve the same function as lactation amenorrhoea. The human neonate is a fragile exterogestate foetus (p. 4), needing prolonged, close maternal care and nutrition. Biological family planning — in the sense of child spacing — from lactation amenorrhoea is as 'old as mankind'. It is 'Nature's prescription' designed to ensure an optimal period of 2–3 years for the child to mature between births (Ratner 1970).

7   Economics and convenience

> *An unusual depletion in the crude-oil reserves of an oil-producing country of Asia or Latin America would be termed a crisis. Its economic and social implications would be so apparent that actions to reverse the trend would be awarded high priority. Yet going virtually unnoticed is a comparable crisis in many of the poor countries of the world, involving a valuable natural resource and losses in the hundreds of millions of dollars.*
> Alan Berg (1973)

In addition to the biological consequences of breast-feeding, various social and economic considerations have to be taken into account, in particular its convenience, acceptability, and economic significance in different socio-cultural circumstances.

1. Convenience and acceptability

The convenience of any practice depends in some measure on culturally defined priorities and alternatives. The Western concept of domestic convenience is related to shortening the time and decreasing the physical work needed to carry out particular tasks, especially those which are repetitive, boring, and strenuous, thus permitting increased time for other activities, including those which are more financially rewarding or diverting, and less menial and physically exacting.

Plainly, 'trade-offs' and different balances of benefits and risks occur, often with much wider social and cultural effects than could have been anticipated. For example, in industrialized countries, the increased incidence in obesity in recent decades is partly the result of over-eating and sedentary jobs and partly the result of labour-saving household appliances, leading in turn to the need for such compensatory 'forced-labour' as jogging, or costly spa regimens.

Nevertheless, the attraction of domestic 'convenience' in the Western sense is also very appealing to poorer mothers in less developed countries, not only because of the prestigious modernness of such methods, but also because 'time-and-motion' studies usually show their lives to be full of hard, grinding, physical work.

From a practical point of view, questions concerning the relative convenience of breast-feeding and bottle-feeding may be considered in relation to preparation and availability, to feasibility outside the home, to the financial significance for working women, and to effects on the parents' sleep at night.

(i) *Preparation and availability*. In most parts of the world today, interest centres increasingly on 'convenience foods' — that is, processed foods that are pre-cooked, ready-to-eat (possibly after initial warming), and requiring little apparatus to prepare or clean up afterwards. Less appreciated are the numerous 'natural convenience foods' that can also be incorporated without cooking into the weaning diet in some parts of the world — for example, ripe bananas, avocado pears, papayas, etc (D.B. Jelliffe 1968*b*). Even less often is it recognized that human milk represents the original ready-to-serve 24-hour convenience food, representing an unique supply-and-demand system (D.B. Jelliffe 1968*b*), with output related to the sucking stimulus (p. 17) and need as expressed by appetite and thirst.

The convenience of breast-feeding becomes apparent immediately after delivery when the baby is put to breast. No mathematical formula has to be devised; there is no need for anxiety that the milk may not agree with the baby. 'At home, the obvious advantages are even greater. With the bottle-feeding mother, there is the constant problem of formula buying and making, worry over whether there is enough (formula) in the house and if the bottles are sterile enough and the holes in the nipple the right size. She has to warm bottles and then cool them if they get too hot. The breast-feeding mother is free from these worries and harassments. Her milk is always right and it is always there' (Tompson 1976).

(ii) *Outside the home*. The convenience of breast-feeding outside the privacy of the home depends particularly on its cultural acceptability and the availability of methods for the mother to take the baby with her. In non-Western traditional cultures (including Europe and North America until the recent decades), no problems usually exist, as breast-feeding is a normal activity in almost any situation. Babies are often (but not always) carried by their mothers in a variety of devices (D. B. Jelliffe 1975*d*) and the range of movement from the house is usually relatively small, except with migrant, pastoralist or hunter communities.

By contrast, the nursing mother in Westernized communities faces essentially two different situations outside the home — travelling (both locally and on longer journeys) and going out to work. Both are related in part to cultural attitudes to breast-feeding, which can range from unconcern with a normal unnoticed activity to accusations of 'indecent exposure'. In fact, 'travelling is especially convenient with a nursing baby. The secret here is wearing clothes that make discreet nursing possible where people might be shocked at the sight of a partially bared bosom' (Tompson 1976). With minor modification in clothing (including nursing brassières) discreet unobtrusive nursing can be inconspicuously undertaken anywhere (Fig. 7.1). In addition, as discussed later (p. 301), cultural attitudes towards breast-feeding in the Western world are changing, as mirrored, for example, on television and in films. With appropriate dress, nursing can be undertaken without those around being aware that it is happening.

Other conveniences while travelling on longer journeys are that the mother has no supplies of formula or bottles to carry around, and has no problems of preparation in strange surroundings, with uncertain water supplies.

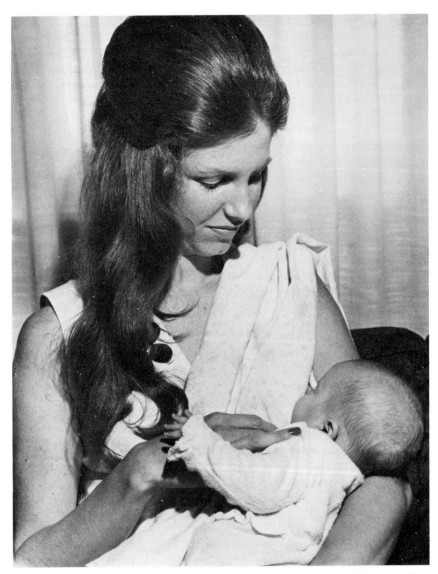

Fig. 7.1. Unobtrusive, culturally acceptable nursing made possible by minor modification of clothes (La Leche League International, Franklin Park, Illinois)

(iii) *Working mothers*. In Westernized societies, the socio-cultural and economic situation of the working mother with a young baby is difficult and has not generally been considered adequately nor resolved satisfactorily.

On one hand, the financial earnings may be highly significant to the family budget and the career outside the home important to the woman's self-esteem, and, indeed, as much her right as the man's. On the other hand, the possible ill-consequences of the disruption of the mother–infant dyad, as epitomized by breast-feeding, becomes more significant as the advantages of this close union emerge, and the financial, logistic, and staffing difficulties required to develop sufficient numbers of day-care centres or crèches of adequate quality, especially for young babies, become evident (p. 335).

Basically, the question is how culturally appropriate opportunities for biological infant feeding and child-rearing, particularly breast-feeding and general close continuous mother–infant contact, can be made available in modern mechanized urbanized societies, at least for those parents who wish to do so, and without financial loss or jeopardization of career.

That such reconsideration is necessary and possible is indicated, for example, by the spontaneous efforts of some women in the U.S.A. and other industrialized countries to continue working while breast-feeding their babies. Analyses of such developments are urgently required, as an indication of a spontaneous 'felt-need', as giving insight into the practical management of lactation and as indicating principles for potential regimens for more general application. Preliminary results of recent studies in Los Angeles have shown that 'reverse rhythm' feeding (i.e. with most feeds at night) and with the use of refrigerated expressed breast-milk in the day, given by bottle or feeding cup by a relative or appropriate available person, is a common pattern. Some women appear to prefer to combine their two careers for some months, by a part-time job and breast-feeding. Possible options for newer approaches are given later, when considering potential future programmes (p. 346).

The situation in the People's Republic of China has been outlined by Wray (1975):

Given the devastating effect of maternal employment on breast-feeding that has been observed in other parts of the world, the measures taken by the Chinese to facilitate breast-feeding are worthy of note. All mothers employed in factories, are given two months maternity leave, with pay, following the delivery of an infant, in order to be sure that breast-feeding can be well established. Thereafter, special provisions are made in order to make the continuation of breast-feeding possible. In factories, infant nurseries or crèches are routinely provided. Mothers arriving for work leave their babies in the nurseries and, in the course of an 8-hour shift, will be given, and expected to take, two half-hour breaks during which they go to the nursery and breast-feed their infants. In the rural communes, maternity leave varies and is generally without pay, but breast-feeding is no less routine. There the work pattern is such that special provisions are not necessary. Although the pattern varies by region and season, farmers traditionally arise at day-break and go to the fields to work for a few hours. At around 9 a.m., they return to their homes for breakfast, then work for two or three more hours, until noon. Lunch is followed by a long rest period, especially during the hot summer months, and then another work period of approximately three hours in the late afternoon. Nursing mothers thus breast-feed their babies on awakening in the morning, when they return home for breakfast, at lunchtime, and after their late afternoon work period.

(iv) *Parents' sleep*. In Westernized cultures in particular, interference with the parents' sleep, including the father's, is rightly emphasized in any consideration of infant feeding. Clinical lore and a recent study in the U.S.A. suggest that what has been termed 'night waking' is commoner in breast-fed than in bottle-fed babies (Carey 1975). However, the phenomenon appears to be mis-termed and in many, or most, instances it can better be related to biologically normal 'night feeding'.

As noted elsewhere, as far as lactation is concerned, man can be classified as a 'continuous-contact, frequent suckling' species with low-protein, low-solute milk, compared, for example, with the rabbit which has milk with some 12 per cent protein and often feeds her young only once daily. Formula feedings with a higher nutrient density are similar to milk of 'intermediate contact species' feeding at more spaced intervals. In the U.S.A. until quite recently (Southworth 1906) and currently in traditional cultures, breast-feeding at night has been recognized as usual. A basic problem in Western linear culture may be the rigidly clock-defined division of the day and night with specific tasks allocated to definite times, for example, meals both adult and infant.

The nutritional significance or importance of night feedings for the breast-fed baby appears to be unknown — although obviously it can increase the amount of sucking stimulus (as compounded by the number of times × length of breast contact on each occasion) (p. 17). Also, growing awareness of the influences of feeding patterns on metabolic circadian rhythms in man and in experimental animals, such as rats, may be relevant (Girard-Globe *et al*. 1975). Chronobiological investigations of the interrelationships of times of feeding and their metabolic consequences are only at early stages (Halberg *et al*. 1975).

The inconvenience of successful breast-feeding at night or in the early morning is less than that of bottle-feeding, provided the infant is near to the mother. He can then be picked up and nursed, with little sleep lost by anyone, both at home and in the maternity ward. By contrast, fetching the formula and feeding the baby is more time-consuming, although the father can do this as well as the mother. However, breast-feeding is least disruptive of the sleep of both parents, and the husband's assistance in child care can better be enlisted in other ways than feeding.

At the same time, the potential for sleep disruption of parents (and paediatricians) of unsuccessful or difficult breast-feeding is plainly considerable. However, this may be expected to become increasingly less likely with the spread of modern knowledge of the practical psychophysiology of lactation both to health personnel and to interested mothers and fathers.

2. Economics

The Westernized world is essentially a competitive, acquisitive, numerate culture. It is a numbers-dominated society, in which everyone spends much time glancing at watches, working out income-tax returns, and giving screeds of numbers as personal identification. In this mathematically oriented society, the well-named 'gloomy science' of economics looms large, and it is plain that it influences the foods available for all age-groups, including those for young children.

In the numerophilic Western culture, it may seem strange that the cost–benefit of human milk has not been adequately perceived until very recently (Berg 1973, D.B. Jelliffe 1968c). However, this is perhaps not really surprising as human milk has not usually been considered or classified as a food by planners or agronomists as it is neither grown agriculturally nor purchased in a can. Food balance-sheets giving estimated production of food in a country, together with exports, imports, etc., have given no attention to the significance of human milk in this regard. No mention of human milk was made, for example, an important 1968 United Nations publication entitled 'International action to avert the impending protein crisis'. This was concerned exclusively with other admittedly extremely important approaches, such as genetic seed improvement, processed foods with new technologies, food fortification, and so on. However, changing awareness may be indicated by a 1975 issue of the journal *Science* on 'Food' in which a paper on 'Human milk, nutrition, and the world resource crisis', was included among other request contributions largely on recent developments in more orthodox agro-economic subjects (Jelliffe and Jelliffe 1975a).

Neither, for that matter, have many food-composition tables, widely used by nutritionists, included the composition of human milk until very recently. In fact, human milk has economic significance on three different, overlapping levels (D.B. Jelliffe 1975): the large scale (national or community level), the family level, and the commercial level.

National level

Human milk has an economic significance on the national level for several different reasons. First, if breast-feeding declines on a large scale, then the need exists for a replacement — a liquid, usually based on cow's milk. Under these circumstances, it is necessary either to produce, process, and distribute such formulas on a wide scale from resources within the country, or, alternatively, to import them from overseas. The first, in almost all developing countries, is impractical for agricultural, economic, and technological reasons. For example, it has been calculated that to supply cow's-milk formulas for all women with young babies in India would require the immediate development of an additional herd of 114 million lactating cows (D.B. Jelliffe 1968c). Alternatively, importing formula from overseas is likewise impossible, especially due to fiscal problems, such as limited foreign exchange and balance-of-payment considerations, and the continually rising cost of so-called 'double-cycle' foods — that is, animal products, such as cow's milk. In a sense, human milk forms part of the usual earth–animal food chain, with the mother acting as the last link in the chain, as biological transmuter.

In less developed countries, loss of national and family revenue also occurs through expenditure on health services to deal with the increasing numbers of infants with marasmus and diarrhoea (p. 287), and through the family-planning services needed to compensate for the loss of lactation contraception (p. 125). In more prosperous technically advanced countries, consideration also needs to be given to the financial cost of services for the treatment of other 'cow's-milk bottle-feeding syndromes', such as infantile obesity (p. 242), and cow's-milk allergy (p. 96).

Nutritionally, the situation is increasingly paradoxical in that a major and correct preoccupation of many international nutritionists is the attempt on a global scale to increase traditional and unconventional foods, and to discover new sources of food, particularly protein-rich foods suitable for young children. At the same time, there has been inadequate appreciation that a decline in breast-feeding is not only a loss from the point of view of affected children, but is also a nutritional retreat, increasing the so-called 'world protein gap' — or, more accurately, the world's food gap (D.B. Jelliffe 1968c). It is not appreciated that human milk has been calculated to comprise about *one-quarter of total milk production in developing countries* (18 million tons compared with 66 million tons of cow's milk) (Helsing 1976).

Family-level cost of feeding

Putting aside all other considerations, comparison needs to be made between the cost of cow's-milk formula for the infant and the corresponding extra expense for the additional foods required by the nursing mother.

Older textbooks suggested that the cost of feeding the mother was greater than the funds needed for purchasing formula. This is not correct. The basic fallacy of these early figures was that they were related to the suggested use by pregnant and lactating mothers of diets that were made up of overly expensive foods, particularly animal products. In fact, it is cheaper to feed a lactating mother than to use formula, particularly the more expensive, convenient, ready-to-feed brands, provided it is realized that the extra nutrients required by the nursing mother can be obtained easily from appropriate mixtures of less costly, locally available, and culturally acceptable everyday foods (particularly using the 'principle of multi-mixes', based on cereal–legume mixtures), together with inexpensive vitamin supplements, if necessary.

In addition, recent studies have shown that the efficiency of conversion of nutrients by the lactating mother is much greater than previously believed — for calories, 90 per cent or more; for protein, 40–60 per cent. Also, there had been an under-appreciation of the importance to lactation of the physiological calorie reserve laid down in pregnancy in the form of subcutaneous fat. This means that additional calorie requirements are only half previous estimates (500 kcal/day) and the protein needs only 20 g/day (Thomson *et al.* 1970).

In terms of everyday foods in the U.S., the protein and calories can be obtained from a whole-wheat bread and peanut-butter sandwich and a glass of milk, and in Indonesia, from an increased intake of two regular foods — rice and *tempeh* (fungus-digested soya preparation) (Rohde 1975*b*).

The financial saving to families breast-feeding their young infants, as opposed to using cow's-milk formulas, is a universal phenomenon, found even in relatively affluent industrialized countries. However, the differences in costs depend on the foods taken by the mother and the type of milk used for the baby (Buss 1975). Thus, a 'luxury diet' to furnish the extra nutrients could be within a similar price-range to the most economical formula — evaporated milk, sugar, and water.

In the American economic context, a comparison in southern California in 1975 showed that, for feeding a 3-month-old child, the cost of everyday foods (plus the least costly daily vitamin–mineral supplement) for the lactating woman was 17–21 cents compared with 50–75 cents for a widely-used, ready-to-feed formula — a ratio of about 1:2 or 1:3 (Jelliffe and Jelliffe 1975*a*, 1976*b*). However, in some ways in well-to-do circumstances such calculations are theoretical. The increased appetite during lactation is automatically adjusted physiologically and in well-to-do families can be taken care for the most part by somewhat larger helpings of usual foods, which may already be available and wasted. However, even in well-fed communities, calories seem the most critical nutrient and, in the U.K. successfully lactating mothers who tried to 'diet' to lose weight were found to have 'an immediate reduction in milk supply' (Whichelow 1975).

The cost of infant formulas has to cover packaging, transport, storage, and advertising, as well as the ingredients and their processing. Domestic expenses include feeding-bottles, nipples, and cleaning apparatus, and usually fuel. Unappreciated costs at the manufacturing end include expenditure on research and development of new products. The basic cost of preparing infant formulas varies very greatly, but most expenditure is for advertising, packaging, transport, and research and development. Conversely, in Western cultures, the cost of a 'nursing' brassière and laundry need consideration in the breast-feeding budget.

Even in resource-rich countries, and especially among the disadvantaged sections of their populations, the situation has become more marked, with the rapid rise in price of all goods especially 'double-cycle' animal products, such as cow's milk. At the consumer level, this has been reflected in the U.S.A., for example, by a near doubling of the supermarket price of some better-known brands of infant formula in recent years. Main factors responsible for the rapidly rising costs of cow's milk are largely related to the high price of cattle-feed and of agricultural and industrial labour. Even dried skim-milk — the basic ingredient of most formulas — has *quadrupled* in price in some countries since 1969 (p. 316). By contrast, there has been no rise in labour or production costs in the maternal processing plant, although the price of the extra foods needed by the lactating woman has increased with inflation.

The situation in technically less developed countries is infinitely more serious. To be able to bottle-feed adequately three things are needed: adequate funds to purchase sufficient formula, reasonable home hygiene, and some degree of cultural conditioning towards domestic mathematics. In less developed countries, it is impossible for the general population to bottle-feed young babies adequately in most situations. The arguments concerning the relative costs of human lactation versus purchased cow's milk formulas are, in fact, almost theoretical and certainly academic. This is clear when one notes the high percentage (up to $40 \cdot 8$–$63 \cdot 3$ per cent) of the minimum wage, (usually the minimum urban wage) that would have to be spent to buy adequate quantities of formula (Table 7.1). Indeed, with more recent rises in food costs, in 1975 investigation in some countries showed that as much as 93 per cent of a basic wage would be needed (Cameron and Hofvander 1975). However, the percentage of wage needed varies from country to country with the salary level of the particular job and the economic level of the country (Table 7.2).

In fact, such purchased baby milks have of necessity to be over-diluted or 'stretched'. For example, in a 1972 study in Barbados, only 18 per cent of poorer mothers were using a 1-lb tin of powdered milk for 4 days or less, as indicated nutritionally, whereas the majority (82 per cent) extended the use of the milk for from 5 days to 3 weeks (Pan American Health Organization 1972).

Relative costs of mother working
It is plain that considerations of the relative costs of formula versus breast-milk, and of the expenses arising from their effects on health, do not take into account the full economic consequences of women working outside the house in salaried employment in relation to the well-being of both mother–child dyad and the family, as opposed to working in the home or in agricultural labour in the family garden or fields.

The complicated effects on the nutrition and health of very young children of women participating in the labour-force do not appear to have been investigated adequately anywhere. From an economic point of view alone, 'time and money' considerations need to be analysed in relation to the mother with young infant. The *income effect* will depend on the net earnings of the mother, after subtraction of any expenditure needed for travel, meals away from home, special work clothes, any form of day care service, the financial loss of breast-milk, the cost (and availability) of adequate quantities of cow's-milk formula, the existence of functioning legislation benefits

TABLE 7.1 *Cost of artificial feeding in some countries and percentage of minimum wages* (from Cameron and Hofvander 1975)

Country	Minimum wage per week U.S. $	Cost per day at 3 months U.S. $	Percentage of wage	Cost per day at 6 months U.S. $	Percentage of wage
United Kingdom	39·20	0·84	2·1	1·30	3·3
Burma	5·01	0·53	10·6	0·81	16·2
Peru	5·60	0·84	15·0	1·30	23·2
Philippines	9·69	1·67	17·2	2·59	26·7
Indonesia	5·60	1·05	18·8	1·62	28·9
Tanzania	7·62	1·57	20·6	2·44	32·0
India	4·62	1·05	22·7	1·62	35·1
Nigeria	5·18	1·57	30·3	2·44	47·1
Afghanistan	2·80	1·05	37·5	1·62	57·9
Pakistan	5·18	2·09	40·3	3·23	62·4
Egypt	4·09	1·67	40·8	2·59	63·3

*Accurate information on wages and costs of food is difficult to find. Here they are expressed as U.S. $ for comparative purposes. It is assumed here that the artificial food, a full-cream modified milk supplies the infant's total daily need for food.

TABLE 7.2 *Cost of complete formula feeding expressed as a percentage of monthly salaries for selected occupations in different countries* (from Cameron and Hofvander 1975)

Age of infant in months	Hospital cleaner/orderly 0–2	3–5	Ministry clerk 0–2	3–5	Junior staff nurse 0–2	3–5
Egypt	28	39	18	26	14	19
Liberia	20	29	7	10	6	9
Malawi	66	93	57	80	10	14
Pakistan	18	25	12	16	8	11
United Kingdom (London)	3	4	4	5	2	3

Salaries were at the basic rates in each country
The formula costed was a popular brand sold
Daily energy requirements were: 550 kcal for 0–2 months
                                 770 kcal   3–5 months
Costs and salaries refer to February 1975

for lactating women (including salaried leave, crèches, etc.), and whether the extra income is spent on food or other items, and whether this food is for the young child. The *time effects* will be greatest on those household activities which are 'time-intensive', such as food preparation and particularly breast-feeding, which also has to be spaced through the day. (Two Filipino studies (Popkin 1975) showed that infants were fed 7–8 times/day with each period lasting 15–30 minutes.)

Studies of this type have been begun in the Philippines by Gill and Popkin (1975), in which breast-feeding behaviour is analysed within the context of the interaction between household time and income constraints. As expected, it was apparent that the working status of the mother led to declines in breast-feeding. Again as expected, negative effects of switching from breast to bottle are much greater if the household is very poor. For example, it was found that among the children of the bottom income quartile, the weight-for-age of those breast-fed is about 10 per cent greater than those bottle-fed.

In poor urban circumstances in the Philippines, Popkin and Solon (1976) have shown that only $0·24 was spent weekly on milk. The unskilled and semi-skilled jobs obtained by working mothers gave annual incomes of from $76 to $130, of which 15–36 per cent would be needed to purchase adequate quantities of canned milk for the first year of life. In fact, 'the key effect nutritionally was on the items which require much of the mother's time, including breast-feeding. This income–time interaction may suggest an imperfect substitution between the goods provided by the mother's additional income and her time contribution both to child-care and home production'.

Similarly in very poor families in urban India, Reutlinger and Selowsky (1975) carried out investigations into the amount of mothers' earnings that would be needed to purchase adequate quantities of cow's milk nutritionally 'equivalent' to the breast-milk lost. This figure — 'marginal propensity' in economists' terms — was calculated based on current information on salaries for unskilled workers and the cost of milk at that time. Results are given in Table 7.3 and included figures for required (or theoretical) marginal propensity. In Table 7.4 the observed or actual marginal propensity was calculated among low-income groups in Calcutta.

Essentially, the required marginal propensity for children less than one year was 0·52 (e.g. about half the mother's salary), and differences between the observed and required marginal propensity would support the notion that, 'even under optimistic assumptions, a decline in breast-feeding as a result of the mother's participation in the labour-force could have an important negative effect on the nutritional status of the child.' (Reutlinger and Selowsky 1975).

Such considerations do not take into account the economics of other aspects of breast-feeding, including the prevention of infections (p. 84), the

TABLE 7.3 *Required marginal propensity to spend on milk to maintain the nutrition status of the child, Ubgan, India (from Reutlinger and Selowsky 1975)*

	Infant's age, months				
	0–6	7–12	13–18	19–24	0–24
1. Monthly potential breast-milk, litres*	25·9	15·2	15·2	6·1	15·6
2. Cow's-milk equivalent, litres*	30·5	17·5	17·5	7·0	18·2
3. Cost of milk equivalent, Rupees†	91·5	52·5	52·5	21·0	54·6
4. Monthly income of unskilled woman in 1973, Rupees‡	120	120	120	120	120
5. Required marginal propensity to spend on milk	0·53	0·30	0·30	0·12	0·32

* From Berg (1973)
† Using a price of 3 Rupees per litre; price as of October 1972 in Bombay and Madras.
‡ Corresponds approximately to the monthly wage of a woman in domestic service in large urban areas.

TABLE 7.4 Calcutta   *Marginal propensity to spend on children's food per child in low-income groups* (from Reutlinger and Selowsky 1975)

Mean monthly *per capita* expenditures, Rupees	15·2	30·7	50·9	81·3
Mean family size	7·3	6·8	6·3	6·0
Monthly family expenditure, Rupees	110·9	208·7	320·6	487·8
Monthly expenditure per child, Rupees				
Age of child: 0–6 months	10·0	14·0	17·0	17·9
7–12 months	14·5	19·9	25·8	36·7
12–24 months	13·7	21·5	29·9	38·4
Marginal propensity to spend on Children's Food (per child), Rupees				
0–6 months		0·04	0·05	0·08
7–12 months		0·03	0·05	0·08
12–24 months		0·01	0·06	0·05

contraceptive effect (p. 118), and the need for close, continuous mother–infant interaction (p.142). In particular, the quality of care and attention received by infants left at home or in ill-equipped, poorly staffed day-care centres is of concern with regard to health, nutrition, and emotional development (p. 335). The need for further studies in this area is crucial, especially if appropriate legislation and child-care services are to be developed to cover both infant feeding and other aspects of child rearing, as well as the need or wish of some women to work out of the home (Popkin and De Jesus 1976).

Human milk as a saleable commodity
As noted earlier, one reason that human milk has not been regarded as a food is because it has not usually been a saleable commodity, with the exception of the more direct and 'invisible' purchase from wet-nurses and the availability of purchasable liquid (or even dried) milk in some breast-milk banks in North America and Europe in the period 1920–40.

Recently there has been a resurgence of interest in breast-milk banks (p. 362), to which milk can be sold. Thus, in Britain in 1973, a pint of expressed breast-milk sold to newborn nurseries for the equivalent of U.S. $0·72 and one particularly abundant lactator was reported to have earned some $1500 during one year by supplying a bank with breast-milk not required by her own baby.

Recently in India, Rao (1975) has made the strange-seeming suggestion that human milk could be collected commercially by breast pump and pasteurized, or even spray-dried. As he points out, cattle in India produce only 250 litres per year, whereas it has been estimated that poorly nourished Indian women can secrete almost 200 litres in the first year of lactation. Such women might receive part of their earnings in food and meals, and part as cash.

The idea initially seems bizarre, as human milk is usually considered a non-profit-making commodity. However, it may be noted that other body tissues are sold, including blood and sperm. It would, in fact, only institutionalize and mechanize the age-old wet-nursing principle, and conform to the concept of using human resources as a national economic asset, especially in highly populated, less industrialized circumstances.

8   Mother–infant interactions

For the truth is, that for babe or man, there is no warmth or security to be found in a bottle. There is only one thing to do with it, and that is to empty it. It cannot be toyed with, caressed or stroked. It is not warm or soft. A bottle is stone, is sand fused and processed into a vaguely breastlike shape for the holding of liquids, but to the infant it is a mockery.
Stuart Cloete (1957) *The curve & the tusk*

Are mammals with more highly developed nervous systems than the mouse equally sensitive to perinatal environmental disturbance?
Niles Newton (1972)

Recent investigations into various animals, including mammals, have shown the special significance of maternal–infant behavioural interaction and bonding especially in the newborn period. As Kaufman (1973) notes, 'for higher organisms that begin life with a long period in which independent functioning is not possible, normal development depends on continuous parental care.'

Likewise, it is increasingly apparent that the interaction of the human mother and her neonate, including that resulting from the method of infant feeding, varies greatly in diverse cultures, with very different immediate psychophysiological results and possible long-term outcomes.

Interaction in Animals

As with other aspects of child-care, potentially valuable information may be obtained by the investigation of behaviour in other species, especially non-human mammals. While great caution is needed in extrapolating findings to man, the possibility of their being relevant probably increases when behavioural patterns are found in many species (Klaus *et al*. 1970, Vaughan 1976).

Perinatal behaviour and imprinting

All animals demonstrate distinct species-specific maternal perinatal behaviour, such as nesting, exploring, grooming, and retrieving. Such behaviour conforms to a pattern which is specific for the particular species, but can be severely altered and deranged if the mother herself received abnormal perinatal care in her own infancy (Harlow and Harlow 1962, Harlow and Zimmerman 1958, 1959).

In recent decades, the work of ethologists and others has clearly indicated the importance in animals of the reflex action and interaction between mother and offspring in the newborn period — the 'care-soliciting' behaviour of the baby, and the 'care-giving' behaviour of the mother.

Imprinting. Evidence in animals suggests that certain reflex behaviour depends on the presence or absence of appropriate stimuli, especially during specific and critical periods, affecting both mother and offspring and leading to bonding or attachment between them. This imprinting can only occur when a young animal is exposed to a particular stimulus at a sensitive period. It leaves a permanent impression, so that henceforth the individual will react in a particular way to the situation. For example, the cormorant becomes imprinted with the mother's cry while still within the egg, so that after hatching the young bird accepts only its own mother out of thousands of others. Conversely, for the mother sheep, the critical period appears to be 5–10 minutes after birth when her licking of the foetal membrane leads to an intense maternal–filial bonding. Sheep-rearers attempt to induce a non-related female to adopt an orphan lamb by rubbing it with the afterbirth of the mother's own dead infant. However, this requires delicate arrangements of timing to prevent the mother from destroying the strange newborn (Klaus and Kennell 1970, Klaus *et al*. 1970). In other species, such as rodents, when offspring are separated from the mother in the first few hours after delivery and then reunited, the mother will care for the young, but not so skilfully (Rosenblatt and Lehrmann 1963).

Neonatal isolation. Experimental work on mammalian neonatal isolation indicates that so-called 'maternal social deprivation' is multi-sensory, but is much related to lack of skin-to-skin contact (somatosensory deprivation), as well as to absence of body warmth, the auditory stimulation of the heart-beat, and even possibly the rocking motion to which the foetus has become accustomed in the uterine amniotic fluid. The paramount role of contact-comfort in one species was reported in 1958 and subsequently by Harlow and colleagues in pioneer experiments on infant Rhesus monkeys isolated from their mothers (Harlow and Harlow 1962, Harlow and Zimmerman 1958, 1959). The preferred inanimate mother-surrogate was made of terry cloth, with a light behind radiating heat, and supplying soft contact and warmth to which the orphaned infant monkey could cling.

The effects of such somatosensory deprivation in infant monkeys persisted into adulthood. Violent, aggressive and hyper-excitable behaviour, psychosexual aberrations, and abnormalities in social and emotional conduct were common phenomena in such deprived animals in later life, as well as abnormalities in the pattern of species-specific perinatal care and mothering in affected female monkeys. In other words, the patterning of behaviour in the neonatal period can crucially affect subsequent behaviour of the mother and infant, on both short-term and long-term bases.

Separation in infancy

The immediate effects of separation in infancy after the perinatal period have been described, and vividly depicted by Kaufman (1973) in 19–24-week-old pig-tail macaque monkeys. The initial response was agitated protest, with constant searching and obvious intense distress. The change was dramatic after 24–36 hours separation from the mother when the baby monkey sat hunched into an immobile ball, with head hanging between legs and with an utterly dejected face. However, after some days, the depression gradually lifted, and by the fourth week of separation the infant appeared alert and active a great deal of the time. The long-term consequences of such separation are difficult to assess, but Kaufman notes the possibility of developing a proneness to depression.

Development of the central nervous system
Certain kinds of stimulation have been shown to affect the morphological and functional development of the central nervous system in experimental animals. Gentling, handling, and patting appear to enhance central nervous system development; while somatosensory deprivation in experimental animals at the sensitive period following birth can inhibit the development of the neurochemistry (and even the number of cells) of the brain, and cerebral electrophysiology (Altman 1968). Thus, newborn rats handled for 15 minutes daily for 11 days showed a much higher rate of brain-cell proliferation than unhandled, but otherwise similar, controls. For example, the mean number of cells in the corpus callosum was 62 per cent higher than in unhandled animals.

Interaction in man

In the human, it is plain that the relationship between mother and neonate is close and intense. Specifics of such interactions and their effects are much more difficult to analyse in man, because of the obvious impossibility of most forms of experimentation, and because so many variables occur in the neonatal period, infancy, childhood, and adulthood in different cultures in such a long-lived species. As Ainsworth (1974) has commented, cultural variables in rearing practices that possibly influence infant development may be interlocked to such an extent that analytic efforts cannot tease them apart. These include, for example, degrees of accessibility and responsiveness, levels of security, and differences between demand and scheduled feeding. In addition, many variable, and possibly traumatic, customary procedures can take place in different cultures in the newborn period, during weaning, and in later childhood, including 'social operations' (circumcision, scarification), head moulding, use of heat (exposure to strong sun or fire smoke) or cold (baths), and enemas (Jelliffe and Bennett 1962).

However, recent studies have brought to light increasingly suggestive evidence that the dyadic mother–infant interaction is highly important biologically to *both mother and neonate, both immediately and subseqently* (Benedek 1956, Bernal and Richards 1970, Blurton-Jones 1972, *Developmental Psychology* 1972, Kazda 1970, Leifer *et al.* 1970, Richards 1975, Sousa, Barros, Gazalle, Begeres, Pinheiro, Menezes, and Arruda 1974).

Attention has particularly focused on the meaning and significance of somatosensory stimulation, on maternal responses to her newborn, and on the effect on mother and child of different methods of puerperal care, especially the degree of contact or separation.

Neonatal behaviour pattern

Key questions with regard to human neonates are, first, '*Is there a sensitive period in the human mother where it is important for the mother to be near her baby for the later development of mothering behaviour?*', and, secondly, '*What is or is likely to be psychologically advantageous or unique to the infant in having been successfully breast-fed?*' (Klaus 1975). The following recent studies increasingly answer these complex issues.

The work of Klaus and colleagues has demonstrated that a specific pattern of behaviour seems to occur in human mothers at first contact with their full-term infants. Quantitative analysis of serial photographs taken each second demonstrates an orderly progression of behaviour in mothers of full-term babies born in hospital (Klaus *et al*. 1972). This commences with fingertip contact and moves to increasing contact (Fig. 8.2). Mother-to-infant eye-to-eye *en face* viewing (Fig. 8.2) appears to be an important exchange. The mothers of 'normal' premature infants permitted to touch them in the first 3–5 days of life followed a similar sequence, but at a slower rate (Fig. 8.3).

It has been suggested that the stroking of the baby parallels the licking of the newborn characteristic of other mammals, and that it represents a continuation of dermal stimulation begun in foetal life by the amniotic fluid and massively reinforced by uterine massage during delivery (Leboyer 1975). Montagu (1971) has stressed that the skin is the body's largest and most extensive sensory organ, and that 'proximity senses' — touch, taste, and smell — are more evolved at birth than are 'distance senses' — sight and

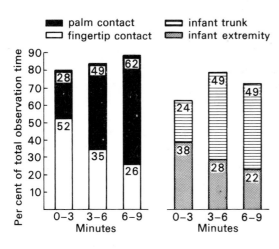

Fig. 8.1. Progression from fingertip contact to palm contact in mothers of normal full-term infants at the first contact 3–12 hours after delivery (Klaus, M. and Kennell, J. H. (1970). *Pediat. Clins. N. Amer.* **17**, 105)

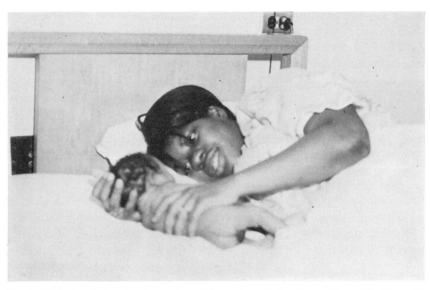

Fig. 8.2. Mother in 'en face' position with newborn baby (from Klaus, M., Kennell, J. H., Plumb, N., and Zuehlke, S. (1970). *Pediatrics* **46**, 187)

Fig. 8.3. Mother in 'en face' position stroking premature newborn baby (from Klaus, M., Kennell, J. H., Plumb, N., and Zuehlke, S. (1970). *Pediatrics* **46**, 187)

hearing — which show more development later. At the same time, the sensory and communicative potential of the neonate has been underappreciated, as emphasized by Brazleton *et al.* (1975), who noted:

Right out of the uterus (1) he can and does turn his head to the human voice repeatedly, and his face alerts as he searches for its source; (2) he will attend to and choose a female vocal pitch over any other; (3) humanoid sounds are not only preferred to pure tones in an equivalent range of pitch but when he is tested with continuous sucking as a response system, he stops sucking briefly after a pure tone, then goes on sucking steadily, whereas to a human tone he stops sucking and then continues in a burst–pause pattern of sucking (as if he were expecting more important information to follow, and as if the pauses in the sucking were designed to allow for attention to this further infomation); (4) he will attend to and follow with eyes and full 90°, head turning a picture of a human face, but will not follow a scrambled face, although he will look at it wide-eyed for a long period (in the delivery room and before any care-taking has been instituted); (5) he will turn to and prefer milk smells above water or sugar-water; (6) he can taste and respond to with altered sucking patterns the difference between human milk and a cow's-milk formula designed to exactly reproduce the contents of breast-milk.

The main means of mother–newborn interaction is by touch (tactile stimulation) and by facial movements, especially the eyes. Difficulties have been noted with a congenitally blind mother who did not customarily 'talk with her face' (Brazleton *et al.* 1975). The reciprocal eye movements have been suggested as being analogous in importance for bonding as 'following' in other species, such as geese (Vaughan 1976).

The rhythmic nature of the interactions has been emphasized by several workers: 'dance-like synchrony of movements, facial expression, and vocalizations' (Hofer 1975), 'dances in rhythm with the mother's words' (Klaus and Kennell 1976), and 'a kind of swan's mating dance' (Brazleton *et al.* 1975). The similarity with the bonding process of adult love is obvious, as emphasized by a quotation from Dante's *Divine Comedy* used by Kennell (1976):

> How does the fire of love endure
> If the eyes and touch are not to kindle it.

As noted earlier, the pattern of mother–infant neonatal behaviour is species-specific in non-human mammals. For example, as Klaus has noted, the domestic cat in Russia, the U.S.A., or England behaves in a characteristic way at the time of birth of her kittens (Klaus *et al.* 1975). However, in man, recent studies by Klaus and colleagues have shown that the orderly progression observed after hospital delivery in the U.S. mothers studied was noted in only half of a series of Guatemalan women delivered in hospital. Even more striking is the variation in the pattern seen in Californian women having their babies at home. The main findings from film studies of such home deliveries have been summarized as follows (Klaus *et al.* 1975):

1. The mother is an active participant. 2. She immediately picks up the infant after birth. 3. She begins to stroke its face with her fingertips and moves to palm contact of the body and head within a few minutes. 4. A striking elevation in mood is observed in association with great excitement of the other participants. 5. Everyone is drawn to look at the infant for prolonged periods. 6. The mother is groomed. 7. Breastfeeding starts within five to six minutes beginning with prolonged licking by the infant.

The question of existence of imprinting in the human mother–neonate dyad is difficult to answer. The Cleveland school suggests that there may be 'a special attachment period for an adult woman — special in the sense that what happens during this time may alter the later behaviour of the adult toward a young infant for at least as long as one month after delivery. It would be useful to have a special term for this period, such as "maternal sensitive period".'

Alternatively, 'the concept of "canalization" may be broader and more serviceable than imprinting . . . It does not imply one-shot learning, nor does it assume the wired-in prepotency of a particular stimulus. Rather, it deals with the establishment of strong preferences, based on familiarization, for one among many stimuli.' (Klaus and Kennell 1970, Klaus *et al.* 1970).

Current work suggests that the sensitive period lasts from the first minutes up to about 12 hours. Newer investigations also suggest the possibility of father–infant bonding.

Various stimuli
The newborn and the infant receive from the mother various stimuli, including skin contact, the auditory perception of the maternal heart-beat, a blend of stimulation in the form of games and play (Call and Marshack 1966), and, above all, the presence of a continuing, identifiable source of care and affection.

The work of Salk (1960) suggests that the sound of the mother's heart-beat, previously perceived constantly *in utero*, is comforting to the neonate, influencing weight-gain and crying. Furthermore, a tendency to hold the baby on the left side, near the heart-beat, has been demonstrated in both right-handed and left-handed mothers in American culture. The rocking movements of the foetus floating in the amniotic fluid can be re-created after birth by various forms of postnatal rocking in many cultures. Indeed, in some societies, the stimulation of both the sound of the heart-beat and the soothing uterine rocking are continued as infants are carried on by their mothers with various types of back-carrier (E.F.P. Jelliffe 1975 *d*).

In many cultures, rocking of the cradle is practised whether or not the child is carried during the day on the mother's back. However, this age-old practice came much under attack in the late nineteenth century in the U.S.A. In a booklet entitled *The care and feeding of children: a catechism for the use of mothers and children*, the well-known paediatrician Emmett Holt stated that rocking was 'a habit easily acquired, but hard to break and a very useless and sometimes an injurious one.' He stated further that 'rocking was both an unnecessary and vicious practice which should not be carried on.' These strong attacks on rocking brought about the advent of the stationary crib (E.F.P. Jelliffe 1975 *d*).

The degree of skin-contact between mother and newborn varies greatly. In most traditional cultures, the baby remains by the mother's side and, often after a period of ritual seclusion (p. 176), will be carried with her in the closest of contacts. By contrast, modern Western culture has been alone in routinely separating mother and neonate.

Back-carriers extend the length and intimacy of contact between mother and infant, introduce children to spatial relationships and continue the pattern of movements to which the infant has become accustomed during intrauterine life, as well as ensuring probably important aural, vestibular, and tactile stimulation.

Methods of carrying babies have been studied both in women in present-day cultures and through the art medium encompassing many generations of mothers. As mentioned earlier, Salk (1960) studied 225 right-handed mothers and found that 83 per cent of them carried their infants on the left side, and among 32 left-handed women a preponderance of left-sided carriers was also found. In a further investigation, a comparison was made of the method of carrying packages, as opposed to babies. No particular preference for either side was demonstrated by the package carriers, but the majority of mothers attending clinics held their babies on the left side. Adult women requested to hold a pillow representing a baby also had the tendency to carry it on the left side. In the realm of art, a study of 446 works of art found that in 80 per cent of the paintings babies were depicted carried on the left side. Illustrations from non-Western culture showed the same trend (Salk 1960).

In yet another experiment, which contrasted mothers separated for a prolonged period from their infants at birth and a control group of mothers who had experienced a normal delivery and had immediate access to their children, the following results obtained: mothers who had been separated from their infants showed no preference for either the right or left side. Among the control group of mothers however, 77 per cent of women showed a preference for carrying children on the left side. Salk concluded that the interval shortly after birth was a sensitive one, and during this period the maternal instinctual pattern of child-holding is similar to the imprinting pattern in birds (Salk 1962).

Many workers are of the opinion that mothers hold their infants instinctively on the left side as their heart-beat, which the foetus has been exposed to during the intrauterine period, will continue to comfort and reassure their infant post-partum with its familiar sounds. This concept was put into practice in a metropolitan hospital in New York. Two groups of newborn infants were considered. The study group was exposed to the recording of a human heart-beat; the control group was not, and showed a median weight-loss of 20 g, whilst the study group gained 40 g in weight during the same 4-day interval following birth. No significant difference in food intake existed among these two groups of infants (Salk 1962).

If one were attempting to devise a method which would encompass the beneficial effects of early tactile stimulation, as well as rocking and the comforting sound of the mother's heart-beat, it would be difficult to find a simpler and less expensive solution that the baby-carrier (Salk 1960).

Other aspects of the continuing interaction between mother and her young child are the games developed spontaneously between the two in all cultures. Call, who has investigated this topic most thoroughly (Call and Marshack 1966), notes that in addition to the infant receiving the right nutrients and being gratified sufficiently, the parent's style of handling the baby and the spontaneous games played are part of the interaction. These are partly culturally defined, but vary with the temperament and personality of the mother and father, and with opportunities available. In addition, in relation to infant feeding, the mother's style and method appears to be important, particularly her manner of holding the infant, the presentation of the breast or bottle, and the speed and consistency of her actions.

In the human infant, the effect of complete separation from the mother in the first months of life does not appear to be as clear-cut as in the latter part of the first year. Spitz (1945) first drew attention to the problem of separated human children, describing two syndromes in institutionalized infants. One syndrome, which he called 'anaclitic depression', arose in the second half of the first year of life when the mothers, who had reared the infants from birth, were removed (Spitz and Wolf 1946). After an initial period of apprehension and crying, the infants showed withdrawal, rejection of the environment, retardation of reaction to stimuli, slowness of movement, loss of appetite, increased finger-sucking, insomnia, 'an obvious distaste for assuming an erect posture or performing locomotion', and a 'physiognomic expression ... difficult to describe ... (which) would, in an adult, be described as depression'. If the mother returned within 3–5 months, there was an immediate dramatic effect. The infants 'suddenly were friendly, gay, approachable' and subsequently recovered fully. If the mother did not return, the other, more malignant syndrome developed. The latter, which Spitz called 'hospitalism', was first seen in infants who lost their mothers permanently and were cared for by very busy nursing personnel. It was characterized by massive failure in development, both mental and physical, frequent illness, marasmus, cachexia, and often early death. Spitz (1945) commented on the importance of locomotion and motility after 6 months of age and thought that, among other things, the loss of mother interfered with the opportunities for locomotion and its important role in development. As commented by Kaufman (1973), the picture is similar to that seen when the infant pig-tail macaque is separated from its mother.

In the newborn period in Westernized societies, the degree of neonatal separation and consequent deprivation of maternal interaction varies with the birth situation. This has been summarized by Barnett and colleagues (1970) for six possible situations (Table 8.1). It seems likely that the greater the separation, especially on the first day of life, the more the likelihood of 'mother–infant asynchrony'.

Breast-feeding

All aspects of feeding of all age-groups have deep and subtle psychological overtones, meanings, and consequences. This is especially so with methods of nurturing, caring for, and handling young infants, and the subject of human milk obviously cannot be considered realistically apart from the process of breast-feeding. Plainly, this is not merely a mechanical fuelling procedure for supplying nutrients to the baby. but also a psychosocial communication, a sociocultural behavioural exchange between the mother–baby dyad (Newton 1953, 1972*a*).

From the maternal viewpoint, as Newton (1972*b*) has pointed out, it needs to be appreciated that there are three human interpersonal acts, reproductive in nature, occurring between two individuals — coitus, child-birth, and breast-feeding. Full understanding of female sexuality (as opposed to male) requires consideration of responsiveness in all three forms of behaviour. Women have a more varied heritage of sexual enjoyment than men (Newton 1972*b*, Francis 1975).

The similarity of behaviour in uninhibited, undrugged childbirth, such as occurs in 'natural childbirth or in labour with psychoprophylaxis, and in coital orgasm seems increasingly clear, as judged by many characteristics, ranging from breathing to uterine reactions to emotional response.' (Newton 1972*b*).

Likewise, marked psychophysiological similarities are found between lactation and coitus, and have been listed by Newton in a recent review in which full references are given: (i) uterine contractions occur both during suckling and sexual excitement; (ii) nipple erection occurs during both activities; (iii) breast stroking and nipple stimulation both occur during breast-feeding and sexual foreplay; (iv) emotions aroused by sexual contact and by breast-feeding both involve skin changes (vascular dilation and raised temperature); (v) milk let-down (or ejection) reflex can be triggered not only by breast-feeding, but by sexual excitement; (vi) the emotions experienced during sexual arousal and the emotions experienced during uninhibited, unrestricted breast-feeding may be closely allied; (vii) an accepting attitude towards sexuality may be related to an accepting attitude to breast-feeding (and vice versa).

Masters and Johnson (1966) have observed that for the first 3 months after delivery, the highest level of sexual interest was noted by nursing mothers, and, as a group, they reported interest in as rapid a return as

TABLE 8.1   *Maternal separation and deprivation levels over time, related to birth situation* (from Barnett *et al.* 1970)

Birth situation	Deprivation levels, time postpartum					
	Day 0	Day 1	Day 3	Day 7	Week 8	Week 9
Home, full term	II, partial deprivation	I, no deprivation	I, no deprivation	I, no deprivation	I, no deprivation	I, no deprivation
Hospital, full term, rooming-in	III, moderate deprivation	I, no deprivation	I, no deprivation	I, no deprivation	I, no deprivation	I, no deprivation
Hospital, full term, regular care	III, moderate deprivation	II, partial deprivation	II, partial deprivation	I, no deprivation	I, no deprivation	I, no deprivation
Premature, mother allowed into nursery	V, complete deprivation	IV, severe deprivation	III, moderate deprivation	II, partial deprivation	II, partial deprivation (discharge nursery)	I, no deprivation (home)
Premature, regular care (separated)	V, complete deprivation	IV, severe deprivation	IV, severe deprivation	IV, severe deprivation	II, partial deprivation (discharge nursery)	I, no deprivation (home)
Unmarried mother, refuses contact	V, complete deprivation	V, complete deprivation	V, complete deprivation	V, complete deprivation	V, complete deprivation	V, complete deprivation

possible to sexual intercourse with their husbands.

The sensuous nature of breast-feeding is seldom recognized in Western society (Newton 1973). As Newton (1972b) has commented:

> Current social patterns are very effective in inhibiting the psychophysical reciprocity of lactation. Mother and infant are usually separated except for brief contacts during their hospital stay. Rigorous rules about duration and timing of each sucking period have been invented and are enforced by persons who usually have never successfully breast fed even one baby. Probably most people in our society would be willing to concede that we would cause coital frigidity if we prescribed the act only at scheduled times and laid down rules concerning the exact number of minutes intromission should last. Mother–baby interactions can be similarly disturbed by similar types of rules.

Sexual stimulation occurs to varying degrees in women who are nursing their young. It has been difficult to assess the commonness or level of stimulation, partly because of culturally defined guilt-feelings in the Western culture, and more indirect questions are usually needed (Masters and Johnson 1966, Newton 1969). That breast-feeding is psychohormonally pleasurable is not surprising. The survival of mankind has depended upon the satisfactions gained by two voluntary acts in the reproductive cycle — coitus and breast-feeding.

Human reproduction through the millennia has depended on the successful sequence of coitus, parturition, and breast-feeding. Linking all are three basic characteristics (Newton 1969): 1. They are based in part on closely related neurohormonal reflexes. 2. They are sensitive to environmental stimuli, being easily inhibited in their early stages. 3. Under certain circumstances, all three trigger care-taking behaviour which is an essential and important part of mammalian reproduction.

The susceptibility of these three reproductive acts to inhibition relates to the vulnerability of the two participants to danger during coitus, parturition, and breast-feeding. 'Mother and offspring, united in the nursing act, are not in an optimum position for fight or flight. It is not surprising that folkways and cultural patterns have long recognized that coitus, parturition, and lactation proceed most smoothly when the surroundings are particularly sheltered or considered to be relatively safe (Newton 1969).

Effects of breast-feeding

Difficulties in estimating the effects of breast-feeding on the behaviour of mother and baby, individually and together, include the existence of other cultural variables referred to earlier, differing aspects of maternal personality and behaviour (including reasons for selection of method of feeding), and variations in techniques, methods, and definitions for breast-feeding, bottle-feeding, and 'weaning'.

Between the two extremes of *token breast-feeding* — limited number of timed, scheduled feeds, complementary bottle feeds, early semi-solids, usually short lactation, and *unrestricted or 'biological' breast-feeding*, there are marked differences in sucking time and in amount of mother–baby contact. There is a distinct psychological, as well as physiological, difference between unrestricted or 'biological' breast-feeding, such as practised by many traditional cultures, in which sucking is freely allowed from birth during the day and night and continued for many months or several years, and the token breast-feeding often currently seen in Europe and the U.S.A. (in which sucking is regulated, only occurs during the day-time and is limited in duration at each feed). Moreover, with an apprehensive, uninterested, and ill-informed 'forced' mother, whose let-down reflex has become impaired, the interaction can be minimal and even of negative value.

Strangely, it is a common assumption in present-day Western urbanized society that the bottle-fed baby held in his mother's arms is receiving an experience emotionally and behaviourally equivalent to that of breast-feeding. This culturally determined belief has become so prevalent that Bowlby's (1969) book on *Attachment and loss*, covering in detail the consequences of different patterns of mother–infant relationships, contains no references to breast-feeding, lactation, or nursing, and uses the word 'sucking' to apply equally to bottle- and breast-feeding from a psychological point of view.

However, to make a fair comparison, it needs to be noted that artificial feeding also has many gradations in relation to the care, tenderness, and the time and intimacy of contact between mother (or attendant) and baby. This can indeed, range from bottle-feeding with close contact and cuddling by the care-taker (Fig. 8.4), to the propped bottle left in the child's mouth in the crib, to the most mechanical delivery of nutrients, sometimes needed in certain diseases — that is, tube-feeding with an indwelling catheter, permitting formula to be delivered directly into the child's stomach.* Differences between the extremes of unrestricted breast-feeding and tube-feeding are plainly emotionally and psychobiologically very great — a parallel might be between sexual intercourse and artificial insemination.

Nevertheless, in the bottle-culture of the present-day Western world, differences between the two methods, which seem completely self-evident and obvious, may not be considered sufficiently scientifically exact or mathematically proven. Strangely, the burden of having to produce proof that differences exist and are significant falls paradoxically on those advocating the natural method tested over millennia — that is breast-feeding.

In fact, mother–infant interactions are very different in breast-feeding and bottle-feeding. Nursing the baby has a profound effect on the secretion of maternal hormones, such as prolactin, which is absent in artificial feeding,

---

* Recent studies by Dowling and de Monterice (1974) have been carried out in babies with unrepaired oesophogeal atresia fed via gastrostomy. Marked deficiency of oral experience, especially without oesophageal swallowing, appeared to be associated with gross motor retardation.

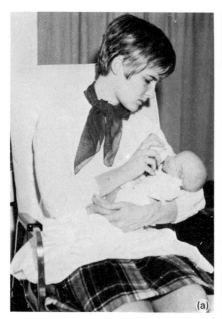 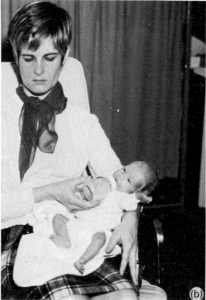

Fig. 8.4. A posed mother shows two different caretaking positions (from Klaus, M. and Kennell, J. H. (1970). *Pediat. Clins. N. Amer.* **17**, 105)

and the pleasurable response to repeated nipple-stimulation has been mentioned (p. 19). Sucking activities by the baby are mechanically dissimilar in quality and duration in the two processes (p. 109). In particular, formula is obtained more easily, rapidly, and with less sucking activity — with consequently less time and opportunity for contact with the mother. In breast-feeding, the mother and baby will of necessity be in skin-to-skin contact, which will not usually be the case with the bottle-fed. There will, therefore, be more prolonged, intimate bodily contact in breast-feeding with a different form of olfactory, tactile, thermal, and auditory stimulation from the more easily-heard maternal heart-beat. The calming effect of the last has become more appreciated in recent years and, bizarrely, but characteristically for Westernized man, a mechanical device — 'Somnitone' — has been produced which reproduces the sound of the mother's heart-beat. Even more recently, a recording — 'The Sound of the Womb' — has been made in Japan which incorporates the other sounds of the intrauterine orchestra, including the *souffle* of the blood pulsing through major vessels.

In fact, the foetus *in utero* is exposed to continued low-pitched but variable sounds ranging from about 85 to 95 decibels from the foeto-maternal cardiovascular systems, from intestinal borborygmi, and from distant respiratory breath sounds, and to tactile, vestibular, and proprioceptive stimulation from a variety of foetal and maternal movements (Kramer and Pierpoint 1976). The minimally handled newborn separated from the mother, especially in an incubator, can be compared to a prisoner in solitary confinement, with little, and different, stimulation, as, for example, with the constant machinery hum of some 77 decibels.

The value of auditory and rocking stimuli has been shown by enhancement of growth of pre-term babies, who were stimulated by periods of gentle rocking, together with the playing of the sounds of a simulated heart beat at 72 per minute and a woman's voice (74–84 decibels) (Kramer and Pierpoint 1976).

The specificity of the signals between mother and newborn suggested by the baby's ability to recognize its own mother's breast is indicated by head-turning prior to contact and initiation of the rooting reflex, and is a recognition of the individualized 'chemical signature' of the scent of the mother's breast, which a newborn can differentiate by the tenth day of life. Conversely, there is the specifically greater thermovascular response in the mother's breast to the cry of her own baby (Lind *et al.* 1971) (Fig. 2.8).

Also, in many instances, bottle-feeding in the newborn period is more usually associated with a physical separation between feeds when infants are housed in a central nursery than is often the case with breast-fed babies. Apart from the reduction (and its possible ill-effects) in opportunity for somatosensory contact, this means that the mother is unable to respond easily to the infant's crying — 'this acoustic umbilical cord between helpless neonate and caretaking environment' (Ostwald 1972).

In brief, breast- and bottle-feeding are different in very many ways for both mother and baby — neurohormonally and as regards tactile, auditory, olfactory, oral stimulation and as regards the mother's fantasies (Newton *et al.* 1968, 1972, Patton and Gardner 1963, Thoman *et al.* 1970, Winter 1970). Bottle-feeding has its main concern with nurturing; breast-feeding is as much concerned with love and affection.

The symbiotic, dyadic nature of breast-feeding needs re-emphasis. The mother reacts to the sight, smell, cry, and closeness of the baby, and, via cutaneous, hormonal, and psychological channels, responds pleasurably to the nipple stimulation of breast-feeding and to the hormonally stimulated uterine contraction and rise in mammary skin temperature. Apart from such operant conditioning to the pleasurable sensations resulting from the infant's sucking, hormonal differences, including increased levels of prolactin, may also affect the woman's 'motherliness' and her attachment to the baby. Likewise, continuing eye-to-eye contact is more likely if the infant is being held at the breast level rather than bottle-fed on the mother's lap (Fig. 8.5).

To the newborn baby, unrestricted breast-feeding represents a more similar continuation of intrauterine placental nutrition, tactile contact, warmth, support, and security than does bottle-feeding. It represents the least traumatic, early transition for the exterogestate foetus, when, in old-world phraseology, the baby is 'welcomed to the bosom of the family' with the immediate availability of warm milk, responsive attention for discomfort

Fig. 8.5. 'Maternity' by Pablo Picasso (1905). Mother and baby in eye-to-eye contact, almost '*en face*' © by S.P.A.D.E.M., Paris 1977

and fears, and much greater sucking activity by the baby. At the same time, early and continuing contact between mother and newborn facilitates the initiation and successful maintenance of lactation for numerous physiological reasons noted elsewhere (p. 17).

The human neonate's need for tactile stimulation is not perhaps obvious to Western highly machine-oriented, technological societies, especially as these are mainly 'non-touch' cultures, endorsing individuality and separateness. The need for close contact between mother and neonate is also suggested indirectly by the fact that 'if patterns of contact between mother and young of various mammal species are compared, a correlation is found between the protein content of the milk and the interval between feeds, a relationship which cuts across taxonomic relationships. The protein content of human milk would place humans among the continuous-contact species.' (Richards and Bernal 1975).

Certainly, usual characteristics of traditional cultures — such as those of Europe and north America until recently — included continuing close contact between mother and baby after birth, including almost universal breast-feeding (p. 161). While details could (and do) vary greatly in different cultures, basically most have the effect of gradually acclimatizing the exterogestate foetus to his new circumstances, and of signalling most effectively a continuation of uterine safety and security.

From the infant's side, lack of somatosensory stimulation occurring in differing degrees of separation from the mother in maternity nurseries means that the neonate is in some degree thrust from the security of the uterus into an uncertain, unresponsive world. The absence of the tangible security of the mother may possibly make more difficult the development of basic trust in human relationships later in life.

The psychological satisfaction and enriched neonatal stimulation inherent in breast-feeding have been summarized recently by Call (1975):

1. *Successful nursing of the infant means satisfaction for both the infant and the mother*. The manner of achieving satisfaction is somewhat different in breast and bottle fed infants. The mother's success at breastfeeding the infant is related to her capacity to identify with the infant. In so doing, the mother must become acquainted with her particular infant and must be able to adapt herself to the behavior and needs of the baby. To do so means that she is supported in the task by other members of the household and by the social milieu which determines her child-rearing attitudes and practices. *Hospital care has by and large tended to be more disruptive than helpful in establishing such a feeling of connectedness between the mother and the infant.*

2. *The breast fed infant is exposed to a wide variety of bodily stimuli*. These are patterned around the infant's needs and provide a richer sensorimotor context in which learning can occur. This is shown by the greater tendency of breast fed infants to demonstrate behavioral anticipation of the feeding as contrasted to those who are bottle fed. Thus, the infant's early adaptive capacity is more readily exercised in relationship to breastfeeding than to bottle feeding.

Conclusions

The particularly close physical, physiological, and psychological links between mother and her breast-fed baby might perhaps have been considered as being completely obvious and apparent. Certainly through the centuries in the Christian world, art has often used the symbolism of the nursing Madonna. As Francis (1975) comments:

The post-Renaissance artists who painted so many mother-and-child pictures instinctively understood the relationship with a vision that the present technological age has lost. Looking at the warm flesh tones of a smugly satisfied Rubens infant bouncing on its mother's knee, or a Murillo "madonna" with her naked baby snuggled up to her soft breasts one can see how incongruous it would be to include a hard bottle in the picture or even to inquire how many mils. (of milk) the baby got.

Likewise, the close emotional links between the nursing woman and the baby on the breast seem to have been partly the basis for the searching enquiry into the temperament, physique, health, and virtue of women being selected as wet-nurses in many ancient cultures (p. 166). Plainly, there are many degrees and forms of mother–neonate contact between more traditional methods of handling the human newborn in which characteristically the first contact with the outside world is the warm alive mother by the baby's side, responsive to touch and satisfying hunger, and the abruptly separated, isolated nursery neonate usual in Western-style maternity units, whose only contact with the mother would be at short, clock-regulated intervals when brought for bottle-feeding.

However, as noted earlier, there are many different forms and qualities of both bottle- and breast-feeding. To caricature the situation, not all breast-fed babies grow up to be saints, nor all bottle-fed babies to be sinners. Nevertheless, characteristic of the present-day scene is the increase in senseless, destructive, vindictive, purposeless violence, including child abuse in the Western world (the 'battered child'). Undoubtedly, many varying factors must be responsible — social, psychological, technical, and economic. Early, close, and continuing mother–newborn contact, facilitated by breast-feeding, may be one remediable factor in the Western culture. While proof is lacking and research required, the following editorial advice (*British Medical Journal* 1972) seems sound:

We need to pay more thought to anything which severs the natural bond between the newborn and his mother — bottle feeding instead of breastfeeding, separations of the baby by putting him in a nursery, discouragement of the mother from picking the baby up when he cries or feeding him when he is hungry — or anything which prevents her enjoying him or his enjoying her.

In the human, evidence is more difficult to obtain which clearly differentiates the effects of the different forms and multiple components of mother–infant interaction. Brody (1956) notes rather caustically that much information at that time was based on 'publications which exemplify a type of study in which the effects of infantile experience on the personality is investigated by relating subject statements of unknown accuracy and relevancy to a partial and/or partially understood theory.' However, as a recent *British Medical Journal* (1972) editorial rightly comments: 'Human studies of the effect of such instincts and of the interference with them are fraught with difficulties because of all the variables involved, but, in the present state of our knowledge, it is wise to respect these instincts.'

Much new and persuasive scientific information has come to light in the past 20 years, notably that of Call, Klaus, and Newton. At the same time, still further investigation is needed. However, desirable and important as such additional research is, it is also in a sense academic and unnecessary (Hofer 1975, Vaughan 1976). There are no particular developmental or psychological advantages to be claimed for Western methods of neonatal care in maternity units, which were introduced for quite different and probably invalid reasons. Indeed, as discussed later, the consequences on physical and mental health of unbiological practices in the neonatal period have reached such a level as strongly suggests the need for modification in practices in maternity wards (p. 304).

Montagu (1971) views the scene more positively and emphatically when he says:

It should be evident that, in the development of the person, tactile stimulation should begin with the newborn baby. The newborn should, whenever possible, be placed in his mother's arms, and allowed to remain by her side as long as she may desire. The newborn should be put to nurse at his mother's breast as soon as possible. The newborn should not be removed to a 'nursery' nor placed in a crib. The cradle should be restored to universal usage as the best auxiliary and substitute for cradling in the mother's arms ever invented. Fondling of the infant can scarcely be overdone — a reasonably sensible human being is not likely to overstimulate an infant — hence, if one is to err in any direction it were better in the direction of too much rather than too little fondling. Instead of baby carriages, infants should be carried on their mother's backs, and also on their father's backs, in the equivalent of the Chinese *madai* or Eskimo *parka*.

Recently, leaders in the health field have begun to show an awareness of the emotional significance of close mother–child relationships, especially in the immediate neonatal period, currently often minimized in more old-fashioned and stereotyped mechanistic hospitals of industrialized countries. The role of close mother–baby contact is becoming appreciated, especially in pre-term neonates, in relation to the preventive care of mothers likely to be at high risk of abusing children (Kennell and Klaus 1971), and of psychogenic 'failure to thrive' in infants (Klaus and Kennell 1976). The role of the mother's presence in moulding the development of the newborn, including the premature, is being reappraised in relation to health-service practice, and pregnancy and childbirth may perhaps cease to be approached as diseases, but rather as physiological family events with particular, but occasional, risks. Too frequently, hospitals, including children's wards and maternity units, seem to have been designed primarily for asepsis and the technological aspects of medicine, for the quasi-regimentation of patients, and for the convenience of medical staff, rather than for families in distress; too seldom is there much understanding of human relationships and emotional needs. Modification and compromise can be inexpensive and easy. All that is needed is to take the intellectual jump out of technological blinkers to a perception of the psychobiological needs of the neonate, the mother, and the rest of the family.

9   Traditional societies

His mother beareth him and his weaning is two years.
Koran, 31,14

May four oceans, full of milk, constantly abide in both your breasts, you blessed one, for the increase of the strength of the child!
Drinking of the milk, whose sap is the sap of immortal life divine, may your baby gain long life, as do the gods by feeding on the beverage of immortality!
Suśruta, III,10

In the past million years or so of man's existence, his way of life has developed from huntsman to agriculturist to herdsman and to city-dweller. The imprecise term 'traditional societies' obviously, therefore, covers a very wide range of different cultures and communities. It includes such diverse, complex, pre-literate societies as the Gauls of ancient Europe, the American Indians of North America, and others; the ancient civilizations of India, China, Egypt, and South America, and the pre-industrial revolution patterns of living in Europe (Ryerson 1961). It also includes to varying extents present-day rural communities in developing countries of Africa (D.B. Jelliffe 1953, Thompson 1967, Vis and Hennart 1974). Asia (Rao *et al*. 1959, Yung-En Kao 1948), and Latin America (Menchu *et al*. 1972), although 'these are altering in different degrees under the influence of Western culture.

Traditional societies are usually characterized by slowly changing customs and practices, and by limited mechanization. All have complex systems of cultural sanctions and proscriptions for all aspects of life, particularly such special, potentially hazardous, and clear-cut episodes as pregnancy, childbirth, and early childhood (Gonzalez and Behar 1966).

Review accounts of different aspects have been given by D.B. Jelliffe (1968*b*), Jelliffe and Bennett (1972), Mead and Newton (1967), and Raphael (1966). Information is also available in the over 200 cultures included in the Human Relations Area Files (available from 755 Prospect Street, New Haven, U.S.A.). The history of infant feeding has been outlined by Hill (1967), Hymanson (1934), D.B. Jelliffe (1968*b*), Levin (1962, 1963), and particularly by Wickes (1953).

In any discussion of breast-feeding, it is necessary nutritionally to consider the whole overlapping, interconnected sequence from mother and foetus to exterogestate foetus to transitional (p. 4). The present-day medical breaking of the reproductive cycle in the middle, with the first portion the responsibility of the obstetrician and the second that of the paediatrician is a relatively new development (Mead and Newton 1967). In the nineteenth century, obstetrics and paediatrics were frequently combined. The *American Journal of Obstetrics and Diseases of Women and Children* was founded in 1869 and stopped publication in 1919. In 1920, its editor assumed the same role of the newly founded *American Journal of Obstetrics and Gynecology* (Packard 1931).

1. The foetus

The nutrition of the mother and foetus is a dyadic process (p. 2). The size and the nutrient stores of the newborn, and the calorie resources laid down by the mother for lactation, all reflect the maternal diet in pregnancy. Customs and practices regulating the foods taken in pregnancy are relevant to lactation. These vary greatly. Sometimes additional or special items may be included. However, not infrequently such practices are restrictive — that is they limit the diet, often with a view to producing a small baby with the hope of an easier delivery (Ebrahim 1976).

2. The newborn

Breast-milk was (and is) the bulwark of infant feeding for the exterogestate foetus (especially the neonate) in traditional societies. It is virtually imperative if the survival of the baby is to be ensured.

The newborn is usually put to the breast very soon after delivery (Breetveld 1972), and remains and sleeps by the mother's side (Fig. 9.1). Colostrum is often regarded as important.* However, in some communities, such as parts of northern Pakistan, colostrum was considered to be poisonous, and was expressed and discarded. In this situation, the newborn may be fed for a few days by a lactating relative or wet-nurse, or given gruels, which often lead to diarrhoea. Colostrum is often considered to have laxative properties.

Some cultures have tests for the suitability or even harmfulness of the mother's milk (Niehoff and Meister 1972). For example, the 'fingernail test' of Soranus, in which the suitability of breast-milk was judged by the way a drop spread when put on a fingernail, was used in Europe for hundreds of years. At present, in some rural areas of Africa, a woman may be seen nursing her baby with one breast only, because 'poisonous' milk has been diagnosed in the other breast.

Most often the initial feeding of the baby is with breast-milk alone, but in some cultures, 'pre-lacteal feeds' may also be given prior to nursing. For example, in parts of Malaysia, mashed ripe banana is fed to the breast-fed baby in the first days of life. Often this is undertaken in part to 'clean out the meconium'.

---

* This is indicated, for example, by the ancient Latin endearment *Meum mel, meum cor, mea colostra* (My honey, my heart, my colostrum) — Maccius Plautus, *c*. 184 B.C.

Fig. 9.1. Exterogestate foetus on mother's back: Hong Kong (courtesy of UNICEF)

Different children

Babies born who are abnormal to a lesser or greater degree are often treated with culturally defined behaviour. For example, in some African communities, breach births, newborn with teeth, albinos, and twins may be neglected to varying extents. Alternatively, as among the Baganda of East Africa, twins may be welcomed as a blessing of the gods and looked after particularly carefully, with titles for life given to the parents.

Preference for male or female children may exist, partly related to whether bride-price or dowry is the local practice. This can be expressed overtly or subconsciously by the degree of attention given, including feeding.

Alternative sources of breast milk

Culturally acceptable survival techniques have often evolved to employ alternative sources of human milk when mothers died in childbirth, such as lactating relatives, induced lactation (Cohen 1971, Jelliffe and Jelliffe 1972*a*, Wieschhoff 1940), and employment of wet-nurses. For example, among the Yoruba of Nigeria, a technique of inducing lactation was carried out using herbal infusions by mouth, mammary massage, and repeated frequent suckling at the breast (D.B. Jelliffe 1968*b*).

Endocrinological explanations are now available for this phenomenon (p. 17), but, prior to this, Western-trained physicians have had great difficulty in accepting the feasibility of such a practice, previously termed 'abnormal lactation' (Foss and Short 1951, Marieskind 1973). Such an experience has been summarized by Mead (1957):

> In 1933, when I returned from New Guinea and reported that women, some of whom had never borne children and others who had not lactated for many years, could suckle newborn children, I was challenged with the query: How do you know they produced milk? I could only reply that it was a substance, white in colour, emitted by the maternal breast, on which the infant lived and thrived. My evidence consisted of two pairs of identical twins; in each case, one twin was fed by its own mother and the other twin was fed by an adoptive mother in whom lactation had been induced by the combination of the infant's suckling, forced fluids, and a definite intention. These observations, made among the Mundugumor of New Guinea, have been corroborated since then by observations made on other peoples; but the scepticism with which my original observations were met exemplifies the blindness induced by habituation within our own cultural pattern.

In a very few communities, the hopeless situation of the newborn deprived of mother's milk, if no alternative was available, was clearly recognized by the practice of burying the live baby with the mother, if she died in childbirth (D.B. Jelliffe 1968*b*, Krzywicki 1934).

Galactogogues
The commonness of true physical inability to breast-feed adequately, labelled agalactia and hypogalactia, is impossible to assess; it is certainly very rare, except as a secondary consequence of such abnormalities as severe cleft palate or maternal insanity. The absolute necessity for successful breast-feeding must have led to the breeding out of genetically poor lactators with some anatomical abnormality, such as inadequate secretory tissue or defective nipple structure, which would have prevented adequate milk production or suckling. Usually lactation failure is related to interference with the let-down-reflex (p. 19).

Many communities have various techniques and preparations, religious ceremonies and rituals intended to stimulate the flow of breast-milk (Ainsworth 1974, Weisler-Aall 1973), especially for the first-born. Little scientific work has been undertaken in this matter. Some traditional galactogogues may have as yet unrecognized pharmacological effects (Ebrahim 1976). Often these methods seem to be based on 'sympathetic magic', with the use of milk-like substances, or charms depicting large breasts (such as the Venus of Willendorf amulets), thereby reassuring the mother and enhancing the let-down reflex. For example, in ancient Polynesian Hawaii,

Fig. 9.2. Ancient Egyptian figurine of cat nursing kittens, sacred to the cat-headed goddess Bast (courtesy of the Trustees of the British Museum)

prayers were made to the gods, Ku and Hina, while strands of freshly plucked vine, dripping with milky sap, were hung on either side of the woman's chest (Jelliffe and Jelliffe 1964).

Although pharmacological effects may sometimes be responsible, it seems more likely that these procedures were more often confidence-inducing procedures — in modern parlance, reinforcers of the let-down reflex (p. 19). Sometimes dietary alteration can be culturally defined during lactation. This can be restrictive or can add to the diet, sometimes with calories, as with *gur* (village sugar) in parts of India.

It has been suggested that the rituals and galactogogues found in some cultures indicated that inadequate lactation may have been a common problem. This seems unlikely, although anxiety-induced failure of the let-down reflex can result from fears of bewitchment or guilt over non-observance of taboos, especially of a sexual nature.

Reasons for breast-feeding
Apart from breast-feeding being the cultural norm and, indeed, the only practical option in traditional cultures, the maternal fertility role is dominant for women. Religious sanction is also often obvious — for example, among the Yoruba of West Nigeria the goddess of fertility is Odudua, depicted as a woman nursing twins. In ancient Egypt one of the mother-goddesses was Bast, represented as a cat nursing kittens (Fig. 9.2), and Philistine goddess of fertility, Astarte, was shown with uplifted breasts. In Aztec culture, infants dying while still being nursed went to a special after-life *chichihuacuauhco*

depicted as a tree of breasts dropping succour into the babies' mouths (Bustamente 1968) (Fig. 9.3). By Talmudic Law, Jewish babies were to be breast-fed for 24 months. Lactation could be continued longer than this, provided it was not stopped and restarted. Conversely, in the Old Testament, the most severe punishment for the erring Israelites was noted: 'Give them, O Lord: what wilt thou give them? Give them a miscarrying womb and a dry breast.' (Hos. 9:14).

Likewise, the symbolism of the female breast in various cultures includes security ('the bosom of the family'), fertility, sacrifice, love, food, succour, etc., in addition to its sexual symbolism; at the same time breast-feeding is always carried out naturally and without embarrassment (Figs 9.4, 9.5, 9.6).

Wet-nurses
In some traditional breast-feeding communities, a paradox must be noted as of possible significance in relation to present-day patterns of declining lactation. In some sophisticated ancient and more modern civilizations (Sussman 1975) it was common for the wives of the aristocracy and the wealthy to give their own babies to wet-nurses to be suckled, enabling these women to take part in political activities, to become involved in a wider range of sexual activities, to cement relationships and ties with lower-class women, whose loyalty could be a useful source of information, and sometimes because of contemporary medical advice. For example, Soranus in the second century A.D. recommended that mother's milk was often 'unclean'

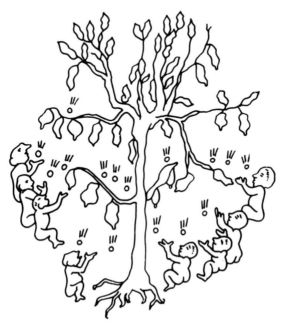

Fig. 9.3.
Chichihuacuauhco: ancient Aztec heaven for children who died while nursing, depicted as a breast-tree from which succour is falling (from Bustamente, M. E. (1968). *Gac. med. mex.* **98**, 1208)

Fig. 9.4. Uneventful breast-feeding, without embarrassment: rural Egypt (courtesy of WHO)

for some days after parturition, so that a wet-nurse had to be found for this period.

Wet-nursing represented a profound change in fundamental human behaviour, although it was still biologically based. Interestingly, the close attachment between wet-nurse and baby was well appreciated; for example, a wet-nurse was judged by strict criteria with regard to temperament, morals, and health, and in some societies social 'milk relationships' were formed between those suckled by the same wet-nurse, as in the French *frères de lait*.

As recent as 1938, Platt and Gin described the arrangements customary in hiring a wet-nurse in China:

(The wet-nurse) attaches herself to a shop in the city which is run as a general servants' agency. The proprietor supplies a baby in order to maintain the milk secretion. The wet-nurse pays for the room and board provided by the agent, and, if she succeeds in obtaining employment, she pays a fee of half her first month's wages to the agent, and the customer pays an amount to the agent of 80 per cent of the wages. The employer is expected to pay two months' wages in advance to the wet-nurse when she is engaged, and he agrees to pay a bonus of an extra month's wages after the child is weaned. She is expected to serve a probationary period of three days to a week in the home. After her wet-nursing duties are completed in the one family, she may be taken on as a servant, she may seek further employment as a wet-nurse, or she may return to her own home. It is considered desirable that the wet-nurse should have certain qualities. She should be young, healthy, of pleasant

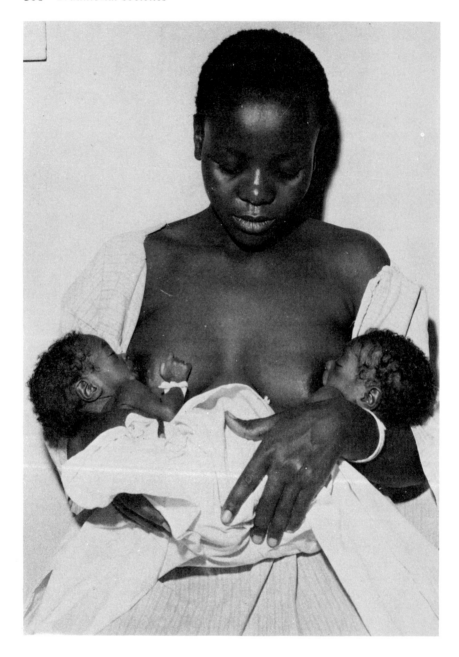

Fig. 9.5. Uneventful breast-feeding of low-birth-weight twins (3½ lbs): Kampala, Uganda

Fig. 9.6. Uneventful breast-feeding: rural Borneo (courtesy of Prof. H. A. P. C. Oomen and the photographic Documentation Centre, Royal Tropical Institute, Amsterdam)

disposition, and if possible of pleasing appearance. A primiparous woman is preferred. Her breast development should be ample, and her attention is paid to the areola of the nipples, which should be black as an indication of the recent delivery of the nurse's own infant. It is recognized that the milk must be white and thick; yellow milk, and bluish, thin milk is not good. A test employed is to drop milk on to the table; the drop formed must be round and raised, and it should not be possible to blow it into smaller drops. A recognized method of determining the quality of milk is by weighing a sample on a special scale which is used for weighing gold; one pan when full should weigh two 'chien' and eight 'li'. Another consideration recognized in the choice of a wet-nurse is the behaviour of the baby, which should not cry if the milk is satisfactory.

Sixteenth-century European guidance for the selection of a wet-nurse, probably derived largely from classical Latin sources, was as follows (D.B. Jelliffe 1968*b*):

She should be of healthy lineage, good behaviour, sober, even-tempered, happy, chaste, wise, discreet, careful, observant, understanding, conscientious, and always willing to give the breast. She should be physically healthy, with a pleasing counte-

Fig. 9.7. Feeding young deer on human milk: Rupununi, Guyana, 1960 (courtesy of Dr. A. Giglioli)

nance, 'ruddie mouth', and rosy complexion, and she should have 'verie white teeth' and broad but not pendulous breasts with good nipples; she should play with her charge and change him often.

Under many circumstances, the original offspring of the women who became wet-nurses were 'hand-reared' or 'dry nursed' — and often died. This was, for example, usually the case with the often illegitimate infants of wet-nurses in eighteenth-century Britain, who were left at foundling homes or 'baby-farms', where the mortality was almost total (Hymanson 1934).

Special celebrations
The extreme danger of the neonatal period is recognized in some cultures by

feasts or celebrations after a defined period, such as 'when the cord is off', 'when the ritual seclusion is finished', or 'after 40 days' (Raphael 1966).

3. The exterogestate foetus (p. 4)

Continuing lactation

In traditional societies, the initiation and maintenance of lactation is usually successful and uncomplicated, with close continuing contact with the mother facilitating demand or opportunity feedings, at any time, place, or position during both day and night, thus ensuring maximal prolactin secretion.

Close mothering, with continuing proximity, is made easier in many cultures by traditional methods of baby-carrying (Fig. 9.1), which have in the past 15 years or so become popular in the U.S.A., Europe, and Australia. Interestingly, some African languages have the same word for both the amniotic membranes and the back-cloth used for carrying the baby — for example, *nkozi* in Luganda.

The mother–baby closeness often seen in traditional cultures has been described among the Aymara of Bolivia in this way (Tichauer 1963):

> Wherever the mother goes, even to a dance, the baby will go with her, little head close to hers and easily slung forward in front of her in case of need . . .. No modesty is attached to nursing even in public places . . .. At night the child sleeps next to his mother. This continues until he is about 2 years old until the next child is born. Nursing has precedence over any other activity in which the mother may be engaged, such as selling her vegetables in the market, for instance, although she may be extremely anxious to make the sale.

Role of animal milk

The milk of many domesticated animals has been used by man in various parts of the world, including that of the cow, goat, sheep, buffalo, camel, yak, reindeer, etc. (p. 27). It is only in the past 10 000 years, following the domestication of various milch animals, that the possibility arose of using animal milk in infant feeding — at least in those societies where milk-drinking was culturally acceptable. However, despite the fact that many different forms of feeding bowl or cup or horn have been discovered in different parts of the world and in various archaeological sites, such forms of artificial feeding of babies were never widely practicable as a substitute for breast-feeding for hygienic reasons.

The high risk of death from diarrhoea and marasmus is clear in such communities, and even as recently as the late nineteenth century in the U.S.A. (McCollum 1958):

> The women in Kansas at that time were convinced that if a baby were fed cow's milk it should surely die. Their belief was fully justified. If you could go back with me and see our cows, or barn, the milk pails and cans, and our lack of facilities for keeping milk cold, you would doubtless have been convinced that no baby could

survive such unsanitary milk. It is my belief that I could have survived being fed on milk contaminated with stable filth. It was the cloth strainer which a baby could not compete with by his defence mechanisms. We rinsed the strainer after pouring the morning's milk through it, and hung it up to dry. In summer fifty or more flies would alight on it within a minute and feed upon the milk residues, speckling it with fly-specks. In the evening, the fresh milk was poured through this fly-excrement-laden cloth. A baby could scarcely ever fail, when fed such contaminated milk, to suffer from diarrhoeal infection and die.

It needs to be re-emphasized that, on a world basis, the drinking of animal milk is a minority food practice, as endorsed physiologically by the recent discovery that the majority of adult mankind (or other adult mammals) do not show the enzyme lactose in intestinal secretions (McCracken 1971). Even when the domestication of milk-producing mammals, such as buffaloes, was part of these cultures, they were used for other purposes, such as for agricultural work and for transport.* In China, Mongolo-Malaya, most of Africa, Polynesia, and Melanesia, no milk — other than human — has ever been used in the diet. Although a good food, rich in protein and calcium, cow's milk is not *necessary* at any age; in fact, biologically liquid milk can be considered as an 'unnatural' item in the diet of adult mammals. Western man has developed a degree of 'cow's-milk emotionalism'.

Artificial feeding
Feeding devices, such as horns and cups, have been used occasionally throughout history, usually for infants without available breast-milk, particularly if the mother died in childbirth. Because of the inadequate nutritional composition of these feedings, which often consisted of dilute animal milk or gruels, diarrhoeal disease often resulted and such babies usually died. For example, in 1660 in England, Sloan noted that over half those 'hand-reared' died in infancy — that is an infant mortality of over 500 per 1000 live births — correctly labelled 'died for want of breast-milk'. By contrast, only one-fifth of breast-fed babies died (Wickes 1953).

For the ultimate neonatal emergency of a dead mother, various methods were used by different cultures: a wet-nurse, a lactating relative, induced lactation (p.163), 'hand-rearing' with feeding devices (using animal milk or gruel), 'direct feeding' on animals' udders, or infanticide.

4. The transitional (p. 4)

The length of breast-feeding and the culturally correct time for weaning, both in the sense of introducing other foods and of the stopping of breast-feeding (*sevrage*), vary from one community to another. Often the reason

---

* Occasionally in a few cultures, human milk was used in breast-feeding baby animals — for example, puppies in ancient Polynesian Hawaii (Jelliffe and Jelliffe 1964), piglets in the New Guinea Highlands (Jelliffe and Maddocks 1964), and deer in the Rupununi hinterland of Guyana (Jelliffe and Maddocks 1964) (Fig. 9.7).

for *sevrage* is a subsequent pregnancy; in some societies, particularly in parts of Africa, the birth-spacing effect of the lactation amenorrhoea (p. 118) resulting from 'biological breast-feeding' was reinforced by sexual abstinence during breast-feeding. In other communities, the time for removal from the breast was locally defined — for example, when a certain number of teeth had erupted or the child could walk. However, in some cultures, such as the San Blas Indians of Panama (Jelliffe *et al*. 1961) or the Karamajong of Uganda (Jelliffe *et al*. 1964), breast-feeding was continued throughout pregnancy.

Most usually what occurs in traditional circumstances is currently termed 'prolonged lactation' — that is continuing for two or more years. The introduction of non-breast-milk foods varies greatly — in some communities the pre-lacteal feeds commenced in the newborn period may be continued with from the time, or softer items of the adult dietary (or less commonly specially prepared items for young children) are introduced earlier or later in the second six months of life or, lastly and not rarely, foods other than human milk may not be introduced until the second year of life.

All cultures have complex food classifications, which may limit the range of items available for infant feeding. In particular, foods considered appropriate or unsuitable for young children, the age at which they can be introduced, and the occurrence of ceremonies at these occasions are of importance to the infant's nutritional transition. The 'cultural superfood' is of considerable significance. If this is low in protein and calories and high in water and cellulose, such as yams or plantain, it places the transitional at greater risk than in communities where a cereal grain is the cultural superfood (e.g. rice, wheat). Essentially, cultural attitudes in infant feeding need to be considered in relation to their potential as 'protein blocks' — that is as practices which facilitate or make more difficult the use of locally available protein-rich foods (Jelliffe 1959*a*, 1962).

The transitional diet has much relevance to breast-feeding in traditional communities. First, the foods taken need to be considered as being complemented nutritionally by the small, but significant, continuing amount of breast-milk secreted (p.65). Secondly, the age at which foods are introduced is relevant to milk production as they have the effect of decreasing sucking stimulus and prolactin secretion, and hence diminishing milk output and reducing lactation amenorrhoea.

Weaning is a curious process common to all mammals in which the young animal's life depends on 'bridging the biologically momentous period, when it changes from a milk-drinking to a starch- and flesh-eating creature.' (Jelliffe 1968*b*). In many human communities, its nutritional, infectious, and psychological dangers and social significance are clearly mirrored by the preference for certain seasons of the year (such as spring or autumn in Europe) and by special ceremonies and *rites de passage*. For example, the Hindu culture has the important *annaprasam* (rice-feeding ceremony), which serves both to widen the infant's diet and to initiate him into orthodox society (Jelliffe 1959a).

Methods of separation of the baby from the mother's milk (*sevrage*) vary considerably in the age at which undertaken, the suddenness, the 'compensation' (if any), and the degree of physical geographical separation of mother and infant at this time. For example, among the Baganda of East Africa, the child is taken from the breast abruptly and sent to stay with a relative, often the grandmother, which can be a potent psychosocial aetiological factor in the development of kwashiorkor ('disease of the displaced child'). In some cultures, the separation may be forced by the application of bitter and unpleasant substances to the breasts, such as aloes, red pepper, or soot. By contrast, other communities have less psychologically traumatic methods, with a more gradual process and with the child receiving special foods as a form of compensation (Namboze 1967).

Pregnancy and family size
Most, or perhaps all, traditional cultures prize large families, despite (or because of) high child mortalities. In such circumstances, many children represent power, as work-force (for fighting or as agricultural strength), or economically (as earners of bride-price or dowries, depending on custom). They are also considered as real or spiritual continuity with the future, and sometimes in cultures with concepts about rebirths into a family, they may also be an actual spiritual link from the past. For example, among traditional Yoruba names indicate this belief, such as *Babatunde* ('father or grandfather comes again').

However, the idea of spacing of pregnancies and babies at not too short intervals is sometimes endorsed by custom and practice. For example, in the central African country of Rwanda, the question 'How many children do you want?' usually leads to the answer 'As many as possible'; whereas the question 'At what intervals?' produces the response 'Two to three years' (Van Balen and Ntabomvura 1976).

Concepts of fertilization and pregnancy vary widely in different communities. Some African cultures use verbal imagery which fits well into modern ideas. For example, among the Rwandese, the placenta and amniotic membranes have the same word, *ingobyi*, as the sheep's skin used to carry the infant on the mother's back. Foetal movements are described as *umwana aronka* ('taking the inside breast'). At birth, they speak of the baby 'moving from the womb to the back'. There is an expression of disapproval, *inda liakana*, for children born at too short an interval from the preceding sibling, locally defined as 'before the earlier child can carry a baby' (Van Balen and Ntabomvura 1976).

After delivery, there may be dietary restrictions or the opposite. Thus, in Malaysia, there is traditionally a 40-day period of limitation of maternal diet after childbirth (*pantang*); while in rural Burma, a special high-protein soup (*ringa*) is culturally approved in the puerperium (Jelliffe and Bennett 1962).

In traditional communities, there is usually little specific breast prepara-tion during pregnancy, in the Western sense of massage of the nipples, expression of milk, etc. However, there is a great deal of subconscious practical and psychological preparation for breast-feeding. Under tradi-tional circumstances, the new mother will be in a community where breast-feeding is the norm. During her own girlhood, she will have observed relatives and others breast-feeding uneventfully, and will have learnt sub-consciously from such observation. In addition, the supportive environment supplied in the perinatal period engenders the confidence and certainty that leads to an unimpaired let-down reflex.

Childbirth
A great range of different practices may be followed during childbirth in various cultures, many of significance to the well-being of both newborn and mother. In relation to breast-feeding, the time the umbilical cord is tied is of importance to the infant's iron stores (p. 47), and the method in which the baby is put to the breast and the attitude towards colostrum are related to the ease (or otherwise) of initiation of lactation.

Perinatal care
Recent work by Raphael has emphasized the key significance of the perinatal period — that is the last months of pregnancy, childbirth, and the first few weeks after delivery — as being of critical importance in relation to the successful initiation and continuation of breast-feeding.

The doula concept
Analyses have recently been carried out by Raphael on the behaviour of social mammals, such as dolphins and elephants, and in traditional human societies, including the Western world until recently, in relation to childbirth and the neonatal period (Raphael 1966, 1969). As a result, she has drawn attention to the fact that it is usual for one or more individuals, usually a female, to be available to assist during the pregnancy, childbirth, and neonatal period. This individual, termed by Raphael a *doula* (from the ancient Greek word for female assistant), supplies traditional information and gives physical help and emotional support. For example, in rural India a girl is brought up surrounded by breast-feeding relatives and learns by cultural osmosis that this is the normal way to behave. She gains intimate knowledge of the art of breast-feeding subconsciously by observation, and she learns how to handle babies by caring for younger siblings. In addition, during later pregnancy, childbirth, and the neonatal period, traditional cultures have *doulas* to assist in this time of psychosocial and physiological transition. In some parts of India there are two *doulas*. For example, during later pregnancy, a young woman moves to stay with her own mother, who

acts, therefore, as a *doula*. In turn, she is reinforced by a second *doula*, the traditional midwife (*dai*), who not only helps with the delivery, but also with the ritual seclusion wisely prescribed by this culture for some weeks after the birth. During this time, the mother can rest and become adjusted to the baby and her new role, and breast-feeding becomes firmly established.

Such *doulas* are usually mature women with their own children and well known to the young mother. Their role is especially significant with the first baby, and the success of 'the lactation-suckling process has to be seen in the matrix of social support.' (Raphael 1966). Knowledge of the art of breast-feeding has traditionally been part of female culture, and, as with other aspects of child rearing, is taught by observation and participation in stable cultures.

Postnatal adjustment

Many traditional cultures have special perinatal *rites de passage*, such as the month-long ritual seclusion following delivery in the New Guinea Highlands (Jelliffe and Maddocks 1964). These have the function of reassurance during this obviously hazardous time, and also of initiating the woman into 'matrescence' in Raphael's terminology. They also serve to accustom the rest of the family to the new roles that they will all be expected to play after the baby has been born.

Traditional cultures never separate mother and newborn — in fact the two are usually kept together continuously. If postnatal seclusion for the mother and her child is the custom, during this period she will only be attended by a limited number of individuals. Although undertaken for religious or ritualistic reasons, this period plainly has the physiological and nutritional advantage of permitting the mother to rest, to become adjusted to her new baby, to permit the cord to heal, and to initiate lactation.

Conclusion

Allowing for much variation, traditional child-rearing practices probably usually lead to relatively little malnutrition, and indeed, to excellent growth for the first six months or so of life — that is for most of the exterogestate foetal period when breast-feeding is usually successful. During the second six months of life, breast-milk continues to be of importance, but as a supplement to other dietary items introduced during this period (Omololu 1974, 1976).

Despite this, infant mortality rates — that is deaths during the first year of life — were exceedingly high in most traditional circumstances; as were death rates in all age-groups, particularly in childbirth and the perinatal period. However, these high rates were in large measure from diseases due to environmental and infective factors (such as respiratory infection, malaria, and accidents), together with infections and injuries associated with the birth process (such as tetanus, septicaemia, and cerebral damage).

Without breast-feeding in traditional societies, the infant mortality becomes almost total, as can be seen with the extremely high mortality rate in artificially-fed babies in village circumstances or in orphanages at the present day in many less technically developed countries (Wickes 1953).

In traditional communities, the peak period of nutritional risk was during the transitional or weaning period — most often, or at least in many communities, in the second year of life. This period of the young child's early life has long been widely recognized as one of particular danger from malnutrition and infection, manifest even in less marked instances by growth failure (Fig. 9.8). Because of this, a special term has been suggested for the 'second-year transitional' — the secotrant (Jelliffe 1969*b*) (Fig. 9.9).

During this period, the young child has to struggle to adjust to a variety of bacterial and parasitic infections and often to the psychological trauma of separation from the mother's breasts (*sevrage*) (Cravioto *et al.* 1967, *The Lancet* 1974*b*, Malcolm 1970). At the same time, the nutrient needs are high in view of the rapidity and complexity of growth and development, and the diet is likely to be inadequate in quantity, quality, and preparation. In addition, this is the period when 'weanling diarrhoea' occurs principally, as an epidemiological entity in traditional societies, largely as a result of the

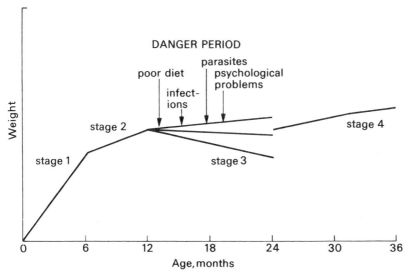

Fig. 9.8. Weight curve often found in traditional communities. Stage 1 — good growth and protection from infections on breast-milk; stage 2 — inadequate growth on breast-milk plus often small quantities of bulky, ill-cooked, largely carbohydrate foods; stage 3 — poor growth or failure to grow or weight loss or protein–calorie malnutrition (kwashiorkor) on small amounts of breast-milk (or none), defective weaning diet, multiple infections, and sometimes psychological ill-effects of weaning (from Jelliffe, D. B. (1974*b*). In *Medicine in the tropics* (ed. A. Woodruff), Ch. 27. Churchill Livingstone, London)

Fig. 9.9. Inadequate weight gain in secotrant (second year of life). Two children of same weight in West Bengal village: right, breast-fed baby 6 months old; left, 17-month-old child, breast-fed with inadequate semi-solids

interaction of malnutrition, intestinal infection, and ill-absorption of inadequately prepared foods (Gordon *et al.* 1963). It is also the time when kwashiorkor is particularly likely to develop, if low-protein, calorie-containing foods are introduced, either with or without the continuance of small quantities of breast-milk, together with the added burdens of the procession of microbial, parasitic, and viral infections and, sometimes the psychological trauma of separation from the mother (Figs: 9.8, 9.9).

Alternatively, and less appreciated perhaps, it is also a period when so-called 'late marasmus' can also occur as a result of 'breast starvation'. This can develop if the young child is continued on breast-feeding into the second year of life unsupplemented even with inadequate transitional foods.

Fundamentally, there is a long transition from total physiological dependence in the uterus to complete physiological independence following *sevrage*. As opposed to many babies in Western countries where this may be completed in minutes, in traditional cultures the process is prolonged for 2–3 years, or more.

As Mead and Newton (1967) note: 'It involves a set of interdependent patterns, which include physical closeness to the mother by day and sleeping

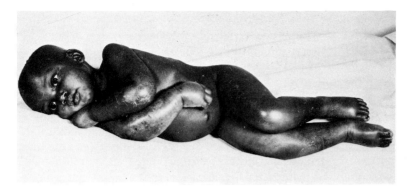

Fig. 9.10. Kwashiorkor in Uganda: almost always a disease of the 'transitional', commonly affecting the secotrant, mainly caused by a carbohydrate low-protein weaning diet, with a small amount or no breast-milk, together with continuous infections

with the mother at night, soothing of all crying, prolonged and frequent sucking at the breast, and the spacing of children so that maternal attention and energy are not quickly divided.

Basic to the whole process is what may be termed 'biological breast-feeding' in which unscheduled nursing occurs as required during the day and night, commencing shortly after birth. This continues unsupplemented for 6–9 months, and thereafter for 2–3 years, when the milk becomes a small but valuable supplement. Other foods are not introduced early, so that there is no competition as regards sucking stimulus; in particular, no bottle-feeds can be given as feeding-bottles in the modern sense do not exist. Such a method permits the mother to care for the child for several years and the lactation amenorrhoea (p. 118) assists in spacing births at 2–4-yearly intervals.

Adaptive suckling

During the millions of years of human history mankind has, until the past two generations, reared his young offspring almost exclusively on human milk during the exterogestate early months of life. Cattle were only domesticated 10 000 years ago (Levin 1963) and canning of cow's-milk formulas on a large scale only has taken place in the last 50 years or so. In the course of that vast period of time, it seems reasonable to assume that selection and modification occurred to ensure that adaptive suckling developed to suit the needs of the human infant and to promote the survival of the species ('teleonomy'). Success in human lactation must have become the rule in view of the breeding out of genetic abnormalities making for difficulties (such as abnormal nipples), by the development of instinctive reflex behaviour involving both mother and newborn, reinforced by a complex interchange of signals ('sign-stimuli'), by information gained by observation during childhood, and by appropriate social and cultural support during the perinatal period.

From the point of view of adaptive suckling, man can be considered as a continuous-contact species needing frequent feedings day and night. The 'lactatory apparatus' in the form of two female mammae is capable of catering for more than 99 per cent of offspring — that is singletons and twins (Fig. 9.5).

The wandering hunting life of early man* and the immaturity of the large-headed exterogestate foetus made speedy recovery from childbirth and rapid bonding between mother and neonate, via hormonal and behavioural interchange, essential for survival of the helpless baby, who had to be carried, defended from predators, cared for, and fed by the mother under difficult conditions of movement following game or in flight. Such close care, carriage, and supply of milk were required throughout the exterogestate-foetal stage of life and for the early transitional. In pre-mechanical hunting communities, no apparatus was available for mashing foods, so that semi-solids for the infant were either pre-chewed by the mother or were naturally soft foods, such as bone marrow. The mother's protective role was needed through the transitional phase, until the child could walk, talk and masticate and have achieved immunity to the main local infections. As Klaus (1975) has emphasized: 'There is an immediate inter-locking and reciprocal set of behaviors for attachment which must quickly operate because of the infant's precarious state following delivery. The infant requires a devoted caretaker to provide warmth and protection. Feeding is also an early necessity.'

The prolonged period of highly dependent infancy in the human may also have adaptive advantages: 'Compared to any other species, the human neonate is relatively helpless in the motor sphere and relatively complex, even precocious, in the sensory sphere. This enforces a kind of motoric dependence and a freedom for acquisition of the many patterns of sensory and affective information that are necessary to the child and adult human for mastering and surviving in a complex world.' (Brazleton *et al*. 1975).

Unlike other mammals, man had no biological birth-spacing technique as a result of mating or oestrus season, but rather spaced offspring at 2–3-year intervals by means of lactation amenorrhoea (p. 118), mainly mediated through the anterior pituitary hormone prolactin, secreted as a result of suckling.

Biologically, the main characteristic of man is his complex biological computer, the brain. Human milk contains an abundance of those nutrients known to be important in the biochemical development of the central nervous sytem. For example, the uniquely high lactose (7 per cent) (metabolized to galactose needed for galactolipids), cystine, cholesterol,

* Studies of twentieth-century hunting communities, such as the Hadza in northern Tanzania (Jelliffe *et al*. 1962), can give much insight (Coon 1962).

specific polyenoic fatty acids, and thromboplastin appear to be key items needed for rapid brain growth — the prime characteristic of the newborn of *Homo sapiens*. The low solute, low protein levels of human milk are appropriate for the relatively slow growth of the human infant and for the satisfaction of fluid needs as well as of nutrients.

Immunologically, the neonate is only half-protected passively by antibodies acquired transplacentally. The positive protective effect of human milk, especially during the early months of life, is increasingly endorsed by recent work (p. 84), and colostrum can be considered as a concentrated immunological bolus. Particularly is this the case with regard to immunity to the organisms of the infant's closest environment — his mother (p. 90).

The dyadic nature of breast-feeding as a mutual exchange and interaction between mother and baby is paramount. For example, the early and frequent sucking of the breast by the infant leads to be a 'supply-and-demand' situation of milk secretion, to lactation amenorrhoea and, in the puerperium, to uterine contractions and early involution. Likewise, the mutual pleasurability of breast-feeding, psychological and hormonal, increases the mother–neonate bond and facilitates continuation of the process.

With this very ancient background of adaptive suckling, the phenomenon of rapid change in the Westernized world to bottle-feeding with cow's-milk formulas in the last 50 years is extremely curious, and needs examination in relation both to technologically advanced, resource-rich countries (p. 182) and in less technically developed, non-Western countries (p. 211).

10 Technological urban societies

An excellent substitute for mother's milk.

Take half an ounce of fresh mutton suet, cut into small pieces, and tie them in a muslin bag, taking care that they are not pressed upon; boil in a pint of cow's milk, to which half an ounce of good oatmeal and a teaspoonful of powdered sugar-candy have been added.

William Pearce (1853) *Plain advice for the management and diet of infants*, London

Things are seldom what they seem,
Skim milk masquerades as cream.

W. S. Gilbert (1878) *H.M.S. Pinafore*

If you give a bottle to your baby twice a week, simply accept the fact that he will be totally bottle-fed by the time he is three or four months old. It just works out that way most of the time. The bottle-feeding deprives the breasts of some stimulation and teaches the baby to suck less hard.

Niles Newton (1957)

The patterns of infant feeding seen in present-day Europe and America date back to changes deriving from the Industrial Revolution. Prior to this, as noted earlier (p. 161), breast-feeding by the mother was the normal and virtually universal method for the exterogestate foetus, apart from the employment of wet-nurses, particularly for some wealthier women.

In the early nineteenth century in North America and Western Europe the situation was similar to other traditional, slowly changing cultures (p. 161), that is with the main nutritional danger-period likely to affect the transitional during weaning, and with an extremely high mortality from diarrhoeal disease and marasmus for such babies as had to be 'hand-reared' because breast-milk was not available. Society was largely rural and families were 'extended' and made up of close-knit interdependent members. Women were direct and indirect economic contributors in their own right in agricultural activities, in the storage and preparation of food, and in the bearing and rearing of children needed for the families' work-force. In other words, in these circumstances breast-feeding was not only a normal unquestioned and irreplaceable female function, but an economic essential for the prosperity and survival of the family.

Changing patterns

During the past 125 years or so, very great changes in patterns of infant feeding have occurred. For convenience, this time-span can be considered in three arbitrarily separated, over-lapping phases: (i) late Industrial Revolution (1850–1910), (ii) 1910–60, and (iii) 1960 to the present.

Late Industrial Revolution (1850–1910)

The full material effect of the Industrial Revolution in the mid-nineteenth century resulted from the harnessing of scientific technology, particularly steam power, for the production of food, for the manufacture of goods, and for their widespread distribution. In Europe and America, it was the development of new industries and mechanized agriculture which both initiated and made urbanization possible — with rapid growth of huge cities, often located at the site of primary products or fuel needed for the particular industry (Jelliffe and Jelliffe 1970*a*).

This initial rapid urbanization brought with it complete changes in ways of life — in particular dependence on a cash economy, little or no opportunity for growing food, and overcrowding and poor hygiene in slums of the nineteenth century. Likewise, the family structure and mores altered as the extended family ties of rural society were fragmented into the more isolated nuclear families of the town. Roles of men, women, and children all changed, and a new kind of family instability emerged. Illegitimacy increased, with an additional impact on the infant mortality rate, as such infants were often abandoned and artificially fed (Lomax 1972).

With the exploitation customary with early industrialization and the low wages offered, it became necessary for many women (and children) to work in factories as well as men, although their wages were even lower than for males. Widespread employment of women in industry at this time had many effects, notably a change in women's role and status, away from her more traditional, almost exclusively home-centred functions. At the same time, the feeding and rearing of young children became more difficult for working mothers, particularly the nursing of their infants. Urban problems with breast-feeding for working mothers were paralleled by increasing attempts at bottle-feeding young infants, but were very frequently disastrously unsuccessful in the impoverished circumstances and poor hygiene of the ill-educated new urban masses (Jelliffe and Jelliffe 1970*a*).

For example, Routh (1863) reported that in Manchester in northern England about 60 per cent of breast-fed babies were 'well developed' — that is well-nourished-looking — during the first nine months of life, compared with only 10 per cent of bottle-fed babies from the same slum community. The poor nutrition and higher infant mortality of young children of the working population in Western cities, particularly related to a decline in breast-feeding, was emphasized by numerous reports from European cities in the early years of the twentieth century, for example, The Hague, Netherlands, in 1908 (Wennen 1969) (Table 10.1) and Derby, England, in 1903 (Harworth 1905) (Table 10.2).

TABLE 10.1   *Infant mortality per 1000 for breast-fed and bottle-fed children, The Hague, Netherlands, 1908* (from Wennen 1969)

Prosperity	Breast-fed	Bottle-fed
High	17	70
Low	63·5	311

TABLE 10.2   *Percentage of infant deaths according to method of feeding, Derby, England, 1900–3* (from Harworth 1905)

	Percentage of all infants	Percentage dying before one year of age
Breast-fed only	63·3	7·0
Mixed feeding (breast and bottle)	17·3	9·9
Never breast-fed	19·5	19·8

The general picture, most fully documented by Newman in his illuminating book written in 1906, entitled *Infant mortality — a social problem*, was in many ways similar to the present-day conditions seen affecting young children increasingly in urbanizing areas of the Third World, with diarrhoea and marasmus predominating (p. 287). The protective effect of breast-feeding was clear, as indicated by the almost three-fold infant mortality in 'hand-fed' babies compared with those nursed by their mothers. The majority of infant deaths at that time were labelled 'diarrhoea and enteritis' and 'atrophy and debility', which could, in modern parlance, be translated as 'weaning diarrhoea' and 'marasmus'. The dangerous role of feeding-bottles under such circumstances was also recognized. One particularly difficult-to-clean model was termed at the time in the medical press the 'murder bottle' and 'bacterial paradise'.

Wickes (1953) summarizes the general problems and responsible factors in the following way:

The general ignorance of slum mothers with regard to hygiene and the correct methods of artificial feeding, and the appalling lack of standards of cleanliness for cow's milk, particularly in the towns are important factors. In London, in the middle of the century, cows were kept in a truly disgusting condition in crowded, ill-ventilated, underground hovels where their food and dung were inadequately separated and disease was rampant. Furthermore, in order to bolster up the naturally very poor yield, the milk was watered and chalk was frequently added. Even as late as 1895 an analysis of 30 samples of milk from working class areas in London revealed that 24 were 'sophisticated', either by removal of the cream to a level below 3%, or by dilution, or by the addition of boric acid as a preservative, and these tests of course took no account of the bacterial content of the samples. The water supply was also liable to be heavily contaminated and this was no doubt responsible for many infant deaths.

The Industrial Revolution was only one manifestation in Europe and America of new scientific knowledge and technology increasingly affecting almost all aspects of life, including many concerned with methods of infant feeding. Scientific technology appeared to be overwhelmingly successful and universally benign and 'right' — for example with mechanized transport, with lighting with gas and electricity, and with the canning of food. The machine-manufactured increasingly dominated as symbols of enlightenment, progress, and modernness, as opposed to seemingly archaic, out-of-date traditional methods and biological practices, of which breast-feeding was one.

Medical science
The spectacular advances of medical science during this period were principally concerned with such vital fields as bacteriology (and consequent development of antisepsis and asepsis in surgery), anaesthetics and radiology. Prior to these events, hospitals had mainly been refuges for the destitute, sick, and dying, often under religious auspices. By contrast, late-nineteenth-century hospitals developed as centres in which the equipment and laboratories needed for these technological achievements could be best carried out, guided by the physician in his newly emerging role as high-priest scientist-healer.

Mathematical infant feeding
Partly in response to the plainly disastrous methods of bottle-feeding then being undertaken by the poor in urban slums, and partly as an overall cultural accompaniment of the technical advances of the period, various developments occurred, which together increased the safety and practicability of artificial feeding of young infants with cow's-milk preparations. Discoveries in bacteriology and the microbial cause of infection led to increasing realization by paediatricians of the need for clean, uncontaminated milk for infant feeding. The emerging science of biochemistry began to clarify the need of young infants for different nutrients (an important part of the commencement of modern nutrition), and also to suggest how cow's milk could be modified by boiling, dilution and the addition of sugar to improve its safety and nutritional suitability for human babies. Other important

technological inventions which made widespread bottle-feeding practicable included the canning of milk (initially condensed milk by Nestlé in 1866), and the vulcanization of rubber by Goodyear in the first half of the nineteenth century. Prior to this, feeding with cow's milk was most usually undertaken with a feeding cup ('bubby pot'), 'sucking bag' or similar device, as earlier attempts at feeding-bottles were largely limited by absence of suitable material for use as teats or nipples, although linen and sponge had been employed. Earlier feeding-bottles were rather over-elaborate, sometimes with a long rubber tube attached; these were superseded by the two-ended boat-shaped bottle ('pocket nurser').

These newer scientific advances in paediatric nutrition were often channelled through health services for mothers and children and guided by legislation designed to distribute various free or subsidized clean milk products to poorer working mothers, together with supervision and weighing of infants, in response to the recognized problem of diarrhoea and malnutrition in bottle-fed babies of families without adequate income or home sanitation. Examples include the *Consultations de nourrissons* of Budin and the *Gouttes de lait* movements in France at the end of the last century, and parallel endeavours in the U.S.A. and Britain. In England, the first such 'infant milk depot', usually with non-medical staff, was opened in 1899, and was more concerned with issuing clean subsidized milk than with breast-feeding, which had less scientific appeal. Additionally, there was no knowledge of the psychophysiological basis for lactation. All in all, it may be surmised that the atmosphere and activities would often directly or subtly favour bottle-feeding as the economical, modern option.

The 'Infant Welfare Movement' of North America, Western Europe, and Australia had its roots in such beginnings and lead on to regular health surveillance at centres (including immunization and weighing), and to home-visiting by public-health nurses or health visitors. Education in breast-feeding was always a stated goal, but the emphasis on the distribution and proper use of the cow's-milk preparation distributed would have appeared to be the more modern activity and an apparent bargain. As was to happen in developing countries 50 years later, often only perfunctory attention may have been given to breast-feeding.

From the distribution of comparatively simple cow's-milk preparations to poorer working women, increasingly complex bottle-feeding began to be used by the élite, although wet-nurses continued to be employed. The cultural appeal of formula feeding to paediatricians and parents in this enthusiastically science-dominated period is obvious. The optimistic certainty and exuberant assurance of such developments is indicated, for example, by the 1867 book by Liebig, entitled: *A food for infants: a complete substitute for that provided by nature*.

Plainly, artificial feeding with cow's milk had the mathematical advantage of being measurable; while the elaborate formulas of percentage feedings were visible, tangible, and numerate 'magical' reassurance of modern scientific infallibility. In retrospect, such ultra-precise approaches appear not only immensely complicated, but also completely impractical and pseudoscientific in the extreme. For example, Dr. Thomas Rotch (1849–1914) of Boston, the founder of the 'percentage system', reduced infant feeding to an intricate mathematical exercise (Rotch 1907). He taught that 'formulas' should be tailored to the needs of the individual baby, and for this purpose established milk laboratories where 'mixtures were compounded and dispensed as carefully as medical prescriptions or dangerous drugs.' Minute variations in the composition of a feed (even $0 \cdot 1$ per cent of a single food element) was believed to make the difference between being digested or not. Attempts by such methods to incorporate slide-rule precision in infant formulas also led to rigid timing of the feeding intervals (rigidly regular feeding is a cultural by-product, only possible after the invention of the clock) and to volumetric estimations of individual feedings based on measurements of stomachs of infant cadavers. The modern American mother does not realize the origin of the everyday word 'formula': it dates from the earnest efforts of the early algebraic school, which conceived of infant feeding as an exercise in mathematical biochemical engineering, to such an extent that a paediatric text in 1904 had 2½ pages of formulas for calculating a healthy baby's feeds (Wickes 1953).

Medical education
Paralleling these developments, the education of medical students, nurses, and midwives moved from their undoubtedly ill-controlled and unlicensed apprenticeship type of training towards a necessarily more supervised and licensed process. However, at the same time, the dramatic successes of scientific allopathic medicine* — for example in anaethesia or the treatment

$$M = \frac{Qb - bC}{b} \qquad C = \frac{L(b^1F - a^1P)}{ab^1 - a^1b} \qquad C = (2F + S + P) \times 1\tfrac{1}{4}Q$$

Fig. 10.1. Highly complicated early formulas used in infant feeding (quoted by Levin 1963)

---

* The currently dominant philosophy and practice of Western medicine basically concerned with 'reacting in opposition' to a disease process. Examples include the use of penicillin in pneumococcal pneumonia and the removal of the infected organ in appendicitis (Jelliffe and Jelliffe 1975 *d*).

of syphilis with complex arsenicals — lead to an education process that was dominated by laboratory and hospital-based training (including obstetrics). It was almost completely pathology-oriented and understandably concerned with the therapy of current priority disease problems. Comparatively little emphasis was given to the significance of prevention (including non-medical considerations such as housing, sanitation, and diet) and still less to understanding of social and psychological aspects of normally successful physiological events, such as childbirth and lactation.

The mother–neonate dyad was particularly affected, with the newborn falling between the 'zones of influence' of the obstetrician (concerned mainly with the 'navigation of the birth canal' and the prevention of puerperal sepsis and haemorrhage), and the paediatrician, principally trained to diagnose and treat sick children. With the understandable concern with obstetrical abnormalities and with puerperal sepsis as a major killing disease, childbirth came to be regarded almost as an illness. Methods adopted, such as the operating-theatre-like delivery room and the exclusion of the family from maternity units, were geared to disease, particularly the prevention of infection, and towards delivery procedures oriented to the health staff, such as the lithotomy position during childbirth and obstetrical induction of labour. Little understanding of the psychophysiology of childbirth was apparent, nor of its biosocial significance in the family setting.

1910–60

Difficulties always exist with the collection of statistics concerning breast-feeding, largely related to definition of success, which can include estimates of length of time continued after birth, whether complete or partial, and the effect on the infant's growth. Nevertheless, all evidence clearly shows that during recent decades in the Western world, there has been, until very recently, a continuing decline in breast-feeding (Bain 1948, Douglas 1950, Newsom and Newsom 1962, Newton 1966, Ross and Herdan 1951, Strom 1948). For example, in America, the neonatal breast-feeding rate fell by half during the 10 years from 1946 to 1956. In 1911, 58 per cent of American infants were still nursing at 12 months, while in 1967 only 25 per cent of newborn babies were breast-fed on leaving the hospital. In 1939 in Bristol, England, the number of 3-month-old breast-fed infants dropped from 77 per cent to 33 per cent in the preceding 20-year period (Jelliffe 1968*b*).

Data collected by Meyer (1958, 1968) at 10-year intervals on the incidence of breast-feeding on discharge from representative hospitals in the U.S.A. show declines from 38 per cent (1946) to 21 per cent (1956) to 18 per cent (1966) (Fig. 10.2). From Europe, Vahlquist (1975) has collected statistics from three countries with different social systems, namely Sweden, Poland, and the U.K. (Figs. 10.3, 10.4, 10.5). All the studies show a continuing decline.

The decline of breast-feeding in Western industrialized countries in recent decades has been due to the same forces as earlier in the Industrial Revolution, reinforced by some newer factors. For example, various feminists movements developed at the beginning of the present century, initially involving the socially well-to-do. These included the suffragette movement and earlier family-planning associations with new methods of birth control. All tended to emphasize the need for women to strive for further economic, political, and sexual equality with men and to endorse this by encouraging more emancipated roles, especially working outside the home. As with cigarette smoking, bobbing the hair, and the contraceptive diaphragm, the feeding-bottle was often visualized by the 'flapper' of the 1920s as a symbol of such liberation and freedom. The rise of bottle-feeding also meant that the always dual role of the female breasts veered more towards their sexual–aesthetic function, with in turn increased cultural emphasis on the need to breast-feed only in privacy. Also more recently, the Western cult of ultra-cleanliness, fostered by commercially inspired anxieties over various real or imagined body odours, and the general visual and actual avoidance of human secretions, including urine, tears, sweat, nasal mucus, etc., can make breast-milk be considered as messy and even an unclean bodily discharge (or an 'exuvia' in anthropological terms), which can be 'noisome to one's clothes' (Wickes 1953).

The potent and speedy influence of a changed 'self-image' is further suggested by the rapid decline in breast-feeding that occurred later when

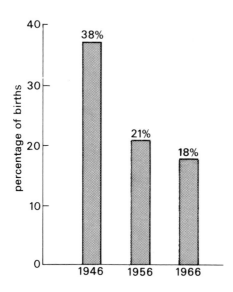

Fig. 10.2. Breast-feeding on discharge from maternity ward in hospitals in the U.S.A. in 1946, 1956, and 1966 (from Meyer, H. F. (1968). *Clin. Pediat.* **7**, 708)

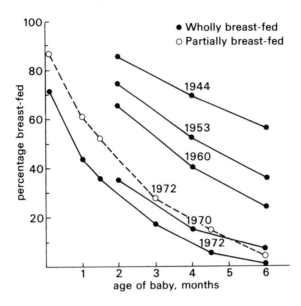

Fig. 10.3. Breast-feeding in Sweden, 1944 to 1972 (from Vahlquist, B. (1975). *J. trop. Pediat. env. Chld Hlth* **21**, 11)

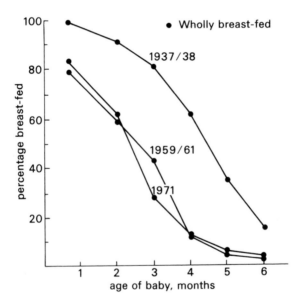

Fig. 10.4. Breast-feeding in Poland, 1937–8 to 1971 (from Vahlquist, B. (1975) *J. trop. Pediat. env. Chld Hlth* **21**, 11)

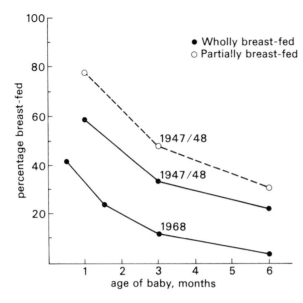

Fig. 10.5. Breast-feeding in the United Kingdom, 1947/8 to 1968 (from Vahlquist, B. (1975). *J. trop. Pediat. env. Chld Hlth* **21**, 11)

Pakistani women emigrated to Britain in the 1950s, bottle-feeding under these circumstances symbolizing their new way of life, as well as appearing to be easier economically and hygienically.

In Westernized urban societies, the economic significance of mothers going out to work in salaried employment with no culturally acceptable facilities available for nursing has plainly been a major impetus to bottle-feeding, but can be over-emphasized. As Vahlquist (1975) notes, 'It cannot explain the fast downward trend in breast-feeding of recent times which has been taking place essentially *before* the baby has reached 3 months of age. In a number of European countries, mothers receive financial support up to 6 months in connection with delivery. In Sweden a housewife will under these circumstances get a minimum of 25 Swedish krona a day (about $5) and, if otherwise working professionally outside home, 90 per cent of her salary. Thus there is no pressing need for financial reasons to start work prematurely'.

Western, and perhaps especially American, attitudes to the whole process of childbirth are relevant. As Mead and Newton (1967) comment, this physiological episode is likely to be almost equated with a sickness. Certainly, labour itself is staged as a surgical procedure and, with the strong Western medical cultural values associated with operative techniques, these may sometimes be used without need. Also, the value of older women personally experienced in childbirth as attendants is often muted in modern maternity units. The whole process has tended to be rather secretive and taboo, with overtones of both mystery and repugnancy, the latter being especially associated with the hastily discarded placenta.

In contrast with traditional societies (p. 161), in modern industrialized Western-type societies, the young woman often receives little information on breast-feeding during childhood, particularly from observation, but is bombarded with formula advertising. Also, with the often geographically widely separated nuclear family, the information obtainable from older female relatives, as well as the routine in maternity units, frequently have what may be realistically termed an 'anti-*doula*' effect (p. 175) as far as supplying the information and support that is so necessary. Likewise, in modern practice the new mother is often unprepared, isolated, and returned rapidly and prematurely to her full domestic responsibilities, including looking after the rest of the family. At home, in view of the little practical experience of breast-feeding by older women in her community, she may be exposed to a wide range of attitudes and beliefs concerning breast-feeding, some of which can be as bizarre as in any distant culture.

The cultural uncertainty, if not confusion, makes for major difficulties (N. Newton 1976):

> The confusing demands of a complex, undirected society, coupled with the lack of support (often even negative support) that is provided for new parents by our present nuclear family system, leave most parents insecure and at the mercy of tremendous internal and external pressures. They have been told that their infant's outcome is to be shaped by them and their parenting; at the same time, there are few stable cultural values on which they can rely for guidance in setting their course as new parents.

At best the usual vacuum in information and support has to be overcome. Woody and Woody (1966) note this lack when they say: 'At birth, processes are at work which are designed to enable a baby to draw his sustenance from his mother's breasts; both mother and baby are physiologically prepared for this transformation. The stages of maternal lactation, the behaviour of the nursling, and the nature of the required maternal responses to the baby's demands were once common knowledge.'

Even more serious is the fact that many of the practices in routine Western maternity hospitals have, until recently, been such that they are likely to increase the mother's anxiety (Burchell 1964), and certainly are not geared to enhancing the prolactin and let-down reflexes. Factors tending to make the initiation and maintenance of lactation difficult have been listed by Haire (1973) in a review provocatively titled: *The cultural warping of childbirth* (Table 10.3).

It is not surprising, therefore, that even in mothers who wish to breast-feed, success may be elusive. Call (1975) has indicated that, as might be expected, 'primiparas are more sensitive than multiparas to psychological action which inhibits milk ejection. Such would include: (a) rigid 4-hour feeding schedules, (b) subjective pain from initial breast engorgement and sucking stimulation, and (c) hospital routines, professional, and cultural attitudes which discourage the mother from nursing and, as a result, diminish her self-confidence and increase her anxiety.'

TABLE 10.3 *Some aspects of stereotyped Western maternity care likely to make the initiation and maintenance of lactation more difficult, via interference with the let-down reflex (anxiety) and/or the prolactin reflex (diminished sucking)* (modified from Haire 1973)

Ambivalent prenatal counselling
Requiring all mothers to give birth in hospitals
Elective induction of labour
Separating the mother from familial support during labour and birth
Withholding food and drink from normal unmedicated woman in labour
Overdependence on medication for relief of pain
Moving normal mother to a delivery room for birth
Delaying birth until physician arrives
Requiring mother to assume lithotomy position
Routine use of forceps and/or episiotomy
Separating the mother from her newborn infant
Use of stilbestrol for suppression of lactation
Delaying first breast-feeding
Offering water and formula to the breast-fed newborn
Restricting newborn infants to a 4-hourly schedule
   (and withholding night-time feedings)
Preventing early father–child contact
Assigning nursing personnel to mother or babies
   (rather than to mother–baby couples)

An obstetrician's view of the situation was given by Tylden (1976) concerning the maternity unit in the U.K.:

Nowadays, mother and baby face difficult processes of readjustment in the first few days after birth. Both are usually confused and slightly drowsy with the drugs used in labour. Attendants still fail to recognise that it is the mother who has achieved the baby, and who will have to nurture it for so many years. Separation at birth is no trivial matter. If a mother does not see her baby at the first possible moment, she cannot imagine what the relationship should be like. Instead, she worries and phantasises that the baby is dead, that it is abnormal, or it hasn't been born. The baby also gets used to different places and different ways of feeding and holding. The longer the separation, the more the two grow apart, though it has been proved that mothers of babies under 3 pounds can breast feed successfully if they can see the baby as soon as possible and be given suitable care and encouragement. Less carefully tended mothers and babies can develop an estrangement after separation which the years cannot heal, and which requires a lot of time and patience to overcome.

One reason for the decline in breastfeeding is undoubtedly that the postnatal period is not regarded as medically interesting. Caesarian section, forceps delivery and breach delivery are interesting. So is labour, particularly when it requires an epidural anaesthetic, or an episiotomy, or a pitocin drip.

Alternative sources of human milk
During this period, wet-nursing became less frequently used, although a *Directory of wet-nurses* was available in the U.S.A. in 1921. The situation in France appears to have been unique in the nineteenth century. Private and public placement bureas (*Bureaux de nourrices*) were available and used by the well-to-do and by working women between 1769 and 1876. Mortality was high among wet-nursed infants, especially as this often took place without surveillance, so that premature weaning and artificial feeding was common (Sussman 1975).

In North America and in Europe from the 1920s to the 1940s, breast-milk banks were to be found widely, with numerous publications in the medical and nursing literature on breast-milk dairies (Chapin 1923), dried human milk (Emerson 1925), maternal milk banks (Laws and Skelley 1938), and methods of preserving mother's milk, including freezing (Laws and Skelley 1938*b*); in 1943 the American Academy of Pediatrics published *Standards for the operation of mother's-milk banks*. An early breast-milk bank was started in Boston in 1910. Such banks were primarily concerned with the feeding of premature babies. They were usually attached to maternity units and collected pooled milk samples, which were preserved by heating or in some other way (Dynski-Klein 1946).

In addition, the revolution in dairying and rapid improvements in food technology lead to the development of many varieties of new cow's-milk formulas, leading to — in Wickes's (1953) words — a bewildering number of 'synthetic masterpieces'.

Breast-feeding advocacy
While general medical opinion was lukewarm or indifferent concerning breast-feeding, several major advocates appeared on the scene, including Truby King, Housden (1932), Waller (1938, 1943, 1946, 1947, 1957) and others. In retrospect, they had little influence on the prevalence of breast-feeding at large, but, as will be discussed later they clearly demonstrated that marked local alterations in the pattern can be effected, which can have considerable significance and guidance in planning community programmes (p. 346).

Infant feeding and mortality
From 1910 to 1960, environmental and home hygiene improved, including water supply and sewage, as well as refrigeration and the development of scientific dairy farming and food technology (including the pasteurization of milk, and the canning, processing, and distribution of cheap, easily available, and bacterially safe evaporated, powdered, and very recently 'ready-to-use' formulas based on cow's milk); and these improvements facilitated the spread of safer bottle-feeding. These changes were associated with much decrease in diarrhoeal disease and marasmus, but with a temporary increase

in infantile scurvy, until it was advised that bottle-fed babies need ascorbic-acid supplementation. However, such general changes do not apply to disadvantaged minority groups, such as for example the Navajo Indians of the U.S.A. (Van Duzen *et al*. 1969) or Australian aborigines (Moodie 1973) among whom diarrhoea and marasmus are still highly prevalent.

Likewise, the fact that infants could grow well, as judged by external assessment, on cow's-milk preparations seemed at the time to indicate that bottle-feeding was little different from breast-feeding and, indeed seemed more in accord with technological modern Western urban living. Nevertheless, only 40–50 years ago in the U.S.A., the protective effects of breast-feeding against childhood infections were very marked (Sedgwick and Fleischner 1921), particularly for respiratory infections and diarrhoeal disease (Woodbury 1922) (Table 10.4). Likewise, Raphael (1966) has noted that:

It is not widely remembered that in the United States many babies died from contaminated milk before the widespread introduction of electric refrigeration some 30 years ago. The adage — "that dangerous second summer" — was coined to express the danger of feeding babies cow's milk that was delivered unrefrigerated during the summer months. Milking by milkers hired off the street was done in the filthy basements of breweries where the cows could be fed cheaply from the left-over grains. Thus, the milk was bacteriologically dangerous in wintertime as well.

However, the infant mortality rates in Sweden (Fig. 10.6) have shown a more-or-less steady decline since the early nineteenth century long before the widespread use of bottle-feeding, or, for that matter, the introduction of most of the potent modern paediatric practices, such as chemotherapy, immunization, or intravenous rehydration. As Vahlquist (1972) notes, the infant mortality rate had dropped to well below 2 per cent when the mean duration of breast-feeding began to show a more marked and fast decline (Fig. 10.7).

Likewise, infant mortality rates elsewhere in the Western world also dropped progressively in the period 1910–60 despite declining rates of breast-feeding. These remarkable changes have sometimes been interpreted as being related in part to the superiority of bottle-feeding over breast-feeding but closer scrutiny indicates that this is an 'ahistorical historical comparison'. In fact, the changes reflect the results of numerous interlocking social developments, particularly improvements in environmental sanitation (especially clean, safe water and waste disposal), in education, in knowledge of infant nutrition (modification of curd tension of high-casein cow's milk, need for vitamin C for the bottle-fed, improved bottles and teats (Drake 1948, Haskell and Lewis 1971, Wood 1955), and methods of cleaning them), in the production, storage, handling, and processing of cow's milk (and formulas), in prosperity, in home storage (notably ice boxes), and in legislation and health services geared to the benefit of mothers and children, of which the improved availability and often subsidized distribution of clean, reliable, appropriately modified cow's milk preparations,

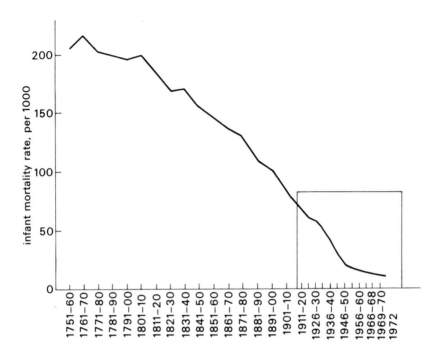

Fig. 10.6. Infant mortality in Sweden, 1751–1970. Box indicates bottle-feeding 'period' (from Vahlquist, B. (1975). *J. trop. Pediat. env. Chld Hlth* **21**, 11)

especially to poorer mothers, was a part.

The relationship between mortality in infancy and method of feeding was striking in the U.S.A. in 1922, especially in the first months of life (Fig. 10.8). The protective effect of breast-feeding against many common infections (and hence mortality) was still very marked in 1934 as shown by a study by Grulee and colleagues (Table 10.4).

However, with improving 'levels of living' in Western countries, these overt dramatic effects became less striking, although still significant. Such investigations were reported from Norbotten, Sweden, by Mellander *et al.* (1959), and from the city of Liverpool in England by Robinson (1951). Major findings relating to mortality, morbidity, and type of infections in infants with form of feeding are clear-cut (Tables 10.5 and 6). Notably, the mortality of the breast-fed (4·6 per cent) was less than half that of the bottle-fed (10·0 per cent), and the case mortality from all infections was

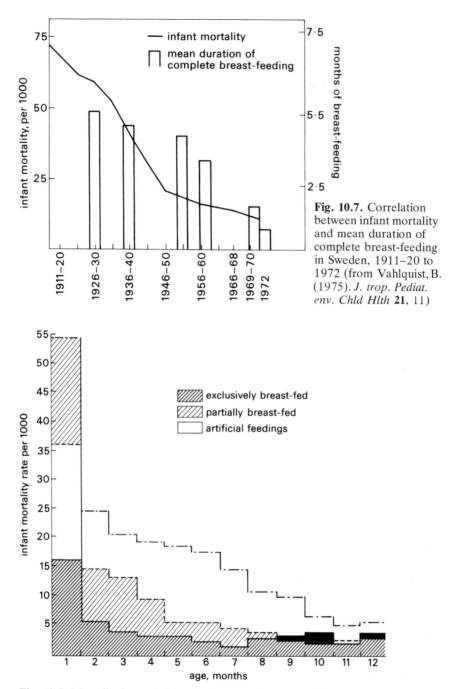

Fig. 10.7. Correlation between infant mortality and mean duration of complete breast-feeding in Sweden, 1911–20 to 1972 (from Vahlquist, B. (1975). *J. trop. Pediat. env. Chld Hlth* **21**, 11)

Fig. 10.8. Mortality by month in the first year of life according to method of infant feeding in the U.S.A. (from Woodbury, R. M. (1922). *Amer. J. Hyg.* **2**, 668)

almost three times as high in the bottle-fed ($9 \cdot 2$ per cent) compared with the breast-fed ($3 \cdot 7$ per cent).

Difficult as it may be for the medically trained to accept, the death rates from respiratory tuberculosis, diphtheria, whooping cough, measles, and other major infectious disease, were already declining progressively sometimes decades before the causative organism was recognized, or modern immunization or therapy discovered (McKeown 1976). In fact, 'before antibiotics and before contemporary methods of control (of infectious diseases), the infant mortality rate in royal families was lower than that which is found in the best national rates now being recorded in any country of the world.' (Kass 1971). Many aspects of life, jointly labelled 'standard of living', are responsible, including environmental hygiene, education, economics, and housing.

TABLE 10.4   *Infections and mortality in infants in the U.S.A. in 1934* (from Grulee et al. 1934)

	Total infection	Percentage incidence of infection		Percentage deaths
		Respiratory	Diarrhoea	
Entirely breast-fed 9749 (48%)	37	28	5	7
Partially breast-fed 8605 (43%)	54	34	13	27
Artificially fed 1707 ($8 \cdot 5$%)	64	39	16	66

TABLE 10.5   *Relation between feeding and mortality and morbidity in Liverpool, England* (from Robinson 1951)

	Number of infants	Mortality, per 1000	Morbidity, per 1000	Case-mortality per cent
Breast-fed	971	$10 \cdot 2$	$223 \cdot 4$	$4 \cdot 6$
Partly bottle-fed	1441	$25 \cdot 7$	$464 \cdot 2$	$5 \cdot 5$
Bottle-fed	854	$57 \cdot 3$	$573 \cdot 7$	$10 \cdot 0$
Total	3266	$29 \cdot 3$	$421 \cdot 3$	$6 \cdot 9$

TABLE 10.6 *Type of feeding in relation to infections in Liverpool, England* (from Robinson 1951)

	Breast-fed	Partly breast-fed	Bottle-fed	Total
No of infants	971	1441	854	3266
Respiratory infections:				
Morbidity	102·9	167·9	170·9	149·4
Mortality	8·2	15·9	31·6	11·7
Case-mortality	8·0	9·5	18·4	11·8
Gastro-enteritis:				
Morbidity	6·1	38·8	78·4	39·8
Mortality		2·0	7·0	2·7
Case-mortality		5·3	8·9	6·9
Otitis media:				
Morbidity	12·3	26·3	45·6	27·2
Mortality		2·0	8·1	3·0
Case-mortality		7·8	17·9	11·2
Percentage chronic	8·3	23·6	23·0	21·3
Mastoid:				
Percentage		5·2	12·8	7·8
Case-mortality			40·0	28·5
Infectious fevers:				
Morbidity	38·1	71·5	74·9	62·4
Mortality			1·1	6·3
Case mortality			1·5	0·4
Unclassified infections:				
Morbidity	59·7	156·8	200·2	139·3
Mortality		2·7	4·6	2·4
Case-mortality		1·7	2·3	1·7
All infections:				
Morbidity	219·3	461·4	570·2	417·9
Mortality	8·2	22·8	52·8	26·6
Case-mortality	3·7	4·9	9·2	6·3

1960–present

The social structure of urban life in the past 15 years has become characterized increasingly by the small, mobile nuclear family with little contact
with older generations. Information on behaviour is more likely to be
influenced by the mass media and by social models, particularly such cultural
'super-people' as film stars, rather than relatives.

Processed infant foods

During this time, the influence of commercial formula and baby-food companies has increased greatly through widespread advertising via many channels and through the lack of interest of the health professional in infant
feeding, in turn related in part to the minimal emphasis on nutrition in
general in medical and nursing curricula. Apart from the influential publications of a few physicians, notably Benjamin Spock, infant-food manufacturers have filled in large measure the vacuum in nutrition education, both for
parents and for physicians via advertising and promotional literature.

An editorial in *The Lancet* (1961) makes the same general point in
relation to Britain:

> The continued lack of interest of paediatricians as a whole in the subject of infant
> feeding has meant that the advice mothers have needed has come to be supplied by
> others, more often by nurses and health visitors, by women's magazines, and by
> commercial firms. Paediatricians, having in effect abrogated their responsibilities in
> this field, must accept responsibility for the present state of affairs.

Similarly, Widdowson *et al.* (1974) comment that 'mothers rely to a
greater extent than formerly on instructions on the packet and on manufacturer's booklets, which are given free, and less on professional advice.'

In recent decades in Western countries, semi-solids (termed *beikost*, i.e.
foods other than milk or formula, by Fomon), have been introduced into the
diets of infants at earlier and earlier ages. The medical literature of fifty years
ago suggested that these be 'introduced cautiously at the beginning of the
child's second year of life'. Current paediatric texts vary, but often advise
2–4 months. In practice, many mothers commence in the first weeks of life.
Reasons for this trend include the persuasion of advertising and maternal
competitiveness in relation to the growth and development of their offspring. Early *beikost* can be tolerated from the first weeks of life, but there are
no nutritional or other reasons for this early introduction. The disadvantages
are the danger of calorie overload because of their usually high sugar content
and low 'diluting fibre', assisting in the aetiology of infantile obesity, the
increased risk of food allergy, and the blunting of the infant's appetite, and
hence sucking stimulus, with decreased milk secretion for babies who are
being breast-fed.

This extreme change has been commented on recently by Vahlquist (1975) as follows:

In the 1920's it was still customary for pediatricians to recommend semi-solids only at the end of the first year. It came almost as a shock when the renowned Swedish pediatrician Jundell proposed in 1921 in an article in the first volume of the *Acta Paediatrica* that such food might and indeed preferably should be introduced as early as at 6 months of age. Since then, as we know, the introduction of semi-solids has taken place at progressively earlier ages; today this is usually *recommended* from 3 months, and *in practice* is often introduced even earlier.

Advice taken from various paediatric textbooks is given in Table 10.7. The impression is given of a rather *laissez-faire* posture, with increasing opportunity for acquiescence to maternal pressures for very early introduction, in considerable measure generated by commercial persuasion. A recent study near Los Angeles (Hollen 1976) showed that about one-third of obstetricians and paediatricians felt semi-solids to be indicated in the first 6 weeks of life, and almost two-thirds within the first three months (Table 10.8).

TABLE 10.7 *Recommended age of introduction of semi-solids according to some standard textbooks, 1942–75* (from Jelliffe and Jelliffe 1975 *b*)

Hutchinson, R. and Moncrieff, A. (1944). *Lectures on diseases of children*, 9th edn. Edward Arnold, London.	'. . . a start with mixed feeding should conveniently be made when the infant reaches about 6 months of age.'
Griffith, J.P. and Mitchell, A.G. (1942). *Textbook of paediatrics*. W.B. Saunders Co., Philadelphia and London.	'. . . spoon feeding with cereals at 4–6 months.'
Bogdan, A. (1964). *Artificial feeding in early infancy*, 2nd edn. Tutorial System Publications, Leeds.	'Spoon feeding — when infant weighs 10 lbs., but probably not before three months (despite recent trends). . .'
Spock, B. (1972). *Baby and Child care*, 17th edn. Pocket Books, New York.	'*Adding solid foods*. There is no set age. Nowadays doctors customarily recommend the first solid food between 2–4 months. There is no great advantage in extreme earliness.'
Lightwood, R. and Brimblecombe, F.S.W. (1963). *Sick children: diseases and treatment*, 8th edn. Cassell and Co., London.	'. . . from about the fifth month . . .'

Mitchell, R.G. (ed.) (1970). *Child life and health*, 5th edn. J. and A. Churchill, London.

'It has become fashionable to introduce cereals from the age of 2–3 months or even younger.... The majority of infants thrive on milk alone until 4–5 months . . .'

Bartram, J.B. (1959). Infant feeding. In *Nelson's Textbook of Paediatrics*, 7th edn. W.B. Saunders and Co., Philadelphia and London.

'There is little evidence that addition of any of these foods to the normal infant's diet before 3–4 months contributes in any significant way to his well being . . .'

Hold, L.E., McIntosh, R., and Barnett, H.L. (1962). *Pediatrics*, 13th edn. Appleton-Century-Crofts, Inc., New York.

'The time at which solid foods are introduced varies greatly in American practice. As more and more prepared infant food became available, the tendency has been to introduce them earlier.
. . .Competition has developed between mothers and even many physicians in this respect.
'. . .on the whole, the policy of exclusive milk feedings for the first 3–4 months of life appears to have no disadvantages and distinct advantages from the point of view of convenience. The earlier introductions of solid foods may be regarded as a fad, though in no sense a harmful one.'

Advertising of formulas and baby foods, based in some measure on partial truth ('just like mother's milk'), on non-nutritional motivation (such as with 'gourmet' labels of status appeal for weaning foods 'Dutch Peach Cobbler Baby Dinner'), and association of ideas, has been and continues to be a major factor in moulding the behaviour of mothers in feeding their offspring. The text of many such advertisements are apparently supportive, yet insidiously destructive ('Breast milk is best, but when you can't breast-feed use . . .'). In addition, the medical and nursing professions can sometimes be very naïve in their interactions with commercial companies, so that mixtures of 'manipulation by assistance' (free samples; assistance with research funds; hospitality at meetings) and 'endorsement by association' (advertisements in news-letters and journals of professional associations; sponsorship of conferences) are very frequently and successfully used promotional methods, usually unperceived, minimized, or tolerated as such by the physicians, nurses, and nutritionists concerned (p. 313).

TABLE 10.8 *Answers received from sample of obstetricians and paediatricians in the San Fernando Valley, Los Angeles, in 1976 to the question: 'At what age do you advise your patients to introduce solids or semi-solids into their infant's diets?* (from Hollen 1976)

	Obstetricians ($n = 18$)	Paediatricians ($n = 51$)	Total sample* ($n = 69$)
Less than 1 week	0·0%	0·0	0·0%
1–6 weeks	38·9	27·5	30·4
6 weeks to 3 months	33·3	35·3	34·8
3–6 months	22·2	31·4	29·0
After 6 months	5·6	5·9	5·8
	100·0	100·0	100·0

* A further 28 obstetricians and 1 paediatrician were asked but did not answer.

Legislation and working women

The vulnerability of working women has been recognized for decades because, as the International Labour Organization (1965, 1969, 1975) of the United Nations notes, of the need for 'protective standards which provide them with the special protection they require because of their biological function of maternity and motherhood.'

The International Labour Organization's *Standards relating to women's employment* covers a wide range of legislation including non-discrimination against women in employment and occupation ('equal remuneration for work of equal value'), work at night, underground and in hazardous situations (lead, ionizing radiation, heavy loads, etc.), maternity protection, and employment of women with family responsibilities.

The last two categories are related to the mother's opportunity to nurse her baby without being dismissed or interrupting her employment or interfering with her chances of promotion or professional advancement. Examination of Interational Labour Organization publications show that legislation for pregnant women and mothers with young babies has been ratified by a wide range of countries. However, the intention of most of such laws appears to be maintaining the female labour-force, and they are concerned more with maternity protection in pregnancy than infant welfare. Various parts of the world, including some countries in Europe, have developed laws and edicts to encourage breast-feeding in past historical times, with uncertain effects. Likewise, the degree of implementation of existing legislation and its usefulness is virtually unknown. In view of the apparent need to review the feasibility of breast-feeding for working women in the modern world, consideration of the potential for practical modification of older and more modern legislation, including the possible roles of crèches, paid 'nursing breaks', and lactation bonuses, will be considered later in relation to programmes designed to promote breast-feeding on a community or national basis (p. 381).

Reasons for decline in breast-feeding
The decline in breast-feeding in technological urban societies is due to a variable blend of interacting socio-cultural factors. Some of these have been noted elsewhere. They can be summarized from a practical point of view, as with the following modification of classifications of Dwyer and Mayer (1975), Vahlquist (1975), and others.

1. Rapid urbanization, industrialization, and change in status of women
— Increased numbers of women working for salaries outside the home (money economy, rising cost of living, new emancipated female role)
— Altered family structure (small nuclear two-generation family with few siblings and less *doula* support from older women)
— Alleged convenience of bottle-feeding (mother need not be present at all feeds; social mobility)
— Emphasis on superiority and social acceptance of the technical and scientific (formula = scientific; breast-feeding = old-fashioned)
— Western urban attitude to female breasts (sex–aesthetic dominance; privacy mandatory for breast-feeding; clothes increase difficulties)

2. Insufficient action by governments to promote breast-feeding
— Failure to provide crèches for working women
— Inadequate attention to appropriate legislation (and its implementation) to support lactation (e.g. leave, bonuses, etc.)
— Nutrition welfare programmes that tend to diminish breast-feeding (e.g. widespread supply of subsidized formula through health services and other outlets)
— Minimal or absent effective health education, especially via mass media
— Lack of attention to human milk as national food resource (e.g. in country-wide food balance sheets)

3. Negative effect of health and nutrition professionals*
— Lack of knowledge or interest in nutrition generally, including breast-feeding (e.g. advice minimal and confused, often over-influenced by information from commercial companies)

* Vahlquist (1975) uses the more rigorous expression 'indolence of health personnel'. He also notes that the medical profession is 'far away from the 1930s when a well-known periodical found it reasonable to devote a 50-page article to disturbances of lactation and their treatment. Health personnel working within or outside hospitals — doctors, nurses, midwives, and auxiliaries — have in recent times mainly been passive spectators of the development, or at times even active promoters of early introduction of artificial feeding. Little has been observed of planned action in defence of breast-feeding.

— Increasing hospital deliveries, with indifferent or disruptive regimens, and confusing advice in maternity unit

— Lactation-inhibiting contraceptive pills

— Lack of emphasis on diet of pregnant and lactating women

4. Marketing, advertising and promotion of formulas
— Manipulative advertising with inadequate legal control via mass media and through health services directly (e.g. emphasis on status, modernness, science, convenience)

— Influencing health personnel, particularly physicians, by various forms of assistance (e.g. free or subsidized samples, research funds).

Changing formulas
Great changes have occurred in the food technology of formula preparation, epitomized, for example, in the U.S.A. by the move in the past decades from evaporated milk mixtures to sterile disposable bottles of ready-to-use preparations in most hospitals, supplied in bulk by commercial formula services (Filer 1971, Fomon 1971, 1974, 1975, Fomon and Anderson 1972, Fomon *et al.* 1969). This has been entirely related to increased convenience and to saving of hospital staff time and space previously used for 'milk-kitchens'. Changes in composition of formulas continue in attempts to modify products to conform more with human milk, or to accommodate to new nutritional knowledge (Wharton and Berger 1976, Hambraeus 1977), or to make good an unrecognized inadequacy (p. 205), or to have a technological promotional advantage over rivals, or to economize on a more costly ingredient. Over recent decades, the curd tension has been decreased, lactose increased, and fatty acids and minerals modified. Cow's milk has been 'modified' to produce an isocaloric product of equal protein value; whole so-called 'humanized' — now termed 'adapted' — formulas have been developed in which attempts have been made to adjust some of the nutrients to levels more comparable to breast-milk particularly protein and minerals (Cooper *et al.* 1976), notably sodium (p. 43).

In Britain in 1974–5, controversy concerning National Dried Milk, a powdered cow's-milk product dating back to World War II and available subsidized at government health centres (Dunn and Pollnitz 1975), has been resolved by the removal of the product from the market. However, it is possible that current rapidly rising costs of living may mean a return to a modified version of valuable, but unglamorous, product. Similarly, in the U.S.A., it is possible that there may be a move back to the least costly method of artificial feeding, that is with evaporated milk, sugar, and water.

The health professional's usual minimal training in the field of nutrition has lead to a widespread lack of awareness of the variations between different present-day commercial cow's-milk formulas and, in turn, their differences from 'parent' cow's milk.* Levin (1963) puts this well when he says:

Cow's milk has been modified in every conceivable manner in order to substitute for human milk. These milks have been termed a "nutritional armamentarium" and "treatments in search of a disease". Additives and subtractives have illustrated the truth of the Slobbovian aphorism: "Of making many milks, there is no end". The additives include all the ordinary constituents of milk: water is the standard addition; sugar and vitamins are almost routinely added, while protein or amino acid powder, and even certain minerals are occasional supplements. In earlier years, it was common to add cream; today it is more fashionable to stick to unsaturated oils as additions to milk. In contrast to the ordinary additives, there are also the extraordinary ones, e.g. lactic acid, starches, proteolytic ferments and even bananas. Current fashion has shifted to subtractives. Some or all of the water may be removed, while fat, protein, and electrolytes may suffer similar fates.

Comparing modern pre-modified processed milk foods for babies with home made formulas of earlier decades, Levin (1963) also notes:

It is not so obvious that the use of the pre-modified milks also involves a good deal of arithmetic, if not advanced mathematics. If they require but dilution with water in order to produce a ready-made formula, it does not follow that they have not undergone algebraic sophistication of the highest order. The earliest tortured concoctions of milk were a process, the current products a *fait accompli*. Though marketed under the guise of simplicity, the mathematics, the slide rules are hidden within the tins. Like so much else these days, the mathematics is supplied "pre-cooked".

The confusing situation is highlighted by a 1974 analysis of 32 dried-milk preparations designed for infant feeding obtained from seven European countries (Ford *et al*. 1974). The composition of the milks differed considerably. Some were full-cream dried milks. Many had carbohydrate added in the form of lactose, sucrose, or dextrimaltose. Some were 'half-cream', others had had all the milk-fat removed and replaced by a mixture of animal and vegetable fats or, in one instance, by maize oil alone. The fatty-acid composition of these milks varied considerably, and linoleic acid accounted for up to 58 per cent of the total fat in one as compared with 9 per cent of the fat in human milk and 1 to 2 per cent of that in cow's milk. All the milks contained considerably more calcium and phosphorus per 100 g solids than human milk; some of them four times as much. Some milks had had an iron salt added during manufacture, and a few contained added copper.

In the U.S.A., ingredients of one popular brand were listed as 'electrodialyzed whey, non-fat cow's milk, a mixture of vegetable and oleo oils, lactose, vitamins and minerals'. In different brands, varying blends of veget-

* The ancestor of present-day 'adapted' formulas was reported by Gerstenberger and Ruh in 1919, as S.M.A. (Synthetic Milk Adapted), composed of skimmed milk, potassium chloride and a fat blend of 'tallow oil, coconut butter, cod liver oil, tallow, etc.', which was stated to be 'similar to breast-milk in its protein, carbohydrate, salt, and water.'

able oils are used, including coconut, soy, corn, and hybridized sunflower, with added soy and lecithin.

Crawford (Crawford *et al.* 1973) has termed modern cow's-milk-based formulas a 'collection of proteins, minerals, vitamins, and some vegetable oil foisted on an uninformed public as being as nutritious as human milk.' In practice, these processed preparations usually have added vegetable oil as source of lipid; the ratio of casein to lactalbumin is often adjusted by fractionation; and the blend of minerals manipulated. The nutritional effects of these changes are quite uncertain. Moreover, relatively little is understood of the interaction and interdependence of nutrients, known and otherwise. As Lowe has remarked (Lowe *et al.* 1969), knowledge of the interrelation between folate and ascorbic acid developed following the occurrence of cases of megaloblastosis, and the lack of iodine in soya formulations was only discovered after a number of infants developed goitre. Recent investigations in Sweden (Hambraeus *et al.* 1975) showed normal breast-milk to have a considerably lower protein content than previously thought, again making for uncertainty regarding the protein content of past (and future) formulas.

Despite continuing modifications (Montreuil 1971, Owen 1969), even the addition of a culture of *Lactobacillus acidophilus* to prevent diarrhoea ('Enpac'), or of lysozyme to milk intended for debilitated babies ('Galliazyme'), the food industry's claims that their products are 'humanized' or 'just like mother's milk' are biochemically and nutritionally incorrect. Indeed, in view of inherent differences in physicochemical structure of even the main constituents and the complex mixture of other ingredients, this objective is literally unattainable, just as it would be impossible to bovinize human milk. In this regard, the 1950s and 1960s have rightly been termed the 'naïve period' by Rolles (1976), who also points out a common confusion between mimicking the composition of human milk and its nutritional effects.

Despite continuing generally low levels of breast-feeding in Westernized industrial countries,* including the involvement of such relatively recently industrialized nations as Japan (Wako and Hatakeyama 1976, Hayashi 1972) (Tables 10.9 and 10), and the extremely dangerous export of bottle-feeding to resource-poor, non-industrialized countries (p. 00), a counter-trend has also begun to develop since about 1960 in the U.S.A., in parts of Europe, and in Australia.

---

* Up-to-date statistically representative figures on the prevalence of breast-feeding are surprisingly sparse. For example, in the U.S.A., *estimates*, based on rather uncertain facts, have been suggested that about 20 per cent of women are breast-feeding at 1 month and only 5 per cent from 5 to 6 months (Fomon 1975). Great differences in various geographical and socio-economic groups may be expected. For example, a study in Los Angeles recently showed that 50 per cent of mothers were breast-feeding on discharge from a hospital with a 'middle class' clientele, compared with only 5 per cent in another maternity hospital catering for a lower socio-economic community (Fleiss 1976).

TABLE 10.9   *Breast-feeding at 3 months of age in Japan in 1960 and 1970* (courtesy of Dr. Michaiki Hayashi)

	1960	1970
Breast-feeding	53·4%	31·0%
Artificial feeding	15·6%	40·9%
Mixed feeding	25·6%	28·1%

Reasons for this resurgence of interest and concern with breast-feeding by such women's self-help organizations as La Leche League International in the U.S.A., the Nursing Mothers' Association of Australia, and *Ammehjel-pen* in Norway appear to include (i) a general reaction against the overemphasis on technology in modern life, (ii) a realization that health professionals (including paediatricians and obstetricians) have usually had little or no training (or much interest) in this field, (iii) awareness of recent investigations indicating that previously unappreciated metabolic, anti-allergic, and emotional advantages of human milk and breast-feeding compared with bottle-feeding and cow's-milk formulas, especially in view of uncertainties and proven difficulties with recent formulas, which appear to become an increasingly complex (and, hence, unpredictable) mixture of ingredients, and (iv) economic considerations.

TABLE 10.10   *Prevalence of breast-feeding near Iwate, Japan in 1970* (from Wako and Hatakeyama 1976)

	3 months	6 months
Village	53%	45%
Urban	32%	28%

Such essentially 'grass-roots' concerns with a less mechanistic approach to childbirth and infant feeding constitute major trends influencing paediatrics in Westernized countries, and, in turn, may help in the situation that is resulting in poorer, technically less-developed regions of the world (p. 211). The methods pioneered by such voluntary groups have real relevance to public-health programmes to promote breast-feeding on a community basis, and their effects to date are given later (p. 306).

The need to reappraise the role of modern medical philosophy and practice in infant feeding has been well summarized by Ratner (1973), himself a physician:

The understanding of the mother–nursing relationship is not the unique province of the biological scientists or practising physician. On the contrary, their specialized education and experience handicaps them. The scientist suffers from a subordination of sense to instrumentation, from a preoccupation with the quantitative to the neglect of the qualitative, and, in general, from the limiting horizon and artificial setting of the laboratory. The physician, similarly, suffers from the myopic confines of office and hospital. He is a victim of his habit of catering to the stylish preferences of his patients, of his lack of reflection characteristic of contemporary, routinized, assembly-line medicine, and of his habitual preoccupation with the specifics and minutiae of curative medicine. Consequently, both scientist and physician miss Nature's *gestalt*. They forgo the macroscopic and holistic for the microscopic and atomic. Both end up viewing the nursing couplet as a mechanical feeding arrangement capable of mechanical replacement. They neglect the multidimensional inter-relationship, the good of which is the total and optimum growth and maturation of infant and mother alike.

The man-made nature of many recorded problems of infant feeding seems clear. As Aldrich noted in 1941: 'Many of the difficulties encountered in caring for young children are due to the disarrangement caused by the impact of new techniques on the child's ancient mechanism.' Likewise, Wickes (1953) concludes his survey of the history of infant feeding as follows:

> In some ways this historical review might be regarded as a chronicle of man-made errors, for many of the ideas in the writing that have been quoted were intended to be an improvement upon Nature though few have succeeded. Those who have heeded Nature anyway, namely the nursing mothers, have seldom found it necessary to put pen to paper. To some extent, however, lactational failure is to blame, for it has been in the search for a suitable substitute for breast-milk that so much artificiality has been unnecessarily introduced and this has even spread to engulf the simple act of successful breast-feeding itself.

Conclusion

As Ellis (1975) notes: 'Milk is a food evolved by nature to feed young mammals — man is the only animal that utilizes this infant food in adult life.' The present-day, rather bizarre situation has been summarized by the Uppsala investigators (Hambraeus *et al*. 1977) as follows: 'It has been said that the introduction of infant formula as breast-milk substitute represents by far "the largest *in vivo* experiment without a control series". What are the long-term effects and what do we know today about the optimal way of feeding a newborn?'

The situation in Europe and in North America has been that modern cow's-milk-based formulas and an improving social setting have given good results compared with the serious picture in previous decades of widespread marasmus or diarrhoeal disease resulting from inadequate, over-diluted, contaminated cow's-milk feeding in poor social circumstances. This has lead to the general extrapolation that 'in some parts of the world, the health of infants is improving in spite of a reduction in breast-feeding'. (Dugdale 1971).

In fact, the results of the decades-long *in vivo* experiment seem to be beginning to emerge, with a pattern of ill-health in childhood and possibly in adult life which is, in considerable measure, attributable to feeding human infants with the bottle and cow's-milk formulas rather than nursing with breast-milk. The consequences appear to be large in resource-rich countries, and will be presented later (p. 241), together with the different, but even more serious, picture of ill-health that is resulting in resource poor, developing countries (p. 270).

11 Recent changes in non-Western countries

Civilized Western infants are still treated in a highly impersonal manner relative to those elsewhere in the world – born in hospitals, separated from their mothers at birth, given minimal body contact in their early years, isolated a great deal, and so on. Fronted by the glamor of Western medicine, furthermore, these barbarities are rapidly being diffused to other cultures.
Philip Slater (1974) *Earth walk*

Advertisements of cow's-milk preparations bombard the population, especially the nursing mothers, from all quarters; billboards, posters, magazines, radio and TV all show in glowing color the sturdiness and attractiveness of babies (and their mothers) fed with this or that product. This is such that it has been found, particularly in developing countries, that artificial feeding becomes a manifestation of status, used by those who would belong to the higher social levels, and breast feeding is only for those who cannot afford and for the lower strata of the population.
Felix Estrada (Editorial, *Journal of the Philippine Medical Association*, 1972)

Earlier developments in the spread of artificial feeding to non-Western countries do not seem to have been documented to any extent. Exceptions include an account (McLaren 1966*a*) of the use of feeding-bottles, imported from Austria, in what was then German East Africa in 1912, and the associated high incidence of resulting 'underfeeding and (intestinal) catarrh'. More recently, Williams (1939) wrote prophetically concerning the dangers of bottle-feeding among poorer families in Singapore, especially in relation to the then common use of condensed skimmed milk and the special extra risks of vitamin-A deficiency (keratomalacia) associated with its use. (The title of one of Williams's addresses (1939) was provocatively direct: *Milk and murder*, although in the text she suggests that 'legal purists' may insist that, as murder is 'the producing of death with malice', the title of the address might be changed to *Milk and manslaughter*.)

However, it is principally after World War II that these changes have become increasingly marked and today are occurring at an accelerating pace in those areas of the world loosely labelled as 'technically less developed' — that is mainly the poorer, often more highly populated, less industrialized, less well sanitated, more disease-ridden countries usually, though not always, situated in the sub-tropics and tropics.

Many of these areas have only recently become independent after varying periods of colonial rule and are still dependent on major industrialized countries for the sale of their main national products, usually agricultural crops. Such products have, until very recently, tended to be competitively produced in various parts of the world and have been highly dependent on fluctuations in world prices, previously mainly laid down by industrialized countries processing these raw materials.

Resource classification of nations

Although at first glance remote from the question of infant feeding (and breast-feeding in particular), national classification based on resources is relevant to the present situation and more so to future alternative approaches and programmes. In such a classification, at least four major forms of national resource need to be considered:

1. *Natural resources*: Power (petroleum, coal, water); Minerals; Foods — especially key international foods (cereals, legumes, beef, milk human and bovine).
2. *Industrial resources*: Ability to produce widely-needed consumer goods at competitive world prices.
3. *Human resources*: Manpower, appropriately trained for local needs.
4. *Morale resources*: Cohesiveness, unity, and certainty of purpose of majority of population.

As recent events have shown, ratings according to this scale will change as alternative resources become available or as industrial marketing potential fluctuates, or as human and morale resources alter in quantity and quality. With this type of classification, a wide range of different mixtures of resources become apparent. For example, the central African country of Burundi has virtually no natural resources, no industrial resources, very limited trained human resources, and negative morale resources, as a result of long-standing bitter and unresolved inter-tribal antagonism and warfare between the two main African communities. By contrast, the countries of the Persian Gulf are technically underdeveloped, but with increasing financial surpluses from oil and its products which are in short supply on a world basis. Under the latter circumstances, questions of economics in infant feeding may not have as much significance — depending in large measure on how widespread and equitable the distribution of the national income. For such countries, the tendency may be to follow the technological road to infant feeding presently taken by industrialized countries, which would be harmful for reasons covered later (p. 241). For countries like Burundi, the situation is, of course, much more critical and to move towards unaffordable bottle-feeding can only be disastrous, with an increasing incidence of diarrhoea and marasmus (p. 287).

The élite

As would be expected, practices of infant feeding imported from Western countries, particularly trends towards bottle-feeding, first involved a small percentage of the population, the élite — that is those well-to-do families in positions of political power and economic control. Initially, in many cases at least the husbands in such families would have been educated abroad in Europe or North America. Likewise, such families are often the successors in terms of power and authority to departing foreigners, at least in previously colonial countries. Under these circumstances, bottle-feeding can be perceived not only as an index of modern scientific twentieth-century living, but also in some ways as associated with authority. It can also be an indication of affluence — the use of cow's-milk feedings rather than available breast-milk is an unappreciated example of 'conspicuous consumption'.

Additionally, bottle-feeding may be considered as important socially and culturally, as not only does it seem to be convenient, but it also permits mothers a wider range of activities outside the home, both in the form of work and other social involvement. Breast-feeding, by contrast, can be considered not only old-fashioned and lower class, due to 'misinformed sophistication which regards breast-feeding as animal behaviour and beneath the dignity of liberated women', but also as primitive behaviour, with unwelcome memories and links with a less affluent or perhaps even subservient past (Mead and Newton 1967).

The majority
Despite great differences from one part of the world to another and despite recognized difficulties in definition (e.g. fully versus partially breast-fed; mixed milk feedings; night feedings), there is increasing evidence of changing patterns of infant feedings, particularly moves towards early weaning, in most (but not all) technically developing countries. Both resource-poor and resource-rich countries have been involved, particularly in urban and peri-urban areas. The process of change has usually been rapid, with an infinitely shorter time-lag than in the Western world during the preceding 50 years.

Examples of declining breast-feeding rates may be quoted from many regions of the world (Fig. 11.1, Tables 11.1 and 11.2), and widely diverse cultures and ecologies (Obgeide 1975a,b, Obgeide and Goyea 1975). For example, in Costa Rica (Central America) 40 per cent of infants are weaned from the breast by the age of 4 months; in modern Fiji, 30 per cent of babies are receiving bottle-feeds by the time they are 6 weeks of age. In a village 65 miles south-west of Mexico City, 91 per cent of infants were fully breast-fed at the age of 6 months in 1960, but only 9 per cent were fully breast-fed at the same age in 1970 (Berg 1973). In Uganda, among Baganda infants living near the capital Kampala, the use of supplementary bottle-feedings before the age of 6 months increased from 14 per cent to 30 per cent in only 5 years from 1950 to 1955 with an average age of weaning of 12·7 months in unsupplemented infants, as against 6·6 months in supplemented infants (Welbourn 1955, 1958). In this context, special difficulties with 'mixed milk feeding' (*allaitement mixte*) in the early months of life need noting, in particu-

TABLE 11.1　*Worldwide trends in breast-feeding* (from E.F.P. Jelliffe 1975*a*)

Country	Study	Pattern of breast-feeding	Rate
Latin America and Caribbean:	Interamerican Investigation of Mortality in Childhood (35 095 deaths) (Puffer and Serrano 1973)	*Breast feeding* for 1 month or over	
1. Bolivia, Cartagena, Chaco Province. Kingston (St. Andrew), Jamaica			1. Over 70%
2. El Salvador, São Paulo Recife			2. Less than 40%
3. San Juan Province. Cali Monterey. Chile. Project Ribeiro Preto			3. between 47·3 and 60·1%
St. Vincent	Antrobus (1971) (300 children)	*Weaning age* range 4–15 months (median 9·6 months)	—
Jamaica	McGregor and Back (1970) University hospital (300 infants)	*Bottle feeding* at 6 weeks	23%
Jamaica	Jelliffe, E.F.P. (1971*b*) Prospective study hospital maternity wards (85 women)	*Intended breast-feeding*: for 1 week not more than 6 weeks up to 3 months between 4–6 months as long as possible not at all	4·7% 11·8% 63·5% 11·7% 5·9% 2·4%

Barbados	National Food and nutrition survey (Pan American Health Organization 1972) (311 interviews)	*Weaning* at: 3 months — 25·3% 4–6 months — 23·0% 7–9 months — 34·5%
Guyana and Trinidad	Gurney (1971) (Interview studies)	*No breast-feeding*: Guyana — 7% Trinidad — 4% *Weaning* at 4 months — 10% of all breast-feeders
Chile	Donoso and Mönckeberg (1965)	*Weaning* at 6 months — 80%
Colombia (Antioquia Province)	Orbendorfer and Mejia (1968) (Interviews 200 mothers)	*No breast feeding* — 5·1% *Weaning* at: 1 month — 11·1% 2 months — 12·9% 3 months — 13·0% 4–6 months — 19·7% 7–11 months — 20·5% 12 months or more — 17·7%
Colombia (Candelaria)	Wray and Aguirre (1969) (1094 children)	*Weaning* at: 3 months — 15·9% 4–6 months — 13·8% 7–9 months — 12·4% 10–12 months — 23·7%
Uganda	Namboze (1967) (73 mothers)	*Weaning* at: 3–12 months — 64·4% 12–24 months — 35·6%

Country	Reference		
Ethiopia	Knutsson and Melbin (1969) (3 regions Ethiopia)	*Weaning at 19 months or longer:* Tigre Sidamo Arussi — weaning at 7–12 months	64% 32%
Philippines	Balderrama-Guzman and Tantengo (1971) (589 children)	*Breast-feeding* up to 6 months	75%
Philippines	Cabucan-Dulay (1970)	*Breast-feeding:* for 2 months	20%
Lebanon	Harfouche (1965) Prospective study (379 mothers)	*Complete weaning* at: 1 month 3 months 6 months	3·2% 15·0% 32·1%
Iran (Teheran)	Sadre et al. (1971)	*Bottle feeding only:* at 1 month at 3 months at 6 months	10% 33% 40%
Singapore	Wong Hock Boon et al. (1963)	*Breast-feeding* for 1 month: 1951 1960	83·5% 62·6%
Korea	Yoon (1970) (304 children)	*Breast-feeding* for 7 months	99·7%

TABLE 11.2   *Changes in percentages of fully breast-fed infants from birth to 6 months (1940–74) in southern Brazil* (from Sousa 1975)

Year	Age in months						
	0	1	2	3	4	5	6
1940	98·0	96·0	86·4	—	—	—	68·0
1974	76·0	39·2	27·4	20·0	16·0	15·0	12·0

TABLE 11.3   *Contrasts between breast-feeding in urban and rural areas* (from Berg 1973)

Country	Urban breast-feeding		Rural breast-feeding	
	Per cent of babies	Duration in months	Per cent of babies	Duration in months
India	92	at least 6	100	at least 6
Gujarat	96	at least 6	100	at least 6
Maharastra	80	at least 12	88	at least 18
West Bengal	88		100	
Indonesia	70	12 to 24	90	12 to 24
China		'only 2 to 3'		'as long as necessary'
Taiwan	61		97	
Iran	52	at least 6	85	at least 12
Nigeria		6 to 9		12 to 24
Guatemala	57	at least 12	77 to 98	at least 12

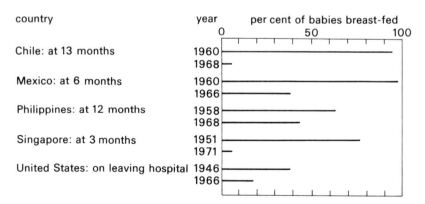

Fig. 11.1. Extent of breast-feeding in selected countries and years, 1946–71 (from Berg, A. (1973). *The nutrition factor*. Brookings Institution, Washington)

lar the change to 'bacteriologically dangerous infant feeding', and the psychological and physiological interference with both the prolactin and let-down reflexes and hence with the maintenance of lactation. Mixed milk feeding may be especially appealing to mothers, as an apparent doubling of nutritional protection and, in some communities, as a prepared insurance in case she wishes to work or finds employment. The immediate risk of diarrhoeal disease and the interference with breast-milk production are not adequately appreciated.

Evidence of a progressive decline in breast-feeding had been noticed in many other areas (Fernando 1963, Grantham-McGregor and Back 1970, Guthrie 1967, Hermelo *et al.* 1968, *The Lancet* 1974*b*, Omolulu 1972), and particularly endorsed by Schaefer (1971*a*) from studies among Eskimos of northern Canada. He employed a retrospective questionnaire among different age-groups, which showed the following increasing previous use of bottle-feeding: adults 4·2 per cent, adolescents 28·6 per cent, and children (1–10 years) 65·9 per cent.

Probably the most thorough prospective studies carried out by one observer are the repeated surveys undertaken by Wong (1971) over a 20-year period in both well-to-do and poor Chinese women in Singapore. The decline has affected both groups, but most recently poorer families have become increasingly involved (Fig. 11.2).

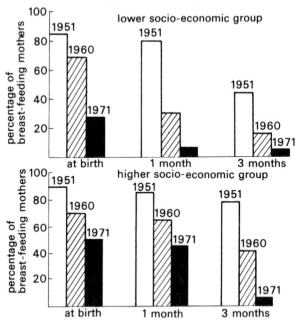

Fig. 11.2. The falling percentage of mothers breast-feeding at birth, 1 month, and 3 months of age, in 1951, 1960, and 1971 (by courtesy of Prof. Wong Hock Boon, (1971). *Breast-feeding in Singapore*. Choon Kee Press, Singapore)

All investigations have also shown that the decline is mainly, but not entirely, an urban phenomenon (Table 11.3). For example, a recent study in the Philippines demonstrated that breast-feeding was continued in rural areas for about 15 months and in towns for nine months. In New Delhi, it was reported that 37 per cent of urban and 2 per cent of rural mothers wean their babies from their breasts by one year of age. In Western Nigeria, breast-feeding of infants during early months of life was observed in 100 per cent of rural mothers living outside Ibadan, while among low- and high-income groups in the city area, the figure was 55 per cent and 12 per cent respectively, and in families of the academic staff at the University campus the percentage was less than one (Berg 1973). Contrasting figures for rural and urban areas are given for both Chile and Iran in Figs 11.3 and 11.4 (Sadre *et al.* 1971).

Reasons for change

There is a great need for further comparative studies into the detailed epidemiology of lactation success or failure in different ecologies. One such large-scale international study is currently under way in eight or more countries, co-ordinated by the World Health Organization and the International Children's Centre, Paris (p. 325). At the same time, there is already evidence available to indicate that the main factors apparently responsible in different degrees in various parts of the world can be suggested. Basically, they are similar to the causes in Western countries, but in different economic, social, and cultural contexts. With the complex and variable

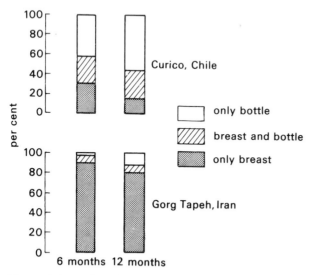

Fig. 11.3. Duration of breast-feeding in rural areas of Chile and Iran (from Sadre, M., Emami, E., and Donoso, G. (1971). *Ecol. Food Nutr.* **1**, 55)

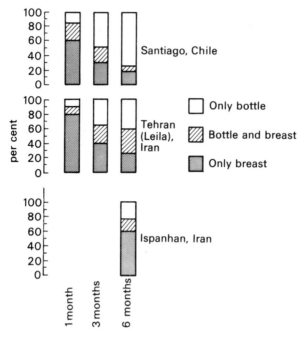

Fig. 11.4. Duration of breast-feeding in urban areas, Iran and Chile (from Sadre, M., Emami, E., and Donoso, G. (1971). *Ecol. Food Nutr.* **1**, 55)

interplay of social and psychological factors involved, it is often difficult to measure their relative effects or to adjudge prime responsibility.

Stated reasons

One approach has been to obtain the mother's stated reasons for not breast-feeding her baby or for lactation failure. Apart from obvious severe physical reasons, such as marked maternal illness or abnormality of the newborn, such answers are at best only indirectly informative and frequently include such statements as 'insufficient milk', 'milk didn't suit baby', 'child weaned himself', 'milk too thin', 'breast not big enough' etc. They mainly represent the mother's anatomical or physiological interpretation of the final outcome of various socio-cultural pressures leading to psychological interference with the let-down and prolactin reflexes (pp. 17, 19). For example, in Pelotas, Brazil, Sousa and co-workers (Sousa, Gazalle, Barros, Begeres, Pinheiro, and Pinto 1974) have described that they term the 'weak-milk syndrome', in which mothers worry that their milk is 'thin and weak'. Equally, to obtain a complete picture of the situation in a particular society, it is also necessary to find the reasons why some mothers bottle-feed their babies.

Alternatively, failure to breast-feed in individual mothers can be classified

as 'inability', 'unwillingness', or 'impossibility'; while yet another classification is into reasons that are apparently 'avoidable', 'not avoidable', or
'avoidable but understandable'. However, these labels are not very useful,
as they fail to emphasize the complex socio-cultural factors responsible.

Socio-cultural factors

Essentially, failure of lactation in the modern scene in non-Western countries is 'occidentogenic' — that is derived from Western cultural influences
seen most markedly in an urban context. Many factors are involved, but for
practical purposes, the following overlapping influences and situations will
be considered separately — Western linear culture, urbanization, attitudes
towards the breasts, commercial influences, effect of health services, and
wage-earning working women.

Western linear culture

The last two centuries or more have been associated with a spread of modern
Western culture into all parts of the world, perhaps particularly into countries previously under colonial control. This new Westernism can be
described as 'linear', and characteristically can be thought of as direct,
efficient-seeming, numerically provable, speedy, impatient, narrow-
spectrum, and technology-based (Jelliffe and Jelliffe 1975 d). It was until
recently also ebullient, assured, forceful, and aggressive. However, recent
limitations, unexpected side-effects, and failures have led in some quarters
to an over-reactive *anomie*, scientific and social, unthought-of 10 years ago.

General, and visual, examples of Western linear culture include roads
systems — 'freeways' compared with ancient winding streets; the square
concrete-box architecture of modern cities; and calligraphy changed from
medieval curlicues to the perpendicular linearity of present-day typescript.

In the field of nutrition, the linear approach also had successes, some
spectacular. For instance, these included the rapid responses of beriberi and
scurvy to appropriate vitamin administration, and, on a community basis,
the lowered incidence of goitre and rickets respectively following fortification of appropriate foods with iodine and vitamin D.

An important ill-effect of the dominance of linear Westernism has been
the difficulty of having preventive medicine taken seriously and, as a result,
the almost incredibly hard, and as yet unsolved, task of introducing nutrition
into the curricula of medical students and nurses anywhere in the world
(E.F.P. Jelliffe 1974, 1976a). Innumerable instances of a preference for
linear techniques permeate Western-style hospital practice. For example,
there is often a needless emphasis on intravenous feeding when not necessary; on highly elaborate, costly electronic monitoring systems for the birth
process, when only a small percentage of pregnant women are receiving
prenatal care; and on the expensive undertaking of screeds of expensive
laboratory examinations without need or indication ('the work-up'),

together with sparse attention given to the social or dietary history.

Until very recently, all cultures in the world, including those of Western Europe and North America prior to the Industrial Revolution, were what may be termed 'bio-traditional' — that is based on biological adaptations made by the species over millennia, and on practices and customs gradually evolved by the community and handed down from generation to generation.

Bio-traditional cultures may be described as 'curved' — with almost the opposite characteristics of linear Westernism. For example, their approaches tend to be more biologically based, slower, and not so concerned with precise numerical proof, with efficiency, or with speed. They are in considerable harmony with wider aspects of community life, including the family and the spirit world (Jelliffe and Jelliffe 1975 *d*).

The success of much of Western linear culture — for example, the railway, the rifle, and the radio — has been such that there has been a tendency until recently to assume that all technological approaches are automatically superior to bio-traditional ones. This appears to be one reason for the ready acceptance of bottle-feeding all over the world, but especially when introduced into non-Western countries by the health services and practised by the local élite, both indigenous and foreign (Jelliffe and Jelliffe 1975 *d*).

Urbanization
A social factor of great significance in recent decades in developing countries has been the massive, so-far uncontrollable movement of people to urban areas ('urban avalanche' or 'urban implosion'), occurring much faster and on a much vaster scale than corresponding population movements in the nineteenth century during the Industrial Revolution in Europe and North America (Schneider 1972). What has been termed the largest migration in man's history is taking place in many areas *without* the parallel industrialization and increased opportunities for employment which helped support such changes in the Western world.

Speaking particularly concerning the special situation in Iran, it has been emphasized (Sadre *et al*. 1971) that these lemming-like population movements:

. . . are sparked by industrialization in the cities which creates a demand for labor and provokes migration from the village to the town. The overflow of migrants imposes a glut on the labor-market, and means unsteady or scarce jobs. The attraction of the city for the villager is great: it means a flight from boredom of the village life, opportunities for economic and social advancement, cinema and spectator sports, educational facilities, etc. But, for many newcomers, the promise of a better life is not fulfilled; living quarters are crowded and remote from work; commodities must be paid for at higher prices. Lodging and transportation, items that did not have to be considered in the village, consume a significant part of the budget. Even when employment becomes stable, other budget items may drain the already meagre amount of money available for food. Hire-purchase of radios, television and other household goods can be very strong competitors to a balanced food intake.

The rapidity of this change is in considerable measure the result of improved road communications and also because the transistor radio brings the lure of the city within reach. The speed and size of such population movements have led in most developing countries to the mushrooming of peri-urban shanty towns, *favellas*, *bustees*, *bidonvilles*, etc., overwhelming the cities limited social services, environmental hygiene (particularly water supplies and waste disposal), and opportunities for work. In fact, such transitional communities often have the worst of both worlds — the rural traditional and the urban slum.

Examples abound, unfortunately. In Indonesia, the population of Jakarta has risen from 300 000 to 5 million in three decades. The city of Bombay has grown from 1·2 million in 1931 to 5·7 million in 1971. Lima, the capital of Peru, increased its population by nearly 50 per cent in the decade 1940–50, and by a further 100 per cent in the next decade.

Cultural shock often prevails for a period of time following arrival in the city. The anonymity, aggressiveness, and competitiveness of city life may repel or frighten the new arrivals and the transition from a traditional cultural pattern can result in a state of *anomie*, until clear-cut new standards of behaviour and rules of survival in this alien world are established (E.F.P. Jelliffe 1975 *a*).

This unbalanced and precipitate urbanization ('disturbanization'*) means that the new townspeople have to try to adjust to very different values and life styles — to an exclusively money economy, and to the likelihood of a breakdown and disruption of the extended family to a non-kin-dominated nuclear family. It also means that both father and mother may have to seek salaried employment out of the house. It means to varying degrees a loss of contact with the holders of traditional knowledge, including the older generation of women (*doulas*, p. 175), with their practical and culturally approved methods of child-rearing and infant feeding. It is usually followed by loosening of traditional mores and a rise in illegitimacy, unstable homes, and abandoned children. Above all, this transition is associated with the search for a new modern-seeming identity, and bottle-feeding appears as an attainable symbol, endorsed by advertising, the practices of the élite, and the health services. Breast-feeding may, then, be rejected as obsolete and rustic, so that the 'idea that breast-feeding is vulgar, unsuited for civilized people, and animal-like, is strengthened by clever advertising showing healthy babies being reared successfully on the advertised product. The obvious success of bottle-feeding by the more cultured, the wealthier, or the ethnically privileged groups of the population, makes bottle-feeding something desirable as a status symbol. There is insufficient understanding that proper hygiene and adequate economic and educational backgrounds are the keys

---

* In a previous paper, this neologism, intended to imply urbanization with much difficulty, was mistakenly type-set as 'disturbanized', perhaps even more evocative (Jelliffe and Jelliffe 1970 *a*).

to such success' (Raphael 1973).

Failure of attempted breast-feeding in such circumstances, as anywhere, is usually the end-result on the psychosomatic let-down reflex (p. 19), which may often result from the social stress of slum life (p. 80). Also, the following circumstances may lead to decreased *milk secretion*, rather than milk ejection: the early introduction of semi-solids or mixed milk feedings, as a result of diminished sucking stimulus and prolactin production (p. 17); oral contraceptives containing oestrogens (p. 121); and inadequate maternal nutrition and health, from a limited range of unfamiliar, relatively expensive nutritionally inferior foods which have to be purchased with very little income (p. 134), often shrinking with inflation. Such ever-increasing populations have been termed 'disurbanized' or (optimistically) 'transitional'. In Spanish, the evocative but not easily translatable word *marginalidad* refers to their being aside from the mainstream of socio-economic development, as well as to their tenuous and precarious existence (Bengoa 1975).

The physical and emotional environmental–psychosocial stress of shanty-town folk has been underappreciated as responsible for failing lactation, as has maternal subnutrition, anaemia, and general health. Lindblad and his colleagues give a grim picture of the scene in Table 11.4.

TABLE 11.4   *Urbanization and lactation performance in developing countries* (from Lindblad *et al*. 1975)

---

1. A 'disturbanized' mother
    isolated from relatives
    isolated in the urban environment due to language barrier,
    high morbidity and mortality among young children.
    Anxiety and uncertainty

2. Maternal disease
    diarrhoea from poor water supply and hygiene
    congested quarters: tuberculosis abundant
    Maternal mortality

3. Maternal undernutrition
    repeated pregnancies
    milk and vegetables expensive inside city boundaries
    Nutritional anaemia

4. Lactation failure and/or early weaning due to industry work
    nutritional and emotional deprivation of young children
    A vicious circle

Attitudes towards the breasts

A cultural concept which has spread from the Europe and North America world to affect the Westernized élite in developing countries concerns the role and symbolism of the female breasts.

Analysis of anthropological literature dealing with ethno-anatomical concepts suggests that in traditional cultures the female breasts are associated primarily with motherhood — that is with sacrifice, love, food, fertility, and succour, as well as with sex. Westernization is associated with a shift in emphasis from the breasts' nurturing function in infant feeding to a primarily sex–aesthetic function, as emphasized in clothing (which also make nursing more difficult mechanically), advertising, and such visual entertainments as films and television. The infant-feeding function of the breasts becomes an urban taboo, and certainly not to be undertaken in public. Urbanization also implies a change in costume: for women, this is usually towards Westernized dresses which are not designed to make breast-feeding easier.

Commercial influence

Although modern advertising reaches out increasingly into rural areas, particularly through the transistor radio, the highest concentration of advertising is obviously in and around towns and cities. While some of this is helpful, having an educational function for the newly urbanized, most is merely designed to sell goods for profit with no necessary relation to real needs of such communities. In non-Western, less technically developed, resource-poor countries, this is the case with regard to the advertising of most foods designed for young children, including cow's-milk formulas designed to supplant (or substitute for) breast-feeding, high-cost low-nutrient commercial weaning foods, and so-called 'tonic foods'.

Although in the present publication major concern needs to be focused on the significance of the promotion of formulas, the situation with jar or canned processed weaning foods requires mention. This is because they are becoming available increasingly in towns in the developing countries and because the trend towards their introduction in the early weeks of life can have an effect on breast-milk secretion, as a result of decreased appetite and hence sucking stimulation. Inherently, such processed weaning foods have captured a large market in industrialized, resource-rich countries because of their convenience and high visibility as a consequence of extensive promotion. Conversely, they are expensive, especially in regards to their cost–nutrient value (p. 134), and are geared more to the mother's palate and purse than to economical or nutritional considerations. Much controversy has arisen, for example, concerning the over-use of salt and sugar in them; excessive use of both are unnecessary and have the possible later ill-consequences of increased risks of hypertension (as suggested by rat experiments) and of infantile obesity and dental caries, respectively. In some countries with more developed cash economies, for example the West Indies, such processed foods have already made considerable impact. Apart from their undeniable convenience, these products, as currently developed, are usually nutritionally undesirable, especially the relatively less expensive, such as crushed banana or apple puree, which often figure prominently. In many (if not most) cases, they are very poor buys anywhere, especially for mothers with little money to spend. Unfortunately, as with formulas, they have high status and prestige, combined with the mystique of modern living (De Morales and Larkin 1972). As emphasized later, there is a real need in parts of the world with a cash economy, mostly in peri-urban areas, for the development of low-cost, high-nutrient weaning foods, based on the 'concept of multi-mixes', to be sold through stores and purchased by governments and others for sale through health services.

Lastly, the mysteriously-termed 'tonic' foods, must be noted, although one wonders what it is particularly 'toned' and how this is achieved. The very term has a quaintly mediaeval-alchemist ring to it. Again, for the affluent these tonic foods form pleasant flavourings and add a very small amount of nutrients to milk. They do no harm, and perhaps may help psychologically. For the less well-to-do — that is, the majority of the world and especially for their children, they are a disastrous waste of money. High-pressure advertising gives them a mystical quality, so that they are highly prized and used in minute and inappropriate quantities directly or dissolved in teaspoonful doses in water in infant feeding and for other groups.

The pressure of advertising of formulas and other infant foods is very great with undisclosed, but certainly, very large budgets, especially in comparison with funds available for nutrition education. Activities have been channelled pervasively through available mass media, through loud-speaker vans, through the shops and stores, through posters and billboards (Fig. 11.5), through handouts and, regrettably, quite often through health services as well, including items clearly labelled with the name of the firm, such as calendars and diaries, free samples, brochures, some equipment (such as weight charts and tapes for measuring the arm circumference,), as well as indirect motivation by various forms of assistance to health staff (p. 313).

In some countries, such as the West Indies, 'milk nurses' have been employed extensively by commercial milk companies. These women are usually trained nurses, who advise on child health and *pari passu* act as sales promoters. They often gain access to the hospital register, in which are recorded the names of newly-delivered mothers, and they may then bring samples of the milks that they are paid to promote to the mothers' bedside, thus emphasizing at the same time the suitability and ease of bottle-feeding, especially with the particular product (E.F.P. Jelliffe 1971 *b*). The message purveyed fits in only too well with the impoverished disoriented new townswoman striving for what she perceives as the status and modernness of

Fig. 11.5. Roadside billboard with formula advertisement: Nigeria (from Wennen, C. A. M. (1969). *Trop. geogr. Med.* **21**, 93)

mechanical twentieth-century living. Such advertising is usually not only inappropriate, but eventually harmful for the majority (Figs 11.5 and 11.6). It is economically out of context, as the items advertised cannot be purchased in sufficient quantities by most of the population and can have a serious displacement effect on breast-feeding. It is psychologically unwarranted, as it creates previously non-existent and unattainable 'felt needs'. Lastly, the high-pressure advertising of such foods is 'developmentally inappropriate', in that these items have little relevance to, and indeed distort, the country's main developmental needs and objectives including, for example, expenditure of foreign currency on food imports.

The content of advertising and the techniques used are those widely employed in the Western world, with emphasis on status, convenience and fear. The tropical mother is in many cases even more vulnerable to these motivating forces. She needs and appreciates convenience foods in her 'three-stone' kitchen even more than does her sister in Manhattan. She is as anxious to emulate the well-to-do élite, both local and foreign, as is any Western mother. Parents can subconsciously regard these modern foods as a method of instantaneous transport into the twenty-first century of satellites, moon probes, and heart transplants (Fig. 11.7).

Infant-food companies often contend that their advertising has been directed to the affluent Westernized minority who have comparable purchasing power, home hygiene, and educational levels as their counterparts in

Fig. 11.6. Cartoon satirizing advertising of formulas in impoverished areas (courtesy of Richard Wilson, *PAN*, Newspaper of the World Food Conference, Rome, Nov. 1974)

Europe and America. This cannot be so. The illiterate is even more impressed than the well-to-do by the visual message of the large-sized, healthy baby juxtaposed on the advertisement with well-dressed smiling mother and with a background of a modern kitchen and feeding utensils (Figs 11.5 and 11.6). In addition to the fact that most of such advertising is pictorial, written material, such as 'baby-books' and other brochures, is often likely to be read aloud by a literate family member, neighbour, or friend. The radio, using the local language, carries its message to the poor as well as the rich.

A special issue arises with what is rather curiously termed 'ethical advertising' by the pharmaceutical and infant-food industries — meaning that directed to a professional audience, such as physicians, nurses, or nutritionists. Here, it is assumed that the readers will be sufficiently aware of issues to make their own reasoned judgements. With the present lack of nutrition in the curricula of health personnel and with this deficiency made up to a considerable extent by literature from companies, it is difficult to see how this can possibly be so. Also, financially such advertising revenue can be a major, or even main, source of funding for professional journals. At best,

Fig. 11.7. Cartoon depicting prestige 'reaching' by poor mothers for high-priced widely advertised formulas (from *Jamaica Daily News*, 6 June, 1974)

this is an unhealthy situation; at worst, it can influence publication policy, either overtly or subconsciously.

A recent report (E.F.P. Jelliffe 1975*b*) for UNICEF on the impact of the food industry on the nutritional status of infants (and pre-school children) in developing countries points out the contrast between the little or slight information often received regarding the techniques or benefits of breast-feeding with the 'wealth of information endorsing bottle-feeding that is constantly available':

Endorsement from both physicians and nursing personnel and close relatives, and the constant flow of information regarding the ease of use, convenience, and excellence of milk products on the market via the radio, newspapers, women's magazines and television programs, imprint the message daily on mothers in search of nutritional guidance. The lavishly illustrated baby-books distributed by commercial firms to public places where mothers will congregate, clinics, maternity hospitals and pediatric wards and even in private areas (physicians' consulting rooms and the family homes) emphasize daily the availability of products.

The range of promotional techniques employed is wide, as indicated, for example, by Wennen (1960) in Nigeria:

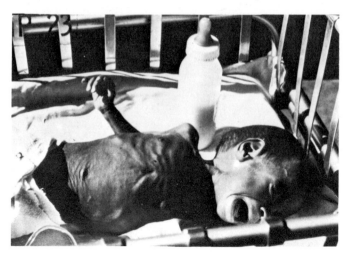

Fig. 11.8. '*Chupa-itis*' (literally 'inflammation of the bottle' – *chupa* = bottle in Swahili): the actuality of bottle-feeding without resources (e.g. sufficient money, home hygiene, parental education). (East Africa).

(1) *The radio*: slogans like "lactogen is good for baby" put on catchy rhythms, in English and in the vernacular, are broadcast several times a week, if not several times a day. It may even be heard in smaller villages where many people now have radio rediffusion.

(2) *The company's African professional "health nurses"*: These girls go around not only in the towns but also in rural areas advertising milk products. They often make friends with Government Health Sisters who are employed in the Child Health Services, by giving small gifts, such as beautiful diaries and, of course, milk. In this way they gain access to government institutions, wandering from clinic to clinic. Consequently, although these nurses claim that they also inform the mothers on the dangers of the feeding-bottle, much loose teaching goes on.

(3) *A free-milk scheme for doctor's babies*: the idea behind it is "Doctor gives it to his own children".

(4) *Good public relations* with the top figures in the medical profession. Thus, a refrigerator was donated by a well-known milk firm to the University Teaching Hospital, Ibadan, on the occasion of the opening of a new Children's Emergency Room.

(5) *Glamorous calendars, brochures, and posters*.

A study undertaken in two hospitals in Jamaica in 1971 emphasized the confusion of mothers released after a short stay in the hospital following delivery (E.F.P. Jelliffe 1971 *b*). Many mothers had been visited by a 'milk nurse' and had received a 'baby-book' published by a commercial firm. These were at times difficult for the often illiterate mother to interpret, and conditions in their homes were very far from adequate as regards efficient sterilization (or even cleanliness) of equipment and mixing of feeds. Some women, however, working as domestics had watched their employers preparing feeds for their own babies. Eight per cent of the women interviewed stated they would ask the help of the chemist (pharmacist), their mother, or close relative regarding the brand of milk to be purchased and 17·7 per cent followed the advice of the commercial milk nurse. At times, nurses from two or more firms vied for the mother's attention, much to her confusion.

The propaganda made for the use of commercial milks among breast-feeding mothers has been much deprecated by concerned paediatricians and nutritionists. Ashworth and Waterlow (1970), for example, reviewing the state of nutrition in the island of Jamaica noted that in a survey undertaken in 1970, 23 per cent of babies born at the University hospital were being totally bottle-fed at 6 weeks and when mothers were asked the reason for starting bottle-feeding, 14 per cent stated that a proprietary 'milk nurse' had either given them a free milk sample or had told them to bottle-feed despite the fact that they were breast-feeding satisfactorily at that time.

To reiterate, under usual circumstances in developing countries, there is no chance of the majority being able to purchase adequate quantities of cow's-milk formulas (p. 136). Attempts to bottle-feed with insufficient resources, with a grossly contaminated home environment (Fig. 11.9) and with mothers unskilled in domestic mathematics, leads to the use of homoeopathic quantities of milk with heavy doses of bacteria, resulting in the downward spiral of marasmus–diarrhoea (Fig. 11.10). This type of syndrome is *increasing* in many peri-urban areas in developing countries (p. 287). It is in part 'commerciogenic' — that is related to the unethical and inappropriate promotion of products by commercial infant-food manufacturers in communities where the majority of the population cannot purchase them in adequate quantities.

Denials of harmful practices by such companies are based on the view that, far from having a displacement effect, they are filling a need as breast-feeding inevitably declines with urbanization, and, at the same time, are gratuitously assisting by bringing services to mothers which cannot be afforded by governments. In fact, as will be discussed later (p. 313) the needs for the feeding of young infants in such urban societies are usually quite different — including crèches and other measures to permit working women to nurse their babies, and the *unadvertised* availability of *low-cost formula* for those really unable to breast-feed. This is a quite different situation from the aggressively advertised expensive milk formulas promoted with modern sales techniques in areas where there is no chance of them being afforded in sufficient amounts, especially where breast-feeding is the norm.

At the 1974 World Food Conference, Blythe (1974) summarized some of the main issues:

Lacking the money to buy substitute milk in the right quantities, impoverished parents "economize" by purchasing less and making it last longer. Medical workers

Fig. 11.9. Bottle-feeding in poor home: Sarawak (courtesy of UNICEF)

have found that in some areas canned milk is being diluted up to three times the recommended amount.

Exhortations to "sterilize bottles for ten minutes in clean boiling water" or to "keep your unopened baby-foods in the 'fridge" are meaningless to people who cannot read, who cook on hot embers, and have only seen refrigerators on advertising boardings in the towns.

On such a grossly inadequate diet millions of babies lose weight, exhibit symptoms of marasmus and die before the age of six months. Those who are not killed outright by wasting away become vulnerable to infection.

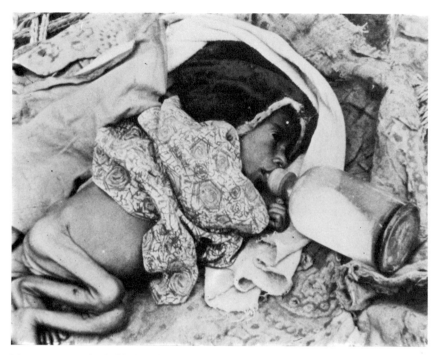

Fig. 11.10. Bottle-fed baby with marasmus–diarrhoea syndrome: India (courtesy of Dr. G. J. Ebrahim, Institute of Child Health, London)

Diarrhoea is prevalent and this has the added effect of reducing the capacity to absorb the small amount of food such infants are receiving.

The bottle itself becomes a source of dangerous infection.

A similar *cri-du-coeur* has been made by Van Balen and Ntabomvura (1976), in relation to the disruption of both infant nutrition and pregnancy-spacing in central Africa as a result of what they term 'bottle-disease':

The bottle's interference with maternal lactation has jeopardized the "external pregnancy" (and) . . . in some instances has lead to a really catastrophic situation . . . The pitiful situation in the big cities of South America or even Africa, with ever-crowded slums, ill-nourished children, "bottle-diarrheas", biologically and mentally exhausted mothers, and the high ratio of abortions, carrying a high maternal mortality rate, particularly among mothers already having many children.

Effects of health services (Iatrogenic effects)
The health services in most developing countries have played a conspicuously negative role in sustaining lactation. It is increasingly apparent that the types of training and of services have most often been imported from elsewhere, particularly from Europe and North America, and that they are,

in fact, far from what is required anywhere, but especially unsuitable in a poor, largely rural developing country. As noted earlier, such services are the outcomeof the linear Western scientific revolution of the last century (p. 185). They are technology-centred, hospital-dominated, and clinically-oriented, both in structure and in staff training. Recent studies, such as those reported in the Zagreb Guidelines (1973) sponsored by the International Union of Nutrition Sciences, increasingly indicate the obvious fact that real need is for the opposite — that is for adequate low-cost maternal and child health services reaching into rural areas (Morley 1973), as well as into peri-urban slums and shanty towns, and with a combination of prevention and basic treatment undertaken by auxiliaries and the people themselves (Mahler 1975 *a,b*, Newell 1975).

Health services can affect the pattern of breast-feeding in resource-poor, less technically developed countries in a variety of ways. Most directly, the widespread distribution of milk powder through such health services has had the obvious effect of displacing breast-feeding by bottle-feeding. The classical case-study in this regard was the socially enlightened policy in Chile (Monckeberg 1968, 1969, 1970), where he widespread and well-intentioned distribution of milk powder through health centres for some decades has been associated with improvement in the pre-school age mortality rate, but with a decline in breast-feeding, a rise in diarrhoea and marasmus, and low benefit as far as the infant mortality rate was concerned.

Similarly, with the facile extra knowledge of hindsight, it was a nutritional tragedy that the well-intentioned, widespread feeding programmes in developing countries in the late 1940s and 1950s should have been primarily concerned with the distribution of dry skimmed-milk powder designed to be reconstituted as liquid milk, and little too with associated health education. As far as mothers of young children were concerned, this can only have appeared as endorsement of bottle-feeding, with a resulting displacement effect on breast-feeding. As far as the health centres, such activity dominated the clinic's work, with inadequate time for other duties (Fig. 11.11).

Bengoa (1974) has emphasized that the main public-health dangers of early weaning — that is a decreased period of breast-feeding — can be correlated anywhere in the world with low 'standards of living', including purchasing power, environmental sanitation, and parental education. He has suggested diagrammatically the need to consider trends in early weaning in relation to trends in standards of living, and the obvious need at least to 'decelerate' the rising incidence of early weaning. However, Bengoa's concerns are only related to major causes of death and severe illness related to early weaning in developing countries (e.g. marasmus and diarrhoea), and he does not take into account other universal considerations related to breast-feeding, such as child spacing (p. 118) or more specific nutritional aspects (p. 26). Moreover, the 'probable trend of improving the standard of living' seems highly optimistic for some countries, especially for the

Fig. 11.11. Large-scale distribution of dried skimmed milk: Addis Ababa, Ethiopia (courtesy of UNICEF)

extremely poor countries of the newly labelled 'Fourth World', where, unfortunately, levels of living may be deteriorating.

The structure, function, and staffing of hospitals, including maternity units

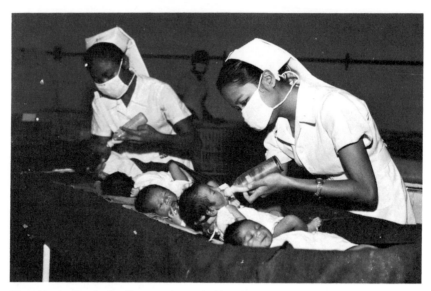

Fig. 11.12. Bottle-feeding newborn babies in Western-style nursery: Indonesia (courtesy of UNICEF)

and paediatric wards, in developing countries have been based on imported models from industrialized countries, where they are usually even less appropriate to the needs and cultures into which they have been transplanted (Jelliffe and Jelliffe 1973 *d*). In particular, maternity units, including the attached premature-baby units, have followed the same pattern as in Europe and North America, with the separation of mothers and neonates, the introduction of 'complementary' bottle feeds to newborn babies (Fig. 11.12) and other Western techniques commented on elsewhere (p. 185). Very many of such practices tend to interfere with the psychophysiology of lactation and increase the practical problems of initiating breast-feeding.

In present-day urban circumstances, the young, inexperienced, *doula*-less mother may have little knowledge concerning breast-feeding, nor, quite frequently, have the medical or nursing staff, although they are meant to be the experts. The crowded, regimented, unprivate atmosphere of many maternity wards means that the mother has limited time to receive individual advice and guidance, even if anyone really knows what to advise. Her baby is often separated from her and put in the nursery — an extraordinary and inhuman travesty of obvious physiological needs. Not surprisingly, the mother is anxious, apprehensive, and uncertain. Her let-down reflex is likely to be inhibited, so that the baby receives little milk and is dissatisfied. He protests by crying and thus further increases the mother's apprehension. The overworked nurse or midwife galloping around the ward makes the instant diagnosis of 'not enough milk' or 'milk doesn't suit the baby'. The recipe is either complete removal to artificial feeding, or, at best, a 'temporary' complementary bottle-feed, which increases the mother's lack of confidence and is the worst possible sabotage of the vigorous sucking needed for successful lactation. Appropriate nutrition education on infant feeding is rarely given, even if time in the ward permits, and mothers often are discharged more confused than on admission.

Likewise, bottle-feeding in the children's ward can be undertaken lightly and with no apparent recognition of the hospital's role as molder of opinion and behaviour. For example, commonplace examples could include a baby with tetanus of the newborn admitted without the mother for prolonged costly treatment over a period of several weeks, only to be discharged home to succumb to diarrhoea and marasmus as a result of failure of maternal lactation and inadequate, contaminated bottle-feedings. What is more, all too frequently, the children's wards in tropical hospitals are continually overflowing with sick children, most of whom are suffering from malnutrition, diarrhoea, various infections, or who have mixtures of these (Jelliffe and Jelliffe 1970*b*). In many places, the pressure on limited beds increases — with chaotic results. Mothers, even those with breast-fed babies, may be excluded from the ward by policy, and the young children admitted may then be crowded two or three in a cot, with an obviously increased likelihood of cross-infection. In extreme cases, the press of circumstances is such that the harried nurses have great difficulty in finding time even to feed the children adequately, but rather concentrate on injections and medication.

In addition, very frequently health services can unwittingly act as unpaid advertisers for processed infant foods, as, for example, by the display of posters and calendars, by the acceptance and distribution of free samples, and by permitting the 'milk nurses' employed by some formula companies to work in hospitals and health centres. Health personnel are very ill-informed or gullible with regard to age-old psychosocial mechanisms employed cheaply and effectively by commercial concerns, including both pharmaceutical companies and infant-food manufacturers. As mentioned earlier, basic methods are combinations of 'manipulation by assistance' and 'endorsement by association'. The value of assistance with funding of meetings, travel, etc., needs careful balance in relation to outcomes in relation to conscious or subconscious modification of policy. In any case, the assistance is not a gift, but comes from the high cost of sales and is, in effect, very inexpensive advertising.

Also until recently, health staff, particularly physicians, were often trained in industrialized countries or, indeed, from textbooks more concerned with clinical diagnosis of rarities in the temperate zone than in the problems of developing countries and their prevention. As in Western countries, little emphasis, if any, is given to the known facts concerning the psychophysiology of lactation, or, indeed, nutrition in general. The staff of health services — physicians and nurses — often act as subconscious and unaware 'casual disruptors' of breast-feeding. For example it seems likely that the reported decline in prevalence of breast-feeding in rural Cuba can in large measure be related to lack of awareness by physicians and nurses, and to the too widespread distribution of dried milk, as advertising would play no part in that country.

On a more general level, the content and implementation of nutrition education through the health services is usually inadequate in amount, and often viewed as a troublesome ritual. It is sometimes not appreciated that this should be inherent and osmotic — that is, occurring following observed practice, as well as following planned activities. Also, despite a realization of the problem for twenty years or more (Jelliffe 1968*b*), culturally, economically, and nutritionally inappropriate activities too often masquerade as health education in centres and clinics, with much waste of time and effort, and much counter-productive confusion as inappropriate information becomes dogma:

> Too frequently one found the pediatrician in a tropical, sun-drenched country, exhorting mothers to use cod-liver oil to prevent non-existent rickets. Or, one found the physician or public health nurse from Europe advising mothers to feed their babies on orange juice when infantile scurvy did not exist, when oranges were unobtainable, when there was a real danger of unclean orange juice producing diarrhea and when the infant would be receiving adequate ascorbic acid through his mother's milk.
>
> Likewise, the earnest unacculturated Western home economist could be demonstrating the preparation of infants needs with no consideration of their cost or of the limited kitchen possibilities in the mothers' homes.

Wage-earning working women
For the new townsmen, urban life is dominated by the need for employment in a cash economy. This usually involves primarily the man of the family, but may also affect women, or women alone in some circumstances, including those with illegitimate babies. In this case, in modern urban situations, the working mother may find it impossible, or not currently culturally permissible, to breast-feed her baby (except at night) in factory, office, or domestic employment, unless she works as a market woman, as in parts of west Africa, or unless crèches are available in or near industry. In rural areas, labour is likely to be agricultural and in most (but not all) of such activities mothers may be able to have their infants with them.

This has a variable significance, however. Studies in some developing countries have indicated that working women often constitute a rather small percentage of bottle-feeding mothers and are often only a minor cause for the decline in breast-feeding in newly urbanized communities. However, this varies considerably. In Colombia, 47 per cent of a series of mothers had stopped breast-feeding because they were working, while in another study in

New Delhi, only 6 per cent were doing so (Berg 1973).

What is more, with rising populations, increasing urbanization, and limited industrialization in less technically developed countries, employment opportunities in cities may decrease in the future. This may affect women more than men — except for more specifically and traditionally female jobs, such as maids.

However, the real need is more than a general view of the wage-earning capacity of such working women, but a deeper assessment of the effect on the mother–infant dyad, and also on the welfare of the whole family. Analysis is required of 'the greatest total benefit or perhaps least total harm' (Dugdale 1971). Such will be complicated even at an immediately tangible economic level, as has been mentioned earlier (p. 134); even more so are decisions concerning potential long-term outcomes that are currently uncertain or difficult to prove.

Conclusion

The suddenness of the change from breast-feeding to bottle-feeding in many urban areas in developing countries, as, for example, in Singapore (Fig. 11.2) (Wong 1971), clearly indicates that biological genetic changes cannot be responsible. Even more rapid alterations in behaviour have been noted in Pakistani women who had migrated to Britain (Aykroyd and Hossein 1967, Evans et al. 1976). The main factors responsible are undoubtedly social, cultural, and economic influences on the parents' attitudes and behaviour in relation to their new self-image.

The selection of life-styles for new townsmen are much influenced by the example of the local élite, the influence of advertising, and the methods and procedures of health services. The élite, as noted earlier, may, to a very considerable extent, have moved from breast-feeding to bottle-feeding, paralleling similar earlier changes in the Western world. Again, the example of foreigners from industrialized countries living in developing countries, usually in cities, also seems to endorse the modernness of artificial feeding. As has been noted by Raphael (1973b), the health and large size of such people also have tended to endorse the 'mystique of the megamen', who, until recently at least, could also be perceived as controlling ultimate world economic, political, and military power.

As noted earlier (p. 185), it seems most probable that a prime reason for changing from breast-feeding to bottle-feeding is in part a subconscious attempt to move from the bio-traditional 'curved' culture of the rural village to the more mechanical, measurement-oriented 'linear' Westernism of the city. Hence, breast-feeding is subconsciously equated with old-fashionedness, primitiveness, and backwardness, while bottle-feeding symbolizes urban life and, therefore, everything which is modern, scientific, and desirable. Also, as a particularly recent phenomenon, pressures towards urban life-styles are no longer confined to cities, but are tending to spread out to rural areas in some countries by word of mouth, and particularly through the channel of the transistorized radio. This process of 'mental urbanization' has already tended to affect ways of life, including ability to breast-feed in some rural parts of the world, and may be expected to do so increasingly in the future, unless the apparent risks and dangers of these developments are appreciated and countered.

However, the situation is far from uniform in different parts of the world with varying levels and types of resource (p. 212). This is especially so in relation to what Wray (1976a) has perceptively contrasted as 'traditional', 'transitional' and 'modern', with differing levels of 'quality of maternal care' (including breast-feeding) and 'environmental quality'. In this scheme, discussed later (Fig. 14.13), it is the 'transitional community' — that is the newly urbanized poor — who have the worst of both worlds. With low levels of both maternal care and environment, they have the highest infant-mortality rates and an increasing number of marasmus–diarrhoea syndrome (p. 287).

In very recent years, for example, the economics of importing infant foods has changed, with rising costs of ingredients, production, and transport. This is leading in some places to reconsideration of import policies (p. 311). Awareness of the significance of breast-feeding is on the increase among health professionals, nutritionists, and educated parents (p. 324). Much attention has been drawn to the impact of the infant-food industry in developing countries in the past few years, including some factual analyses of advertising (p. 320) (Greiner 1975) and legal action (p. 320). Likewise the formula-manufacturing companies have begun to respond to what are perceived by them as recent ill-considered and ill-informed attacks on their integrity (p. 321). In fact, a number of major trends and influences can be identified, which may tend to make breast-feeding more, or less, likely to be the norm in the future, both in resource-poor and resource-rich countries. These are considered later (p. 300), but prior to this it is necessary to consider the consequences of inadequate breast-feeding in terms of health, economics, and resources on a world basis, including the varying circumstances in technically less developed countries with different levels of resources, and in such relatively well-to-do countries as those in Europe, North America, and Australasia, and Japan.

12 World consequences of early weaning

> *If a frog is placed in hot water, it will make frantic efforts to escape; but, so it is said, if the animal is put in cold water which is slowly heated, it may after passing through various stages of phylogenetic maladjustments be boiled to death without so much as a struggle. In modern civilization, we may be exhibiting pathological responses to adverse conditions, yet consider these responses normal and be unaware that they are pathological.*
>
> The Boiling Frog Principle, B. A. and E. J. Mobbs (1972)

> *Against an environment almost uniformly hostile to his continued existence man, of all animals, is singularly ill-equipped to fend for himself. His lengthy gestation, his much longer period of infantile dependence, his scant body hair, and poor sense of smell, all militate against successful survival under natural conditions. Moreover, he lacks the speed, strength, and agility of most predators of comparable size and has no natural camouflage from his enemies. Only his reason, his superior intelligence, has saved him from extinction eons ago. It is true that many animal species show intelligence of a sort and that some, the whale and dolphin for example, have larger brains, but none appear to have the complex structure and peculiar circuitry that confers to great in advantage on the brain of* Homo sapiens.
>
> In Defence of the Mind, Arnold Pearce (1975)

Evidence has already been presented showing recent widespread declines in breast-feeding in many areas of the world and the use of cow's milk formulas instead (p. 214). The fundamental question is the significance of this change. In other words, what are the proven and potential consequences to human health and resources in differing ecologies in the world, particularly in the contrasting circumstances found in resource-rich and resource-poor communities, and in rural and urban areas.

RESOURCE-RICH COMMUNITIES

In relatively resource-rich countries, such as the U.S.A., Japan, and those of Western Europe and Australasia, bottle-feeding with cow's-milk formulas has become the usual way of feeding babies in recent decades. Under the economic, hygienic, and social conditions found in the majority of families in such countries, this practice is now considered to be as safe and effective as breast-feeding as regards the growth, nutrition, and health of such infants, and, indeed, as most appropriate economically and culturally for modern urban life-styles. The same assumptions have also spread to the Westernized élite minority in resource-poor countries. However, recent evidence suggests that there may be particular, previously unsuspected and underappreciated problems or side-effects associated with bottle-feeding, which are less common in the breast-fed, and which may constitute significant health concerns or ecological issues.

Actual or potential consequences of bottle-feeding babies with cow's-milk formulas may be reviewed under the following headings: nutritional–metabolic, allergic, sudden-infant-death syndrome, infective, emotional, alimentary, and economic. The detailed background has largely been given earlier, so that the present account will be more concerned with the numerical significance and dimensions of such consequences in communities.

1. Nutritional–metabolic consequences

Investigations in the last ten years or so suggest that four possible areas of concern have emerged, which can be labelled: (a) 'cow's-milk bottle-feeding syndromes', (b) 'formula-deficiency syndromes', (c) optimal growth, and (d) adult health.

'Cow's-milk bottle-feeding syndromes'
Six nutritional–metabolic disorders are seen more frequently in infants who are bottle-fed on cow's-milk formulas — infantile obesity, iron-deficiency anaemia, hypernatraemia, neonatal hypocalcaemia, amino-acidaemia in prematures, and acrodermatitis enteropathica.

Infantile obesity. In recent years, it has become recognized that obesity in infants and young children is a problem, which appears to be increasing in prevalence. Large numbers of reports have appeared in the medical literature of Western Europe and North America (*Archives of Diseases of Childhood* 1973, *British Medical Journal* 1973*b*, 1975*a*, Brook *et al.* 1972, Knittle 1972, Lloyd *et al.* 1961, Mayer 1968) and, to a lesser extent, of Japan and Eastern Europe. A similar situation occurs in the infants of the well-to-do minority in resource-poor communities (Jelliffe and Jelliffe 1975*b*).

Difficulties of definition and diagnosis are still unresolved, although 120 per cent or more of standard weight-for-weight-for-age is often used as an approximate indicator, preferably associated with fat-fold measurements (Jelliffe and Jelliffe 1975*b*). Community surveys do not appear to have been undertaken, but the high prevalence in babies attending child-health clinics has been documented in various parts of the world. A number of studies have so reported from England and these are summarized in Table 12.1. Taitz noted an apparently increasing tendency to excessive weight-gain even in the first weeks of life. In a well-baby clinic, Shukla *et al.* (1972) reported that 44·4 per cent of infants were either overweight or obese.

Similar concern has also been voiced in the medical literature from the U.S.A., continental Europe, and Japan. For example, a report from Labrador, Canada indicated that some 70 per cent of infants under one year old attending a clinic were either overweight or obese (Jelliffe and Jelliffe 1975*b*).

TABLE 12.1 *Summary of some obesity studies in England* (from Department of Health and Social Security, 1974)

Authors	Number of babies	Age	Findings
Hutchinson-Smith (1970)	200	under 1 year	35% were over 20% overweight
Taitz (1971)	240	six weeks	59·6% exceeded 90th centile for weight
Shukla *et al.* (1972)	300	under 1 year	16·7% were over 20% overweight 27·7% in addition were between 10% and 20% overweight

Undoubtedly, many socio-cultural factor and family emotional factors can play a part in the aetiology of infantile obesity, as well as genetic influences. These include the age-old plump 'ideal' body-image for infants, the degree of restraint on movement (e.g. swaddling), maternal competitiveness as regards growth, development, and precocity of their babies (and age of introduction of foods other than milk), emphasis on weight curves in monitoring child growth and health (without consideration of upper limits), and persuasion by baby-food companies towards ever earlier feeding with semi-solids. Also, individual variations in physiology, and even temperament, undoubtedly are relevant, as reflected, for example, by differences in metabolic rate, absorption of nutrients, and spontaneous physical activity, such as kicking and moving in the crib (see p. 389).

Nevertheless, the direct cause of infantile obesity must be primarily related to caloric overdosage, with disbalance between the intake and expenditure of calories. The recently developed Western pattern of infant feeding seems largely responsible — that is, the use of cow's-milk-based formula, with the introduction of semi-solids in the first weeks or months of life. This has, in effect, introduced a form of calorific 'double-feeding' from early infancy, instead of the traditional sequence of milk:weaning (transitional period):adult diet.

Bottle-feedings are under the mother's control as regards volume and, in some instances, concentration. Because of maternal anxiety, economy, and competitiveness, babies may be coaxed to take more than their basic needs indicated by appetite. More concentrated mixtures than needed may be prepared intentionally, or, probably more usually, inadvertently, especially with powdered-milk products (Ringel and Renner 1973). That this can lead to additional caloric intake has been demonstrated by Fomon *et al.* (1975) who showed that more calories were taken with high-concentration formulas (100 kcal/100 ml) than with less 'calorie-dense' mixtures (54 kcal/100 ml). In addition, too concentrated foods can lead to increased thirst (p. 00) and in turn to further increased intake of formula and hence, of additional calorie load (Taitz and Byers 1972): 'the restless, fractious, always hungry baby may well in truth be the over-stuffed baby with a great thirst.'

By contrast, breast-milk is virtually an 'invisible food' without the possibility of overconcentration, and with the intake under the control of the infant's appetite and thirst, as a form of biological supply-and-demand system. In addition, it has been suggested that the breast-fed baby has various inherent biochemical, metabolic mechanisms controlling the volume taken when feeding. For example, the hind-milk (p. 56) contains concentrations of 4–5 times as much fat and somewhat more protein than found in fore-milk, and one of the cues curbing the appetite and limiting feeding may be the changed taste and viscosity of hind-milk (Hall 1975, D. P. Davies 1975).

Infantile obesity can occur in the exclusively breast-fed baby. It is much less common, as indicated by the data reported by Taitz (1971) from Sheffield, England, where 59·6 per cent of artificially fed babies were overweight by six weeks of age, compared with only 19 per cent of the breast-fed. Both groups were also being given semi-solids. Elsewhere, an investigation of 'well babies' attending a clinic found 7·3 per cent of them to be obese — all of whom were bottle-fed. Weight gains of the breast-fed averaged about 155 g (5½ oz) per week, compared with 185 g (6½ oz) per week for those on formula (Jelliffe and Jelliffe 1975b). The effect of reducing the calorie intake by breast-feeding and delaying the introduction of solids on the prevalence of overweight in infants has been shown by Taitz (1977) (Table 12.2). In Los Angeles, doubling of birth-weight occurs much earlier in the bottle-fed than in breast-fed infants (Neumann and Alpaugh 1976).

Also, it is possible that infantile obesity in the breast-fed baby may be a different syndrome biochemically from that seen in the bottle-fed. Certainly, the fatty-acid composition of the subcutaneous fat can vary with the detailed biochemistry of the infant's diet (p. 32), as does retention of water and electrolytes (p. 42).

An additional cause of the calorie overdosage leading to infantile obesity is the practice of unnecessarily introducing semi-solid foods in the early weeks of life (p. 201), while also bottle-feeding. Shukla and associates (1972) found that infants with this type of reinforced 'double-feeding' received 13–24 per cent extra calories above the recommended dietary allowance.

Although most babies can tolerate a wide range of puréed foods from the first week or so of life, there is no proof of any advantage or benefit to infant health or development. On the contrary, there is increasing evidence that the practice may be harmful not only as regards to calorie intakes, but also in relation to increased metabolic mineral load and to the incidence of allergy (p. 42).

TABLE 12.2 *Trends in infant feeding in Sheffield, 1971–6* (from Taitz, 1977)

	1971*	1974*	1976*
Number	100	100	100
Breast-fed	8	29	41
Unmodified milk powder	90	67	0
Modified powder	2	4	59
Solids	80	20	10
Above 50th centile	79	55	43

* Successive full-term infants at 6 weeks of age

For example, some 'junior dinners' contain approximately 3 g sodium per 100 kcal, compared with some 230 mg/100 kcal in human milk. Also, the early introduction of wheat products, with short periods of breast-feeding, have been associated in some parts of the world with a rising incidence of gluten enteropathy (coeliac disease) (Department of Health and Social Security, U.K. 1974).

However, it is the combination of cow's-milk-formula feeding *and* the very early introduction of semi-solids which cumulatively increases the likelihood of infantile obesity developing. The two practices are likely to go together. In present-day circumstances in Western countries, mothers breast-feeding their babies usually introduce semi-solids later.

Infantile obesity is a health hazard even in early childhood. There is an increased tendency to respiratory infections. For example, Tracey *et al.* (1971) reported 39·9 per cent of a series of infants weighing more than 120 per cent of standard weight to have one or more respiratory infections during the study period compared with 21·1 per cent of babies whose weights were within normal limits. In addition, obese infants have more difficulty in dealing with severe respiratory infections, partly because of the increased mechanical burden while breathing.

The over-fat baby also has greater difficulty in dealing with skin diseases and infections. If these occur, the creases and folds of fat can make treatment a problem, because of irritation of adjacent surfaces, and because of the sogginess of skin that is inadequately ventilated.

Lastly, obesity in infancy, as in any other age group, can have a double vicious-cycle effect calorifically. First, the increasingly fat baby tends to become less mobile, with consequently further reduced expenditure of energy. At the same time, the heavier infant may be assumed to need more food because of his larger size. Both can contribute to the imbalance between the energy taken in and the energy used up.

In addition, it seems likely that overfeeding of babies may condition the individual to an abnormally large appetite, and that obesity in childhood, especially infancy, may lead to multiplication of fat cells, which can be retained permanently throughout life (Brook *et al.* 1972, Jelliffe and Jelliffe 1975*b*, Knittle 1972). This, in turn, may pose problems of obesity-proneness in later life, as well as a higher risk of diabetes (Baum *et al.* 1975). Although it is not known what percentage of very fat babies are saddled with a life-long tendency to obesity and for how many the condition is transitory ('puppy-fat'), limited studies have shown that 80 per cent of obese children are obese in adult life (Eid 1970). Investigation of 260 obese school children by Asher (1966) showed that 44 per cent of these had been overweight in infancy.

The long-term public-health significance can be far reaching. Obesity in older children and adults is now the most important nutritional problem in well-to-do communities (Mayer 1968). One study in 1956 in the U.S.A. showed 10 per cent of school children to be obese (Johnson *et al.* 1956); in Western technically more developed countries, obesity occurs in about 7–25 per cent adults. In one survey in the U.S.A., 50 per cent of women over 50 years of age were obese (Jelliffe and Jelliffe 1975*b*). In countries where food is relatively abundant, such as the U.S.A. and Western Europe, obesity is more common in the less well-to-do (Pan American Health Organization 1972). The obese have increased risks from surgery and accidents (including burns). They also have psychological and economic, employment difficulties, and decreased life expectancy as a result of associated cardiovascular disease, diabetes, etc., major causes of death in Western man. Not all obesity in adults can be linked to obesity in infancy, but sufficient evidence exists to confirm the likelihood of a connection in a substantial number. As Mayer (1968) comments, 'obesity is most malignant when it commences early.'

Iron-deficiency anaemia. What is currently considered to be haematological evidence of iron deficiency is a 'relatively common occurrence among pre-school children regardless of socio-economic status' in the U.S.A., according to the interpretation of the 1970 National Pre-school Nutrition Survey by Owen and colleagues (1971); Robson (1972) found that from 25 to 30 per cent of young children aged 3–36 months have haemoglobin concentrations of less than 10 g per 100 ml. Despite some uncertainty over haematological standards and their meaning, a similar situation is considered to exist in other industrialized countries. However, this is mainly an overt problem of the exterogestate foetus, with the main incidence of iron-deficiency anaemia usually between 9 and 24 months, except in special circumstances such as neonatal haemorrhage, multiple births, or prematurity.

The adequacy of iron supplies in early childhood needs to be considered as an aggregate from all sources, that is the early diet (milk), the later diet (semi-solids and the utensils in which they are cooked) (Lowe *et al.* 1969), the placental transfusion, and the foetal hepatic stores, balanced against potential losses, as for example, from intestinal microhaemorrhages and in diarrhoea (Elian *et al.* 1966). The interaction of these variables on iron sufficiency has been discussed earlier (p.46).

Briefly, the breast-fed baby, who has received optimal stores transplacentally from a well-nourished mother and from the placental transfusion resulting from late clamping of the umbilical cord, needs no iron supplementation until semi-solids are introduced at 4–6 months of age, when iron-containing foods should be included. The use of iron supplement may need to be discouraged for the solely breast-fed because of possible saturation of the antibacterial lactoferrin present in human milk.

The iron content of cow's milk is low, as is that of breast-milk. However, the iron needs may be greater in some bottle-fed infants, as feeding with some cow's-milk preparations has been shown to be associated with intestinal micro-haemorrhages. As with the breast-fed, iron-containing non-milk foods need to be introduced at 4–6 months of age in babies reared on cow's-milk formulas. In later infancy and in the second year of life, iron deficiency is so well recognized as being associated with a cultural over-emphasis on cow's milk as a 'complete, perfect food' that is has been labelled 'milk anaemia'. Interestingly, a similar severe chronic iron-deficiency anaemia — Bahima disease — has been described in older children of pastoralist cattle-keeping people in Uganda, who prefer to live on large amounts of cow's milk without other foods (Jelliffe and Blackman 1967).

In view of the commonness of iron-deficiency anaemia in largely bottle-fed communities in the U.S.A., iron-fortified formulas (containing 18 mg/l) have recently been introduced and have been endorsed by the American Academy of Paediatrics for use from birth (Pearson 1971). Currently, no significant ill-effects of the much larger intake of iron in fortified formulas during early infancy are apparent. They certainly have the advantage of adding iron 'silently' for the artificially fed and increasing stores that can be drawn on in the second year of life. The use of iron-fortified milk for the transitional as part of the weaning diet seems advantageous in both the breast-fed and the bottle-fed, when available and affordable. Present evidence suggests that those preparations are non-toxic and well absorbed.

Iron-deficiency anaemia has long been considered to be less common in breast-fed babies. However, as emphasized earlier (p. 46), this depends on the iron available from the milk used (breast-milk; form of cow's-milk preparation), from the foetal stores, and from the placental transfusion for the exterogestate foetus, and the iron content and its availability in the weaning diet for the transitional. The interrelationship of all of these factors has often not been considered sufficiently in haematological studies, and, indeed, they are difficult to measure quantitatively or comprehensively.

Relatively few limited studies have been undertaken on small series of patients. In an early report from Britain, McKay (1931) demonstrated higher haemoglobin values in infants fed on breast-milk, when compared

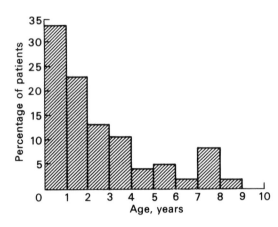

Fig. 12.1. Age incidence of
iron-deficiency anaemia in
108 children admitted to the
paediatric ward, University
Hospital, Singapore. The
highest incidence was in children under one year old, all of
whom were artificially fed
(by courtesy of Prof. Wong
Hock Boon (1971). *Breast-
feeding in Singapore.*
Choon Kee Press, Singapore).

with infants fed on reconstituted dried cow's milk. In Singapore, Wong
(1971) analysed 108 children admitted to hospital with iron-deficiency
anaemia. One-third of these were in the first year of life, all of whom were
artificially fed (Fig. 12.1).

However, practical testing of the adequacy of iron derived from foetal
stores, placental transfusion, and human milk for the first 4–6 months of life,
with the introduction of semi-solids thereafter, has been undertaken
recently by several investigators in the U.S.A. Good (1974) followed 105
unselected consecutive healthy full-term babies who were solely breast-fed
for four months; some had solids started during the next 4 months, and all
were on solids and breast-milk at one year. Most were on multiple vitamins
with fluoride by 8 to 12 months. At 4 months, the average haemoglobin was
$12\cdot4\,\mathrm{g}/100\,\mathrm{ml}$ (range $10\cdot2$–$15\cdot1\,\mathrm{g}/100\,\mathrm{ml}$). At both 8 months and 12
months, the mean haemoglobin was $11\cdot6\,\mathrm{g}/100\,\mathrm{ml}$ (Fig. 12.2). White
(1974) studied 30 solely breast-fed infants at 6 months of age and found
averages of $12\cdot0\,\mathrm{g}/100\,\mathrm{ml}$ in boys and $11\cdot7\,\mathrm{g}/100\,\mathrm{ml}$ in girls. In a recent

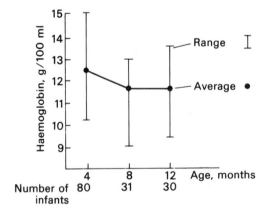

Fig. 12.2. Haemoglobin levels in
breast-fed infants 4 months to 1
year of age (from Good (1974).
Personal communication)

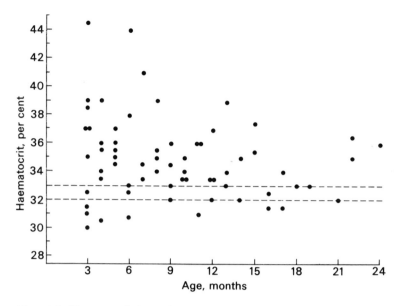

Fig. 12.3. Haematocrit levels in breast-fed children in first two years of life (from Coulson, K. M., Cohen, R. L., Coulson, W. F., and Jelliffe, D. B. (1975). *Proceedings of the International Nutritional Congress*, Kyoto, Japan)

study in Los Angeles (Coulson *et al.* 1975), haematocrit levels were measured on babies whose method of feeding has consisted of breast-feeding continued until about 12 months: other factors, particularly the placental transfusion, was not known. Results in the large majority of infants were within normal limits. Of the lower figures from 6 to 12 months of age, 2 were twins and 2 were babies who had not received solid food at 6–9 months.

Recently, four infants were followed up when *solely* breast-fed for 8–18 months (mean 10·9 months) without added vitamins or food supplements. All laboratory tests of iron status were normal, although they had almost tripled their birth-weight (average 2·9 times), and customary clinical teaching is that iron stores are no longer adequate after the baby has doubled the birth-weight (McMillan *et al.* 1976).

While further more detailed haematological studies of iron metabolism in mothers and their breast-fed infants are urgently needed, the evidence suggests that the long-standing 'clinical-impression' of the lower incidence of iron deficiency in breast-fed babies is largely correct. The value of breast-feeding as *one* approach to the prevention of iron-deficiency anaemia in early childhood needs stress.

Hypernatraemia. The higher solute load of cow's milk, and most formulas, is mainly due to their mineral and protein contents (Keen 1969). As noted earlier (p. 42) babies fed on cow's milk-based formulas have to deal with a different and increased metabolic load. Indeed, they have a different body composition, as noted by Davies and Saunders (1973) in Britain, who found that 75–88 per cent of apparently normal, healthy bottle-fed babies have blood urea levels above what is normally considered the upper limit of normal (40 mg/100 ml). Likewise, a relatively sudden change from breast- to bottle-feeding can be accompanied by a rapid gain in weight due to water retention associated with increased body sodium (McCance and Widdowson 1957). Whether these differences are of no consequence in healthy, non-dehydrated infants, who can adapt without harm, or whether metabolic loads ('chronic hyperelectrolytaemia') have current or later ill-effects is unknown.

However, the risk of metabolic overload with mineral and protein can easily be increased to dangerous levels either inadvertently or by design, as a result of mothers using too much powdered milk or inadequately diluting 'double-strength' liquid formula (Chamber and Steel 1975). The high solute load of sodium imposes an extra stress on the kidneys in the event of increased loss of water and dehydration, as in hot weather, fever, diarrhoea, or vomiting. There is the real risk of seriously high levels of serum sodium (hypernatraemic dehydration), which can lead to permanent brain damage, even after rehydration. This likelihood is increased as the thirst characteristic of early hypernatraemia can further add to the metabolic load, if the mother responds by giving additional 'drinks' of high-solute formula. The unexplained finding of very high levels of electrolytes in the vitreous fluid of some young children dying suddenly also needs noting (Emery *et al.* 1974).

The frequency and public-health significance of such 'solute-load syndromes' is difficult to ascertain, but numerous publications have appeared in recent years. That they are a justifiable cause for general concern is suggested by the changes made in this regard by formula manufacturers and by the recommendation in Britain that the powdered 'National Dried Milk' available through government health services should be modified 'to reduce the content of phosphate, sodium, and protein . . . nearer to that of breast milk'. (Department of Health and Social Security, U.K. 1974, 1975).

Neonatal hypocalcaemia. Despite much higher levels of calcium in cow's milk than in human milk, absorption is poor because of the formation of insoluble calcium palmitate in the intestines (p. 33) and the lower level of lactose. Also, the high phosphate intake from cow's milk diminishes the serum calcium level; while the levels of magnesium are also marginally reduced (Department of Health and Social Security, U.K. 1974).

So-called 'late neonatal hypocalcaemia', with hyperphosphataemia, infantile convulsions, and tetany, occurs in the first two weeks of life (Watney *et al.* 1971). It is primarily a condition of babies who are fed with cow's milk formulas (Bakwin 1937, Barltrop and Oppé 1970, 1973), as has been recognized for 25 years. Fatality from heart failure can occur (Troughton and Singh 1972), and, in addition to immediate risks, hypoplasia of the dental enamel has been reported subsequent to neonatal hypocalcaemia (Stimmler *et al.* 1973). Those affected were all bottle-fed. The risks of both hypocalcaemia and enamel hypoplasia may be reduced if babies can be breast-fed for at least 1–2 weeks. Also, in order to minimize the risk of neonatal hypocalcaemia, more recently formulas have been modified so that the calcium, phosphorus, and sodium components and the calcium–phosphorus ratio are nearer to human milk. However, 'such demineralized milks are expensive and are not without a possible risk since in the process of demineralization as yet unidentified nutrients may be removed.' (Department of Health and Social Security, U.K. 1974).

Estimates on the incidence of this condition in the U.S.A. were not readily available, but reports suggest that some 5000 cases occur annually in Britain. In 1969, $8 \cdot 7$ per 1000 newborn babies were reported to have convulsions in Manchester, of which cases 34 per cent were attributed to hypocalcaemia alone (Keen 1969). Recent analysis (Stimmler *et al.* 1973) in the country have shown that about 14 per cent of babies affected subsequently show severe defects of dental development (enamel hypoplasia).

Amino-acid metabolism in premature babies. The amino-acid profiles of cow's milk and human milk are quite different. The lower level of cystine in bovine milk has special significance for premature babies, as the enzyme cystothianase (which alters methionine to cystine) is absent in the livers and brains of foetuses and premature babies. Cystine appears therefore to be an essential sulphur-containing amino acid for prematures and is possibly 'semi-essential' for young full-term babies, and may have special significance for brain growth and liver function.

In addition, neonates, especially premature babies, have limited ability to metabolize tyrosine or phenylalanine, which are present in cow's milk in 3 and 4 times respectively the amount found in human milk. In prematures fed on cow's-milk formulas, amino-acidaemia can result with serum levels of tyrosine 10–20 times higher than in adults. This can produce lethargy, poor feeding, and impaired weight-gain — a similar picture to generalized septicaemia (Mamunes *et al.* 1976).

The incidence of 'transient tyrosinaemia' is difficult to compare from one centre to another, in view of different ages of babies tested, proportions of immature, levels of protein in the formula, methods of analysis, and definitions of abnormal levels of blood tyrosine. In 1967, Wong *et al.* investigated 652 newborns (excluding those premature by gestational age) of 10–21 days old, and found 4 per cent with tyrosinaemia in the breast-fed and 80 per cent in the bottle-fed. Menkes and Avery (Menkes *et al.* 1972) found 88 per cent in low birth-weight babies. Mamunes and colleagues (1976) suggested that transient tyrosinaemia is found in $0 \cdot 5$ per cent of all bottle-fed babies over 1 week of age, using 13 mg/100 ml or more as the critical blood level. They stress that commonly preparations of evaporated

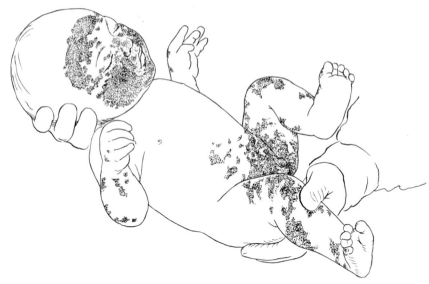

Fig. 12.4. Acrodermatitis enteropathica: characterized
by diarrhoea and skin rash in non-breast fed infant. Fatal
without treatment, curable with oral zinc or breast milk.
Illustration shows typical distribution of blistering
vesicular eruption, commencing around the mouth and
anal opening and involving face and legs.

milk (12 milk:19 water) are high in protein, and hence particularly likely to
lead to marked tyrosinaemia.

There is also evidence that high concentrations of amino acids in the blood
may cause neurological and intellectual sequelae in prematures and in
full-term low birth-weight babies (Goldman *et al.* 1974, Menkes *et al.* 1972),
including specific learning disabilities (Mamunes *et al.* 1976). The long-term
significance of such metabolic changes need further study, but they suggest
caution in the amount of protein, and particularly certain amino acids, fed to
young babies, especially if premature, and a reappraisal of the usually
relatively high-protein formulas advocated.

Acrodermatitis enteropathica. This is a rare syndrome characterized
mainly by a blistering vesicular eruption, especially around body orifices and
distal parts of the limbs (Fig. 12.4) and by diarrhoeal attacks. The disease,
which is fatal if untreated, occurs only in infants fed on cow's-milk formulas.
In most cases, cure was previously achieved by switching the baby to fresh or
stored expressed breast-milk, or by administering oral diodoquine. Recently, cures have been reported following treatment with zinc by mouth. The
condition is due to an inborn error of metabolism, previously considered to
be related to an inability to metabolize tryptophan, present in much larger

amounts in cow's milk than human milk; currently, it is considered that zinc metabolism is affected.

The zinc content of cow's milk and human milk have been variously reported. It seems certain that absorption from breast-milk is very efficient, as has been used therapeutically. This may be related to a lower zinc:copper ratio, or to other nutrients or factors in human milk. Colostrum is rich in zinc, and in mice zinc deficiency can be precipitated in newborn who do not receive colostrum (Nishimura 1953).

'Formula-deficiency syndromes'

Modern research endorsing the complex uniqueness of human compared with the equally, but different, complexity of the milks of other mammal species, has been several times inadvertently endorsed by unexpected nutritional and metabolic anomalies and imbalances produced in commercial attempts to produce 'humanized' processed cow's-milk-based formulas.

The first recognized of such 'formula-deficiency syndromes' was the occurrence of pyridoxine (vitamin B_6)-deficiency convulsions in the 1950s, when a change in manufacturing process reduced the vitamin B_6 content of one formula below the critical level needed by the central nervous system (Coursin 1954). Other nutritional deficiencies produced by manipulation of the ingredients contained in cow's-milk formulas include the skin lesions of severe linoleic-acid deficiency (Hansen *et al.* 1947, 1962) and the haemolytic anaemia due to lack of vitamin E (Oski and Barness 1967, Ritchie *et al.* 1968). As soon as recognized, these deficiencies were corrected by the manufacturers, but the probability of a continuing sequence of such imbalances is unavoidable. Current realization of the possible significance of zinc may be noted, with attention being given to the need for this mineral in formulas (Walravens and Hamidge 1975). The future situation with other trace elements and micronutrients is wholly unknown. Indeed, each further adaptive manipulation poses new risks.

Difficulties with attempts at modification in the preparation of cow's-milk formulas are illustrated by recent experiments (Willis *et al.* 1973) designed to develop a breast-milk substitute which would be bifidogenic — that is, encourage the growth of *Lactobacillus bifidus* in the same way as human milk (p. 86). The result was successful in this regard. However, this typically monovalent approach had put aside any adequate consideration of even the major nutrient composition of the product, let alone the detailed balance of micronutrients. As all mammal milks are different, complex biological systems of large numbers of interacting constituents, the modification of one nutrient potentially affects an unknown range of other ingredients, of known or as yet unknown significance.

To some, an increasing awareness of the approximations of infant formulas to nutritional and metabolic needs suggest that 'until human milk can be simulated in every way there is much need for active research' (Lonnerdal *et al.* 1975). To others, it suggests the impossibility of transubstantiating cow's milk into human milk, except at the grosser level, and certainly not in relation to the finer balance of micronutrients nor, of course, with similar anti-infective and anti-allergic properties (pp. 84 and 96). For example, in relation to the sodium content alone, a recent publication (Department of Health and Social Security, U.K. 1974) notes: 'Only by demineralization and addition of electrolytes can a food based on cow's milk be prepared which has a sodium-ion concentration near to that of breast-milk. But during this process all minerals are removed including, for example, known trace elements and perhaps others as yet unknown. When trace elements are replaced in the form of soluble inorganic salts, there is no certainty that they are then present in physiologically ideal form'.

It is insufficiently realized that present-day formulas are varying and changing blends of ingredients which are 'cow's-milk-based' — that is, with dried skimmed milk (low-fat milk) as their basic core. The choice and blend of other ingredients is dictated by economic considerations, by the claims of rival concerns, and by attempts to approximate the additional qualities of human milk, or to make good some newly recognized ill-effect of the previous mixture. It is therefore difficult indeed to be sure that advertisements claiming a particular formula to be 'congruent with' or 'more like' mothers' milk are true. The detailed ingredients given on one well-known product, for example, are said to consist of water, non-fat milk, lactose, soy, coconut and corn oils, mono- and diglycerides, soy lecithin, carrageenan, ascorbic acid, ferrous sulphate, zinc sulphate, α-tocopheryl acetate, niacinamide, potassium citrate, cupric sulphate, vitamin-A palmitate, calcium pantothenate, thiamine chloride hydrochloride, pyridoxine hydrochloride, riboflavin, manganous chloride, vitamin D_3 concentrate, cyanocobalamin, and folic acid.

'Optimal growth'

Apart from the more immediate effects of the use of cow's-milk-based formulas in infant feeding, the question of providing a positive nutritional milieu for optimal growth needs consideration and further research. In the case of the human neonate, rapid brain growth is *the* characteristic of the species. Various factors in human milk may facilitate this by supplying the nutrients required in abundant supply, including *lactose* (which is metabolized into galactose) (p. 40), *specific fatty acids* (p. 31), and even perhaps *thromboplastin* (p. 51), used in the biochemical growth and development of the galactolipids and other biochemical components of the brain (p. 31) (Crawford and Willmott 1971, Crawford and Sinclair 1972, Crawford *et al.* 1973, 1974, Crawford, Hassam, Hall, and Laurance 1976, Crawford, Laurance, Hall, Berg-Hansen, and Munhambo 1976, Fumagalli *et al.* 1969, Galli *et al.* 1973). In addition, the cystine:methionine ratio is such that cerebral development may be assisted, especially in the low-weight

newborns in whom the enzyme cystothianase, is absent or at a low level
(p. 37).

The specific blend and digestibility of nutrients in breast-milk may be such
that they facilitate growth of bone, via efficient absorption of calcium
(p. 33), and of muscle and other protein-rich tissues, because of enhancement of protein utilization in part possibly related to the specific pattern of
polyamines and nucleotides. Conversely, as noted earlier, the composition
of human milk and the supply-and-demand mechanism of breast-feeding
make overgrowth, in the form of infantile obesity, very much less likely to
occur.

Adult health
There is considerable evidence that coronary heart disease can commence in
the early years of life and that prevention should be considered in childhood
(Mitchell 1973, Strong and McGill 1969). The observation of atheromatous
streaks in aortas of young children suggest that factors in very early life may
be contributing to the increasing problems of coronary heart pathology in
adult life. Information suggests that breast-feeding may have a protective
role. For example, Osborn (1967) measured the coronary arteries of 109
persons up to the age of 20 years and found the greatest reduction of lumen
size in those who had not been breast-fed.

Although dealing with a condition of complex, multiple aetiology, one
cannot but agree with Bradshaw (1973) who speculates that coronary disease or ischaemic heart disease (IHD) may well be essentially the cumulative by-product of the 'pathogenic life-style of Western man': 'IHD is the
biggest single killing disease in Western countries... The chief factors
commonly thought to be involved in producing it are cigarette smoking, lack
of exercise, stress, hypertension, abnormalities of diet (non-breast-feeding
in infancy), and later excess of cholesterol and saturated fat ... obesity and
softness of water.'

Factors in human milk which may have a protective role include the *higher
levels* (Darmady *et al.* 1972) of cholesterol than in cow's milk, the specific
pattern of fatty acids, non-antigenic protein (Davies 1946, Ellis 1974, Ross
and Oster 1975) and the much lower zinc:copper (Zn:Cu) ratio. The last
consideration is based on a study by Klevay (1974) in 47 cities of the U.S.A.
in which the mortality rate from coronary heart disease was found to
correlate with the Zn:Cu ratio in 'market milk', higher prevalence rates
being found with higher ratios. The author emphasizes that the concentration of cholesterol in the serum is greater in experimental animals consuming a high ratio of Zn:Cu. The Zn:Cu ratio in cow's milk is 6–8 times as high
as in human milk, and apparently these levels have existed for several
decades.

Plainly with so many variables in the aetiology and with a very prolonged
period of development, it is difficult to isolate different contributing factors

and their interrelationships. Nevertheless, the crisis situation in indus-trialized countries where more and more people are at risk of an early death is strikingly different from traditional societies, and may be related to the method of feeding the exterogestate foetus, as well as to other factors, such as the subsequent diet, lack of exercise, stress, etc. Certainly, this possibility warrants further scientific, epidemiological investigation (Scott *et al.* 1976).

Also, the rise in incidence of mammary cancer in recent years when breast-feeding has declined suggests the need for further research (Lynch *et al.* 1976).

2. Allergic consequences

In urban Westernized societies, different forms of allergic disease appear to be particularly common, and can occur in response to a wide range of different allergens, including foods (Gerrard *et al.* 1973, Glaser 1966, 1973, Halpern *et al.* 1973). In infants and young children, the commonest food allergy is to cow's-milk protein, or rather to the more than 20 different proteins present. Probable mechanisms responsible have been discussed already (p. 98), with special relation to the considerable active and passive protective effects of breast-feeding.

Current estimates of the commonness of intolerance or allergy to cow's-milk proteins vary with definition used and diagnostic technique, but range from $0 \cdot 4$ to $7 \cdot 5$ per cent in infants in Western communities, with an approximate average of $0 \cdot 5$–$1 \cdot 0$ per cent (Woodruff 1976). The incidence in older children and adults is less certain.

In communities in which cow's milk is culturally a recent introduction to the diet, such as Japan, it has been suggested that allergy to bovine milk proteins may be particularly common (Matsumura *et al.* 1972). The use of soya-protein-based formulas for infants who are allergic to cow's milk has a quite different range of usefulness in communities where soya products are part of the habitual diet.

A recent very detailed and painstaking study by Goldman (1975) has thrown considerable light on the prevalence, aetiology, and prevention of cow's-milk allergy. In his practice, 700 infants with symptoms developing in the first few months of life (Figs. 5.5 and 5.6), who were suspected of allergy to cow's milk, were carefully tested by the 'cumbersome dietary-elimination–oral-challenge method'; lactoglobulin 62 per cent, 'casein' 60 per cent, α-lactalbumin 53 per cent, and bovine serum albumin 52 per cent.. As can be seen from the results, multiple allergens were common. Also, it is notable that β-lactoglobulin and bovine serum albumin are not present in human milk, while, as mentioned elsewhere (p. 38), cow's-milk 'casein' is composed of a different blend of the four main caseins, which in any case each have different physicochemical properties.

From this important investigation, Goldman makes the following conclu-sions:

If one accepts that the incidence of cow milk sensitivity is of an order of $0 \cdot 3$–$1 \cdot 0$ per cent, it would be estimated that 10 000 to 30 000 newborn infants may be affected annually in the United States. Therefore, it is medically important to apply any practical methods that are available for the prevention of this problem. Because many of the major proteins in cow milk are potentially allergenic, it is not practical to produce a processed cow milk which is hypoallergenic. Furthermore, processing of cow milk may possibly lead to the formation of new allergens. Therefore, it follows that cow milk should be avoided during the greatest period of susceptibility.

The treatment of cow milk sensitivity is limited to symptomatic therapy and to the dietary elimination of cow milk. The prevention of these sensitivities in infants could be accomplished by encouraging breast feeding and thereby avoiding exposure to cow milk (Goldman 1975).

In addition, two serious diseases of adult life may be related to sensitivity to cow's milk related to method of infant feeding. According to Agranoff and Goldberg (1974), *multiple sclerosis* has a geographical distribution which is suggestive; and some cases of the syndrome *ulcerative colitis,* appear to be sensitivity responses to cow's milk (Acheson and Truelove 1961). Further epidemiological studies are needed, including detailed considera-tion of methods of infant feeding, including information on 'partial' breast-feeding or 'mixed milk feeding' or neonatal 'complementary feeding', in which cow's milk may have been used.

3. Sudden infant-death syndrome

The sudden-infant-death syndrome, or cot death, is now the leading cause of mortality in babies between one month and one year of life in Western Europe and North America (Camps and Carpenter 1972, Raring 1975). Its approximate incidence per 1000 live births for three countries has been described by Tonkin (1974): New Zealand $1 \cdot 9$, U.S.A. $2 \cdot 0$, and U.K. $2 \cdot 9$. In Britain, 2000–3000 deaths are reported annually (*The Lancet* 1975e). Whether it is increasing in such resource-rich, technically developed coun-tries or becoming more apparent is not certain. Its prevalence in poorer, developing countries is not known, but the impression is that it may be uncommon or even rare.

Seventy per cent of cases of cot death occur between the ages of 4 weeks and 4 months (Fig. 12.5), and during the third and fourth months of life the numbers of children dying are equal to those from all other causes com-bined.

The aetiology is debatable, sometimes covered by the term 'obscure natural causes' in legal phraseology. Possibilities have included suffocation (bed clothes, position, 'overlaying'), infection ('overwhelming virus', intes-tinal endotoxin absorption), allergy (hypersensitivity), and developmental maladjustment (apnoea, immature sleep rhythm). (Tonkin 1974).

A protective effect of breast-feeding has been noted by some inves-tigators, although the details are not usually sufficiently specific (e.g. token

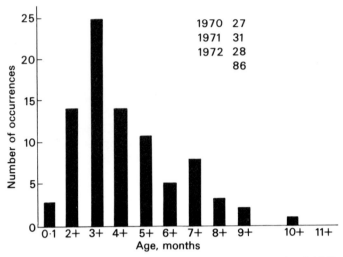

Fig. 12.5. Age of 'cot deaths' in Auckland, New Zealand 1970–72 by complete calendar months. Those under one month of age were all in the fourth week (from Tonkin, S. (1974). In *SIDS* 1974, p.169)

or biological breast-feeding (p. 154), mixed milk feeding, last feed before death, use of semi-solids). For example, Johnstone and Laway (1966) reported that in 46 cases where the type of feeding was definitely known, all but two were given formula based on dried cow's milk. The two exceptions were aged 4 and 8 days. However, the most clear-cut results were those of Tonkin (1974) from Auckland, New Zealand (Table 12.2). Of 86 babies dying with sudden-infant-death syndrome, 83 (96 per cent) were bottle-fed and 3 (4 per cent) breast-fed.

TABLE 12.2   *Sudden-infant-death syndrome and types of feeding in Auckland, New Zealand* (from Tonkin 1974)

	Number	Breast-fed	Artificially fed
'Cot deaths' 1970–2	86	3 (4%)	83 (96%)
1972 controls at 2 weeks of age	800	360 (45%)	440 (55%)
1972 controls at 3 months of age	800	205 (25%)	595 (75%)

The protective effect of human milk and breast-feeding could be related to several potential aetiologies (or to combinations):

Infection. Transplacental immune bodies in the infant's blood are waning at the time that cot death occurs. It has been estimated that these are 75 per cent lost by three months of age, while active immunity has not yet developed. Also, the increased risk of the bottle-fed to respiratory infection is well documented, especially in poorer circumstances.

Gunther (1975) has recently drawn attention to what she aptly terms the neonate's 'immunity gap' which is greater when human milk is not available to the baby, and which coincides with the peak incidence of cot death. In pre-mechanical times in man's early history when infants were brought up without foods prepared 'by grinding, sieving, bottle and teat making, spoons and cups, the period of obligatory mammary feeding imposed by built-in behaviour more than covers that when most cot deaths occur.' Some cases of sudden-infant-death syndrome could therefore be related to silent and overwhelmingly rapid infection in babies during a phase of physiological immunodeficiency, exacerbated by the absence of the immunological protection afforded by breast-milk.

Endotoxaemia. As has been reiterated by Reisinger (1974), sudden death syndrome also occurs in calves, piglets, and other mammalian species, where a major factor in mortality has been considered since the 1920s to be endotoxaemia, with the responsible toxins absorbed from the intestine (Smith and Orcutt 1925). As noted earlier (p.53), the intestinal flora of the breast- and bottle-fed are absolutely dissimilar, with bifidobacteria predominating in the former and with gram-negative organisms, such as *E. coli*, Klebsiella, and bacteriodes, in the latter (Bendig and Haenel 1970). In calves, the main organism responsible for the suggested endotoxaemia is *E. coli*. In the artificially-fed human infant, there may not only be what has been termed a 'dysbiotic' intestinal flora and an absence of local antibodies (notably secretory IgA), but also possibly a parallel immaturity of intestinal reticuloendothelial cells.

Reisinger (1974) considers that the endotoxaemia mechanism is the most likely 'unifying concept' to explain sudden death syndrome in a variety of infant mammals, including man. His conclusion is that: 'Prevention can best be accomplished by breastfeeding, in order to maximize natural immunological defenses and minimize numbers of *E. coli* in the digestive tract.'

Hypersentivity. The age-range of sudden-infant-death syndrome corresponds to a considerable extent with that of the onset of infantile allergy to cow's milk. It is known that deficiency of secretory IgA is found in the secretions of the respiratory tract as well as the intestine. Sudden foetal collapse of an anaphylactic hypersensitivity type can be induced in the newborn of various species, including the guinea pig, by introducing small quantities of foreign milk, such as cow's milk, into the respiratory tract (Gunther 1975, Parish, Barret, Coombs, Gunther, and Camps 1960, Parish, Barrett, and Coombs 1960). A similar process may sometimes occur in the human baby.

Hyperelectrolytaemia. Investigations in a few cases in England have shown very high electrolyte levels, as judged by autopsy estimations of the vitreous fluid of the eye (Emery *et al.* 1974).

Sleep rhythm. Another theory of the causation of cot death is that it may be related to apnoea occurring while the baby is in the process of adjusting to a diurnal sleep rhythm, which presumably does not occur *in utero*. It may be noted speculatively that the normal feeding pattern of 'low-solute, continuous-contact species', such as man, is for several feedings during the night, compared with a lower number with higher-solute feedings (e.g. formula), especially if accompanied by the early introduction of semi-solids (p. 201).

Present opinion seems to suggest that cot death may represent 'a whole range of diseases lumped together' that are attributable to various 'bodily and social ills' (*The Lancet* 1975*e*). Epidemiological factors of significance include a low birth-weight, bottle-feeding, and a low parental income. Recent studies have shown some cases to be associated with minor clinical illness in the previous days, suboptimal medical care, and microscopical lung lesions at autopsy (*The Lancet* 1975*e*).

Despite its still uncertain and probably variable aetiology, the condition often appears to have possible general aetiological points of similarity with 'weanling diarrhoea' (p. 285) — low levels of immunity and an excessive reaction to organisms (or foreign protein) usually considered to be of little pathogenicity in later life. Both conditions appear to be preventable in the majority by breast-feeding.

Recent work by Emery and colleagues in Sheffield, England, has suggested that some cases of cot death can be prevented by rather simple methods of health supervision and advice to mothers on the care and feeding of their babies, particularly breast-feeding (Emery and Carpenter 1974). During the last two years, while these measures were taken, the incidence in Sheffield of sudden unexplained deaths in infants has dropped by about half. Likewise, in Sweden in 1968–72, the rate of sudden infant deaths was only between $0 \cdot 4$ and $0 \cdot 8$ per 1000 live births. Petersson and Von Sydow (1975) speculate that the intensive child supervision in Sweden, with most of the infant population having an average of $11 \cdot 7$ contacts with the doctor or nurse in the first year of life, and the rather high rate of unsupplemented breast-feeding ($30 \cdot 7$ per cent for 2 months) may have been responsible.

4. Infectious consequences

It is frequently believed that the anti-infective properties of human milk are of relevance only to poorly sanitated, resource-poor countries, and not to more affluent industrialized nations under present-day circumstances. Plainly, the active and passive functions of breast-milk increase in significance with low levels of both environmental hygiene and parental education. The dramatic public-health value of breast-feeding in these circumstances was easily seen in Europe and North America in the early decades of the present

nowadays in most of the world, in developing countries. More modern investigations clearly indicated a significant, but less obvious, protective effect of breast-feeding at that time. For example, the investigations of Mellander *et al.* (1959) in Sweden and of Robinson (1939, 1951) in Britain in 1951 gave clear-cut results in relation both to mortality and morbidity (mostly infections) (p. 84). However, very recent reports in the U.S.A. have shown only slight differences in incidence of infections in middle class relatively well-to-do American infants who were breast-fed or bottle-fed (Adebonjo 1972), in part because of improved environmental circumstances. Nevertheless, a study of well-nourished Japanese babies in the city of Iwate showed an incidence of 31·4 per cent with respiratory illness in the bottle-fed compared with 16·0 per cent in those who were breast-fed (Wako 1975). Also, Cunningham (1976) found 'significant illness' — mainly acute lower respiratory infection, otitis, vomiting, and diarrhoea — to be three times as common in bottle-fed babies in rural New York State in 1976.

That the anti-infective properties of breast-milk are more significant than appreciated in industrialized countries is indicated by Downham *et al.* in a recent (1976) paper from Newcastle upon Tyne in England with the positive title of 'Breast-milk protects against respiratory syncytial virus infection'. In this, they report high levels of respiratory syncytial virus neutralizing antibody in colostrum. Of 115 young children admitted with this common infection 8 (7 per cent) had been breast-fed, compared with 167 control children admitted for other reasons among whom 46 (30 per cent) had been breast-fed.

More importantly, it seems probable that the anti-infective value of human milk in relatively resource-rich countries is not currently appreciated because of lack of attention to the age group most protected — the neonate. A basic problem in this regard is that the newborn is too often regarded as an immunological 'isolate', rather than being part of the interacting mother–infant dyad, with human milk supplying continuing oral passive immunity (Gotoff 1974). In fact, some infections in young babies can, in modern terminology, be regarded as 'opportunistic' with the host 'compromised' by the immunodeficiency that results from the failure to supply the host resistance factors present in human milk. Likewise, prevention of neonatal infection is viewed over-exclusively in 'linear' technological terms (p. 225), such as the selection of the form of antibiotic chemoprophylaxis that is least likely to meet with resistant bacteria or the most efficient antiseptic for handwashing by staff.

An apparent recent increase in infections with gram-negative bacteria, particularly in the newborn, is a serious developmentas has been the increased occurrence of septicaemia (Overall 1970, Speer, Taser, Yow, Rudolph, Urtega, and Waller 1976) and of 'hospital staphylococci', often insensitive to many antibiotics (*British Medical Journal* 1974*e*, Overall 1970, Speer *et al.* 1976). Additional risks of neonatal infection in maternity units can occur because of difficulties of sterilizing incubators adequately (Kelsey 1975), because of the separation of the mother and baby that often forms part of the regimen (p. 142), and because of the movement of nursing staff between different infants and mothers. It has become realized that the modern maternity unit's neat regimentation and chromium equipment do not automatically remove infections, and may sometimes increase certain risks.

The rise in incidence of infections with gram-negative organisms, such as bacterioides, has been documented in America and Europe (Cooke 1975). In 1972, 10 per cent of bacteria reported causing septicaemia in Britain were *E. coli*, particularly in cases of septicaemia and meningitis in young babies. Studies in the Karolinska Institute in Stockholm (Winberg and Gothefors 1976) have indicated the protective effect of breast-milk against neonatal septicaemia, seemingly related to the quantity taken.

So-called epidemic neonatal diarrhoea, also due to infection with specific pathogenic *E. coli*, increased in New York from $0 \cdot 73$ per 1000 live births in 1926 to $1 \cdot 79$ per 1000 live births in 1936. Recent outbreaks, such as the one in 1974 in Arizona, indicate that this infection of the newborn still needs consideration (Boyer *et al.* 1975). The protective effect of breast-feeding has been known for decades. Essentially, *E. coli* diarrhoea in the newborn is a bottle-feeding disease.

In addition, the relationship between host resistance provided by human milk and the present-day possibly increasing prevalence of serious virus infections in young infants, especially generalized *Herpes hominis* (Nahmias *et al.* 1970) and cytomegalic inclusion virus, is speculative, but needs investigating. So does the considerable increase in *Haemophilus influenzae* infections in the last 3–4 decades, mainly in infancy and early childhood (*The Lancet* 1974*b*). The role of the interferon and other host resistance factors in human milk may play a part in the control of such virus disease (De Clercq *et al.* 1975).

Of particular and striking importance is the recent recognition that acute necrotizing enterocolitis is a not uncommon condition in special-care units for low-birth-weight babies in the U.S.A., with 1–7 per cent reported to be affected and with a high mortality rate (Barlow *et al.* 1974, Santulli 1974). Current views on aetiology are given elsewhere (p. 93). Infection of a damaged intestinal wall with *Klebsiella* organisms appears to play a major role (Berdon *et al.* 1964, Swarmer and Barnes 1976) (Figs. 12.7–10).

There are striking clinical parallels with the condition known in pidgin English as *pigbel*, mainly an intestinal infection with *Clostridium welchi*, with gangrene of the bowel wall. It occurs in largely vegetarian New Guinea Highlanders, especially children, following rare feasts during which large quantities of partly cooked, possibly infected, pork are eaten, presumably with changes in the intestinal flora (Jelliffe and Maddocks 1964, Radford and Basset 1968). One case of necrotizing enterocolitis with clostridial

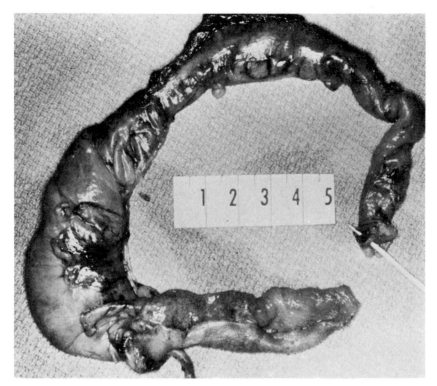

Fig. 12.6. Acute necrotizing enterocolitis, showing multiple perforations including one in the distal sigmoid (scale in cm) (from Santulli, T. V. (1974). *Hosp. Pract.* Nov., p.129)

infection has been reported (Pederson *et al* 1976).

The protective effect of maternal rat milk has been clearly demonstrated in experiments on young rats. A similar protective effect is being sought in human neonates; those fed fresh human milk seem to gain some protection, as studies by Mata (Mata and Urrutia 1971) in Guatemala some years ago showed that colonization of the intestines with *Klebsiella* did not occur in the breast-fed, in whom the intestinal flora was predominantly made up of bifidobacteria (p. 86). It may well be that necrotizing enterocolitis may be partly iatrogenic, related to methods of caring for low birth-weight neonates; it is therefore parallel with retrolental fibroplasia seen some years ago, which was due to oxygen overdosage. It is extremely uncommon in the University Children's Hospital intensive-care unit in Helsinki, where *all* premature babies are given breast-milk (Raiha 1975).

In older infants, it seems possible that diarrhoeal disease of infectious origin is not a condition of the past, as often believed. In the U.K., for example, recent publications (Ironside 1973, Jamieson 1972) have stressed that acute gastroenteritis is still a major cause of morbidity during early

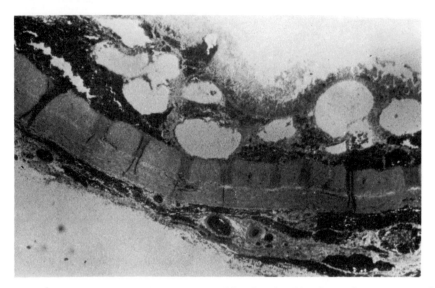

Fig. 12.7. In acute necrotizing enterocolitis, showing histology of acute mucosal necrosis and ulcerations, submucosal haemorrhage, and pneumatosis (from Santulli, T. V. (1974). *Hosp. Pract.* Nov., p.129)

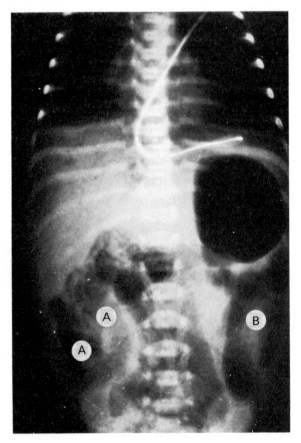

Fig. 12.8. Acute necrotizing enterocolitis: typical roentgenogram of an infant with acute necrotizing enterocolitis, showing pneumatosis of the intestinal wall (A), and ballooning portal vein gas (B) (from Santulli, T. V. (1974). *Hosp. Pract.* Nov., p.129).

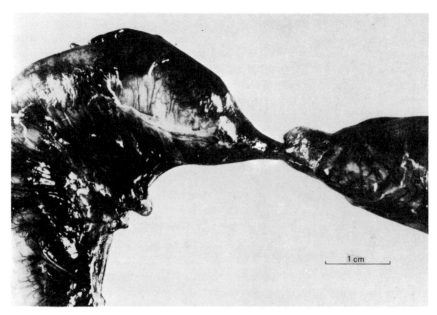

Fig. 12.9. Acute necrotizing enterocolitis, showing benign strictures which may be found among those who survive and require resection to eliminate the obstruction. This surgical specimen taken five weeks after disease shows severe stenosis of the bowel (from Santulli, T. V. (1974). *Hosp. Pract.* Nov., p.129)

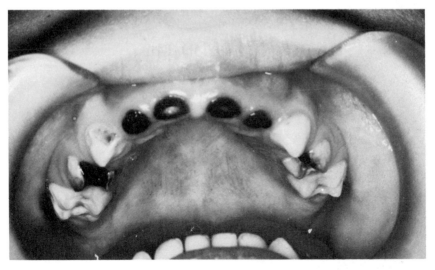

Fig. 12.10. 'Nursing-bottle syndrome' showing rampant caries of the front teeth of the upper jaw, especially the incisors, with no involvement of the teeth of the lower jaw (courtesy of Dr. A. Nizel, School of Dental Medicine, Tubs University, Boston)

childhood, and Addy summarizes the situation as follows: 'over 14 000 infants were admitted to hospital in England and Wales in 1972 with gastroenteritis. Of these, 306 died and the infant mortality rate from this cause was 0·4 per 1000 live births or about 1 in 40 deaths in the first year of life. The disease is much more common in bottle-fed babies. In a recent hospital series from Manchester only one of 339 infants, of whom 170 were under 6 months, was breast-fed.' (D.P. Addy 1976).

The aetiological field has been increased recently by the discovery of the probably causative role of newly recognized viruses, including orbiviruses and rotaviruses, which had previously been known to produce diarrhoea in calves (*British Medical Journal* 1974 *d*, 1975 *b*, Bryden *et al.* 1975, Davidson *et al.* 1975, Flewett *et al.* 1974, *The Lancet* 1975 *a*, Middleton *et al.* 1974, Paver *et al.* 1973, Yamashita *et al.* 1975). Whether human milk has a protective role is not known, but the fact that it has effects against other enteroviruses, including those of poliomyelitis, suggests the need for further investigations. At St. Thomas's Hospital, London, Banatuala (1976) found that of 71 babies who excreted rotaviruses in their stools 41 were bottle-fed, whereas of 51 non-excretors only 12 were bottle-fed.

From a different point of view, the apparent ease of bottle-feeding may lead to careless, ill-controlled preparation of feedings, as regards cleanliness as well as composition (p. 00). For example, in Rome a study showed 42 per cent of bottles and 60 per cent of teats to be microbiologically unsatisfactory, as indicated by substantial findings of coliforms, streptococci, staphylococci, and *Candida albicans* (Darca Simonetti 1972). Similarly an investigation in Sweden (Soderhjelm 1972) found 17 per cent of feeding bottles to be contaminated.

Plainly, infections in the newborn and in young children are still a problem in resource-rich countries, probably more than sometimes appreciated. Equally, they are related to numerous environmental and biological circumstances. However, it is also certain that many old or new infections can be reduced in incidence and mortality by breast-feeding. A relationship of other infections to breast-feeding seems probable and certainly needs further investigation.

5. Emotional consequences

As noted earlier (p. 142), it is difficult to disentangle the numerous factors that can affect mother–child relationships, and even more so the complex forces responsible for subsequent personality development and the psychological balance considered appropriate by different cultures. Nevertheless, a characteristic of the present-day scene is the rise in senseless, destructive, vindictive, purposeless violence all over the world, including the U.S.A. Undoubtedly, many and differing factors and forces must be responsible in various regions — social, psychological, technical, and economic. In this confusion, it is difficult to disentangle the moulding forces that may be operative in the changing pattern of child rearing, including the possible emotional effects of a decline in breast-feeding in recent decades, together with altered patterns of mother–infant somatosensory contact (Lewis and Rosenblum 1974). Similarly, the question of possible relationships with the increasing problem of child abuse needs further investigation (Fomufod *et al.* 1975, Heifer and Kempe 1968, Holman and Kanwar 1975). Certainly, studies in monkeys show that females who have not been adequately 'mothered' in their own infancy are later likely to neglect or abuse their own babies (Rheingold 1963).

With a long-lived species such as man, and with so many variables in each family within each culture and with changes in society occuring rapidly and continually, it is indeed difficult to dissect out all aspects of mother–baby interaction in different cultures and to weigh their relative merits and efforts. Plainly, not all bottle-fed babies grow up to be maladjusted, nor all breast-fed babies to be emotionally balanced citizens.

Recently, Prescott has attempted to correlate behaviour in different communities showing varying degrees of closeness between mother and young child (and other indications of affectionate behaviour), with cultural acceptance of extreme forms of cruelty, such as killing, torturing, or mutilating captured enemies (Prescott and McKay 1972).

The hypotheses of Prescott are far-reaching in relation to the effects on the infant's subsequent development of 'maternal social deprivation' or 'interactional deprivation' — least likely to occur in the permissively breast-fed (Prescott 1970*a,b*, 1972, 1975, Prescott and McKay 1972). He postulates that the human brain is highly immature and vulnerable at birth and that sensory stimulation is necessary for its development — 'like a nutrient'. The effects of somatosensory deprivation in the young infant may be both psychological and anatomical, especially affecting vestibular–cerebellar brain structures, and may perhaps be related to subsequent violence and aggressive activity.

In a recent study, Lynch (1975) found that early separation of mother and baby was one of the main factors associated with subsequent child abuse by the mother concerned. However, she emphasizes the complex and varied aetiology when she notes: 'Child abuse cannot be seen as simply "caused". It is the cataclysmic end of a stochastic process.'

The size of the child-abuse problem is particularly difficult to determine. It is obviously likely to be concealed and the varying syndromes produced may be misdiagnosed medically. It has been suggested that 6 per 1000 babies born may be at risk in Westernized societies (R.Wigglesworth 1975).

Evidence suggests that 'disorders of mothering' or 'bonding failure' can be responsible in part. Barnett *et al.* (1970) have outlined schematically factors that may play an aetiologic role, indicating those which are ingrained (or inherent) and those which may be altered or changed (Table 8.1, p. 152). Most significantly, the last one is mother-and-infant separation (especially perinatal) and other aspects of the hospital regimen. All can be easily altered and can be most satisfactorily arranged by keeping the breast-fed baby by its mother.

6. Alimentary consequences

Dental caries

As noted earlier (p. 110), it has been suggested that a lower prevalence of dental caries in the primary dentition may be in part related to breast-feeding, through uncertain mechanisms. There is a need for better controlled investigations, particularly in view of the high incidence of caries, even in primary teeth, and the many variable factors in its aetiology.

A special form of rampant caries of the deciduous teeth, involving the upper incisors (Figs. 12.10 and 11) has been termed 'nursing-bottle syndrome'. Its incidence on a community basis does not seem to be known, but in a dental clinic in a London borough, investigation of 602 children aged 1–4 years showed 8 per cent to have such rampant caries (Robinson and Naylor 1963). In the U.S.A., Nizel (1975) has estimated that the average child of 4 years of age has $2 \cdot 5$ decayed or filled teeth, whereas with the nursing-bottle syndrome there were 10 or more decayed or filled teeth. At his clinic at the School of Dental Medicine, Tufts University, Boston, 5–10 per cent of the problem patients referred in this non-fluoridated area have this syndrome.

Malocclusion

Varying degrees of malocclusion are common in children in some parts of the world, and especially so in the U.S.A. Malocclusion is also expensive to deal with and severe cases are stated to lead to prolonged ill-consequences, if orthodontic correction with braces is not undertaken. As noted earlier, the different oral and nasopharyngeal mechanics of bottle-feeding compared with breast-feeding may have an aetiological role (Simpson and Cheung 1976). Certainly, in view of the commonness of malocclusion and the cost, discomfort, and time for its correction, additional attention needs to be given to the investigation of details of early feeding practices in its aetiology, with particular reference to breast-feeding and to thumb-sucking.

Intestinal

Alimentary obstruction. The dense curd of cow's milk, made up largely of precipitated casein, calcium, and fat, can lead to 'milk-bolus obstruction' even with modern formulas, if the mixture is prepared without adequate dilution. The condition has been reported to account for 6 per cent of neonatal intestinal obstructions in one leading children's hospital in England. In particular, inspissated formula milk causing intestinal obstruction is a well-recognized problem in the premature infant (Dickson *et al.* 1974,

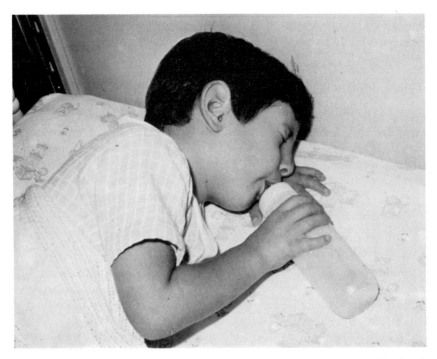

Fig. 12.11. Child sleeping with feeding bottle in mouth, leading to 'nursing-bottle syndrome' (courtesy of Dr. D. Powell, Assistant Professor of Paedodontics, University of Southern California, Los Angeles)

Steiner 1972). In the U.S.A., Majd and Lopresti (1972) have described a case and reviewed 4 others, in whom overconcentrated powdered milk and water produced a radiologically visible coagulum, a 'lactobezoar', in the stomach.

Recently, a case of an infant vomiting a 'curious curd' has been reported. This was due to feeding with warm undiluted Jersey milk, which has a higher fat and calcium content than ordinary cow's milk. A large, rather dense curd formed in the infants stomach, and subsequent vomiting through the oesophagus lead to the curd's sausage-shape (Bennett and Herman 1975, J. P. Davies 1975).

Intussusception. It has been suggested that some cases of intussusception may be related to hypertrophied Peyer's patches and mesenteric lymph glands as part of an antigenic response to cow's-milk protein (Truelove and Jewell 1975).

7. Economic consequences

As noted earlier (p. 134), it is two or three times as expensive to bottle-feed a baby with ready-to-use formula than to feed a lactating mother with the necessary extra nutrients from everyday, less costly foods, as judged by estimates in Los Angeles in early 1975. This would mean, in effect, a saving of about $59–97 in a six-month period. This could be significant in less well-to-do families in poorer communities, but economic analyses need to be much more sophisticated and comprehensive, and to take into account wider present and future financial outcomes (p. 134).

On a national scale, the failure to use human milk is a more considerable waste than appreciated, even in resource-rich countries. For example, in the U.S.A., a bottle-fed baby uses about 150 tins of ready-to-feed formula in six months. With an estimated 3 million births per annum in the U.S.A., this implies not only the loss of large quantities of milk, but at the same time, the use of 450 million usually non-recyclable tins, or about 70 000 tons of tin-plate each year (Jelliffe and Jelliffe 1975 *a*).

RESOURCE-POOR COMMUNITIES

Evidence from a wide variety of different parts of the world all indicates that a decline in breast-feeding performance, associated with early weaning, is appearing increasingly frequently in many resource-poor communities in developing countries, especially in cities and in peri-urban areas (p. 211). As noted earlier (p. 219), the main impetus for this spread appears to be the symbolism of bottle-feeding as the modern, mechanical twentieth-century way of living, together with the efforts of ill-informed health services (p. 233), the pressures of urban slum living (p. 222), forceful and inappropriate advertising of infant foods (p. 225), and usually to a lesser extent only, women having to go out to paid work away from home (p. 238).

The consequences of declining breast-feeding in such communities include all those conditions discussed earlier as occurring in resource-rich areas of the world. However, in addition, the ecological background produces special problems and risks in resource-poor communities.

Ecological background

Economically and technically less-developed, resource-poor communities all over the world are characterized by poverty, demonstrated domestically by small family incomes, and nationally by a low *per capita* gross national product, usually derived mainly from a limited range of agricultural products, with prices widely influenced by fluctuations in the international market (Bryant 1969). Educational levels are usually low, with high rates of illiteracy and with inadequate numbers of technically trained professional staff, including health workers, and with totally insufficient funds or training facilities to make improvements rapidly. At the same time, unemployment and underemployment are widespread, not only among the uneducated, but also for an increasing number of school drop-outs, and in certain countries, for expensively educated university graduates, whose training has often been ill-adapted to the local context and need. The population of underdeveloped countries is largely rural (70 to 90 per cent). However, with the trend towards rapid urbanization (p. 222), the development of spreading shanty towns is increasing (Force 1975). Standards of environmental hygiene, including water supplies and disposal of excreta, are often rudimentary. The age structure shows a high child population, often with approximately 20 per cent of the population below 5 years of age, that is, twice as many as in industrialized countries. Families are large, with consequent increased perinatal and infant mortality rates, due to malnutrition and infectious disease. Despite considerable mortality in early childhood and short life-spans, population size increases rapidly (2–4 per cent per annum). The culture pattern for the rural majority is for the most part traditional and non-Western, with quite different concepts of food classification and beliefs concerning the causation and cure of illness, including malnutrition.

There will be high disease death rates in early childhood, with an infant mortality of up to 10 times, and of 1–4-year-old children 20 to 50 times, those of well-to-do technically developed countries. Malnutrition, particularly associated with dietary deficiency and defective absorption of protein and calories, and interacting microbial and parasitic infections dominate the picture of illness and death in the vulnerable first years of life. Maternal ill-health is widespread, with very high mortality rates in childbirth, made worse by malnutrition, poor environmental surroundings, overwork, and defective prenatal care. There will be a high incidence of low birth-weight immature neonates.

The situation is little related to the tropical or sub-tropical circumstances of most developing countries. The same picture was found in Europe and North America in the nineteenth century and earlier. The principal factors responsible are economic, educational, hygienic, and cultural, and the final community picture as far as mothers and children are concerned is mainly the end-result of the interaction of malnutrition and infections, combined with too many, too frequent pregnancies. Similar, but much less marked, circumstances are also to be found in disadvantaged communities in industrialized resource-rich countries, as, for example, immigrant slum-dwellers in Europe and the U.S.A., migrant workers, and some indigenous peoples (e.g. Indians in America (French 1967, Gonzalez 1972, Grantham-Cumming 1967), aborigines in Australia (Moodie 1973)).

Under these circumstances, the same basic metabolic, biochemical, emotional, and other problems can occur with methods of infant feeding as in resource-rich countries. However, these are entirely subsidiary compared with the large-scale public-health consequences, mainly associated with the poverty, poor hygiene, and lack of education, in the fields of nutrition, infectious disease, population growth, and economics.

1. Nutritional consequences

A wide range of forms and degrees of malnutrition occur in early childhood in resource-poor communities, including some that are general problems throughout the world, such as iron-deficiency anaemia, and some that are more localized geographically and are related to specific dietary patterns, for example, infantile beriberi or vitamin-B_{12} deficiencies in communities consuming polished rice or limited vegetarian diets respectively. However, the group of conditions known collectively as 'protein–calorie malnutrition of early childhood' (also termed 'protein–calorie deficiency disease', 'protein–joule malnutrition', 'energy–protein malnutrition', 'protein–energy malnutrition') constitute the most widespread and serious nutritional public-health problem in the world, involving millions of young children.

The term 'protein–calorie malnutrition of early childhood' was introduced to cover all categories from the severe syndromes of kwashiorkor and nutritional marasmus, to the much more numerous mild–moderate cases (Jelliffe 1959*b*). This group label also has the advantage of emphasizing the importance of calories, both in infant feeding concerned with prevention, and in the treatment of established cases. In addition, the time-span covered by 'early childhood' is designedly imprecise, covering both infancy (exterogestate foetus) and the 1–4-year pre-school period (transitional), as the age-prevalence of the various forms of protein–calorie malnutrition is not the same in different regions of the world and, as noted later, seems to be changing in urban circumstances.

The various syndromes covered by this general diagnostic label can be envisaged as the 'tip of the iceberg' of protein–calorie malnutrition. This emphasizes the fact that the major clinical syndromes of kwashiorkor and nutritional marasmus are easily identifiable, while the much more numerous mild and moderate forms are 'subclinical', need anthropometry for their recognition, and occur much more commonly than the severe syndromes.

Mild–moderate protein–calorie malnutrition
As noted earlier (p. 177), mild–moderate degrees of protein–calorie malnutrition cannot be identified clinically. For this reason, they are usually under-recorded in health services, when the accompanying infection, such as diarrhoea or pneumonia, is given as 'the' diagnosis in the ward or at autopsy. They are usually detected by body measurements (anthropometry), including various combinations of weight, height, and arm circumference (Jelliffe 1966*a*).

Mild–moderate cases of protein–calorie malnutrition have a clear risk of developing into severe syndromes, and they are also more susceptible to infections and have a high mortality from them. Preventive services need to focus on the detection of early cases when still at mild–moderate levels.

In resource-poor countries, poor weight gains and hence mild–moderate protein–calorie malnutrition, occur more commonly in bottle-fed babies

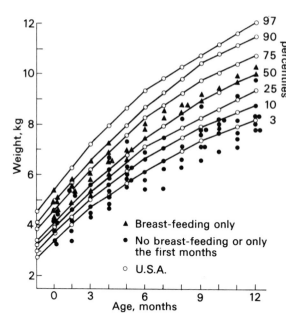

Fig. 12.12. Weight of infants of the Province of Curico, Chile, related to those of the U.S.A., showing lower weight and higher incidence of malnutrition (under 3rd percentile) in children with no breast-feeding (or only the first months) (from Mönckeberg, F. (1969). *Proceedings of the Western Hemisphere Nutrition Congress* II, San Juan, Puerto Rico. S. Karger A.G., Basel.)

than in those who are breast-fed. This has, for example, been reported from Chile (Monckeberg 1970) (Fig. 12.12), from Uganda in East Africa (Welbourn 1958), and many other places. It can best be understood by the four-stage weight curves commonly seen in these circumstances, and described earlier (Fig. 9.8, p. 177). For the first 6 months or so (stage 1), the breast-fed infant usually gains weight well and is protected from infections by maternal antibodies acquired transplacentally. In the second semester of the first year of life (stage 2), growth is often less good, as the diet frequently comprises decreasingly adequate quantities of breast-milk, together with small amounts of largely carbohydrate gruels or pastes. This inadequate and imbalanced nutrient intake is associated with waning passive immunity to infections. The third phase of growth (stage 3) is usually a feature of the second year of life. Breast-feeding may have been stopped, or if lactation is continuing, the quantity of mother's milk received is inadequate for the child's needs, and other foods will often consist of low-protein, mainly carbohydrate foods. At the same time, the non-immune child is exposed to a wide, cumulative and continuing burden of bacterial, viral, and parasitic infections of nutritional consequence (Fig. 12.13), and, in some cases, to the psychological trauma of often abrupt separation from the breast (*sevrage*). During this dangerous phase, the weight curve may remain flat, or decline, and, in severe instances, kwashiorkor develops. In the less affected, subsequently the child's weight gradually starts to increase in the third or fourth years of life (stage 4), although the curve usually remains below standard levels.

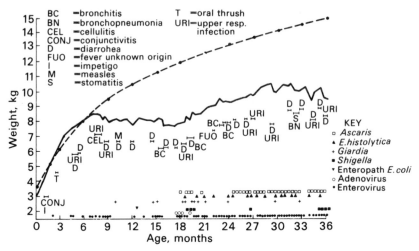

Fig. 12.13. Serial growth curve in Guatemalan village child, showing inadequate weight gain and multiple, repeated infections (from Behar, M. (1975). *Bull. Pan Amer. Hlth Org.* **9**, 1)

Kwashiorkor

In many traditional communities, kwashiorkor is the main severe syndrome of protein–calorie malnutrition (Fig. 12.14), and is principally a disease of the transitional, often the secotrant — that is the child in the second year of life (Jelliffe 1969 *b*). The aetiological background is a transitional diet low in protein (but containing carbohydrate calories), repeated infections (Fig. 12.15), and sometimes the psychological trauma of 'weaning' from the mother's breast (*sevrage*). It is especially likely if the child's main food is a high-bulk staple, such as cassava, with a considerable content of water and cellulose and with a consequent low calorie density, as well as a low protein content. In addition, associated defective intakes of various vitamins and minerals may be present in different combinations.

The time of onset of kwashiorkor may be much earlier, if the baby is not breast-fed for long, if diarrhoea is avoided, and if a high-carbohydrate source of calories is fed to the young infant. Such, for example, was the case in Trinidad 15 years ago when *infantile* kwashiorkor, with a peak incidence at 5–7 months, was reported in babies bottle-fed on arrowroot (*Maranta arundinacea*). This was used as a white, milk-like suspension which was culturally considered very suitable (strengthening and binding) for babies, although virtually a starch devoid of protein (Jelliffe *et al.* 1960).

Breast-milk plays a minor, but still significant, role in the prevention of kwashiorkor commonly seen in the secotrant, as a small protein–vitamin–calorie supplement to a mixed diet from 4–6 months to the second year of life or later (Rohde 1975 *b*).

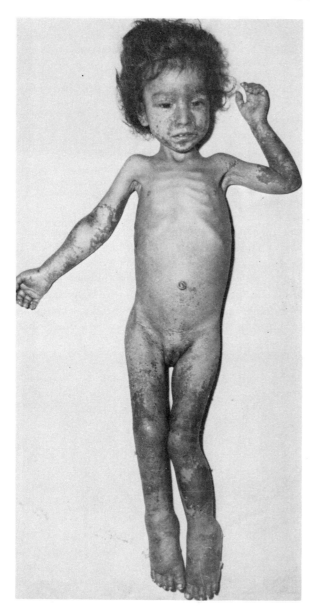

Fig. 12.14. Kwashiorkor in a 'transitional' in Guatemala, showing characteristic oedema, apathy, wasted muscles with presence of subcutaneous fat, and 'flaky-paint rash' (courtesy of the Institute of Nutrition of Central America and Panama)

Nutritional marasmus

This is the other main syndrome of severe protein–calorie malnutrition. It is characterized by growth failure (notably a weight of 60 per cent or less of that expected for age), and very wasted muscles and subcutaneous fat (Fig. 12.16). It is due to a diet that is extremely low in both protein and calories, but is *especially associated with an insufficiency of energy-*

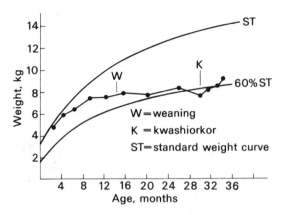

Fig. 12.15. The development of kwashiorkor in an infant in an Iranian village. The weight curve was within the normal range until 8 months of age, then remained almost flat until an episode of diarrhoea precipitated the onset of kwashiorkor at 28 months (from Sadre, M., Emami, E., and Donoso, G. (1971). *Ecol. Food Nutr.* **1**, 55)

containing foods. Marasmus most usually occurs in the first year of life (early marasmus). Low birth-weight babies and prematures are specially at risk. It is mostly due to attempts to rear the baby artificially with dilute, contaminated bottle-feeds, leading to a downward spiral of starvation and infective diarrhoea (Fig. 12.17). It can also occur as a result of inadequate lactation, mainly insufficient breast-milk production because of maternal malnutrition, overwork, and environmental psychosocial stress when diminished

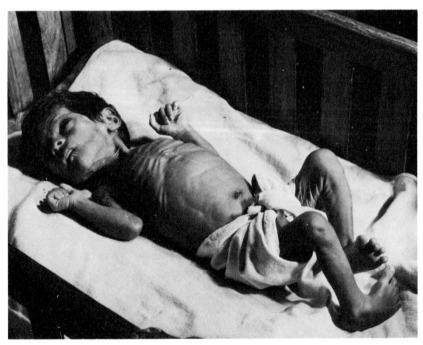

Fig. 12.16. Nutritional marasmus in five-month-old non-breast-fed infant in India, with repeated attacks of diarrhoea (courtesy of the World Health Organization)

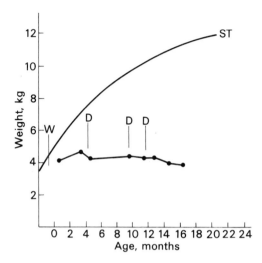

Fig. 12.17. The development of marasmus in a child in Tehran, Iran. Weaning from the breast shortly after birth is followed by flat and declining weight curve, with associated episodes of diarrhoea. W, weaning; D, episode of diarrhoea; ST, standard weight curve (from Sadre, M., Emami, E. and Donoso, G. (1971). *Ecol. Food Nutr.* **1**, 55)

milk output can result. This can occur in rural, traditional communities, as in areas of the New Guinea Highlands (Jelliffe and Maddocks 1964), where there may be a background of poor maternal nutrition, physical over-work, large families, and cultural food restrictions in pregnancy or the puerperium. It is obviously more likely in disruptive disasters, such as in the recent Sahelian drought and famine in parts of Africa, with the associated loss of cattle, diminished agriculture, and movement of population. However, it is more common, and probably increasing, in urban slums and shanty towns where maternal malnutrition and environmental psychosocial stress are likely to be marked (p. 62), and where increased influence from the commercial promotion of formulas (p. 225), and from ill-adapted health services (p. 233) are most prominent (Fig. 12.18).

The aetiology of 'early marasmus' is most usually associated with bottle-feeding with cow's-milk formulas by parents who are unable to purchase more than token quantities and who administer totally inadequately diluted, usually contaminated feeds; over-diluted feedings may also be given because of cultural anxieties concerning the danger of the 'strength' or 'heat' of undiluted milk for young infants (Jelliffe 1968*b*). For example, Kanaaneh (1972) has reported a much higher incidence of infants below the third percentile of weight-for-age in bottle-fed babies than with 'mixed-milk feedings' or breast-feeding (Table 12.3). Also, interference with milk secretion occurs with oestrogen-containing oral contraceptives which can lead to malnutrition ('contraceptive marasmus', p. 121), especially if their effects are compounded by poor maternal nutrition and environmental psycho-social stress.

A usually less common form of this severe syndrome of protein–calorie malnutrition is 'late marasmus', which is characteristically seen in the secot-

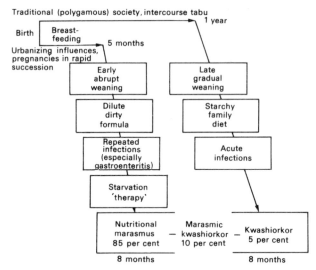

Fig. 12.18. Paths leading from early weaning to nutritional marasmus and from protracted breast-feeding to kwashiorkor (from McLaren, D. S. (1966*b*). *Lancet* **ii**, 485)

rant, or less commonly in the later pre-school child. It is usually due to breast-feeding continued after six months of age *without* additional food ('breast starvation'). Diarrhoea and/or tuberculosis may be present at the time. In addition, marasmus can occur at all ages, including adults, if prolonged source of food shortage occurs, as in famines. Late marasmus may be increasing in some parts of the world, as a result of inflationary price increases.

The protective role of breast-feeding has also been demonstrated by an investigation by Van Duzen *et al* (1969) among the Navajo Indians (Table 12.4). Of 114 children with severe protein–calorie malnutrition with known feeding histories, 76 per cent of infants with marasmus were bottle-fed or received 'mixed milk feedings', as were all children diagnosed as kwashiorkor.

TABLE 12.3   *Weight of six-month-old boys attending mother-and-child-health stations in three Arab villages in Israel, analyzed by feeding schedule* (from Kanaaneh 1973)

	Weight, kg	Below 3rd percentile (Harvard)
Breast-fed (6 months)	7·997	1·6%
Mixed fed (3 months)	7·256	17·9%
Bottle-fed (6 months)	7·040	28·6%

TABLE 12.4 *Relationship between breast-feeding and severe pro-tein–calorie malnutrition in young children (Navajo Indians)* (from Van Duzen *et al.* 1969)

	Marasmus 29 cases		Kwashiorkor 94 cases	
	Number	per cent	Number	per cent
Breast-fed only	5	17	0	0
Breast-fed and other feeds	1	3	0	0
Not breast-fed	15	52	14	93
Unknown	8	28	1	1

Vitamin deficiency
The move from breast-feeding to necessarily inadequate feeding with over-dilute cow's-milk formulas in resource-poor countries increases the risk of two vitamin-deficiency syndromes. First, infantile scurvy is virtually never seen in the breast-fed, presumably partly because sufficient ascorbic acid is received by the baby in mother's milk; but it is a well recognized hazard of artificial feeding, unless supplements of vitamin C in the form of fruit juice or ascorbic acid itself are added, as processed or boiled cow's milk has had its vitamin C (and folic acid) destroyed. Secondly, if, as has been the case in the past, skimmed milk preparations are used for feeding young babies because of their relative cheapness, risks of avitaminosis A, particularly keratomalacia, increase greatly. Fortunately, most dried skimmed milk has nowadays been fortified with vitamin A.

Public-health significance of protein–calorie malnutrition
The size of this public-health nutrition problem is very large, as can be seen by the large number of publications on the subject and by various approximate estimates compiled by workers from different sources of information (Bailey 1975, Bengoa 1974, Bengoa and Donosa 1974, Jelliffe 1975c, and Rao 1974). For example, recent data from Africa emphasize that severe protein–calorie malnutrition (PCM) — that is kwashiorkor and marasmus — is a major problem *in hospitals*. Bailey (1975) has recently reported on hospital data from 14 African countries:

Although the populations served by these hospitals are not necessarily representative of the whole country, in each case the data do indicate that nutritional problems are an important reason for admissions of children, from 65% to over 50% (median 15%) of such admissions being due to malnutrition. Fatality rates among malnourished children are relatively high (21–24%), as is the percentage of child deaths due to malnutrition (median 20%). These figures certainly underestimate the importance of malnutrition among hospitalized children, since only overt cases of PEM (kwashiorkor and marasmus) are included. A study in the Congo revealed that, in addition to the 17% who were frankly malnourished, 70% of children suffered from diarrhoeal or respiratory disorders in which malnutrition played a very important role; 87% of children admitted to hospital were in fact malnourished. Apart from the 20% of deaths directly due to malnutrition, PEM was a contributory factor in at least a further 53% of deaths. Even from the hospital standpoint, therefore, PEM's a major public-health problem.

Also in Africa, the 1–4-year mortality rates which are often used as an age-specific indicator of transitional protein–calorie malnutrition (PEM) averaged 27·5 per cent as compared with 0·9 per cent in U.K. and U.S.A. (Bailey 1975). In 12 countries associated with the Eastern Mediterranean Regional Office of the World Health Organization, community surveys from the late 1960s up to 1972 showed protein–calorie malnutrition to be common, although with very different degrees of emphasis on severe and mild–moderate degrees of malnutrition (Rao 1974) (Fig. 12.19).

Most striking are Bengoa and Donoso's (1974) recent estimates based on community surveys carried out in various parts of the world. Essentially, some 98·4 million children aged between birth and 4 years are considered to be suffering from severe or moderate protein–calorie malnutrition in Latin America, Africa, and Asia (excluding China) (Table 12.5).

TABLE 12.5 *Estimated number of children aged 0–4 years suffering from protein–calorie malnutrition in 3 areas of the world* (Bengoa 1974)

Region	Severe protein–calorie malnutrition	Moderate protein–calorie malnutrition	Total
Latin America	700 000	9 000 000	9 700 000
Africa	2 700 000	16 000 000	18 700 000
Asia (excluding China)	6 000 000	64 000 000	70 000 000
Total	9 400 000	89 000 000	98 400 000

Changing pattern

The neglected attention given to marasmus compared with kwashiorkor was first emphasized by McLaren (1966b). In retrospect, it seems likely that kwashiorkor received major attention because it was the main problem in rural Africa where much early work was undertaken and because of the exotic-seeming nature (and name) of the condition, compared with marasmus. However, in numerous areas of the world experiencing precipitate urbanization, a changing pattern of protein–calorie malnutrition appears to be occurring in young children, often with a probable increase in overall incidence, with a 'move to the left' (towards the first year of life), and with a rising incidence in marasmus. For example, data collected recently by Khanjanasthiti and Wray (1974) in Thailand show marked differences between

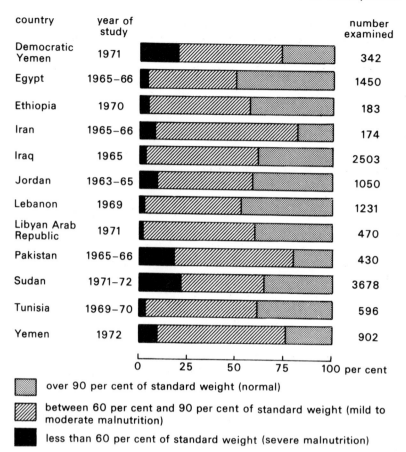

country	year of study		number examined
Democratic Yemen	1971		342
Egypt	1965–66		1450
Ethiopia	1970		183
Iran	1965–66		174
Iraq	1965		2503
Jordan	1963–65		1050
Lebanon	1969		1231
Libyan Arab Republic	1971		470
Pakistan	1965–66		430
Sudan	1971–72		3678
Tunisia	1969–70		596
Yemen	1972		902

0   25   50   75   100 per cent

☐ over 90 per cent of standard weight (normal)

▨ between 60 per cent and 90 per cent of standard weight (mild to moderate malnutrition)

■ less than 60 per cent of standard weight (severe malnutrition)

Fig. 12.19. Prevalence of protein–calorie malnutrition of early childhood in certain countries in or near the Eastern Mediterranean, based on community surveys collected by the World Health Organization (from Rao, K. S. (1974). *Chron. Wld Hlth Org.* **28**, 172)

the nutritional status of young children in Bang Pa-In villages, where breast-feeding was practised, and Makkasan slum, where bottle-feeding dominated (Figs. 12.20 and 12.21). The overall incidence of protein–calorie malnutrition of early childhood was higher, but the more striking finding was the high incidence of third-degree malnutrition (below 60 per cent of standard weight) in the first year of life in Makkasan. In the 0–5 month age-group, over 70 per cent showed some degree of protein–calorie malnutrition and over 15 per cent showed marasmus in the urban slums while in Bang Pa-In villages, less than 10 per cent showed mild–moderate degrees of protein–calorie malnutrition and no children were found with marasmus.

The report of Sadre *et al* (1971) in Iran contrasts findings between Leila, a poor urban area of Iran, and the village of Gorg Taipeh. Twenty-six per cent

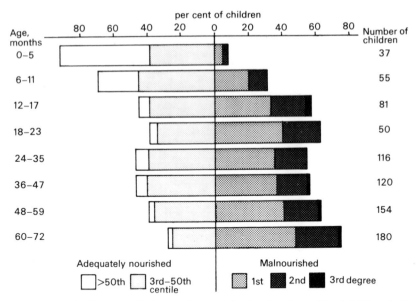

Fig. 12.20. Distribution of adequately nourished and malnourished children in Bang Pa-In villages Thailand (from Khanjanasthiti, P. and Wray, J. D. (1974). *J. med. Ass. Thailand* **57**, 468)

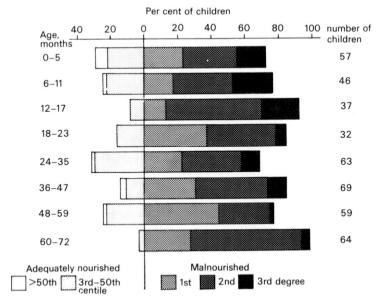

Fig. 12.21. Distribution of adequately nourished and malnourished children in Makkasan slum, Bangkok, Thailand (from Khanjanasthiti, P. and Wray, J. D. (1974). *J. med. Ass. Thailand* **57**, 468)

of babies in the first year of life were marasmic in the urban area, while none were affected in the rural village (Table 12.6).

TABLE 12.6 *Severe protein–calorie malnutrition in young children in urban and rural areas of Iran* (from Sadre *et al.* 1971)

Locality	Age, months	Percentage of the population under 60 per cent standard*
Urban	0–6	26
(Leila-Teheran)	6–24	32
Rural	0–6	0
(Gorg Tapeh)	6–24	17

* Median for weight for age, Harvard School of Public Health

The dominance of marasmus in urban Iran has also been emphasized by Sadre and colleagues: the majority of children admitted to hospital with protein–calorie malnutrition were bottle-fed infants in the first year of life suffering from marasmus. In Teheran hospitals, 42 per cent of the cases of malnutrition were children below one year of age with marasmus. Bottle-feeding was the single most important cause, with dilute contaminated feedings another probable one. The mortality was particularly high in children with malnutrition in the first year of life (Fig. 12.22).

The numerical frequency of marasmus in the first year of life is also indicated by the Latin American study on childhood mortality undertaken by Puffer and Serrano (1973, 1975) under the auspices of the Pan American

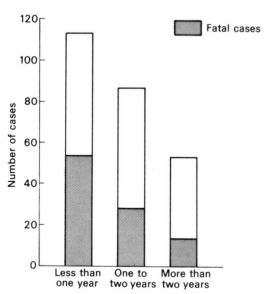

Fig. 12.22. Age-incidence of malnourished children admitted to hospital in the city of Tehran, Iran, showing high morbidity and mortality in those less than one year old (from Sadre, M., Emami, E., and Donoso, G. (1971), *Ecol. Food Nutr.* **1**, 55)

Health Organization. In infants below the age of one year, 26 per cent of the deaths were due to marasmus and 5 per cent to kwashiorkor. Between 1 and 4 years of age, 31 per cent of deaths were due to kwashiorkor and 18 per cent to marasmus.

A few years ago, the following prediction was made by Sadre *et al.* (1971): 'It seems inevitable that ecological factors operating in the developing nations will shift the prevalence of malnutrition from the pre-school kwashiorkor type to the infant-marasmic type.' Although precise figures of changes are not available, this does seem to be occurring. Thus, speaking of *recent* experience in tropical Africa in general, Bailey (1975) concluded in a recent review that 'it is clear that almost everywhere (except perhaps in cassava areas), marasmus is several times more frequent than kwashiorkor.'

A move from the kwashiorkor pattern in a community to a higher prevalence of early marasmus has a special significance. Firstly, the condition has a high mortality (approximately 40–60 per cent), often higher than kwashiorkor (approximately 10–30 per cent). Also, as it occurs in infancy, quite often in the earlier months of life, there is an increased danger of permanent brain damage, as this appears to be the most vulnerable and critical period of brain development as regards damage from malnutrition (Cravioto *et al.* 1974, *The Lancet* 1972 *b*, Winick *et al.* 1972). From the point of view of medical economics, marasmus is often slow to respond to even the best treatment, in which attention has been given to a generous calorie intake. It is therefore an expensive disease financially, capable of 'blocking' a bed in the paediatric ward for weeks, when such exists.

Finally, the condition is preventable with a potentially immediately available food — human milk from an adequately fed mother, which requires no expertise in food technology, no agronomic forecasts, and no apprehensions concerning preservation and distribution.

2. Infections

Bottle-feeding in resource-poor countries increases the risks of certain infections greatly, especially diarrhoeal disease.

Diarrhoeal disease

In the prevailing socio-economic and hygienic circumstances in most technically less-developed countries, bottle-feeding is a highly hazardous process, and most likely to lead to diarrhoeal disease, with a greater severity and mortality in the younger infant ('cholera infantum'). The extent of this problem is indicated by Rohde and Northrup's (1976) estimate of incidences in 1975: 97·5 million episodes in children in the first year of life, and 113·7 million episodes in the second year.

A contaminated water supply, inadequate fuel, poor storage facilities, and usually only one inadequately cleaned bottle and teat make the preparation of uncontaminated, bacteriologically safe feeds extremely difficult, if not impossible, even when attempted for trial purposes by trained health staff in the real-life circumstances of most tropical homes (Phillips *et al.* 1969). Risks become still greater, of course, when feeds are prepared by poorly educated mothers, with little conditioning in the domestic mathematics needed for formula preparation, and with no understanding of the connection between unclean feeding-bottles and teats and the risk of alimentary infection.

Bailey (1975) summarized the situation as follows: 'Bottle-fed infants are particularly prone to diarrhoeal diseases, which are almost unavoidable in the hygienic conditions of households of modest income. A vicious circle sets in: diarrhoeal disease, reduced intake (due to semistarvation or a starvation diet), early malnutrition, reduced appetite, reduced resistance, further diarrhoea.'

Practical difficulties of bottle-feeding in resource-poor countries cannot be over-stressed: 'The possibility of producing an uncontaminated feed is almost nil, when a mother may have only one feeding bottle and nipple, no storage space (let alone electricity or a refrigerator), water from a near-by pond or stream, and because of minimal education, difficulty in following advice on preparing feeds properly. Under these circumstances in very many cases homeopathic doses of milk are administered with large quantities of bacteria — the result is starvation and diarrhoea, too often leading to death with the label of marasmus.' (Jelliffe 1972*b*).

In addition to the much greater cleanliness and lesser bacterial contamination of human milk, a change from breast-milk to cow's milk also means the loss of the active protective, host resistance factors of human milk, which seem particularly designed to counter enteral infections (p. 84).

The protective effect of breast-feeding has been known since ancient times and was dramatic in Europe and North America until very recent decades (p. 183). This has again been re-emphasized recently by Kanaaneh (1972), who recorded the incidence of infants hospitalized for diarrhoeal disease from three Arab villages in Israel in relation to the method of feeding used. Differences were striking (Table 12.7), with contrasting rates of 0·5 per cent for those solely breast-fed for 6 months compared with 24·8 per cent admissions in children bottle-fed only for three months.

TABLE 12.7 *Incidence of infants hospitalized for severe diarrhoea from three Arab villages in Israel analyzed by feeding schedule* (from Kanaaneh 1972)

Method of feeding	Hospitalization, rate per cent
Breast-fed only (6 months)	0·5
Breast-fed only (3 months, <6 months)	2·9
Mixed >3 months	7·0
Bottle only (3 months)	24·8

Often the changing pattern of infant feeding towards cow's-milk formulas is mirrored by the development of 'rehydration centres', which have been evolved to deal with the increased incidence of diarrhoeal disease which inevitably results. As Rohde (1976) comments, fluid–electrolyte malnutrition can be considered as the most acute, prevalent, and fatal form of malnutrition in the world.

In addition, 'epidemic neonatal diarrhoea' (p. 262) appears to be uncommon in traditional tropical circumstances despite much worse environmental hygiene 'as compared with the unphysiological aggregation of neonates in hospital accompanied by exposure to strange *E. coli* strains', and can be negatively correlated with breast-feeding and close mother–newborn contact. However, if a Western-style neonatal regimen is instituted outbreaks can occur. For example, in Jogjakarta in Indonesia, Ismangoen (1957) reported such an epidemic in a hospital nursery. Of the newborn at risk, 2·6 per cent of the breast-fed and 44·4 per cent of the bottle-fed were affected. The apparent recent emergence of this condition in the 1940s in Western countries, the protective effect of human milk, and indeed successful use of breast milk therapeutically in those affected suggest strongly that the neonatal *E. coli* diarrhoea is to a considerable extent a 'bottle-feeding, cow's-milk infection', easily made epidemic when non-breast fed infants are unbiologically removed from their mothers and concentrated away from them in a nursery.

Weanling diarrhoea. The link between 'weaning' — in the sense of the introduction of other foods than breast-milk — and diarrhoeal disease in infancy has been well recognized since the earliest paediatric writings. 'Weanling diarrhoea', as it has been termed by Gordon *et al.* (1963), is, in fact, an epidemiological entity and the end-result of the interaction of several factors during the transitional or weaning period — notably enteral infection (with classical pathogens occasionally, or more usually with a sudden change in intestinal microflora or with large doses of environmental bacterial contaminants), together with the effects of malnutrition (such as diminished intestinal enzymes), and sometimes a diet of indigestible, ill-cooked foods, which may be poorly absorbed or even irritant (Britt *et al.* 1973, Jelliffe 1970).

Recent results from various developing countries endorse this clear-cut association. Strongly affirmative findings were recorded by Gordon *et al.* in their original investigations into weanling diarrhoea in the Punjab, India. The death rate in the first six months was relatively low: 20·6 per 1000 infants of that age per year. In the second six months, it was 53·6 per 1000. In the second year, the rates were 34·8 in the initial half and 7·4 in the second. In the third year, with weaning largely completed, deaths were far fewer — about 2 per 1000 among children of that age. The connection with the weaning process (that is the introduction of foods other than breast milk) was very clear (Scrimshaw *et al.* 1968).

Shigella *infections*

Detailed longitudinal studies have been undertaken by the Institute of Nutrition of Central America and Panama in a village in Guatemala into intestinal colonization by enterobacteria, including pathogens, in small children from birth to 3 years of age. The rates of positive stools and of *Shigella* diarrhoea were minimal during the first nine months of life, but increased rapidly thereafter (Table 12.8), especially after the first year of life when the children had begun to receive a fair amount of food besides their mother's milk. They reached a maximum in the third year, when practically all the children had been completely weaned (Behar 1975).

TABLE 12.8   *Percentages of diarrhoea cases associated with* Shigella *in children 0–3 years of age, by age group, in Santa Maria Cauqué, Guatemala (1964–7)* (from Mata *et al.* 1971).

Age, months	Percentage of diarrhoea cases associated with *Shigella*
0–5	1·2
6–11	9·2
12–17	19·0
18–23	39·0
24–29	41·6
30–35	55·5

The effectiveness of the protection afforded by breast-milk against diarrhoeal disease in less developed countries is endorsed by general clinical experience of tropical paediatricians with breast-fed babies in slum and poor rural areas. It is clinically obvious that they have ability usually not only to survive in the most grossly contaminated environments, but also to grow well in the first months of life with a relatively low incidence of diarrhoea infections. It may be noted that ingestion of environmental microbacteria from dust, dirty hands, and the mother's skin are inevitable under these circumstances, even in the breast-fed infant.

Behar (1975) summarizes the situation in Latin America when he notes 'the high level of contamination found in milk formulas prepared at home and the feeding bottles and other implements used for their administration', and concludes 'that where poor socio-economic and cultural conditions prevail, both early weaning and artificial feeding of infants are dangerous practices. They limit a child's natural defences against enteric infections and greatly increase his exposure to an unhealthy environment.

'Marasmus–diarrhoea syndrome'

Basically, the association of marasmus with diarrhoeal disease in non-breast-fed infants is so frequent in less developed countries that the two interacting conditions can be jointly considered as the 'marasmus–diarrhoea syndrome'.

A 1975 WHO publication (*World Health* 1975) puts the situation clearly:

> The alarming decline in breastfeeding among the low socio-economic urban communities in recent years and its replacement by bottle feeding with unsatisfactory milk substitutes, prepared and given in the most unhygienic manner, have produced serious health problems. The incidence of malnutrition and gastro-enteritis has jumped during the early months of infancy.
>
> The feeding bottle is indeed a dangerous instrument in low socio-economic communities and should be avoided. For supplementary feeding of breast-fed babies the cup and spoon can and should be used.

For example, in one year (1972–3) in the paediatric ward in Freetown Hospital, Sierra Leone, there were 611 deaths: 13·8 per cent diagnosed as protein–calorie malnutrition and 13·8 per cent as gastroenteritis. However, of 137 cases of protein–calorie malnutrition aged 12 months or less, 123 were marasmus and 64 showed gastroenteritis as an associated infection (Robin-Coker and Jalloh 1975).

The interaction of the breast-feeding and episodes of diarrhoeal disease in the aetiology of marasmus is well recognized, for example, in the Navajo Indian study of Van Duzen *et al.* (1969). It is graphically portrayed in a weight-curve of an Iranian infant published by Sadre and colleagues (1971) (Fig. 12.17). Conversely, the increased incidence and severity of diarrhoea in young children with poor nutritional status is evident from longitudinal studies undertaken in the village of Santa Maria Cauqué in Guatemala (Table. 12.9) (Gordon *et al.* 1964).

TABLE 12.9   *The relationship between nutritional status* and the incidence and severity of diarrhoea in children under five years of age at Santa Maria Cauqué, Guatemala (1961–2) (from Gordon et al. 1964)*

Nutritional status	Rate of attack (diarrhoea cases/year/100)	Severe cases (per cent of total)
Normal	98·8	22·9
First-degree malnutrition	164·1	37·8
Second-degree malnutrition	252·5	29·1
Third-degree malnutrition	274·5	40·0

* Gomez classification

The path leading to marasmus in the Lebanon is contrasted with that of kwashiorkor. The former is characteristically urban, with early weaning from the breast and repeated infections (especially gastroenteritis, often treated with starvation). (Fig. 12.18).

Mortality rates

The effects of the method of feeding on mortality in the neonatal and post-neonatal periods, and in infancy are well demonstrated by Scrimshaw *et al.* (1968) (Table 12.10) in data collected in seven Punjab villages in the years 1955–9. The infant-mortality rate in the artificially fed was 950 per 1000 live births compared with 120 in the breast-fed. Differences were in large measure related to diarrhoeal disease and malnutrition, but also include other conditions, such as respiratory-tract infections, whose effects are often underemphasized.

TABLE 12.10 *Deaths and death rates by feeding regimen in seven Punjab villages 1955–59* (from Scrimshaw *et al.* 1968)

Feeding regimen	Newborn infants		Neonatal deaths, 0–28 days inclusive		Postneonatal deaths, 29 days to 11 months inclusive		Infant mortality, 0–11 months inclusive	
	Number	Per cent of total	Number	Deaths per 1000	Number	Deaths per 1000	Number	Deaths per 1000
No food given	16	2·1	16	1000·0	—	—	16	1000·0
Artificial feeding from birth	20	2·6	15	750·0	4	200·0	19	950·0
Breast-fed at birth	739	95·3	34	46·0	555	74·4	89	120·4
Total	775	100·0	65	83·9	59	76·1	124	160·0

The recent 11-country Inter-American Investigation of Mortality in Childhood organized by the Pan American Health Organization showed that 'nutritional deficiency' was the most serious health problem, with nutritional marasmus having high rates in 2–6-month-old babies and with 'protein malnutrition' (kwashiorkor) having its peak at 12–17 months of age. Malnutrition was the underlying cause of death in 7 per cent of all children and associated cause in 43 per cent. Associated disorders of greater importance were infectious diseases, especially diarrhoea and measles, and low birth-weight. Among breast-fed infants, lower proportions of deaths were due to diarrhoeal disease and 'nutritional deficiency' than in those never breast-fed (Puffer and Serrano 1973).

Figures obtained in the city of São Paulo in the course of this investigation showed the highly significant relationship between lack of breast-feeding and both diarrhoeal disease and 'nutritional deficiency' (Tables 12.11–12).

TABLE 12.11   *Deaths from diarrhoeal disease as underlying cause according to breast-feeding of infants dying at 1–5 months of age, São Paulo* (from Puffer and Serrano 1973)

	Per cent of deaths	Total number
Breast-fed, never weaned	31·4	16
Breast-fed one month or longer	49·2	155
Breast-fed less than one month	49·5	242
Not breast-fed	47·3	149

TABLE 12.12   *Infant deaths (1–5 months) from nutritional deficiency as underlying or associated cause according to breast-feeding, São Paulo* (from Puffer and Serrano 1973)

	Per cent of deaths	Total number
Breast-fed, never weaned	35·3	18
Breast-fed one month or longer	45·4	143
Breast-fed less than one month	52·1	255
Not breast-fed	48·9	154

Overall in some developing countries, the infant-mortality rate has dropped in recent years. Such figures are difficult to analyze and need to be disaggregated into social groups, into rural or urban dwellers, into causes of death, and into other factors, including feeding practices. According to Bengoa (1974), at least in some Latin American countries, this has been accompanied by higher mortality rates from nutritional deficiency disease. Major factors in producing these lowered infant-mortality rates are the more widespread availability of effective management of infectious diseases, such as antibiotics in pneumonia and 'sepsis', rehydration in diarrhoeal disease, and immunization. Such services reduce mortality from infectious diseases which were often the final episode in poorly-nourished children. As a result, it has been suggested that some parts of the world may be moving from 'the era of great mortality to the era of increasing numbers of "surviving children" with some handicaps in their biological and social development' (Bengoa 1974); or to a situation characterized by 'death of the weakest and survival of the weakened' (Helsing 1976).

Disaggregation of data on infant-mortality rates is not usually available, and needs to be undertaken more, when possible. For example, urban infant mortality in Brazil may be increasing, at least as reflected by the city of São Paulo where the infant-mortality rate has risen: 1961 — 60·2 per 1000 live births; 1963 — 69·9; 1967 — 74·3; and 1969 — 83·0 (Shellard 1975). This trend seems to parallel the rising infant mortality in the poor in towns in Europe at the beginning of the Industrial Revolution (p. 194).

Analysis by feeding pattern also needs to be made, as in the preceding pages. The protective effect of breast-feeding was noted by Plank and Milanesi (1973), who found that the infant-mortality rate was much higher in bottle-fed compared with wholly breast-fed babies in rural Chile.

Otitis media

Otitis media is commoner in bottle-fed babies in the first six months of life. This has been noted in the U.S.A., but seems particularly marked in certain communities, such as Eskimos. Among the latter, a study of 120 infants showed 65 per cent to have had at least one episode (Schaefer 1971 *b*). The association seems clear, but the aetiology is debatable. It may be in part allergic, infectious (perhaps related to lowered host resistance), or 'positional', that is, resulting from the flow of milk from the pharynx to the middle ear, via the short, relatively straight Eustachian tubes of early infancy, especially if a propped bottle is used.

Chronic otitis media, with a persistently discharging perforated ear-drum is often a common problem in resource-poor communities. This seems to be especially the case among Eskimos in Alaska and Northern Canada (Hildes and Schaefer 1973). For example, in 489 children aged to 10 years, 76 per cent had had one or more attacks of otitis media, perforation or scarring of the ear-drum was present in 41 per cent, and hearing loss in 16 per cent. In this group, 78 per cent of the first attacks of middle-ear infection had occurred in the first two years of life (Kaplan *et al.* 1973). In another study in a similar Eskimo community, otitis media was found to have affected 15–30 per cent of children, compared with 3–5 per cent in the U.S.A. or Britain (Johonnott 1973). In fact, the condition seems to be so common in infants and young children that it is reported not to be considered as a disease (Maynard 1969).

Acute middle-ear disease can be related to many factors. However, Schaefer has noted an inverse relationship between the incidence of chronic middle-ear disease and the duration of lactation in 'traditional' and 'acculturated' Canadian Eskimos, with a minimum incidence found in those breast-fed for more than 12 months (Schaefer 1972) (Table 12.13). The preventive effect may be related to protection against infection, absence of allergy, or the impossibility of a positional aetiology, as it is not possible to 'prop a breast'.

TABLE 12.13 *Incidence of severe chronic otitis media in traditional living and 'acculturated' Canadian Eskimos related to past infant feeding* (from Schaefer 1972)

	Breast-fed, per cent	Bottle-fed, per cent
Traditional	0·8	8
Acculturated	3·7	29·3

3. Population growth

The contraceptive effect of biological breast-feeding (p. 118) and consequent lactation amenorrhoea is now well recognized, proven, and with an understandable endocrinological explanation (p. 118). However, the dimensions of this effect has only recently been appreciated, largely as a result of the work of Rosa (1976c). In fact, the 'couple–years protection' provided by breast-feeding in developing countries may be as high as 35 million annually (Table 12.14). This provides one-third more fertility protection than afforded by current family-planning programmes.

TABLE 12.14 *'Couple–years protection' provided by breast-feeding in developing countries** (from Rosa 1976c)

Area	Total population	Fertility protection from breast-feeding	Annual birth rate per 1000	Couple–years protection
Rural	1 378 500 000	8 months	40	31 300 000
Urban	459 500 000	4 months	30	3 400 000
Total	1 838 000 000	—	—	34 700 000

* Excluding China, North Korea, North Vietnam, and Cuba

Conversely, a widespread community change from breast-feeding to bottle-feeding can be expected to have a demographically significant anticontraceptive effect. Thus, in regions of high fertility and of successful, unsupplemented, and prolonged lactation, such as in rural parts of Taiwan (Jain 1970) or the Philippines (Del Mundo and Adiao 1970), lactation contraception may be responsible for a reduction of as much as 20–5 per cent of expected births. The effect of declining breast-feeding on birth interval has been strikingly illustrated by Hildes and Schaefer (1973) in the Igloolik Eskimos (Fig. 12.23). Older women aged 30–50 years had breast-fed their babies for 2–3 years, with the next conception occurring 20–30 months later. In young women (17–29 years old), bottle-feeding was increasingly common and the next conception occurred 2–4 months after

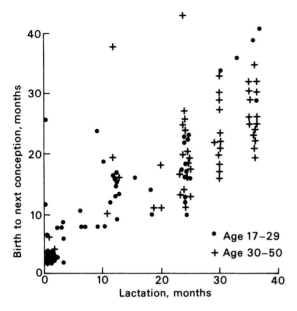

Fig. 12.23. Correlation of length of lactation with period from birth to next conception, contrasting shorter periods in younger women aged 17–29 years and in older women aged 30 years: Igloolik Eskimo population (from Hildes, J. A. and Schaefer, O. (1973). (*J. human Evol.* **2**, 241)

the birth of the previous child. Schaefer (1971*a*) is of the opinion that the main factor increasing the birth rate from 40 to 64 in the Canadian Eskimos with whom he worked was the introduction of bottle-feeding. The increase in birth rate could even be correlated with the proximity to the nearest trading centre providing tinned milk.

As is well known already, the world's most extreme increases in population are envisaged for less developed countries where resources are least available. However, such predictions do not usually take into account the anti-contraceptive effects of declining breast-feeding in accelerating such population increases.

The increase in the number of births and in family size that can occur following removal of the biological child-spacing effect of breast-feeding plainly has impact on food available *per capita*; the pressure on limited health and social services, housing, and employment increases the potential for malnutrition in families, both because of the large number of individuals and because of too closely spaced childbirths, with nutritional ill-effects for both mother and offspring. In newly urbanized families in shanty towns and slums, an increase in the 'diarrhoea–marasmus syndrome' may be predicted as another ill-consequence.

However, as Rosa (1976*a*) emphasizes:

Breast-feeding is more a reason for contraception than an alternative to it, since a new pregnancy is the most common ultimate reason for discontinuing breastfeeding in developing countries. Usually about the sixth month following delivery, supplemental infant feeding is started, reducing lactation and the fertility protection provided by it and increasing the likelihood of conception. Under these circumstances the nursing infant, the weary mother, and the baby just conceived all face a nutritional crisis which undoubtedly contributes to the high infant-mortality rates that prevail in countries with high birth rates. Kwashiorkor, for instance, is a West African word which means 'displaced, or deposed, child'. A basic issue is to devise a program in which the contraceptive effect of breastfeeding can be reinforced by inexpensive, although acceptable, technological methods, without impairment of the yield or composition of human milk, and preferably even with their enhancement.

4. Economics

Comparisons of breast-feeding or bottle-feeding anywhere need to consider economic costs (p. 132). This is plainly particularly so in less well-to-do communities all over the world, *including disadvantaged groups in resource-rich countries.* Breast-feeding has economic significance both on a family and on a national basis. Some aspects have been considered earlier (p. 132), but the broader national implications need further emphasis.

For example, Berg (1973) has calculated the possible effects of the changing scene in Chile. In this country 20 years ago, the majority of mothers breast-fed their children beyond the first year. By 1969, the figure had dropped to 6 per cent with only 20 per cent of the babies being nursed for as long as two months. The potential breast-milk production in Chile in 1950 was 57 700 tons, of which all but 2900 tons, or only 5 per cent, was realized; by 1970, 78 600 tons or 84 per cent of 93 200 potential tons, was unrealized. The output of a herd of 32 000 Chilean milk cows would be required to compensate for the 1970 loss of breast-milk.

In other parts of the world, similar losses can be estimated. Thus, in Kenya a few years ago, the 11·5 million dollars annual loss in breast-milk is equivalent to two-thirds of the national health budget or one-fifth of the average annual economic aid (Berg 1973). Likewise, in the Philippines, 31 per cent fewer mothers nursed their babies in 1968 than a decade earlier. The $33 million waste for that year is nearly double the $17 million loss in 1958. In Singapore between 1951 and 1960 there was a decrease from 71 per cent to 42 per cent of children in low-income families breast-fed for at least three months (Wong 1971). This implied an annual loss of U.S. $1·8 million (Berg 1973). More recently, analysis by Reutlinger and Selowsky (1975) estimates the cost of replacing breast-milk with powdered milk in India, Philippines, and Mexico (Table 12.15).

Berg (1973) has also emphasized the particular importance of declining lactation in urban areas. He has noted that an estimated 80 per cent of the world's babies are born in developing countries, about one quarter in urban areas. Therefore, the estimated 27 million mothers in urban areas of developing areas are potential producers of milk. If 20 per cent of these women do not breast-feed, the loss to the developing world is $365 million. If half of the other urban mothers do not continue to breast-feed after the first six months, the total loss reaches $780 million.

TABLE 12.15   *Cost of replacing breast-milk at world prices of powder milk — India, Philippines, and Mexico, urban areas* (modified from Reutlinger and Selowsky 1975)

Item	Age, months			
	0–6	7–12	13–18	19–24
India				
Total population in age-group, × 1000	10 538	9924	9626	9436
Corresponding urban population (18·8%), × 1000	1981	1865	1809	1774
Cost of milk replacement, × million U.S. $	23·7	12·7	12·3	4·9
Philippines				
Total population in age-group, × 1000	764	749	734	719
Corresponding urban population (23·2%), × 1000	177	173	170	167
Cost of milk replacement, × million U.S. $	2·1	1·2	1·1	0·5
Mexico				
Total population in age-group, × 1000	929	922	912	905
Corresponding urban population (61·8%), × 1000	574	569	563	559
Cost of milk replacement, × million U.S. $	6·8	3·9	3·8	1·5

Very recently, Rohde (1975b) in Indonesia has computed the economic value of human milk for children in the second year of life ('secotrants' Jelliffe 1969b), a previously neglected aspect of the subject. Results of this analysis show the sum of $87 million per year for this large country alone.

The dimensions of the food loss that can result from widespread declines in breast-feeding have not been fully appreciated by the politician, the national planner, the paediatrician, or the nutritionist. In fact, it has been suggested that at the present day the yield of human milk in developing countries is about one-quarter of that produced by cows. For example, past food balance-sheets showing food imported, exported, and produced within a country have never considered including human milk. In fact, these important ledgers demonstrating, as it were, profits and losses, and balances and reserves of food availability on a national basis, have until now been concerned entirely with foods grown or processed. Perhaps characteristically of modern man such a fundamentally biological food as human milk has received no consideration.

Other macro-economic considerations include the rapidly *rising* cost of dairy production, the world grain, soya-bean, and oil crisis, the increasing international difficulties with regard to currency exchange, the need for all countries to conserve limited relatively hard currency, and the general rising cost of manufactured goods — including processed foods — from industrialized countries. Under these circumstances, the need to import large quantities of costly processed cow's-milk-based breast-milk substitutes (and expensive commercial weaning foods), has to be scrutinized carefully and the feasibility reviewed. It seems more likely that governments will increasingly have to adjust their import expenditure to necessities and priorities, and, in relation to infant foods, to screen out all imports, except those which are really needed in the local economic, cultural, and developmental priorities of the particular country.

Family and national costs due to childhood malnutrition also require consideration (Cook 1968). This is a complex undertaking, but an analysis by Cook (1971) showed that in 1968 in the small island of Jamaica the financial loss due to child wastage and treatment of malnutrition could be 'conservatively estimated to be $1·5 million each year'. Probably about one-third to one-half of this could be related to the nutritional and infective consequences of inadequate lactation in children in the first year of life. Lastly, the economic cost to the state of damaged 'survivors' of malnutrition in early childhood is difficult to estimate, but must be considerable in, for example, possible mental inability to gain sufficient benefit from school education and contribute to national development.

Until recently, the current world decline in breast-feeding has been a strange and silently unappreciated phenomenon. Quite correctly, there is global concern with developing new sources of protein food, with improving the quantity and quality of existing foods (as, for example, by the genetic selection of improved corn), and with devising what are hoped to be low-cost processed weaning foods. However, at least as much attention needs to be given to the disappearance of human milk (and to making the best of other foods already available in the village), and to investing as much in the way of funds and ingenuity in trying to devise programmes to deal with this major nutritional retreat, as with other programmes designed to improve the problem of childhood malnutrition.

Conclusion

Bottle-feeding in the type of circumstances found in rural and urban areas of resource-poor, less developed countries is extremely difficult, if not impossible, to undertake adequately because of extremely small purchasing power, defective environmental hygiene, and low levels of maternal education. Under such circumstances, infants usually receive dilute, contaminated feeds containing homoeopathic doses of nutrients and massive quantities of bacteria. The resulting effects on child health, particularly the marasmus–diarrhoea syndrome, were well recognized in similar circumstances in the Industrial Revolution in the past in Europe and North America. Moreover, the main problems of maternal and child health in general in developing countries in both mothers and their young offspring can be summarized as a 'formula':

maternal and child health $\propto$ nutrition $\times$ infection $\times$ hazardous, excessive pregnancies

When breast-feeding is replaced by the necessarily inadequate bottle-feeding found in developing countries, *all of the factors* in this equation are affected adversely for biological and economic reasons. Nutrition deteriorates, infections (particularly diarrhoeal disease) increase, and pregnancies become more frequent, closely-spaced and hazardous, with greater risk of maternal mortality.

In fact, as emphasized by both Mönckeberg (1970) and Bengoa (1974), for bottle-feeding to be 'successful' in the sense of producing satisfactory infant growth and survival, it is absolutely necessary to have an adequate economic, hygienic, and educational infrastructure. This accounts, for example, for the ill-effects of bottle-feeding in Chile, even when free powdered milk was made easily available at health services, but education and environmental health remained unchanged. Conversely, it helps to explain why bottle-feeding was undertaken uneventfully by Pakistani immigrant mothers to Britain in recent years (Aykroyd and Hussain 1967, Hussain and Wadsworth 1967). Without such an infrastructure, bottle-feeding with cow's milk cannot be undertaken by the vast majority in less developed resource-poor parts of the world and methods of trying to decelerate the present trend away from breast-feeding must be considered as a major world public-health concern.

The size of the public health problems related to the availability (or otherwise) of human milk are huge, increasing, and almost completely

TABLE 12.16 *Some preventive advantages of biological young-child feeding*

	Developing areas	Industrialized areas
1. Nutrition	Marasmus and diarrhoeal disease (10 million cases per year)	Infantile obesity (1 million cases per year) Metabolic overload syndromes of newborn
2. Infections		Necrotizing enterocolitis (? 3500 deaths per year)
3. Allergy	———	Cow's-milk allergy of infancy (100 000 cases per year)
4. Child-spacing effect	Highly significant (more protection then technological programmes)	Slight (with widespread technological contraceptives)
5. Economic consequences	Billions of dollars annually needed for breast-milk substitutes	

unappreciated. While different problems occur in resource-poor and resource-rich countries, all of the conditions mentioned are universal and world-wide, but are found in very different proportions. For example, malnutrition and diarrhoeal disease affect children in disadvantaged communities in the resource-rich countries; conversely infantile obesity and cow's-milk allergy affect the Westernized élite minority in resource-poor nations.

In less technically developed, resource-poor countries, Bengoa (1974) has estimated that there are 9·4 million cases of severe protein–calorie malnutrition annually. It is not known how many are suffering from kwashiorkor or from marasmus. Assuming, conservatively, that only half have marasmus related to bottle-feeding or to inadequate lactation, this means that 4·7 million children could be protected wholly or in part by breast-feeding by adequately fed mothers. The numbers of children with diarrhoea associated with bottle-feeding in such countries is difficult to calculate. However, the condition is common and if a somewhat higher figure (5·3 million) than for marasmus is postulated, then the partial or complete protection of some 10 million infants annually may be available. With an assumed 30 per cent mortality, this would mean 3 million lives saved, and with an arbitrary figure of $100 per child for treatment, a yearly expenditure of one billion dollars avoided.

Parallels between the causation of the main nutritional syndromes of early childhood in different parts of the world can be clarified by delineating the main effects of protein–calorie malnutrition at different stages of early life — foetus, exterogestate foetus, and transitional (Figs. 12.26–30), and their relationship to maternal nutrition and breast-feeding.

In technically more developed, resource-rich countries of the world, there are more than 11 million births annually, and the partial or complete preventive effect of breast-feeding can also be highly significant in these communities. If obesity is assumed conservatively to occur in 10 per cent of infants, then an annual total figure of 1·1 million babies could receive protection if they were breast-fed and if semi-solids were introduced at 4–6 months of age rather than earlier. If a similar incidence of cow's-milk allergy throughout resource-rich countries is found as in the U.S.A. — that is about 1 per cent of newborns — then the avoidance of cow's milk in the early months of life by breast-feeding could prevent (or, at worst, delay the onset of) some 100 000 new cases of infantile cow's-milk allergy *each* year.

If about 4 per cent of newborns are of very low birth-weight, and if a minimum figure of 1 per cent incidence of enterocolitis is assumed to occur among them, evidence suggests that the use of human milk might prevent 4400 cases annually or, with 80 per cent mortality, might avoid 3520 neonatal deaths. If recent evidence of an at least partial protective affect of breast-feeding against cot death is considered to be at only a 10 per cent level of effectiveness, and if the lower annual incidence figure for the world given by Tonkin (1974) is accepted (200 000), breast-feeding may lead to the saving of 20 000 sudden, unexpected, and especially emotionally traumatic infant deaths. The potential role of breast-feeding and human milk can also be noted in relation to the 5000 cases of neonatal hypocalcaemia seen annually in Britain.

These figures are, it must be stressed, approximate and, in some countries, must be an underestimate. Likewise, the public-health value of breast-feeding and human milk in relation to the avoidance of various severe man-made metabolic stresses in the newborn and in early infancy, especially in premature babies, such as amino-acidaemia* and hypernatraemia, is difficult to calculate, as prevalence figures for these conditions are not available. Similarly, the partial protective value of breast-feeding in iron-deficiency anaemia is difficult to express numerically, especially in a condition of such complex aetiology.

It is increasingly realized that infant nutrition may affect subsequent health in both school-children and adults. Breast-feeding may protect against some cases of adult obesity rooted in infantile obesity. The effect of infant feeding practices, including breast-feeding, on atheroma, ulcerative colitis, multiple sclerosis, and cancer of the breast is in need of further investigation.

From a family-planning point of view, breast-feeding currently affords 35 million couple–years protection annually (Rosa 1976c). Improvement of lactation in less developed countries would increase this. Further decline would lead to a loss of this protection, an increase in birth rate, and the need for funds and facilities to increase family-planning services.

Economically, as noted earlier, Berg (1973) has calculated that if only one-fifth of the mothers in urban areas in developing countries do not breast-feed, this means a direct loss of $365 million per year to those nations. What is more, this figure has to be *doubled*, at least in theory, as it would have to be matched by a similar expense on purchasing breast-milk substitutes.

The ill-consequences of bottle-feeding rather than breast-feeding are widespread, of very large dimensions, and can involve millions of infants throughout the world. In the 'adaptive and maternal and child health services' (p. 356) urgently required in all countries, breast-feeding obviously should play a major role. There is no need for a 'double-standard approach' to infant feeding (Hirschorn 1976, Jelliffe 1976a). In practical terms, breast-feeding is a key prophylactic against both marasmus *and* infantile obesity, against infective diarrhoea *and* acute necrotizing enterocolitis, as well as the perfect promoter of physical growth and emotional development.

---

* Using the suggested figure of 0·5 per cent of all bottle-fed newborn (Mamunes *et al.* 1976), up to 15 000 neonates with transient tyrosinaemia may be expected annually in the U.S.A., if none are breast-fed.

13 Trends and influences

Stewingly warm in their cushion of peritoneum and gorged with blood surrogate and hormones, the foetuses grew and grew. . . With a faint hum and rattle the moving racks crawled imperceptibly through the weeks and the recapitulated aeons to where, in the Decanting Rooms, the newly unbottled babes uttered their first yell of horror and amazement.

Brave New World, Aldous Huxley (1932)

I do not believe in the noble savage and I am not advocating any brand of bucolic romanticism. I do not want to put an end to machines, I only want to remove them from their position of mastery, to restore human beings to a position of equality and initiative.

The Pursuit of Loneliness, Philip Slater (1970)

The present world situation with regard to the feeding of young children has itself come about as a result of many socio-economic developments and cultural changes. Most have been unplanned, especially the dominance of Western influences in philosophy and practice, including those resulting from the dramatic technological successes of the past 100 years and from the process of urbanization itself. The acceptance or rejection of breast-feeding seems to have been mainly influenced by perceptions of convenience, family economics, and, above all, the community's attitude to the process, as being old-fashioned or modern, culturally acceptable or not. The success of those wishing to breast-feed appears to be mainly the outcome of a balance between psychological factors (p. 225) and methods of social support by the community (p. 175), mediated physiologically through effects on the let-down and prolactin reflexes (pp. 17, 19). The role of severe maternal mal-nutrition and environmental psychosocial stress in inadequate lactation seems to be increasing, especially in shanty towns and slums (p. 62).

The precipitate declines in breast-feeding in many urbanized com-munities in recent years, and the increase in prevalence quite rapidly pro-duced by the influence and activities of such women's organizations as La Leche League (Fig. 13.1) indicate that the pattern of breast-feeding is labile and changeable by spontaneous social forces and, so far on a limited scale, by organized action.

Before considering possible practical programmes (p. 346), it will be help-ful to review some of the social forces and trends which may be likely to effect both community behaviour and the attitudes of professional groups (such as health personnel, nutritionists, economists, national planners, and administrators) with regard to breast-feeding in coming years. Apart from anything else, effective programmes will need to reinforce positive trends and attempt to neutralize, circumvent or counteract negative influences.

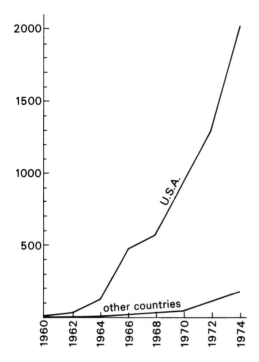

2000 —

1500 —

1000 —

U.S.A.

500 —

other countries

1960 1962 1964 1966 1968 1970 1972 1974

Fig. 13.1. Growth of La Leche League in the period 1960–74 in the U.S.A. and other countries

The selection and classification of social forces given here which favour breast-feeding or otherwise are an oversimplification, with other classifications possible. The significance and magnitude of such social forces obviously will vary from one part of the world to another, depending on many circumstances, such as degrees of Westernization and urbanization, and the availability of different types of resources. Moreover, the unaltered continuation of existing social influences need not necessarily occur. As Toffler (1970) notes, sudden, often dramatically unpredictable and widely pervasive changes in ways of life and patterns of human organization are already occurring almost uninterruptedly and can be expected to continue to do so. These include the development (and discarding) of technologies, changes in priorities with regard to politics, economics, and world resources, and social psychological pressures as culture patterns and priorities alter. Nevertheless, at the present time, the following overlapping, interacting social forces currently seem to favour either breast-feeding or bottle-feeding, though degrees of emphasis vary from society to society, and from culture to culture.

SOCIAL FORCES FAVOURING BREAST-FEEDING

1. Naturalism

In recent years, in some industrialized countries, especially the U.S.A., a large number of manifestations have developed as a form of disquiet or protest against the overmechanization, impersonality, and 'unnaturalness' of modern urban life. These new life-styles and ideologies, loosely termed 'naturalism', have ranged from extreme to minor, from the bizarrely irrational to understandable ecological concern. Indicators of protest have ranged widely through such social phenomena as the hippies, the 'flower children', nudism, and food faddism of innumerable varieties. With regard to the diet, apart from anything else, 'the consumer is in search of symbols to remind him of his Nature' (Périssé 1972). However any of these particular individual movements may be viewed, and however transient or long-lasting their effects, they seem at core to mirror an understandable concern by modern urban man to develop a benign cultural, psychological, and physical symbiosis between his over-dominant technology and his neglected biological and traditional inheritances — in fact, a 'curvilinear compromise' (Jelliffe and Jelliffe 1975e) (p. 225).

Child-rearing
In seeking for a balance in which man benefits by technology, but is not dominated by it, the role of more biological and traditional methods of child-rearing have been sought after, often by parents themselves. Various forms of 'natural childbirth'**, home deliveries (*Maternal and Child Health Information* 1973), the significance of mother–infant interaction after birth, biological methods of family planning (including the 'basal body temperature', 'sympto-thermal', and 'ovulation' methods (Martin 1975)), the back-carrying of babies, home-made weaning foods (including emphasis on the use of 'table foods' (Hipsley 1975)), and breast-feeding have recently received increasing attention by informed trend-setting parents and concerned professionals, and will undoubtedly continue to do so in the future (Davis 1974, Dyal and Kahrl 1967, Guthrie and Guthrie 1966, Jolly 1975).

Attitudes to female breasts
In Westernized communities, the dual role of the female breasts — sexual–aesthetic and nurturing — has lead to bizarre situations. For example, a few years ago, a woman was arrested for breast-feeding her baby outside the John F. Kennedy Center for the performing arts.

In discussions on breast-feeding in predominantly male technical groups, ambivalence or embarrassment is very frequently manifest by tension-relieving jokes ('comes in such cute containers', etc.). Despite loudly proc-

---

*These include the methods of Dick-Read, Kitzinger, and Bradley, and the Lamaze Technique and Psychoprophylaxis. Recently, Leboyer (1975) has moved the emphasis in the 'birthing couple' to include greater consideration of the emerging baby. His concept of 'birth without violence' refers to the neonate, and how with simple, no-cost alterations in management at delivery the transition to extra uterine life may be made smoother and less physiologically and emotionally traumatic for the baby.

laimed changes in sexual mores ('the sexual revolution'), Newton (1972*b*) has noted 'strange reversals in areas of prudishness', which 'make exotic sexual acts of all sorts acceptable', while single beds and pyjamas for both sexes have come into vogue. In addition, current concern with the increasing commonness of mammary cancer means that the breasts have also become organs that are to be feared. In Britain, the 'breast group' is an association of surgeons concerned with the detection and management of mammary cancer.

However, probably as part of the movement towards naturalism, there has been a definite and obvious increase in visual presentations of breast-feeding infants, for example, on television and in films in very recent years. There has been more fashionable freedom to show the female breasts ('the bra-less look' rather than the cantilevered appearance of 1950s films). This has, to some extent, been accompanied by greater liberty to use them for infant feeding in public with greater socio-cultural acceptance.* However, that this is not universally so, is indicated by a recent instance of a young married teacher at a college in Southern California being suspended by the authorities for discreetly breast-feeding her 4-month-old baby on campus.

Acceptance in the family
For older siblings, there is always jealousy of some degree, transient or more lasting for the new baby. In Western circumstances, the breast-feeding mother is intriguing for the older children, and can perhaps lead to a break in the chain of practical inexperience that has developed in modern times.

For a husband, the convenience of breast-feeding at night is apparent, with opportunities to help and support his wife in many other ways. The realization of the numerous advantages of breast-feeding will be persuasive, including the slimming effect of lactation, the lack of evidence that this leads to loss of the 'figure', and the nursing woman's increased sexuality (Masters and Johnson 1966). Studies do not seem to have been carried out on the significance of the husband's jealousy to the baby, who has usurped his wife's breasts. In view of humankind's past experience in other cultures,

---

*This attitude is well illustrated by the following question and answer in the popular newspaper column 'Dear Abby' (*Los Angeles Times*, 14 Sep 1975):
'Dear Abby:
 I'll soon be having my first baby and I plan to breastfeed it.
 I'd like to know how you and others feel about seeing a mother nursing her baby in doctors' offices, waiting rooms, shopping-center malls, restaurants, etc.?
 With the increased popularity of breast feeding, plus women's lib, I have seen more and more public breast feeding.
 Does it make some people uncomfortable to witness it? Should I hide from house guests and visitors?'
Mother-to-be

'Dear M-T-B:
 Breast-feeding a baby is natural and beautiful, but if you have a choice, do it privately. If you do nurse your baby in public, wear a shawl that can be lightly tossed over your bosom while your baby nurses and be as inconspicuous as possible.'

this cannot often be of major significance. Probably it is important that the man be more part of the 'delivery end' of reproduction than previously, so that he is as much involved in outcome — birth and breast-feeding — as with input — coitus.

However, as Weichert (1975) notes, the overlap between the nurturing and erotic functions of the breasts can lead to conflict and anxieties which can be responsible for negative attitudes. Primarily, as she caustically notes:

> ... a functional castration of women has occurred. They have aquiesced to a combination of forces, medical and cultural, which have eventuated in the use of the breast as the primary sex symbol and yardstick of feminine desirability, divorced from its nurturing role. Women in a critical period of their life cycle have become divorced from themselves and from the ability to confirm their identity fundamentally. In this instance, the degree of concern of the medical profession might be described as inversely proportional to the dimension of the problem. To draw an analogy, would the professional distance of physicians be maintained were it routinely recommended that all insemination be accomplished artificially? Would anybody suggest, seriously, that males abstain from intercourse, bind themselves, take drugs to relieve congestion, or be mechanically relieved routinely, and that it would be as good?
> The apparent absurdity of the analogy goes to the heart of the problem. If one sees lactation as part of a psychosexual continuum in women, the analogy can be taken seriously.

She also is of the opinion that: 'To deal with anxieties that lactating women express concerning their 'normality', because of the sensual relationship they share with the infant, one must confront the relationship between lactation and sexuality, not deny it'.

Changes in health services
One aspect of this apparent trend is beginning to become manifest in the modification of health services, particularly for mothers and children, in which the focus is on biological and emotional needs, as well as technical medical considerations. Such developments include, for example, attempts at the reorganization of wards for prematures and infants and of maternity units geared to family-centred care. Similarly, the interest and concern of parents themselves, especially mothers, appears to be slowly modifying the practice of obstetrics and paediatrics, as practitioners respond to new awareness by their clientele of alternatives in matters of childbirth and infant feeding, which can modify the extent, as well as the type, of their practices, and ultimately the medical curriculum.

An additional reason for changing emphasis in prenatal service is the realization that what is needed is greater attention to education in general health, to nutrition, to preparation for parenthood, especially motherhood (or, as Raphael (1973 a) has termed it, 'matrescence'), to child-care, and to family living, not only to skilled technical obstetrical management. Childbirth is being reappraised not as a disease or pathological condition, but as a normal physiological process, which, however, needs supervision and prompt skilled obstetrical attention for occasional complications and emergencies.

Also, within the health professions, it is becoming increasingly apparent that Western mainstream medicine ('allopathy') has many areas of spectacular success, but also blind spots or areas of failure (p. 225), as well as more serious and more frequent hazards than previously recognized, as is evidenced by the large number of papers in the medical press concerning iatrogenic disorders. Hopefully, this may be leading to a wider view of healing and possibilities of synthesis of allopathic and other systems ('synpathy'), taking into account the practices and techniques, and the successes and failures of other systems, both outside the Western world and within.

That such conceptual elasticity has developed is indicated, for example, by a paper published in 1975 in the *Journal of the Royal Society of Medicine* by Inglis on 'Fringe medicine', referring to non-allopathic systems in Western countries at the present day. He also summarizes ancient philosophical differences:

> Current medical orthodoxy stems from what used to be known as Mechanism. It was rational and materialist in its attitude and tended to be allopathic in its techniques, in the belief that diseases are, or at least are caused by, entities that make war on man, and that have to be fought off with whatever clinical weapons are available. Fringe practices, on the other hand, are derived from the old Vitalist tradition. Even when an illness could actually be traced to specific germs or toxins, Vitalists would still be found arguing that the sick man would not have succumbed if his life force had been in working order.

In particular, a widening of medical perspectives may permit non-technological methods of prevention and cure by psychological (Morris 1972) and physical support and by enhancement of the 'life force' (the 'host resistance' in modern semantics) to be given more prominence in training and practice, thus strengthening the modern medical armament. The roles of optimal nutrition and emotional harmony at all ages, but especially in infancy, are particularly relevant, and most likely to be achieved by breast-feeding.

Another inadequately appreciated trend is for health services in Western countries to adopt methods used for years in developing countries because of tradition or heavy pressure on very limited resources (e.g. auxiliaries, mothers being admitted with children, etc.). This trend is indicated, for example, by a recent publication of the United States National Institute of Mental Health entitled *The family in hospital: lessons from the underdeveloped countries* (Bell 1969); by the theme on *Lessons from developing countries* of the Dag Hammarskjöld Conference in *The quantity, quality, and cost of child services in Africa* (Nordberg et al. 1975) in Addis Ababa in 1973; and by the title of an exhibit at the 1973 American Public Health

Association Annual Conference, entitled *International health: a two-way street.*

Unfortunately, at the same time, hospitals, and particularly maternity wards, in technically less developed, resource-poor countries have been adopting the seemingly unbiological, certainly outmoded and probably harmful systems of dealing with (and usually separating) the mother and her newborn baby, which have so unfortunately and unnecessarily dominated the scene in the Western world in the past century.

Voluntary groups

As part of such trends towards naturalism in childbirth and infant rearing, various organizations have emerged in some technically more developed countries of the world in the past fifteen years or so. These include *Ammeh-jelpen* (Norway), the Association for the Improvement of Maternity Services (U.K.), International Childbirth Education Association (U.S.A.), Lamaze Technique, La Leche League International (U.S.A.), the National Childbirth Trust (U.K.), the Nursing Mothers' Association of Australia, and the Parents' Clubs of Australia.* All have somewhat different emphases and goals, but, as regards breast-feeding, they all try to supply scientifically accurate information based on research and experience, and to reinforce the individual and group support so necessary psychophysiologically for successful lactation. Similarly, other associations have recently started in various parts of the world — for example, the Singapore Breast-feeding Mothers' Group; while La Leche League International has developed over 200 overseas groups.

Such organizations were initiated with little or no general support or enthusiasm from the health professions, although this is now beginning to change in some respects. Their rapid spread has been indicated by statistics given elsewhere. Interest in such activities is also suggested by popular articles published in the U.S.A. in the last 2–3 years in such widely read magazines as *McCalls, Glamor,* and *Time*, by the appearance of a number of excellent non-technical low-cost books†, and, in 1975, by a new magazine intended as an 'interdisciplinary forum devoted exclusively to supporting the working mother and infant' entitled *Keeping Abreast Journal.*

---

*Addresses are given in Appendix A.

---

†*The complete book of breast-feeding* by M. Eiger and S. Olds (1972); *Nursing your baby* by K. Pryor (1973); *The tender gift: breast-feeding* by D. Raphael (1973*a*); *Boken Om Amning* by E. Helsing (1974) (in Norwegian); *Please breast-feed your baby* by A. Gerard (1972); *The womanly art of breast-feeding* by the La Leche League International (1958) (in English, Spanish, French, and Japanese); *Successful breast-feeding* by V. Phillips (1975); and *Discovering childbirth and the joy of breast-feeding* by P. O'Brien (1974).

Women's groups concerned with promoting 'good mothering through breast-feeding' initially have mainly involved the 'middle-class' educated, and in some communities, despite difficulties in a bottle-feeding culture, breast-feeding has changed from the 'less available option' to the modern — even fashionable — way to rear babies. Interestingly, it seems that the main body of the Women's Liberation movement is supportive, as permitting the mother the choice as to how she wishes to rear her child (Helsing 1975 *a*) For example, in Norway, *Ammehjelpen* comments that their organization 'does not see any contradiction between the liberation of women and the voluntary fulfilment of women's biological role.'

Similarly, the philosophy of the Nursing Mothers' Association of Australia has been expressed as follows (E. C. Wigglesworth 1975):

Surely the principles of the feminist movement apply to a mother too; that she may have:
— equal opportunity — the opportunity to learn about her tasks, to develop the capacity for skilled and loving mothering, to obtain help and support when needed,
— equal choice — to choose, regardless of economic or social pressures, how to bring up her children, based on the knowledge she has gained; the right to participate in decision making in her community, state and country,
— equality of respect — for the job she is doing is surely a worthwhile one.

The numerical influence of the La Leche League is indicated by the growth in number of groups in the U.S.A. from 16 in 1960 to almost 2000 in 1974, and in other countries to over 150 (*Pédiatrie* 1976). The League currently reaches more than a million people annually through group meetings, correspondence, telephone conversations, and League publications. The *La Leche League News,* a bi-monthly journal, goes to some 35 000 paid subscribers. More than two million brochures, pamphlets, and information-sheets are distributed annually. Key publications have been translated into French, Spanish, Portuguese, Italian, German, Swahili, and Eskimo. *The womanly art of breast-feeding,* the basic League manual, was first issued in a printing of 1000 in 1958. Over 500 000 copies of the revised edition have been sold.

A review article in the *Journal of Paediatrics* in 1968 (Hill 1968) made the following comment on La Leche League: 'That its program is meeting a need is clearly demonstrated by its rapid growth and by the recognition it has achieved in the short time it has been in existence.'

The key activities of La Leche League International have been summarized by an outside observer as follows (Murrow 1974):

The usual La Leche group consists of 10–30 mothers from a geographic area. Members learn of the organization through doctors, nurses, friends, and newspaper announcements. There is a series of four highly structured meetings which is repeated several times during the year. The topics of these meetings are (1) the advantages of nursing; (2) overcoming difficulties in nursing; (3) baby arrives and joins the family (including a discussion of labor and birth); (4) nutrition and weaning (including understanding of toddler and sibling rivalry). Attending the meeting are pregnant women, new mothers with infants, and those with several older children.

After the formal part of the meeting there is much informal conversation about specific problems and solutions. Each group maintains a full library of articles and books on childbirth, nursing, and child-rearing. Each member receives a regular newsletter. Group leaders are available for telephone consultation at any time, and in turn may receive advice from other knowledgeable people within the system. Referrals are made, on occasion, to doctors and other professionals. Women are encouraged to consult with others in their own situation.

New group leaders are chosen carefully, after their functioning within the group and relationships with their own children are observed over a period of time. They then enter into a period of training which involves reading, and discussions with experienced leaders, as well as workshops. The system is very well organized, and maintains central control with regional and state coordination, and a central office in Chicago.

The basic counselling role in such women's organization has been stated by Hapke (1975) of the Nursing Mothers' Association of Australia, as follows:

Because of this the mother learning to care for her child is faced with two problems. On the one hand she may lack information that could help her (e.g. that feeding her baby more frequently will increase her milk supply if it is too low). On the other hand she may be faced with too much information and advice (e.g. when she comes to decide how much sleep her child should have, or when to introduce solids). Much of this advice may be conflicting, some of it may be wrong, some she may be unable to interpret in the way it could apply in her situation.

The role of the counsellor is to give the mother the information she needs (which sometimes includes passing her onto someone else) without adding to the confusion she may already feel. Her role is not to take the place of the professional expert — usually an expert on one aspect of child development. Her role is to help the mother see, that while she is still at time dependent on advice from others, she is nevertheless the expert on her child (if not on children generally) and that she must interpret the advice she is given according to what seems best in her situation. It is to help her to see mothering as an evolving, learning process, and not as a series of rules that can be learnt and applied by rote.

In Australia, membership of the Nursing Mothers' Association of Australia has increased from 33 in 1965 to 11 500 in 1974 to 20 000 in 1975 (Smibert 1975) (Fig. 13.2). In Norway, membership of *Ammehjelpen* rose from 17 in 1968 to 100 in 1974. During this period, 20 000 copies of their Norwegian language booklet entitled *Breast-feed your baby* were purchased — a considerable figure in relation to the 60 000 annual births in this relatively small country.

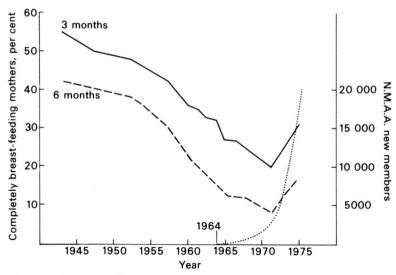

Fig. 13.2. Breast-feeding of children attending 'Baby Health Centres' at Victoria, Australia, and increase in membership of the Nursing Mothers' Association of Australia (courtesy of N.M.A.A.)

TABLE 13.1 *Breast-feeding perspectives* (from Marshall and Knafl 1974)

Problematic situation	La Leche League perspective	American middle-class and/or medical perspective
Timing of feedings	Feed infants when they indicate hunger	Feed infants at 3–4 hour intervals
Nursing outside the home	Feed hungry infants outside the home using techniques of discreet nursing	Breast-feeding outside the home is in most cases immodest and improper
Introduction of solid foods	Feed breast-milk *only* for first 4–6 *months* of infant's life	Begin feeding solid foods at 4–6 *weeks* of age
Duration of nursing	Continue breast-feeding as long as mutually agreeable, often for 1–3 years	Wean infant from the breast at any time; frequently recommended times are 3, 6, or 9 months
Manner of weaning	Wean from the breast in a gradual manner co-operatively determined by mother and child	Weaning process is directed by the mother
Initial breast-feeding	Breast-feed as soon after delivery as possible	Breast-feed no sooner than 6 hours postpartum and often after 24 hours
Room accommodations in hospital	Mothers care for their infants in their hospital room, a practice called rooming-in	Medical personnel care for infants in a newborn nursery

The main features of the La Leche League International perspective on infant feeding have been contrasted by Marshall and Knafl (1974) with what they term the 'American middle-class and/or medical perspective' (Table 13.1).

The general affects of methods employed by La Leche League International have been analyzed by Ladas (1970*a*, 1970*b*, 1972) and give much insight for the development of practical programmes (p. 342). The main benefits appear to be the result of counselling — that is by the supply of accurate information and by the individual and group support. In other words, such associations supply 'a social and sociable environment in which breast-feeding is the norm' (Marshall and Knafl 1974). Experienced mothers in the League have similar roles towards new members as *doulas* (p. 175) towards young primiparas in traditional societies (Raphael 1973*a*). Their effectiveness is explicable in terms of modern knowledge of the psychophysiology of lactation, and the prolactin and let-down reflexes in particular (pp. 17, 19). They fill the gap in modern society, supplying support for the confused, uncertain, isolated new urban mother (Ladas 1972).

A recent review of Nursing Mothers' Association of Australia activities notes the following kinds of help: discussion groups at members' homes at which fathers are welcome; round-the-clock telephone counselling and letter counselling; literature (some in migrant languages); mothering and lactation aids (e.g. baby sling, breast-pump); local milk banks; a newsletter; a library; a research department (Australian Commission on Health 1976).

Plainly the activities of such voluntary groups and associations may provoke antagonism and criticism from more conservative elements in the medical profession ('fanatical amateurs'), especially if such activities are largely successful (E. C. Wigglesworth 1975):

In a paper on the role of the Nursing Mothers' Association of Australia in the community, given at our first national conference, the idea was expressed: 'as we become a stronger force within the community — in fact in the precise measure that we do become a stronger force — so the pressures against us will build up. Our success threatens people's livelihood or, at least their authority, and those who feel most threatened will be most antagonistic.' As a general principle, this remains true, but I feel that our Association, by its quiet strength and restrained presentation of the facts, by its attempts to join forces and co-operate with possibly threatened authority, by its support of professional opinion and emphasis on medical approval of its suggestions and literature has pursued a policy which has gathered a hidden strength unto itself, which is quietly and serenely diverting the hostility against it.

For the most part, La Leche League International, the Nursing Mothers' Association of Australia, and *Ammehjelpen* have attempted to blend technical information ('science') with practical knowledge based on experience ('art'). They all have medical advisers, and a defined standard of behaviour, as, for example, the Nursing Mothers' Association of Australia's 'Code of

Ethics and Behaviour'. Their educative role is conceived of as both 'to make available medically-approved, professionally researched information' and 'to pool ideas and experiences of many successful problem-solvers' — that is mothers who have themselves breast-fed their infants (E. C. Wigglesworth 1975). In relation to lactation, 'knowledge is confidence' (Helsing 1976).

Investigations of the impact of organizations such as La Leche League International on the overall pattern of breast-feeding in communities are difficult to undertake in view of the many changing aspects of modern life, but such research urgently needs to be done. However, in the U.S.A. a recent study showed that the breast-feeding rate on discharge from hospital had risen from 18 per cent in 1966 to 25–30 per cent in 1973 (Ross Laboratories 1974, Sehring 1975). Also, in Norway in which *Ammehjelpen* has a similar role, the 6-month-old breast-feeding rate in 1974 was 20–30 per cent, as opposed to 4 per cent in Sweden where such an organization did not exist. In the State of Victoria in Australia, where both the Nursing Mothers' Association of Australia and the government network of infant-welfare centres are very active the rate of *solely* breast-fed babies attending such clinics has risen in recent years. In 1971, the figures showed 21 per cent breast-feeding at 3 months and 9 per cent at 6 months; in 1974, the corresponding results had risen to 28 per cent and 15 per cent (Department of Health, Victoria, Australia, 1975).

2. Economic considerations

Present universal rapid rises in cost of living are influencing feeding patterns in general, including the diets of young children. Such greatly increasing prices have particularly involved 'double-cycle', animal protein foods, including cow's milk, which has often risen in cost while declining in volume produced (*Foreign Agriculture* 1972, Krostitz 1974). In addition to current very high costs of bovine milk production, including feed, labour, and transport, various other factors have entered the picture, including the new markets of Japan, and the oil-rich OPEC countries, most of which are traditional milk-drinkers. Recent figures for North America on the production and cost of dried skimmed milk, and its declining use in overseas food aid, indicate some aspects of the situation clearly (Table 13.2). In these few years, the price of dried skimmed milk increased by almost 250 per cent. At the same time, the U.S.A. production declined, so the country became an importer for the first time in 1972.*

---

*The present-day lability of world food supplies is indicated by an upsurge in milk production in the last few years, so that, temporarily, the European Economic Community has accumulated a 'powder mountain' of 3000 million lb of dried skimmed milk and the U.S.A. 430 million lb (*Business Week* 1976)

TABLE 13.2   *Dried skimmed milk in North America* (courtesy of U.N. Food and Agriculture Organization)

	1966–70	1973
Production (millions of tons)	857	574
Food aid (millions of tons)	128	54
Cost per ton ($)	257	632

More recent figures kindly supplied by UNICEF show the price increases from 1967 to 1975 for three major food items: wheat, soyabeans, and non-fat dry milk (dried skimmed milk). Analysis shows that the dried skimmed-milk price increased by three times, compared with soyabeans (twice) and wheat (2½ times) (Table 13.3).

TABLE 13.3   *Price changes ($) in soyabeans, non-fat dry milk, and wheat (1967–75)* (courtesy of Mr. A. J. Parrenti, Chief, Operational Service Unit, UNICEF)

Commodity	Basis	1967	1968	1969	1970	1971	1972	1973	1974	1975
Soyabeans, U.S. No.2 yellow	per bushel (27 kg; 60 lb), export value	2.89	2.75	2.69	2.91	3.24	3.65	7.43	6.97	5.68 (Sep.)
Non-fat dry milk, export grade	per pound, value ex U.S. plant	0.1992	0.2236	0.2351	0.2631	0.3074	0.3306	0.4638	0.5862	0.6136 (Sep.)
Wheat, U.S. No.1 hard winter, 15–12% protein	per bushel (27 kg; 60 lb), export value	1.79	1.71	1.59	1.50	1.68	1.92	3.78	4.54	4.35 (Aug.)

These considerable changes may be expected to reinforce the economic reasons for breast-feeding. Such considerations, it must be stressed, will need to be viewed on a world basis and in relation to the economic impact and cultural and logistic feasibility of working mothers breast-feeding or not, and the cost of extra nutrients needed by the lactating woman (p. 59). The poor will be particularly affected, *including disadvantaged communities in resource-rich countries.*

On a national basis, consumer interests have sometimes become involved, partly for economic reasons. For example, in 1974 the Housewives Association of Trinidad and Tobago was responsible for the developing of a breast-feeding campaign (A. White 1974) (p. 400). Also, universal concerns with the balance of payments and expenditure of foreign currency may be expected to lead to government scrutiny of imports, and of the limitation, selection, or restriction of locally unneeded or low priority items, accompanied by activities to promote the production of local import substitutes. In many countries, it is becoming realized slowly that breast-milk is, in fact, a locally produced 'import substitute' for expensive processed cow's-milk formulas purchased from overseas, leading to the following agro-economic questions: Who will pay for human milk substitutes at the family, community, or national level? How will this affect foreign-currency reserves, the balance of payments, and the availability of funds for other development projects?

3. Conservation of resources and ecological concerns

The last two decades have shown an increasing awareness throughout the world of the need to avoid wasting resources, including foods (Berry 1975). One of the four main objectives of the U.N. Food and Agriculture Organization (F.A.O.) has been to try to minimize the often very great loss of foodstuffs by rodents, insects, fungi, etc. Although not usually considered in this connection, a major change in a community from breast-feeding to bottle-feeding represents both the waste of a potentially existing food and also an unnecessary squandering of resources as ingredients for an appropriate human-milk substitute, usually based on cow's milk, will need to be produced, processed, and distributed, with the energy consumption that this will entail.

Additionally, serious consideration is now being given everywhere to questions of the production and disposal of tins, bottles, and other containers, as a part of attempts to minimize environmental pollution and to save resources. As noted earlier (p. 270), with artificial feeding, the U.S. infant population would use about 45 million tins of ready-to-feed formula annually, which need to be disposed of. This is plainly not the case with breast-feeding.

4. Critical scrutiny of the infant-food industry

Recent years in many industrialized countries, including the U.S.A., have clearly given indications of public concern with the need for close critical scrutiny of the food industry. As with all market-place transactions, *caveat emptor* ('let the buyer beware' — or, at least, be alert) applies as much in the modern technological world as in ancient Rome, if not more so. With formulas, the situation is further complicated because, as noted by Müller (1975): 'Knowledge is still very limited with respect to the metabolism of the various nutrients and their long-term affects on the development of the child.'

The continued appearance of new processed foods, including formulas, with varying blends of ingredients and additives, and with the deployment of persuasive modern marketing skills, present-day problems of devising workable legislation and acquiring funds for staff and equipment for adequate scrutiny and testing are considerable. Also, manufacturers in a competitive free market society can have genuine concerns over divulging information of value to rivals, although this has also been used as an argument to block analysis and labelling.

In the U.S.A., activities of the food industry, concerned with the feeding of children have been under critical debate, including, for example, controversy over the intense coverage of children's television programmes with advertisements for nutritionally undesirable foods (such as snacks, sweets, and breakfast foods with a very high sugar content), and concern over inadequately labelled baby foods, including those with unnecessary and possibly harmful ingredients added (such as excessive salt and sugar, and monosodium glutamate) to appeal to the mother's taste. In America, two agencies have been involved — the Food and Drug Administration which controls the labelling of food products, and the Federal Trade Commission which regulates the advertisement of food products on the mass media (Richardson 1976).

Disquiet has been mirrored by the rise of consumerism with attempts to draw the attention of the public and of legislators to pricing in relation to content and composition, to harmful products, and to advertising which misleads. In the U.S.A., critical scrutiny is undertaken by various non-Governmental groups, including consumer associations such as 'Action for Children's Television', community-oriented nutritionists (notably the Society for Nutrition Education), and by such organizations as the Center for Science in the Public Interest, which produced a 'White Paper' on Infant Feeding Practices in 1974 (Center for Science in the Public Interest 1974). The latter, for example, was critical of many current practices with regard to the promotion, contents, and cost of formulas and of processed foods for infants, particularly because 'the composition and marketing have been guided largely by economic factors'. The report also noted that: 'Manufacturers of formulas and bottles advertise their products in literature aimed at new mothers and doctors. *No comparable promotion reminds mothers and their physicians of the benefits of breast-feeding.* Formula salespeople visit doctors regularly, leaving behind free samples and literature to encourage use of their products. Giving free formula to new mothers when they leave the hospital — a "service" of the manufacturers — is an additional deterrent to breast-feeding.'

Recommendations made in this 'White Paper' can form the basis for the development of more rational programmes of biological, rather than overly commercialized, infant feeding and will be discussed later. Basically, the activities of informed consumer and other non-governmental groups focus attention on issues for the public and for legislators.

Most industrialized countries have regulating agencies to watch over food products for substances considered to be harmful or toxic, and to take appropriate legal action when indicated. In the U.S.A., for example this is the function of the Food and Drug Administration.

However, in the U.S.A., with the exception of regulations to exclude some possibly harmful additives from baby foods (notably monosodium glutamate), governmental regulation of the marketing of baby foods is usually much more difficult to achieve, particularly advertising purporting to support breast-feeding, while subtly undermining confidence. In addition, governmental financial support for continuing efforts to supply information to the public regarding the advantages of breast-feeding have to date been almost nil.

Any considerations of monitoring of the infant-food industry must take into account relations that can develop between the companies concerned and the health professions. In this regard, the controversy concerning the influence of the pharmaceutical industry and the medical profession (which was discussed by the 1974 U.S. Senate Subcommittee on Health) may be a parallel. In the hearings, the Chairman, Senator Edward Kennedy, reported that the records of the 20 largest drug companies in the U.S.A. showed that they had given away more than 2 billion pills to physicians, had spent almost $13 million on other gifts for doctors and nurses, and had given away 45 million less lavish 'reminder items' as part of their promotional and sales efforts.

In the same year, the President of the American Medical Association, Dr. Malcolm Todd, suggested that dropping advertising — largely pharmaceutical — from the Association's 14 publications, despite the loss of $9 million annual advertising revenue, might make the journals 'credible and influential in these abusive times' (Nelson 1974). Similarly, in a recent book, Silverman and Lee (1974) note that the flood of advertising and drug promotion has often been 'unobjective, incomplete, or misleading', and they suggest that editors of medical journals can be reluctant to comment on misleading drug promotion because the journals are supported by advertising that is almost solely by drug companies.

Ignatius (1973) quotes a comment by Harvard medical students which is at the heart of the matter: 'The medical profession is largely responsible, because it does not maintain proper distance from the industry. This distance is essential for the doctor's objectivity. Since the doctor is in a unique economic position, namely that of directing what the consumer will buy, strict objectivity is his obligation to the patient.'

As with the pharmaceutical industry, the infant-food industry is highly competitive and profitable, and puts particular emphasis on professional approval. Thus, a recent directive on 'Responsibility for Infant Feeding' from a major American infant-food company has the following seemingly unexceptional advice to mothers (Stewart 1975):

The final decision for or against breast-feeding should rest with the mother and her doctor.

Your baby's doctors should prescribe the specific formula, technique of preparation and appropriate schedule for artificial feeding. His directions will be based on your baby's own nutritional and digestive needs.

Starting solids. Ask your doctor. Just as you follow the doctor's advice on your baby's formula and vitamin D and C supplements, you will let him direct the addition of solids. He should decide when your baby is ready for them, suggest what should be served, and the order in which they should be added.

Unfortunately, most physicians and nurses have received minimal training in nutrition (including the wider issues of infant feeding) in the curricula of their schools, and their education in this regard is to a considerable extent supplied by publications and promotional material from the infant-food industry directed specifically to health professionals, so that they may lack sufficient information to be able to make critical judgements and comparisons.

In addition, as with the drug industry, opinion-moulding and product selection may be facilitated by a continuing supply of professional and social financial assistance, ranging from free samples to research grants to entertainment at scientific meetings. All tend at least to make independent judgement less likely, if not to inhibit action because of the need for continuing support.

Most usually, physicians and nurses seem unaware of the psycho-dynamics of such age-old techniques of opinion-moulding. In fact, it represents a very low-cost form of advertising and promotion, being both relatively economical and, anyway, absorbed by increased product cost. It is a potent way of influencing the influentials, with the bonus of fostering a benign image by assisting in scientific and professional activities. Moreover, because of their clinical training without emphasis on social and community aspects of medicine, health professionals may see no appropriate role in modifying such practices — or may be overawed by the size, influence, and power of the companies concerned.

In the U.S.A., recent criticisms made concerning the infant-food industry appeared to have been met with much consternation by the manufacturers, partly because they had become main arbiters on nutritional matters because of lack of interest and training by health personnel.

However, partly in response to questions raised by consumer groups and non-official bodies, some changes have been made — for example, labelling of baby foods with nutrients and lesser emphasis on their salt and sugar content.

The motives of such critics have been questioned, as witness a recent circular letter to paediatricians in the U.S.A. from the chief executive officer of one of the major infant-food firms: 'Activist groups are attempting to undermine confidence in our food supply with inaccurate and unfounded changes.' The situation, in fact, is very different. In urban technological societies, processed foods will play an important role in feeding such populations. The question is how to ensure that such processed foods are used optimally, together with non-commercial foods, such as breast-milk and home-made weaning mixtures, principally for infant nutrition, as well as for profit by the manufacturers. Conflicts of interest for infant-food companies between the need for maximum sales and for nutritional and social benefit obviously can occur, especially in a highly competitive field.

Again, as noted by a major infant-food company, 'valid, authoritative opinions on the formulation of these (infant) foods' has been sought from: 'the Food and Nutrition Council of the American Medical Association, the Committee on Nutrition of the American Academy of Paediatrics, the Food and Nutrition Board and the Food Protection Committee of the National Academy of Sciences, the Food Research Institute, the Nutrition Foundation, and the Food and Drug Administration.' This implies that there needs to be a 'search for sound advice'.

This may be best obtained from an appropriately structured, independent body, governmental or otherwise, with a surveillance function, and with professional membership, where no conflict of interest exists, and with participation from appropriate consumer groups.

The situation in Sweden and Britain may be noted. In both countries, the decision-making apparatus with regard to paediatric nutrition policy is independent of the infant-food industry, with whom, however, cordial relations are maintained and from whom consultation is obtained. This can, for example, be seen in the recent authoritative publication of the Committee on Medical Aspects of Food Policy of the U.K. Department of Health and Social Security (1974) entitled *Present-day practice in infant feeding.* The membership of the Working Party involved in discussions, decisions, and drafting the Report were all paediatricians, nutritionists, or technical representatives of appropriate governmental ministries. A considerable number of senior technical and research persons 'greatly helped by giving evidence before them, by making available unpublished information, or by reading and commenting on parts of the Report in draft form'.

The situation in relation to the role of the infant-food industry overseas in less developed, usually resource-poor countries has been a matter of concern for some paediatricians for many years, as the disruptive effects on the local pattern of breast-feeding of the promotion of unaffordable formulas has been readily apparent in areas where parents had neither the funds, nor the home hygiene (especially water supply), nor the conditioning in the domestic mathematics needed to be able to use the powdered formulas available in sufficient strength or in a clean fashion. The rising problem of the marasmus–diarrhoea syndrome in infancy has paralleled these changes, as has been emphasized earlier (p. 287). Earlier reports* expressing anxiety about the impact of the advertising of infant formulas in less developed countries appeared in the late 1950s and the 1960s (Adeniyi-Jones 1955, Jelliffe 1962, Symonds 1958). For example, Ellis (1962) observed that: 'It would be disastrous if rapid industrialization and commercial propaganda were to lead to a widespread decline in breastfeeding among native populations where neither hygiene nor milk production were within measurable distance of rendering artificial feeding safe, reliable, or desirable.'

Writing about Nigeria in 1969, Wennen (1969 *a*) made the following critical comments:

> For the last ten years, a new disease has been appearing in many developing countries; it threatens the lives of children in the first years of their existence; namely, unnecessary artificial feeding. More and more mothers start buying powdered milk for their infants even when breast-milk is abundant. Incessant commercial propaganda has convinced them that "this is good for baby"; also the example of the "elite mother, the fashion leader, whose babies are healthy and strong . . . The results of the vicious circle of infectious diarrhoea–malnutrition–infections, etc., might be summarized in the word "bottle-disease".

In 1970, a paper was presented at the annual conference of the American Society of Food Technologists in the apparent ill-effects of both health services and the commercial promotion of formulas (Jelliffe 1971 *a*):

> It seems, therefore, that an objective outside observer could make a case that Western nutrition influence, both from health services and from the much more potent forces of advertising, have done little good in many less developed tropical areas in the past quarter century, and indeed probably on balance have produced more harm than benefit. There is a real need to reconsider where nutrition education and persuasion is going, and this includes both the medical fraternity and also the world of commerce.

> For example, is it ethical to advertise, using modern techniques of motivation and persuasion, infant foods in a population that has no chance financially or hygienically of being able to use them in adequate quantities? Should infant milk foods be widely advertised in regions where breastfeeding is currently practised?

Such comments in the scientific, professional literature produced no apparent impact on the practices of the infant food industry in developing countries, and the first major concerted attempt to highlight the concern of paediatric nutritionists was made by the Working Party of the Protein Advisory Group of the United Nations on *Feeding the pre-school child* in Geneva in October 1971. At this meeting, the causes of failure to breastfeed were discussed including, among other factors, inappropriate health services. The following statement on 'Commercial Persuasion' was approved by the Working Party:

*The sequence of events leading to current criticism of the infant food industry has been given by Cottingham (1976) in a booklet *Bottle babies: a guide to the baby-foods issue*, available from the Christian Medical Council, 150 rue de Fernay, Geneva, Switzerland.

During the last two decades the increased availability and consumption of expensive proprietary brand infant foods within developing countries, stimulated by commercial firms and in many countries also by the nature and scale of advertising campaigns which they have implemented, have seriously aggravated the trend towards breast-milk displacement. The passive attitude of many governments towards regulating the flow and use of such goods according to their nutritional value and potential benefit to consumers is also deplored.

Particular devices used by commercial companies to induce support from health services must be especially censured, e.g. the employment by some firms of "milk nurses" to make home visits and attend clinics to promote sales of specific products, the issue of free samples, posters, calendars, etc., as an incentive to favour particular brands or companies. Insufficient discrimination has been shown by companies in the content of their advertising communications, and the extensive use of mass media as a channel for such communications may have multiplied any detrimental effect of commercial advertising efforts on nutrition of the preschool child.

The extensive introduction and indiscriminate promotion of expensive processed milk-based infant food in some situations may constitute a grave threat to the nutritional status of the infants for whom they are intended. The sophisticated luxury and fashionable appeal of such products to the mother may lead to the undesirable effect of displacing the child from the breast, in circumstances where the mother may have no access to affordable alternative foods which can be given safely and without risk of alimentary infection and diarrheal disease.

Subsequent meetings were held by this Working Party with representatives of the food industry in Bogota, Colombia, in Paris, in New York, and in Singapore. The major intention of these conferences, from the viewpoint of tne Working Party, was to exchange information with the food industry and to see if a mutually supportive compromise could be achieved.

As noted elsewhere (p. 316), the benign self-image of the companies concerned made it difficult for them to appreciate that many, probably most, tropical paediatricians were of the opinion that they were often contributing to malnutrition in young children rather than helping. Moreover, the decline in breast-feeding was felt by manufacturers to be unrelated to the promotion of formulas, but rather that these products could be considered as filling a 'felt-need' with the 'inevitable' falling away from breast-feeding with urbanization (p. 194).

The complexity of the situation became apparent as it became increasingly clear that various interacting factors were responsible for declining lactation. The blame is impossible to apportion. Nevertheless, the comment by Sutedjo (1974) concerning Indonesia appears valid: 'Nowadays, economically less favoured mothers in bigger as well as in smaller towns start to give artificial milk formula to their infants. Many reasons have been put forward to explain this unlucky phenomenon. One thing is for sure — that is that the intensive propaganda of milk factories, associated with incentives to medical as well as paramedical personnel and the mothers themselves, make the situation worse.'

Difficulties in assessing the impact of one factor, such the effect of x units of advertising, is difficult to disentangle from other variables. Moreover, as Greiner (1975) comments, details of methods and extent of advertising and their effectiveness are trade secrets:

Does advertising "cause" low-income mothers in developing countries to buy commercial infant foods? A fairly accurate answer might be found by watching the sales response of an isolated population to an isolated advertising campaign. Most large companies which advertise carry out such market studies, but do not make results available.

However, we may assume that such statements as the following one from the Nestlé 1963 Annual Report are backed by extensive research: "Despite the somewhat unfavourable situation in Latin America, intensive promotional and advertising efforts brought about a marked improvement in sales of our brands of milk products."

In 1973, a journalistic approach to the situation was launched by the War on Want in London in a booklet entitled *The baby killer: an investigation into the promotion and sale of powdered baby milks in the Third World* (Muller 1974). Essentially, this reported in dramatic terms the ill-effects of the widespread promotion of formulas in developing countries (Muller 1973, 1975*a, b*), as has been covered in the present publication. This booklet was translated into German, French, Italian, and Spanish in Switzerland by the *Arbeitsgruppe Dritte Welt* (1974)* and all language versions have attracted much attention and debate in the press, including newspapers (Crittenden 1975, Power 1975) and journals such as *Science, N.Y.* in the U.S.A. (Wade 1974), and the *Lancet* (1974), *New Internationalist* (1975), and the *New Humanist* (Turner 1974) in Britain.

A similar critical account of the infant-food and pharmaceutical industries has been written by Ledogar (1975) for the Consumers Union. It is concerned with Latin America and the Caribbean, and is entitled *Hungry for profits*.

More recently, in the U.S.A., the Inter-Faith Center on Corporate Responsibility, a sponsored movement of the National Council of Churches, New York, has become concerned at the activities of major American infant-food companies overseas in which they are substantial stockholders. Recently (July 1976) four religious organizations, led by the Sisters of the Precious Blood of Dayton, Ohio, and associated with the Center, are suing Bristol–Myers, the parent company of Mead Johnson, to obtain details of their marketing practices with infant formulas overseas, in areas where 'chronic poverty would lead to misuse or harmful effects' (Community Nutrition Institute Report 1976).

In addition, endorsement of the major importance of breast-feeding and

---

*An English-language film has been made and is available from Teldok Films, 504 Bruhl, Chlodwigstrasse 29, Cologne, West Germany.

of the need for scrutiny of the activities of the infant-food industry have been endorsed by international agencies, such as the World Health Organization (p. 325).

The situation with regard to the ill-effects of the promotion of costly formulas in resource-poor, developing countries is increased not only by the poverty and poor home hygiene in such countries, but also by the lack of sophistication of mothers, the absence of consumer associations, and, very often, by the power of large, often multi-national companies in relation to many aspects of small countries' economy and development.

The effect of the different types of protest over the past few years has varied. Basically, it has drawn to the issue the attention of the paediatric and nutritional world, of the infant-food industry, of various international agencies, and a segment of the educated public, both in industrialized and less technically developed countries.

Response by infant-food companies has varied and is often difficult to discover. Most drastically, Nestlé has sued the *Arbeitsgruppe Dritte Welt* for libel; and the outcome of the case has been reported in some detail (Community Nutrition Institute Report 1976):

A Swiss court last week found 13 defendants — mostly students, teachers, and clergymen — guilty of having libeled Nestle, the multinational food company, with a pamphlet on infant formula marketing in developing countries titled "Nestle Kills Babies".

However, the court told Nestle to "carry out a fundamental reconsideration" of its sales techniques in the Third World. The verdict is "not an acquittal of Nestle", said Judge Juerg Sollberger, warning the company to "reconsider its advertising policies to avoid being accused of immoral conduct" and to change its marketing procedures "if it does not want its products to become lethally dangerous".

The defendants, members of a so-called Third World Working Group, had accused Nestle of contributing to infant malnutrition in developing countries by promoting expensive and easily-misused formula products. The judge found the pamphlet title, "Nestle Kills Babies", clearly defamatory because it suggests infant deaths are caused by the formula itself, not by poor hygiene or misuse of the product.

The decision was clearly a phyrrhic victory for Nestle. The firm had sought unsuccessfully to prevent the defendants from calling witnesses on their behalf, arguing that the entire proceedings were "against national interests". When the final hearing began last week, Nestle withdrew three of its four libel charges, effectively conceding that it had used so-called "milk nurses" and other questionable practices in marketing formula abroad.

Written protest and denial is usual, and often mention is made of 'some unethical companies', 'other manufacturers, notably those of Europe and Britain', 'while taking note of the actions of competitors', etc. Indeed, varying standards of ethics do pose problems in a competitive field, with those least scrupulous gaining most benefit. Likewise, more obviously inappropriate advertising campaigns directed at less well-to-do parents in developing countries have been attributed to advertising abuses by small local distributing companies. A typical example, reported by Greiner (1975), is the advertisement in the newspaper *Cong Lam* in Vietnam, 12 May 1972: 'The first year of life is the decisive year in the life of a baby. And only you can decide your baby's life. Right on the day of birth, feed it with Similac powder.' The radio advertising of the same product to the general public in pidgin English on the radio in Sierra Leone ('E milk good for my pikin when e sick-sick so?' 'Yes! Dis milk no make pikin vomit so!') received the following reply from the Public Relations Department, Abbott Laboratories: 'The incident came to our attention two months ago when the same subject was referred to in another publication. The matter was immediately investigated through our regional management. We learned that the local distributor undertook this campaign entirely on his own — without our knowledge, consent, or financial support. The Sierra Leone distributor was instructed to immediately cease and desist in his public advertising efforts under pain of losing the agency. A policy is now being instituted to prevent a recurrence of this situation.' (Isham 1975).

Likewise, it is often stated that their products are channelled via physicians and the health service, that company 'milk nurses' are extensions of inadequate health services, and that advertising is directed only to the affluent, literate segment of the population. However, this is obviously not the case when products have been promoted directly to mothers (Fig. 13.3) on the radio in the local language, and visually in vernacular newspapers and on posters in stores. Under these circumstances, literacy is not needed to receive the message.

Despite denials, some responses endorse the fact, obvious to the paediatrician with long tropical experience, that the promotion of infant formulas has been undertaken in a way likely to lead to disruptive effects on the pattern of breast-feeding and without consideration of the feasibility of their safe usage. For example, a recent editorial in the *New Internationalist* (1975) notes:

First we applaud and congratulate the Cow and Gate company for changing its advertising policies throughout Africa. It is almost two years since the *New Internationalist* began this campaign against the promotion of tinned baby-foods to poor mothers who did not need them and who could not afford them. But the widespread advertising of artificial baby milk in underprivileged and often illiterate communities has continued to lead to the use of over-dilute feed and unsterilized bottles. Untold hundreds of babies have died as a result.

Last month, the Public Affairs Manager of Unigate, of which Cow and Gate is a subsidiary, announced that 'the decision was made not to continue advertising in Africa, until copy was cleared with local paediatricians. The reason . . . was that we were satisfied that there could be a danger of our products being misused, as a result of a radio advertisement script being misunderstood. . . The cessation of advertising has, in effect, meant cancelling some contracts and allowing others to lapse.'

Fig. 13.3. Distribution of free samples. Caption from Nestlé Century Publication (1967) ran: 'Family celebrations — in our picture a baptism — frequently offer an opportunity for welcome gifts.'

Likewise, a recent paper by Benton (1975) presented at the 1974 Protein Advisory Group Regional Seminar, Singapore, on 'The role of the food industry in promoting desirable policies and practices in feeding of infants and children' noted that there should be a reduction in the advertising that is intended to encourage unnecessary bottle-feeding.

However, in addition to the question of advertising directly to the public, which some manufacturers seem to have agreed to discontinue in developing countries, the issues related to what is rather strangely termed 'ethical advertising' — that is, advertising directed at health professionals, largely through journals and various direct means — are just as wide-ranging. A major consideration is the 'endorsement by association' of advertisements for economically and culturally inappropriate infant foods in general medical or, especially, paediatric journals intended for developing countries. Likewise, the question of patronage and the subsequent moulding of medical opinion and influencing of decisions is an issue of greater significance to paediatrics than an intimate knowledge of metabolic pathways, but scarcely ever discussed. Important developments on this front include the devising by the Ross Laboratories of Abbot Laboratories of an 'International Code of Marketing Ethics: with Reference to Infant Feeding', and the initiation in Zurich in 1975 of an International Infant Formula Council.

inly, a major recent trend making breast-feeding more likely has
e critical scrutiny of the activities of the infant-food industry, espe-
erseas. The possible role of the 'International Code' and the Council
I to remains to be seen (p. 401).

5. Recent scientific knowledge

A recurrent theme in the present publication is that a great deal of new,
scientifically important information has been discovered and published in
recent years, concerning both the biochemical (p. 26), anti-allergic (p. 96),
anti-infective (p. 84), and metabolic uniqueness of human milk, and the
emotional (p. 142) and contraceptive (p. 118) effects of breast-feeding
compared with artificial bottle-feeding with formula. They have been
detailed at length earlier, as have problems with inaccuracies of formula
preparation, especially using powdered milk (p. 42).

The picture in various areas of the world is beginning to become clearer
and in some places, such as Brazil (Sousa 1975 b), regional reviews have
been brought together giving available information on the prevalence of
breast-feeding, ecological factors involved, and other information.

Recent information also suggests that some older health programmes on
lactation, notably the very widespread distribution of powdered milk
through child health services (p. 356) had an adverse effect, and conversely,
that plans for the future should include emphasis in paediatric units on the
positive and multiple values of human milk for the premature (p. 304), and
the setting up of 'new style', fresh breast-milk banks (p. 362).

Likewise, recently acquired knowledge makes clear the basic endocrinology of breast-feeding, and, incidentally, validates many traditional practices, such as, for example, putting the baby to the breast as soon as possible
after birth and frequently thereafter (p. 161). Also, sociological studies have
shown the effectiveness of social support systems (Caplan 1974), such as the
various voluntary groups designed to promote breast-feeding (p. 306).

6. International concern

Initially because of the grave problems of protein–calorie malnutrition and
associated infections in resource-poor countries, particularly the rising incidence of the marasmus–diarrhoea syndrome in urban areas, international
agencies and organizations have become increasingly aware of the need to
tackle the serious issue of declining breast-feeding. Similarly, the importance of breast-feeding has been endorsed by some national or nutritional
associations in resource-rich nations.

World Health Organization
WHO has always appreciated the significance of breast-feeding in infant
nutrition in resource-poor countries, as has been clearly emphasized by their
publications over the past 20 years (Jelliffe 1968 b). However, recently their

concern has mounted, as indicated by the considerable emphasis given to breast-feeding in their messages for World Health Day in 1973 — 'Health Begins at Home' and in 1974 'Better food for a Healthier World'.

In May 1974, at its twenty-seventh annual meeting, the World Health Assembly in Geneva took the unusual step of proposing and adopting a specific resolution:

INFANT NUTRITION AND BREAST-FEEDING
The Twenty-seventh World Health Assembly,

Reaffirming that breast-feeding has proved to be the most appropriate and successful nutritional solution for the harmonious development of the child:

Noting the general decline in breastfeeding, related to socio-cultural and environmental factors, including the mistaken idea caused by misleading sales promotion that breastfeeding is inferior to feeding with manufactured breast-milk substitutes;

Observing that this decline is one of the factors contributing to infant mortality and malnutrition, in particular in the developing world; and realizing that mothers who feed their babies with manufactured foods are often unable to afford an adequate supply of such foods and that even if they can afford such foods the tendency to malnutrition is frequently aggravated because of lack of understanding of the amount and correct and hygienic preparation of the food which should be given to the child,

1. RECOMMENDS strongly the encouragement of breast-feeding as the ideal feeding in order to promote harmonious physical and mental development of children;

2. CALLS the attention of countries to the necessity of taking adequate social measures for mothers working away from their homes during the lactation period, such as arranging special work timetables so that they can breast feed their children;

3. URGES Member countries to review sales promotion activities on baby foods and to introduce appropriate remedial measures, including advertisement codes and legislation where necessary;

4. URGES the Director-General to intensify activities relevant to the promotion of breast-feeding, to bring those matters to the notice of the medical profession and health administrators and to emphasize the need for health personnel, mothers and the general public to be educated accordingly; and

5. REQUESTS the Director-General to promote and further support activities related to the preparation and use of weaning foods based on local products.

Fourteenth Plenary Meeting, 23 May 1974

Lastly, in recent years, WHO has developed a research project on various aspects related to breast-feeding, in collaboration with the International Children's Centre, Paris. The study is a collaborative one initiated in various countries (Chile, Guatemala, Hungary, India, Lebanon, Niger, Nigeria, and Sweden), and has two main parts which will be implemented in two stages (Fig. 13.4). The first stage is a basic study of the frequency and duration of breast-feeding and factors influencing it in rural and urban poor, and in the urban well-to-do. This is at present being carried out in eight countries and

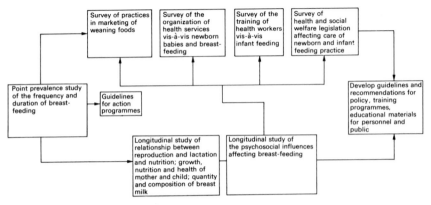

Fig. 13.4. World Health Organization collaborative studies on breast-feeding

practices, social policy, legislation, problems of working mothers, training and organization of health care and their influence on breast-feeding behaviour, biological aspects such as lactation and reproduction, and nutrition: quality and quantity of breast-milk. The purpose of all these studies is to have more factual data on major factors influencing the trends in breast-feeding behaviour in order to guide action programmes in primary health care and maternal and child care.

United Nations Children's Fund (UNICEF)
The general recommendations on *Priorities in child nutrition in developing countries* (Mayer 1975) was drawn up by a group of consultants, under the direction of Dr. Jean Mayer, for presentation to the UNICEF Executive Board. The following section is relevant:

Protection and promotion of breast-feeding
It is essential that every effort be made to protect and promote breast-feeding, particularly in the urban slums, where it is showing its most rapid decline:

Education of health personnel — doctors, nurses, auxiliaries, etc. on the necessity for prolonged breastfeeding and the introduction of solid foods at six months of age to supplement, *not* supplant it. Practical examples should be set in health centers and hospitals to encourage breastfeeding and actively discourage bottle feeding.

Educational materials and aids should be provided to health personnel to prepare expectant mothers for correct breastfeeding, educate them on the advantages of breastfeeding, the dangers of bottle feeding and the correct type of solids to add at four to six months. The introduction of solid food at six months is preferable in tropical countries, as there is a risk of contamination of these foods in hot climate.

Public awareness should be aroused through the mass media, e.g. posters, newspapers, radio, and television, about the benefits of breast-feeding and the dangers of bottle feeding. Such a campaign spearheaded by a respected or well-known figure, like the wife of the President or Prime Minister, well-known actresses, and community leaders, could be most effective.

There should be governmental control on the advertising and marketing of infant formulas and infant weaning foods, in order to protect the public from some unscrupulous commercial concerns.

Food and Agriculture Organization (FAO)

At a recent general assembly of FAO, the significance of human milk in world food supplies was brought up by the Norwegian delegate, with subsequent endorsement of the move for attention to be given to this previously neglected resource:

The 17th Session of the Food and Agriculture Organization of the United Nations. The Statement by Mr. Thorstein Treholt, Minister of Agriculture, Norway, in the General Debate on 14 November 1973.

Under Item 12B of the Agenda, a report of the Ad-Hoc Committee on increasing the production and use of edible proteins is to be considered. In this connection the Norwegian Delegation would welcome reactions concerning mother's milk. In Norway, and in most of the industrialized parts of the world, mother's milk is of small importance now compared to earlier times. Nutrition physiologists regret this state of affairs. Mother's milk supplements are no substitute for mother's milk. In particular, nutrition physiologists regret this trend in the developing countries and maintain that this constitutes a threat to human health in these countries.

If today we should have to find substitutes for the protein which through mother's milk is available for the growing generation, we should be faced with immense problems. In the industrialized countries, it is possible to give babies processed cow's milk somewhat similar to human milk. But in the developing countries for various reasons it would be quite impossible to substitute mother's milk with untreated cow's milk — not to mention processed cow's milk.

I have been informed of the conditions which arose in this respect in a developing country where some years ago they started a costly programme for the distribution of dried milk to families to remedy malnutrition of children. Evaluation of the programme showed that only about 25 percent of the milk was used for the benefit of the children. At the same time, when the dried-milk distribution was effected a great many mothers stopped breastfeeding their children.

The transition to artificial foodstuffs for babies results in many parts of the world in the children being supplied with polluted water in their food, and the lack of fuel for heating or cooking means that infants' milk generally becomes heavily infected with bacteria. Thus the standard of hygiene deteriorates.

We are interested in being informed as to whether FAO has noted this unfortunate development and of what the Organization may be able to do to counteract it. Is the policy pursued by FAO, WFP and other UN Institutions the right one in this important field?

Subsequently, FAO-sponsored assistance programmes to (i) increase the use of human milk and (ii) explore the relative effectiveness of different kinds of educative and promotional activities are under consideration with the governments of Malaysia and Sri Lanka (Food and Agricultural Organization 1975, Helsing 1975 b). Additionally, an FAO study is underway into 'human milk as a food commodity and its economic value', and in the

Organization's 1975 report on 'Population, food supply, and agriculture' attention is given to declining breast-feeding in relation to world food supplies.

International Labour Organization (ILO)
The International Labour Organization (1965, 1969) has developed a range of recommendations concerning protection in pregnancy and after childbirth. The present situation has been received recently at both sessions of the International Labour Conference in 1975 in the general topic 'equality of opportunity and treatment of women workers' (International Labour Organization 1975).

Protein Advisory Group
The Protein Advisory Group (now renamed the Protein–Calorie Advisory Group) of the United Nations' Ad-Hoc Working Group on Feeding the Young Child has repeatedly emphasized the great importance of breast-feeding and the dangers of currently declining rates. They have supervised four important, but inconclusive, meetings between the infant-food industry and paediatric nutritionists from resource-poor countries.

At a meeting in 1973, a tentative Code of Practice was drafted for advertising of infant foods, with special reference to developing countries. The following is extracted from this code:

No food should be advertised as being a food suitable for or to be given to an infant of three months or less. Local conditions may require national authorities to extend this restriction to six months.

No claim shall be made in an advertisement implying that any food including infant formula, is equivalent or superior to mother's milk, nor shall statements be made in advertisements which would, directly or indirectly, encourage a mother not to breast feed her infant.

No advertisement shall state or imply that the product advertised has medical or other professional support.

Advertisements and samples of branded infant foods should not be distributed or displayed.

Joint WHO/FAO Expert Committees.
In 1975, a Joint WHO/FAO Expert Committee met in Geneva to discuss the *Methodology of nutritional surveillance*, as had been recommended by the 1974 World Conference in Rome. In addition to advising surveillance of vulnerable groups, particularly young children, simple monitoring of food availability, including breast-feeding, was recommended.

International Paediatric Association
In 1970, the International Paediatric Association organized a 'workshop' in Vienna just prior to the Thirteenth International Paediatric Congress on the subject of 'New Urban Families', with particular emphasis on resource-poor countries (*Australian Paediatric Journal* 1971).

More recently, the International Paediatric Association organized a seminar for professors of Paediatrics from English-speaking Africa at Ahmadu Bello University, Zaria, Nigeria on 'Practical Difficulties in Applying Existing Knowledge about Nutrition and Infections', in which the role of declining lactation in urban areas was a recurrent theme. At the Fourteenth International Congress of Paediatrics held in Buenos Aires in October 1974, a full plenary symposium was organized on 'Human Milk and Breast-feeding: Recent Scientific Advances and Practical Programme', which was published as a monograph in the Journal of Tropical Paediatrics in 1975. In 1975, the International Paediatric Association organized a seminar for paediatric leaders from various parts of the world in Montreux, France on programmes to deal with the breast-feeding situation. The following recommendations have been published widely:

RECOMMENDATIONS FOR ACTION PROGRAMMES TO ENCOURAGE BREASTFEEDING

A. *Educational activities*
1. *Directed at the Medical Profession*
Pediatric societies should actively disseminate information about breast-feeding, including recent advances in knowledge that provide scientific validation for the superiority of breast-milk over any other type of infant food. Our primary efforts must be directed at those within the profession who are indifferent to or ignorant of the importance of the subject. Special efforts should also be made to apprise obstetricians, general practitioners, public health personnel, nurses and midwives and all cadres of paramedical personnel of current thinking. Particular attention must be directed at medical students and where medical curricula are deficient in the emphasis given to teaching on breast-feeding, every effort be made to make good such deficiencies.

2. *Education of the general public*
Through every medium available, press, radio, television, word of mouth, etc., the public must be made aware of the advantages of breast-feeding, and the emphasis must be given to the enlightenment of men as well as women. In this context, the importance of organizations like La Leche League should be mentioned. The creation of such organizations on a national basis should be supported. All medical personnel and all medical institutions should remove from their places of work any material, in whatever form, that may encourage bottle feeding and substitute material that promotes breast-feeding. The International Paediatric Association should undertake to provide suitable material, designed by professionals, to give publicity to breast-feeding.

3. *Education of those with special influence within the community*
In every community there are those whose opinions carry special weight with the general public. Every effort should be made to enlist the active support of these leaders of thought in promoting public education. The support of such people will also weigh heavily in bringing about reforms that require action at the local or central government level.

4. Education of boys and girls at school
The nutritional value of human milk and the advantages of breast-feeding for the infant should be taught at school as part of health and nutrition education and of preparation for family life and responsible parenthood. To this end there is an urgent need to educate the teachers and to provide them with the materials for inclusion in their syllabus.

B. *Curtailing promotion of artificial feeding*
   1. Sales promotion activities of organizations marketing baby milks and feeding bottles, that run counter to the general intent expressed in this document, must be curtailed by every means available to the profession, including, where necessary and feasible, legislation to control unethical practice.
   2. Dissemination of propaganda about artificial feeding and distribution of samples of artificial baby foods in maternity units should be banned immediately.

C. *Health services – reorganization to maintain breast-feeding*
   1. Every effort should be made to facilitate close mother and child relationships in obstetrical units and the practice of removing infants to 'well baby nurseries' must be actively discouraged.
   2. Breast-fed babies admitted to hospitals must not be separated from their nursing mother in order that breast-feeding not be interrupted.
   3. Preparation for motherhood must be viewed as an integral function of health-care systems and the nutrition of pregnant and lactating mothers, preparation for breast-feeding, initiation and continuation of breast-feeding must be given appropriate emphasis in practice.
   4. Special consideration must be given to the support of primary health-care units as channels for promoting breast-feeding at the grass-roots level.

D. *Facilities for working mothers who breast-feed*
Economic and social pressures will mitigate against breast feeding unless existing regulations and working conditions for nursing mothers can be modified to suit their requirements. Both government and the private sectors of commerce and industry should be approached to provide facilities and modify labor laws to:
   1. Provide facilities at places of work for breast-feeding.
   2. Modify the working day to fit in with breast-feeding requirements.
   3. Extend the period of maternity leave to allow for breast-feeding requirements.
   4. Provide appropriate allowances for payment to nursing mothers.

E. *Agreed policy on weaning*
We recommend that the introduction of cereals and other solid foods to the diet of fully breast fed infants before 4 months of age should be strongly discouraged and that in situations where environmental sanitation poses specially hazardous conditions that introduction of additive foods be delayed until the fifth or sixth month.

There is a great need to provide information related to weaning foods and a special need for attention to be directed to home prepared weaning foods based on locally available ingredients. In this context reference should be made to the PAG/WHO manual on infant and young-child feeding (Cameron and Hofvander 1975)

F. *Child spacing and Breast-feeding*
Breastfeeding traditions have achieved sensible child spacing in many societies, and

cognizance should be taken of the beneficial effects thereof for family health. Contraceptive pills containing substances that are likely to suppress lactation or which may adversely affect the infant if excreted in breast-milk, must not be distributed to lactating women.

G. *Research*
We recommend that active surveillance be maintained on trends in feeding practices at local and national levels and that research be directed at discovering factors that motivate change. We also recommend that research continue on 'fundamental' aspects of breastfeeding, including studies in the field of immunology, endocrinology, psychosocial adaptation and reproduction. Comparative studies of morbidity patterns in breastfed and artificially fed infants should also be undertaken on a longitudinal basis.

International Children's Centre (ICC)
In 1973, the International Children's Centre in Paris organized a Colloquium in the French language in Abidjan, Ivory Coast in West Africa on Breast-feeding ('Colloque sur l'Allaitement Maternel') and, as noted earlier, is currently co-sponsoring a multi-national investigation into lactation in eight countries, in collaboration with the World Health Organization. Péchevis and colleagues (1975) have produced a report in French entitled *Etudes sur les measures sociales et educatives en matière d'allaitement maternal.*

7. National concern

U.S.A. White House Nutrition Conference. At a national level, at the White House Nutrition Conference, held in Washington in 1971, the Panel on the Family as a Food Delivery System wrote:

It is recommended:
1. That more support for the breastfeeding decision and educated assistance be given to the vast majority of women who are physically and emotionally capable of nursing their babies, re-emphasis in medical schools, schools of nursing and in all other allied health training programs, including education in how to help a mother be successful in nursing her child.
2. That maternal and child health services (both federal and local) be directed to give high priority to doing all possible to assure an adequate food supply to low-income pregnant and nursing mothers and their families on inadequate diets.

U.S. Senate Committee on Nutrition and Human Needs (1973). The Chairman, Senator C. Percy, in his summing up of the sessions on mothers and young children noted: 'The seventh point is an interesting one: In summary, there is a low-cost nutritious food that can perhaps reduce malnutrition among infants to next to nothing and that is mother's milk through breastfeeding.'

Society for Nutrition Education. The following Resolution was adopted at the 1974 Annual Convention:

(V) *Information and encouragement on breastfeeding*
Whereas only a small minority of American women is breastfeeding their babies; and
Whereas breast fed babies appear to be more resistant to disease and allergies than bottle fed bablies; and
Whereas there is evidence that breastfeeding is conducive to a healthy psychological relationship between mother and baby; and
Whereas the promotional efforts of manufacturers of canned formula encourage bottle-feeding rather than breastfeeding; and
Whereas it is the responsibility of public health officials and private and governmental agencies to encourage measures that optimize the public's health;
Be it therefore resolved that the Society for Nutrition Education recommend that the Federal government, hospitals, obstetricians, · pediatricians, and state and local health departments provide every pregnant woman with objective information describing the relative merits of breastfeeding and bottle feeding and urge new mothers to consider breastfeeding their infants.

U.S. National Academy of Sciences. The U.S. National Academy of Sciences (1975) issued the following statement on policy development concerning nutrition and fertility:

The sharp decrease in breastfeeding is a matter of widespread concern. It compounds the serious deficits in food availability and the high incidence of infant disease and death among many marginal populations. There should be established under suitable auspices a world program to sponsor education on human lactation and to provide nutritional and social support that will enable more women to breast feed their babies successfully and for adequate periods.

U.K. Department of Health and Social Security.
In Britain, a report of a Working Party of the Panel on Child Nutrition of the Department of Health and Social Security entitled *Present-day practice in infant feeding* was published in 1974. Four reprintings, comprising 30 000 copies were sold in one year, and a popular version is in preparation. Relevant recommendations were:

6.1 General
6.1.1. Because we are convinced that satisfactory growth and development after birth is more certain when an infant is fed an adequate volume of breast milk, we recommend that all mothers be encouraged to breast feed their babies for a minimum of two weeks and preferably for the first four to six months of life.
6.1.2. We are concerned that women do not always receive adequate advice and encouragement to breast-feed their babies and we recommend that steps be taken to remedy this situation.
6.1.3. We are aware that lactation will not always be successfully established and we therefore recommend that the provision of modified cow's milk feeds, at a reasonable cost, should be continued.
6.1.4. We recommend that young babies should be weighed regularly so that an assessment of growth by comparison with standard centile charts can be made, and that as much attention should be paid at an early stage to excessive as to inadequate weight gain.

6.2 Encouragement of breastfeeding.
6.2.1. We are of the opinion that breastfeeding should be encouraged by education of (a) boys and girls in school and in the home; (b) parents in prenatal clinics and classes; and (c) mothers in the maternity-units of hospitals and at home.
6.2.2. We think that adequate instruction in the principles of nutrition, including infant feeding, should be given in the training of all professional personnel who are to be concerned with infant feeding — medical student, dietitian, midwife, health visitor and nurse.
6.2.3. We suggest that the principles and practice of infant feeding should be agreed by all concerned. We hope that in the newly integrated National Health Service there will be appointed in each district somebody with suitable qualifications and experience to coordinate education in nutrition, including infant feeding.
6.2.4. We are of the opinion that the period during which the maternity allowance is payable should be more adaptable to the requirement of the mother and child — i.e. that those mothers who, with the approval of the doctor in charge of ante-natal care, wish to continue at work during the third trimester of pregnancy should be able to receive the allowance for a longer period after parturition than at present.
Such an arrangement would encourage breastfeeding without the likelihood of great financial loss to the mother.
6.2.5. We think that the mass media could with benefit be used in educating the public in the principles of infant feeding which we have stated in this Report, and we disapprove of their use of an advertisement to promulgate ideas about infant feeding which are contrary to those principles.

Conversely, this report reiterates the lack of feasibility of producing formulas with similar composition to human milk:

5.2.1. Attempts to manufacture 'artificial' milk feeds which, of scientific knowledge, are both chemically and physiologically equivalent to human milk, are governed by such factors as cost of production, problems of packing and storage, palatability, acceptance by mothers, and by the fact that the compostion of breast-milk changes, especially during the early days of lactation. At the same time the advice which can be given by scientists to manufacturers is hampered by large areas of ignorance.

Scandinavia
A 'Breast-feeding Task Force' of the Swedish Ministry of Social Affairs has just completed a study and its recommendations will be available shortly. Likewise, the Swedish Nutrition Foundation is planning a Symposium 1977 for the 500th anniversary of Uppsala University on the topic: *'The Mother–Child Dyad'*. Also, a Working Group of the Norwegian Ministers of Social Affairs is preparing a comprehensive *Report on conditions and prerequisites for breast-feeding*.

Other countries
Various other countries have become concerned about this problem. For example, in Japan, a government-funded investigation is commencing into the situation with regard to breast-feeding and its significance in modern

Japan. Inclusion of revised emphasis on breast-feeding, and on proposals for actual campaigns, have been under discussion in Costa Rica, Venezuela, Chile, Spain, and the city of São Paulo, Brazil.

8. 'Times of trouble'

During what Toynbee has called 'times of trouble', breast-feeding rapidly and of necessity becomes the norm. For example, Williams (1947) found this to be the case among the offspring of European women in a Japanese internment camp in Malaya during World War II. As throughout history, natural disasters, including floods, droughts, and famines, continue to occur. In fact, with rising population pressure and with recent problems of world food production and possible climatic changes, it is likely that these may become more frequent, more extensive and, in some cases, more prolonged. At the same time, regrettably, in the turbulent and uncertain present-day world, man-made 'times of trouble' in the form of local or general economic difficulties, or 'limited' wars or civil strife occur almost continuously.

The modern world situation is, of course, not advanced as an argument in favour of breast-feeding, but as a sad fact of life. However, in such times of crisis and disaster, it is important not to bring in cow's-milk formulas for the emergency feeding of young babies (unless orphaned), with all the particular difficulties of transport and hygienic preparation under such circumstances, but to direct food to breast-feeding mothers and to start 'lactation centres' (p. 364).

SOCIAL FORCES FAVOURING BOTTLE-FEEDING

1. Family structure and role of women

In Westernized urban communities, extended types of family structure have become replaced increasingly by less stable, more mobile nuclear families, and, in some areas, single-parent families, where one parent (usually the mother) is left alone as a result of divorce, desertion, or death of the partner. Summarizing an analysis of the past 25 years, Bronfenbrenner (1975) emphasizes 'the progressive fragmentation and isolation of the family in its child-rearing role.'

Characteristic of such societies has been an increasing tendency for some women to work out of the home, partly for economic reasons and partly for self-fulfilment as independent individuals, made possible by smaller families because of contraception. Such changes plainly have the potential for marked and far-reaching effects on methods of child-rearing, especially breast-feeding. However, as noted earlier, the extent of female participation in the labour force varies in different parts of the world, perhaps especially when they have small children. For example, in 1971, U.S.

Labour Statistics showed that only 16 per cent of mothers with children under 3 years of age and with husbands, were full-time workers, although this figure is rising annually (Bernard 1974). Essentially, as Bernard notes, 'motherhood in a modern industrial society is a phenomenon quite different from motherhood in pre-literate and pre-industrialized societies.' Even with modern home technology, women may find themselves with a double burden of both 'mother work' and 'industrial work'.

Economics
The additional income from working mothers obviously supplies a high motivation in cash economies, especially when associated with continuous commercial stimulation towards increased consumption and upward social mobility. Its relevance becomes even greater in times of inflation or if the husband becomes unemployed.

Dugdale (1971) has emphasized that the overall objective should be the welfare of the whole family. However, this is difficult and, in some circumstances, the economic advantages to a family of a working mother may, in fact, be less than considered at first sight. As Popkin and Solon (1976) have commented, detailed socio-economic studies in urban areas in the Philippines give evidence of negative relations between mothers' participation in the labour force and the health and nutrition of their young children, as well as difficulties in being able to make use of any social services, such as child health clinics, because of the mothers' absence at work. In addition to 'out-of-house' expenses by working mothers, such as transport and meals, questions of the cost and availability of day-care centres, or 'child-minding' facilities for young children are the central issues. In a study undertaken a few years ago, Mead (1970) stated that in the U.S.A. at that time the annual cost of a well-run day-care centre service per child was about $1 500. The psychosocial significance to both mothers and offspring, especially young infants, of day-care centres has not really been defined. Again, as Mead has emphasized, evidence suggests that the stability, continuity, and quality of care for children under three years of age has importance in emotional development and adjustment. Leaving young children at a day-care centre with changing staff, even when highly motivated and affectionate, plainly cannot supply one individual as a 'stable point of reference'. With often limited personnel, babies tend to be left alone with things rather than a person, although this can also occur at home (Mead 1970).

Realistically, many thousands of day-care centres would be needed and that appears to be a financial impossibility for governments in most parts of the world. This is particularly true with the extra facilities and staff needed for the young infant at the exterogestate-foetal stage. 'It is impossible to provide really adequate services for infants and small children at a cost that the ordinary working mother can pay. Similarly, governmentally supported centres, which reach ideal standards, are ruinously expensive for the tax-payer.' /Mead 1970). The likelihood of low-quality, ill-supervised centres developing into 'dumping grounds for children and easy outs for women and for society unwilling to face real problems of women and needs of children' has been suggested by Mead, together with a warning that 'commercialized baby-tending could verge on the horror of the old baby farms'.

In some parts of the world, including the U.S.S.R., China, and Israel, crèches in industry permit working mothers to breast-feed their babies. This can be a simple room with cots and basic equipment for infant care, super-vised by a nursery nurse. Mothers can leave their babies and return to them at intervals, often 3-hourly.

Legislation in those countries has been geared to the provision of appropriate 'nursing breaks' (*pauses d'allaitement*), of two half-hour breaks per day, as well as to adequate maternity and lactation leave or bonuses, with guaranteed return to employment without loss of seniority (International Labour Organization 1969). Such legislation exists in a large number of countries but may not often be followed in practice. It is geared more to retaining women in the labour force than to infant health but may not often be followed in practice. Plainly the cost of equipping and staffing factory crèches would pose problems in private industry, as would payment for the one hour's work 'lost' by nursing mothers daily (International Labour Office 1975, International Labour Organization 1965). Likewise an unofficial comment by U.S. Labour-union leaders was reported by Lowe (United States Senate Committee on Nutrition and Human Needs 1973): 'They felt that if there were a national movement favouring breast feeding that women would return to work at an increased period of time after delivery, and only if industry could be encouraged to develop day care programs or places where the infant could be kept so that the woman could be both at work and breast feed were they willing to endorse a national program in favor of this.'

In some parts of the world, for example Scandinavia, a greater sharing of home-making and child-rearing duties and of outside employment between both parents may be becoming accepted, although of course this does not affect the unique biological roles of the female in child-bearing and in breast-feeding.

A variety of other adaptations have been used by working mothers who wish to breast-feed their babies, including temporary part-time work, 'night feedings' (p. 17) and expressing milk in the morning. None is always satisfactory. The real question is the need to consider providing opportunities for biological child-rearing, including close mother–infant contact and breast-feeding, for working mothers wishing to do so in Westernized technical urban societies. This is a complex subject which has not been adequately addressed. Current rising interest in this area may be expected to focus further attention and consideration is given to the matter later in discussion of potential programmes (p. 342).

Self-fulfilment

Another important social world trend, especially in Western countries, has been women's move towards equality with men, including the individuality and independence acquired by gainful employment out of the house. Apart from the economic considerations, salaried work permits women who so wish to fulfill their role as equal citizens in the wider world. This was stressed for example, in a recent study on the 'misuse of medical womanpower' in the U.K. where the inequity and wastefulness of the situation strongly suggested that attention needed to be given to special career structures (Bewley and Bewley 1975).

The Feminist or Women's Liberation Movement is made up of many different groups of opinion. To some, breast-feeding may be considered as a part of the role of the unliberated house-bound wife of the past, adding a further period of time to that already lost to an outside career as a result of pregnancy. The mainstream of the movement, however, appears to feel that the important issue is that the woman can have the right to choose her sexual and reproductive activities, and that lactation, and also pregnancy, is a particular, specific, and uniquely female activity, beyond the biological capacity of the male sex. This point of view has, for example, been stressed in a recent publication (Eiger and Olds 1972) on breast-feeding: 'This book is for today's woman, who values the natural way, is proud of her body and its special functions, is assertive in considering her special needs, and is free to choose to combine motherhood and career.'

Plainly, to achieve a balance between the roles of both parents which is psychologically equitable, biologically feasible, economically sound, and emotionally optimal for the whole family, especially the young baby, is something which Westernized urban '*Homo technologicus*' has yet to manage. Changes in attitude by men, women, and society will be necessary, as well as imaginative reconsideration of legislation and social services for mothers, fathers, and their young offspring, and of full-time and part-time career structures for women in which continuity of employment and seniority are not jeopardized by pregnancy and lactation. Methods can be (and have been) evolved by some women and in some societies by which a blend of women's two roles can be achieved. Aspects of such programmes will be discussed later (p. 342).

2. Increasing urbanization

All over the world, but particularly in many developing countries, uncontrolled urbanization, often without parallel industrialization or opportunities for employment, is an ever-increasing problem. This is associated with changes which make breast-feeding difficult, including Westernized cultural influences (advertising, health services, example of the élite, cash economy), changing family patterns (illegitimacy, women working out of the house), and the general environmental psychosocial stresses, both emotional and physical, of slum living (for a fuller account of these influences see Chapters 4 and 11).

In particular, under these circumstances the socio-cultural pressures to change and to achieve at least symbolic modernness mean that the presently seen moves from breast-feeding to bottle-feeding in new townsfolk may continually escalate, unless non-punitive methods of slowing the present urban avalanche are found (which seems very difficult) or unless governmental authorities concerned realize the serious ill-consequences of such changing patterns of child-rearing and infant feeding and attempt to introduce priority programmes to reverse, or, at least, to decelerate, this adverse trend (p. 342).

3. Dominant commercialism

All over the world, including developing countries, commercial infant-food companies compete with each other for markets, so that the relevance of the products in the particular social, cultural, or economic contexts may have to become a secondary consideration after business opportunity. Indeed, the very fact of intense competition makes it difficult for the companies to use other than the same tactics as their competitors in relation to ingredients used and to their promotional and advertising techniques.

Resource-rich countries.
The magnitude of sales-promotion activities is indicated by the estimated number of 1500 sales persons active in this field in the U.S.A. Sales-promotion practices are wide-ranging, including the provision of the product at subsidized rates to health services, as, for example, noted in a recent issue of the *New York Times* (14 Sep. 1975):

>   *Baby formula to be given free to city hospitals by 1979*
> IN a few years, it will cost the city nothing to provide infant formula to babies born in city hospitals.
>
>   Under a three-year contract with Ross Laboratories of Columbus, Ohio, the company is sharply cutting the cost of its formula, Similac, in the first two years and will supply the hospitals at no charge in the third, Dr. John L. S. Hollomon Jr., president of the Health and Hospitals Corporation, announced yesterday. At the list price, about $300 000 a year was spent on formula products.
>
>   Last year, under a competitive contract program, the corporation got Ross to supply the hospitals for less than $100 000 and the contract reached slashes last week that amount further, a spokesman said.
>
>   He ascribed the supplier's willingness to charge less now and nothing in the third year to business acumen, since parents usually keep their 25 000 infants a year on hospital formula, paying the regular price.
>
>   'For the company it's an investment,' the spokesman said. 'They hope to get the future business.'

Direct advertising has extensive coverage for both the public and for the health professionals. In fact, as Newton (1968) notes:

There is great pressure on each of us to bottle feed. Demonstrate this to yourself by looking over baby care magazines. How many pictures are there of formula equipment and bottle feeding babies as compared with pictures of breast-feeding babies? Then, if you have the chance, look over a medical journal when you next go to the library. You will be surprised to see the number of full-page advertisements there are for artificial feeding compounds. No one spends thousands of dollars a year advertising breastfeeding.

A similar message put with a slightly different emphasis, was emphasized recently in Britain (Malvern 1976):

The rejection of breastfeeding by many people is partly due to our attitudes towards sex, and partly to the fact that this aspect of breast function, together with the virtues of dried milk have thousands of pounds in advertising money spent on them. Breasts are erogenous zones, and their shape is an important part of sex symbolism. Adolescent girls have their attention focussed on this by the literature about figures and brassieres they read. Budding breasts are a sign of womanhood, a source of both pride and shame. Young girls are extremely self-conscious about their breasts — anxious for older people not to tease them on the one hand, on the other, competing with their contemporaries over who can wear a brassiere earliest. All womens publications, and underground stations advertise multiple adolescent uptilted breasts as a sex symbol. A family doctor leaflet carried five double-page spreads about dried milk, and there was only one picture, with an article, of a baby at the breast.

In a recent paper, Gussow (1974) has given the following analysis of the role of advertising in the U.S.A.:

The purpose of advertising, at this time, in this country, is to stimulate wants and to instill needs — a fundamental purpose which the most influential of our media, television, never brings into question. Advertising promotes consumption beyond need — i.e. overconsumption. This is true whether the potential customer is a housewife who is being convinced that her private parts require deodorizing, or a child who is being convinced that the last set of plastic people he acquired were nothing compared to the new improved version now available.

Yet we are coming into a time — we are, indeed, in the midst of a time — when overconsumption (translated as waste) of any of the world's increasingly scarce resources is wrong. What do we do about the habits of overconsumption which advertising has encouraged and continues to encourage, now that the world is beginning to run short of many of the things it needs to survive? How do we help our children learn the real consumer wisdom — which is how not to consume, how to put the minimum burden on the planet Earth?

To change the pressure of advertising of infant foods easily will be difficult, as has been suggested by difficulties with altering advertising of another commodity, tobacco (*The Lancet* 1975b). It is more likely that there will be increased advertising directed at the health professionals, as well as at mothers, with token support of breast-feeding, but actual undermining of confidence, leading to complementary bottle-feeds and consequent decline in milk secretion as a result of the decreased prolactin production.

Speaking of advertising, Gussow (1974) makes a similar point:

> I think it is perfectly clear to any attentive — dare I say perceptive — observer, that we are on the verge of a burst of 'pro-social' or 'consumer education' efforts on the part of advertisers, networks, and advertising agencies who feel themselves under siege. Child-oriented PSA's [Public Service Advertisements] are coming, however — indeed, some are already here. What concerns me is that what will be produced is a good deal of very inoffensive so-called 'consumer education' stuff — all of it absolutely guaranteed not to change consumer behaviour in any significant way whatsoever.

That such approaches are likely is endorsed by the self-justificatory and self-complimentary posture of the infant-food industry (Sehring 1975):

> I am of the opinion that the prepared formula industry played a significant role in solidifying a base for breast-feeding. For over 20 years, industry has praised breast milk as the ideal feeding and that which provided the model for humanized milk. This message has been transmitted to physicians and mothers through promotional literature. Humanized milk formulas owe their success to having been promoted as close equivalents to breast-milk, and providing comparable clinical benefits. These factors have fostered a positive attitude toward breastfeeding in the minds of many prospective mothers.

Resource-poor countries
The problems faced by the infant-food industry include climbing costs of materials and labour, and mounting competition. Also, in the major markets of the U.S.A. and Western Europe, declining birth rates and increasing breast-feeding have lead to diminished markets for formulas. In the U.S.A., there were about 4·3 million births in 1957, and only 3·1 million in 1974. As a consequence, companies marketing infant-food products, including formulas, are diversifying their activities. To compensate for declining sales in the U.S.A., and Europe, an increasing drive has developed for sales overseas in resource poor countries, where marketing surveillance is negligible and large populations using small quantities could still add substantial sales. By creating a need, sales can be expanded down the income ladder.

Techniques employed in sales promotion include 'milk nurses' (p. 226), 'formula banks', free samples to mothers and to health services widespread distribution of 'educational' promotional material (posters, calendars, brochures, baby books, vaccination cards, formula slips), prizes, contests, lotteries, contrived news items, displays at 'point of purchase' and on labels, and assistance to health professionals, as well as advertising through the mass media (Zaltman *et al*. 1971).

As noted earlier (p. 311), economic forces may be developing which may make it advisable for governments to introduce import restrictions in resource-poor countries for unnecessary items, such as overly expensive formulas, and to scrutinize critically the cultural and socio-economic appropriateness of advertising with regard to its effects on infant health and nutrition. However, difficulties in this regard must not be under estimated. Infant-food companies have an inherent, long-standing, and carefully pre-served benign image 'as instruments in the service of health and nutrition'. Queries as to the suitability or harmfulness of such products are likely to be misconstrued as faddist, and, in resource-poor countries, suggestions con-cerning the limitation of importation of infant formulas may be charac-terized as crank behaviour by Westernized senior government officials or foreign residents, whose wives may often be using them for their own children.

In many cases, foreign infant-food companies are also involved in other aspects of industry or agriculture in developing countries, for example, dairying or cocoa plantations. These will increase their weight in influencing decision-making in the country. Additionally, advertising by such concerns through government-owned mass media, particularly the radio and press, or through newspapers or magazines, may represent a major or only source of revenue for these enterprises (as in many industrialized countries). Changes may then be difficult to effect, as has been the case with the advertising of tobacco (*The Lancet* 1975c).

Also, the sheer size, complexity, and influence of some of the multi-national food corporations can be gauged by the comparison of their gross annual sales with the gross national products of some developing countries. A few years ago, for example, Nestlé ranked ahead of Ghana, or of Uganda and Tunisia combined (Berg 1973).

However, Margulies (1975) points out that conflicts of interest between governments of resource-poor countries and multi-national companies are beginning to be appreciated:

> Third World governments know that human priorities tend to get lost when decisions are based on corporate needs, and are formulated at distant corporate headquarters in New York, Geneva or Tokyo. Nevertheless, they risk their autonomy and buy in. Underneath this uneasy alliance is a very real and very basic time conflict of interests. For corporations, development means creating needs the corporations products can fill. For the people in the Third World countries, however, development means fulfilling needs that are already there. These urgent needs are the goods and services, and industry that is tailored to their national priorities.

Nevertheless, although the forces, as regards time, money*, and expertise in public relations, available to those concerned with public health aspects of paediatric nutrition in developing countries have been very slight in relation

---

*In the U.S.A., there are about 74 000 deaths from lung cancer annually. It can be calculated that this means that the tobacco industry spends about $2800 per lung cancer death compared with about $14 per death spent by the government-funded anti-smoking campaign. Similar figures could be calculated per death from marasmus and diarrhoea.

to those of the food industry, some changes have developed in recent years, and may be fostered by future programmes.

4. Conservatism of western medicine

A major factor in relation to infant feeding is undoubtedly the often ill-informed and/or ambivalent, 'vague and dispirited' (Richardson 1976) attitude of the medical and nursing professions towards breast-feeding (Hollen 1976, Johnston 1975). Very frequently this takes the form of a general ritual endorsement, with neither up-to-date knowledge nor aware-ness of the factors that make for success or failure, and consequently with actual regimens which can unwittingly make successful lactation more difficult. This problem has been stated in the following way (Jelliffe and Jelliffe 1973*b*):

> Unfortunately, unbiased consideration concerning causes of the current decline in breast-feeding performance in many parts of the world, including developing coun-tries, has clearly shown that activities by more usual forms of health service have often played a detrimental role. Obviously, this depends ultimately on senior administrators and educators of health staff being made aware of modern knowledge in this field and becoming adequately convinced.

> Very often health staff, including doctors, health nurses, and mid-wives, may, at best, endorse breast-feeding passively by the ritual repetition of a list of ten advan-tages of breast-milk compared with cow's milk. At the same time, because of lack of conviction and inadequate knowledge of the psychophysiology of lactation, mothers may, in fact, be dealt with in a way in maternity units that makes the successful initiation of lactation very difficult indeed.

The conservatism of medical (and nursing) education is in part at fault; 'current educational practices are curiously resistant to rational change' (Simpson 1974). From a cultural viewpoint, prestige always lies with ultra-scientific departments in Western-type training schools. For example dis-proportionate status will be given to such specialist fields, as molecular biology and brain surgery, and with inadequate emphasis allowed for more holistic, preventive subjects such as nutrition and community medicine. Students learn more about total parenteral nutrition than lactation. Indeed, a recent survey of paediatricians and obstetricians in an area of California showed that over half had never seen a baby being breast-fed either in their childhood or in their medical training (Hollen 1976). In Pasay in the Philip-pines, up-to-date knowledge of breast-feeding was very slight among health personnel. For example, an understanding of the basic reflexes controlling lactation was found in only 35 per cent of physicians, 6 per cent of midwives, and 0 per cent of nurses (Burgess 1976).

Clinical and laboratory training over-dominate the curricula. One aspect of such bias has been termed the '*Myth of the basic sciences*' — or perhaps it is rather a series of interlocking myths, like some gloomy Norse saga. One part of it is what has been called *Physico-chemical reductionism* — the attitude that denies that man is anything more than a fortuitously elegant arrangement of molecules (Simpson 1974). Similarly, the emphasis in higher paediatric education is almost always on the diagnosis of rare conditions.

All over the world in most medical schools nutrition is taught minimally and is fragmented between various disciplines, such as biochemistry and paediatrics (American Medical Association 1972). Infant nutrition has often been complacently considered as of only historical interest in industrialized countries, with current methods regarded as optimal and simple, only needing occasional minor modification to be incorporated as a result of research findings.

Present-day deficiencies in training of nursing personnel in nutrition are also very great, as indicated, for example, by results of a study of 742 Schools of Nursing throughout the world undertaken for the International Union of Nutritional Sciences. Results showed that the coverage with regard to nutrition was almost always inadequate and that real-life aspects of the subject such as cultural attitudes, composition of commoner foods, and particularly the significance of human milk rarely formed part of the curriculum. (E. F. P. Jelliffe 1974, 1976*a*). Lastly, the training of nutritionists in some parts of the world is concentrated too much with biochemistry and metabolism, rather than providing a blend or spectrum running from cellular considerations to community applications.

A lack of up-to-date information and a 'damned with faint praise' ambivalence towards breast-feeding have often been evident in medical attitudes, as for example, in two recent brief notes in leading British journals:

Breast milk has some psychological and physiological advantages. A possible disadvantage is underfeeding, and another that iron and vitamins cannot be put into the feed. (*British Medical Journal*, 1974).

Compared with canned formulas, breast milk is cheaper, cleaner, and (presumably) ideally suited to the nutrition of the human infant. (*The Lancet,* 1961)

Another attitude is that of the lost cause. This is exemplified in the reply received by an author who had sent a paper on breast-feeding to a leading Canadian journal: ' . . . while important in the Arctic as you maintain, in the more settled parts of Canada [breast-feeding] is a lost cause and no longer generates interest among obstetricians, paediatricians (despite the lip service they are always careful to pay it), or, most important, mothers.' (Schaefer 1973).

The iatrogenic background to lactation failure and its potential for change has been emphasized by Creery (1973):

The whole subject of the natural feeding of human infants is surrounded by an aura of abject defeatism. Many members of the professions concerned with child health appear to regard the promotion of breast-feeding as a lost cause, and much thought and effort are spent in concocting more elegant and expensive unnatural substitutes for human milk. There are clearly many factors in determining why women refuse to recognize that 'breast is best' for their children; one factor at least in their denial of breast milk for their children is a widespread lack of knowledge of the benefits of human milk for human babies and of the demerits of cow's milk as an infant food. Another is the obvious lack of interest in a support for natural feeding shown by many doctors (family doctors, obstetricians, and paediatricians alike), midwives, and health visitors. If one can manage to rekindle or arouse interest and enthusiasm among health professionals, the results can be startling and the situation can be transformed in a very short time.

On the other hand, some changes are also occurring quietly in medical education. For example, the leading paediatric textbook in the U.S.A., and probably the world, has completely rewritten its influential section on infant feeding with much increased emphasis on breast-feeding, including up-to-date and accurate coverage of the psychophysiology, and the address of La Leche League is provided for mothers needing practical assistance with nursing (Laupus 1975). In addition, the American Medical Association now sponsors an annual course for physicians, organized by the medical advisory group of La Leche League. In Britain, the recent production of the important *Present-day practice in infant feeding* by the Department of Health and Social Security (1974) may be expected strongly to influence philosophy, practice, and paediatric training in that country. Also, in both the U.S.A. and Britain, other recent publications have clearly indicated the need for a fresh look at infant-feeding methods (D. P. Addy 1976, *Dairy Council Digest* 1976, D. B. Jelliffe 1976*a*, Neumann and Jelliffe 1977).

Fundamentally, there often appear to be two polarized extremes in modern medical thinking, the ultra-technological, epitomized by some intensive care units for the newborn (Swyer 1975) and the excessive use of parenteral 'elemental' nutrition, and a questioning of some of these mechanistic methods as being harmful and used unnecessarily. The latter viewpoint is indicated in a recent conference on iatrogenic problems in neonatal intensive care (Johnson 1976) and by a paper entitled 'Obstetric delivery today: for better or for worse (Dunn 1976), in which the 'Gordian Knot' approach and the routinely over-active management of labour are criticized.

The immediate need is for a blend between the technological and the bio-traditional, towards what has been termed a 'curvilinear compromise' (Jelliffe and Jelliffe 1975*d*, 1976*d*). From a broader viewpoint, there is a world need to realize that Western linear allopathy does not have all the answers, and that other medical systems (Jelliffe and Jelliffe 1976*e*) have powerful contributions to what has been termed 'syn-pathy' — an amalgam of the beneficial from diverse medical systems.

Conclusion

Plainly, the various moulding forces touched upon briefly in the present chapter vary considerably from one area of the world to another. Some are potentially modifiable with relative ease; some represent world changes, such as trends to urbanization and rising costs of food, over which even economists and planners seem to have little control.

Especially in the welter of present-day rapid and often unexpected change, it is impossible to predict future developments for man, including the methods he will employ for rearing and feeding his children. Some would say this would be towards the ultra-scientific dehumanization satirized by Aldous Huxley in *Brave New World* (p. 300), or propounded recently in apparent seriousness by Elizabeth Borghese (1973):

> *Homo sapiens* is the last mammal. There won't be other mammals after him. His baby, far from perfect, is helpless, unfinished, like the little marsupial. But the mother, to whom he is so long attached, is at the end of her mammality. Especially in the higher classes, in the cities, among intellectual and professional women — that is among the most evolved specimens — breast-milk is scarce. So lactation is being externalized. And mothers go to work, and the more work there is for mother, the more hazardous becomes gestation. Premature births are common. Mothers's physical build — tall and slender — does not seem particularly suitable for childbearing and childbirth labor. But premature births are no longer as dangerous as they used to be. There are incubators. Thus, gestation is externalized; and the incubator-plus-formula corresponds to the egg.

From an opposite viewpoint, few would have predicted the spontaneous resurgence of concern with 'naturalism', including breast-feeding, which has developed in the last 15 years in mechanized America and Western Europe.

Fundamentally, if it is considered that the present modern scientific evidence supports the superiority of breast-feeding compared with formula feeding, then it becomes valid to consider ways of promoting programmes to ameliorate the situation. A common response to this type of suggestion is that such programmes have failed in the past. This is not the case. They have never been tried, especially with the very new information on the psychophysiology of lactation and on its practical application. The development of such programmes, specifically adapted to the ecological circumstances in different areas, is a world priority as regards infant health and nutrition.

14 Practical programmes

We are made sharply aware of discrepancies when an attempt is made to introduce modern ideas of hygiene to a people who have no idea of bacterial contamination; but the difficulties are no less apparent when an attempt is made to introduce into the regime of a modern hospital elements of greater autonomy for the parturient woman, or an opportunity for greater spontaneity between mother and child, or a greater tolerance for different styles of relationship within the family. These attempts to widen the allowance for variation violate the tradition of the hospital, which is organized to deal with the sick, and clashes between old and new, established and innovative, elements in medical practice are bound to occur.

Margaret Mead and Niles Newton (1967) Cultural patterning of perinatal behavior

There are two views to be taken of the catastrophic decline of breast-feeding in recent decades. One is that further decline is inevitable and will be rapid and very widespread. According to this view, it is better to anticipate the unavoidable: that is, to concentrate on producing, testing, packaging, and distributing breast-milk substitutes, probably based on cow's milk with added plant-protein foods. The other view is that the trend towards artificial feeding and early weaning can be reversed, or at least decelerated.

Inevitable-decline approach

This point of view is based on the failure to affect trends in breast-feeding in the Western world previously and on recognized improvements in overall general child nutrition, mortality, and health which have coincided in the past with the development of reliable clean sources of cow's milk-based formulas in Western countries (Aykroyd 1971).

It is correct that the widespread introduction of economical, easily available, clean supplies of various forms of cow's milk were associated with lowering of the very high infant mortality rates in already hand-fed babies in the slums of cities produced by the industrial revolution in Europe and North America (p. 183). However, to carry this analogy to present circumstances in tropical developing countries is an 'ahistorical historical comparison'. Improvements in infant mortality rates in general in the present century in Europe and North America have coincided with and been paralleled by highly significant improvements in environmental hygiene, in housing, in education, in general food production and distribution, and in economic levels. All of these affected the health and nutrition of young children directly and indirectly, and made artificial feeding safer and more feasible economically and practically.

In fact, although infants can grow adequately with artificial feeding under good conditions of hygiene, income, and parental education, these rarely exist in most resource poor, developing countries, and cannot be expected to alter for the better in the near future (and may worsen), especially in the increasing urban slums.

The concept that low-cost breast-milk surrogates may in the near future be largely based on plant-protein mixtures may, indeed, have to be correct — for economic and agronomic reasons. At the same time, a whole new area of as yet unexplored biochemical and metabolic problems will emerge as attempts are made to juggle such relatively untried ingredients into an approximate blend for babies without metabolic side-effects (Lowe 1972).

Additionally, the 'inevitable-decline' approach ignores the fundamentally important new work that has emerged in recent years on the unique and universally relevant properties of human milk and breast-feeding responsible for the revival of interest by both mothers and health professionals.

Even if abundant cow's milk were available for the preparation of formulas, it would be a retrograde step biologically from a health and nutrition point of view to make this change. Inadequate food supplies and increasing costs mean that there is little chance of the ingredients of such formulas being available on a world-wide basis, let alone economically enough for resource-poor countries.

Another argument of the 'inevitable-decline' school is that previous campaigns to promote breast-feeding have been failures. In fact, various small-scale programmes have been undertaken successfully. Larger community or national campaigns of the past, which seemed to have had little effect, were carried out without the benefit of modern knowledge of the causes of lactation failure, were usually narrowly unimaginative and confined to single or limited range approaches — for example, via posters, or maternity benefits only — and were not evaluated adequately.

Some past programmes were mentioned by Berg (1973) who noted that as early as the eighteenth century the French government printed posters encouraging mothers to nurse; Finland assessed penalties on non-nursing mothers whose infants died; the British government mounted a campaign to encourage breast-feeding in the early 1900s.

Imperfect as present knowledge still is, recent investigations into the psychophysiology, endocrinology, and social dynamics of lactation and breast-feeding, as well as the successes of such 'information-and-support' organizations as La Leche League, mean that new methods, techniques, and practical approaches are now available for campaigns and programmes to promote breast-feeding. To assist the formulation of such programmes, appropriate to different regions, there is a great need for further epidemiological studies into the social, cultural, economic, psychological, and other factors responsible for success or failure in lactation in different communities. Currently, such research is under way in various parts of the world, including a large-scale multi-national study planned under the auspices of World Health Organization and the International Children's Centre, Paris. At the same time, sufficient information, much of it new and often unfamiliar to persons in the health and nutrition fields, has become available in recent years and permits the main components of such a practical programme to be suggested.

Briefly, the 'inevitable-decline' scenario cannot be contemplated, and there is an urgent need to devise appropriate approaches to problems of maternal and child nutrition, both in rural and increasingly in urban areas in all parts of the world. It is not known whether practical programmes to reverse, or produce a decelerated decline, in breast-feeding are feasible on a large scale in present-day communities or not. There is an urgent need to try, using available modern knowledge, modified by information gained by research.

If, however, it proves impossible to halt or at least to decelerate the present decline, current information indicates clearly that it will not be possible to produce, distribute, and use safely the vast quantities of breast-milk substitute that will be required. This will be impossible agriculturally from projected world food supplies, and economically, logistically, and hygienically. In resource-poor countries, it is not feasible within the constraints of national and family budgets, with very limited distribution outlets (such as health centres), and with existing low levels of household hygiene. Results will include a widespread worsening of infant health and nutrition, especially in poorer less technically developed countries, together with increased population pressure and unnecessary added strains on already limited national and world economic and agricultural resources.

Community programme approach

Many experienced paediatric nutritionists are becoming much concerned with the consequences of the present trends in infant feeding on child health and nutrition, and are striving to devise programmes designed to reverse or at least to decelerate the trend towards early weaning and artificial feeding, and to prevent its spread to areas as yet unaffected. In addition, the situation is arising when national and international concern is more frequently beginning to be channelled towards the possible organization of such programmes, and advice is being sought for their development. This will be a matter of considerable difficulty in the present-day 'bottle-feeding culture' where breast-feeders are a minority group (Richards and Bernal, 1975). It will need to take into account many complex interacting social and economic factors. Success may sometimes only be partial. However, as Berg (1973) has remarked, 'benefits from even modest improvements, such as the increase by a few percentage points of the proportions of mothers who elect to breast-feed, or extension of nursing by a few weeks or months for those who already do, could be translated into millions of dollars and, more importantly probably millions of lives.

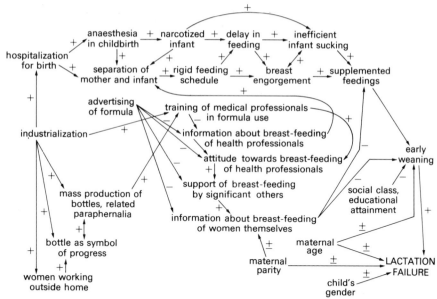

Fig. 14.1. Suggested relationships between ecological, clinical, and sociological variables which contribute to world-wide lactation failure, illustrating wide range of factors which could be included in a highly detailed community analysis (from Auerbach, K. G. (1975). Proceedings of the Fourth International Congress of Psychosomatic Obstetrics and Gynaecology, p.415–18, Karger, Basel)

A practical programme, specifically designed to meet the requirements of each individual community, will need to be devised based on information obtained by a community diagnosis.

Community diagnosis

Details of national or community programmes to promote breast-feeding will plainly need to vary greatly with the situation and the many factors which can influence matters (Fig. 14.1). Information will be needed, in particular, concerning current methods of infant feeding and community influences on breast-feeding in the particular society. This will enable 'at-risk' factors in the country to be identified, and specially vulnerable communities to be selected. Such information will have to include the situation of the élite, including foreign families in developing countries, as being influentials and trend-setters. Community diagnosis can vary greatly in complexity (Tables 14.1 and 2) and often it may only be possible to collect relatively limited data.

Pattern of infant feeding.

The existing pattern of infant feeding needs to be investigated, in relation to relevant aspects of the social background and, if feasible, to the major outcomes as regards health and nutrition in early childhood. In some special circumstances, it may be possible to collect longitudinal data. More usually, approximate but useful information on the infant feeding practices in a community can be obtained rapidly, inexpensively, and simply from the results of cross-sectional 24-hour recall questionnaires administered to mothers.

Knowledge and attitude studies need to be undertaken among young women, older women, school girls, husbands, and health service personnel. Information is needed concerning the variation with social background, particularly between the urban poor, the urban élite, and the rural poor. Subsampling might be needed to include major ethnic, religious, and other groups.

TABLE 14.1   *Representative data to be collected in a community diagnosis*

Pattern of infant feeding

Maternal diet:	pregnancy and lactation (especially cultural food restrictions)
Breast-feeding:	when commenced; prelactal feeds; frequency (including night feeds); scheduled or not; customs interfering with lactation (traditional or modern)
Introduction of semi-solids:	when, how, what
Use of pacifiers (dummies):	
Removal from breast (sevrage):	when, how, compensatory actions

Community Influences   (1) HEALTH SERVICES

Prenatal care:	information; breast preparation; dietary advice
Puerperal care:	practices interfering with lactation reflex (Table 14.2); cultural dietary practices; routine inhibition of lactation (e.g. oestrogens); cutting umbilical cord (at once or delayed)
Premature unit:	use of breast-milk (especially colostrum); breast-milk bank; mother–baby contact; nearby accommodation for mothers
Children's ward:	opportunity for breast-feeding; admission of mothers; hospital policy to formula purchasing and distribution
Health centres:	supplementary food distribution policy
Health education:	formal and informal; 'ill-health education' (advertising etc.)
Family-planning services:	methods advised (in relation to lactation)
Staff training:	curriculum content (nutrition, infant feeding, psychophysiology, modern knowledge on properties of human vs. cow's milk, practical management in theory and practice; relationships with food industry)

(2) FOOD INDUSTRY

Advertising: (shops, press, radio, television):	coverage (time space); motivation; relevance (income, domestic hygiene, present infant feeding practices)

| *Promotion (via health services):* | direct (posters, calendars, brochures; free samples; professional journals) |
| | indirect (funding of meetings, hospitality, prizes, research) |

(3) ROLE OF WOMEN

Working women:	percentage working for wage out of home; types of jobs; facilities for breast-feeding; cost–benefit to family
Voluntary groups (concerned with breast-feeding):	name, size, activities, and methods
Legislation:	maternity protection laws (with special reference to lactation)
Attitudes to breasts and breast feeding:	information from women, husbands, young girls, grandmothers and health workers; status, modernness, acceptability in public.

TABLE 14.2 *Puerperal practices interfering with lactation via the prolactin and let-down reflexes* (modified from Haire 1973).

Practice	Effect on lactation (via maternal reflexes)
Delaying first breast-feed	
Sedated newborn (excess maternal anaesthesia)	
Supplying prelacteal and complementary feeds	Limitation of suckling and
Regular, limited feeds (4 hours) (with no or limited night feeds)	prolactin secretion
Mother and infant separated ('nurseries')	
Uninformed, confused mother	
Tired mother (no food or drink in labour)	
Routine episiotomy (pain)	
Weighing before and after (test feeds)	Anxiety and intereference
Restricting visitors	with let-down reflex
Unsympathetic or ambivalent health staff ('anti-*doula* effect')	
Lack of privacy	

The 'success' of methods of infant feeding used can be roughly gauged by growth — minimally by weight gain compared with appropriate standards, but optimally with other anthropometric parameters included, such as length and subcutaneous fat, and by the prevalence of the more important local forms of malnutrition (such as obesity or marasmus); and of infections (such as weanling diarrhoea) (p. 285).

Variations in community programmes
Community programming need to vary greatly in different parts of the world. For example, in some rural areas of Asia, Africa, or New Guinea, traditional breast-feeding and weaning practices are still the norm, and programmes should be geared to avoiding deterioration (Jelliffe and Maddocks 1963). Conversely, in particular developing countries where lactation has already diminished in varying degrees, the decline may be attributed more to one particular cause — for example, the spread of health services in Cuba; the effect of advertising in Cairo; the widespread free distribution of powdered milk in Chile. Yet again, the situation is very different in industrialized countries in Europe or America where bottle-feeding has been common for one or two generations.

Community lactation patterns
Analyses and discussion presented in earlier chapters suggest that four main categories of lactation patterns can be identified on a community basis, with certain general common features which can be summarized briefly. These categories, modified from Raphael (1973*b*), are:
   1. *Traditional, pre-industrial (total breast-feeder).* In this type of traditional community (p. 161), breast-feeding is the norm and is prolonged for one to three years or more. Feedings are on demand, including during the night, when the baby sleeps by the mother's side.
   2. *Recently urbanized poor (emerging bottle-feeder).* By contrast, in recently urbanized poor communities, such as shanty towns and slums all over the world, there is usually a rapid decline in prevalence of breast-feeding for reasons noted elsewhere (p. 214). Breast-feeding is often only undertaken for a short period of time, frequently for only a few weeks or months; it is sometimes followed by 'mixed milk feeding', in which breast-feeding and cow's-milk formula from a bottle are both employed.
   3. *Urban educated well-to-do (élite bottle-feeder).* Breast-feeding is carried out by a small, but varying minority. Bottle-feeding with cow's milk-based formula has become the norm, either from birth or from a few weeks after birth. Likewise, there has been a move from the preparation of home-made infant weaning foods towards commercial processed infant foods of high convenience.
   4. *Naturalist urban educated (neo-élite breast-feeder).* An increasing percentage of more educated women in Western countries are becoming actively concerned with nursing their babies on the breast and with promoting breast-feeding as an important aspect of mothering (p. 142).

Vulnerable points
The prior community analysis will also enable specific cultural, as well as general, 'vulnerable points' in lactation to be identified. For example, in Brazil, Sousa and colleagues identified the following four points: (1) the first

minutes and hours, (2) post-hospitalization, (3) 6 weeks after delivery (when intercourse was often resumed), and (4) at the time of the first menstrual period (Sousa 1975).

Characteristics of programmes

All preventive programmes need certain characteristics. They should be based on information obtained in the community diagnosis. They need to be based on educational measures — both to professional groups and to the public — that include the supply of up-to-date information, persuasion and motivation. *In general, they need to be concerned with strengthening enhancing influences and minimizing inhibiting forces, using motivational appeals appropriate to the country, having particular emphasis on influentials in the 'modern life-styles'.* They need to bear in mind constantly the key fact that maternal confidence and nutrition are the essential ingredients for successful breast-feeding. They need to be made with awareness that Western and non-Western cultures have much to learn from each other, and that there are grave dangers for resource-poor countries imitating inappropriate or universally questionable patterns of infant care from the Western world, which are often in the process of changing.

Educational component

The educational component of a community programme would have to be aimed at supplying information about breast-feeding to a wide audience (Jelliffe and Jelliffe 1973b), ranging from governmental planners and policy makers and trend-setting élite, to professional nutritionists and health workers (particularly leaders, teachers, and students in general medicine, obstetrics, paediatrics, nursing, and midwifery (Jelliffe and Jelliffe 1973a, 1973d, Mobbs and Mobbs 1972, Newton 1969)), to school-teachers and schoolchildren of both sexes, and to women themselves (and, very importantly, to their husbands). Up-to-date practical information for parents and for health and nutrition professionals is a paramount need (p. 404).

In addition, information needs to be supplied concerning other aspects of parent education and child-rearing, but especially infant feeding (such as the age of introduction to solids), and techniques of breast-feeding, including anatomy, psychophysiology, and practical pre-natal and post-natal management, particularly low-cost maternal diets and preparation for child birth. This is especially needed by women themselves during girlhood, pregnancy, and the puerperium, and by health workers concerned with the supervision of mothers and young babies (and by training schools for such workers).

Messages and motivation

These should have similar Madison Avenue appeals as commercial advertisements — that is motivation through modernness, wealth, success, and

Mother's milk is best

Fig. 14.2. Counter-productive breast-feeding poster: Uganda, 1959. The message is correct in that the milk of each species is the most appropriate for its offspring, but there is also an unfortunate implication that nursing is an animal-like function

sexual attractiveness*, as well as health and nutritional advantages, and entertainment value. In some circumstances, traditional religious sanction or nationalism ('negritude' for example) may be an extra motivation.

As an example of misguided effort, a poster prepared in Uganda some ten years or more ago showed various animals such as zebras and elephants suckling their offspring (Fig. 14.2); although this was technically correct, the perceived message was probably that breast-feeding was an animal-like function. Conversely, the sex-glamour approach was used in a breast-feeding campaign in Trinidad (White 1974) (Fig 14.3).

The message with regard to breast-feeding is both specific and yet paradoxical. It is not a new practice to be introduced, but rather an ancient one to be endorsed by modern science and endowed with a fashionable image. Motivation is easier if assistance can be obtained from famous and attractive women from the same community, who have themselves breast-fed their infants. For example, at their 1971 Convention the La Leche League had Princess Grace of Monaco as their guest speaker.

A major issue is sometimes the degree of persuasion permissible — too much being felt to be likely to lead to guilt and unhappiness in the mother unable or unwilling to breast-feed. While this is true, recent new findings make the reasons to breast-feed much more valid and proven than in past

*For example, the following slogan was suggested at a recent conference 'Breast-feeding for slimmer babies, sexier mothers, and less pollution'; or a Californian bumper-sticker: 'Breast-feeding — ecology with love'; or the title of the 1976 Convention of the Parents' Centres of Australia: 'Breasts — a sensational feeding device'.

YOU CAN GET YOUR FIGURE BACK TOO

During pregnancy, the womb stretches and expands to accommodate your baby. Breast feeding helps to retract the womb and bring it back to its normal size. So breast feeding is actually a pretty marvellous way to put yourself back in shape. It is too, the most natural way, since breast feeding uses up the fat laid down during pregnancy in readiness for lactation. That way you lose weight and get back your figure, naturally.

"This is part of the Consumers Education Programme designed and sponsored by the Housewives Association of Trinidad and Tobago, The Advertising Agencies Association of Trinidad and Tobago and the Trinidad and Tobago Publishers and Broadcasters Association"

every baby deserves the breast

Fig. 14.3. Breast-feeding poster employing modern motivations: Trinidad, 1974 (from White, A. (1974). *Cajanus* **7**, 205)

decades. The mother (and paediatrician) should be able to make an informed choice, but there is no way that equivalence of breast-feeding and bottle-feeding can be presented; the attempt to do so has undoubtedly formed part of the *laissez-faire* posture that has developed in infant feeding in the Western World.

Channels of information

Basically, the need is to understand the target of population to be reached, to supply correct information (adjusted to the audience), to motivate, and to engender confidence. The channels through which such a programme could flow would vary, but in all instances would include the mass media, the health service, schools, and women's groups.

All over the world, the mass media would include particularly the transistorized radio, newspapers, and magazines (with visual messages and with a text which, if necessary, could be read out to a group by a literate villager). Where available, television also has a role. Promotion also needs to be undertaken via posters (Fig. 14.4), bill-boards, and hand-outs, even in the village shop. Slides and films can assist, and are becoming increasingly available (p. 396).

In many developing countries, though not all, and some industrialized countries, revenue to finance radio and television systems, newspapers, and magazines may be largely derived from commercial advertising. Under these circumstances, it is difficult, but necessary, to try to introduce the idea of critical scrutiny of the advertising and to suggest the desirability of screening infant foods which conform to the special nutritional, economic, and cultural needs of the country (p. 373).

From a postive point of view, a largely unexploited field remains for the use of mass media, particularly the radio, for health, and nutrition education (Manoff 1972, 1975), including messages concerned with the promotion of breast-feeding. However, the basic problem is the lack of funds for such activities; possibly a more informed international agency could direct substantial funds to such programmes, in addition to other approaches to nutritional improvement, such as the search for new processed foods or genetically improved crops.

In largely literate countries, popular non-commercial booklets on infant feeding are required, but with sufficient appeal to be read with enjoyment Library lists are available from La Leche League International and the Nursing Mothers Association of Australia.

Health services

The supplying of correct information and the increasing of confidence in mothers can be sought through modification in the functions and regimens of the health services (Bjerre and Ekelund 1970, Burden 1959, De Chateau *et al.* 1973, Illingsworth and Stone 1952, Lind and Jaderling 1964, Mobbs 1973, Osorio *et al.* 1975, Richardson 1925). These will obviously depend on

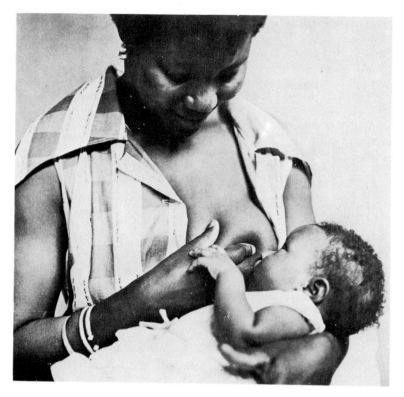

The perfect baby food – BREAST MILK

1972

JANUARY
SUN MON TUES WED THUR FRI SAT

SUN	MON	TUES	WED	THUR	FRI	SAT
🌑	🌓	🌕				1
2	3	4	5	6	7	8
9	10	11	12	13	14	15
16	17	18	19	20	21	22
23 30	24 31	25	26	27	28	29

FEBRUARY
SUN MON TUES WED THUR FRI SAT

SUN	MON	TUES	WED	THUR	FRI	SAT
		1	2	3	4	5
6	7	8	9	10	11	12
13	14	15	16	17	18	19
20	21	22	23	24	25	26
27	28	29	🌑	🌓	🌕	

MARCH
SUN MON TUES WED THUR FRI SAT

SUN	MON	TUES	WED	THUR	FRI	SAT
🌑	🌓	🌕	1	2	3	4
5	6	7	8	9	10	11
12	13	14	15	16	17	18
19	20	21	22	23	24	25
26	27	28	29	30	31	🌕

MINISTRY OF HEALTH, JAMAICA
PRODUCED & DISTRIBUTED BY BUREAU OF HEALTH EDUCATION
IN COLLABORATION WITH CARIBBEAN FOOD & NUTRITION INSTITUTE

Fig. 14.4. Wall calendar (courtesy of Ministry of Health, Jamaica)

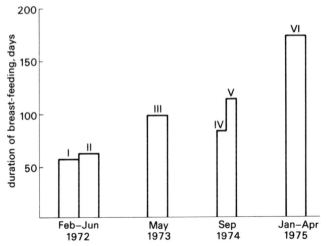

Fig. 14.5. The mean duration of breast-feeding in groups of mothers with different post-partum care: I, routine care; II, no weighing of infant before and after breast-feeding and no supplementary feeding (n=203); III, as II, one year later (n=68); IV, additional and prolonged information (father not present at information (n=23); V, additional and prolonged information (father present at information) (n=20); VI, naked skin-to-skin and suckling contact immediately after delivery (n=21) (from de Chateau, P. (1976). *Neonatal care routines.* Umea University Medical Publications No. 20, Umea, Sweden)

the findings of the community diagnosis and the structure of the local health services. Some of these are summarized in Table 14.3. All require little or no additional expense.

The effectiveness of certain limited programmes on the rate of breast-feeding is shown in Table 14.4 and 14.5. Others have been reported recently from the U.K. (Coles and Valman 1976, Smart and Bamford 1976, Burne 1976, Jepson *et al.* 1976). These are based on minor changes in ward routine, and advice and encouragement, but are undoubtedly affected by the enthusiasm of the health workers (and, hence, mothers) and by diminution of maternal anxiety (e.g. with rooming-in).

Prenatal care
Necessary information and confidence should be initiated and engendered during pregnancy, for both wife and husband. Particularly useful as a visual aid can be a woman who is already successfully breast-feeding her baby. Also, simple demonstrations and appropriate and written handouts can be useful. Information can often be on a single card as only the most motivated mothers will read booklets; this card should have on it simply and briefly, the advantages of breast-feeding, for both mother and baby. It should also deal with common fallacies (such as that breast-feeding is related to the size of the mother's breasts) and it should emphasize that a woman who breast-feeds gets her figure back more quickly (Tylden 1976). However, it is most

important to ensure that the balance is attempted between supplying essential information and adding unnecessary complexities, which can themselves induce anxiety.

In all parts of the world, especially in poorer developing communities, priority attention also needs to be given to the *maternal diet* (p. 59), both in pregnancy and in lactation (Pitkin *et al.* 1972, Rosa 1974).

Childbirth and the puerperium

During and after childbirth, those responsible, more usually the midwife or maternity nurse, must have been trained to realize her *doula* role (p. 175 — that is as supplier of information, giver of physical and emotional support, and engenderer of confidence (Figs 14.6 and 7). In the maternity unit itself,

TABLE 14.3 *Possible modifications in health services designed to promote breast-feeding in a community.*

Health service	Modifications
Prenatal care	Information on breast-feeding (preferably from breast-feeding mothers). Breast preparation. Maternal diet. Emotional preparation for labour.
Puerperal care	Avoid maternal fatigue/anxiety/pain (e.g. allow to eat in early labour; avoid *unnecessary* episiotomy; husband permitted during delivery; relatives and visitors allowed; privacy and relaxed atmosphere; organization of day with breast-feeding in mind). Separate mother and newborn as little as possible. Stimulate lactation (e.g. no prelacteal feeds; first breast-feeding as soon as possible; avoid *unnecessary* maternal anaesthesia; permissive schedule; rooming-in). Lactation 'consultants' (advisers — preferably women who have breast-fed). Adequate 'lying-in' period. In hot weather, extra water by dropper on spoon.
Premature unit	Use of expressed breast-milk (preferably fresh). Contact between mother and baby with earliest return to direct breast-feeding.
Children's wards	Accommodation in hospital (or nearby) for mothers of breast-fed babies.
Home visiting	Encourage, motivate, support.
Health Centre	Supplementary food distribution (e.g. formula and weaning foods) according to defined, locally relevant policy.
General	Supportive atmosphere from all shifts. Avoid promotion of unwanted commercial infant foods (e.g. samples, posters, calendars, brochures, etc). Adopt minimal bottle-feeding policy and practical health education concerning 'biological breast-feeding.

TABLE 14.4   *Results from selected hospital or practice-based programmes designed to improve breast-feeding*

Author	Method	Results
Waller (1946)	Antenatal: Woolwich nipple shield, expression colostrum in late pregnancy Puerperal: avoid overdistension	Percentage breast-feeding at 6 months 42% (controls): 83% (regimen)
McBryde (1951)	Rooming-in	Percentage breast-feeding on discharge 35% (controls): 58·5% (rooming-in)
Blaikely et al. (1953)	Antenatal: Woolwich nipple shield, expression Puerperal: avoid overdistension	Percentage breast-feeding at 6 months 26% (controls): 51% (regimen)
Rawlins (1961)	Prenatal: reading material, demonstration of breast-feeding prenatally by lactating mother	Percentage breast-feeding at 5 months (1958) (1961) 17% : 57% (Multips.) 13% : 44% (Primips.)
Sloper et al. (1975)	Minimal education of midwifery staff	Percentage breast-feeding on discharge 27% (before): 40% (after.)
De Chateau (1976)	No weighing or complementary feeds. Information to mother and father. Naked skin–skin contact and immediate sucking	Length of breast-feeding 60 days (before change) 170 days (after change)

numerous procedures may interfere with the initiation of lactation. A number of minor-seeming, but important, adaptations of procedure of proven scientific value can be introduced without much difficulty or cost to form an important part of any practical education and action programme. For example, various widespread obstetrical practices need to be used *only when indicated clinically*, including the withholding of food and water in labour, maternal anaesthesia (or analgesia), elective induction, episiotomy, and forceps (Bowes 1970, *British Medical Journal* 1974*b*). It should be assumed that mothers will probably wish to breast-feed. Routine oestrogen suppression, prelacteal bottle feedings and the routine issue of formula to the mother prior to discharge should be forbidden. The baby should be put to the breast as soon as possible, should sleep near the mother, and should suckle the breast as often and as long as he desires. If the climate is *extremely*

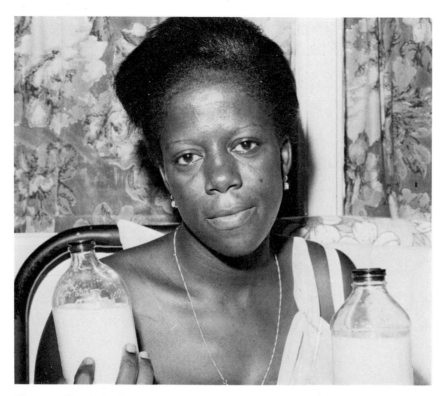

Fig. 14.6. Psychological support in recently delivered woman showing amount of milk she will be producing (Maternity Unit, Jamaica)

hot and dry, boiled water can be given after breast feeds *with a spoon*.

The ideal hospital *doula* is the midwife or the female physician who has breast-fed her own children. The possibility of using women who are suckling their own babies for practical nutrition education in the wards should be considered, whenever possible (Fig. 14.6). The value of a quiet comfortable breast-feeding room, perhaps with a rocking chair and relaxing music, can be considerable, especially in view of possible embarrassment by women in Westernized cultures.

Paediatric hospitals
The mother's role is particularly vital when her baby is still being breast-fed. To exclude her can be an added impetus to malnutrition of the child, and, in less technically developed countries, it is possible for a baby to recover from, say, septicaemia of the newborn only to die of marasmus later, as a result of hospitalization-induced lactation failure. All hospitals, in the tropics or elsewhere, should have at least some facilities for mothers to be admitted with their offspring, not only for breast-feeding but also to assist with the general care and feeding of infants and to supply emotional support.

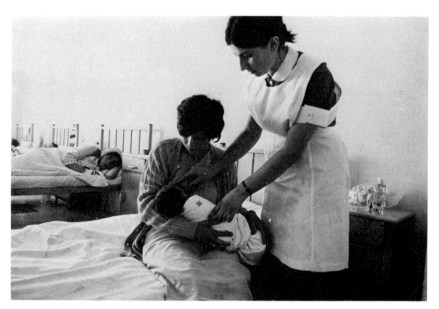

Fig. 14.7. Nurse assisting mother with breast-feeding her newborn baby in maternity unit in Turkey (courtesy of World Health Organization)

Hospitals as centres for health education
The hospital's role as a focal point for health and nutrition education is rarely developed, or even considered. In fact, this needs to be stated as part of hospital policy, including written endorsement that breast-feeding will be encouraged by all means.

If mothers are present (preferably admitted to the ward but also when parents are visiting), various situations can be utilized for motivation and persuasion. The malnourished child's clinical improvement, particularly if reinforced by a rapidly rising weight curve, is the most vivid teaching aid, especially if this improvement has been seen to be achieved mainly by feeding. Also, mothers whose children are recovering would seem to constitute a particularly receptive group, both for individual discussion and for demonstrations on various locally important aspects of child health and nutrition, including breast-feeding.

Conversely, the hospital can unwittingly become a centre of 'ill-health education' by using, and hence endorsing, methods that mothers are not advised to follow (including widespread bottle-feeding), and by permitting the advertisement of artificial foods, both directly by printed material and free samples, and indirectly via the activities of 'milk nurses' (p. 226).

Breast-milk banks
Recent investigations into the metabolic and anti-infective significance of human milk for premature babies (p. 369), have suggested the value of

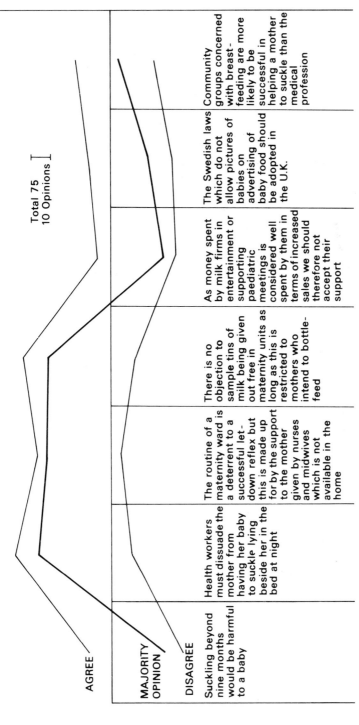

Fig. 14.8. Results of questionnaire on attitudes used on hospital housestaff in London, as part of series contrasting attitudes in different groups (from Liebrich, V. A. and Morley, D. (1976). *J. trop. Pediat. env. Chld Hlth* (in press))

re-establishing breast-milk banks, and, indeed, this has commenced in some paediatric centres. It seems likely that colostrum and human milk will become routine chemoprophylaxis and diet for all prematures, especially those 'at risk' of infection.

The particular value of fresh, unheated, unrefrigerated breast-milk (particularly colostrum) poses new practical problems of storage; and fresh milk may be used from a donor mother with symptomless excretion of viruses (virolactia), in which case legal problems may arise. Cultural problems also may occur with reluctance by mothers to permit their milk to be used for someone else's baby.

Important approaches to practical procedures include studying methods used in the past with old-style breast-milk banks of earlier decades of the century (Davy 1975, Duncombe 1975, Emerson 1921, Illman 1973, Laws and Skelley 1939, Quinby *et al.* 1976, Seleste 1953), such as questions of source of donors (including consideration of payment), methods of collection, pooling, methods of distribution, etc., and also currently successful practices employed by breast-feeding mothers, who are working away from home during the day.

Lactation units

Units concerned with re-establishing, reinforcing, or initiating lactation, and demonstrating the effectiveness of breast-feeding, can play a role in various circumstances. For example, a 're-establishment-of-lactation unit' was operative in Mulago Hospital, Kampala, Uganda for seven years. This was for healthy, less well-to-do African mothers who had misguidedly started their babies on bottle-feeds; the regimen employed is given in Table 14.5. Major factors responsible for success were undoubtedly the sucking and prolactin release, and the confidence-enhanced let-down reflex (p. 19) resulting from support from the staff and from other mothers in whom lactation had already been re-established. Chlorpromazine (50 mg three times daily for 7 days) was given because of its known hypothalamic effect and initiation of lactation in some women, and because of its tranquilizing property. 'Syntocin' (synthetic oxytocin) was administered occasionally, if required, as a nasal spray above five minutes before nursing, in order to enhance the let-down reflex. The unexpected type of procedure and its rapidly observable effect were often dramaticaley impressive for anxious mothers. In fact, in retrospect, it seems that the drug therapy used was mainly supportive and of psychological value. In Chile, recent preliminary investigations have used oral thyrotropin-releasing hormone in women to initiate lactation (Tyson *et al.* 1975). In Brazil, Sousa has been trying out the effect of oral metoclopramide, a phenothiazine derivative known to be a potent stimulator of prolactin (Sousa 1975, Sousa *et al.* 1975). The dose used has been 10 mg three times daily for 9–10 days.

TABLE 14.5 *Regimen for re-establishment of lactation, used at Makerere Hospital, Kampala, Uganda (1961–6)*

	Procedure	Hormonal effect in mother
Baby	Frequent sucking at breast (at least 2-hourly)	
	Complementary feeds by cup or by spoon	Increase prolactin secretion
	Treat dehydration or infection (especially oral moniliasis)	
Mother	Reassurance, information, and confidence (from staff and by other mothers in whom breast-feeding had been re-established)	Facilitate let-down reflex
	One pint of cow's milk daily	
	'Syntocin' nasal spray, if required	Hypothalamic effect — prolactin secretion
	Chlorpromazine	

Crawford and Hall (1975) have expressed anxiety that 'a pharmacological forcing of the mammary gland would not be in the best interests of the mother and child'. Certainly, the main factors responsible for successful lactation are an uninhibited let-down reflex, maximal prolactin secretion from nipple stimulation, and an adequate plane of maternal nutrition. Nevertheless, although 'the pharmacology of milk production and ejection is built into the human female endocrinological system, the use of metoclopramide may perhaps be of value for indirect reasons. First, it may help in initiating the flow of prolactin and thus possibly be an external pharmacological booster for a few days for what would anyhow result from normal inherent reflex mechanisms. Also, in our Western medical philosophy the respectability of any procedure increases immediately with a chemical therapeutic approach, or some similar dramatic and approved method, is instituted, with consequent enthusiasm by the physicians and nurses, and, by contagion, the mother.' (Jelliffe and Jelliffe 1976*b*).

Lactation units could very easily be incorporated in hospital wards or out-patient departments in various parts of the world, including industrialized countries. In addition, special situations exist in some resource-poor countries, where such units could be a part of existing low-cost 'mothercraft centres' or 'nutrition rehabilitation units', which are currently mainly concerned with malnutrition in the transitional.

A special role for a lactation centre could be found during a relief operation for famine (Fig. 14.9). Under these circumstances, as noted by Brown (1972) in Bangladesh, the correct approach is through the re-establishment of lactation, including feeding the mother, rather than distributing pow-

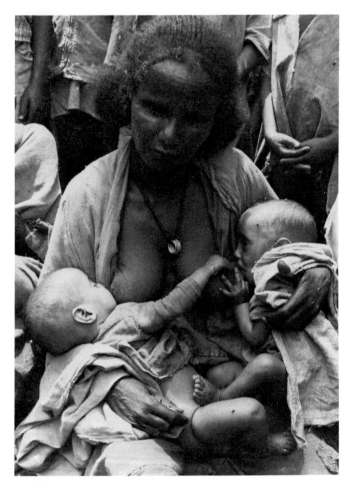

Fig. 14.9. Lactating woman in Ethiopian famine (courtesy of UNICEF)

dered milk for babies, with its high risks of producing diarrhoea and marasmus.

In recent years, women in some richer countries, notably the U.S.A., have
adopted babies and wish to breast-feed them. The women concerned
were not lactating at the time, and, in some cases, may have had no children
of their own in the past. Regimens for the establishment of 'adoptive
breast-feeding' are often successful. Basically, they work via confidence and
the let-down reflex, and, even more importantly, the sucking stimulus and
the consequent secretion of anterior-pituitary prolactin. As the process
takes some weeks to become adequate by itself for the baby, a problem
always exists with methods of supplying additional food, in the form of cow's
milk, without interfering with the process. This can be done by using a

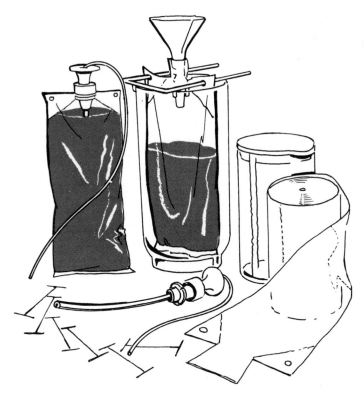

Fig. 14.10. Lact-Aid Nursing Supplementer showing plastic-bag container for formula, filled and with filling funnel (courtesy of Mrs. Jimmie Avery)

feeding cup, preferably of an old-fashioned boat-shape, or a cup and spoon, but is time-consuming and tedious. A technological invention — the 'Lact-Aid Nursing Supplementer'* (Figs 14.10 and 11) — ingeniously supplies additional milk, without interfering with sucking. It consists of a small plastic bag with formula hung round the neck, from which a thin plastic tube comes which can be taped to the breast. The baby obtains a mixture of breast-milk and formula simultaneously — both obtained by sucking. Adequate lactation occurs after about two weeks (Avery 1972). The supplementation can also be used for women with inadequate lactation from other causes (e.g. following maternal illness, etc.).

Family-centred maternity care
Trends in obstetrical and puerperal management in Western countries have begun to give increased emphasis to psychosocial considerations in relation to delivery, which may, in turn, have physical consequences. Increased

---

*Address: J. J. Avery Inc., P.O. Box 6459, Denver, Colorado 80206, U.S.A.

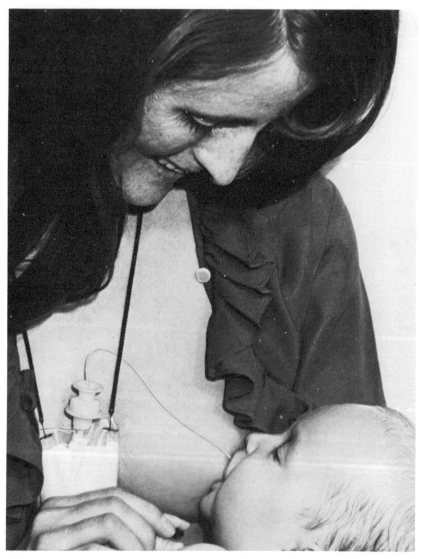

Fig. 14.11. Lact-Aid Nursing Supplementer in use (courtesy of Mrs. Jimmie Avery)

attention has been given to home deliveries, to 'family-centred maternity care' (Bing 1972, Donald 1966, Haire and Haire 1971), and to the use of midwives in the U.S.A. (where, in contrast to most European countries, this is not presently the norm).

In Raphael's maternity centres (or birth centres) mothers could be admitted before delivery and remain for some time afterwards. Mothers would be treated as people delivering human infants, not as dependent patients whose babies belong to the nursing staff. Delivery would be undertaken by experienced midwives, with the obstetrician on call only for abnormal or difficult childbirths, and with emergency facilities available (e.g. blood). Perinatal care of a *doula*-like type, especially in the post-delivery period, could be assisted by currently or formerly lactating mothers (Raphael 1973*a*).

Mead and Newton (1967) have similar concerns and objectives, but query whether it would be better 'to have maternity wards in general hospitals, or should we, instead, attach them to well-baby clinics? Here it would be necessary to take account of the fact that the inclusion of the maternity ward in the hospital helped to alter the definition of a hospital from a wholly terrifying place of suffering and death to a place associated with health and life. Although maternal and child health might gain by the separation of birth from hospitals, the over-all relationship of the community to the hospital and the definition of the hospital as a place for regaining strength and health might well suffer'.

Cultural difficulties exist in Western countries, including the U.S.A., which have been expressed as follows by Haire (1973):

Our culture has created a generation of women who, on the whole, prefer to submit passively to being delivered of their babies, unaware that their reluctance to participate places their babies at a disadvantage. If we are to effect a change for the better we must begin by helping each mother to appreciate the important contribution which only she can make to her child's long-term well-being by availing herself of proper prenatal care and the best possible diet her budget will allow. We must help all mothers to realize the benefits of preparing themselves to cope with the stress and discomfort of childbirth. Childbirth education classes should be an inherent part of hospital maternity care if we are to reduce or eliminate the mother's need for medication during labour and birth.

A 'parent–staff interaction guide' has been developed in the U.S.A. recently to ensure that good mother–neonate contact was considered and augmented, to communicate between the medical and nursing staff, and to assist others interacting with parents such as social workers, liaison nurses, and community health workers to know what parents have been told, and which physicians or nurses have been most involved with particular families (Chamberlin 1975, Cropley and Bloom 1975).

In technically less developed countries, a higher proportion of women have severe obstetrical complications or abnormalities. Under these circumstances, a chain of services needs to be envisaged, varying with local circumstances, including the terrain and transport problems, but often including home deliveries (preferably with trained indigenous birth attendants), village delivery units (several beds at the health centre or midwife's home), 'maternity villages' near to hospitals, and obstetrical units and hospitals, with special facilities (Matland 1966).

Units for premature, low-birth-weight, and 'special care' babies
The feeding of premature and 'small-for-date' low-birth-weight babies has

until recently been concerned very considerably with nutrients alone (Davies 1971), with emphasis on the theoretically too low protein in human milk for the high metabolic needs of such babies.

Recent work referred to elsewhere emphasizes that a wider view has to be taken concerning the low-birth-weight babies need for mother–infant contact (p. 152), to avoid metabolic overload (p. 251), including tyrosine, electrolytes, urea, and ammonia (Raiha *et al.* 1976), and to receive protection against infections (p. 84).

Breast-feeding and human milk supply all of these, together with a biochemical composition which enhances digestion and absorption (e.g. with calcium and fat). This wide holistic view indicates clearly that the balance or risks endorses the advantages of human milk and breast-feeding in more modern 'special-care units' for low-birth-weight babies, and others in all parts of the world, (Jelliffe 1967, Tafari and Sterkey 1974). This is a significant consideration in view of the commonness of low-birth-weight neonates.

Parenthetically, the current vogue for the *excessive* use of so-called total or elemental deep intravenous diet therapy in prematures (Heird and Driscoll 1975, Heird and Winters 1975) and other children can be predicted to lead to a crop of iatrogenic new hazards (*British Medical Journal* 1969). Philosophically, it is classical Western linearism (p. 225).

Hospital as a source of danger
As Mendelsohn (1964) notes: 'The hospital is a necessary form of therapy to be improved, of course; but meanwhile, as in the case of antibiotic drugs, to be used with full appreciation of its side effects and hazards . . . So, two dangers of hospitalization — internal contagion and emotional disturbance — have been identified. The third, and one that practically no one talks about in public, is danger from hospital personnel: from error on the part of house staff, nurses, laboratory technicians, X-ray departments, dieticians, housekeepers, and aides. We tend to excuse these by saying, 'Oh, that was a mistake in this one case.' Yet, when the force of the modern specialized, departmentalized hospital is brought to bear on the patient, with some 20 to 30 people or more usually participating in the care of one patient, the exception in each case becomes the rule.'

In the usually worse circumstances in resource-poor countries, the overcrowding and lack of staffing may be extreme in children's wards. In a paper entitled 'The paediatric ward as a lethal factor' the following picture has been painted (Jelliffe and Jelliffe 1970*b*):

All too frequently the children's wards in tropical hospitals are continually overflowing with sick children, most of whom are suffering from malnutrition, diarrhoea, and various infections, or who have synergistic mixtures of these.

Mothers, even those with breast-fed babies, may be excluded from the ward by policy, and the young children admitted may then be crowded 2 or 3 in a cot, with an obviously increased likelihood of cross-infection. In extreme cases, the press of circumstances is such that the harried nurses have great difficulty in finding time to feed the children adequately, but rather concentrate on injections and medication.

Even though malnourished children respond miraculously to often haphazard feeding, discharge is likely to be premature (because of the shortage of beds), follow-up is undocumented, possibly fatal, relapses are not unlikely after the return home. Under these circumstances, there comes a point when it has to be asked whether the children's ward has become a negative, or even a lethal, factor in the management of malnutrition, rather that a beneficial influence.

Therapy of diarrhoeal disease
The confirmation by Kingston (1973*a*) in Liberia that diarrhoeal dehydration seen in that country is almost always hypotonic suggests that the correct treatment for the moderately affected cases would be the continuation of breast-feeding with doses during the day of 'concentrated diarrhoea formula'* (Kingston 1973*b*). This regimen has the advantages that it does not permit secretion to decline and uses human milk as low-solute repair fluid 'topped up' to make good deficits of electrolytes by concentrated diarrhoea formula.

Lactation-promoting contraception programmes
On a community basis, lactation amenorrhoea can constitute an important part of a family-planning programme. Conversely, the ill-effects of some oral contraceptives on lactation are becoming appreciated (Rosa 1976*b*).

When 'biological breast-feeding' is practised, the questions are when to start a reinforcing technological contraceptive and what this should be. More research is needed and questions of cultural acceptability, cost, simplicity, and availability to mothers have to be considered. The intra-uterine device currently seems most advisable, although condoms and the diaphragm may be appropriate in some communities. If hormonal preparations are employed, orally or by intramuscular injection, progestogens should be selected (*The Lancet* 1971, Rinehart and Winter 1975). Rosa (1976*b*) makes the important point that a main and common maternal objection to the use of progestogens — suppression of the menses — does not apply if they are commenced while the woman is still exhibiting lactation amenorrhoea. However, further investigation into the immediate and long-term effects on both mother and nursing baby of progestogens is needed.

Education of health personnel
There is a great need for modern information on human lactation — in training schools and in refresher courses (or other similar activities) for those in practice in various health fields, including physicians (especially

---

*Composition: sodium chloride 100 mEq/1; potassium citrate 50 mEq/1; sodium benzoate 0·1%; trace of carbol fuchsin for colouring. 200 ml containing 20 mEq of sodium and 10 mEq of potassium were dispensed in beer bottles.

paediatricians and obstetricians), nurses, nutritionists, midwives, and public health nurses (health visitors). In many areas, similar needs may also exist in the curricula of a variety of agencies, universities, etc. In some countries, these will include the agricultural department (especially its extension division) and the agency concerned with community development.

Students need to learn the biological basis of infant feeding, including its mechanisms through the three stages of early human development — the foetus, the exterogestate foetus, and the transitional (p. 4); and hence its dyadic character between mother and offspring (p. 2) (Table 14.6). *The educational programme adapted to local needs has to be based on current information and also should represent a consensus between those working in paediatric nutrition in the area,* including advice to be given on breast-feeding. Such an approach, entitled *Guidelines to young-child feeding in the contemporary Caribbean* (Pan American Health Organization 1970*b*), was made a few years ago in the Caribbean. Much to be learned as 'new' techniques are, in fact, ancient and part of everyday biotraditional practice in some non-Western cultures, but have recently been given scientific respectability by numerate, laboratory proof. Aspects of the practical management of breast-feeding are given in Appendix F (p. 404).

TABLE 14.6   *Main areas to be covered in curriculum on biological basis of infant feeding.*

Foetus	Nutritional requirements
	Maternal diet, cultural factors,
	optional growth
Extero	Nutritional requirements
gestate	*Breast-feeding:* Anatomy and physiology of
foetus	breast development. Psychophysiology
	of lactation. Information and support
	for parents. Recent knowledge concerning
	biochemical, anti-infective, contraceptive,
	anti-allergic, emotional, economic
	comparisons with cow's-milk formulas.
	Community influences on lactation
	(health services, infant-food industry,
	working women, cultural attitudes, women's groups)
	methods and techniques of successful breast-feeding.
	Management of common problems.
	Bottle-feeding: Least-cost formula. Safest
	technique. Risks in different ecologies.
Transitional	Nutritional requirements.
	Duration of breast-feeding for different situations.
	Semi-solids: age of introduction, composition

Infant-food industry

Formulas and processed infant foods

Anywhere in the world, but especially in resource-poor countries, a major need is to reconsider the actual and potential impact of processed infant foods in the light of real nutritional requirements, of available socio-economic resources, and of existing cultural practices.

In general terms, policy needs to be related to the following four principles:

1. Processed infant foods need to be geared to the real nutritional needs of priority ages of young children and mothers in the area.

2. Processed infant foods need to be promoted (or not) with regard to their economic feasibility, within the constraints of the family budgets and the national income of the community concerned.

3. Processed infant foods must not be advertised and promoted if and when they are culturally, socially, and economically inappropriate for the particular community.

4. Processed infant foods must not be promoted if this will lead to the destruction of an existing satisfactory pattern of infant feeding, particularly breast-feeding, which cannot be replaced by the proposed substitute.

Information should be obtained on the brands available and their composition, cost, methods of preparation (including simplicity of instructions), geographical distribution, and outlets (via stores, health services, etc; on sale, subsidized, etc.). Data on volume of imports and of sales should be sought for, but may be difficult to ascertain.

Such an analysis will permit calculation of the *cost/income ratio*, that is the cost to feed a three-month-old baby adequately compared with the basic minimum government wage, usually expressed as a percentage, and the *artificial-feeding/breast-feeding cost ratio*, that is the cost of artificially feeding a three-month baby compared with the cost of locally appropriate foods needed to supply the extra nutrients for the lactating woman, which can be expressed as a ratio.

The ingredients and nutrients in the available formulas need to be compared, as was done, for example, by McKigney (1971) in the English-speaking Caribbean. Also, *cost–nutrient analyses* (Table 14.7) permit a rating to be made in relation to protein and calories, although other considerations need to be taken into account, such as simplicity of preparation, cultural acceptability, continuous availability, keeping properties, protein quality, and the presence of other nutrients (e.g. vitamins, iron).

TABLE 14.7   *Cost–nutrient values: average cost of foods in the West Indies as sources of protein and calories, related to recommended dietary allowances for one-year-old child* (from McKigney 1968)

Cost per 20 grams of protein (Eastern Caribbean $)		Cost per 1000 calories (Eastern Caribbean $)
0·05	Dry skimmed milk	0·25
0·06	Pulses	0·22
0·08	Cornmeal—wheat flour	0·10
0·10	Salt fish	1·20
0·12	Rice	0·13
0·15	Macaroni—rolled oats	0·25
0·18	Sardines	0·60
0·20	Fresh milk	0·55
0·20	Fresh beef, goat, mutton, cheddar cheese	
0·20	Fresh fish	1·80
0·20	Bread	0·25
0·20	Chicken necks and backs	1·10
0·20	Corned beef	1·20
0·22	Peanut butter	0·47
0·23	Dry whole milk	0·55
0·23	Sweetened condensed milk	0·25
0·25	Evaporated milk	0·55
0·25	Minced (ground) beef	0·90
0·28	Ground provisions (root crops)	0·25
0·35	Fresh pork	0·40
0·35	Broiler meat	2·20
0·40	Irish potatoes	0·60
0·40	Frankfurters, sausages	1·10
0·40	Fresh eggs	1·60
0·51	Milk-based, cereal-based, infant foods	0·80
0·56	'Health promoting' foods	0·80
0·59	Plantain, green bananas, ripe bananas	0·29
0·69	Infant foods—strained meats	4·87
2·08	Infant foods—strained vegetables and meat	
13·00	Arrowroot	0·55
—	Sugar	0·09
—	Margarine, cooking oil	0·15
—	Glucose	0·80

Advertising

The scope of the information obtained can include the range, format, and content of direct advertising (including labelling), of indirect advertising (via non-dietary promotional devices, such as competitions, free gifts, lotteries, baby shows, etc), and of motivational methods used to persuade and influence health personnel and others giving advice on infant feeding or making decisions on policy concerning food imports or food purchasing for health and welfare or other services.

Approximate assessment of the geographical, cultural, and socio-economic outreach of advertising of infant foods can be obtained by carrying out a short monitoring of the radio and television (including note of the time coverage), of the measured 'advertisement area' in newspapers, of the situation with regard to bill-boards, and of promotional material in stores and in health services. The study should include journals intended for the medical, nursing, and nutrition professions for what is rather curiously termed 'ethical advertising'.

Advertising of infant foods needs to be viewed in the local context to ensure that claims are not false, deceptive (manipulative), socially harmful or undermining of confidence.

In resource-poor countries in particular, the advertising stated to be aimed principally at the small percentage of affluent people needs to be considered in light of its effects on the less well-to-do, for whom, as noted, the visual message will be apparent and the motivation of status and modernness particularly alluring.

Lastly, advertising in professional journals must also be scrutinized, as it may be plainly promoting an infant food (or, indeed, vitamin preparation or drug) which has no relevance to local needs or even with contrary message to the policy suggested by the consensus of informed paediatric nutritionists, or even the views of the editorial board. Advertising in a professional journal can only be taken to imply endorsement. Editorial policy needs to explore less constricting and compromising sources of revenue.

Legislation

The community diagnosis should include the collection of information (a) on legal specifications for milk products (especially formulas) and for processed weaning foods, (b) on existing laws concerning advertising (including labelling), and (c) on the legal and administrative apparatus to deal with apparent abuses.

Obviously, the situation will vary greatly. In many poorer less developed countries, little will exist — or only on paper. Effective governmental codes and practical legislation concerned with *the importation and promotion of formulas and weaning foods*, will be inherently difficult to prepare and to implement in a free-market economy (World Health Organization 1968). Difficulties will include basic problems of definition, of persuasion of policy makers and, indeed, of tactics with the large multi-national infant-food companies, whose incomes may, in some cases, be larger than those of developing countries in which they are working, and whose influence and financial power will often be very great within any country. Such legislation may perhaps be assisted by a recent proposal by the United Nations ECOSOC (Economic and Social Council) to set up an 'information and research centre' to consider the advantages, problems, and harm due to the activities of multi-national industrial corporations (Somavia 1974).

Legislation also needs to be devised to insure *the exclusion of advertising which is false, deceptive, misleading, or 'socially harmful'.*

Plainly,there is a need for some mechanism for continuing surveillance by some neutral body and for legal action, when and if necessary. Some degree of continuing superficial surveillance can, however, be undertaken by intermittent enquiry (Appendix D) by health services, or by voluntary groups.

Suggested standards of international usage for the composition of infant foods are laid down by the Committee on dietetic and Infant Foods of the FAO-sponsored *Codex Alimentarius Commission*. Their views have been overinfluenced by a majority membership from Western industry; standards for advertising and promotion have not been their concern. The question of the nutritional consequences and regulations for the promotion of infant foods have recently been reviewed by United Nations Protein–Calorie Advisory Group (FAO/WHO/UNICEF 1971). An outline of the major consideration is given in Table 14.8.

TABLE 14.8   *Areas needing consideration in modification of promotion of infant formulas*

General	Eliminate advertising to general public, directly or via health services Eliminate free samples Eliminate activity of 'milk nurses' Modify written and pictorial content of advertising (eliminate false, deceptive, those undermining confidence; indicate breast-feeding superior and first choice; simple instructions appropriate for local situation on labels)
Health and Professions Nutrition	Establish editorial advertising policy (content of advertising as above; do not over estimate similarity; indicate main dangers for community e.g. diarrhoea if water supply inadequate, and malnutrition (marasmus or obesity, if dosage incorrect) Establish health and nutrition service policy (eliminate advertising and free samples; agreed policy on selection, purchase, use, and education on formulas needed) Limitation of free samples and gifts Limitation of infant-food industry assistance to professional and social activities

Areas of emphasis

The role of the infant-food industry should vary in different ecologies. With the more overwhelming problems of developing countries, the following are the main needs.

Formula for use when medically indicated

Limited quantities of formula will be required for abandoned or motherless babies, for some twins, and for babies whose mothers were unable or unwilling to breast-feed them (e.g. severe maternal ill-health, mother working out of the home in paid employment where Westernized cultural attitudes and facilities do not permit nursing). However, such products should be as economical as possible (both for purchase by parents and by governments), without advertising to the public, through the radio or by other means, and capable of simple preparation (Fig. 14.12).

Fig. 14.12. Basic home-feeding kit used by Mulago Hospital, Kampala, Uganda (1959–66) containing feeding cup similar to outer leaf of banana flower used traditionally. The kit was issued and brought back weekly (from Welbourn, H. F. and De Beer, G. (1964). *J. trop. Med. Hyg.* **67**, 155)

The possibility of a two-tier price structure may be feasible — a low-cost version available via health services and a high-priced version via limited stores in major cities for the elite.

A national tender might be made for formulas with certain specifications as regards composition, packaging, and preparation, the two companies with the most appropriate formulas at least cost being both contracted to make supplies available. The specifics required by the country would be the priority (especially cost, and simplicity and safety of preparation). Distribution would be worked out jointly by the company and the government, without advertising.

Appropriate weaning mixtures
Major emphasis on weaning foods in less developed countries will usually need to be based on suitable home-made village-level 'multi-mixes'. However, in addition, there is sometimes a need for a low-cost processed weaning-food mixture, again using the principle of multi-mixes, usually based on a cereal grain–legume blend, preferably with small amounts of dried skimmed milk or other animal product. Such processed food mixtures will be required in severe food shortages and famines and in urban situations. They need to be prepared industrially to be fed by spoon and without the possibility of being given by bottle. They should be easy to cook, suitable for infants from the age of 4–6 months onwards and conform to the local culture. Ideally, they should be manufactured within the country, mainly from locally available ingredients. Sometimes, small-scale 'intermediate technology' approaches may be more practicable at local level.

Problems with such products are well known and most attempts in the past have been failures (Orr 1972). Advertisement and better packaging unfortunately often appear to be highly significant to acceptance. It is most important that the impression of 'food-for-poor' is not created. It may be desirable to initiate the new product through the well-to-do and, later, to introduce a more inexpensive version for sale in poorer circumstances and for guaranteed large-scale use through government health services, child-feeding programmes, etc.

Maternal supplements
Again, improved maternal nutrition will usually be sought through the best use of locally available foods from the family diet, especially as 'multi-mixes' (p. 377). In addition, the use of supplementary iron and folic acid may be recommended during pregnancy (when affordable and feasible), together with other appropriate vitamins in special circumstances in pregnancy and/or lactation.

In some circumstances, a low-cost dietary supplement for the pregnant and lactating woman may be both feasible and a valid approach to the improvement of breast-feeding, quantitatively and qualitatively (p. 59), to lowering the incidence of low-birth-weight babies, and to correcting or preventing nutritional maternal depletion (p. 65). This is an area in which the food industry can play a role, but has shown little apparent awareness or interest to date.

Foods to treat malnutrition
Kwashiorkor (p. 274), marasmus (p. 275), and other syndromes of protein–calorie malnutrition (p. 273) have to be treated. Despite considerable

variation in therapy (Wharton *et al*. 1968) the basis of treatment is dietary. Earlier methods with reconstituted dried skimmed milk have been super-seded by mixtures which have added calories (sucrose, vegetable oil) and in which the lactose is 'diluted' by these added ingredients and by added casein. Such a therapeutic preparation was 'Kwashiorkor Food Mix', tried out successfully in acute cases of severe protein–calorie malnutrition in the Nigerian Civil War by Ifekwunigwe (1975) followed by the use of 'Post-Kwashiorkor Food Mix' when the critical acute stage was over. With present-day continually climbing costs of dried skimmed milk, it seems likely that treatment will have to be attempted with locally prepared mix-tures, and that there is a need for a commercial company to devise low-cost treatment mixtures.

Special formulas
In every country, there are a relatively small number of babies needing special formulas — with, for example, allergy to cow's milk or inborn errors of metabolism. The former group can for practical purposes be avoided or greatly minimized by breast-feeding; the latter group may need a specially adapted formula to survive. Sufficient, relatively small amounts of such formulas are needed in resource-rich countries and for the élite in poor countries. They can be regarded as a form of medicine. Among the majority in resource-poor countries, these conditions have extremely little practical significance. Among the large numbers of sick infants with malnutrition, diarrhoea, and infections, cases are unlikely to be detected, and the economics and the practical difficulties with bottle-feeding make their man-agement of very doubtful value.

Interactions with the infant-food industry
During recent years, various forms of interaction with the infant-food indus-try have developed from different groups concerned with feeding of young children. With paediatric nutritionists, dialogue has been carried out on a national level in the U.K. (Department of Health and Social Security, U.K. 1974) and in an international context with the U.N. Protein Advisory Group (1972). The latter was initiated for the following reasons:
    The overriding need is for a dialogue between these two groups, and for the production and promotion of infant foods truly designed for the economic, cultural and hygienic circumstances of less developed areas — including those within the United States and Europe — which both benefit the nutritional level of the child community and also are successful business ventures.
    In the last three years, criticism has been voiced by voluntary groups concerned with infant feeding — for example, in the U.S.A. by the Center for Science in the Public Interest, Washington (1974). In relation to developing countries the War on Want published a more journalistic

Nader-style exposé booklet *The baby killer* (Muller 1974), subsequently translated into German and French, and the Consumer's Union have published a book concerning Latin America and the Caribbean entitled *Hungry for profits* (Ledogar, 1975).

Such interactions with the infant-food industry, often of an abrasive nature, may be leading to reconsideration of overseas policy by some, but not all, major formula companies. The concept of self-regulation by the infant-food industry with a written code of ethics appears to have been initiated in the course of meeting with the U.N. Protein Advisory Group Working Party on 'Feeding the pre-school child'.

Subsequently, the concept was expanded by Ross Laboratories Division of Abbott Laboratory, under the title of *International code of marketing ethics with reference to infant feeding.* (Appendix G). While the appearance of this Code may be construed as encouraging, certain inherent problems exist with regard to the likelihood of the document being effective both within the present guidelines and even more in their implementation in the competitive markets in countries far removed from headquarters. Of major significance is the fact-of-life competition between different formula companies, especially as some are more unrestrained about, for example, direct advertising to the public.

In part as a result of recent criticism and publicity, a council (the International Council of Infant Food Industries) has been formed with representation from nine of the major international manufacturers of infant foods. The first meeting was held in November 1975 in Zürich, Switzerland. One of the main objectives was to devise and promulgate an international code of ethics, etc., for breast-milk substitutes (Appendix G).

Analysis of these recent codes (Appendix G) shows them to be very ambiguous and there is little doubt that independent observation will be needed, and also that the 'burden of advice' is being moved increasingly (and correctly) by the infant-food industry to the health professionals. The corollary is plainly that the health professionals need to be educated in nutrition, including modern knowledge concerning breast-feeding, which is not usually the case at the moment.

Role of women

Implementation of the segment of a national breast-feeding programme concerned with the role of women is really concerned with the structure, economics, and physical and emotional health of families in the community.

Traditional societies
Breast-feeding was the norm in traditional pre-industrialized societies (p. 161). Women mostly worked in and around the home, including, in some cultures, active involvement in agriculture in the family holdings. Often the baby would be taken with the mother when working in the fields, or some-

times women changed their pattern of work to minimize moving far from the infant during the breast-feeding period. This pattern should be preserved wherever possible.

Paid work in Westernized urban circumstances
A programme to breast-feeding in working mothers for a minimum of 6 weeks, for an average of 6 months, and possibly for longer, needs to be devised. The number and percentage of women working in paid occupations outside the home varies greatly in different countries and towns. The pattern also differs very much from area to area, including jobs in industry, offices, and other people's homes (e.g. maids and other domestic work).

It is often assumed that breast-feeding is impossible for women working in an urbanized society (Brewster 1976, Mobbs 1972). This is not necessarily so, and a recent analysis of working women in Los Angeles showed that, by making conscious and often difficult modifications in their daily life, mothers could evolve a regimen which permitted a blending of paid work and continued breast-feeding. Various techniques were employed, including part-time paid work during breast-feeding. With full-time employment, a 'reverse rhythm', was usually developed; but where feeding was mostly during the day, techniques included expressed breast-milk (kept in the refrigerator or freezer) or formula given by cup and spoon or by bottle by a relative or responsible babysitter, *or*, if employment was very nearby, with mothers returned home to nurse. In a very few instances, mothers were able to make acceptable makeshift arrangements to bring their babies to work with them. This was the case, for example, with a college teacher and a laboratory technician.

Legislation for maternity protection
Another valid approach is to analyse, at least qualitatively, the legislation encouraged by the International Labour Organization since the first Convention on Maternity Protection in 1919. The range and diversity of such legislation is great and has been reviewed by the International Labour Organization in 1965 and 1975. It covers, in general, maternity benefits, maternity protection, facilities for lactation at employment.

Maternity benefits. These include the provision of money to compensate financially for absence from paid work during late pregnancy and after the birth of the baby. This is specified as distinct from and in addition to annual holidays and sick leave. The length of time suggested by International Labour Organization is 12 weeks, which can be split into two parts, prenatal and postnatal, in varying proportions.

In a few countries, a specific lactation bonus is available, in money or free food. Notably in France, in 1974 a *prime d'allaitement* of 42.50 francs was available to mothers nursing fully, and 30 francs for those partially breast-feeding. In Sweden, low-cost assistance (home help) is available for mothers at home during the 'lying-in' period.

Maternity protection. Legislation has been defined to protect women in pregnancy from excessive and harmful forms of work, including those with toxic environments, night duty, and very heavy physical labour. Also basic is legislation to ensure that the woman can have her job guaranteed for her, so that she can return to it after maternity leave.

Facilities for nursing at employment. Such facilities, particularly the provision of crèches and nursing breaks, can be crucial. Adequate facilities, including hygienic surroundings and defined health standards, are obviously needed. Crèches can be quite simple, as suggested by the French term *chambre d'allaitement*. They are more usual in communist countries.

The provision of 'nursing breaks' (*pauses d'allaitement*) is laid down by law in some countries, but not all (Richardson 1975). The basic recommendation by the International Labour Organization is for two half-hour nursing breaks during the working day, but various countries differ considerably from this. The upper age-limit for its continuation varies with the laws which reflect the customary practices of the country. The range is quite wide, from a usual figure of 6 months to, exceptionally, 15 months in some African countries. Nursing breaks are sometimes, but not always, included in the total of paid hours of work.

Trends and targets in women's legislation. A recent International Labour Organization Convention report (1975) notes certain world trends in legislation for maternity protection, notably as follows: (1) extension of maternity protection schemes to new categories of women workers. (2) prolongation of the period of statutory or prescribed maternity leave (or flexibility as to how much is taken before or after the birth), (3) more liberal provision of extended or extra leave during the child's infancy, (4) higher rates of maternity benefit, (5) more effective protection against dismissal during pregnancy and after confinement, (6) greater encouragement of breast-feeding and wider provision of nursing breaks for mothers, (7) more adequate attention to the safety and health of women during pregnancy and lactation (for example, through transfers to lighter work), and (8) establishment by social security schemes or public bodies of day nurseries to care for infants and children of working parents.

For examples, in Bulgaria a working mother, following obligatory paid leave, may take *further* leave for about 8–12 months at a minimum basic wage and still further unpaid leave with employment rights protected until the child is 3 years old. In Austria, within the framework of unemployment insurance, a working mother is granted 1 year of paid maternity leave following childbirth. In Scandinavian countries, there has been a trend towards fathers being eligible for 'maternity' benefits. For example, in Sweden, 'parents' benefits' can be paid to either working parent staying at home during the period of extended leave, or the period can be divided. In France, three days' paid leave is awarded to the father after his wife's delivery. In Norway, it has been proposed that male workers whose wives are in gainful employment should be entitled to 2–4 weeks childcare leave during the first year of the baby's life, and that benefits be paid to men workers during such leave.

Cost–benefit analysis

Without excluding social and emotional considerations, it is particularly necessary to consider cost–benefit analyses of working women breast-feeding from the point of view of the family, the industrial concern, and the nation.

Family. Often such discussions limit themselves to the money earned by the working mother versus the extra cost of formula required if she is unable to breast-feed her baby (Dugdale 1971). The issue is highly complex economically (without considering issues such as the value of continuing mother-infant contact and, conversely, the psychological satisfaction of extra-domiciliary work to the woman) and hidden costs are extensive.

Industry. The economic balance sheet with regard to women breast-feeding in industry or office work (p. 132) is difficult to calculate, and will depend largely on whether the cost of developing and running crèches and the payment to the mother of the commercially 'lost time' spent breast-feeding will be made by the government (via taxation or insurance). It is for this reason, among others, that industrial crèches are more common in centrally directed economies. Also, the International Labour Organization directives suggest the need to 'avoid a heavy burden on the owner of private industry'. A possible economic bonus to management could be the contraceptive effect of breast-feeding, decreasing future maternity leave.

National. On a national basis, the provision of legislation, resources, and organization to facilitate breast-feeding by working females, depends very much on the need for women in the labour-force, particularly, for example, in war-time. In addition, the concept of the relative advantages of breast-feeding by the health profession, nutritionists, and women themselves can influence the situation.

Position of women

In all parts of the world, a key factor is the enhancement of the position of women in their joint roles of mother and worker. In the U.S.A., Bronfen-brenner (1975) sees this in the context of preserving the family:

These concerns bring me to what I regard as the most important single factor affecting the welfare of the nation's children. I refer to the place and status of women in American society. Whatever the future trend may be, the fact remains that in our society today, the care of children depends overwhelmingly on women, and specifically on mothers. Moreover, with the withdrawal of the social supports for the family, the position of women and mothers has become more and more isolated. With the breakdown of the community, the neighborhood, and the extended family an increasing responsibility for the care and upbringing of children has fallen on the young mother. Under these circumstances, it is not surprising that many young women in America are in revolt. I understand and share their sense of rage, but I fear the consequences of some of the solutions they advocate, which will have the effect of isolating children still further from the kind of care and attention they need. There is, of course, a constructive implication to this line of thought, in that a major route to the rehabilitation of children and youth in American society lies in the enhancement of the status and power of women in all walks of life — in the home as well as on the job.

In poor countries, the basic needs of women are still very far from being met. As Wray (1976*b*) notes, for the majority, primary concerns are with 'survival requirements':

A better than minimal diet during pregnancy and lactation.

Simple, but adequate care and assistance during pregnancy, at delivery, and during the postpartum period.

A supportive and stable human environment during pregnancy and the postpartum period, and adequate guidance in child rearing and nutrition. Freedom from excessive physical demands during pregnancy and lactation.

A decent physical environment, with adequate housing, and easily available clean water.

Easy access — geographic, economic, and social — to safe, effective contraceptives to provide a realistic choice in determining how many children they will have, and how often.

Women's groups
The value of voluntary organizations, such as La Leche League International, *Ammehjelpen*, and the Nursing Mothers' Association of Australia, has become increasingly obvious in arousing awareness of the significance of breast-feeding and in increasing lactation performance (p. 306). Their addresses and a list of their publications are found in Appendixes A and B. Recently, similar groups have emerged in various developing countries, such as in Malaysia and Singapore.

It is particularly important that there should be a joining of forces between such voluntary groups and health professionals, including physicians, nurses, and midwives. 'Mixed' conferences have been organized in Australia by the Nursing Mothers' Association of Australia. An ideal consultant combination, for example, could be an experienced La Leche League group-leader and a well-informed health professional, either physician or nurse. It is imperative to have a Medical Advisory Board Committee, both to advise on more technical matters and newly available scientific information, and to avoid a rift developing in which physicians, particularly paediatricians, feel that what they perceive to be their area of expertise is being taken over by 'fanatical amateurs'.

Governmental planners

Data obtained from various sources, particularly from the community survey, will enable plans to be made as to the Ministry group, committee, or other similar body to whom this information (and its interpretation) can be supplied in a suitable brief non-scientific form to initiate and further promote a breast-feeding programme. This will include those concerned with food and nutrition policy, with family planning activities, with educational programmes (both general and medical), with health services, and with national economic planning. Information needs to be selected to highlight the results relating to the special interests of the particular Ministry or group, and also needs to be aired in the local press in an appropriate newsworthy form.

Food and nutrition

Until recently, the thinking of economic planners was exclusively concerned with the gross national product, and agriculturists with economic profit from cash crops alone, rather than with *both* profit and nutrition. It has been difficult to make the mental leap needed to consider human milk both as a national economic resource and as a locally processed convenience food (Platt 1954, Popkin and Latham 1973), but this has now occurred and the Food and Agriculture Organization include this among their concerns and information on breast-feeding is collected as part of 'nutritional surveillance'.

Health programmes

The question of breast-feeding also needs to figure prominently in the health segment of national developments plans, in many ways that have been discussed earlier. The emphasis will vary with local problems — for example, the prevention of infantile diarrhoea in the Caribbean and of obesity in Australia. The evaluation of the effectiveness of any programme needs to be measured in relation to a locally relevant definition of 'successful breast-feeding' (especially its duration), and to its effect on major problems in the particular ecology (e.g. marasmus, infantile allergy).

It has become clear recently that the main 'health' service need everywhere in the world is the development of low-cost basic family health programmes, reaching out into presently unserved rural areas. 'Self-help', the best use of available resources, the prevention of infection and malnutrition in young children, and child-spacing are major concerns. Breast-feeding plays an important role in all of these, and its importance needs to be

Mahler 1975*a*, Newell 1975, Katz and Bender 1976, Belloc and Breslow 1972, UNICEF-WHO Joint Committee on Health Policy 1975, Zagreb Guidelines 1973).

Research

Research needs to be initiated or continued in various aspects of breast-feeding, including epidemiology, specific considerations, and the effect of planned programmes (Table 14.9) The information obtained then needs dissemination widely to a range of disciplines — from health professionals to government planners.

Envoi

The present-day almost pandemic decline in breast-feeding, initially in industrialized Westernized regions, but more recent in peri-urban areas of developing countries, is essentially a twentieth-century phenomenon. In other words, it represents a nanosecond of time in the 200 million years of ancestral lactation history. The strangeness and radicalness of this abrupt and summary discarding of the most fundamental biological aspect of mammalian behaviour has been slow to be appreciated, as have its consequences. In fact, it is in some ways even more bizarre than the test-tube embryos in the hatcheries of Aldous Huxley's *Brave new world*.

TABLE 14.9   *Selected priority research topics*

Epidemiology	*General*: Prevalence of breast-feeding in different ecologies, using internationally agreed definitions, with analysis of associated social, economic, cultural factors *Community factors*: Activities of health services and infant-food industry (including advertising, marketing, promotional techniques, especially motivation); working women (practices, legislation)
Specific considerations	*Family planning*: interactions of contraceptives and lactation (especially progestogens) *Neonatal*: effects on infections, metabolism, mother–baby interaction; organization of milk bank *Pharmacology*: drug excretion in human milk (including pollutants) *Dental*: relation to caries and malocclusion *Nutritional*: longitudinal studies, with varying maternal diet; newly recognized constituents *Psychological*: results of different forms of mother–infant interaction *Adult disease*: obesity, atheroma, mammary diseases (including fibrocystic disease), multiple sclerosis, ulcerative colitis
Planned programmes	Effects of limited and wide-spectrum programming

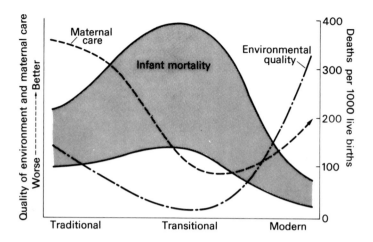

Fig. 14.13. Postulated interaction between quality of maternal care, environmental quality, and infant mortality in traditional, transitional, and modern societies (from Wray, J. D. (1976*a*). *Amer. Acad. Advancement Sci.* (in press))

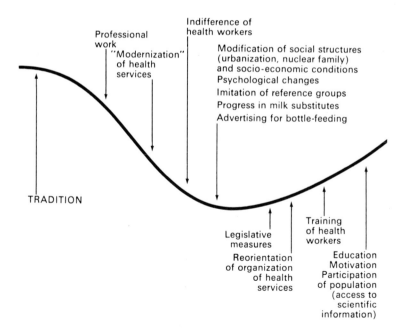

Fig. 14.14. Changing patterns of breast-feeding in relation to major factors of influences: tentative model (from Pechevis, M. (1975). *Assignment Children* **32**, 33)

Man has certainly achieved temporary world dominance because of his inventive gadgetry and scientific mastery, but only recently with the dramatic speed of the electronic revolution has he been brought to halt to consider the possible biological ill-consequences of poorly understood technological change and mechanized *hubris*, and to consider the possibility that he may have become an 'endangered species' (Tiger and Fox 1972). It seems, then, timely to consider the question of infant feeding in this context, and to recognize breast-feeding as much more than a 'less available option', as it has been somewhat derogatorily termed (Ladas 1972).

There is a widening gap between technological 'medical care' and needed 'health care', which, it is increasingly clear, must be based on community 'self-care' (Mahler, 1975). Breast-feeding is a classical example — with the baby's nutrition and health catered for biologically by the mother.

Infant mortality and health can be visualized as the outcome of the interaction of two groups of forces — maternal 'competence' (notably breast-feeding), and environment (including hygiene and food supply) (Wray 1976) (Fig. 14.13). In modern Westernized societies, the environment is relatively benign, but maternal competence, related to social preparation for motherhood, is low, as regards the infant, compared with traditional societies. The ideal for the future is for the combined benefits of both environment and maternal competence — for both adequate environmental hygiene and food supply, together with maternal competence, including breast-feeding.

The time is overdue for the development and active promotion of breast-feeding programmes on national scales, using modern knowledge of the psychophysiology of lactation and marketing techniques, and the value of social support groups (Fig. 14.14). This is a priority in countries of all levels of technical development and of resources. 'Double standards' for infant feeding are not called for. Human milk and breast-feeding has a positive, beneficial effect everywhere, and affords protection against different spectra of ill-health in varying parts of the world.

Man's willingness and ability to achieve a balance between technology and ecology are major concerns for future survival of the species. Newer information leads increasingly to a consensus which points to the need for a system of infant feeding based on blend of modern scientific knowledge, an awareness of time-tested adaptations, and man's ancient biological mammalian heritage.

Addendum

RECENT HIGHLIGHTS

Continuing high levels of interest in breast-feeding and human milk are indicated by the 290 papers listed in the Additional Bibliography (pp. 475 to 488), mostly appearing in the past ten months, and by the 15 recent technical meetings held (p. 392). Selected recent highlights are summarized below:

Interaction

The biology of mother–infant interaction continues to be explored, including the significance of pheromones, ultrasound signals (Smotherman *et al.* 1976), and the effect of increased nipple sensitivity (Robinson and Short 1977). Unappreciated endocrinological interaction may be indicated by the presence of hormones in breast-milk, including thyroxine (Sack *et al.* 1977, Tenore *et al.* 1977), insulin (Čevreska *et al.* 1975), and prostaglandins (Evans and Johnson 1977). Investigations continue into the early relationship of mother and baby, including breast-feeding, as regards both immediate and later consequences (De Chateau and Winberg 1977*a,b*; Klaus and Kennell 1976, Lozoff *et al.* 1977).

Composition

Numerous papers have appeared on the biochemical composition of human milk in different circumstances. It has been shown that high levels of water-soluble vitamin D are present (Lakdawala and Widdowson 1977), that the absorption of zinc (Eckhert *et al.* 1977, Evans and Johnson 1976) and iron (McMillan and Oski 1977, Saarinen *et al.* 1977) are greater than with cow's-milk formulas, and that breast-milk in mothers with premature babies has a different composition (Atkinson *et al.* 1977). The significance of human milk as a source of calories has been emphasized (Rutishauser 1974), and the neglected nutritional (and anti-infective) role of colostrum is realized increasingly, especially as regards vitamin A, carotenoids, vitamin D, zinc, and copper (Widdowson 1977*b*).

Volume

Many investigations in widely differing parts of the world re-emphasize the unique difficulties in assessing the volume of breast-milk produced in relation to optimal infant growth. In general, the effects of various forms of 'environmental psychosocial stress', including culturally defined practices in the perinatal period, are most often responsible for inadequate milk availability, as a result of interference with the prolactin and let-down reflexes. The role of adequate maternal nutrition (Lechtig *et al.* 1975, 1977; Schutz *et al.* 1977), *both* in pregnancy and lactation, is becoming increasingly clear: a good diet in pregnancy reduces the risk of a low-weight 'small for dates' neonate (Swedish International Development Agency 1977).

Host resistance

Major advances have included the demonstration that human milk has anti-viral properties (Emödi and Just 1974, Matthews *et al.* 1976, Modak and Marcus 1977) and, of great importance in developing countries, active protection against intestinal parasites (Mata and Urrutia 1977). Tuberculin sensitivity has been shown to be transmitted via human milk, with the possibility of some protection against tuberculosis (Mohr 1973). Anti-infective effects may be presumed to be related to the amount of host-resistance substances ingested, and, as the concentration diminishes with continuing lactation so the total quantity is maintained by the increased milk volume (McLelland *et al.* 1977).

Excretion of chemicals

A number of papers have been published reporting the presence of various pharmaceuticals in the milk of nursing mothers receiving medication; the drugs investigated have included warfarin (Orme *et al.* 1977), theophylline (Yurchak and Jusko 1976) and theobromine, from chocolate (Resman *et al.* 1977). Newer information has enabled more up-to-date lists to be drawn up, with suggestions concerning the relative risks of different drugs (P. O. Anderson 1977, Forrest 1976, White 1977).

A great deal of attention has been given to concentrations of lipophilic environmental pollutants in breast-milk, including those used mainly in agriculture (Jonsson *et al.* 1977, *Nutrition Reviews* 1977) and in industry, e.g. PCBs (R. W. Miller 1977). No immediate ill-effects are known, except with mothers who are themselves severely poisoned, as with the use of cooking oil that was highly contaminated in Japan. Such pollutants should be removed from the environment for the protection of the community, but it will be a difficult task, especially as some have been in use for years. Studies into dietary modifications in pregnancy and lactation are being undertaken, with special attention to restriction of fattier animal products.

Effects of breast vs. formula feeding

Additional evidence has appeared showing the protective effect of breast-feeding against cow's-milk protein allergy in infancy (Matthew *et al.* 1977) and common infections (including diarrhoea) in industrialized countries (Tripp *et al.* 1977, Vobecky *et al.* 1977) and in disadvantaged communities (Gerrard and Tan 1977). A possible protective effect against mammary cancer has again been suggested by a study of women in Hong Kong who feed with only one breast (Ing *et al.* 1977). The possibility of unsuspected ill-effects from the substances used, or produced, by food technologists in the preparation of processed formulas has been suggested by two recent findings: first the discovery of toxic effects in newborn guinea-pigs from carrageenan (Udall *et al.* 1977), which is almost universally employed to prevent separation and sedimentation; and, second, the recognition of lactulose-induced diarrhoea (Hendrickse *et al.* 1977). Inherent risks of bacterial contamination during manufacture were emphasized by the major outbreak of salmonella gastroenteritis in Australia in 1977 due to infected powdered-milk preparations (*The Age* 1977).

The potential consequences of infant nutrition on health in adult life continues to be an important, but difficult, focus for investigation. The level of sodium intake has been looked at from this angle (Rose 1977). Infantile obesity has been investigated a great deal. Its aetiology seems more complex (Weil 1977) than previously believed; for example, neonatal obesity may be involved and may be linked with an excessive calorie intake by the mother during pregnancy (Swedish International Development Agency 1977). Further problems include the prognosis and significance of the uncommon over-fat solely breast-fed baby, in the light of known differences in the composition of subcutaneous fat (Oakley 1977).

Health services

Interest by health professionals is indicated by the volume of publications in medical literature and by moves to incorporate supportive practices into hospitals and other services. Particular attention has been given to the question of the organization of 'new style' breast-milk banks (Fomon 1977), since it is increasingly considered to be more appropriate for low birth-weight babies to be fed on human colostrum and milk, with their anti-infective properties and superior nutritional values (Räihä 1976).

Governments in some parts of the world, notably Sweden, Indonesia, Malaysia, and Chile, have developed different forms of national effort to support breast-feeding. In one less developed country, New Guinea-Papua, an Act has been introduced which prohibits the advertising or supply of feeding bottles or teats unless authorized by a physician, nurse, or medical assistant (Independent State of Papua New Guinea 1977).

Infant-formula industry

Past and continuing criticism of the promotional activities of infant-formula companies in developing countries has provoked a few of these companies into making concessions. For example, Borden and Abbott have said that they will stop all direct advertising to the consumer in the Third World. The subject is difficult to judge objectively as facts about sales, advertising budget, methods of marketing, and promotional techniques are trade secrets. A new Code of Marketing Ethics has been drawn up by Abbott

Laboratories (1977) in which seven revisions have been made, including the elimination of nurses' uniforms worn by company saleswomen, etc. This is still far from the Swedish Code of Ethics for Marketing Infant Foods (*Acta Paediatrica, Stockholm* 1977) drawn up jointly by the food industry and paediatric authorities, in which direct advertising to consumers and the use of free gifts or samples are banned.

In the U.S.A., the case brought by the Sisters of the Precious Blood against Bristol–Meyers was dismissed on a technical legal issue, but there is to be an appeal (National Council of Churches 1977). Also, a new group INFACT (Infant Formula Action) is organizing a boycott of Nestlé products demanding that this company stop the free distribution of formula and bottles in hospitals and clinics and stop the use of mothercraft nurses in developing countries (*Nutrition Action* 1977).

Working women

Breast-feeding poses practical problems for working women in different parts of the world; as an attempt to find some solutions, a first meeting was held on this matter in 1977 sponsored by the International Planned Parenthood Federation and International Union of Nutritional Sciences. It was attended by representatives of the I.L.O. (International Labour Organization).

RECENT TECHNICAL MEETINGS

The following recent conferences and workshops have been related to different aspects of breast-feeding and were held in 1976 and 1977:

1. Ciba Symposium No. 42. (1976). *Acute diarrhoea in childhood.* Elsevier Press, Amsterdam.
2. *Breast-feeding,* Department of Health and Social Security, London, England, 14 July 1975. Proceedings in *J. Nutr.* (1976) **30**, 223–80.
3. Ciba Symposium No. 45 (1976). *Breast-feeding and the mother.* Elsevier Press, Amsterdam.
4. *Food and Immunology,* Swedish Nutrition Foundation, Saltsjöbaden, Sweden, 9–11 June 1975. Proceedings (1977), eds. L. Hambraeus, L. A. Hanson, and H. McFarlane, published by Almquist and Wiksell, Stockholm.
5. *New concepts in infant feeding,* Symposium at Royal College of Physicians, London, England, 20 September 1976. Proceedings in *Current Medical Research and Opinion* (1976) **4**, Supplement: 1.
6. *Regulation of fertility during lactation,* International Planned Parenthood and Ciba Foundation, London, England, November 1976. Proceedings in 1977 Supplement of *J. Biosoc. Sci.* (in press).
7. *Recent advances in breast-feeding,* George Washington University School of Medicine and Health Sciences, and the National Foundation–March of Dimes, Washington, D.C., 7–8 October 1976. Proceedings in press.
8. *Nutrition and reproduction,* National Institute of Child Health and Human

Development, Bethesda, Maryland, U.S.A., 13–16 February 1977. Proceedings in press.

9. Conference on *Human Lactation,* New York Academy of Sciences, 2–4 March 1977. Proceedings in press.

10. *Natural fertility,* Seminar organized by the International Union for the Scientific Study of Population, Paris, France, 21–24 March 1977. Proceedings in press.

11. *Practical approaches to combatting malnutrition: with special reference to mothers and children,* International Union of Nutritional Sciences, Cairo, Egypt, 25–29 May 1977. Proceedings in press.

12. *The mother–child dyad: nutritional aspects,* Swedish Nutrition Foundation, Uppsala, Sweden, 20–22 June 1977. Proceedings in press.

13. *Lactation, fertility and the working woman,* International Planned Parenthood Federation (IPPF) and the International Union of Nutritional Sciences (IUNS), Bellagio, Italy, 6–12 July 1977. Proceedings in press.

14. *Recent advances in lactation* and *Infant feeding: trends in the 1970s,* International Congress of Pediatrics, New Delhi, India, 23–28 October 1977. Proceedings in press.

15. *Obstetric management and infant outcome,* American Foundation for Maternal and Child Health, 16 November 1977. Proceedings in press.

PROPOSED GLOSSARY OF TERMS†

1. *Breast-feeding*
   Feeding from the breast of the mother or of another woman.
   1.1. *Complete breast-feeding*
      (Synonyms: totally, fully or solely breast-fed)
      Feeding from the breast exclusively, apart from water or fruit juice in very small quantities, or of vitamin concentrates.
   1.2. *Partial breast-feeding*
      Breast-feeding associated with other food provided in significant amounts and on a regular daily basis.
   1.3. *Mainly breast fed*
      Breast milk provides most of the energy in the total diet.
   1.4. *Nibbling*
      The child sucks at the breast for comfort and emotional relief but does not obtain significant amounts of milk.

2. *Weaning from breast*
   The process of withdrawing breast feeding, which may be gradual or abrupt.
   2.1. *Partial weaning from breast*
      The process of weaning has not been completed.
   2.2. *Complete weaning from breast*
      Breast feeding has stopped completely.

3. *Artificial feeding*
   (Often referred to as bottle-feeding)
   Feeding with a substitute for breast-milk.
   3.1. *Complete artificial feeding*
      (Synonym: total artificial feeding, also often referred to as completely bottle fed).
      The breast milk substitute forms the sole diet.
   3.2 *Mainly artificially fed*
      A breast milk substitute provides most of the energy in the child's diet.
   3.3. *Complementary feeding*
      (N.B. In French, *alimentation supplementaire*)
      Breast feeding plus a breast milk substitute ('complement').

4. *Mixed feeding*
   (Synonym: supplementary feeding. N.B. In French, *alimentation complémentaire*)
   In addition to breast milk, infants receive additional solid foods or paps ('supplements') in significant amounts on a regular daily basis.

† Proposed by WHO and reproduced with permission.

Appendix A

The following are the addresses of some groups concerned with modern methods of infant feeding, including breast-feeding:

Ammehjelpen, Postboks 15, Holmen, Oslo 3, Norway.

Arbeitsgruppe and Dritte Welt, Postbach 1007, Bern, 300, Switzerland.

Association for Improvement of Maternity Services, 61 Dartmouth Park Road, London N.W.5, U.K.

Baby Foods Action Group, 103 Gower Street, London, WC1E 6AW, U.K.

Center for Science in the Public Interest, 1779 Church Street, N.W., Washington, D.C. 20036, U.S.A.

La Leche League International, 9616 Minneapolis Avenue, Franklin Park, Illinois 60131, U.S.A.

National Childbirth Trust, Breast-feeding Promotion Group, 9 Queensborough Terrace, London W2 3TB, U.K.

Nursing Mothers' Association of Australia, 99 Burwood Road, Hawthorn, Victoria, Australia 3122.

Parents Centres of Australia, 148 Hereford Street, Forest Lodge, N.S.W., Australia 2229.

International Childbirth Education Association, 2763 N.W. 70th Street, Seattle, Washington 98167, U.S.A.

War on Want, 467 Caledonian Road, London N.7, U.K.

Other groups include: Amninghjaelpen (Sweden), Ñu Ñu (Argentina), PPI (Malaysia), and Singapore Breast Feeding Mothers' Group.

Appendix B

The following publications are available covering various aspects of the subject:

Popular publications

Center for Science in the Public Interest (1976). *Let's give babies a better start*. Washington, D.C. In press.

Eiger, M. and Olds, S. (1972). *The complete book of breast-feeding*. Workman, New York.

Gerard, A. (1972). *Please breast-feed your baby*. Signet Books, New York.

Helsing, E. (1974). *Boken Om Amning*. Bokforlaget Trovi, Oslo (in Norwegian).

Kippley, S. and Kippley, K. (1974). *Breast-feeding and natural child spacing*. Harper and Row, New York.

La Leche League International (1958). *The womanly art of breast-feeding*. Interstate Publishers, Franklin Park, Ill. (In English, French, Spanish, and Japanese).

Matsumura, T. (1972). *Breast-feed your children*. Horiuchi Bunjiro, Tokyo (in Japanese).

Phillips, V. (1975). *Successful breast-feeding*. Down Under Press, Australia.

Pryor, K. (1973). *Nursing your baby*. Harper and Row, New York.

Raphael, D. (1973). *The tender gift: breast-feeding*. Prentice Hall, Princeton, New Jersey.

Technical publications

Applebaum, R. M. (1970). *Pediat. Clins. N. Am.* **17**, 203. The modern management of successful breast-feeding.

Center for Science in the Public Interest (1974). *White paper in infant nutrition*. Washington, D.C.

Haire, D. and Haire, J. (1974). *The nurses' contribution to breast-feeding*. International Childbirth Association, New Jersey.

International Children's Centre, Paris (1972). *Collogue sur l'allaitment maternel*. Abidjan, Côte d'lvoire (in French).

Periodicals

Journal of Tropical Pediatrics, 2A Drayson Mews, Kensington, London W.8, U.K.

Keeping Abreast Journal, P.O. Box 6459, Denver, Colorado 80205, U.S.A.

Lactation Review, Human Lactation Center, 666 Sturges Highway, Connecticut 06880, U.S.A.

La Leche League News, 9616 Minneapolis Avenue, Franklin Park, Illinois
   60131, U.S.A.
Nursing Mothers' Association of Australia Newsletter, 99 Burwood Road,
   Hawthorn, Victoria, Australia 3122.

Appendix C

The following are examples of available audio-visual aids on breast-feeding.

Slides

1. Set available from Nursing Mothers Association of Australia.
2. Breast Feeding Series. 22 slides from Photoview Instructional Aids, Dept. B, Deodera Drive, Los Altos, California 94022, U.S.A.

Films

1. *A better beginning*. 16 mm sound film about the Evanston Premature Babies' Milk Bank. Available on free loan to interested groups. Film Library, Speech Annex, North-western University, Evanston, Ill., U.S.A.
2. *Breast-feeding*. Available from Health Sciences Communication Center, Case Western Reserve University, University Circle, Cleveland, Ohio 44106, U.S.A.
3. *Breast-feeding – a family affair*. 16 mm sound and colour film. Association for Childbirth Education, Mrs. William H. McCafferty (distribution chairman), 2763 N.W. 70th Street, Seattle 7, Washington, U.S.A. Fee, $5 per showing.
4. *Great Expectations*. Society for Nutrition Education, 2140 Shattuck Avenue, Suite 1110, Berkeley, California 94704, U.S.A.
5. *Talking about breast-feeding*. 16 mm sound film, cinema-verité style. A touching, warm glimpse of what it is like to be a nursing mother; good teaching aid or introduction. Polymorph Films, Inc., 331 Newbury St., Boston, Mass. 02115, U.S.A. Rent or purchase.
6. *Bottle babies*. Teldok Films, 504 Bruhl, Chlodwigstrasse 29, Cologne, West Germany.

Appendix D

Scheme B for a non-quantitive inquiry into probably relevant activities of the health services and the food industry; by courtesy of Leah Margulies, Eco-Justice Task Force Interfaith Center on Corporate Responsibility, 475 Riverside Drive, New York, 10027, U.S.A.

1. *Interview local health-care personnel.* Try to analyse to what extent the problem of infant malnutrition related to bottle-feeding exists in your area.

2. *Visit local hospitals and clinics.* See what kinds of literature, posters, and promotional material are there.
   Interview hospital staff. Find out what kinds of formulas, if any, are distributed through that unit.

3. *Visit companies that distribute infant formulas.* What brands do they distribute? If possible, try to get sales figures.
   What are the sales and promotional practices of that particular company and product?
   Do they distribute to pharmacies, supermarkets and general stores, doctors' offices, hospitals (public and private) and clinics?
   Do they visit homes and/or schools?
   What kind of sales personnel do they hire: nurses and/or salesmen?
   Do the sales personnel make home visits?
   Do they receive a set salary? A bonus of any kind? Fringe benefits? In-service training?

4. *Try also some informal investigating, not just interviews.* Collect advertisements and promotional material. Talk to mothers and get their opinions. Use your imagination. Try investigative areas not mentioned if you think they are worthwhile.

Appendix E

NATIONAL PROGRAMMES

Various small-scale, narrow-spectrum programmes to improve breast-feeding in a hospital or medical practice have been outlined earlier, as well as figures showing specific benefits.

On a national scale, concern has been voiced in various different parts of the world, including Chile, Venezuela, Singapore, Malaysia, Indonesia, Trinidad, etc:

Some countries have taken active steps to protect mothers and children from the attention of baby food companies. Niger permits no demonstration or advertising of bottle feeding techniques at mother and child health centers. The Zambian nationalized company which produces 'Dawn' powdered milk states clearly in its advertising: Don't feed your child artificially unless you are sure you have the money to buy the milk. (New Internationalist 1975).

In New Guinea, the government introduced an 'anti-bottle' campaign, preventing the sale of feeding bottles, especially in the Highlands.

Three national approaches need particular emphasis, because of their pioneering nature and likelihood of containing useful examples. The three countries are small, cosmopolitan, urbanized, and insular — Trinidad (950 000 population), Singapore (1·8 million population), and Jamaica (2 million population).

Trinidad campaign

In January 1974, the Association of Advertising Agencies offered their services to the Housewives Association of Trinidad and Tobago to promote consumer education. Since many of the latter's previous efforts had been directed toward nutrition education it was decided to accept the offer and gear the programme to breast-feeding as a local priority agreed to by health workers and nutritionists.

The campaign (described by A. White 1974) was aimed first at providing mothers-to-be with facts on breast-feeding so that they could make a reasoned decision to nurse their babies, and, secondly, to create an awareness in the whole population of the desirability of human milk.

During April, the scientific facts were converted by copy writers and artists into language and images which would inform and 'sell the product'. At this time, the Minister of Health pledged his ministry's support for the campaign and the Trinidad and Tobago Publishers and Broadcasters Association promised cooperation in the form of time and space on radio, television, and in the press for a six-week period. The campaign was launched on 31 May.

Advertising. During June and July, the two daily papers, the Trinidad Guardian and Express, and the evening paper carried once, twice, or three times a week, a series of five advertisements each highlighting a different aspect of breast-feeding, but repeating the same basic information (Fig. 14.3). Some weekly and monthly publications have also included at least one of the series. The radio stations gave at least nine 15- and 30-second 'spots' per day between them, and Trinidad Television one 10-second 'spot' per day at 'prime time'.

Supporting programmes. Early in June, the Housewives Association of Trinidad and Tobago accepted an offer by All Media Projects Ltd. to coordinate the production of material for press articles, releases, radio and TV programmes. They interviewed and recorded nurses and mothers in clinics to provide material for five 15-minute Government Broadcasting Unit features. On their suggestion a film was made in one of the Health Centres. During July they were responsibile for a daily 5-minute radio series which appeared simultaneously in the press. They also arranged a telephone conversation between the President of the Housewives Association of Trinidad and Tobago, Mrs. Faith Wiltshire, and Mrs. Manley, wife of the Prime Minister of Jamaica, who endorsed the programme.

At least nine television programmes have focussed on breast-feeding during this period: an interview on Panorama, the daily news programme; a current-affairs discussion; the film of mothers and nurses in a clinic; and a series of six interviews based on the five advertisements (the President of the Housewives Association of Trinidad and Tobago, a nurse, a mother — a member of La Leche League, a home economist, a medical officer, and a nutritionist).

The Ministry of Health arranged a briefing session for health-service personnel, etc., so that they would have up-to-date information on breast-feeding. They also printed handbills and posters and have been responsible for distribution to health centres. Ministry personnel have assisted with television and radio programmes.

Other activities. These included: (i) talks and discussion with secondary-school children in main towns; (ii) talks to other groups — e.g. Parent–Teacher Associations, church groups, father's clubs, etc.; (iii) the organization by the Central Library of a collection of material on breast-feeding for display in the capital and the outlying districts served by the mobile library; (iv) an endorsement by the Trinidad and Tobago Medical Association and acceptance of an article on breast-feeding for the Association's publication, 'Medinews'.

Comment. This campaign seems to be unique, both as an activity and specifically in obtaining the cooperation of high-priced advertising and media concerns (whose expertise is evident in the 'promotional material' produced) (Fig. 14.3), with consumers and government, through the Ministry of Health. As appreciated by the organizers themselves, this was a *campaign*, lasting only six weeks (June and July 1974), without funds or containing expert assistance for prolonged activities.

Gueri (1975) investigated the effect of the campaign immediately after its completion, and found a highly significant relationship between the 'knowledge score' regarding breast-feeding and frequency of exposure to mass media. A major side-issue of such a short, but quite intensive, campaign may be the 'consciousness-raising' among a wide range of different groups, including politicians and administrators, health workers and nutritionists, and the public.

Singapore programme

Professor Wong Hock Boon of the Department of Paediatrics of the University of Singapore has been monitoring the status of breast-feeding in Singapore since 1951; and in 1971, the mothers from the higher socioeconomic group showed a fall of 85 per cent to 28 per cent in initiating breast-feeding over the two decades, and only 4 per cent were breast-feeding by 3 months. The corresponding fall for mothers in the lower income group was 90 per cent to 51 per cent, and only 5 per cent were breast-feeding by 3 months though 77 per cent had done so in 1951. Because of this alarming fall, and the rise in infant and childhood malnutrition, efforts were made to check this.

An on-going programme to promote breast-feeding was therefore initiated and has been outlined by Wong Hock Boon (1975*b*), as follows:

Public forums, talks, use of the mass media (radio, TV, newspapers, etc.) all highlighted this severe set-back, but, the impact on the mothers was minimal. In 1974, the campaign waged by the Department was intensified, and a Singapore Breast feeding Mothers' Group was formed. This was affiliated to the Consumers' Association of Singapore, and a large number of breastfeeding mothers rallied to the meetings. Forums and teaching seminars were held, and for the latter, certificates were issued to those who attended. The mass media became intensely interested and the activities of the Group were highlighted almost weekly, and the newspapers assisted in contacting more mothers for the Group.

The Protein–Calorie Advisory Group of the United Nations System chose Singapore for the venue for a Seminar on Infant & Child Nutrition with special emphasis on breast-feeding in November 1974, where paediatricians from S.E. Asia as well as representatives from the commercial milk firms attended.

The deliberations and recommendations have since been published in the Protein Advisory Group Bulletin Vol. V. No. 1, March 1975. Following on this, the Department of Paediatrics, called a meeting of paediatricians and representatives of milk firms to a meeting, to implement the recommendations made at this Seminar. A small sub-committee was then formed and this group has been dealing with unethical advertising and sales promotion for canned cow's milk. There is no doubt that this sub-committee has been responsible for the raising of ethical standards. By now, most mothers in Singapore realize that breast-feeding is best for their babies. However, rapid urbanization and assimilation of Western cultural attitudes in such a short time, have militated against the attainment of higher percentage of breast-feeding mothers.

In 1975, the Department with the assistance of the Breast-feeding Mothers' Group started a Breast-milk Bank to cater to those infants with problems due to cow's milk feeding, and for those mothers who are finding initial difficulty in breast-feeding their babies. This is the first such bank in S.E. Asia. It has already saved the lives of some infants with severe allergy to cow's milk resulting in malignant refractory diarrhea.

The Breast-feeding Mothers' Group operates in smaller groups catering to the various areas in Singapore. These are zoned, and the mothers receive phone calls from prospective mothers who wish to breast-feed, or are finding difficulties in breast-feeding. Each zone leader is also responsible for collection of milk for the Milk Bank. The Group is now in the process of writing a book of breast-feeding for distribution to women in Singapore.

There is no doubt that all the above activities have resulted in arresting the further fall in breast-feeding, and indeed they have converted many mothers to breast-feed their babies.

The Department and this Breast-feeding Mothers' Group work very closely with the Infant Welfare Clinics where antenatal mothers are motivated and taught how to breast-feed. Mothercraft nurses have now been banned from visiting Government Hospitals and Infant Welfare Clinics.

It is hoped that this philosophy of breast-feeding will be taught to school children, and efforts have now been made in this direction. School texts on infant nutrition should be re-written so that mother's milk should receive pride of place and not cow's milk. The education of schoolgirls in this direction before they become mothers will be our aim for the future.

Jamaica programme

In 1976, a three-phase programme is being initiated by the Government of Jamaica with assistance from the World Bank, and will cover breast-feeding, weaning foods, and the best utilization of services for maternal and child health, nutrition, and family planning. Phase I, lasting 9 months, will be directed at the health services; phase II, at the public; and phase III, at evaluation. The programme will be carried out through the mass media, the health services (including a six-weeks home visiting period after delivery) etc.

Appendix F

ASPECTS OF THE MANAGEMENT OF LACTATION

Special attention should be given to practical consideration of the methods and techniques needed for successful breast-feeding, together with the management of common problems, such as covered by Applebaum (1970, 1974, 1976), in various La Leche League publications or in the 1975 edition of Nelson's *Textbook of pediatrics* (see Laupus 1975).

Some techniques may be culture-bound (e.g. precise positioning and 'burping' in the Western world); the mechanism, or even effect, of others may be disputed (e.g. expression of colostrum in later pregnancy (Ingelman – Sundberg 1958)), except as an assurance-giving procedure of importance in promoting confidence and, hence, an unimpaired let-down reflex. The techniques advised should be as simple as possible, agreed to by all in the field locally, and should fit in with indigenous cultural concepts and attitudes.

Important modern points that have emerged as scientifically valid in the last two decades are prenatal preparation (counselling; breast support with brassière; nipple care — including nipple massage for inversion and the use of a nipple shield, if needed; possibly expression of milk in the last six weeks of pregnancy), demand (or flexible demand) feedings (from soon after delivery, with rooming-in at the hospital and home, giving both breasts at each feeding, modification in clothes to permit inconspicuous nursing); nursing for varying length of time depending on the ecology (as will be discussed later), introducing semi-solids at 4–6 months and weaning from the breast gradually and cooperatively ('lead by the weanee', onto cup and spoon without intermediate feeding bottle).

Problems and contra-indications. The great majority of women can breast-feed successfully. The commonest practical problems with breast-feeding are *engorgement*, often related to inadequate emptying which can be dealt with by expression (manually or by electric breast pump*), and *nipple trouble* (inverted, retracted, or cracked) which can be prevented in the majority of cases by prenatal care and by practices which facilitate the let-down reflex. Breast infection, both mastitis and abscess, are nowadays not usually regarded as a reason for stopping, in fact the pumping effect of the baby assists in relieving engorgement, together with a short course of appropriate antibiotic for the mother (Newton and Newton 1950). An exception is an abscess caused by antibiotic-resistant bacteria.

Severe illness in the mother may be a rare contra-indication to breast-

*Probably the most effective is the widely used Egnell Breast Pump (Pilling Co.). Address: Delaware Drive, Fort Washington, Pa 19034, U.S.A.

feeding — for example, with congestive heart failure, eclampsia, typhoid, or puerperal mania. However, the situation will vary from one ecology to another. Thus, in less technically developed countries, maternal pulmonary tuberculosis or leprosy are *not* contra-indications to breast-feeding (D. B. Jelliffe 1968*b*). In the former, active treatment is indicated for the mother (plus advice on the disposal of sputum), together with oral isonicotinic acid hydrazide (INH) chemotherapy for the baby, with immunization with BCG vaccine (preferably with the INH-resistant strain). In the baby of the woman with leprosy, ideally the infant should be kept apart from the mother (especially for close prolonged skin-to-skin contact), giving diamino-diphenyl sulphone by mouth and returned to mother for nursing. This will only be a practicable regimen in a leprosarium. With breast-feeding and these precautions there is a slight chance the baby will become infected; without breast-feeding, he will die.

A short cessation (48 hours) is indicated in babies with pregnanediol jaundice, if the direct bilirubin level rises above 15 mg/100 ml (p. 108). The situation with regard to chemicals in human milk is complex and has been discussed elsewhere (p. 101). Essentially, all drugs should be avoided for lactating women. If necessary, the drug with the least potential for toxicity should be used for the shortest period of time to be effective. In some cases, temporary removal of the baby from the breast (with expression of milk and feeding with cow's-milk formula) may be necessary for a few days. Occasionally, with certain drugs, especially if they have to be used in high dosage for a long period may be an indication for ceasing to breast-feed, difficulties may occur from the neonatal end of the dyad. These include weakness and poor sucking vigour in the newborn as a result of maternal anaesthesia, or of prematurity and low birth-weight (including twins), severe jaundice, septicaemia, cerebral birth injury, mechanical defects from marked cleft palate or harelip, or absence of the swallowing reflex in pre-maturity. These may mean temporary inability to breast-feed although expressed milk may be used and 'relactation' commenced later. Twins can be breast-fed in many instances. (H. L. Addy 1976, Nursing Mothers' Association of Australia 1972).

Anywhere, the main difficulties are related to matters of technique and, above all, to emotional interference with the let-down reflex; 'non-thrivers' in the breast-fed usually have this type of aetiology (Fleiss 1976*a*). In some parts of the world, fear of bewitchment may be a primary cause of anxiety. In others, the lack of knowledge and socio-cultural uncertainties, or environmental psychosocial stress, or the effects of oral contraceptives are root causes. In the present-day, small family, bottle-feeding culture anxiety is likely to be high.

Techniques for improving declining lactation will depend on the causes, but will include consideration of increasing prolactin production (by increased sucking stimulation of the breast), enhancing the let-down reflex (by decreasing anxiety), and improving the mother's nutrition.

Duration of breast-feeding. In traditional societies, including the Western world until the present century, breast-feeding was usually continued for 2–3 years or more. Often the signal for discontinuance was a subsequent pregnancy, related to the waning effect of biological 'lactation contraception' (p. 118).

Secondly, differentiation needs to be made between human milk as the *sole* food for the exterogestate foetus in early infancy, and its role as a decreasing, but significant supplement for the 'transitional', especially in poorer countries with limited food supplies.

The optimal duration of breast-feeding *alone* needs to take into consideration (1) the metabolic adequacy (volume and composition) of human milk for growth and nutrient needs of the increasingly large baby, (2) probable depletion of foetal stores (e.g. hepatic iron, etc.), (3) development of immunity to infections previously protectable by transplacental antibodies and by the active and passive effects of breast-milk, (4) decline in allergy-prone phase of early infancy, characterized by absorption of protein macromolecules, (5) appearance of indicators of physiological maturity (e.g. deglutition reflex, eruption of first 'milk teeth', increase in starch-splitting intestinal amylase), and (6) endocrinological considerations in mother, especially understanding that the amount of nipple stimulation is related to prolactin secretion, and hence to the volume of milk produced and to the anovulatory contraceptive effect.

Socio-cultural factors also affect locally acceptable decisions, whether custom (e.g. when child has reached certain developmental level), or economics, such as the mother's need to return to salaried work in Western-type urban circumstances, in which facilities for breast-feeding are not yet available.

In relatively resource-rich countries, with well-fed mothers and with good foetal stores, breast-feeding *alone* for 4–6 months (Jelliffe and Jelliffe 1975e) offers the baby (a) excellent growth (with less opportunity for infantile obesity), (b) optimal protection against cow's milk allergy, neonatal hypocalcaemia, and various other metabolic conditions, (c) special opportunities for mother–infant interaction, and (d) a supply of the unique blend of nutrients adapted to the needs of human offspring over millennia (including, in particular, an abundant supply of nutrients needed for the growth and development of the central nervous system in the young baby, e.g. high lactose, cystine, and cholesterol and a species-specific pattern of fatty acids (p. 26). At the same time, a short period of breast-feeding (e.g. 1–2 months) still appears to have important nutritional, emotional and anti-infective advantages for the neonate (MacKeith 1969). Even a short period of 2 weeks breast-feeding is valuable in relation to the prevention of metabolic imbalances (hypocalcaemie, tyrosinaemia) and infection in the newborn (Department of Health and Social Security, U.K. 1974).

The desirability of breast-feeding *alone* for 4–6 months applies in general to resource-poor countries for similar reasons, but is even more important because of (a) the protection against the interrelated syndromes of marasmus and diarrhoeal disease, and (b) the child-spacing contraceptive effect (Jelliffe and Jelliffe 1975*e*). In all circumstances attention needs to be turned to maternal nutrition in pregnancy and lactation, using low-cost, locally available foods.

In resource-poor countries, breast-feeding to 1–2 years supplies small, but important, dietary supplement to the transitional (weaning) diet and continuing, but declining biological contraception. In resource-rich countries, lactation prolonged after 6 months does not currently appear to have nutritional advantages, and may be stated to be optional.

Appendix G

INDUSTRY CODES OF ETHICS

In recent years, two codes of ethics have been introduced by the infant-food industry: (A) from Ross Laboratories (p. 408), and (B) from the International Council of Infant Food Industries (p. 411).

A. INTERNATIONAL CODE OF MARKETING ETHICS with Reference to Infant Feeding

Because good nutrition is an essential consideration in proper health care, we believe that supervision of the infant's diet should be the responsibility of medical and paramedical personnel whose training, experience and understanding of local needs best qualify them to provide this guidance. We attempt to conduct our business in a manner so as to become an adjunct to local health personnel, supporting their efforts through the provision of appropriate products and services. We further believe that this alliance is especially important in developing countries, where delivery of primary health care to major segments of the population is complicated by unfavourable living conditions. Within this context we are keenly aware of the responsibilities of Ross for making a positive contribution to the health and well-being of infants in developing countries.

We set forth below guidelines for ethical behaviour through which we fulfill these responsibilities.

1. We believe that breast-milk of healthy, well-nourished mothers is the best feeding for infants up to 6 to 9 months of age. We believe that mothers in general — and mothers in the lower income and nonmoney sectors of the economy in particular — should be encouraged to feed their infants at the breast as long as quantity and quality of milk remain minimally adequate.

2. We believe our products have a valid place in the economy of developing countries and we want to restrict their use to that place — infants of affluent parents when breastfeeding is not chosen, or of working mothers who cannot breastfeed because of separation from their infants, and of mothers who cannot breast-feed for any other reason. Perhaps some form of public assistance is the best way to aid mothers who can neither breast-feed nor afford a suitable replacement.

3. For those infants who cannot be fed at the breast or who need supplemental nutrition, we offer SIMILAC Infant Formulas, which are patterned as closely after the nutritional qualities of human milk as current knowledge and technology permit. In presenting these products to the medical and paramedical professions, our goal is to promote awareness and acceptance of physiologic nutrition as the most desirable alternative when breast-feeding is not available.

4. We wish to co-operate in every way with local health authorities in preventing misuse of our products because of poverty, ignorance or lack of proper hygienic conditions. And we do not encourage use of our products where private purchase would impose a financial hardship on the family, or where inadequate facilities for preparation constitute a hazard to infant health.

5. Our product label will carry a statement that breast-milk is the preferred feeding for young infants, and a warning that proper proportions in mixing formula are necessary and that overdiluted formula may not provide adequate nutrition for the infant.

6. We work with professional and governmental agencies, and industry to standardize instructions for mixing all powdered products, i.e., 1 scoop (provided in tin of product) to the same quantity of water for each powder product, each scoop individually designed to provide the proper caloric density set by the manufacturer for his product. Such standardization should facilitate educational efforts of public health personnel to create parental awareness of proper mixing of formula.

7. We assist in health education of mothers through appropriate media to (a) promote good nutrition; (b) encourage breastfeeding; (c) improve infant and child care; (d) improve sanitation; (e) stress proper preparation of infant formula.

8. We represent accurately the cost of proper infant feeding so that professional personnel can better advise mothers according to their economic status.

9. We resist the practices of using direct advertising and offering special inducements to encourage mothers to act independently of professional advice in the care and feeding of their infants. We prefer to direct our resources toward extending the coverage and increasing the effectiveness of qualified local health personnel. Further, we believe that no communication to the general public should encroach in any way on the responsibility of health care professionals to provide guidance as their judgment and experience dictate.

10. Our advertising is directed to medical, paramedical and other professionals (physicians, midwives, nurses, nutritionists, etc.), and seeks to provide better understanding of the proper role for our products, of their proper preparation, and of our willingness to be of assistance in their practice.

11. Whenever possible we choose as our representatives experienced paramedical personnel who understand local needs. They are thoroughly taught the knowledge and application of our products, the value of breast-feeding, and the social pressures that lead to unwise purchases and practices by those who cannot afford to buy infant formula. They are schooled to perform their duties in a professional manner and with integrity. Deception and other unethical practices are expressly forbidden.

12. These representatives are reimbursed through adequate salary, with monetary incentive given only for true service rendered to the customer and not directly derived from measurement of sales impact. Their functions are to develop product understanding, to render services that facilitate application of our products, and to make available other health care aids, without attempt to incur obligation for services.

13. The activities of the representatives are co-ordinated with those of professionals responsible for infant and mother care. We want them, in concert with clinic personnel, to furnish genuine mothercraft outreach services where practical, in support of instructions and counsel received in clinic. In this way our representatives can greatly increase the numbers of mothers and infants receiving good care, and extend the range of care to include many for whom clinics are not readily available.

14. We want medical and governmental health professionals to advise industry on training representatives and establishing the range of their mother-craft activities.

15. We welcome critical review of these guidelines by all concerned with the health of infants. We want suggestions for their extension, elaboration, modification.

Within the Code, it will surely be difficult 'not to encourage use of our products where private purchase would impose financial hardship on the family, or where inadequate facilities for preparation constitute a hazard to infant health' (para. 4) without excluding them from poorer countries altogether.

Representing 'accurately the cost of proper infant feeding so that professional personnel can better advise mothers according to their economic status' (para. 8) may pose innovative problems in copy writing and preparation of promotional material. And to 'resist the practices of using direct advertising' (para. 9) does not ensure that this will be completely jettisoned.

The comment on formulas 'patterned as closely after the nutritional qualities of human milk as current knowledge and technology permits' (para. 3) may be correct, although biochemical and metabolic considerations given elsewhere indicate how unbridgeably far apart the products are. However, this narrows the issue only to the important, but limited, field of nutrition. *It takes no cognizance whatsoever of the overlapping effects of human milk and breast-feeding as a birth-spacing contraceptive and as a chemoprophylactic anti-infective 'system', none of which are present in any way whatsoever in formulas.*

The choice of representatives who are 'experienced paramedical personnel' (para. 11) who are 'reimbursed through adequate salary, with monetary incentive given only for true service rendered to the customer and not directly derived from measurement of sales impact' (para. 12) in practice pose irreconcilable conflicts of interest, even if such staff have distinct uniforms. Cook (1974) summarizes this as follows: 'There is really no place for the continued combined function or role of sales agent and adviser to mothers on infant feeding. These are two roles, not one. By all means have sales agents, but do not clothe them in the prestige and trust accorded to the nursing profession. The nurse is believed by the mother to give advice directed *solely* to the welfare of the child and its mother with no commercial consideration at all involved; and the sales agent/nurse cannot do this.'

Moreover, such 'milk nurse' positions are usually better paid than government posts and have valued fringe benefits. Even when bonuses are not related to sales, lack of sales cannot but be related to continuation of services and promotion. Under these circumstances, it is difficult to imagine more than token support — or persuasion to use the rival product — human milk.

CODE OF ETHICS AND PROFESSIONAL STANDARD FOR ADVERTISING, PRODUCT INFORMATION AND ADVISORY SERVICES FOR BREAST-MILK SUBSTITUTES

In recognition that sound nutrition during infancy is essential for normal growth and development, the members of the INTERNATIONAL COUNCIL OF INFANT FOOD INDUSTRIES subscribe to the principles and the primacy of the medical and paramedical professions' roles in supervising the dietary intake of infants. These principles affirm that the milk of healthy mothers is the preferred form of nutrition for normal infants, and support the recommendations of the United Nations Protein–Calorie Advisory Group and of the World Health Organization.

Breast-milk substitutes meet essential needs when used appropriately in the feeding of infants. Breast-milk substitutes are intended to supplement breast-milk and for use when mothers can not or elect not to breast-feed for medical or other reasons.

Therefore, the members of the INTERNATIONAL COUNCIL OF INFANT FOOD INDUSTRIES hereby pledge that:

1. As providers of essential supplies for infant nutrition, the members of ICIFI accept responsibility for the diffusion of information which supports sound infant feeding practices and for services consistent with the application of this Code.

2. Product information for the public will always recognize the milk of healthy, well-nourished mothers as the feeding of choice with the recommendation to seek professional advice when a supplement or alternative may be required.

3. Product labelling will affirm breast-feeding as the first choice for the nutrition of normal infants.

4. Product claims will reflect scientific integrity without implication that any product is superior to the breast milk of healthy mothers.

5. To insure optimal nutritional intake, explicitly worded instructions and demonstrations for product use will be provided for the hygienic and correctly measured preparation of breast-milk substitutes.

6. In cooperation with health authorities, professional communications and educational materials will be provided to caution against misuse and to inform mothers on the importance of and methods for obtaining safe water for the preparation of breast-milk substitutes.

7. Members' personnel will observe professional ethics and established rules of conduct in medical/nursing centres, maternities, and physicians' offices and in all contacts.

8. Members will employ nurses, nutritionists and mid-wives whenever possible to perform mothercraft services. When professionally trained personnel are not available, high educational standards and experience commensurate with prevailing condition will be required. Training of these staffs will be in keeping with scientific standards for infant nutrition to emphasize the importance of breast-feeding and the appropriate use of breast-milk substitutes.

9. Individual contacts by mothercraft personnel and issuance of complimentary supplies of breast-milk substitutes will be in consultation with medical or nursing personnel in the institution or the area.

10. Mothercraft personnel will support doctors' and nurses' prerogatives in counselling mothers on infant feeding and will not discourage mothers from establishing or continuing breast-feeding.

11. Nurses' uniforms will be worn only by persons who are professionally entitled to their use. The attire worn by mothercraft personnel will bear the identification of the respective ICIFI member. It is recommended that an ICIFI emblem be worn.

12. Compensation of mothercraft personnel will be on a basis of quality and level of services performed and without relationship to sales.

13. Adherence to this Code will be obligatory on all members of ICIFI except when precluded by the laws or regulations of a given country.

The Code is prepared in recognition of the responsibilities shared by all who guard the health and welfare of the world's children and who play a role in their feeding.

Much of the document is ambiguous and highly general. For example, para. 4 — 'without implication that any product is superior to the breast-milk of healthy mothers' — circumvents the issue of false advertising as 'just like mother's milk'. Again, para. 6 — 'to inform mothers on the importance of and methods for obtaining safe water for the preparation of breast-milk substitute' — is laughable in the vast majority of circumstances in poor developing countries; such water supplies usually do not exist. Para. 7 — 'professional ethics and established rules of conduct in medical/nursing centres, maternities, and physicians offices and in all contacts' — is so vague as to be meaningless.

Para. 8 — 'Mothercraft personnel' . . . 'will not discourage mothers from establishing or continuing breast-feeding' — implies at best a negative, and certainly a non-supportive, role.

The emphasis on the use of 'milk nurses', or mothercraft personnel, is unacceptable for the same reasons mentioned earlier — basically a completely unavoidable and inherent conflict of interest and purpose.

It is understood that the Council has Working Parties examining priorities. In its present form, it is virtually meaningless on a practical and specific level, without more detail. Even should such be forthcoming and be acceptable to concerned, experienced paediatric nutritionists, similar endeavours in other industries have already indicated obvious difficulties. For example, the failure of the Advertising Standard Authority to monitor advertisements in Britain does not give rise to optimism (Medawar and Hodges 1973). The recent decision of the alcohol industry in U.K. to introduce a code of advertising, plainly with conflicting interests between sales and health, will be a parallel test-case (Rix 1975). In relation to more general issues in advertising, Medawar and Hodges are of the following opinion: 'We do not believe that any voluntary control scheme can substitute for the stringent and comprehensive statutory controls over advertising that are so clearly needed.'

The likelihood of the International Council of Infant Food Industries being an effective mechanism for self-regulation is further decreased by the fact that not all major infant food companies are members. In December 1975, the list was Japan 4 companies, Europe 3, and the U.S.A. 1 (with one to be added).

Bibliography

(Consulted in preparation of text, but not all referred to directly.)

ACHESON, E. D. and TRUELOVE, S. C. (1961). *Brit, med. J.* ii, 929. Early weaning in the aetiology of ulcerative colitis.

ABBOTT, D. C., GOULDING, R., and TATTON, J. O. G. (1968). *Brit med. J.* iii, 146. Organochlorine pesticide residues in human fat in Great Britain.

ADDY, D. P. (1976*a*). *Brit. med. J.* i, 1268. Infant feeding: a current view.

—— (1976*b*). *Brit. med. J.* ii, 742. Breast is best.

ADDY, H. L. (1976). *J. trop. Pediat. env. Chld Hlth* **21**, 231 The breast-feeding of twins.

ADEBONJO, F. O. (1972). *Clin. Pediat.* 11, 25. Artificial vs. breast-feeding. Relation to infant health in a middle class American community.

ADENIYI-JONES, O. (1955). *J. trop. Pediat.* **1**, 123. The ethical and medical significance of breast-feeding.

AGRANOFF, B. W. and GOLDBERG. D. (1974. *Lancet* **ii**, 1074. Diet and the geographical distribution of multiple sclerosis.

AINSWORTH, M. D. S. (1974). 'Culture and social influences in infancy and early childhood'. Infant development and mother–infant interaction among Ganda and American families.

ALDRICH, C. A. (1941). *Amer. J. Dis. Childh.* **64**, 714. Ancient process in a scientific age: feeding aspects.

ALEXANDER, G. (1975). *Brit. med. Bull.* **31**, 62. Body temperature control in mammalian young.

ALLARDYCE, R. A., SHEARMAN, D. J. C., McLELLAND, D. B. L., MARWICK K., SIMPSON, A. J., and LAIDLAW, R. B. (1974). *Brit. med. J.* iii, 307. Appearance of specific colostrum antibodies after clinical infection with *Salmonella typhimurium*.

ALTMAN, J. (1968). Effect of early experience on brain morphology. In *Malnutrition, learning, and behaviour* (ed. N. S. Scrimshaw and J. E. Gordon), p. 332. Colonial Press, Boston.

AMBROSE, A. (ed.) (1969). *Stimulation in early infancy*. Academic Press, London and New York.

AMERICAN ACADEMY OF PEDIATRICS (1943). *Pediatrics* **23**, 112. Recommended standards for the operation of mother's milk bureaux.

——(1974*a*). Report of the Committee on Infectious Diseases, p. 57. *Escherichia coli* diarrhea. Evanston, Illinois.

—— (1974*b*). *Pediatrics* **53**, supplement. The susceptibility of the fetus and child to chemical pollutants.

—— (1974*c*). *Pediatrics* **53**, 137. Committee on Nutrition Review. Lead.

—— (1974*d*). *Pediatrics* **53**, 115. Committee on Nutrition. Salt intake and eating patterns of infants and children in relation to blood pressure.

—— (1975). *Pediatrics* **52**, 484. Committee on Infant and Preschool Child: Statement on Day Care.

AMERICAN MEDICAL ASSOCIATION (1972). *Conference on guidelines for nutrition education program*. Williamsburg, Virginia.

AMIN-ZAKI, L., ELHASSANI, S., and MAJEED, M. A. (1974). *Proceedings of the*

XIVth International Pediatric Congress, Buenos Aires. Vol. 3, Section 17, p. 54. Prenatal methylmercury poisoning in Iraq.

ANKE, B. (1971). *Swed. dent. J.* **64**, 617. Prolonged sucking habits related to feeding methods in infancy.

ANSELL, C. J. (1975). *Lancet* **ii**, 978. Milk for babies.

ANTONOV, A. W. (1947). *J. Pediat.* **30**, 250. Children born during the siege of Leningrad, 1942.

ANTROBUS, A. C. K. (1971). *J. trop. Pediat. env. Chld Hlth* **17**, 188. Child growth and related factors in a rural community in St. Vincent.

APPLEBAUM, R. M. (1970). *Pediat. Clins N. Am.* **17**, 203. The modern management of successful breast feeding.

—— (1974). Breast feeding and care of the breasts. In *Davis' Gynecology and obstetrics*, Vol. I, Chapter 32, p. 1. Harper and Row, Hagerstown, Maryland.

—— (1976). *J. trop. Pediat. env. Chld Hlth* **21**, 273. Techniques of breast feeding.

ARBEITSGRUPPE DRITTE WELT BERN (1974). *Nestle totet kinder*. Bern, Switzerland.

—— (1976). Export-interessen Gegen Muttermilch. Rowolt, Hamburg.

ARCHAVSKY, I. A. (1952) *Vop. Pediat.* **20**, 45. Immediate breast feeding of newborn infants in the prophylaxis of so-called physiological loss of weight. (Original in Russian)

Archives of Diseases of Childhood (1973). **48**, 495. Infant malnutrition in a developed country.

ARENA, J. (1970). *Nutr. Today* **5**, 2. Contamination of the ideal food.

ARROYAVE, G., BEGHIN, I., FLORES, M., DE GUIDO, C. S., and TICAS, J. M. (1974). *Archivos Socieda Latin Americana Nutricion* **24**, 485. Efectos del consumo de azucar fortificada con retinol en las madres embarazadas y lactantes.

ASHER, P. (1966). *Arch. Dis. Childh.* **41**, 672. Fat babies and fat children.

ASHWORTH, A. and WATERLOW, J. C. (1970). Nutrition in Jamaica, 1966–70. Tropical Metabolism Research Unit, Extra-mural Department, University of the West Indies, Jamaica.

ASSOCIATION FOR THE WELFARE OF CHILDREN IN HOSPITAL (1975). *Med. J. Austral.* 9 August, supplement 5. Health care policy relating to children and their families.

AUERBACH, K. G. (1975). *Proceedings of the Fourth International Congress of Psychosomatic Obstetrics and Gynecology*, p. 415–18, Karger, Basel.

AUSTRALIAN COMMISSION ON HEALTH (1976). *N.M.A.A. Newsletter* **1**, 15. Sabin vaccine — a review.

Australian Pediatric Journal (1971). Supplement 2, p. 45. New urban families: conclusions and recommendations.

AVERY, L. J. (1972). *The Lact-Aid nursing supplementer*. Denver, Colorado.

AXEL, R., SCHLOM, J., and SPIEGELMAN, S. (1972). *Nature (Lond.)* **235**, 32. Presence in human breast cancer of RNA homologous to mouse mammary tumour virus RNA.

AYKROYD, W. R. and HUSSAIN, M. A. (1967). *Brit. med. J.* i, 42. Diet and state of nutrition of Pakistani infants in Bradford, Yorkshire.

—— (1971). *Amer. J. clin. Nutr.* **24**, 480. Nutrition and mortality in infancy and early childhood: past and present relationship.

BACON, C. J. and WYLIE, J. M. (1975) *Brit. med. J.* i, 308. Mothers' attitudes to infant feeding at Newcastle General Hospital in Summer 1975.

BADER, M. B. (1976). *Int. J. Hlth Services* **6**, 609. Breast-feeding: the role of the multi-national corporations in Latin America.

BAILEY, K. V. (1962). *Trop. geog. Med.* **14**, 11. Rural nutrition surveys in Indonesia. (6) Field surveys of lactating women.

—— (1965).*J. trop. Pediat.* **11**, 35. Quantity and composition of breast milk in some New Guinean populations.

—— (1971). Personal communication.

—— (1975). *Wld Hlth Chron.* **29**, 354. Malnutrition in the African Region.

BAIN, K. (1948). *Pediatrics* **2**, 213. The incidence of breastfeeding in hospitals in the United States.

BAKKEN, A. F. and SEIP, M. (1976). *Acta Paediat. Scand.* **65**, 535. Insecticides in human breast-milk.

BAKWIN, H. (1937). *Amer. J. Dis. Childh*. **54**, 1211. Pathogenesis of tetany of the newborn.

BALDERRAMA-GUSMAN, V. and TANTENGO, V. O. (1971).*J. Philipp. med. Ass.* **47**, 323. Effect of nutrition and illness on the growth and development of Filipino children (0–4 years) in a rural setting.

BAMFORD, F. N. (1971). *Brit. med. J*. i, 276. The immigrant mother and her child.

BANATVALA, J. E. (1976). Ciba Foundation Symposium No. 42. *Acute diarrhoea in children*. Discussion, p. 233. Elsevier, Holland.

BARLOW, B., SANTULLI, T. V., HEIRD, W. C., PITT, J., BLANC, W. A., and SCHULLINGER, J. N. (1974). *J. pediat. Surgery* **9**, 587. An experimental study of acute neonatal enterocolitis — the importance of breast milk.

BARLTROP, D. and OPPE, T. E. (1970). *Lancet* ii, 1333. Dietary factors in neonatal calcium homeostasis.

—— and —— (1973). *Arch. Dis. Childh.* **48**, 580. Calcium and fat absorption by low birth weight infants from a calcium-supplemented milk formula.

BARNES, A. (1975). *Brit. med. J*. ii. 265. Reorganization of a nutrition unit in Papua-New Guinea.

BARNESS, L. A. (1975). *Clins Perinatol*. **2**, 345. Nutrition for the low birth weight infant.

BARNET, R. and MULLER, R. (1974). *New Yorker* 2 Dec. and 9 Dec. Global reach.

BARNETT, C., LEIDERMAN, P., and GROBSTEIN, R. (1970). *Pediatrics* **45**, 1970. Neonatal separation: the maternal side of interactional deprivation.

BARRIE, H. (1976). *J. Maternal Chld Hlth* **1**, 30. Modified milk for babies.

——, MARTIN, E., and ANSELL, C. (1975). *Lancet* i, 1330. Milk for babies.

BARSIVALA, V. M. and VIRKAR, K. D. (1973). *Contraception* **7**, 307. The effect of oral contraceptives on concentrations of various components of human milk.

BASSIR, O. (1956).*J. trop. Pediat.* **59**, 138. Breast milk in Nigeria.

—— (1958).*J. trop. Pediat.* **4**, 3. Nutritional studies on the breast milk of Nigerian women.

—— (1959). *Trans. roy. Soc. trop. Med. Hyg.* **53**, 256. Nutritional studies on breast milk of Nigerian women.

—— (1975). *West. Afr. J. biol. Chem.* **1**, 15. Nutritional studies on breast milk of Nigerian women. Determination of the output of breast milk.

BATEMAN, M. (1975). *Sunday Times* (Lond.) 16 Mar. Baby big and the magic milkmen.

BAUM, J. D., OUNSTED, M., and SMITH, M. A. (1975). *Lancet* ii, 866. Weight gain in infancy and subsequent development of diabetes mellitus in childhood.

BEAL, V. A. (1957). *Pediatrics* **20**, 448. On the acceptance of solid foods, and other food patterns, of infants and children.

—— (1970). Nutritional intake. In *Human growth and development* (Ed. R. W. McCammon), p. 61. Thomas, Springfield.

—— (1969). *J. Amer. diet. Ass.* **55**, 31. Breast and formula feeding of infants.

BEASLEY, R. P., STEVENS, C. E., SHIAO, I. S., and MENG, H. C. (1975). *Lancet* **ii**, 740. Evidence against breast feeding as a mechanism for vertical transmission of hepatitis.

BEAUREGARD, W. G. (1971). *J. Pediat.* **79**, 294. Positional otitis media.

BECROFT, T. (1967). *Med. J. Aust.* **2**, 598. Child-rearing practices in the Highlands of New Guinea: a longitudinal study of breast feeding.

BEER, A. (1975). Proceedings of Ross Laboratories 68th Conference on Pediatric Research: Necrotising enterocolitis in the newborn infant, p. 53.

—— and PARMELY, M. J. (1976). *Pediat. Res.* **10**, 356. Analysis of the immunocompetence of human milk lymphocytes.

BEGGOTT, J. (1974). Personal communication.

BEHAR, M. (1975). *Bull. Pan Amer. Hlth Org.* **9**, 1. The role of feeding and nutrition in the pathogeny and prevention of diarrheic processes.

—— (1976). *Pan Amer. Hlth* **7**, 17. A potent medicine.

BELAVADY, B. (1963). Studies on human lactation. *Ind. Council Med. Res.* Spec. Rep. Ser. **45**, 1–17.

—— (1969) *Ind. J. med. Res.* **57** (supplement), 63. Nutrition in pregnancy and lactation.

—— and GOPALAN, C. (1959). *Ind. J. med. Res.* **47**, 234. Chemical composition of human milk in poor Indian women.

—— and —— (1960). *Ind. J. med. Res.* **48**, 518. Effect of dietary supplementation on the composition of breast milk.

BELL, J. E. (1969). *The family in the hospital: lessons from developing countries.* National Institute of Mental Health, Chevy Chase, Maryland.

BELL, K. and McKENZIE, H. A. (1964). *Nature (Lond.)* **2**, 1275. Beta-lactoglobulins.

BELLOC, N. B. and BRESLOW, L. (1972). *Prev. Med.* **1**, 409. Relationships of physical health status and health practices.

BELSEY, M. A. (1973). *Bull. Wld Hlth Org.* **48**, 1. The epidemiology of favism.

BENDIG, J. and HAENEL, H. (1970). *Proceedings of the Eighth International Congress of Nutrition*, Prague, 1969. Gastrointestinal microecology in sudden unexpected death of infants.

BENEDEK, T. (1956). *Amer. J. Orthopsych.* **26**, 272. Psychobiological aspects of mothering.

BENGOA, J. M. (1972). Nutritional significance of monthly statistics. *Proceedings of the Western Hemisphere Nutrition Congress III*, p. 270. Future Publishing, New York.

—— (1974). *WHO Chron.* **28**, 3. The problem of undernutrition.

—— (1975). *Archives Socieda Latin americana Nutricion* **25**, 243. Nutricion y marginalidad.

—— and DONOSO, G. (1974). *Protein–calorie Advisory Group Bulletin 4*, 24. Prevalence of protein–calorie malnutrition, 1963–1973.

BENNETT, P. and HERMAN, S. (1975). *Lancet* ii, 1430. A curious curd.

BENTON, D. (1975). *Protein–calorie Advisory Group Bulletin* **5**, 20. The role of the infant food industry in promoting desirable policies and practices in feeding of infants and children.

BERCOVICI, B., GEDALIA, I., and BRZEZINSKI, A. (1960). *Obstet. Gynec.* **16**, 319. Fluorine in human milk.

BERDON, W. E., GROSSMAN, H., BAKER, D. H., MIZRAHI, A., BARLOW, O., and BLANC, W. A. (1964). *Radiology* **83**, 879. Necrotizing enterocolitis in the premature infant.

BERG, A. (1973). *The nutrition factor*. Brookings Institution, Washington.

BERGQVIST, G. (1974). *Acta paediat. (Uppsala)* **63**, 858. Viscosity of the blood in the newborn infant.

BERNAL, J. and RICHARDS, M. P. M. (1970). *J. psychosomat. Res.* **14**, 247. The effects of bottle and breast feeding on infant development.

BERNARD, J. (1974). *The future of motherhood*. Dial Press, New York.

BERRY, R. S. (1975). *Bull. atom. Sci.* **31**, 31. Crisis of resource scarcity.

BESSER, G. M. and EDWARDS, C. R. W. (1972). *Brit. med. J.* **ii**, 280. Galactorrhoea.

BETTELHEIM, B. (1969). *The children of the dream*. MacMillan, London.

BEWLEY, B. R. and BEWLEY, T. H. (1975). *Lancet* **ii**, 270. Hospital doctor's career structure and the misuse of medical woman power.

BIERMAN, J. M. (1957). *Quart. Rev. Pediat.* **12**, 137. Infant feeding in the U.S.S.R.

BILLAR, H. (1976). The father–child relationship: some crucial issues. In *The family – can it be saved?* (ed. V. C. Vaughan and T. B. Brazleton). Year Book Medical Publishers, Chicago.

BING, E. D. (1972). Psychoprophylaxis and family-centered maternity. In *Psychosomatic medicine in obstetrics and gynecology* (ed. N. Morris). Karger, Basel.

BISSETT, G. W. (1968). In *Handbuch der experimentellen Pharmakologie*, Vol. XXIII: Neurohypophysial hormones and similar polypeptides. The milk-ejection reflex and actions of oxytocin, vasopressin and synthetic analogues on the mammary gland. Springer Verlag, Berlin.

BJERRE, J. and EKELUND, H. (1970). *Acta paediat. (Uppsala)* Supplement **206**, p. 125. Breastfeeding and postpartum care.

BLAIKLEY, J., CLARKE, S., MCKEITH, R., and OGDEN, K. M. (1953). *J. Obstet. Gynaec. Brit. Emp.* **60**, 657. Breast feeding: factors affecting success.

BLAND, R. D. (1972). *Pediatrics* **49**, 187. Otitis media in the first six weeks of life.

BLAXTER, K. L. (1961). Lactation and growth of the young. In *Milk: the mammary gland and its secretion*, p. 305. Ed. S. Kon and A. T. Cowie. Academic Press, N.Y.

—— (1971). The comparative biology of lactation. In *Lactation* (ed. I. R. Falconer). Butterworths, London.

BLURTON-JONES, N. (1972). In *Ethological studies of child behaviour*. Comparative aspects of mother–child contact. Cambridge University Press, London.

BLYTHE, C. (1974). *PAN* (Newspaper of the World Food Conference). No. 9, 14 Nov. The great baby food scandal.

BOEDIMAN, D., ISMAIL, D., and IMAN, S. (1975). *Proc. 2nd Asian Congress of Pediatrics*, Jakarta. Quality of milk beyond one year.

BOLLINGER, A. and GROSS, R. (1960). *Austral. J. Sci.* **22**, 292. Nutrition of the marsupial suckling.

—— and PASCOE, J. V. (1953). *Austral. J. Sci.* **15**, 215. Composition of kangaroo milk.

BONNAR, J., FRANKLIN, M., NOTT, P. N., and MCNEILLY, A. S. (1975). *Brit. med. J.* iii, 82. Effect of breast feeding on pituitary-ovarian function.

BOOK, S. J., HERBST, J. J., ATHERTON, S. O., and Jung, A. L. (1975). *J. Pediat.* **87**, 602. Necrotizing enterocolitis in low birth weight infants fed on elemental formula.

BONTE, M. and VAN BALEN, H. (1969). *J. biosoc. Sci.* **1**, 97. Prolonged lactation and family spacing in Rwanda.

BORGHESE, E. M. (1973). *Center Magazine* March, p. 4. Human nature is still evolving.

BOSTOCK, J. (1962). *Lancet* i, 1033. Evolutionary approaches to infant care.

BOURNE, F. J. (1973). *Proc. Nutr. Soc.* **32**, 205. The immunoglobulin system of the suckling pig.

BOYER, K. M., PETERSEN, N. J., FARZANEH, I., PATTISON, C. P., HART, M. C., and MAYNARD, J. E. (1975). *J. Pediat.* **86**, 919. An outbreak of gastroenteritis due to *E. coli* 0142 in a neonatal nursery.

BOWERS, C. V., FRIESEN, H. G., HWANG, P., GNYDA, H. J., and FOLKERS, K. (1971). *Bioch. biphysic. res. communicat.* **5**, 1033. Prolactin and thyrotropin release in man by synthetic pyroglutanyl-histidyl-prolinainide.

BOWES, W. A. (1970). *Monogr. Soc. Res. Chld Dev.* **35**, 3. Obstetric medication and infant outcome.

BOWLBY, J. (1969). *Attachment and loss.* Hogarth Press, London.

BRADSHAW, S. (1973). *Brit. med. J.* i, 349. The pathogenic life style of Western man.

BRAMBLETON, T. B. (1956). *Pediatrics* **17**, 400. Sucking in infancy.

BRANDT, T. (1936). *Acta derm.-venereol. (Stockholm)* **17**, 513. Dermatitis in children with disturbances of general condition and absorption of food elements.

BRAY, G. W. (1928). *Trans. roy. Soc. trop. Med. Hyg.* **22**, 9. Vitamin deficiency in infants.

BRAZLETON, T. B., TRONICK, E., ADAMSON, L., ALS, H., and WISE, S. (1975). Early mother–infant reciprocity. In *Parent–infant interaction*, p. 137. Ciba Foundation Symposium No. 33. Elsevier, Amsterdam.

BREETVELD, J. P. (1972). *Psychology Today* February, p. 63. Mother and child in Africa: a brief conversation with Thomas Lambo.

BRENNEMAN, G. and FORTUINE, R. (1966). *Alaska Med.* **8**, 56. Enteropathic *Escherichia coli* diarrhoea in Western Alaska.

BREWSTER, P. (1977). Breast feeding under unusual circumstances. (In press).

British Medical Journal (1968). ii, 411. Fluoride in pregnancy.

—— (1969). iv, 633. New hazards for the newborn.

—— (1971). iv, 510. Amenorrhoea after the pill.

—— (1972). ii, 419. Mothering the baby.

—— (1973a). i, 437. Problems of iron deficiency anaemia in infancy.

—— (1973b). ii, 727. Fashions in infant feeding.

—— (1974a). i, 48, Any questions? Infant diet.

—— (1974b). ii, 1090. Obstetric analgesics and the newborn baby.

—— (1974c). iii, 134. Breast cancer in Japanese migrants.

—— (1974d). iv, 410. More about D. and V.

—— (1974e). iv, 615. Septicaemia on the increase.

—— (1975*a*). ii, 706. Nature and nurture in childhood obesity.

—— (1975*b*). iii, 555. Virus of infantile gastroenteritis.

—— (1975*c*). iv, 188. Prolactin, pregnancy and lactation.

—— (1976*a*). i, 920. Puerperal mastitis.

—— (1976*b*). i, 1167. Breast-feeding: the immological argument.

—— (1976*c*). iii, 412. Intercepted letter: Breast is best.

BRITT, B., KOURANY, M., and MILLAR, J. W. (1973). *J. trop. Pediat. env. Chld Hlth* **19**, 282. A pilot-search for environmental factors influencing diarrhoeal disease in young children in Panama.

BRODY, S. (1956). *Patterns of mothering*. International Universities Press, New York.

BRONFENBRENNER, U. (1975). Who cares for American children? In *The family – can it be saved?* (ed. V. C. Vaughan and T. B. Brazleton). Year Book Medical Publishers, Chicago.

BROOK, C. D. G., Lloyd, J. K., and Wolf, O. H. (1972). *Brit. med. J.* ii. 25. Relation between age of onset of obesity and size and number of adipose cells.

BROWN, M. L. and ADELSON, S. F. (1969). *Trop. geogr. Med.* **21**, 53. Infant feeding practices among low and middle income families in Honolulu.

—— (1972). *Clin. Pediat.* **11**, 334. Some nutritional considerations in times of major catastrophe.

BROWN, R. E. (1973). *Amer. J. clin. Nutr.* **26**, 556. Breast feeding in modern times.

BRUCKER, M. (1953). *J. dent. Res.* **22**, 315. Studies in the incidence and cause of dental defects in children. IV. Malocclusion.

BRUNN, V. B. (1974). *Courrier* **24**, 461. The care of children of working parents. Trends in some countries. I. Sweden.

BRYANT, G. D. and GREENWOOD, F. C. (1972). *Lactogenic hormones* (ed. G. E. W. Wolstenholme and J. Knight), p. 197. The concentration of human prolactin in plasma measured by radioimmunoassay.

BRYANT, J. (1969). *Health and the developing world*. Cornell University Press, Ithaca and London.

BRYDEN, A. S., DAVIES, H. A., HADLEY, R. E., FLEWETT, T. H., MORRIS, C. A., and OLIVER, P. (1975). *Lancet* **ii**, 241. Rotavirus enteritis in the West Midlands during 1974.

BUCHANAN, R. (1975), *Population Reports*, Series J. No. 4. Breast feeding: aid to infant health and fertility control. Her Majesty's Stationery Office, London.

BUECHLEY, R. (1972). Personal communication.

BULLEN, C. L. and WILLIS, A. T. (1971). *Brit. med. J.* iii, 338. Resistance of the breast-fed infant to gastroenteritis.

BULLEN, J. J., ROGERS, H. J., and LEIGH, L. (1972). *Brit. med. J.* i, 69. Iron-binding proteins in milk and resistance to *Escherichia coli* infection in infants.

—— (1976). *Iron-binding proteins and other factors in milk responsible for resistance to E. coli*. Ciba Foundation Symposium No. 42, p. 149. Elsevier, Amsterdam.

BURCHELL, R. C. (1964). *Obstet. Gynec.* **24**, 272. Predelivery removal of pubic hair.

BURDEN, J. K. (1959). *Med. J. Austral.* **46**, 520. A study of feeding and rooming-in of babies.

BURGEN, A. S. V. (1974). *Proc. roy. Soc. Med.* **67**, Symposium 15. Constraints on the advance of medicine.

BURGESS, A. (1977). Breast feeding in Pasay. Personal communication.

BURNE, S. R. (1976). *Lancet* **ii**, 261 Breast-feeding.

Business Week (1976). 21 April, p. 31. A trade war looms over powdered milk.

BUSS, D. H. (1975). *Lancet* iii, 766. Cost of breast feeding.

BUSTAMENTE, M. E. (1968). *Gac. med. mex.* **9**, 1208. Commentario oficial al trabajo pediatria mexicana prehispanica.

CAGAS, C. R. (1972). *Philipp. J. Pediat.* **21**, 151. On drug company sponsorship of medical society activities.

CALDEYRO-BARCIA, R. (1969). Milk ejection in women. In *Lactogenesis* (ed. M. Reynolds and S. J. Folley). University of Pennsylvania, Philadelphia.

CALL, J. D. (1975). Personal communication.

—— and MARSHAK, M. (1966). *J. Amer. Acad. Chld Psychiat.* **5**, 193. Styles and games in infancy.

CAMERON, M. and HOFVANDER, Y. (1975). *Manual on feeding infants and young children* (second edition). Protein Advisory Group of the U.N., New York.

CAMPBELL, B., SARWAR, M., and PETERSEN, W. E. (1957). *Science (N.Y.)* **125**, 932. Diathelic immunization: a maternal offspring relationship involving milk antibodies.

CAMPS, F. E. and·CARPENTER, R. G. (ed.) (1972). *Sudden infant deaths in infancy (cot deaths): Proceedings of a Symposium.* John Wright, Bristol.

CAPLAN, G. (1974). Support systems and community mental health: lectures in concept development. Behavioural Publications, New York.

CARBALLO, M. (1975). *Wld Hlth* Aug./Sep., P. 34. The need for adaptation.

CAREY, W. B. (1975). *J. Pediat.* **85**, 327. Breast feeding and night waking.

CARNEIRO, T. A. and DUTRA DE OLIVEIRA, J. E. (1973). *J. trop. Pediat. env. Chld Hlth 19*, 384. Nutritional studies in human lactation in Brazil (I). Chemical composition of breast milk.

CARLSSON, B., GOTHEFORS, L., AHLSTED, S., HANSON, L. A., and WINBERG, J. (1976). *Acta paediat. (Uppsala)* **65**, 216. Studies of *E. coli* O antigen specific antibodies in human milk, maternal serum and cord blood.

CARROLL, K. K. and HAMILTON, R. M. G. (1973). *Lipids* **8**, 635. Plasma cholesterol values in suckling and weaned calves, pigs and colts.

CATZ, C. S. and GIACOIA, G. P. (1973). In *Dietary lipids and postnatal development* (ed. C. Galli, G. Jacini, and A. Pecile), p. 247. Drugs and metabolites in human milk. Raven Press, New York.

CENTER FOR SCIENCE IN THE PUBLIC INTEREST (1974). *White Paper on Infant Nutrition.* Washington, D.C.

—— (1975). *Let's give babies a better start, or Babies deserve better: a practical guide on infant feeding for parents and concerned citizens.* Washington, D.C.

CHAJECKA, M., SALAMON-RURARZ, Z., and ZAWIRSKA-ROEFLER, B. (1968). *Courrier* **18**, 1. L'alimentation du nourisson.

CHALMERS, I. (1976). *Pediatrics*, **58**, 328. British debate on obstetric practice.

——, CAMPBELL, H., and TURNBULL, A. C. (1975). *Brit. med. J.* ii, 116. Use of oxytocin and incidence of neonatal jaundice.

CHAMBERLIN, R. W. (1975). *Pediatrics* **56**, 768. Parental use of 'positive contact' in child rearing.

CHAMBERS, T. L. and STEEL, A. E. (1975). *Arch. Dis. Childh.* **50**, 610. Concentrated milk feeds and their relationship to hypernatraemic dehydration in infants.

CHAN, P. C. and COHEN, L. A. (1974). *J. nat. Cancer Inst.* **52**, 25. Effect of dietary fat, antiestrogen and prolactin on the development of mammary tumors in rats.

CHANDAN, R. C., SHAHAMI, K. M., and HOLBY, R. G. (1964). *Nature (Lond.)* **204**, 76. Lysozyme content of human milk.

CHANG, L. L. (1973). *Acta paediat. (Uppsala)* **62**, 173. Storage of iron in foetal livers.

CHANG, W. P. (1974). *J. Ethiopian Studies* **12**, 1. Population studies in Ethiopia.

CHAO, Y-M. (1971). *Int. Nurs. Rev.* **18**, 15. A comparative study of regains of body weight of newborns during the first ten days of life.

CHAPIN, H. D. (1923). *J. Amer. med. Ass.* **81**, 200. The operation of a breast milk dairy.

CHAVEZ, A., MARTINEZ, C., BOURGES, H., CORONADO, M., LOPEZ, M., and BASTA, S. (1975). *Proceedings of the IXth International Nutrition Congress*, Mexico City, August 1972, Vol. 2, p. 90. Child nutrition problems during lactation in poor rural areas.

——, ——, and —— (1976). *Ecol. Food Nutr.* **4**, 159. Role of lactation in the nutrition of low socio-economic groups.

CHEN, L. C., AHMED, S., GESCHE, M., and MOSLEY, W. H. (1974). *Pop. Studies.* **28**, 277. A prospective study of birth interval dynamics in rural Bangladesh.

CHERON, A. (1971). *Ann. Nutr. (Paris)* **25**, A135. Les globulines immunes du lait.

CHOPRA, J. C. (1972). *Amer. J. clin. Nutr.* **25**, 1202. The effect of steroid contraceptives on lactation. Prepared for the Sub-committee on Nutrition and Fertility, Committee on International Nutrition Programs, National Academy of Sciences, Washington, D.C.

CHRISTENSEN, V. (1975). *World Health* Oct., p. 18. Highway conscience.

CLARK, F. LE G. (1953). *Nutrition* **7**, 82. The meaning of the human child: a problem in biological and social evolution.

CLARKE, R. and HINDLEY, G. (1975). *The challenge of the primitives*. Jonathan Cape, London.

COBO, E. (1973). *Amer. J. Obstet. Gynec.* **115**, 817. The effect of different doses of ethanol on the milk-ejecting reflex in lactating women.

—— (1974*a*). In *Lactogenic hormones, fetal nutrition and lactation* (ed. J. B. Josimovich, M. Reynolds, and E. Cobo), Chapter 20. Neuroendocrine control of milk ejection in women. Wiley, New York.

—— (1974*b*). Epidemiologia de la lactancia y su relacion con el uso de anticonceptivos. Simposia sobre lactancia. *VIth Conference of the Latin American Association for the Investigation of Human Reproduction*. Lima, Peru, 1974.

COHEN, R. (1971). *Pediatrics* **48**, 996. Breastfeeding without pregnancy.

COLE, A. P. and HARGREAVES, T. (1972). *Arch. Dis. Childh.* **47**, 415. Conjugation inhibitors and early neonatal hyperbilirubinaemia.

—— and HAILEY, D. M. (1975). *Arch. Dis. Childh.* **50**, 741. Diazepam and active metabolite in breast milk and their transfer to the neonate.

COLES, E. C. and VALMAN, H. B. (1976). *Lancet* ii, 583. Breast-feeding in Harrow.

COMMUNITY NUTRITION INSTITUTE REPORT (1976). Nestle wins libel suit against formula critics.

Consumer Reports (1975). Sep. p. 528. Are baby foods good enough for babies?

COOK, R. (1968). *J. trop. Pediat. env. Chld Hlth* **14**, 60. The financial cost of malnutrition in the Commonwealth Caribbean.

—— (1971). *Ecol. Food Nutr.* **1**, 61. The cost of malnutrition in Jamaica.

—— (1974). Personal communication.

COOKE, R. W. I. (1975). *Arch. Dis. Childh.* **50**, 241. *Bacteroides fragilis* septicaemia in early infancy.

COON, C. (1972). *The hunting people*. Jonathan Cape, London.

COOPER, A. P. (1840). *The anatomy of the breast*. Longmans, London.

COOPER, J. K. (1974). Personal communication.

COOPER, L. V., DE SWIET, M., and FAYESS, P. (1976). *Lancet* i, 421. Dried milk infant foods.

COOPER, R. T. and STEIGER, P. E. (1976). *Los Angeles Times* 27 June. Occupational health hazards.

CORPORATE INFORMATION CENTER (1975). *CIC Brief: Formula for malnutrition*. Consumers Union, New York.

CORSINI, C. A. (1974). *Rivista Fondata da Corrada Gini* **31**, 243. La fécondité naturelle de la femme mariée. Le cas des nourrices.

COTTINGHAM, J. (1976). *Bottle babies. A guide to the baby foods issue*. International Information and Communication Service, Switzerland.

COULSON, K. M., COHEN, R. L., COULSON, W. F., and JELLIFFE, D. B. (1975). *Proceedings of the International Nutrition Congress*, Kyoto, Japan. Hematocrit levels in breastfed babies.

COUNT, E. W. (1967). *Homo* **18**, 38. The lactation complex: a phylogenetic consideration in the mammalian mother–child symbiosis with special reference to man.

COURSIN, D. B. (1954). *J. Amer. med. Ass.* **154**, 406. Convulsive seizures in infants with a pyridoxine-deficient diet.

COWIE, A. T. (1972). *Proc. roy. Soc. Med.* **65**, 24. Induction and suppression of lactation in animals.

—— (1973). *Proc. roy. Soc. Med.* **66**, 861. The physiological actions of prolactin.

—— and TINDAL, J. S. (1971). *The physiology of lactation*. Edward Arnold, London.

CRAFT, I. L., Matthews, D. M., and Linnell, J. C. (1971). *J. clin. Path.* **24**, 449. Cobalamins in human pregnancy and lactation.

CRAVIOTO, J., BIRCH, H. G., LICARDIE, E. R., and ROSALES, L. (1967). *Acta paediat. (Uppsala)* **56**, 71. The ecology of infant weight gain in a pre-industrial society.

——, HAMBRAEUS, L., and VAHLQUIST, B. (ed.) (1974). Early malnutrition and mental development. *XII Symposium of the Swedish Nutrition Foundation*. Almquist and Wiksell, Uppsala.

CRAWFORD, J. and WILLMOTT, J. V. (1971). *Trop. geogr. Med.* **23**, 250. Nutritional status of young Gilbertese children in a transitional economy.

CRAWFORD, M. A., HASSAM, A. G. and HALL, B. M. (1977). *Nutr. Metab.* **21** (Supplement 1), 187. The metabolism of essential fatty acids in the human foetus and neonate.

——, LAURANCE, B. M., HALL, B., and MUNHAMBO, A. (1976). *Curr. Med. Res. Opinion* **4** (Supplement 1), 33. Milk lipids and their variabilities.

—— and SINCLAIR, A. J. (1972). Nutritional influences in the evolution of the mammalian brain, p. 267. In *Lipids, malnutrition, and the developing brain*. Association of Scientific Publishers, Amsterdam.

——, ——, MSUYA, P. M., and MUNHAMBO, A. (1973). Structural lipids and their polyenoic constituents in human milk, p. 41. In *Dietary lipids and postnatal development* (ed. G. Calli, J. Jacini, and A. Pecile). Raven Press, New York.

——, Stevens, P., Msuya, P., and Munhambo, A. (1974). *Brit. J. Nutr.* **31**, 50A. Lipid composition of human milk: comparative studies on African and European mothers.

—— and Hall, B. (1975). *Brit. med. J.* ii, 232. Breast feeding and maternal nutrition.

Creery, R. D. G. (1973). *Brit. med. J.* iv. 299. Breast feeding.

Crittenden, A. (1975). *New York Times*, 11 Sep., p. 556. Baby formula sales in Third World are criticized.

Cron, R. S., Shutter, H. W., and Lahmann, A. H. (1940). *Amer. J. Obstet. Gynec.* **40**, 88. Epidemic infectious diarrhoea of the newborn.

Cronin, T. J. (1968). *Lancet* iii, 422. Influence of lactation upon ovulation.

Cropley, C. and Bloom, R. (1975). *Pediatrics* **55**, 287. An interaction guide for neonatal special care unit.

Cross, B. A. (1955). *J. Endocrin.* **12**, 15. The hypothalamus and the mechanism of sympathetico-inhibition of milk ejection.

—— and Findlay, A. L. R. (1969). Comparative and sensory aspects of milk ejection. In *Lactogenesis* (ed. M. Reynolds and S. J. Folley). University of Pennsylvania, Philadelphia.

—— and Silver, I. A. (1956). *Proc. roy. Soc. Med.* **49**, 40. Milk ejection and mammary engorgement.

Cunningham, A. S. (1977). *J. Pediat.* **90**, 5. Morbidity in breast-fed and artificially-fed infants.

Cutherbertson, W. F. J. (1976). *Amer. J. clin. Nutr.* **29**, 559. Essential fatty acid requirements in infancy.

Dairy Council Digest (1976). **47**, No. 2. Current concepts in infant nutrition.

Dale, G., Goldfinch, M. E., Sibert, J. R., and Webb, J. K. G. (1975). *Arch. Dis. Childh.* **50**, 731. Plasma osmolality, sodium and urea in the breast-fed and bottle-fed infants in Newcastle upon Tyne.

Dale, P. P. (1964). *J. Amer. dent. Ass.* **68**, 530. Prenatal fluorides.

Danks, D. M., Tippett, P., and Rogers, J. (1975). *Acta paediat. (Uppsala)* **64**, 209. A new form of prolonged transient tyrosinemia presenting with severe metabolic acidosis.

Darca Simonetti, A. (1972). *Commun. Med.* **14**, 188. Contamination of infant feeding bottles and teats in Rome.

Darmady, J. M., Fosbrooke, A. S., and Lloyd, J. K. (1972). *Brit. med. J.* ii, 685. Prospective study of serum cholesterol during the first year of life.

Davidson, G. P., Bishop, R. F., Townley, R. R. W., Holmes, I. H., and Ruck, B. J. (1975). *Lancet* i, 242. Importance of a new virus in acute sporadic enteritis in children.

Davies, D. F. (1946). *Amer. Heart J.* **81**, 289. Milk protein and other food antigens in atheroma and coronary heart disease.

Davies, D. P. (1973). *Arch. Dis. Childh.* **48**, 575. Plasma osmolality and protein intake in pre-term infants.

—— (1975). *Lancet* iii, 366. Infant's self-regulation of food intake.

—— and Saunders, R. (1973). *Arch. Dis. Childh.* **48**, 563. Blood urea: normal values in early infancy related to feeding practices.

——, ——, and Gray, O. P. (1972). *Arch. Dis. Childh.* **47**, 946. Weight gain and chemical changes in low birth weight infants after change from human milk to modified cow's milk.

—— and THOMAS, C. (1976). *Lancet* i, 420. Why do some women stop breast feeding?

DAVIES, J. G. (1976). *Lancet* ii, 1468. Encouraging breast-feeding.

DAVIES, F. (1974). *Glamor* Sep., p. 180. Why are more women breast feeding?

DAVIES, J. P. (1975). *Lancet* ii, 276. Curious curd.

DAVIES, P. A. (1971). *Brit. med. J.* i, 351. Problems of the newborn: feeding.

DAVIES, R. V. and HARTREE, A. S. (1973). *Proc. roy. Soc. Med.* 33, 862. Purification of human prolactin.

DAVY, S. T. (1975). *Nursing Times.* 15 May, p. 758. Human milk banks.

DEAN, N. M. B. (1967). *J. trop. Pediat.* 13, 4. General practice paediatrics in the tropical African town of Calabar, Nigeria.

DE CHATEAU, P. (1976). *Neonatal care routines.* Umea University Medical Dissertations No. 20, Umea, Sweden.

——, HOLMBERG, H., and WINBERG, J. (1973). *Acta paediat. (Uppsala)* Supplement 236, p. 33. Relationship between feeding routines at the maternity ward, weight development and duration of breast feeding.

DE CLERCQ, E., EDY, V. G., DE VLIEGER, EECKELS, R., and DESMYTER, J. (1975). *J. Pediat.* 86, 736. Intrathecal administration of interferon in neonatal herpes.

DEB, A. K. and CAMA, H. R. (1962). *Brit. J. Nutr.* 16, 65. Studies in human lactation. Dietary nitrogen utilization during lactation, and distribution of nitrogen in mother's milk.

DEES, S. C. (1972). *Pediatrics* 50, 420. Some unsolved problems in clinical allergy.

DEFOREST, A., PARKER, P. B., DI LIBERTI, J. H., YATES, H. T., MARTEN, S., SIBINGA, M. S., and SMITH, D. S. (1973). *J. Pediat.* 83, 93. The effect of breast feeding on the antibody responses of infants to trivalent oral polio virus vaccine.

DELGADO, H., LECHTIG, A., YARBROUGH, C., MARSHALL, R., and KLEIN, R. E. (1975). The effect of marginal malnutrition on the duration of post partum amenorrhea in moderately malnourished communities. *Proceedings of the Xth International Congress of Nutrition*, Kyoto, Japan.

DELVOYE, P., DELOGUE-DESNOECK, J., and ROBYN, C. (1976). *Lancet* ii, 288. Serum prolactin in long-lasting lactation amenorrhoea.

DE MORALES, A. and LARKIN, F. A. (1972). *Ecol. Food Nutr.* 1, 131. The influence of the availability of commercial infant foods on feeding practices in Jamaica.

DEL MUNDO, F. and ADIAO, A. (1970). *Phillip. J. Pediat.* 19, 128. Lactation and child spacing as observed among 2,102 rural Filipino mothers.

DENNIS, J. K. and BYTHEWAY, W. R. (1965). *J. Obstet. Gynec.* 72, 94. Changes in body weight after delivery.

DEODHAR, A. D. and RAMAKRISHNAN, C. V. (1960). *J. trop. Pediat.* 6, 44. Relation between the dietary intake of lactating women and the chemical composition of milk with regard to vitamin content.

——, RAJALAKSHMI, R., and RAMAKRISHNAN, C. V. (1964). *Acta pediat. (Uppsala)* 53, 42. Effect of dietary supplementation on vitamin contents of breast milk.

DEPARTMENT OF HEALTH AND SOCIAL SECURITY, U.K. (1974). *Present-day practice in infant feeding.* Social Security Report on Health and Social Subjects No. 9. Her Majesty's Stationery Office, London.

—— (1975). *Health services development, baby milks and infant feeding.* Health Circular No. HC (76) 17. London.

DEPARTMENT OF HEALTH, VICTORIA, AUSTRALIA (1975). *Annual Report for Calendar Year 1974 of the Director of Maternal, Infant and Preschool Welfare*, p. 16.

DE SILVA, C. C. (1964). *Advanc. Pediat. 13*, 213. Common nutritional disorders of childhood in the tropics.

Developmental Psychology (1972). **6**, 110. Neonate–mother interaction during breast-feeding.

DICKSON, J. A. S., LEWIS, C. T., and SWAIN, V. A. J. (1974). *Arch. Dis. Childh.* **49**, 825. Milk bolus obstruction in the neonate.

DIXON, J. S. and LI, C. H. (1964). *Metabolism* **13**, 1093. Chemistry of prolactin.

DJOEANDA, P., RUSKANDI, M., and ALISJAHBANA, A. (1976). *Proc. 2nd Asian Pediat. Congress, Jakarta*. A 'rooming-in' programme for mothers and newborn in Dr. Hasan Sadikin General Hospital, Jakarta, Indonesia.

DOLBY, J. M., and HONOR, P. (1975). *Arch. Dis. Childh.* **50**, 823. Bacteriostasis of *Esch. coli*, by milk.

DONALD, I. (1966). *Brit. med. J.* iv, 1327. Visiting in maternity hospitals.

DONOSO, G. and MONCKEBURG, F. (1965). *Rev. chil. Pediat.* **36**, 301. Consideraciones generales y epidemiologicas.

DOUGLAS, J. W. B. (1950). *J. Obstet. Gynaec.* **57**, 335. The extent of breast feeding in Great Britain in 1946, with special reference to the health and survival of children.

DOWLING, S. and DE MONTERICE, D. (1974). *Pediat. Res.* **8**, 343. Motor development in infants with esophageal atresia. The critical importance of oral feeding experience.

DOWNHAM, M. A. P. S., SCOTT, R., SIMS, D. G., WEBB, J. K. G., and GARDNER, P. S. (1976). *Brit. med. J.* ii, 274. Breast-feeding protects against respiratory syncytial virus infections.

DRAKE, T. G. H. (1948). *J. hist. Med. allied Sci.* **3**, 507. American infant feeding bottles, 1841–1946, as disclosed by United States patent specifications.

DRIFE, J. O., MCCLELLAND, D. B. L., PRYDE, A., ROBERTS, M. M., and SMITH, I. I. (1976). *Brit. med. J.* ii, 503. Immunoglobulin synthesis in the 'resting' breast.

DUBOIS-PREVOST, R. (1967). *Sem. Hôp. Paris.* **43**, 612. Le lysozyme et son application en dietetique infantile.

DUGDALE, A. E. (1971). *Brit. J. Nutr.* **26**, 423. The effect of the type of feeding on weight gain and illnesses in infants.

DUNCOMBE, M. A. (1975). *Nursing Times* 15 May, p. 762. A new kind of famine.

DUNN, P. M. and POLLNITZ, R. (1975). *Lancet* i, 269. Subsidising National Dried Milk (N.D.M.).

—— (1976). *Lancet* i. 790. Obstetric delivery today. For better or for worse?

DWYER, J. and MAYER, J. (1975). The demise of breast feeding: sales, sloth or society? In *Priorities in child nutrition*, Vol. II. UNICEF, New York.

DYNSKI-KLEIN, M. (1946). *Brit. med. J.* ii, 258. Breast milk bank in maternity units.

—— (1975). *Atlas of pediatrics*. Yearbook Publishers, New York.

DYAL, L. and KAHRL, L. (1967). *Amer. J. Nurs.* **67**, 12. When mothers breastfeed.

EASTHAM, E., SMITH, D., POOLE, D., and NELLIGAN, G. (1976). *Brit. med. J.* i, 305. Further decline in breast feeding.

EBRAHIM, G. J. (1976). Cross-cultural aspects of breastfeeding. In *Breastfeeding and the mother*. Ciba Foundation Symposium No. 45. Elsevier, Amsterdam.

EDOZIEN, J. C., RAHIM KHAN, M. A., and WASLIEN, C. I. (1976). *J. Nutr.* **106**, 312.

Protein deficiency in man: results of a Nigerian village study.

EGLI, G. E. and NEWTON, M. (1961). *Pediatrics* **27**, 314. The influence of number of breast feedings on milk production.

EID, E. E. (1970). *Brit. med. J.* ii, 74. Follow-up study of physical growth of children who had excessive weight gain during the first six months of life.

EIGER, M. S. and OLDS, S. W. (1972). *The complete book of breast feeding.* Workman, New York.

EKSMYR, R. (1969). *A trial to change infant feeding practices in an Ethiopian village.* Ethiopian Nutrition Institute, Addis Ababa.

ELIAN, E., SHULAMITH, B. S., LIBERMAN, A., and MATOTH, Y. (1966). *J. Pediat.* **69**, 215. Intestinal blood loss: a factor in the calculations of body iron in later infancy.

ELLIS, F. R. (1974). *Lancet* iii, 400. Food antibodies and myocardial infarction.

ELLIS, R. W. B. (1975). *Pediatrics* **20**, 1041. Social change and child health.

ELWIN, V. (1948). *Man in India* **28**, 1. Notes on the Juangs.

ELY, F. and PETERSON, W. E. (1941). *J. Dairy Sci.* **24**, 211. Factors involved in the ejection of milk.

EMERSON, P. W. (1921). *J. Amer. med. Ass.* **78**, 641. The collection and preservation of human milk.

—— (1925). *Amer. J. Dis. Child.* **30**, 719. Dried human milk.

EMERY, J. L. and CARPENTER, R. G. (1974). *Proceedings of the F. E. Camps International Symposium on Sudden Death Syndrome*, p. 97. Toronto, Canada.

EMERY, J., SWIFT, P. G. F., and WORTHY, E. (1974). *Arch. Dis. Childh.* **49**, 686. Hypernatraemia and uraemia in unexpected death in infancy.

ENBERSDOBLER, H. and GROPP, J. (1973). *Proc. Nutr. Soc.* **32**, 223. Aspects of protein quality in calf nutrition.

ENTWISTLE, B. R. (1965). *Austral. J. Dermat.* **8**, 13. Acrodermatitis enteropathica. Report of a case in a twin with dramatic response to expressed human milk.

ERICSSON, Y. (1969). *Caries Res.* **3**, 159. Fluoride excretion in human saliva and milk.

—— and RIBELIUS, U. (1971). *Caries Res.* **5**, 78. Wide variations of fluoride supply to infants and their effects.

ESTRADA, F. E. (1972). *J. Philipp. med. Ass.* **48**, 32. Editorial: The case for breast feeding.

EVANS, G. W. and JOHNSON, P. E. (1976). *Lancet* ii, 1310. Zinc-binding factor in acrodermatitis enteropathica.

EVANS, N., WALPOLE, R., QUERESCHI, M. V., MENUON, M. H., and JONES, H. W. E. (1976). *Arch. Dis. Childh.* **51**, 608. Lower breast-feeding and early weaning in infants of Asian immigrants in Wolverhampton.

EWY, D. and EWY, R. (1975). *Preparation for breast feeding.* Doubleday Dolphin Books, New York.

FAHIM, M. S., BENNETT, R., and HALL, D. G. (1970). *Nature (Lond.)* **228**, 1222. Effect of DDT on the nursing neonate.

FALCONER, I. R. (ed.) (1971). *Lactation.* Butterworths, London.

FAO/WHO/UNICEF PROTEIN ADVISORY GROUP (PAG) (1971). *Feeding the pre-school child: Report of a PAG Ad Hoc Working Group.*

FASS, E. N. (1962). *J. dent. Child.* **29**, 245. Is bottle feeding a factor in dental caries?

FEIGIN, R. D. and SHEARER, W. T. (1975). *J. Pediat.* **87**, 677. Opportunistic infection in children. (II) The compromised host.

FEILEIB, M. and GARRISON, R. J. (1969). *Cancer* **24**, 1109. Interpretation of the vital statistics of breast cancer.

FELTMAN, R. and KOSEL, G. (1961). *J. dent. Med.* **16**, 190. Prenatal and postnatal ingestion of fluorides. Fourteen years of investigations.

FERNANDO, M. A. (1963). *Ceylon J. Chld Hlth* **9**, 17. Breast-feeding in Ceylon.

FILER, L. J. (1971). *Pediatrics* **74**, 489. Infant feeding in the nineteen seventies.

—— (1975). *Clins Perinatol.* **2**, 353. Maternal nutrition in lactation.

FINDLAY, A. L. R. (1971). Neural and behavioural interactions with lactation. In *Lactation* (ed. I. R. Falconer). Butterworths, London.

—— (1974*a*). *Res. Reprod.* **6**, 6. Lactation.

—— (1974*b*). In *Lactogenic hormones, fetal nutrition and lactation* (ed. J. B. Josimovich, M. Reynolds, and E. Cobo), Chapter 21: The role of suckling in lactation. Wiley, New York.

FINDLAY, J. B. C. and BREW, K. (1972). *Europ. J. Biochem.* **27**, 65. The complete amino-acid sequence of human lactalbumin.

FLATZ, G. and ROTTHAUWE, H. W. (1973). *Lancet* ii, 76. Lactose nutrition and natural selection.

FLEISS, P. M. (1976*a*). *The "non-thriver" in breast fed infants under six months.* Personal communication.

—— (1976*b*). Personal communication.

——, JELLIFFE, D. B., and JELLIFFE, E. F. P. (1976). 'Human milk — a biological system.' Paper presented at the American Academy for the Advancement of Science, Boston, February 1976.

FLEWETT, T. H., BRYDEN, A. S., DAVIES, H., WOODE, G. N., BRIDGEN, J. C., and DERRICK, J. M. (1974). *Lancet* iii, 61. Relation between viruses from gastroenteritis of children and newborn calves.

FLUGE, G. and FINNE, P. (1975). *T. Norske Laegeforen* **95**, 769. Neonatal feeding of infants of low birth-weight.

FOLLEY, F. J. (1969). *J. Endocr.* **44**, 10. The milk ejection reflex: a neuroendocrine theme in biology, myth and art.

FOMON, S. J. (1971). *Bull. N.Y. Acad. Med.* **47**, 569. A pediatrician looks at early nutrition.

—— (1974). *Infant nutrition* (second edition). W. B. Saunders, Philadelphia.

—— (1975). *Pediatrics* **56**, 350. What are infants fed in the United States?

—— and ANDERSON, T. A. (ed.) (1972). *Practices of low-income families in feeding infants and small children*. U.S. Department of Health, Education and Welfare, Washington, D.C.

——, FILER, L. J., THOMAS, L. N., ROGERS, R. R., and PROKSH, A. M. (1969). *J. Nutr.* **98**, 241. Relationship between formula concentration and rate of growth of normal infants.

——, ——, ——, ANDERSON, T. A. and NELSON, S. E. (1975). *Acta paediat. (Uppsala)* **64**, 172. Influence of formula concentration on caloric intake and growth of normal infants.

—— and MAY, C. D. (1958). *Pediatrics* **22**, 101. Metabolic studies of normal full term infants fed pasteurized human milk.

—— and WEI, S. H. Y. (1976). Prevention of dental caries. (In press)

FOMUFOD, A. K., SINKFORD, S. M., and LOUY, V. E. (1975). *Lancet* iii, 549. Mother–child separation at birth: a contributing factor in child abuse.

FOOD AND AGRICULTURE ORGANIZATION (1970). *Nutritional studies: aminoacid content of foods*, p. 134. Rome, Italy.
—— (1975). In defense of breast feeding. Food and Nutrition Division, Rome (Mimeo)
—— (1975). *Population, food supply and agricultural development*, p. 17. Rome, Italy.
FORCE, R. W. (1975). *Amer. J. trop. Med. Hyg.* **24**, 721. Health-related effects, consequences, and results of social change in the Pacific.
FORD, J. E. (1974). *Brit. J. Nutr.* **31**, 243. Some observations on the possible nutritional significance of vitamin B_{12} and folate-binding proteins in milk.
FORD, J. E. LAW, B. A., MARSHALL, V. M. E., and REITER, B. (1976). **90**, 29. *J. Pediat.* Influences of the heat treatment of human milk on some of its protective constituents.
——, SCOTT, K. J., SANSOM, B. F., and TAYLOR, P. J. (1975). *Brit. J. Nutr. 34*, 469. Some observations on the possible nutritional significance of vitamin B_{12} and folate-binding proteins in milk.
——, ——, THOMPSON, S. Y., LE MARQUAND, J., and TRUSWELL, A. S. (1974). *Arch. Dis. Childh.* **49**, 974. Comparisons of dried milk preparations for babies on sale in 7 European countries. II, Folic acid, vitamin B_6, thiamin, riboflavin and vitamin E.
Foreign Agriculture (1972). Apr. p. 6. The nonfat milk story.
FORSIUS, H. (1973). *Acta paediat. (Uppsala)* Supplement 239. The Finnish Skolt Lapp children.
FORSUM, E. (1974). *J. Dairy Sci.* **57**, 665. Nutritional evaluation of whey protein concentrations and their fractions.
FORSYTH, F. (1969). Primate prolactins and placental lactogens. In *Lactogenesis* (ed. M. Reynolds and S. J. Folley). University of Pennsylvania Press, Philadelphia.
FORSYTH, I A. (1973). *Proc. roy. Soc. Med.* **33**, 862. Bioassay of prolactin.
—— and EDWARDS, C. R. W. (1972). *Clin. Endocrinol.* **1**, 293. Human prolactin, its isolation, assay, and clinical applications.
FOSS, G. L. and SHORT, D. (1951). *J. Obstet. Gynaec. Brit. Fmp.* **58**, 35. Abnormal lactation.
FOWLER, M. (1974). 'Human milk and lactation'. 46th ANZAAS (Australian and New Zealand Association for the Advancement of Science) Meeting, Melbourne, Australia, Dec. 1974.
—— (1976). *J. Pediat. env. Chld Hlth* **22**, 34. A new era in breast feeding.
FRANCIS, B. (1975). 'Successful lactation: an overlooked function of woman's sexuality'. Paper presented at a conference on woman's health in a changing society, University of Queensland, Brisbane, Australia.
—— (1976). *Parents Centre of Australia J.* Feb./Mar. p. 7. Successful lactation.
FRANT, S. and ABRAMSON, H. (1937). *J. Pediat.* **11**, 772. Epidemic diarrhoea of the newborn (II). Control and prevention of outbreaks in hospital nurseries.
FRAUMENI, J. F. and MILLER, R. W. (1971). *Lancet* ii, 1196. Breast cancer from breast feeding.
FREED, D. (1976). *Brit. med. J.* i, 961. Bottle feeding and 'tummy ache' in infants.
FREIER, S. (1974). In *Clinical immunology–allergy in paediatric medicine* (ed. J. Brostoff): Paediatric gastrointestinal allergy, p. 107. Blackwell, Oxford and London.

FRENCH, J. G. (1967). *Amer. J. clin. Nutr.* **20**, 375. Relationship of morbidity to feeding patterns of Navajo children from birth through twenty-four months.

FREUDENBERG, E. (1953). *Jb. Kinderheilk.* **54**, 1. Die Frauenmilch-Lipase.

FRIEDMAN, G. and GOLDBERG, S. J. (1975). *Amer. J. clin. Nutr.* **28**, 42. Concurrent and subsequent serial cholesterols in breast- and bottle-fed infants.

FRIEDMAN, K. M. (1975). *Amer. J. publ. Hlth* **65**, 979. Cigarette smoking and public policy.

FRIESEN, H. G. (1976). *Res. hum. Reprod.* **8**, 3. Prolactin and human reproduction.

FULTON, A. A. (1945). *Brit. med. J.* **ii**, 693. Incidence of puerperal and lactational mastitis in an industrial town of some 43,000.

FUMAGALLI, R., SMITH, M. E., URNA, G., and PAOLETTI, R. (1969). *J. Neurochem.* **16**, 1329. The effect of hypocholesteremic agents on myelinogenesis.

FÜRER, A., MAURON, J., and MÜLLER, H. R. (1975). *Nestle and baby food in the Third World*. Vevey, Switzerland.

GABUCAN-DULAY, M. L. (1970). *Philipp. J. Pediat.* **19**, 95. Current feeding patterns as observed among 1000 Filipino infants.

GAIRDNER, D. (1974). *Proc. nutr. Soc.* **33**, 119. The effect of diet on the development of the adipose organs.

GALLI, C., JACINI, G., and PECILE, A. (ed.) (1973). *Dietary lipids and postnatal development*. Raven Press, New York.

GANZIN, M. (1974). *PAN* (Newspaper of the World Food Conference). No. 9, 15 Nov. The real food.

GARDNER, L. I., MacLACHLAN, E. A., PICK, W., TERRY, M. L., and BUTLER, A. M. (1950). *Pediatrics* **5**, 228. Etiologic factors in tetany of newly born infants.

GARNG, G., WINKLER, R., and POLAND, R. L. (1976). *Pediat. Res.* **10**, 424. A survey of human milk samples for inhibitors of bilirubin UDP glucuronyl transferase.

GARROW, D. H. and SMITH, D. (1976). *Proc. roy. Soc. Med.* **69**, 4. Modern practice of separating the newborn baby from his mother.

GEBRE-MEHDIN, M., VALQUIST, A., HOFVANDER, Y., UPPSÄLL, L., and VAHL-QUIST, B. (1976). *Amer. J. clin. Nutr.* **29**, 441. Breast milk composition in Ethiopian and Swedish mothers. (I) Vitamin A and beta-carotene.

GEISSLER, C., GALLOWAY, D. H., MARGEN, S., and KENNEDY, B. (1975). *Fed. Proc.* **4**, 896. Lactation adequacy, pre and post-natal nutritional status and serum hormonal levels in Iranian women of low and middle socio-economic status.

GERARD, A. (1972). *Please breast feed your baby*. Signet Books, New York.

GERRARD, J. W. (1974*a*). *Pediat. Ann.* **3**, 9. Allergy in infancy.

—— (1974*b*). *Pediatrics* **54**, 757. Breast feeding: second thoughts.

——, MACKENZIE, J. W. A., GOLUBOFF, N., GARSON, J. Z., and MANINGAS, C. S. (1973). *Acta paediat. (Uppsala)* Supplement 234. Cow's milk allergy: prevalence and manifestations in an unselected series of newborns.

GERSTENBERGER, H. J. and RUH, H. O. (1919). *Amer. J. Dis. Child.* **17**, 1. Studies in the adaptation of an artificial milk to human food.

GILL, H. and POPKIN, B. (1975). The health and nutritional implications of women's participation in the labor force. *Proceedings of the Xth International Congress of Nutrition*, Kyoto, Japan, August 1975.

GINDRAT, J. J., HANSON, L. A., GOTHEFORS, L., and WINBERG, J. (1972). *Acta paediat. (Uppsala)* **61**, 587. Antibodies in human milk against *E. coli* in the serogroups most commonly found in neonatal infections.

GIOBBI, S. A., KEMP, J. P., MELLON, M., ORGEL, H. A. and HAMBURGER, R. N. (1976). 'Milk sensitivity in breast fed infants'. Paper presented at American Academy of Allergy Conference.

GIOSIA, R. (1955). *Amer. J. Obstet. Gynec.* **70**, 162. The incidence of pregnancy during lactation in 500 cases.

GIRARD-GLOBE, A. BOURDEL, G., and FORESTIER, M. (1975). Regulation of circadian rhythm in hepatic enzymes by schedule of food ingestion. *Proceedings of the Xth International Congress of Nutrition*, Kyoto, Japan, August, 1975.

GLADE, B. E. and BUCHANAN, G. R. (1976). *Pediatrics* **58**, 548. The bleeding neonate.

GLASER, J. (1966). *J. Asthma Res.* **3**, 199. The dietary prophylaxis of allergic disease in infancy.

—— (1973). The prophylaxis of allergic disease in infancy and childhood. *Allergy and immunology in childhood* (ed. F. Speer and R. S. Dockhorn), Chapter 32, p. 403. Thomas, Springfield.

—— (1975). *Annal. Allergy* Intra-uterine sensitivity and allergy in the newborn and breast fed infant. (In press)

GOLDBLUM, R., AHLSTEDT, S., CARLSSON, B., and HANSON, L. A. (1976). *Nature (Lond.).* Antibody forming cells in human colostrum after oral immunization. (In press)

GOLDMAN, A. S. (1977). Cow milk sensitivity: a review. In: *Food and Immunology*, p. 99, ed. L. Hambraeus, L. Hanson, and H. Macfarlane. Almquist and Wiksell, Stockholm.

—— and SMITH, C. W. (1973). *J. Pediat.* **82**, 1082. Host resistance factors in human milk.

GOLDMAN, H. I., GOLDMAN, J. S., KAUFMAN, I., and LIEBMAN, O. B. (1974). *J. Pediat.* **85**, 764. Late effects of early dietary protein intake on low-birth-weight infants.

GOLDSTEIN, G. B. and HEINER, D. C. (1970). *J. Allergy* **46**, 270. Clinical and immunological perspectives in food sensitivity.

GOLNICK, A. L. and MATHEWSON, R. J. (1967). *J. Mich. State dent. Ass.* **49**, 261. Nursing bottle syndrome: more can be done.

GONZALEZ, N. L. (1972). In *Nutrition, growth and development in North American Indian children* (ed. W. M. Moore, M. J. Silverbeg, and M. S. Read). Changing dietary patterns of North American Indians. DHEW Publication No. NIH 72–26.

—— and BEHAR, M. (1966) *Milbank memo. Fd Quart.* **64**, 77. Child rearing practices, nutrition and health status.

GOOD, J. (1974). Hemoglobin levels in breastfed infants. Personal communication.

GOOSE, D. H. (1967). *Caries Res.* **1**, 167. Infant feeding and caries of the incisors.

GOPALAN, C. (1958). *J. trop. Pediat.* **4**, 87. Studies on lactation in poor Indian communities.

—— and BELAVADY, B. (1961). *Fed. Proc.* **20**, No. 1, part 3. Nutrition and lactation.

—— and NAIDU, A. N. (1972). *Lancet* **ii**, 1077. Nutrition and fertility.

—— and NARASINGA RAO, B. S. (1971). *Indian J. med. Res.* **59**, 111. Nutritional constraints on growth and development in current Indian dietaries.

GORDON, J. E., CHITKARA, I. D., and WYON, J. B. (1963). *Amer. J. med. Sci.* **245**, 345. Weanling diarrhea.

——, GUZMAN, M. A., ASCOLI, W., and SCRIMSHAW, N. J. (1964). *Bull. Wld Hlth*

Org. **31**, 9. Acute diarrheal disease in less developed countries. 2. Patterns of epidemiological behavior in rural Guatemalan villages.

GOTHEFORS, L. (1975). *Studies of antimicrobial factors in human milk and bacterial colonization of the newborn.* Umea University Dissertations, Larsson, Umea.

——, CARDSSON, B., AHLSTEDT, S., HANSON, L. A., and WINBERG, J. (1976). *Acta paediat. (Uppsala)* **65**, 225. Influence of maternal gut flora and colostral and cord serum antibodies and the presence of *E. coli* in faeces in the newborn infant.

GOTOFF, S. P. (1974). *J. Pediat.* **85**, 149. Medical progress: neonatal immunity.

GRABER, T. M. (1966). *Orthodontics: principles and practice*, Chapter 6: Etiology of malocclusion. Saunders, Philadelphia.

GRANTHAM, E. (1973). *Arch. Dis. Childh.* **48**, 568. Sore bottoms in the newborn.

GRANTHAM-CUMMING, G. (1967). *Canad. J. publ. Hlth* **58**, 391. Infant care in Canadian Indian homes.

GRANTHAM-McGREGOR, S. M. and BACK, E. H. (1970). *Arch. Dis. Childh.* **45**, 404. Breastfeeding in Kingston, Jamaica.

GREBBENIKOV, E. P. and SOROKA, V. R. (1963). *Pediatrija* **6**, 16. Contents of trace elements in breast milk.

GREENFIELD, H. (1975). The energy needs for pregnancy and lactation. *Xth International Congress of Nutrition*, Kyoto, Japan, August, 1975.

GREINER, T. (1975). *The promotion of bottle feeding by multinational corporations: how advertising and the health professions have helped.* Cornell International Nutrition Monograph Series No. 2. Ithaca and New York.

GRIFFITHS, M. (1965). *Comp. Biochem. Physiol.* **16**, 383. Rate of growth and intake of milk in a suckling echidna.

GRIMMONPREZ, L. (1966). *C. R. Acad. Sci. (Paris)* **263D**, 1269. Isolement et composition de six nouveau polyosides du lait du femme.

—— (1971). *Ann. Nutr. (Paris)* **25**, A39. Les glucides du lait.

GROSCLANDE, F., MERCIER, J. C., and RIBADEAU DUMAS, B. (1973). *Ned. Melk. en Zuiveltijdschr.* **27**, 328. Genetic aspects of cattle casein research.

GROSSMAN, E. R. (1975). *J. Pediat.* **86**, 840. More on the prophylactic dose of fluoride.

GROSVENOR, C. E., MENA, F., and SCHAEFGEN, D. A. (1967). *Endocrinology* **8**, 449. Effect of nonsuckling interval and duration of suckling on the suckling-induced fall in pituitary prolactin concentration in the rat.

——, and MENA, F. (1974). *Lactation: a comprehensive treatise* (ed. B. L. Larson and V. R. Smith), Vol. 1, Chapter 4: Neurologic and hormonal control of milk secretion and ejection, p. 227. Academic Press, New York.

GRULEE, G. G., SANFORD, H. N., and HERRON, P. H. (1934). *J. Amer. med. Ass.* **103**, 735. Breast and artificial feeding.

GUERI, M. (1975). Evaluation of a breast feeding campaign in Trinidad. Unpublished document.

GUGLER, E. and MURALT, G. V. (1959). *Schweiz. med. Wschr.* **89**, 925. Uber immunoelektrophoretische Untersuchungen an Frauenmilchprotein.

GULLBERG, R. (1974). *Scand. J. Gastoenterol.* **9**, 287. Possible influence of vitamin B_{12}-binding protein in milk on the intestinal flora in breast-fed infants.

GUNTHER, M. (1952). *Brit. J. Nutrit.* **6**, 215. The composition of human milk and factors affecting it.

—— (1955). *Lancet* i, 575. Instinct and the nursing couple.

—— (1975). *Lancet* **i**, 445. The neonate's immunity gap, breast feeding and cot death.

GUNTHER, M (1976). A new mother's view of herself. In *Breast feeding and the mother*. Ciba Foundation Symposium No. 45. Elsevier, Amsterdam.

——, CHEEK, E., MATTHEWS, R. H., and COOMBS, R. R. (1962). *Int. Arch. Allergy* **21**, 257. Immune responses to cow's milk proteins taken by mouth.

—— and STANIER, J. E. (1951). *Spec. Rep. Ser, med. Res. Coun. (Lond.)* **275.** Studies of undernutrition, Wuppertal.

GURNEY, M. (1976). *Lancet* ii, 1467. Establishment of lactation.

GURNEY, M. J. (1971). *West. Ind. med. J.* **20**, *227.* Weaning practices from Guyana, rural Trinidad, Grenada, Montserrat and Antigua.

GUSSOW, J. (1974). *American Academy of Pediatrics News and Comments*, Vol. 25, p. 10. T.V. and children: consumer education for kids.

GUTHRIE, H. A. (1967). *Trop. geogr. Med.* **19**, 48. Infant feeding practices in a corn-eating area of the Philippines.

—— and GUTHRIE, G. M. (1966). *Clin. Pediat.* **5**, 481. The resurgence of natural child feeding. A study of 129 middle class mothers in a college community.

GYÖRGY, P. A. (1953). *Pediatrics* **11**, 98. A hitherto unrecognised biochemical difference between human milk and cow's milk.

—— (1971). *Amer. J. clin. Nutr.* **24**, 976. Biochemical aspects of human milk.

—— (1973). *Fourth Wyeth Nutrition Symposium*, p. 1–7. Human milk differences.

HABITCH, J. P., DELGADO, H., YARBROUGH, C., and KLEIN, R. E. (1975). *Proceedings of the IXth International Nutrition Congress*. Mexico City, August 1972, Vol. 2, p. 106. Repercussions of lactation on nutritional status of mother and infant.

HADJIMARKOS, D. M. (1963). *J. Pediat.* **63**, 273. Selenium content of human milk: possible effect on dental caries.

HAENEL, H. (1970). *Amer. J. clin. Nutr.* **23**, 1433. Human normal and abnormal intestinal flora.

HAIRE, D. (1973). *J. trop. Pediat. env. Chld Hlth* **19**, 171. The cultural warping of childbirth.

—— and HAIRE, J. (1971). Implementing family-centred maternity care with a central nursery. ICEA, Washington.

—— and —— (1974). (I) *The nurse's contribution to successful breast feeding*. (II) *The medical value of breast feeding*. International Childbirth Education Association, New Jersey.

HALBERG, J., HALBERG, E., and HALBERG, F. (1975). Non-obese mammals pair-fed or on free-choice diets. *Proceedings of the Xth International Congress of Nutrition*, Kyoto, Japan, August 1975.

HALL, B. (1975). *Lancet* **i**, 779. Changing compostion of human milk and early development of an appetite control.

—— (1976). The uniformity of human milk. (In press)

HALES, D., KENNELL, J., and SOSA, R. (1976). *Pediat. Res.* **10**, 448. How early is early contact? Defining the limits of the sensitive period.

HALPERN, S. R., SELLARS, W. A., JOHNSON, R. B., ANDERSON, D. W., SAPERSTEIN, S., and REISCH, J. S. (1973), *J. Allergy clin. Immunol.* **51**, 139. Development of childhood allergy in infants fed breast, soy and cow's milk.

HAMBERG, L. (1971). *Lancet* **i**, 441. Controlled trial of fluoride in vitamin drops for the prevention of caries in children.

HAMBIDGE, K. M. (1977). The role of zinc and other trace elements in pediatric nutrition and health. *Pediat. Clins N. Amer.* **24**, 95 (ed. C. Neumann and D. B. Jelliffe).

—— (1977). *Pediat. Clins N. Amer.* Infant feeding (ed. C. Neumann and D. B. Jelliffe). (In press)

HAMBRAEUS, L. (1977). Proprietary milks versus human breast milk. A critical approach from the nutritional point of view. *Pediat. Clins. N. Amer.* **24**, 17 (ed. C. Neumann and D. B. Jelliffe.

——, FORSUM, E., and LÖNNERDAL, B. (1975). Nutritional aspects of breast milk and cow's milk formulas. In: *Food and Immunology*, p. 116, ed. L. Hambraeus, L. Hanson, and H. Macfarlane. Almquist and Wiksell, Stockholm.

HANAFY, M. M., MORSEY, M. R. A., SEDDICK, Y., HABIB, Y. A., and EL LOZY, M. (1972). *J. trop. Pediat, env. Chld Hlth* **18**, 187. Maternal nutrition and lactation performance. A study in urban Alexandria.

HANEBERG, B. and FINNE, P. (1974). *Acta Paediat.* **63**, 588. Lysozymes in feces from infants and children.

HANNA, J. C. (1967). *J. Dent. Child.* **34**, 243. Breast feeding versus bottle feeding in relation to oral habits.

HANSEN, A. E., KNOTT, E. M., WIESE, H. F., SHAPERMAN, E., and McQUARRIE, I. (1947). *Amer. J. Dis. Child.* **73**, 1. Eczema and essential fatty acids.

——, STEWART, R. A., HUGHES, G., and SODERHJELM, L. (1962). *Acta Paediat.* **51**, Supplement 137. The relation of linoleic acid to infant feeding.

HANSON, L. A. (1961). *Immunological studies of human milk*. Orstadius Boktryckeri, Goteborg, Sweden.

—— and WINBERG, J. (1972). *Arch. Dis. Childh.* **47**, 845. Breast milk and defense against infection in the newborn.

—— and JOHANSSON, B. G. (1970). Immunological studies of milk. In *Milk proteins: chemistry and molecular biology* (ed. H. A. McKenzie). Vol. I, p. 45. Academic Press, New York.

——, CARLSSON, B., AHLSTEDT, S., SVANBORG, C., and KAIJSER, B. (1975). *Mod. Prob. Pediat.* **15**, 63. Immune defense factors in human milk.

HANSSON, O. (1969). *Amer. J. Dis. Child.* **117**, 72. Acrodermatitis enteropathica.

HAPKE, A. (1975). *Nursing Mothers of Australia Newsletter* Aug. p. 13. The counsellor's role.

HARFOUCHE, J. K. (1965). *Feeding practices and weaning patterns of Lebanese infants*. Khayats, Beirut.

—— (1970). *J. trop. Pediat.* **16**, 135. The importance of breast feeding.

HARGREAVES, T. and PIPER, R. F. (1971). *Arch. Dis. Childh.* **46**, 195. Breast milk jaundice.

HARLOW, H. and HARLOW, M. (1962). *Bull. Menninger Clin.* **26**, 213. The effect of rearing conditions on behavior.

—— and ZIMMERMAN, R. R. (1958). *Proc. Amer. Philosoph.* **102**, 501. The development of affectional responses in infant monkeys.

—— and —— (1959). *Science (N.Y.)* **130**, 421. Affectional responses in the infant monkey.

HARTFIELD, V. J. (1972). *Int. Planned Parenth. Fedn med. Bull.* **6**, 1. Contraception and lactation.

HARWORTH, W. J. (1905). *Lancet* **ii**, 210. The influence of feeding on the mortality of infants.

HASKELL, A. and LEWIS, M. (1971). *Infantilia: the archaeology of the nursery*. Dennis Dobson, London.

HATSUNO, K. (1975). *Acta paed. jap.* **79**, 16. A comparative study of serum lipid fractions and fatty acid patterns between breast fed and bottle fed healthy infants.

HAWORTH, W. N. and LONG, C. W. (1927).*J. Chem. Soc.* **1**, 544. The constitution of disaccharides. Part XII. Lactose.

HAYASHI, M. (1972). Personal communication.

HAYES, W. J. (1971). WHO Document WHO/VBC/71.251, Geneva.

——, DALES, W. E., and PINKLE, C. I. (1971).*Arch. env. Hlth* **22**, 119. Evidence of safety of long-term, high, oral doses of DDT for man.

HAYES, K., DANKS, D. M., GIBAS, H., and JACK, I. (1972). *New Eng. med. J.* **287**, 177. Cytomegalovirus in human milk.

HEALY, C. E. (1972). *Pediatrics* **49**, 910. Acidosis and failure to thrive in infants fed Nutramigen.

HEDENSTEDT, S. and HEIJKENSKJOLD, F. (1965). *Ann. Allergy* **22**, 76. Intravenous milk infusion in children.

HEER, J. (1966). *World events 1866–1966. The first hundred years of Nestlé*. Rivaz.

HEIRD, W. C. and DRISCOLL, J. M. (1975). *Clins Perinatol.* **2**, 309. New methods of feeding low birth weight infants.

—— and WINTERS, R. W. (1975).*J. Pediat.* **82**, 2. Total parenteral nutrition — the state of the art.

HEIFER, R. E. and KEMPE, C. H. (1968). *The battered child*. University of Chicago Press, Chicago and London.

HEINER, D. C., SEARS, J. W., and KNIKER, W. T. (1962). *Amer. J. Dis. Child.* **103**, 634. Multiple precipitins in cow's milk in chronic respiratory disease.

HELSING, E. (1974). *Boken Om Amming*. Glydendal, Norsk Forlag, Oslo.

—— (1975*a*).*J. trop. Pediat. env. Chld Hlth* **21**, 210. Woman's liberation and breast feeding.

—— (1975*b*). Some notes and ideas concerning the role of FAO in the promotion of breast feeding. Unpublished document.

—— (1977). How to assist mothers in dealing with breast feeding. (In preparation).

HENRIPIN, J. (1960). *Population Studies* **61**, 84. La Fecondite des menages cana-diens au debout du XVIII siècle.

HENSCHEL, M. J. and COATES, M. E. (1974). *Brit. med. J.* **iii**, 112A. The toxicity of cow's milk to infant rabbits.

HERMELO, M., AMADOR, M., HERNANDEZ, P., GONZALEZ, M. E., GONZALEZ-CELAA, F., and TUDELA, J. (1968). *Rev. cuba. Pediat.* **40**, 299. Los tipos de lactancia y el destete como factores determinantes de diarrhea aguda y desnutri-cion en el lactante menor de seis meses.

HEYNDRICKX, G. V. (1962).*Arch. paediat.* **198**, 356. Investigations on the enzymes in human milk.

HEYWOOD, P. and HEYWOOD, A. (1974).*Cajanus* **5**, 95. Please breast-feed the baby and keep the bottle for yourself.

HEYWOOD, R. (1974). *Proc. Nutr. Soc.* **33**, 87. Some observations on growth and development of *Macaca mulatta*.

HILDES, J. A. and SCHAEFER, O. (1973).*J. human Evol.* **2**, 241. Health of Igloolik Eskimos and changes with urbanization.

HILL, L. F. (1967). *Pediat. Clins N. Amer.* **14**, 255. Infant feeding: historical and current.

—— (1968). *J. Pediat.* **73**, 161. A salute to La Leche League International.

HINDLEY, C. B. (1968). *Dev. Med. Chld Neurol.* **10**, 715. Growing up in five countries.

——, FILLIOZAT, A. M., KLACKENBERG, G., NICOLET-MEISTER, D., and SAND, E. A. (1965). *J. Child Psychiat.* **6**, 179. Some differences in infant feeding and elimination training in five European longitudinal samples.

HIPSLEY, E. (1975). *Proceedings of the 13th Pacific Science Congress*, Vancouver, Canada. One of the family — do children need special foods?

HIRSCHMAN, C. and SWEET, J. A. (1974). *Soc. Biol.* **21**, 39. Social background and breast feeding among American mothers.

HIRSCHORN, N. (1976). *Arch. Dis. Childh.* **76**, 326. Hyperetraemia and milk formulas.

HOFER, M. A. (1975). Summing up. In *Parent–infant interaction*. Ciba Foundation Symposium No. 33. Elsevier, Amsterdam.

HOFVANDER, Y. and SJÖLIN, S. (1972). Quoted by Vahlquist (1975).

HOLLEN, B. K. (1976). *J. Pediat. env. Chld Hlth.* **20**, 288. Attitudes of physicians to breast-feeding and its management.

HOLMAN, R. R. and KANWAR, S. (1975). *Arch. Dis. Childh.* **75**, 50. Early life of the 'battered child'.

HOMING, M. G., NOWLIN, J., HICKERT, P., STILWELL, W. G., and HILL, R. M. (1973). In *Dietary lipids and postnatal development*, p. 257. Identification of drugs and drug metabolites in breast milk by gas chromatography-mass spectrometry.

HONDA, T., KAWAKAMI, T., KOHNO, H., MORISHIMA, N., and OSUMI, K. (1975). A study of aurantiasis in Japanese children. *Proceedings of the Xth International Congress of Nutrition*, Kyoto, Japan, August 1975.

HOOPER, P. D. and ALEXANDER, E. L. (1971). *Practioner* **207**, 221. Infant morbidity and obesity.

HORMANN, E. (1972). Relactation: a guide to breast-feeding an adopted baby. Unpublished document.

HORROBIN, D. F., BURSTYN, P. G., LLOYD, I. J., DURKIN, N., LIPTON, A., and MIURURI, K. L. (1971). *Lancet* **ii**, 352. Action of prolactin on human renal function.

HORWITT, M. (1974). *Amer. J. clin. Nutr.* **27**, 960. Selenium-glutathione peroxidase and vitamin E.

HOUSDEN, L. G. (1932). *The breast-fed baby in general practice*. H. K. Lewis, London.

HUGHES-DAVIES, T. H. (1975). *Brit. med. J.* **i**, 586. Baby feeding.

HUNTINGTON, G. E. and HOSTETLER, J. A. (1970). *Population Studies* **24**, 321. A note on nursing practices in an American isolate with a high birth rate.

HUSSAIN, M. A. and WADSWORTH, G. R. (1967). *Proc. Nutr. Soc.* **26**, 212. Nutritional status of Asian infants.

HUTCHINSON SMITH, B. (1970). *Med. Offr* **123**, 257. The relationship between the weight of an infant and lower respiratory infection.

HWANG, P., GUYDA, H., and FRIESEN, H. (1971). *Proc. nat. Acad. Sci. (Wash.)* **68**, 1902. A radioimmunoassay for human prolactin.

——, HARDY, J., FRIESEN, H., and WILANSKY, D. (1971). *J. clin. Endocrinol.*

Metab. **33**, 1. Biosynthesis of human growth hormone and prolactin by normal pituitary glands and pituitary adenomas.

HYMANSON, A. (1934). *Arch. Pediat.* **51**, 1. A short review of the history of infant feeding.

HYTTEN, F. E. (1954). *Brit. med. J.* **i**, 175. Clinical and chemical studies in human lactation.

—— (1954). *Brit. med. J.* **i**, 175. Collection of milk samples.

—— (1954). *Brit. med. J.* **i**, 176. Variation in major constituents during a feeding.

—— (1954). *Brit. med. J.* **i**, 179. Diurnal variation in major constituents of milk.

—— (1954). *Brit. med. J.* **i**, 912. The functional capacity of the breast.

—— (1954). *Brit. med. J.* **ii**, 844. Relationship of the age, physiologic and nutritional status of the mother to the yield and composition of milk.

—— (1954). *Brit. med. J.* **i**, 1410. The effect of differences in yield and composition of milk on the infant's weight gain and duration of breast feeding.

—— (1954). *Brit. med. J.* **ii**, 1447. Breast feeding in hospital.

—— and LEITCH, I. (1971). *The physiology of human pregnancy* (second edition). Blackwell Scientific Publications, Oxford.

IBRAHIM, A. N. and EL TAWIL, N. Z. (1968). *Int. Surg.* **49**, 561. The effect of a new low dosage oral contraceptive pill on lactation.

IFEKWUNIGWE, A. E. (1975). *Amer. J. clin. Nutr.* **28**, 79–83. Emergency treatment of large numbers of children with severe protein-calorie malnutrition.

IGNATIUS, D. (1973). *Washington Monthly* Oct. p. 21. Health: the morality of medicine.

ILLICH, I. (1974). *Medical nemesis*. Calder and Boyars.

ILLINGSWORTH, R. S. and STONE, D. G. H. (1952). *Lancet* **i**, 683. Self-demand feeding in a maternity unit.

ILLMAN, J. (1973). *Sunday Times* (London) 18 Nov. Mother's milk in short supply.

INGALLS, T. H., DRAPER, R., and TEEL, H. M. (1938). *Amer. J. Dis. Child.* **56**, 1011. Vitamin C in human pregnancy and lactation.

INGELMAN-SUNDBERG, A. (1958). *J. Obstet. Gynaec. Brit. Emp.* **65**, 448. The value of antenatal massage of the nipples and expression of colostrum.

INGLIS, B. (1975). *J. roy. Coll. Physns* **9**, 347. Fringe medicine.

INSULL, W., HIRSCH, J., JAMES, T., and AHRENS, E. H. (1959). *J. clin. Invest.* **38**, 443. The fatty acids of human milk II. Alteration produced by manipulation of caloric balance and exchange of dietary fats.

INTERNATIONAL LABOR OFFICE (1975). International Labor Conference. 60th Session. Report VIII. Equal opportunity and treatment for women workers.

—— (1965). International Labor Conference. 49th Session. Report of the Committee of Experts on the Application of Conventions and Recommendations 160. Geneva.

—— (1969). *Ratification outlook after fifty years: Seventeen Selected Conventions*. Geneva.

INTERNATIONAL PEDIATRIC ASSOCIATION (1976). *Acta paediat. (Uppsala)* **65**, 275. Recommendations for Action Programmes to Encourage Breast Feeding: IPA Seminar, Montreux, August 1975.

INTERNATIONAL UNION OF NUTRITION SCIENCES (1975). *J. trop. Pediat. env. Chld Hlth* **21**, 345. Report of the second meeting of the IUNS Committee V/II. Nutrition education in nursing.

IRONSIDE, A. G. (1973). *Brit. med. J.* i, 284. Gastroenteritis of infancy.

ISHAM, J. C. (1975). *New Internationalist* 8, 30. Letters: Baby Foods.

ISMANGOEN (1957). *J. trop. Pediat.* 3, 13. Neonatal gastroenteritis due to pathogenic *Escherichia coli* and/or *Salmonella Worthington*.

IVERSEN, R. (1974). *Courrier* 24, 567. The care of children of working parents. II. Principal solutions. Family day care in Denmark.

IYENGAR, L. and APTE, S. V. (1972). *Brit. J. Nutr.* 27, 313. Nutrient stores in human foetal livers.

―――― and SELVARAJ, R. J. (1972). *Arch. Dis. Childh.* 47, 411. Intestinal absorption of immunoglobulins by newborn infants.

JACKSON, E. B., WILKIN, L. C., and AUERBACH, H. (1956). Pediatrics 17, 700. Statistical report on incidence and duration of breastfeeding in relation to personal social and hospital maternity factors.

JACKSON, R. L. (1977). Long term consequences of feeding practices in early life. *Pediat. Clins. N Amer.* 24, 63 (ed. C. Neumann and D. B. Jelliffe).

――――, WESTERFELD, R., FLYNN, M. A., KIMBALL, E. R., and LEWIS, R. B. (1964). *Pediatrics* 33, 642. Growth of 'well-born' American infants fed human and cow's milk.

JACOBS, L. S. and DAUGHADAY, W. H. (1974). Physiologic regulation of prolactin secretion in man. In *Lactogenic hormones, fetal nutrition and lactation* (ed. J. B. Josimovich, M. Reynolds, and E. Cobo). John Wiley, New York.

JACOBSON, H. N. (1975). *Clins Perinatol*. 2, 233. Weight and weight gain in pregnancy.

JACOBSON, M. (1976). Personal communication.

JADHAV, M., WEBB, J. K. G., VAISHNAVA, S., and BAKER, S. J. (1962). *Lancet* ii, 903. Vitamin B_{12} deficiency in Indian infants. A new syndrome.

JAIN, A. K., HSU, J. C., FREEDMAN, R., and CHANG, M. C. (1970). *Demography* 7, 255. Demographic aspects of lactation and post-partum amenorrhea.

JAMES, P. M. C. (1975). *Brit. med. Bull.* 31, 146. Epidemiology of dental caries: the British scene.

――――, PARFITT, G. J., and FALKNER, F. (1957). *Brit. dent. J.* 103, 37. A study of the etiology of labial caries of the deciduous teeth in small children.

JAMIESON, S. R. (1972). *J. roy. Soc. Hlth* 4, 211. Infantile gastroenteritis — a preventable disease.

JANSEN, A. A. J., LUYKEN, R., MALCOLM, S. H., and WILLIAMS, J. J. L. (1960). *Trop. geogr. Med.* 12, 138. Quantity and composition of breast milk in Biak Island. (Netherlands New Guinea).

JANSSEN, F. (1975). *Mschn. Kinderheilk* 123, 34. Diseases caused by drug therapy in newborn babies (in German).

JANZ, A. J., DEMAYER, E. M., and CLOSE, J. (1957). *Ann. Nutr. (Paris)* 11, 33. Nutrition et lactation chez la femme.

JARVIS, A. A., BROWN, J. R., and TIEFFENBACH, B. (1963). *Canad. med. Ass. J.* 88, 136. Strontium 89 and strontium 90 in breast milk and in mineral supplement preparations.

JATHAR, V. S., KAMATH, S. A., PARIKH, M-N, REGE, D. V., and SATOSKAR, R. S. (1970). *Arch. Dis. Childh.* 45, 236. Maternal milk and serum vitamin B_{12}, folic acid and protein levels in Indian subjects.

JELLIFFE, D. B. (1952). *Brit. med. J.* ii, 1131. The protein content of breast milk of

African women.

—— (1953). *West Afr. med. J.* **2**, 114. Infant feeding among the Yoruba of Ibadan.

—— (1956). *Courrier* **6**, 191. Breast feeding in developing countries: with special reference to West Bengal.

—— (1959*a*). *J. Pediat.* **54**, 227. Cultural blocks and protein malnutrition in West Bengal.

—— (1959*b*). *J. Pediat.* **54**, 277. Protein-calorie malnutrition. A review of recent literature.

—— (1962). *Amer. J. clin. Nutr.* **10**, 19. Culture, social change and infant feeding.

—— (1966*a*). *The assessment of the nutritional status of the community.* WHO Monograph No. 53. Geneva, Switzerland.

—— (1966*b*). *J. Pediat.* **69**, 161. La Leche League as an influence in tropical pediatrics.

—— (1967). *Obstetrics and gynecology in the tropics* (ed. J. B. Lawson and D. B. Stewart), Chapter 15: Prematurity, p. 253. Edward Arnold, London.

—— (1968*a*). *Child health in developing regions.* U.S. Government Publication No. 1822. Government Printing Office, Washington, D.C.

—— (1968*b*). *Infant nutrition in the subtropics and tropics* (second edition). WHO Monograph No. 29. Geneva, Switzerland.

—— (1968*c*). *Clin. Pediat.* **7**, 2. Breast milk and the world protein gap.

—— (1969*a*). *Amer. J. clin. Nutr.* **22**, 1159. Letter to editor.

—— (1969*b*). *J. Pediat.* **74**, 808. The secotrant — a possible new age category in early childhood?

—— (1970). Diarrhoeal disease of early childhood. In *Alimentary and haematological aspects of tropical disease* (ed. A. Woodruff). Edward Arnold, London.

—— (1971*a*). *Food Technol.* **25**, 55. Commerciogenic malnutrition?

—— (1971*b*). *J. trop. Pediat. env. Chld Hlth* **17**, 171. Approaches to village-level infant feeding. VI The essential characteristics of weaning foods.

—— (1972*a*). *Lancet* **ii**, 760. Intolerance to lactose in mother's milk?

—— (1972*b*). *Nutr. Rev.* **30**, 199. Commerciogenic malnutrition? Time for a dialogue.

—— (1972*c*). *World Rev. Nutr. Diet.* **16**, 1. Nutrition in early childhood.

—— (1974*a*). 'Human milk: unique gift of love and world resource.' Address to La Leche League Convention, Chicago, July 1974.

—— (1974*b*). *Medicine in the tropics* (ed. A. Woodruff), Chapter 27: Protein–calorie malnutrition of early childhood. Churchill Livingstone, London.

—— (1975). *J. trop. Pediat. env. Chld Hlth* **21**, 267. Nutrition and economics in the modern world.

—— (1976*a*). *Amer. J. clin. Nutr.* **29**, 1227. World trends in infant feeding.

—— (1976*b*). Community and socio-political considerations of breast feeding. In *Breast feeding and the mother.* Ciba Foundation Symposium No. 45. Elsevier, Amsterdam.

—— (1976*c*). *New York Times* 23 Jun. Letter to Editor: Food for infants — a wrong emphasis.

—— and BENNETT, F. J. (1962). *Clin. Obstet. Gynec.* **5**, 64. World wide care of the newborn.

—— and —— (1972). *J. trop. Pediat. env. Chld Hlth* **18**, 25. Monograph No. 19. Aspects of child rearing in Africa.

——, ——, JELLIFFE, E. F. P., and WHITE, R. H. R. (1964). *Arch. env. Hlth* **9**, 25. The ecology of childhood disease among the Karamojong of Uganda.

—— and BLACKMAN, V. (1967). *J. Pediat.* **61**, 774. Bahima disease.

——, GURNEY, M., and JELLIFFE, E. F. P. (1975). Unsupplemented human milk as the sole food of the exterogestate fetus. *Proceedings of the IXth International Nutrition Congress*, Mexico City, Vol. 2, p. 77. August 1972.

——, IFEKWUNIGWE, A. E., and JELLIFFE, E. F. P. (1975). *Ecol. Food Nutr.* **4**, 53. Recommended dietary allowances for infants.

——, ——, and —— (1976). *Breast feeding and weaning foods: an annotated bibliography of recent publications*. USAID. (In press)

—— and JELLIFFE, E. F. P. (1970a). *J. Amer. diet. Ass.* **57**, 114. The urban avalanche.

—— and —— (1970b). *J. Pediat.* **77**, 895. The children's ward as a lethal factor?

—— and —— (ed.) (1971a). *Amer. J. clin. Nutr.* **24**, 968. The uniqueness of human milk.

—— and —— (1971b). The effects of starvation on the function of the family and society. In *Nutrition and relief operations in times of disaster*, p. 54.

—— and —— (1971c). *J. trop. Pediat.* **18**, 62. How breast feeding really works.

—— and —— (1972a). *Pediatrics* **50**, 169. Non-puerperal induced lactation.

—— and —— (1972b). *J. Pediat.* **81**, 829. Lactation, conception, and the nutrition of the nursing mother and child.

—— and —— (ed.) (1972c). *Amer. J. clin. Nutr.* **25**, 595. Nutrition programs for pre-school children.

—— and —— (1973a). *J. trop. Pediat. env. Chld Hlth* **19**, 258. The role of the midwife in child nutrition.

—— and —— (1973b). *Ecol. Food Nutr.* **2**, 127. Education of the public for successful lactation.

—— and —— (1973c). *J. Pediat.* **83**, 893. Pacifist factors in human milk?

—— and —— (1973d). Stereotyped hospital wards and child nutrition. In *Nutrition programs for pre-school children* (ed. D. B. Jelliffe and E. F. P. Jelliffe). p. 46. Institute of Public Health, Zagreb, Yugoslavia.

—— and —— (1974). *J. Pediat.* **84**, 462. *Doulas*, confidence and the science of lactation.

—— and —— (1975a). *Science (N.Y.)* **183**, 557. Human milk, nutrition and the world resource crisis.

—— and —— (1975b). *J. trop. Pediat. env. Chld Hlth* **21**, 123. Monograph No. 41. Fat babies: prevalence, perils and prevention.

—— and —— (1975c). Inter-relations of lactation, conception and the nutrition of the nursing couple. *Proceedings of the IXth International Nutrition Congress*, Mexico City, August 1972.

—— and —— (1975d). Cultural interaction and young child nutrition. Towards a curvilinear compromise? In *Nutrition and agricultural development* (ed. N. S. Scrimshaw and M. Behar). Plenum Press, New York.

—— and —— (1975e). *Lancet* **i**, 752. Duration of breast feeding.

—— and —— (1976a). *Lancet*. Cost of breast feeding. (In press)

—— and —— (1976b). *Lancet*. Breast feeding and maternal nutrition. (In press)

—— and —— (1976c). Early child nutrition. (a) Breast feeding. In *Nutrition and development* (ed. M. Winick). Plenum Press, New York. (In press)

—— and —— (1976*d*). *J. trop. Pediat. env. Chld Hlth* **22**, 203. Obstetric delivery tomorrow: towards a curvi-linear compromise?

—— and —— (1976*e*). *Lancet* **ii**, 635. Breast is best.

—— and —— (1976*f*). *Postgrad. Med.* **60**, 153. Nutrition and human milk.

—— and —— (1976*g*). *Ecol. Nutr.* **5**, 249. Adaptive suckling.

——, D. B. and J. ——, E. F. P. (1978). *Amer. J. Clin. Nutr.* **31**, 492. The volume and composition of human milk, its special relation to poorly nourished communities.

——, ——, GARCIA, L., and DE BARRIOS, G. (1961). *J. Pediat.* **59**, 27. The children of the San Blas Indians of Panama.

—— and MADDOCKS, I. (1964). *Clin. Pediat.* **3**, 432. Ecologic malnutrition in the New Guinea Highlands.

——, SYMONDS, B. E. R., and JELLIFFE, E. F. P. (1960). *J. Pediat.* **57**, 922. The pattern of malnutrition in Southern Trinidad.

——, WOODBURN, J., BENNETT, F. J., and JELLIFFE, E. F. P. (1962). *J. Pediat.* **50**, 907. The children of the Hadza hunters.

JELLIFFE, E. F. P. (1971*a*). *J. trop. Pediat. env. Chld Hlth* **17**, 135. Monograph No. 16. A new look at weaning multimixes for the Caribbean.

—— (1971*b*). *West Ind. med. J.* **20**, 3. Nutrition education in the maternity ward.

—— (1974). *J. trop. Pediat. env. Chld Hlth* **20**, 149. Nutrition in nursing curricula: Historical perspectives and present-day trends.

—— (1975*a*). In *The changing pattern of malnutrition in the Third World. Priorities in child nutrition* (ed. J. Mayer), Vol. III, p. 40, UNICEF, New York.

—— (1975*b*). The impact of the food industry on the nutritional status of infants and preschool children in developing countries. In *Priorities in Child Nutrition*, (ed. J. Mayer), Vol. II, p. 253. UNICEF, New York.

—— (1975*c*). *Protein-calorie malnutrition of early childhood: two decades of malnutrition. A bibliography*. Commonwealth Bureau of Nutrition, Aberdeen, Scotland.

—— (1975*d*). *J. trop. Pediat. env. Chld Hlth* **21**, 94. Recent trends in infant carrying.

—— (1976*a*). *J. trop. Pediat. env. Chld Hlth*. Further analysis of nutrition education. (In press)

—— (1976*b*). *J. trop. Pediat. env. Chld Hlth* **21**, 280. Introducing breast feeding into modern health services.

—— (1976*c*). Maternal nutrition and lactation. In *Breast feeding and the mother*. Ciba Foundation Symposium No. 45. Elsevier, Amsterdam.

—— and JELLIFFE, D. B. (1964). *Clin. Pediat.* **3**, 604. Children in ancient Polynesian Hawaii.

JENNESS, R. (1974). The composition of milk. In *Lactation. A comprehensive treatise*, Vol. III, p. 3. Eds. B. Larson and V. R. Smith. Academic Press, New York.

JEPSON, M. E., SMITH, B. A. M., PURSALL, E. W., and EMERY, J. L. (1976). *Lancet* **iii**, 426. Breast-feeding in Sheffield.

JOHN, T. J., DEVARAJAN, L. V., LUTHER, L., and VIJAYATHAN, P. (1976). *Pediatrics* **57**, 47. The effect of breast feeding on seroresponse of infants to oral polio virus vaccination.

JOHNSON, J. D. (1976). Infant feeding and feeding methods. In *Iatrogenic problems in neonatal intensive care*. 69th Ross Conference on Pediatric Research. Columbus, Ohio.

JOHNSON, E. J., GOYEA, H. S., OMAGHOMI, E., OGEBEIDE, M. I. (1975). Breast milk intake of infants in Benin City, Nigeria.

JOHNSON, M. L., BURKE, B. S., and MAYER, J. (1956). *Amer. J. clin. Nutr.* **4**, 231. The prevalence and incidence of obesity in a cross-section of elementary school children.

JOHNSON, P. and SALISBURY, D. M. (1975). Breathing and sucking during feeding in the newborn. In *Parent–infant interaction*, p. 119. Ciba Foundation Symposium. Elsevier, Amsterdam.

JOHNSTON, E. M. (1975). Maternal and infant nutrition. Attitudes and practices of physicians in British Columbia. Ph.D. Thesis, University of British Columbia.

JOHNSTONE, J. M. and LAWAY, H. S. (1966). *Brit. med. J.* **i**, 706. Role of infection in cot deaths.

JOHONNOTT, S. (1973). *Clin. Pediat.* **12**, 415. Differences in chronic otitis media between rural and urban Eskimo children.

JOLLY, E. (1975). *Nursing mothers' association of Australia. Newsletter*. Aug. p. 2. Editorial: Mothers of a changing world.

JORDAN-MARSH, M. (1976). Role of educational systems in community lactation programs. Unpublished.

JOSIMOVICH, J. B., REYNOLDS, M., and COBO, E. (ed.) (1974). *Lactogenic hormones, fetal nutrition and lactation*. John Wiley, New York.

KADER, M. M. A. and KAMAL, I. (1969). *Amer. J. Obstet. Gynec.* **105**, 978. Clinical, biochemical and experimental studies on lactation. III. Biochemical changes induced in milk by gestagens.

KAGAN, B. M., STANINCOVA, V., FELIX, N. S., HODGMAN, J., and KALMAN, D. (1972). *Amer. J. clin. Nutr.* **25**, 1153. Body compositon of premature infants: relation to nutrition.

KAKKAR, B. (1976). The impact formula food companies in infant health: answering the question 'so what?'. Unpublished.

KAMAL, I., HEFNAWI, F., GHONEIM, M., TALAAT, M., YOUNIS, N., TAGUI, A., and ABDALLA, M. (1969). *Amer. J. Obstet. Gynec.* **105**, 324. Clinical, biochemical and experimental studies on lactation.

KANAANEH, H. (1972). *J. trop. Pediat. env. Chld Hlth* **18**, 302. The relationship of bottle feeding to malnutrition and gastro-enteritis in a pre-industrial setting.

KAPLAN, G. J., FLESHMAN, J. K., BENDER, T. R., BAUM, C., and CLARK, P. S. (1973). *Pediatrics* **52**, 577. The long-term effect of otitis media. A ten year cohort study of Alaskan Eskimo children.

KARLE, S. (1972). Personal communication.

KARMARKAR, M. G., RAJALAKSHINI, R., and RAMAKRISHNAN, C. V. (1963). *Acta paediat. (Uppsala)* **52**, 473. Studies on human lactation: 1. Effect of dietary protein and fat supplementation on protein, fat, and essential amino acid contents of breast milk.

KASS, E. H. (1971). *J. infect. Dis.* **123**, 110. Infectious diseases and social change.

KATZ, A. H. and BENDER, E. I. (1976). *The strength in us: self-help groups in the modern world*. New Viewpoints, New York.

KATZ, M. and PLOTKIN, S. A. (1968). *J. Pediat.* **73**, 267. Oral polio immunization of the newborn infant; a possible method for overcoming interference by ingested antibodies.

KAUFMAN, C. (1973). Mother-infant separation in monkeys. In *American Associa-*

tion for the Advancement of Science Symposium on 'Separation and Depression', p. 33. Washington, D. C.

KAZDA, S. (1970). The relationship between the suckling period and later development in man. In *The post-natal development of the phenotype*. Butterworths, London.

KEE, T. S. (1975). *Med. J. Malaysia* **30**, 175. Breast-feeding in a rural area in Malaysia.

KEEN, J. H. (1969). *Arch. Dis. Childh.* **44**, 356. Significance of hypocalcaemia in neonatal convulsion.

KELSEY, J. C. (1975). *Lancet* **i**, 455. Hygiene of babies' incubators.

KENNELL, J. H. and Klaus, M. H. (1971). *Clin. Obstet. Gynec.* **14**, 926. Care of the mother of the high risk infant.

——, ——, SOSA, R., and URRUTIA, J. (1976). *Ped. Res.* **10**, 426. Early neonatal contact: effect on growth, breast-feeding and infection in the first year of life.

——, TRAUSE, M. A., and KLAUS, M. H. (1975). Evidence for a sensitive period in the human mother. In *Parent–infant interaction*. Ciba Foundation Symposium No. 933. Elsevier, Amsterdam.

KENNY, J. F., BOESMAN, M. I., and MICHAELS, R. H. (1967). *Pediatrics* **39**, 202. Bacterial and viral coproantibodies in breast fed infants.

KERPEL-FRONIUS, E. (1972). Quoted by Vahlquist (1975).

KHANJANASTHITI, P. and WRAY, J. (1974). *J. med. Ass. Thailand.* **57**, 468. Early protein–calorie malnutrition (PCM) in slum areas of Bangkok Municipality, 1970–71.

KILDEBERG, P. and WINTERS, R. (1972). *Pediatrics* **49**, 801. Infant feeding and blood acid–base status.

KIMMANCE, K. J. (1972). *J. trop. Pediat. env. Chld Hlth* **18**, 313. Failure to thrive and lactation in Jordanian villages in 1970.

KING, F. (1972). *Lancet* **ii**, 335. Intolerance to lactose in mother's milk.

KING, J. and NEWTON, R. S. (1852). *The eclectic dispensatory of the United States of America*. H. W. Derby, Cincinati.

KING, M. (1975). *The child in the health centre: a component of a child health package* (English Experimental Edition). Lembega Kesehatan Nasional, Jalan Inderpura. Surabaya, Indonesia.

—— (1975). *Pediatrica Indonesiana* **15**, 69. Why package child care?

——, KING, F. M. A., MORLEY, D. C., BURGESS, H. J. L., and BURGESS, A. (1972). *Nutrition for developing countries*. Oxford University Press, Nairobi and London.

KINGSTON, M. E. (1973*a*). *J. Pediat.* **82**, 1073. Biochemical disturbances in breast-fed infants with gastroenteritis.

—— (1973*b*). *J. trop. Pediat. env. Chld Hlth* **19**, 168. Continued breast feeding and concentrated diarrhoea formula in the outpatient treatment of gastroenteritis.

KIPPLEY, S. A. (1974). *Breast feeding and natural child spacing. The ecology of natural mothering*. Penguin Books, New York.

—— and KIPPLEY, J. F. (1972). *J. Obstet. Gyn. Nursing* **1**, 15. The relation between breast feeding and amenorrhea: report of a survey.

—— and —— (1974). Breast feeding and natural child spacing. Harper and Row, New York.

KIRKSEY, A. and WEST, K. D. (1975). Relationship between vitamin B_6 intake and the content in human milk. *Proceedings of the Xth International Congress of*

Nutrition, Kyoto, Japan, August 1975.

KLACKENBERG, G. and KLACKENBERG-LARSON, I. (1968). *Acta Paediat. (Uppsala).* Supplement **187**, 94. The development of children in a Swedish urban community: a prospective longitudinal study.

KLAUS, M. (1975). Personal communication.

——, JERAULD, R., KREGER, W., McALPINE, W., STEFFA, M., and KENNELL, J. (1972). *New Engl. J. Med.* **286**, 460. Maternal attachment: importance of the first post-partum days.

—— and KENNELL, J. H. (1970). *Pediat. Clins N. Amer.* **17**, 105. Mothers separated from their infants.

—— and —— (1976). Parent-to-infant interaction. In *The family –can it be saved?* (ed. V. C. Vaughan and T. B. Brazleton). Year Book Medical Publications, Chicago.

——, ——, PLUMB, N., and ZUEHLKE, S. (1970). *Pediatrics* **46**, 187. Human maternal behaviour at the first contact with her young.

——, TRAUSE, M. A., and KENNELL, J. H. (1975). Human maternal behaviour following delivery. Is this species-specific? In *Parent–infant interaction*, P. 69 Ciba Foundation Symposium. Elsevier, Amsterdam.

KLEBE, J. G. and INGOMAR, C. J. (1974). *Acta Paediat. (Uppsala)* **63**, 65. The influence of the method of delivery and the clamping technique on the red cell volume in infants of diabetic and non-diabetic mothers.

KLEINBERG, D. L. (1975). *Science (N.Y.)* **190**, 278. Human alpha-lactalbumin: measurement in serum and in breast cancer organ cultures by radioimmunoassay.

KLEVAY, L. M. (1974). The ratio of zinc to copper in milk and mortality due to coronary artery disease. An association. In *Trace substances in environmental health* (ed. D. D. Hemphill), Vol. VIII, University of Missouri, Columbia."

KNITTLE, J. L. (1972). *J. Pediat.* **81**, 1048. Obesity in childhood: a problem in adipose tissue cellular development.

KNODEL, J. (1968). *Population Studies* **22**, 297. Infant mortality and fertility in three Bavarian villages: an analysis of family histories from the 19th century.

—— and VAN DE WALLE, E. (1967). *Population Studies* **21**, 109. Breast feeding, fertility, and infant mortality: an analysis of some early German data.

KNOWLES, J. A. (1965). *J. Pediat.* **66**, 1068. Excretion of drugs in milk: a review.

KNUTSSON, K. E., and MELLBIN, T. (1969). *J. trop. Pediat.* **15**, 40. Breast-feeding habits and cultural context: a study of three Ethiopian communities.

KOLODNY, R. C., JACOBS, L. S., and DAUGHADAY, W. H. (1972). *Nature (London.)* **238**, 284. Mammary stimulation causes prolactin secretion in non-lactating women.

KOLTPYN, A., LANGOVAL, N., and VLASOV, V. (1953). *Children's diseases.* Foreign Languages Publishing House, Moscow.

KON, S. K. (1972). *Milk and milk products in human nutrition* (second edition). FAO Nutritional Studies No. 27. Food and Agriculture Organization, Rome.

—— and COWIE, A. T. (ed.) (1961). *Milk: the mammary gland and its secretion*, Vols I and II. Academic Press, New York and London.

—— and MAWSON, E. H. (1960). *Spec. Rep. Ser. med. Res. Coun. (Lond.)* **219**. Human milk.

KORA, J. S. (1969). *Fertil. Steril.* **20**, 419. Effects of oral contraceptives on lactation.

KOTZMANOVA, J. (1974). *Courrier* **24**, 464. The care of children of working parents.

Trends in some countries. II. Czechoslovakia.

KRAMER, L. I. and PIERPOINT, M. E. (1976). *J. Pediat.* **88**, 297. Rocking waterbeds and auditory stimuli to enhance growth of preterm infants.

KRETCHMER, N., ROSSI, E., and SERENI, F. (1975). *Modern problems in paediatrics*, Vol. 15. Milk and Lactation. Karger, Basel.

KROGER, M. (1972). *J. Pediat.* **80**, 401. Insecticide residues in human milk.

KROLL, R. G. and STONE, J. H. (1967). *J. Dent. Child.* **4**, 45. Nocturnal bottle-feeding as a contributory cause of rampant dental caries in the infant and young child.

KRON, R. E., STEIN, M., and GODDARD, K. E. (1966). *Pediatrics* **37**, 1012. Newborn suckling behaviour affected by obstetric sedation.

——, SMITH, M., PHOENIX, M. D., and FINNEGAN, L. P. (1976). *J. Pediat.* **88**, 637. Neonatal narcotic abstinence.

KROSTITZ, W. (1974). *International dairy situation and outlook.* Food and Agriculture Organization Document DDI: G/74/42. Rome.

KRZYWICKI, L. (1934). *Primitive society and its vital statistics.* Longman, London.

KUITUNEN, P., RAPOLA, J., SAVILAHTI, E., and VISAKORPI, J. K. (1973). *Acta Paediat. (Uppsala).* **62**, 585. Response of the jejunal mucosa to cow's milk in the malabsorption syndrome with cow's milk intolerance.

KULLBERG, R. W. and HANSEN, F. S. (1963). *Med. Times* **91**, 621. The family physician should share in dental care.

KURATANI, H. (1966). *Acta Paediat. jap.* **8**, 55. Vitamin E content of milk and serum in children.

LADAS, A. K. (1970*a*). The relationship of information and support to behavior: the La Leche League and breast-feeding. Doctor of Education Dissertation, Columbia University.

—— (1970*b*). *Clin. Pediat.* **9**, 702. How to help mothers breastfeed: deductions from a survey.

—— (1972). *J. trop. Pediat. env. Chld Hlth* **18**, 317. Monograph No. 25. Breast-feeding: the less available option.

LA LECHE LEAGUE (1958). *The womanly art of breast feeding.* Interstate Publishers, Franklin Park, Illinois.

LAMM, S. H., COLE, B., GLYNN, K., and ULLMAN, W. (1973). *New Engl. med. J.* **289**, 574. Lead content of milks fed to infants 1971–2.

—— and ROSEN, J. F. (1974). *Pediatrics* **53**, 137. Lead contamination of milk-fed infants.

The Lancet (1961). **ii**, 813. Fact and fiction in infant rearing.

—— (1971). **i**, 25. Progestagen-only contraception.

—— (1972*a*). **ii**, 1129. Prolactin and breast cancer.

—— (1972*b*). **iv**, 1349. Nutrition and the developing brain.

—— (1974*a*). **ii**, 719. War on baby foods.

—— (1974*b*). **iii**, 462. Haemophilus influenzae infections.

—— (1974*c*). **iv**, 1183. A time to be born.

—— (1975*a*). **i**, 257. Rotaviruses of man and animals.

—— (1975*b*). **iii**, 122. The tobacco act.

—— (1975*c*). **iii**, 316. Immoral earnings.

—— (1975*d*). **iii**, 351. Zinc in human medicine.

—— (1975*e*). **iv**, 1024. Cot death.

—— (1976). **iii**, 407. Lactation, fertility, and contraception.

LARGUIA, A. M., URMAN, J., and CERIANI, J. M. (1974). *Arch. Pediat. Argent.* **72**, 109. Imunidad local en el recien nacido. Primer experiencia con la administracion de colostro humano a recien nacidos pretermino.

——, ——, STOLIAR, O. A., CERIANI, J. M., O'DONNELL, A., BUSCAGLIA, J. C., and MARTINEZ, J. C. (1977). *J. trop. Pediat. env. Chld. Hlth.* Fresh human colostrum for the prevention of *E. coli* diarrhoea. (In press).

LARSON, B. L. and SMITH, V. R. (ed.) (1974). *Lactation: a comprehensive treatise*, Vols I, II, and III. Academic Press, New York.

LATHAM, M. C. (1972). 'The effects of lactation on human fertility.' Paper prepared for the Sub-committee on Nutrition and Fertility, Committee on International Nutrition Programs, National Academy of Sciences, Washington, D.C.

LAWICK-GOODALL, J. VAN (1968). *Anim. behav.* (Monograph) **1**, 161.

LAUPUS, W. E. (1975). Feeding of infants, p. 162. In *Nelson's Textbook of pediatrics* (ed. V. C. Vaughan and R. J. McKay). Saunders, Philadelphia.

LAWRIE, R. A. (1970). *Proteins as human food*. Avi Publications, Westport, Connecticut.

LAWS, C. H. and SKELLEY, E. G. (1938*a*). *Amer. J. Nursing* **38**, 862. A maternal milk laboratory.

—— and —— (1938*b*). *Amer. J. Nursing* **38**, 1003. Preserving maternal milk.

—— and —— (1939). *Amer. J. Nursing* **39**, 381. Manual expression of mother's milk.

LEALMAN, G. T., LOGAN, R. W., HUTCHINSON, J. H., KERN, M. M., FULTON, A. M., and BROWN, C. A. (1976). *Arch. Dis. Childh.* **51**, 377. Calcium phosphorus and magnesium concentrations in plasma during the first week of life and their relation to type of milk feed.

LEBOYER, F. (1975). *Birth without violence*. Knopf, New York.

LECCE, J. G. and MORGAN, D. O. (1962). *J. Nutrit.* **78**, 263. Effect of dietary regimen on cessation of intestinal absorption of large molecules (closure) in the neonatal pig and lamb.

LECHTIG, A., YARBROUGH, L. C., DELGADO, H., HABICHT, J-P., MARTORELL, R., and KLEIN, R. E. (1975). *Amer. J. clin. Nutr.* **28**, 1223. Influence of maternal nutrition on birth weight.

LEDOGAR, R. J. (1975). *Hungry for profits*. IDOC, New York.

LEE, J. A. H. and WEATHERALL, A. F. (1975). *Lancet* **ii**, 713. Incidence of breast cancer.

LEE, K. H. (1975). Promotion of breastfeeding: a persuasive communication approach. (In press)

LEIFER, A., LEIDERMAN, P., and BARNETT, C. (1970). *Child. Develop.* Mother-infant interaction: effects on later maternal behavior.

LEMARQUAND, J. P., MC, M. C. F., and TRUSWELL, A. S. (1974), *Brit. J. Nutr.* **33**, 111A. The vitamin E content of selected infant milk formulas.

LENGEMANN, F. W. (1959). *J. Nutr.* **69**, 23. The site of action of lactose in the enhancement of calcium utilization.

LE PAGE, G. A. (1971). *Cancer Bull.* **23**, 118. Possible viral etiology of breast cancer.

LEVIN, L., KATZ, A. H., and HOLST, E. (1976). *Self care*. Neville Watson Academic Publication Inc., New York.

LEVIN, S. S. (1962). *Med. Proc.* Mar. p. 114. Babyfood ballyhoo: some thoughts on infant feeding.

—— (1963). *A philosophy of infant feeding*. Charles. C. Thomas, Springfield, Illinois.

LEWIS, M. and ROSENBLUM, L. (ed.) (1974). The effect of the infant on its caretaker. John Wiley, New York.

L'HERMITE, M., VEKEMANS, M., DELVOYE, P., NOKIN, J., and ROBYN, C. (1973). *Proc. roy. Soc. Med.* **33**, 864. Prolactin studies in normal subjects.

LIEBIG, J. VON (1867). *Food for infants: a complete substitute for that provided by nature* (second English edition). J. Walton, London.

LIEBRICH, V. A. and MORLEY, D. (1976). *J. trop. Pediat. env.* **22**, 31 *Chld. Hlth.* Attitudes towards breast feeding.

LIGHT, I. J., SUTHERLAND, J. M. and BERRY, H. K. (1973). *Amer. J. Dis. Child.* **125**, 423. Clinical significance of tyrosinemia of prematurity.

LILIBRIDGE, C. B. and TOWNES, P. L. (1973). *J. Pediat.* **82**, 279. Physiologic deficiency and pancreatic amylase in infancy: a factor in iatrogenic diarrhea.

LILIENTHAL, C. M. and LANG, L. P. (1971). *Med. J. Austral.* **2**, 821. The disputed value of fluoride given during pregnancy.

LINNEMAN, C. C. and GOLDBERG, S. (1974). *Lancet* ii, 155. HBAg in breast milk.

LIND, J. and JADERLING, J. (1964). *Acta paediat. (Uppsala)* Supplement 159. The influence of 'rooming-in' on breast feeding.

——, VUORENKOSKI, V., and WASZ-HOCKERT, O. (1971). *Psychosomatic medicine in obstetrics and gynaecology. Third International Congress*, London, p. 293. The effect of cry stimulus on the temperature of the lactating breasts of primipara: a thermographic study.

LINDBLAD, B. S., LJUNGQUIST, A., GEBRE MEHDIN, M., and RAHIMTOOLA, R. J. (1977). The composition and yield of human milk in developing countries. In: *Food and Immunology*, p. 125. Eds. L. Hambraeus, L. Hanson, and H. Macfarlane. Almquist and Wiksell, Stockholm.

—— and RAHIMTOOLA, R. J. (1974). *Acta paediat. (Uppsala)* **63**, 125. A pilot study of the quality of human milk in a lower socio-economic group in Karachi, Pakistan.

LINZELL, J. L. (1971). Techniques for measuring nutrient uptake by the mammary glands. In *Lactation* (ed. I. R. Falconer). Butterworths, London.

LIU, H-Y, TSAO, M. V., and MOORE, B. (1968). *Gastroenterology* **54**, 27. Bovine milk protein induced intestinal malabsorption of fat and lactose in infants.

LLOYD, J. K., WOLFF, O. H., and Whelen, W. S. (1961). *Brit. med. J.* ii, 145. Childhood obesity: a long term study of height and weight.

LOMAX, E. R. (1972). Advances in pediatrics and infant care in nineteenth century England. PhD. Thesis, University of California, Los Angeles.

LÖNNERDAL, B., FORSUM, E., and HAMBRAEUS, L. (1975). *Proceedings of the Swedish Nutrition Foundation Symposium on 'Food and Immunology'*. The protein content of human milk. II. A longitudinal study of Swedish normal material.

——, ——, and —— (1975). The protein content of human milk. *Proceedings of the Xth International Congress of Nutrition*, Kyoto, Japan, August 1975.

——, ——, and —— (1976). *Amer. J. clin. Nutr.* **29**, 1127. A longitudinal study of the protein, nitrogen, and lactose contents of human milk from Swedish well-nourished mothers.

——, ——, GEBRE-MEHDIN, M., and HAMBRAEUS, L. (1976). *Amer. J. Clin. Nutr.* **29**, 1127. The protein content of human milk. III. Breast milk composition in

Ethiopian and Swedish mothers.

——, ——, ——, and —— (1976). *Amer. J. clin. Nutr.* **29**, 1134. Breast-milk composition in Ethiopian and Swedish mothers. II. Lactose, nitrogen, and protein contents.

LOWE, C. V. (1972). *Amer. J. clin. Nutr.* **25**, 245. Research in infant nutrition: the untapped well.

——, COURSIN, D. B., FILER, L. J., HEALD, F. P., HOLLIDAY, M. A., O'BRIEN, D., OWEN, G. M., PEARSON, H. A., and SERIVER, C. R. (1969). *Pediatrics* **43**, 134. Iron balance and requirements in infancy.

LUTZ, P. and PLATT, B. S. (1958). *Proc. Nutr. Soc.* **17**, iii. The amount and distribution of the nitrogenous components of British, Indian and African mothers, with special reference to the curd-whey protein ratio.

LYNCH, H. T., HARRIS, R. E., GUINGIS, H. A., LYNCH, P., MALONEY, K., RANKIN, L., and LYNCH, J. (1976). *Lancet* **ii**, 627. Early age of onset and familial breast cancer.

LYNCH, M. A. (1975). *Lancet* **ii**, 317. Ill-health and child abuse.

LYNCH, W. D. and SURVALY, W. D. (1951). *J. Indiana med. Ass* **44**, 1. Modified infant feeding: a simplified approach.

MACFARLANE, A. (1975). Olfaction in the development of social preferences in the human neonate. In *Parent–infant interaction*. Ciba Foundation Symposium No. 33. Elsevier, Amsterdam.

MACKAY, H. M. M. (428). *Arch. Dis. Childh.* **3**, 1175. Anaemia in infancy: its prevalence and prevention.

MACKEITH, R. (1969). *Develop. Med. Child Neurol.* **11**, 277. Breast feed for the first two months.

MACKLIN, M. T. (1959). *J. nat. Cancer Inst.* **22**, 927. Comparison of the number of breast-cancer deaths observed in relatives of breast-cancer patients and the number expected on the basis of mortality rates.

MACMAHON, B., LIN, T. M., LOWE, C. R., MIRRA, A. P., RAVNIHAR, B., SALBER, E. J., TRICHOPOULOS, D., VALAORAS, V. G., and YUASA, S. (1970). *Bull. Wld Hlth Org.* **42**, 185. Lactation and cancer of the breast.

MACY, I. G. (1949). *Amer. J. Dis. Child.* **78**, 589. Composition of human colostrum and milk.

——, KELLY, H. J., and SLOAN, R. E. (1953). The composition of milks. National Academy of Science National Research Council, Publication No. 254. Washington, D.C.

MAHLER, H. (1975*a*). *Lancet* **iii**, 829. Health: the demystification of medical technology.

—— (1975*b*). *Wld Hlth* Aug./Sep., p. 3. A moral revolution.

MAJD, M. and LOPRESTI, J. M. (1972). *Amer. J. Roentgenol.* **116**, 575. Lactobezoar.

MALCOLM, L. A. (1970). *Growth and development in New Guinea: a study of the Bundi people of the Madang District.* Monograph No. 1. Institute of Human Biology, Madang.

MALVERN, J. (1976). *J. Human Nutr.* **30**, 253. The responsibility of the obstetrician in the establishment of breast feeding.

MAMUNES, P., PRINCE, P. E., THORNTON, N. H., HUNT, P. and HITCHCOCK, E. S. (1976). *Pediatrics* **57**, 675. Intellectual deficits after transient tyrosinemia in the term neonate.

MANOFF, R. K. (1972). *Proceedings of the Western Hemisphere Nutrition Congress* III, p. 155. The role of the communications specialists: the reach-and-frequency use of mass media.

——— (1975). *J. Nutr. Educat.* **7**, 139. Toward a new 'American Mentality'.

MARGULIES, L. (1975). *Christianity and crisis* **35**, 264. Baby formula abroad: exporting infant malnutrition.

MARIESKIND, H. (1973). *J. trop. Pediat. env. Chld Hlth* **19**, 123. Abnormal lactation.

MARSHALL, A. J. (1967). *Nature (Lond.)* **216**, 192. Original of delayed implantation in marsupials.

MARSHALL, B. R., HEPPER, J. K., and ZIMBEL, C. C. (1975). *J. Amer. med. Ass.* **233**, 1377. Sporadic puerperal mastitis. An infection which need not interrupt lactation.

MARSHALL, H. M. and KNAFL, K. (1974). Professionalizing motherhood: La Leche League and breast feeding. Annual Meeting of the American Sociological Association, New York City, August 1973.

MARTIN, M. C. (1975). *Natural family planning*. Human Life Foundation, Washington.

MARTINEZ, C. and CHAVEZ, A. (1971). *Nutr. Rep. Int.* **4**, 139. Nutrition and development in infants of poor rural areas. (1) Consumption of mother's milk by infants.

MASAWE, A. E. J., MUINDI, J. M., and SWAI, G. B. R. (1974). *Lancet* ii, 314. Infections in iron deficiency and other types of anaemia in the tropics.

MASON, W. A. and KENNEDY, M. D. (1974). *Science (N.Y.)* **183**, 1209. Redirection of filial attachments in Rhesus monkeys: dogs as mother surrogates.

MASTERS, W. H. and JOHNSON, V. E. (1966). *Human sexual response*. Little Brown, Boston.

MATA, L. J., FERNANDEZ, R., and URRUTIA, J. J. (1969). *Rev. lat.-amer Microbiol. Parasitol.* **11**, 103. Infeccion del intestino por bacterias enteropatogenas en ninos de una aldea de Guatemala, durante los tres anos de vida.

———, KRONMAL, R. A., GARCIA, B., BUTLER, W., URRUTIA, J. J., and MURILLO, S. (1976). Ciba Foundation No. 42. *Acute diarrhoea in childhood*, p. 311. Breast-feeding, weaning and the diarrhoeal syndrome in a Guatemalan Indian village.

——— and URRUTIA, J. J. (1971). *Ann N.Y. Acad. Sci.* **176**, 93. Intestinal colonization of breast fed children in a rural area of low socioeconomic level.

———, ———, and LECHTIG, A. (1971). *Amer. J. clin. Nutr.* **24**, 249. Infection and nutrition of children of a low socioeconomic rural community.

Maternal and Child Health Information (1973). New interest in home deliveries.

MATLAND, H. (1966). *J. trop. Pediat.* **3**, monograph 2, p. 27. The Ngora maternity annex.

MATSUMURA, T. (1972). *Breast feed your children*, Horiuchi Bunjiro, Tokyo.

———, KUROUME, T., OGURI, M., KOBAYASHI, K., KANBE, V., YAMADA, T., and MATSUMOTO, S. (1972). Demonstration of haemaglutinating antibody against food antigens in the amniotic fluid and cord blood. Personal communication.

MAY, J. (1963). *Postgrad. Med.* **33**, 380. Nutrition and lactation.

MAYER, G. (1966). *J. trop. Pediat.* **12**, 58. Undernutrition, prolonged lactation and female infertility.

MAYER, J. (1968). *Overweight: causes, costs and control*. Prentice Hall, New Jersey.

——— (1975). Priorities in child nutrition in developing countries: general recommendations to UNICEF and governments. Document E/ICEF/L. 1328. (Mimeo)

MAYNARD, J. E. (1969). *Alaska Med.* **11**, 93. Otitis media in Alaskan Eskimo children: an epidemiological review.

MCARTHUR, J. W., O'LOUGHLIN, K. M., BEITINS, I. Z., JOHNSON, L., HOURIHAN, J., and ALONSO, C. (1976). *Mayo clin. Proc.* **51**, 607. Endocrine studies during the refeeding of young women with nutritional amenorrhoea and infertility.

MCBRYDE, A. (1951). *J. Amer. med. Ass.* **145**, 625. Compulsory rooming-in on the ward and private newborn service at Duke Hospital.

MCCABE, M. and CHANG, C. T. (1971). *Lancet* i, 972. Human breast cancer virus and artificial feeding of babies.

MCCANCE, R. A. and WIDDOWSON, E. M. (1957). *Acta Paediat.* **46**, 337. Hypertonic expansion of the extracellular fluids.

MCCOLLUM, E. V. (1958). In *The nutritional ages of man.* Proceedings of the Borden Centennial on Nutrition. Borden Foundation, New York.

MCCRACKEN, R. D. (1971). *Curr. Anthropol.* **12**, 479. Lactase deficiency: an example of dietary evolution.

MCCULLACH, K. G. and WIDDOWSON, E. M. (1970). *Brit. J. Nutr.* **24**, 109. The milk of the African elephant.

MCGREGOR, S. A. and BACK, E. H. (1970). *Arch. Dis. Childh.* **45**, 504. Breastfeeding in Kingston, Jamaica.

MCKAY, H. M. M. (1931). *Spec. Rep. Ser. med. Res. Counc. (Lond.)* **151**, 36. Nutrition anemia in infancy, with special reference to iron deficiency anemia.

MCKENZIE, H. A. (ed.) (1970). *Milk proteins: chemical and molecular biology*, Vols I and II. Academic Press, New York.

MCKENZIE, S. A., SELLEY, J. A., and AGNEW, J. E. (1975). *Arch. Dis. Childh.* **50**, 894. Secretion of prednisolone into breast milk.

MCKEOWN, T. (1976). *The modern rise of population.* Edward Arnold, London.

——, BROWN, R. G., and RECORD, R. G. (1962). *Population Studies* **16**, 345. An interpretation of the modern rise of population in Europe.

MCKIGNEY, J. (1968). *J. trop. Pediat. env. Chld Hlth* **14**, 55. Economic aspects of infant feeding practices in the West Indies.

—— (1971). *Amer. J. clin. Nutr.* **24**, 1005. Economic aspects.

MCLAREN, D. S. (1966*a*). *J. trop. Pediat.* **12**, 50. An early account of infant feeding practices and malnutrition in East Africa.

—— (1966*b*). *Lancet* ii, 485. A fresh look at protein-calorie malnutrition.

—— and BURMAN, D. (ed.) 1976). *A textbook of paediatric nutrition.* Churchill Livingstone, Edinburgh.

MCLEOD, B. E. and ROBINSON, M. F. (1972). *Brit. J. Nutr.* **27**, 229. Dietary intake of manganese in New Zealand infants during the first year of life.

MCMILLAN, J. A., LANDAW, S. A., and OSKI, F. A. (1976). *Pediatrics.* **58**, 686. Iron sufficiency in breast fed infants and the availability of iron from human milk.

MCNEIL, C. (1942). *Brit. med. J.* ii, 271. An alphabet of breast feeding.

MCNEILLY, A. S. (1973). *Proc. roy. Soc. Med.* **33**, 863. Radioimmunoassay of human prolactin.

MEAD, M. (1957). *Int. J. Psychoanal.* **38**, 369. Changing patterns of parent–child relations in an urban culture.

—— (1970). *Manpower.* Jun., p. 11. Working mothers and their children.

—— and NEWTON, N. (1967). Cultural patterning of perinatal behavior. In *Child-*

bearing: Its Social and Psychological Aspects. Williams and Wilkins, Baltimore.

MEADOW, R. (1973). *Brit. med. J.* iv, 546. Personal view.

MEDAWAR, C. and HODGES, L. (1973). *Campaign* 22 Jun., p. 22. How the voluntary system fails.

Medical Journal of Australia (1976). **1**, 730. Nursing Mothers of Australia.

MELLANDER, O., VAHLQUIST, B., and MELLBIN, T. (1959). *Acta Paediat.* Supplement 116, p. 1. Breast feeding and artificial feeding: the Norbotten study.

MELLON, M., GORRIN, H., PRENNER, B., INCAUDO, G., BECHAMN, J., GIOSSI, S., ORGEL, H. A., and HAMBURGER, R. N. (1976). Paper presented at American Academy of Allergy Conference. Effects of environmental modification of atopic disease and IgE levels in infancy.

MENCHU, M. T., FLORES, M., LARA, M. Y. and BEHAR, M. (1972). *Archivos Socieda Latin americana Nutricion* **22**, 83. Lactancia y destete en el area rural de Centro America y Panama.

MENDELSOHN, R. S. (1964). *Child and family* Oct. Whom is the hospital for?

MENKES, J. K., WELCHER, D. W., LEVI, J. S., DALLAS, J., and GRATSBY, N. W. (1972). **49**, 218. Relation of elevated blood tyrosine to the ultimate intellectual performance of premature infants.

MEPHAM, B. (1976). *The secretion of milk*. Institute of Biology. Studies in Biology No. 60. Edward Arnold, London.

MERTON, P. T. (1975). Personal communication.

MEYER, H. F. (1958). *Pediatrics* **22**, 116. Breast feeding in the United States: extent and possible trend.

—— (1968). *Clin Pediat.* **7**, 708. Breast feeding in the United States.

MICKELSON, K. N., HAWKE, J. C., MORIARTY, K. M., NEWSTEAD, D. F., GRAY, I. K., RUMBALL, S. V., and THOMAS, I. (1975). Composition of human milk. *Proceedings of the Xth International Congress of Nutrition*, Kyoto, Japan, August 1975.

MIDDLETON, P. J., SZYMANSKI, M. T., ABBOT, B. D., BORTOLUSSI, R., and HAMILTON, J. R. (1974). *Lancet* i, 1241. Orbivirus acute gastroenteritis in infancy.

MIGASENA, P. (1975). Assessment of nutritional status in the lower Mekong Basin. *Proceedings of the Xth International Congress of Nutrition*, Kyoto, Japan, August 1975.

MILES, D. P. B. (1976). *Lancet* ii, 152. Breast-feeding.

MILL, P. J. (1972). *Proceedings of the Xth roy. Soc. Med.* **65**, 16. Acrodermatitis enteropathica with lactose intolerance.

MILLER, G. H. and HUGHES, L. R. (1970). *Obstet. Gynec.* **35**, 44. Lactation and genital involution effects of a new low dose oral contraceptive on breast feeding and their infants.

MILLER, R. W. and FRAUMENI, J. F. (1972). *Pediatrics* **49**, 645. Does breast-feeding increase the child's risk of breast cancer?

MILNER, R. D. G., DEODHAR, A. D., CHARD, C. R., and GRANT, R. M. (1975). *Arch. Dis. Childh.* **50**, 654. Fat absorption by small babies fed two filled milk formulae.

MINISTERS OF HEALTH OF THE COMMONWEALTH CARIBBEAN ANNUAL CONFERENCE (1973). Resolution No. 7. Strategy for overcoming gastro-enteritis and malnutrition.

MINTZ, M. (1976). *Washington Post*, 13 Sept. Industrial chemical PCB linked to liver cancer.

MITCHELL, S. C. (1973). *Amer. J. Cardiol.* **31**, 539. Symposium on prevention of atherosclerosis at the pediatric level.

MOBBS, E. J. (1973). *Med. J. Aust.* **2**, 339. Breast feeding, rooming-in, demand-feeding, and houses of correction.

—— and MOBBS, G. A. (1972). *Med. J. Aust.* **1**, 770. Breast feeding — success (or failure) due to attendants and not to prevailing fashion.

MOBBS, G. A. (1972). *Med. J. Aust.* **1**, 1163. Breast feeding and the working mother.

—— and BABBAGE, N. F. (1971). *Med. J. Aust.* **2**, 436. Breast feeding adopted children.

—— and MOBBS, E. J. (1972). *Med. J. Aust.* **1**, 829. Breast feeding and the boiling frog.

MOLLER, T. (1972). Quoted by Vahlquist (1975).

MONCKEBERG, F. (1968). *Cuad. Med.-Soc.* **9**, 5. Efecto de la nutricion en medio ambiente sobre el desarrollo psico-motor en el nino.

—— (1969). *Proceedings of the Western Hemisphere Nutrition Congress II*, San Juan, Puerto Rico, 1968. The effect of malnutriton and environment on mental health. American Medical Association, Chicago.

—— (1970). Factors conditioning malnutrition in Latin America with special reference to Chile. In *Malnutrition is a problem of ecology*, p. 23. Karger, Basel and New York.

MONCRIEFF, M. and FADAHUNSI, T. O. (1974). *Arch. Dis. Childh.* **49**, 810. Congenital rickets due to maternal vitamin D deficiency.

MONEY, D. F. L. (1970). *N.Z. med. J.* **71**, 32. Vitamin E and selenium deficiencies and their possible aetiological role in the sudden death in infants syndrome.

MONTAGU, A. (1971). *Touching: the human significance of the skin.* Columbia University Press, New York.

MONTREUIL, J. (1971). *Ann. Nutr. (Paris)* **25**, A.1. La maternisation des laits: etat actuel de la question.

—— and MULLET, S. (1959). *C.R. Soc. Biol.* **153**, 1364. Evolution de la constitution glucidique du lait de femme au cours de lactation.

MOODIE, P. M. (1973). *Aboriginal health.* Australian National University Press, Canberra.

MOORE, D. H., CHARNERY, J., KRAMARSKY, B., LASFARGUES, E. Y., SARKAR, N. H., BRENNAN, M. J., BURROWS, J. H., SIRSAT, S. M., PAYMASTER, J. C., and VAIDYA, A. B. (1971). *Nature (Lond.)* **229**, 611. Search for human breast cancer virus.

MOORE, G. M., RATTRAY, J. B. M., and IRVINE, D. M. (1968). *Can. J. Biochem.* **46**, 205. Composition of milk cephalins.

MORGAN, R. V., VAKIL, D. V., and CHIPMAN, M. L. (1974). *Amer. J. Epidemiol.* **99**, 117. Breast feeding, family history and breast disease.

MORLEY, D. (1973). *Paediatric priorities in the developing world.* Butterworths, London.

—— (1975). *J. trop. Pediat. env. Chld Hlth* **21**, 109. Hospital involvement in community health care.

——, BIDDULPH, J., and JELLIFFE, D. B. (1974). *J. trop. Pediat. env. Chld Hlth* **20**, 183. Editorial: Harmful advertising of infant foods.

—— and CUTTING, W. (1974). *Lancet* ii, 712. Charts to help with malnutrition and overpopulation problems.

MORRIS, N. F. (ed.) (1972). *Third International Congress on Psychosomatic Medicine in Obstetrics and Gynecology*. Karger, Basel and New York.

MORRISON, S. D. (1952). *Human milk: yield, proximate principles and inorganic constituents*. Technical Communication No. 18. Commonwealth Agricultural Bureau.

MOULINIER, J. (1953). *Sem. Hop. Paris* **29**, 448. Breast-feeding infants with hemolytic disease.

MOYNAHAN, E. J. (1974). *Lancet* ii, 399. Acrodermatitis enteropathica: a lethal inherited human zinc deficiency disorder.

MULLER, H. R. (1975). *Mod. Probl. Paediat.* **15**, 213. New quality criteria for infant formula-feeding.

MULLER, M. (1973). *New Scient.* **61**, 530. Milk, money, and marasmus.

—— (1974). *The baby killer*. War on Want, London.

—— (1975). *New Scient.* **63**, 528. Milk, money and the law.

—— (1975). *Guardian* (London) 7 Feb. Milking the poor.

MUMFORD, L. (1961). *The city in history*. Secker and Warberg, London.

MURDOCK, G. P. (1934). *Our primitive contemporaries*. Macmillan, New York.

MURILLO, G. J. and GOLDMAN, A. S. (1970). *Pediat. Res.* **4**, 71. The cells of human colostrum. II Synthesis of IgA and Beta Ig.

MURRAY, A. B. (1971). *Lancet* i, 497. Infant feeding and respiratory allergy.

MURROW, H. (1974). Personal communication.

MURTHY, G. K. and RHEA, U.S. (1954). *J. Dairy Sci.* **54**, 1001. Cadmium, copper, iron, lead, manganese and zinc in evaporated milk, infant products and human milk.

MUSOKE, L. K. (1961). *Arch. Dis. Childh.* **36**, 305. Analysis of admissions to the Pediatrics Department, Mulago Hospital, 1959.

NAGASAWA, T., KIYOSAWA, I., and TAKASE (1973). *J. Dairy Sci.* **56**, 1159. Lactoferr.n and serum albumin of human casein in colostrum and milk.

——, ——, FUKUWATARI, Y., KITAYAMA, T., UECHI, M., and HYODO, Y. (1973). *J. Dairy Sci.* **56**, 177. Alphalactalbumin and serum albumin in human milk.

NAHMIAS, A. J., ALFORD, C. A., and KORONES, S. B. (1970). *Advanc. Pediat.* **17**, 185. Infection of the newborn with *Herpes hominis*.

NAIDOO, S. (1974). *Courrier* **24**, 572. The care of children of working parents. II. Principal solutions. Combined solutions.

NAISMITH, D. G. (1971). *Proc. Nutr. Soc.* **30**, 93A. The role of body fat, accumulated during pregnancy and in lactation in the rat.

—— (1973). *Brit. J. Nutr.* **30**, 567. Kwashiorkor in Western Nigeria: a study of traditional weaning foods with particular reference to energy and linoleic acid.

—— and RITCHIE, C. D. (1975). *Brit. J. Nutr.* **32**, 116A. The effect of breast feeding and artificial feeding on body weights, skin-fold measurements and food intakes of forty-two primiparous women.

NAKAMURA, T., OGASAWARA, C., ARAI, A., and ARAI, M. (1975). *Proceedings of the Xth International Congress of Nutrition*, Kyoto, Japan, August 1975. Malnutrition among adolescent girls on a reducing diet.

NAMBOZE, J. M. (1967). *Trop. geogr. Med.* **19**, 154. Weaning practices in Buganda.

NATIONAL ACADEMY OF SCIENCES (1974). *Recommended dietary allowance* (eighth edition). Washington, D.C.

—— (1975). *Nutrition and fertility interrelationships*. National Research Council,

Washington, D.C.

NELSON, J. D. (1971), *J. Pediat.* **79**, 348. Prop the baby, not the bottle.

NELSON, H. (1974). *Los Angeles Times* 2 Dec., p. 24.

NEUMANN, C. G. and ALPAUGH, M. (1976). *Pediatrics* **57**, 469. Birth weight doubling: a new look.

—— and JELLIFFE, D. B. (editors) (1977). *Pediat. clin. N. Amer.* **24**, 1–272. Nutrition in pediatrics.

NEWELL, K. (ed.) (1975). *Health by the people*. World Health Organization, Geneva.

New Internationalist (1975). **8**, 1. Editorial: Campaign.

NEWMAN, G. (1906). *Infant mortality, a social problem*. E. P. Dutton, New York.

NEWSOM, L. J. and NEWSOM, E. (1962). *Brit. med. J.* ii, 1744. Breast feeding in decline.

NEWTON, D. B. (1966). *Med. J. Aust.* **2**, 801. Breast feeding in Victoria.

NEWTON, M. (1976). The effect of modern obstetric care on the family. In *The family – can it be saved?* (ed. V. C. Vaughan and T. B. Brazleton). Year Book Medical Publishers, Chicago.

—— and NEWTON, N. R. (1950). *Surg. Gynec. Obstet.* **91**, 651. Breast abscess. A result of lactation failure.

—— and —— (1968). *J. Pediat.* **33**, 698. The let-down reflex in human lactation.

NEWTON, N. (1953). *Maternal emotions*. Paul B., Hoeber, New York.

—— (1957). *The family book of child care*. Harper, New York.

—— (1968). *Psychol. Today* Jun., p. 34. Breast feeding.

—— (1969). *Child and Family*. Winter issue, p. 61. The importance of prenatal education.

—— (1972*a*). A woman's view on women's problems. In *Psychosomatic medicine in obstetrics and gynecology* (ed. N. Morris). S. Karger, Basel.

—— (1972*b*). Inter-relationships between various aspects of the female reproductive role. In *Psychosomatic medicine in obstetrics in gynecology* (ed. N. Morris). S. Karger, Basel.

—— (1973). *Contemporary sexual behavior: critical issues in the 1970's* (ed. J. Zubin and J. Money), p. 77, Chapter 5: Interrelationship between sexual responsiveness, birth, and breast feeding. Johns Hopkins Press, Baltimore.

—— (1976). Stability of the family in a transient society. In *The family – can it be saved?* (ed. V. C. Vaughan and T. B. Brazleton). Year Book Medical Publishers, Chicago.

—— and NEWTON, M. (1967). *New Engl. J. Med.* **277**, 1179. Psychologic aspects of lactation.

——, PEELER, D., and RAWLINS, C. (1968). *J. reprod. Med.* **1**, 257. The effect of lactation on maternal behavior in mice, with comparative data on humans.

——, ——, and ——. (1972). Does breast-feeding influence mother-love? In *Psychosomatic medicine in obstetrics and gynaecology* (ed. N. Morris). S. Karger, Basel.

NIEHOFF, A. and MEISTER, N. (1972). *J. trop. Pediat. env. Chld Hlth* **18**, 16. The cultural characteristics of breast-feeding: a survey.

NIMS, B., MACY, I. G., BROWN, M., and HUNSCHER, H. (1932). *Amer. J. Dis. Child.* **43**, 828. Human milk studies. IX Variations in the composition of milk at four hour intervals during the day and night.

——, ——, HUNSCHER, H., and BROWN, M. (1932). *Amer. J. Dis. Child.* **43**, 1062. Daily and monthly variations in milk components as observed in two successive lactation periods.

NISHIMURA, H. (1953). *J. Nutr.* **49**, 79. Zinc deficiency in suckling mice deprived of colostrum.

NIZEL, A. (1975). *Nutr. News* **38**, 1. 'Nursing-bottle syndrome': rampant dental caries in young children.

NOGUEIRA, D. M., BEREZIN, A., PEDROSO, F. I., and STRUFALDI, B. (1966). *O. Hospital* **70**, 91. Folic acid levels (PGA) in human colostrum and milk.

NORA, J. J. and Nora, A. H. (1973). *Pediat. Res.* **7**, 321. Oral contraceptives and birth defects.

NORDBERG, O., PHILLIPS, P., and STERKY, G. (1975). Action for Children: Towards an Optimum Child Care Package in Africa. *Proceedings of the Dag Hammarskjöld Seminar on the Dilemma of the Quality, Quantity and Cost in African Child Care,* Addis Ababa, May 14–19, 1973. Dag Hammarskjöld Foundation, Uppsala.

NURSING MOTHERS ASSOCIATION OF AUSTRALIA (1972). *Two for the price of one: care and breast feeding of twins.*

Nutrition Abstracts (1973). **43**, 3. Nutrition programs for pre-school children: Zagreb Guidelines.

OATES, R. K. (1973). *Brit. med. J.* ii, 762. Infant feeding practices.

OBGEIDE, M. I. and GOYEA, H. S. (1975). *J. trop. Pediat. env. Chld Hlth* **21**, 12. The unfavorable trend in infant feeding.

OBGEIDE, O. (1975a). *Proc. Nutr. Soc.* **35**, 26A. Dietary habits of lactating women and infant feeding practices in the Mid-West State of Nigeria.

—— (1975b). *Amer. J. clin. Nutr.* **28**, 88. Breast feeding in Mid-Western State of Nigeria.

O'BRIEN, P. (1974). *Discovering childbirth and the joy of breastfeeding.* Antipodean Publishers, Sydney.

O'BRIEN, T. E. (1974). *Amer. J. Hosp. Pharm.* **31**, 844. Excretion of drugs in human milk.

OGURI, M., IWASAKI, I., MATSUMURA, T., and KUROUME, T. (1971). *Jap. J. Allergy* **20**, 128. Studies on congenital sensitization. (3) Relationship between the incidence of eczema in breast fed neonates and anti-food antibody titers against various food in the amniotic fluid. (English abstract).

OLIVECRONA, T., BILLSTROM, A., FREDRICKZON, B., JOHNSON, O., and SENNELSON, G. (1973). *Acta Paediat.* (Uppsala) **65**, 520. Gastro lipolysis of human milk lipids in infants with pyloric stenosis.

OLSEN, E. (1949). *Studies on intestinal flora.* Einer Munksgaard, Copenhagen.

OLSON, M. (1970). *Pediatrics* **46**, 538. The benign effect on rabbits' lungs of the aspiration of water compared with 5 per cent glucose or milk.

OLSZYNA-MARZYS, A. E. (1975). *Proceedings of the IXth International Nutrition Congress.* Mexico City, 1972, Vol. 3, p. 283. Pesticide residues and their significance.

OMOLULU, A. (1972). *Children in the Tropics* **82**, 19. Breast feeding in Nigeria.

—— (1974). Information Packet for WHO Day. The importance of breast feeding. World Health Organization, Geneva.

—— (1975). Personal communication.

—— (1976). *J. trop. Pediat. env. Chld Hlth* **21**, 270. Significance of breast feeding in developing countries.

OOMEN, H. A. P. C. (1961). *J. trop. Pediat.* **6**, 103. The Papuan child as a survivor.

—— (1972). *Ecol. Food Nutr.* **1**, 3. Ecology of human nutrition in New Guinea.

—— and MALCOLM, S. H. (1958). Nutrition and the Papuan child. South Pacific Commission Technical Report No. 118.

OPPE, T. E. and REDSTONE, D. (1968). *Lancet* i, 1045. Calcium and phosphorus levels in healthy newborn infants given various types of milk.

ORBERNDORFER, L. and MEJIA, W. (1968). *J. trop. Pediat.* **14**, 27. Statistical analysis of the duration of breastfeeding: a study of 200 mothers of Antioquia Province, Colombia.

ORR, E. (1972). *The use of protein-rich foods for the relief of malnutrition in developing countries: an analysis of experience*. Tropical Products Institute, London.

OSBORN, G. R. (1967). *Colloques int. Cent. nat. Rech. Scient.* **169**, 93. Relationship of hypotension and infant feeding to the aetiology of coronary disease.

OSKI, F. A. and BARNESS, L. A. (1967). *J. Pediat.* **70**, 211. Vitamin E deficiency: previously unrecognized cause of hemolytic anemia in the premature infant.

OSORIO, A., ROSSELLO, J. L. D., and CAPURRO, H. (1975). *Bull. Panamer. Hlth Org.* **9**, 129. A rooming-in program for mothers and newborns.

OSTWALD, P. (1972). *Devel. Med. Child. Neurol.* **14**, 350. The sounds of infancy.

OUNSTED, M. and SLEIGHS, G. (1975). *Lancet* i, 1393. The infant's self regulation of food intake and weight gain.

OVERALL, J. C. (1970). *J. Pediat.* **76**, 499. Neonatal bacterial meningitis.

OWEN, G. M. (1969). *Amer. J. clin. Nutr.* **22**, 1150. Modification of cow's milk for infant formulas: current practices.

——, LUBIN, A. H., and GARRY, P. J. (1971). *J. Pediat.* **79**, 563. Pre-school children in the United States. Who has iron deficiency?

PACKARD, F. R. (1931). *History of medicine in the United States*, Vol. 2. Paul B. Hoeber, New York.

PAN AMERICAN HEALTH ORGANIZATION (1970*a*). *Maternal nutrition and family planning in the Americas*. Scientific Publication No. 204. Washington, D.C.

—— (1970*b*). *Guidelines to young child feeding in the contemporary Caribbean*. Scientific Publication No. 217. Washington, D.C.

—— (1972). *The National Food and Nutrition Survey of Barbados*. Scientific Publication No. 237. Washington, D.C.

PARIS, W. E., BARRETT, A. M., COOMBS, R. R. A., GUNTHER, M., and CAMPS, F. E. (1960). *Lancet* ii, 1106. Hypersensitivity to milk and sudden death in infancy.

——, ——, and —— (1960). *Immunology* **3**, 307. Inhalation of cow's milk by sensitized guinea pigs in the conscious and anaesthetized states.

PARKES, A. S. (1966). *Sex, science, and society*. Oriel Press, Newcastle upon Tyne.

PARSONS, M. P. (1976). *Soho Weekly News*, 21 Oct. Infants are second-class puppies.

PARTINGTON, M. W., DELAHAYE, D. J., MASOTTI, R. E., READ, J. H., and ROBERTS, B. (1968). *Arch. Dis. Childh.* **43**, 195. Neonatal tyrosinaemia.

PASTEELS, J. L., ROBYN, C., and EBLING, F. J. G. (ed.) (1973). *Human prolactin*. American Elsevier, New York.

PATEL, B. D. (1974). *Ind. Pediat.* **11**, 1. Perspectives in pediatrics in India for the seventies.

PATTON, R. G. and GARDNER, L. I. (1963). *Growth failure in maternal deprivation*. Charles Thomas, Springfield, Illinois.

PAVER, W. K., GAUL, E. O., ASHLEY, C. R., and CLARKE, S. K. R. (1973). *Lancet* i, 237. A small virus in human feces.

PAYNE, J. M., DEW, S. M., and MANSTON, R. (1971). The use of a metabolic profile test to determine the nutrition and metabolic status of a dairy herd in relation to its production requirement. In *Lactation* (ed. I. R. Falconer). Butterworths, London.

PEARCE, A. (1975). *Lancet* ii, 1288. In defence of the mind.

PEARCE, C. (1976). *Newsletter NMAA* Apr., p. 1. The isolation of a new mother.

PEARSON, H. A. (1971). *J. Pediat.* **79**, 557. Iron-fortified formulas in infancy.

PECHEVIS, M. (1975). *Assignment Children* **32**, 33. Elements of a policy promoting breast feeding.

——, MASSE, N., BERENBERG, S., and BONNAL, M. J. (1977). *Courrier* (In press). Etude sur les mesures sociales et educatives en matiere d'allaitement maternal.

PEDERSEN, P. V., HANSEN, F. H., HALVEG, A. B., and CHRISTIANSEN, E. D. (1976). *Lancet* ii, 715. Necrotizing enterocolitis of the newborn — is it gas gangrene of the bowel?

Pédiatrie (1976). **12**, 54. XXe anniversaire de la Ligue Internationale pour l'Allaitement Maternal.

PEREZ, A., VELA, P., POTTER, R., and MASNICK, G. (1971). *Population Studies 3*, 491. Time and sequence of resuming ovulation and menstruation after childbirth.

PERISSE, J. (1972). *FAO Nutrition Newsletter* **10**, 1. Is *Homo economicus* going back to stone-age fare?

PETERS, F. E. (1953). *Brit. J. Nutr.* **7**, 208. The chemical composition of New Hebridean human milk.

PETERSSON, P. O. and VON SYDOW, G. (1975). *Brit. med. J.* iii, 490. Cot deaths in Sweden.

PETRAKIS, N. L., MASON, L., LEE, R., SUGIMOTO, B., PAWSON, S., and CATCHPOOL, F. (1975). *J. nat. Cancer Inst.* **54**, 829. Association of race, age, menopausal status, and cerumen type with breast fluid secretion in non-lactating women, as determined by nipple aspiration.

PETROS-BARVAZIAN, A. (1975). *Mod. Probl. Paediat.* **15**, 155. Maternal and child health and breastfeeding.

PHILLIPS, I., LWANGA, S. K., LORE, W., and WASWWA, D. (1969). *J. trop. Pediat.* **15**, 167. Methods and hygiene of infant feeding in an urban area of Uganda.

PHILLIPS, M. J., KNIGHT, N. J., MANNING, H., ABBOTT, A. L., and TRIPP, W. J. (1974). *Lancet* iv, 1176. IgE and secretory otitis media.

PHILLIPS, V. (1975*a*). Breast feeding and the mother. Paper presented at a conference on 'Women's Health in a Changing Society', University of Queensland, Brisbane, Australia.

—— (1975*b*). *Successful breast feeding*. Nursing Mothers of Australia, Victoria, Australia.

PHILPOTT, M. G. (1975). *Lancet* i, 1378. Infant foods and softened water.

PICCIANO, M. F. and GUTHRIE, H. A. (1976). *Amer. J. clin. Nutr.* **29**, 242. Copper, iron and zinc contents of mature human milk.

PILSON, M. E. Q. and KELLY, A. L. (1962). *Science (N.Y.)* **135**, 104. Composition of milk from the California sea-lion.

PINCUS, J. B. and GITTELMAN, J. F. (1936). *Amer. J. Dis. Child.* **51**, 816. Infantile tetany.

PIRIE, N. W. (1976). *Ecol. Food Nutr.* **5**, 1. On terminology and composition.

PITKIN, R. M., KAMINETZY, H. A., NEWTON, M., and PRITCHARD, J. A. (1972). *Obstet. Gynec.* **40**, 773. Maternal nutrition.

PITT, J., BARLOW, B., HEIRD, W. C., and SANTULLI, T. V. (1974). *Pediat. Res.* **8**, 384. Macrophages and the protective action of breast milk in necrotizing enterocolitis.

——, ——, and —— (1976). *Milk leucocytes give passive immunity.* (In press)

PLANK, S. J. and MILANESI, M. L. (1973). *Bull. Wld Hlth Org.* **48**, 203. Infant feeding and infant mortality in Chile.

PLATT, B. S. (1954). *Proc. Nutr. Soc.* **13**, 94. Infant feeding practices. Breast feeding and the prevention of infant malnutrition.

—— (1961). *Fed. Proc.* **20.** supplement 7. Digestion in infancy.

—— and GIN, S. Y. (1938). *Arch. Dis. Childh.* **13**, 343. Chinese methods of infant feeding and nursing.

POEPLAU, W. and SCHLAGE, C. (1969). Nutrition and health — Usumbara. In *Investigations into health and nutrition in East Africa*. Weltform Verlag, Munich.

POHLANDT, F. (1974). *Acta Paediat. (Uppsala)* **63**, 801. Cystine: a semi-essential amino acid in the newborn infant.

POKROVSKY, A. (1972). Personal communication.

POMERANCE, J. J. (1974). *Amer. J. Obstet. Gynec.* **118**, 1149. Effect of contraception on lactation.

POPKIN, B. M. (1975). Income, time, and the working mother and child nutrition. Paper No. 75–9, Institute of Economic Development and Research, School of Economics, University of the Philippines. (Mimeo)

—— and DE JESUS, S. (1976). Determinants of breast feeding behavior among rural Filipino households. Unpublished report on Laguna households study. School of Economics, University of the Philippines.

—— and LATHAM, M. C. (1973). *Amer. J. clin. Nutr.* **26**, 1015. The limitations and dangers of commerciogenic nutritious foods.

—— and SOLON, F. (1976). *J. trop. Pediat. env. Chld. Hlth.* **22**, 156. Income, working mothers and infant nutrition.

Population Reports (1975*a*). Series J, No. 4. Breast feeding: aid to infant health and fertility control.

—— (1975*b*). Series J, No. 8. Effects of child bearing on maternal health.

POWELL, D. (1973). Rampant decay in the toddler: the nursing bottle syndrome. Unpublished pamphlet.

POWER, J. (1975). *New York Herald Tribune* 15 Sep., p. 8. The Third World 'baby killers'.

PRAWIROSUDIRDJO, G. (1976). *Proc. 2nd Asian Congress of Pediatrics*, Jakarta. A survey of breast-feeding practices among mothers of highly selected groups in Jakarta.

PRESCOTT, J. W. (1970*a*). A developmental neural-behavioral theory of socialization. American Psychological Association Symposium, Miami Beach, Florida.

—— (1970*b*). Early somatosensory deprivation as an ontogenetic process in the abnormal development of the brain and behavior. *Proceedings of the Second Conference of experimental Medicine and Surgery of Primates*. New York, 1970, p. 356. Karger, Basel.

—— (1972). *The Humanist* Nov./Dec., p. 19. Before ethics and humanity.

—— (1975). *Bull. atom. Sci.* **31**, 10. Body pleasure and the origins of violence.

—— and McKay, C. (1972). Somatosensory deprivation and the pleasure princi-ple: neurobiological and cross-cultural perspectives of sexual, sadistic, and affec-tional behaviors. Society of Biology and Psychiatry 27th Annual Convention, Dallas, Texas.

Prinsloo, J. G., Wittman, W., Strydom, E. S. P., Devilliers, D. B., Wehmeyer, A. S., Laubscher, F., and Botha, M. A. (1970). *S. Afr. J. Nutr.* **44**, 738. Composition of breast milk from Bantu and white women on the fifth postpartum day.

Prothero, R. (1969). *Med. Offr* **121**, 141. Women who still breast-feed their babies.

Protein Advisory Group of the United Nations (1972). Statement No. 23. Rational promotion of processed foods.

Pryor, K. (1973). *Nursing your baby*. Harper and Row, New York.

Puffer, R. R. (1975). *J. trop. Pediat. env. Chld Hlth* **21**, 273. Mortality from nutritional deficiency: editorial.

—— and Serrano, C. V. (1973). *Patterns of mortality in childhood*. Scientific Publication No. 262. Pan American Health Organization, Washington, D.C.

—— and —— (1975). *Courrier* **25**, 367. Challenging problems from the Inter-American investigation of mortality in childhood.

Pynnonen, S. and Sillanpaa, M. (1975). *Lancet* iii, 563. Carbamazepine in human milk.

Quek, K. K. (1976). *J. trop. Pediat. env. Chld Hlth* Growth in breast-fed infants. (In press)

Quick, A. J. (1974). *The hemorrhagic diseases and the pathology of hemostasis*. C. C. Thomas, Springfield.

Quinby, G. E., Armstrong, J. F., and Durham, W. F. (1965). *Nature (Lond.)* **207**, 726. D.D.T. in human milk.

——, Newak, M. N., Lega, R. E., and Andrews, B. F. (1976). *Ped. Res.* **10**, 359. Bacterial colonization of human milk.

Radbill, S. X. (1976). *J. Pediat.* **89**, 3. Colonial pediatrics.

Radford, A. and Basset, H. (1968). *Papua New Guinea med. J.* **11**, 3. Enteritis necoticians in the Northern District of Papua.

Raiha, N. C. R. (1974). *Pediatrics* **53**, 147. Biochemical basis for nutritional man-agement of pre-term infants.

—— (1975). Personal communication.

——, Heinonen, K., Rassim, D. K., and Gaull, G. E. (1976). *Pediatrics* **57**, 659. Milk protein quantity and quality in low birth weight infants (1). Metabolic responses and effects on growth.

Rajalakshmi, R. and Ramakrishnan, C. V. (1969). Gestation and lactation performance in relation to nutritional status. Biochemistry Department, Baroda University Baroda (Mimeo)

——, Subbulakshmi, G., and Kothari, B. (1974). *Baroda J. Nutr.* **1**, 117. Ascorbic acid metabolism during pregnancy and lactation.

Rao, A. R. (1977). *J. trop. Pediat. env. Chld. Hlth.* **23**, 286. Human breast milk as a commercial infant food.

——, Swaminathan, M. C., Swarup, S., and Patwardhan, U. N. (1959). *Bull.*

Wld Hlth Org. **20**, 603. Protein malnutrition in South India.

RAO, K. S. (1974). *Chron. Wld Hlth Org.* **28**, 172. Malnutrition in the Eastern Mediterranean Region.

RAPHAEL, D. (1966). The lactation-suckling process within a matrix of supportive behavior. Ph.D. Thesis, Columbia University, New York.

—— (1969). *Persps biol. Med.* **12**, 290. Uncle rhesus, auntie pachyderm, and mom: all sorts and kinds of mothering.

—— (1973*a*). *The tender gift: breastfeeding*. Prentice-Hall, New Jersey.

—— (1973*b*). *Ecol. Food Nutr.* **2**, 121. The role of breast feeding in a bottle-feeding world.

RARING, R. H. (1975). *Crib deaths*. Exposition Press, New York.

RASMUSSEN, F. (1973). In *Dietary lipids and postnatal development* (ed. C. Galli, G. Jacini, and A. Pecile), p. 231: The mechanism of drug excretion into milk. Raven Press, New York.

RATCLIFF, J. D. (1972). *Readers Digest* May, p. 48. I am Jane's breast.

RATNER, H. (1970). *Child and Family* **9**, 99. Childspacing: Nature's prescription.

—— (1973). Child and family reprint booklet series. *The nursing mother*. Historical insights from art and theology.

RAWLINS, C. (1970). Information from La Leche League International.

READ, W. W. C., LUTZ, P. G., and TASHJIAN, A. (1965). *Amer. J. clin. Nutr.* **17**, 180. Human milk lipids. II. The influence of dietary carbohydrates and fat on the fatty acids of mature milk. A study in four ethnic groups.

REDMAN, C. W. G., BONNAR, J., BEILIN, L. J., and McNEILLY, A. S. (1975). *Brit. med. J.* i, 304. Prolactin in hypertensive pregnancy.

REINA, D. (1975). *Clins Perinatol.* **2**, 373. Infant nutrition.

REISER, R. and SIDELMAN, Z. (1972). *J. Nutr.* **102**, 1009. Control of serum cholesterol homeostasis by cholesterol in the suckling rat.

REISINGER, R. C. (1974). Paper presented at Conference of Research Workers in Animal Disease, Chicago, December 1974. Sudden death syndrome in young mammals: a unifying concept.

REUTLINGER, S. and SELOWSKY, M. (1976). Malnutrition and poverty, magnitude and policy options. World Bank Staff occasional papers, No. 23. Johns Hopkins University Press, Baltimore.

REYNOLDS, J. W. (1974). *Developmental nutrition*, No. 10. Water. Ross Laboratories, Columbus, Ohio.

REYNOLDS, M. and FOLLEY, S. J. (ed.) (1969). *Lactogenesis: the initiation of milk secretion at parturition*. University of Pennsylvania Press, Philadelphia.

RHEINGOLD, H. L. (ed.) (1963). *Maternal behavior in mammals*. John Wiley, New York.

RIBADEAU-DUMAS, B. (1971). *Ann. Nutr. Paris* **25**, A181. Les proteines du lait autres que les immunoglobulines et les transferrines.

——, GROSCLANDE, F., and MERCIER, J. C. (1975). *Mod. Probl. Paediat.* **15**, 46. Primary structure of the polymorphs of casein.

——, MERCIER, J. C., ADDEO, F., GARNOT, P., and PELISSIER, J. P. (1975). *Proceedings of the Xth International Congress of Nutrition*, Kyoto, Japan. Implications of the knowledge of the primary structure of the caseins in the assessment of their physiological and nutritional role.

RICHARDS, M. P. M. (1975). *Mod. Probl. Paediat.* **15**, 143. Feeding and the early growth of mother–child relationship.

RICHARDS, M. and BERNAL, J. (1975). *Parents Centres of Australia Newsletter* Aug./Sep., p. 3. Breast feeding mothers: a minority group.

RICHARDSON, J. (1925). *J. Amer. Med. Assoc.* **85**, 668. Universalizing breast feeding in a community.

RICHARDSON, J. L. (1975). *J. trop. Pediat. env. Chld. Hlth* **21**, 249. Legislation regarding nursing breaks.

RICHARDSON, J. L. (1976). Actions to limit infant-formula advertising. Unpublished.

RICHARDSON, K. C. (1949). *Proc. roy. Soc. Biol. B* **136**, 30. Contractile tissue in the mammary gland: with special reference to myoepithelium in the goat.

RIDDLE, O., BATES, R. W., and DYKSHORN, S. W. (1932). *Proc. Soc. exp. Biol.* **29**, 1211. A new hormone of the anterior pituitary.

RINEHART, W. and WINTER, J. (1975). *Population Reports* Series K, No. 1. Injectable progestagens: officials debate but use increases.

RINGEL, K. P. and RENNER, E. (1973). *Ecol. Food Nutr.* **2**, 201. The real amounts of dried milk formulas given by mothers.

RITCHIE, J. H., FISH, M. B., MCMASTERS, V., and GROSSMAN, M. (1968). *New Engl. J. Med.* **279**, 1185. Edema and hemolytic anemia in premature infants. A vitamin E deficiency syndrome.

RIX, K. J. B. (1975). *Lancet* i, 986. Alcoholism education and alcohol advertising.

ROBERTS, S. A., COHEN, M. D., and FORFAR, J. O. (1973). *Lancet* iv, 809. Antenatal factors associated with neonatal hypocalcaemic convulsions.

ROBIN-COKER, D. J. O. and JALLOH, M. A. S. (1975). *J. trop. Pediat. env. Chld Hlth* **21**, 14. Infant feeding and protein-calorie malnutrition in Freetown.

ROBINSON, M. (1939). *Arch. Dis. Childh.* **14**, 258. A review of twenty years of breast feeding in Liverpool.

—— (1951). *Lancet* i, 788. Infant morbidity and mortality: a study of 3 266 infants.

ROBINSON, S. and NAYLOR, S. R. (1963). *Brit. dent. J.* **115**, 250. The effects of late weaning on the deciduous incisor teeth.

ROBSON, J. R. K. (1972). *Malnutrition: its causation and control*, Vols I and II. Gordon and Breach, New York.

ROHDE, J. E. (1975*a*). *Lancet* **i**, 853. Pregnancy spacing by child weight.

—— (1975*b*). *Paediat. Indonesiana* **14**, 198. Human milk in the second year: nutritional and economic considerations in Indonesia.

—— and NORTHRUP, R. S. (1976). Ciba Foundation Symposium No. 42. *Acute diarrhoea in childhood*, p. 338. Taking science where the diarrhoea is. Elsevier, Holland.

ROLLES, C. (1976). Nursing Mothers' Association of Australia Newsletter, **12**, 1. Can we really mimic human milk?

ROMANIUK, A. (1973). Modernization and natural fertility: the case of the James Bay native Indians. In *Natural Fertility*. I.U.S.P., Liege, Belgium.

ROSA, F. W. (1974). *Amer. J. Obstet. Gynecol.* **119**, 1121. Birth weight in Fiji and Western Samoa. A Pacific prescription for pregnancy?

—— (1974). *J. trop. Pediat. env. Chld Hlth* **20**, 1. Breast feeding and family planning.

—— (1976*a*). *People.* **3**, 10. Breast feeding: a motive for family planning.

—— (1976*b*) *Amer. J. pub. Hlth* **66**, 781. Resolving the 'public health dilemma' of steroid contraception and its effect on lactation.

—— (1976*c*). A cumulative total of contraceptive method acceptance reported by developing countries and an estimate of current use. (In press)

—— (1976*d*). *P. A. G. Bulletin* **5**, 5. Breast-feeding in family planning.

ROSENBLATT, J. and LEHRMANN, D. (1963). Maternal behavior in the laboratory rat. In *Maternal behavior in mammals* (ed. H. Rheingold). John Wiley, New York.

ROSENBLOOM, L. and SILLS, J. A. (1975). *Arch. Dis. Childh.* **50**, 750. Hypernatraemic dehydration and infant mortality.

ROSENBURG, O. (1973). *Rev. Saude Publ.* **7**, 381. Aleimento no primeiro ano de Sao Paulo.

ROSENSTEIN, S. H. (1966). *N.Y. St. dent. J.* **32**, 400. Systematic and environmental factors in rampant caries.

ROSS, A. I. and HERDAN, G. (1951). *Lancet* **i**, 630. Breast feeding in Bristol.

ROSS, D. J. and OSTER, K. A. (1975). *Lancet* **ii**, 1037. Milk protein antibodies and myocardial infarction.

ROSS LABORATORIES (1974). Market research data. On file. Columbus, Ohio.

ROSSIER, A. and DENAVIT, M. F. (1976). *Rev. Pract.* **26**, 793. Hyperazotémie des premières semaines par excès de la ration protidique.

ROSSOFF, S. R. and GROTBERG, E. H. (1975). *Courrier* **25**, 1. The care of children of working parents: program and policy in the United States of America.

ROTCH, T. (1907). *N.Y. med. J.* **85**, 432. A historical sketch of the development of percentage feeding.

ROTHBERG, R. M. and FARR, R. S. (1965). *Pediatrics* **35**, 571. Antibovine serum albumin and anti-alpha lactalbumin in the serum of children and adults.

ROTHERMEL, P. C. and FABER, M. M. (1975). *Birth and Family J.* **2**, 76. Drugs in breast milk: a complete chart.

ROTHSTEIN, R. L. (1972). *Pediatrics* **49**, 168. Otitis media in infants.

ROUCHY, R., TAUREAU, M., and VALMYRE, M. J. (1961). *Bull. Fed. Gynec. Obstet. Franc.* **13**, 471. Current trends in maternal breastfeeding.

ROUTH, C. H. F. (1863). *Infant feeding and its influence on life* (second edition). London.

RUSHMAN, R. F. (1975). *Humanizing health care: alternative futures for medicine*. M. I. T. Press, Cambridge, Massachusetts.

RYERSON, A. J. (1961). *Harvard Educ. Rev.* **31**, 302. Medical advice on child rearing, 1550–1900.

SACKETT, W. W. (1953). *South. med. J.* **46**, 358. Results of three years experience with a new concept of baby feeding.

SACKS, S. H., BRADA, M., HILL, A. M., BARTON, P., and HARLAND, P. S. (1976). *Practit.*, **216**, 183. To breast feed or not to breast feed? A survey among primiparae.

SADRE, M., EMAMI, E., and DONOSO, G. (1971). *Ecol. Food Nutr.* **1**, 55. The changing pattern of malnutrition.

SAIGAL, S., O'NEILL, A., SURAINDER, T., CHUA, L., and USHER, R. (1972). *Pediatrics* **49**, 406. Placental transfusion and hyperbilirubinemia in the premature.

SAITO, K., FURNICHI, E., KONDO, S., KAWANISHI, Q., NISHIKAWA, I., NAKAZATO, H., NOGUCHI, Y., DOI, T., NOGUCHI, A., and SHINGO, S. (1965). *Studies on Human Milk*. Snow Brand Milk Products, Tokyo.

SALAZAR, H. and TOBON, H. (1974). *Lactogenic hormones, fetal nutrition and lactation* (ed. J. B. Josimovich, M. Reynolds, and E. Cobo), Chapter 13: Morphologic changes in the mammary gland during development, pregnancy and lactation, p. 221. John Wiley, New York.

SALBER, E. J., FEINLEIB, M., and McMAHON, B. (1965). *Amer. J. Epidem.* **82**, 347. The duration of post partum amenorrhea.

SALK, L. (1960). *World ment. Hlth* **12**, 1. Effects of the normal heart beat sound in the behavior of the newborn infant.

—— (1962). *Trans. N.Y. Acad. Sci.* **24**, 753. Mother's heart beat as an imprinting stimulus.

SAMMOUR, M. B., RAMADAM, M. E. A., and SALAH, M. (1973). *Fertil. steril.* **24**, 301. Effect of chlormadinone on the composition of human milk.

SANCHEZ-MEDAL, L. (1975). *Proceedings of the IXth International Congress of Nutrition*, Mexico City, 1972, Vol. I, p. 149. Iron deficiency in pregnancy and infancy: prophylaxis and treatment. Karger, Basel.

SANDERS, T. A. B. and NAISMITH, D. J. (1976). *Proc. Nutr. Soc.* **35**, 63A. Long-chain polyunsaturated fatty acids in the erythrocyte lipids of breast-fed and bottle-fed babies.

SANGUANSENSRI, J., GYORGY, P., and ZILLUKEN, F. (1974). *Amer. J. clin. Nutr.* **27**, 859. Polyamines in human and cow's milk.

SANJUR, D. M., CRAVIOTO, J., ROSALES, L., and VAN VEEM, A. (1970). *Acta Paediat. (Uppsala)* Supplement **200**, 1. Infant feeding and weaning practices in rural pre-industrial setting: a socio-cultural approach.

SANTULLI, T. V. (1974). *Hosp. Pract.* Nov., p. 129. Acute necrotizing enterocolitis: recognition and management.

SARFF, D., McCRACKEN, G. H. SCHIFFER, M. S., GLODE, M. P., ROBBINS, J. B., ORSKOV, I., and ORSKOV, F. (1975). *Lancet* ii, 1100. Epidemiology of *Escherichia coli* K I in health and diseased newborns.

SAUL, F. P. (1973). Disease in the Maya area: the pre-columbian experience, p. 301. In *The classic Maya collapse* (ed. T. P. Culbert). University of New Mexico Press, Albuquerque.

SCHAEFER, O. (1971*a*). *Nutr. Today* Nov./Dec. p. 8. When the Eskimo comes to town.

—— (1971*b*). *Can. J. publ. Hlth* **62**, 478. Otitis media and bottle feeding.

SCHAEFER, O. (1973). Personal communication.

SCHEVING, L. E. (1976). *Endeavour* **35**, 66. The dimension of time in biology and medicine-chronobiology.

SCHLESINGER, E. R. (1965). *Amer. J. publ. Hlth* **55**, 1123. Dietary fluorides.

SCHLOM, J., SPEIGLEMAN, S., and MOORE, D. (1971). *Nature (Lond.)* **231**, 97. RNA-dependent DNA polymerase activity in virus-like particles isolated from human milk.

SCHMIDT-KOLMER, E. (1974). *Courrier* **24**, 565. The care of children of working parents. II. Principal solutions. Collective day care (nurseries).

SCHNEIDER, K. R. (1972). *Int. Develop. Rev.* **2**, 16. The urban implosion of the population bomb.

SCHOLANDER, P. F. (1963). *Scient. Am.* **209**, 92. The master switch of life.

SCHOU, M. and AMDISEN, A. (1973). *Brit. med. J.* **ii**, 138. Lithium ingestion by children breast-fed by women on lithium treatment.

SCHULTZE, R. R. and WINKELMAN, R. K. (1966). *Mayo Clin. Proc.* **41**, 334. Acrodermatitis enteropathica: report of a patient responding to continued treatment with human milk and diidohygroxyquin.

SCHUTZ, Y., LECHTIG, A., and BRADFIELD, R. B. (1977). *Amer. J. clin. Nutr.* Energy intakes and expenditures of lactating women in rural Guatemala. (In press).

SCHWARTZ, A. M. and GRATZINGER, M. (1966). *Removable orthodontic appliances.* W. B. Saunders, Philadelphia.

SCHWARTZ, C. (1975). *Bull. atom. Scients* **31**, 15. The corporate connection.

SCHWERDTFEGER, E. (1965). *Naturwissenschaften* **52**, 162. Der. Aminosaurengehalt der Muttermilch.

SCOTT, B. B., McGRIFFIN, P., SWINBURNE, M. L., and LOSOWY, M. S. (1976). *Lancet* ii, 125. Dietary antibodies and myocardial infarction.

SCRIMSHAW, N. S., TAYLOR, C. E., and GORDON, J. E. (1968). *Interaction of nutrition and infection.* WHO Monograph No. 29. Geneva.

SEDGWICK, J. P. and FLEISCHNER, E.C. (1921). *Amer. J. publ. Hlth* **11**, 153. Breast feeding and the reduction of mortality.

SEHRING, D. A. (1975). *Mod. Probl. Paediat.* **15**, 231. Infant feeding trends in an industrialized culture.

SELESTE, E. (1953). *Acta fenn. paediat.* **31**, Supplement 8. The keeping quality of cow's milk and mother's milk.

SHANGHAI CHILD HEALTH COORDINATION GROUP (1976). *J. trop. Pediat. Env. Chld Hlth* **21**, 284. Measurement of the growth and development of children up to 20 months in Shanghai.

SHAW, J. C. L., JONES, A., and GUNTHER, M. (1973). *Brit. med. J.* **ii**, 17. Mineral content of brands of milk for infant feeding.

SHEA, J. J., GILESPIE, S. M., and WALDBOTT, G. L. (1967). *Ann. Allergy* **25**, 388. Allergy to fluoride.

SHEEHAN, H. L. and DAVIS, J. C. (1968). *Brit. med. Bull.* **24**, 59. Pituitary necrosis.

SHELLARD, L. N. (1975). Considerations on breast feeding practices in Sao Paolo, Brazil. Unpublished data.

SHINER, M., BALLARD, J., and SMITH, M. E. (1975). *Lancet* **i**, 136. The small intestinal mucosa in cow's milk allergy.

SHUKLA, A., FORSYTH, H. A., ANDERSON, C. M., and MARWAH, S. M. (1972). *Brit. med. J.* **iv**, 507. Infantile overnutrition in the first year of life. A field study in Dudley, Worcestershire.

SHUVAL, H. I. and GRUENER, N. (1972). *Amer. J. publ. Hlth* **62**, 1045. Epidemiological and toxicological aspects of nitrates and nitrites in the environment.

SIDEL, R. (1972). *Women and child care in China.* Hill and Wang, New York.

SIGNER, E. and FRIDRICH, R. (1975). *Acta paediat. (Uppsala)* **64**, 515. Gastric emptying in newborns and young infants.

SILVERMAN, M. and LEE, P. R. (1974). *Pills, profits and politics.* University of California Press, Berkeley.

—— (1976). *The drugging of the Americas.* University of California Press, San Francisco.

SIMPSON, G. G. (1949). *The meaning of evolution.* Yale University Press, New Haven.

SIMPSON, H. W. (1973). *Int. J. Chronobiol.* **1**, 19. Human chronobiology.

SIMPSON, I. A. and CHOW, A. Y. (1956). *J. trop. Pediat.* **2**, 3. The thiamine content of human milk in Malaya.

SIMPSON, M. A. (1974). *Lancet* **i**, 399. A mythology of medical education.

SIMPSON, W. J. and CHEUNG, D. K. (1976). *J. Canad. Diet. Assoc.* **42**, 124. Developing infant occlusion: related feeding methods and oral habits.

—— and TUBA, J. (1968). *J. oral Med.* **23**, 104. An investigation of fluoride concentration in the milk of nursing mothers.

SIMPSON-HERBERT, M. (1975). *Breast feeding and human fertility.* No. 9. Technical Information Service. Carolina Population Center, Univ. of North Carolina.

SIMS, D. G., and NELIGAN, E. A. (1976). *Obstetric. Gynec. Survey* **31**, 369. Factors affecting the increasing incidence of severe non-haemolytic neonatal jaundice.

SINCLAIR, A. J. and CRAWFORD, M. A. (1972). *J. Neurochem.* **19**, 1753. The accumulation of arachidonate and docahexaenoate in the developing rat brain.

—— and —— (1973). *Brit. J. Nutr.* **29**, 127. The effect of low-fat maternal diet on neonatal rats.

SINGARIMBUN, M. and MANNING, C. (1976). *Studies Fam. Pl.* **7**, 175. Breast-feeding amenorrhoea and abstinence in a Javanese village.

SISSON, T. R. C. and LUND, C. J. (1958). *Amer. J. clin. Nutr.* **6**, 376. The influence of maternal iron deficiency on the newborn.

SJOLIN, S., HILLERVIK, C., and HOFVANDER, Y. (1975). Unpublished data from retrospective and prospective breast feeding studies in Uppsala, Sweden.

SLIJPER, E. J. (1962). *Riesen des Meeres.* Springer Verlag, Berlin.

SLOPER, K., MCKEAN, L., and BAUM, J. D. (1974). *Arch. Dis. Childh.* **49**, 749. Patterns of infant feeding in Oxford.

——, ——, and —— (1975). *Arch. Dis. Childh.* **50**, 165. Factors influencing breast feeding.

——, ——, and —— (1975). *Lancet* **ii**, 978. Encouraging breast feeding.

SMART, J. L. and BAMFORD, F. N. (1976). *Lancet* **iii**, 42. Breast-feeding and spontaneous trends and differences.

SMIBERT, J. (1975). *Med. J. Aust.* **2**, 954. Two books on breast feeding published in Australia.

SMITH, B. A. M. (1974). *Brit. med. J.* **iv**, 741. Feeding overstrength cow's milk to babies.

SMITH, C. W. and GOLDMAN, A. S. (1968). *Pediat. Res.* **2**, 103. The cells of human colostrum. (I) *In vitro* studies of morphology and function.

——, ——, and YATES, R. D. (1971). *Exp. Cell Res.* **69**, 409. Interactions of lymphocytes and macrophages from human colostrum.

SMITH, T. and ORCUTT, M. L. (1925). *J. exp. Med.* **41**, 89. The bacteriology of the intestinal tract of young calves with special reference to early diarrhea ('scours').

SODERHJELM, L. (1972). *Acta paediat. (Uppsala)* **61**, 565. Infant feeding hygiene in Sweden.

SOLE, A. (1935). *Klin. Wchschr.* **14**, 1354. Die Muttermilch als Blutstillungmittel.

SOLIEN DE GONZALEZ, N. L. (1964). *Amer. Anthrop.* **66**, 873. Lactation and pregnancy.

SOMAVIA, J. (1974). *Development Dialogue* **2**, 11. Transnational corporations: information-getting by the United Nations.

SOOTHILL, J. F. (1975). *Proc. roy. Soc. Med.* **69**, 439. Some intrinsic and extrinsic factors predisposing to allergy.

—— (1977 Immunodeficiency, allergy and infant feeding. In: *Food and Immunology*, p. 88. Eds. L. Hambraeus, L. A. Hanson, and H. Macfarlane. Almquist and Wiksell, Stockholm.

Sosa, R., Klaus, M., and Urrutia, J. J. (1976).*J. Pediat.* **88**, 668. Feed the mother, thereby the infant.

Soupart, P., Moore, S., and Bigwood, E. J. (1954). *J. biol. Chem.* **206**, 699. Amino acid composition of human milk.

Sousa, P. L. R. (1975). *Brit. med. J.* **i**, 512. Metoclopramide and breast feeding.

—— (1975).*J. trop. Pediat. env. Chld Hlth* **21**, 212. The decline of breast feeding in Brazil.

——, Barros, F. C., Gazalle, R. V., Begeres, R. M., Pinheiro, G. N., Menezes, S. T., and Arruda, L. A. (1974). *Proceedings of the XIVth International Pediatric Congress*, Vol. 3, Section 4, p. 136. Attachment and lactation.

——, Gazalle, R. V., Barros, F. C., Begeres, R. M., Pinheiro, G. N. and Pinto, P. S. (1974). *Proceedings of the XIVth International Pediatric Congress*, Vol. 3, Section 4, p. 139. The 'weak milk' syndrome.

——, Barros, F. C., Pinheiro, G. N., and Gazalle, R. V. (1975).*J. trop. Pediat. env. Chld Hlth* **21**, 214. Re-establishment of lactation with metoclopramide.

—— (1975).*J. trop. Ped. env. Chld Hlth* **21**, 215. Vulnerable periods of lactation — a view of breast feeding practices in Brazil.

Southgate, D. A. T., Widdowson, E. M., Smits, B. J., Cooke, W. T., Walker, C. H. M., and Mathers, N. P. (1969). *Lancet* **i**, 487. Absorption and excretion of calcium and fat by young infants.

Southworth, T. S. (1906). Maternal feeding. In *Practice of pediatrics* (ed. W. L. Carr). Lea Brothers, Philadelphia.

Soysa, P. E. (1975).*PAG Bull.* **5**, 8. Policies and practices recommended in feeding young infants (zero to six months) in countries in the region.

Speer, M. E., Taser, L. H., Yow, M. D., Rudolph, A. J., Urteaga, J., and Waller, S. (1976).*J. Pediat.* **89**, 91. Fulminating neonatal sepsis and necrotizing enterocolitis associated with a 'non-pathogenic' strain of *Escherichia coli*.

Spence, J., Walton, W. S., Miller, F. J. W., and Court, S. D. M. (1954). *A thousand families in Newcastle upon Tyne*. Oxford University Press, London.

Spik, G. (1971). *Ann. Nutr. Paris* **25**, A81. Formes conjugées et assimilation du lactofer par le nourrisson.

Spitz, R. A. (1945). *Psychoanalyt. Stud. Child* **1**, 53. Hospitalism. An inquiry into the psychiatric conditions in early childhood.

—— and Wolf, K. M. (1946). *Psychoanalyt. Study Child* **2**, 313. Anaclitic depression.

Squires, B. T. (1952). *Trans. roy. Soc. trop. Med. Hyg.* **46**, 95. Ascorbic acid content of the milk of the Tswana women.

Staley, T. E., Norris, H. T., and Staley, J. A. (1972). *Lancet* **ii**, 597. E. coli diarrhea.

Stanley, E. M. (1972). *Abstracts Internat.* **33**, 3B. A study of tongue thrust and related factors in breast fed and bottle fed school children.

Steel, R. and Langworth, J. T. (1966). *Can. med. Ass. J.* **94**, 1165. The relationship of antenatal and postnatal factors to sudden unexpected death in infancy.

Steinbels, M. O. (1973). *Who's minding the children?* Simon and Schuster, New York.

STEINER, G. M. (1972). *Proc. roy. Soc. Med.* **65**, 733. Abnormal meconium and 'milk inspissation'.

STEPHENS, T., IRVINE, S., MUTTON, P., GUPTA, J. D., and HARLEY, J. D. (1974). *Med. J. Austral.* **2**, 910. The case of the cataractous kangaroo.

——, ——, ——, ——, and —— (1974). *Nature (Lond.)* **248**, 524. Deficiency of two enzymes of galactose metabolism in kangaroos.

STERN, G. M., JONES, R. B., and FRASER, A. C. L. (1972). *Arch. Dis. Childh.* **47, 468**. Hyperosmolar dehydration in infancy due to faulty feeding.

STEVENS, L. H. (1969). *Med. J. Aust.* **11**, 976. The first kilogram.

STEWART, C. A. (1943). *J. Pediat.* **23**, 310. The use of cereal-thickened formulas to promote maternal nursing.

STEWART, R. A. (1975). *Pediat. Basics* **12**, 3. Responsibility in infant feeding.

—— (1976). *Pediat. Basics* **15**, 3. What is mother's milk?

——, PLATOU, E., and KELLY, V. J. (1958). *J. biol. Chem.* **232**, 777. The alkaline phosphatase of human milk.

STOLIAR, O. A., PELLAY, R. P., KANIECKI-GREEN, E., KLAUS, M. H., and CAR-PENTER, C. C. J. (1976). Secretory IgA against enterotoxins in breast milk. (In STIMMLER, L., SNODGRASS, G. J. A., and JAFFE, E. (1973). *Arch. Dis. Childh.* **48**, 127. Dental defects associated with neonatal sympomatic hypocalcaemia.

STROM, J. (1948). *Acta Paediat.* **35**, 55. Supplement 1. The breast-feeding of mature infants during the neonatal period and the influence of some factors on the same.

STRONG, J. P. and McGILL, H. C. (1969). *J. Atheroscler. Res.* **9**, 251. The pediatric aspects of atherosclerosis.

STUART, J. E. and CONNELHAN, P. (1973). *Aust. Paediat. J.* **9**, 159. Ascorbic acid studies in aborigines.

STURMAN, J. A., GAULL, G., and RAIHA, N. C. R. (1970). *Science (N.Y.)* **169**, 74. Absence of cystothionase in human fetal liver: is cystine essential?

——, RASSIN, D. H., and GAULL, G. E. (1977). *Pediat. Res.* **11**, 28. Taurine in developing rat brain.

SULMAN, F. G. (1970). *Hypothalamic control of lactation*. William Heinemann Medical Books, London.

SUSSMAN, G. D. (1975). *French His. Stud.* **9**, 304. The wet-nursing business in nineteenth century France.

SUTEDJO, R. (1974). *Paediat. Indonesica* **14**, 73. Trends in paediatric nutrition in developing countries.

—— (1975). *PAG Bull.* **5**, 13. Policies and practices recommended in feeding older infants (6–12 months) and young children (12–24 months) in Indonesia.

SVIRSKY-GROSS, S. (1958). *Ann. Paediat.* **190**, 109. Pathogenic status of coli 0111 among prematures and the use of human milk in controlling outbreaks of diarrhoea.

SUTHERLAND, J. M., GLUECK, H. I., and GLASER, G. (1967). *Amer. J. Dis. Child.* **113**, 524. Hemorrhagic disease of the newborn.

SWARMER, O. W. and BARNES, F. M. (1976). *Pediat. Res.* **10**, 432. Necrotizing enterocolitis and klebsiella infection of high risk infants.

SWYER, P. R. (1975). *The intensive care of the newly born: physiological principles and practices*. Monograph in Pediatrics No. 65. Karger, Basel.

SYMONDS, B. E. R. (1958). *J. trop. Pediat.* **5**, 159. Clinical studies in South Trinidadian children. (1) Fetal malnutrition.

SZOKOLAY, A., UHNAK, J., and ROSIVAL, L. (1975). Chlorinated pesticides in the food chain and its influence on man. *Proceedings of the Tenth International Congress of Nutrition*, Kyoto, Japan, August, 1975.

TAFARI, N. and STERKY, G. (1974). *J. trop. Ped. env. Chld Hlth* **29**, 73. Early discharge of low birth weight infants in developing countries.

TAITZ, L. S. (1971). *Brit. med. J.* **i**, 315. Infantile overnutrition among artificially fed infants in the Sheffield region.

—— (1975). *Arch. Dis. Childh.* **50**, 746. Modification of weight gain by dietary changes in a population of Sheffield neonates.

—— (1977). *Pediat. Clins. N. Amer.* Infantile obesity. **24**, 107. (ed. C. Neumann and D. B. Jelliffe).

——, and BYERS, H. D. (1972). *Arch. Dis. Childh.* **47**, 257. High calorie/osmolar feeding and hypertonic dehydration.

TAKAHASHI, K., NISHIDA, N., TAKADO, S., and NAKASHIMA, H. (1974). *Acta paediat. jap.* **78**, 663. Intestinal microflora in young infants with non-specific entero-colitis.

TANK, G. and STORVICK, C. A. (1965). *J. Amer. dent. Ass.* **70**, Feb. Caries experience of children of one to six years old in two Oregon communities. (III) Relation of diet to variation of dental caries.

TANNER, J. M. (1958). The evaluation of physical growth and development. In *Modern times in paediatrics* (ed. A. Holzel and J. P. M. Tizard), p. 235. Butterworth, London.

——, WHITEHOUSE, R. H., and TAKAISHI, M. (1966). *Arch. Dis. Childh.* **41**, 454. Standard from birth to maturity for height, weight, height velocity and weight velocity: British children, 1965.

TARJ-ELDRIN, S. (1971). *Arch. Dis. Childh.* **46**, 121. Favism in breast-fed infants.

TASSOVATZ, B. and KOTSITCH, A. (1961). *Sem. Hôp. Paris* **37**, 1649. Le lait de femme et son action contre les infections intestinales chez le nouveau-né.

TAYLOR, B., NORMAN, A. P., ARGEL, H. A., STOKE, C. R., TURNER, M. W., and SOOTHILL, J. F. (1973). *Lancet*, **ii**, 112. Transient, IgA deficiency and the pathogenesis of infantile atopy.

TENNANT, B. (ed.) (1971). *Ann. N. Y. Acad. Sci.* **176**. Neonatal enteric infections caused by *Escherichia coli*.

THALLER, R. M. (1976). Aspirin and breast feeding. Personal communication.

THOMAN, E. B., CONNER, R. L., and LEVINE, S. (1970). *J. comp. Physiol. Psychol.* **70**, 364. Lactation suppresses adrenal corticosteroid activity and aggressiveness in rats.

THOMPSON, B. (1967). *Matern. Chd Care* **3**, 545. Early Childhood in a West African village.

THOMPSON, M. P. and FARRELL, H. M. (1974). Genetic variants of milk proteins. In *Lactation. A comprehensive treatise*, p. 109. Academic Press, New York.

THOMSON, A. M. and BLACK, A. E. (1976). *Bull. World Hlth Org.* **52**, 168. Nutritional aspects of human lactation.

——, HYTTEN, F. E., and BILLEWICZ, W. Z. (1970). *Brit. J. Nutr.* **24**, 565. The energy cost of human lactation.

THORNER, M. O., MCNEILLY, A. S., HAGAN, C., and BESSER, G. M. (1974). *Brit. Med. J.* **ii**, 419. Long-term treatment of galactorrhoea and hypogonadism with bromocriptine.

Tichauer, R. (1963). *J. Pediat.* **62**, 399. The Amyra children of Bolivia.

Tiger, L. and Fox, R. (1972). *The imperial animal*. Delta, New York.

Toffler, A. (1970). *Future shock*. Bantam Books, New York.

Toivanen, A., Viljanen, M. K., and Savilahti, E. (1975). *Lancet* **iii**, 205. IgM and IgG anti-milk antibodies measured by radioimmunoassay in myocardial infarction.

Tokuhata, G. K. (1969). *Amer. J. Epidemiol.* **89**, 139. Morbidity and mortality among offspring of breast cancer mothers.

Tompkins, R. B. and Livingood, C. S. (1969). *Arch. Derm.* **99**, 190. Acrodermatitis enteropathica persisting into adulthood.

Tompson, M. (1976). *J. trop. Pediat. env. Chld Hlth* **21**, 264. Role of voluntary agencies in promoting breast feeding.

Tonkin, S. (1970). *N. Z. med. J.* **71**, 129. Maori infant health. Trial of intramuscular iron to prevent anaemia in Maori babies.

—— (1974). In *SIDS 1974*, p. 169. Epidemiology of SIDS in Auckland, New Zealand. Canadian Foundation for the Study of Infant Deaths, Toronto.

Toth, R. (1975). *Los Angeles Times* Sunday, 14 December.

Tracey, V. V., De, N. C., and Harper, J. R. (1971). *Brit. med. J.* **i**, 16. Obesity and respiratory infections in infants and young children.

Tronick, E., Wise, S., Als, H., Adamson, I., Scanlon, J. and Brazleton, B. (1976) *Pediat.* **58**, 94. Regional obstetric anesthesia and newborn behavior.

Troughton, O. and Singh, S. P. (1972). *Brit. med. J.* **iii**, 76. Heart failure and neonatal hypocalcemia.

Truelove, S. C. and Jewell, D. P. (1975). In *Clinical aspects of immunology* (ed. P. G. H. Gell, R. R. A. Coombs, and P. J. Lachman). Blackwell, Oxford.

Tsang, R. C. and Glueck, C. J. (1975). *Clins Perinatol.* **2**, 275. Perinatal cholesterol metabolism.

Tsuchiya, S. (1972). *Acta paediat. jap.* **76**, 7. Digestion and absorption of milk in the intestinal tract of the infant.

Turkington, R. W. (1974). In *Lactation: a comprehensive treatise* Vol. II, p. 237. (ed. B. L. Larson and V. B. Smith) Chapter 7: Pathophysiology of prolactin secretion in man. Academic Press, New York.

Turner, J. (1974). *New Humanist* **89**, 401. Hooked on the bottle.

Turner, K. J., Baldo, B. A., and Hilton, J. M. N. (1975). *Brit. med. J.* **i**, 357. IgE antibodies to *Dermatophagoides pteronyssinus* (house dust mite), *Aspergillus fumigatus* and beta-lactoglobulin in Sudden Death Syndrome.

Tylden, E. (1976). The obstetrician's view. In *Conference on Breast Feeding*. Department of Health and Social Security, London.

Tyndale-Biscoe, N. (1973). Quoted by Mepham, B. (1976).

Tyson, J. E., Khojandi, M., Huth, J., and Andreassan, B. (1975). *J. Clin. Endocrin. Metab.* **40**, 764. The influence of prolactin secretion on lactation.

——, Zanartu, J., Perez-Sanchez, A., and Hacker, R. (1975). Puerperal lactation in reponse to oral TRH. (In press)

Udesky, I. C. (1950). *Amer. J. Obstet. Gynec.* **59**, 843. Ovulation in lactating women.

Underwood, B. A., Hepner, R., and Abdullah, H. (1970). *Amer. J. clin. Nutr.* **23**, 400. Protein, lipids, and fatty acids of human milk from Pakistani women during prolonged periods of lactation.

UNGAR, R. (1949). *Kinderartz. Prak.* **17**, 295. Zwiemilchnahrung und Stilldauer.

UNICEF-WHO JOINT COMMITTEE ON HEALTH POLICY (1975). Report on the Twentieth Session Held at the Headquarters of the World Health Organisation, Geneva. Document JC20/UNICEF-WHO/75.6. (Mimeo)

UNITED NATIONS (1968). *International action to avert the impending protein crisis.* Special Report Series No. E/4343/Rev. 1, New York.

UNITED STATES OF AMERICA (1973). *Report of the Senate Committee on Nutrition and Human Needs in the U.S. Senate*, p. 67.

UNITED STATES NATIONAL ACADEMY OF SCIENCES (1975). *Nutrition and fertility: implications for policy and action.* Washington, D.C.

UNITED STATES SENATE COMMITTEE ON NUTRITION AND HUMAN NEEDS (1973). Hearings before the Select Committee on Nutrition and Human Needs, 5 and 6 June, 1973. *Maternal, fetal, and infant nutrition*, Part I: Consequences of Malnutrition. Washington, D.C.

UNITED STATES DEPARTMENT OF LABOR (1971). *Who are the working mothers?* GPO 2916–0007. U.S. Government Printers, Washington, D.C.

UPADHYAY, Y. N. and GERRARD, J. W. (1969). *Ann. Allergy* **27**, 218. Recurrent pneumonia in Indian children.

VAHLQUIST, B. (1972). Coordinated International Study on Socio-cultural Dynamics of Breast-feeding. Unpublished document.

——(1975). *J. trop. Pediat. env. Chld Hlth* **21**, 11. The evolution of breast feeding in Europe.

VAN BALEN, J. and NTABOMVURA, A. (1976) *J. trop. Pediat. env. Chld. Hlth.* **22**, 50. Traditional methods of birth spacing, maternal lactation and post partum abstinence in relation to traditional African culture.

VAN DUZEN, J., CARTER, J. P., SECONDI, J., and FEDERSPIEL, C. (1969). *Amer. J. clin. Nutr.* **22**, 1362. Protein and calorie malnutrition among pre-school Navajo children.

VAN GINNEKEN, J. K. (1974). *Stud. Fam. Planning* **5**, 177. Prolonged breast feeding as a birth spacing method.

VAN HELLEMOND, K. K. and VAN WEERDEN, E. J. (1973). *Proc. Nutr. Soc.* **32**, 231. Milk-protein substitutes in nations for veal calves.

VARGA, L., LUTTERBUCK, P. M., WENNER, R., and ERB, H. (1972). *Brit. med. J.* **ii**, 743. Suppression of puerperal lactation with an ergot alkaloid: double-blind study.

VARMA, S. N., SCHWARZ, V., and SIMPSON, N. (1962). *Biochem. J.* **85**, 546. The role of dietary lactose in the synthesis of brain galactolipids.

VAUGHAN, V. C. (1976). Perspectives from ethology. In *The family – can it be saved?* (ed. V. C. Vaughan and T. B. Brazleton). Year Book Medical Publishers, Chicago.

VENKATACHALAM, P. S. (1962). *A study of the diet, nutrition and health of the people of the Chimbu Area, New Guinea Highlands.* Monograph No. 4. Department of Public Health, Territory of Papua and New Guinea.

VIS, H. L. (1976). *Bull. int. pediat. Ass.* No. 6, p. 26. Influence on maternal health on the volume and quality of breast milk secreted.

—— and HENNART, P. (1974). *Assignment Children* **25**, 87. L'allaitement maternel en Afrique centrale.

VORHERR, H. (1974). *Postgrad. Med.* **56**, 97. Excretion of certain drugs into milk.

—— (1975). *The breast: morphology, physiology and lactation*. Academic Press, New York
WADE, N. (1974). *Science (N.Y.)* **184**, 45. Bottle feeding: an adverse effect of Western technology.
WAISMAN, H. A. and KERR, G. R. (1970). *Feeding and the nutrition of the non-human primate*. Academic Press, New York.
WAKO, W. (1975). Personal communication.
—— and HATAKEYAMA, T. (1976). Personal communication. Infant nursing tendency and growth in recent years.
WALDMAN, T. A., WOCHNER, R. D., and LASTER, L. (1967). *New Eng. J. Med.* **276**, 761. Allergic gastroenteropathy.
WALETZKY, L. R. and HERMAN, E. H. (1976). *Amer. J. Family Physns* **14**, 69. Relactation.
WALKER, A. (1972). Unpublished data.
WALKER, A. R. P., ARVIDSSON, U. B., and DRAPER, W. L. (1952). *Lancet*, **i**, 317. Breast-feeding and diet.
WALKER, W. A. and HONG, R. (1973). *J. Pediat.* **83**, 517. Immunology of the gastro-intestinal tract. Part I.
—— and ISSELBACHER, K. J. (1974). *Gastroenterology* **67**, 531. Uptake and transport of macromolecules by the intestine.
WALLER, H. K. (1938). *Clinical studies in lactation*. Heinemann, London.
—— (1943). *Lancet*, **i**, 69. A reflex governing the outflow of milk from the breast.
—— (1946). *Arch. Dis. Childh.* **21**, 1. The early failure of breast feeding.
—— (1947). *Arch. Dis. Childh.* **22**, 193. Some clinical aspects of lactation.
—— (1957). *The breasts and breast feeding*. Heinemann, London.
WALLGREN, A. (1945). *Acta Paediat.* **32**, 778. Breast milk consumption of healthy newborn infants.
WALRAVENS, P. A. and HAMBIDGE, K. M. (1976). *Amer. J. clin. Nutr.* **29**, 1114. Growth of infants fed a zinc-supplemented diet.
WATNEY, P. J. M., CHANCE, G. W., SCOTT, P., and THOMPSON, J. M. (1971). *Brit. med. J.* **ii**, 432. Maternal factors in neonatal hypocalcaemia: a study in three ethnic groups.
WEICHERT, C. (1975). *Pediatrics* **56**, 987. Breast-feeding: first thoughts.
WEISLER-AALL, L. (1973). *Mokring de Nyfødtes Stell i Nyere Norsk Overlevering*, Utgitt av Norsk Fokmuseum, Oslo.
WEISS, E. (1975). *The female breast*. Bantam Books, New York.
WELBOURN, H. F. (1955). *J. trop. Pediat.* **1**, 34. The danger period during weaning.
—— (1958). *J. trop. Pediat.* **3**, 157. Bottle feeding: a problem of modern civilization.
—— and DE BEER, G. (1964). *J. trop. Med. Hyg.* **67**, 155. Trial of a kit for artificial feeding in tropical village homes.
WELLBY, M., O'HALLORAN, M. W., and WELLBY, M. L. (1973). *Lancet* **i**, 458. Maternal diet and lipid composition of breast milk.
WENNEN, C. A. M. (1969). *Trop. geogr. Med.* **21**, 93. The decline of breast feeding in Nigeria.
—— (1969). *J. trop. Pediat.* **15**, 163. Breast feeding by mothers with flat nipples.
WESTÖÖ, G. and NOREN, K. (1972). *Vår Föda*, **24**, 41. Contents of organochlorine pesticides and polychlorinated biphenyls in Swedish breast milk.

WHARTON, B. A. and BERGER, H. M. (1976). *Brit. med. J.* **ii**, 1326. Problems of Childhood: Bottle Feeding.

——, JELLIFFE, D. B., and STANFIELD, J. P. (1968). *J. Pediat.* **72**, 721. Do we know how to treat kwashiorkor?

WHICHELOW, M. J. (1975). *Arch. Dis. Childh.* **50**, 669. Calorie requirements for successful breast feeding.

—— (1976). *Proc. Nutr. Soc.* **35**, 62A. Success and failure in breast-feeding in relation to energy intake.

WHITE, A. (1974). *Cajanus* **7**, 205. The breast feeding campaign in Trinidad and Tobago.

WHITE, G. (1974). Personal communication.

White House Conference on Food, Nutrition and Health (1970). U.S. Government Printing Office, Washington, D.C.

WHO/FAO/UNICEF (1975). *Methodology of nutritional surveillance.* (In press)

WHYTE, H. M. and YEE, I. (1958). *Austral. Ann. Med.* **7**, 336. Serum cholesterol levels in Australians and natives of New Guinea from birth to adulthood.

WICKES, I. G. (1953). *Arch. Dis. Childh.* **128**, 151. A history of infant feeding.

WIDDOWSON, E. M., SOUTHGATE, D. A. T., and SCHUTZ, Y. (1974). *Arch. Dis. Childh.* **49**, 897. Comparison of dried milk preparations for babies on sale in 7 European countries. I. Protein, fat, carbohydrate and inorganic constituents.

——, DAUNCEY, M. J., GAIRDNER, D. M. T., JONXIS, J. H. P., and PELIKAN-FILIPKOVA, M. (1975). *Brit. med. J.* **i**, 653. Body fat of British and Dutch infants.

WIERNIK, P. H. and DUNCAN, J. H. (1971). *Lancet* **ii**, 912. Cyclophosphamide in human milk.

WIESCHHOFF, H. A. (1940). *Bull. Hist. Med.* **8**, 1403. Artificial stimulation of lactation in primitive cultures.

WIGGLESWORTH, E. C. (1975). *Nursing Mothers Association of Australia Newsletter* Aug., p. 4. The effect of the NMAA on the community.

WIGGLESWORTH, R. (1975). *Roy. Soc. Hlth J.* **95**, 144. Battered babies and their parents. (a) the ecology of child abuse.

WILKINSON, B., MARKS, K. H., GAMSU, H., and CUNLIFFE, A. C. (1976). *Pediat. Res.* **10**, 361. Stool bacteria in low birth weight infants: changes with milk formula.

WILKINSON, P. W., NOBLE, T. C., GRAY, G., and SPENCE, O. (1973). *Brit. med. J.* **ii**, 15. Inaccuracies in measurement of dried milk powders.

WILLIAMS, C. D. (1939). Mimeographed document: address to the Rotary Club, Singapore. Milk and murder.

—— (1946). *Arch. Dis. Childh.* **21**, 37. Rickets in Singapore.

—— (1947). *Proc. Nutr. Soc.* **5**, 127. Nutritional conditions among women and children in internment in the civilian camp in Singapore.

—— and JELLIFFE, D. B. (1972). *Mother and child health: delivering the services.* Oxford University Press, London.

WILLIAMS, M. L., SHOTT, R. J., O'NEAL, P. L., and OSKI, F. A. (1975). *New Engl. med. J.* **292**, 887. Role of dietary iron and fat on vitamin E deficiency anemia in infancy.

WILLIS, A. T., BULLEN, C. L., WILLIAMS, K., FAGG, C. G., BOURNE, A., and VIGNON, M. (1973). *Brit. med. J.* **iv**, 67. Breast milk substitute: a bacteriological study.

WILSON, J. F., HEINER, D. C., and LAHEY, M. E. (1964). *J. Amer. med. Ass.* **89**, 568.

Milk-involved gastrointestinal bleeding in infants with hypochromic anemia.

WINBERG, J. and GOTHEFORS, L. (1976). *J. trop. Pediat. env. Chld Hlth.* **24**, 107. Host resistance factors.

—— and WESSNER, G. (1971). *Lancet* **i**, 1091. Does breast milk protect against septicaemia in the newborn?

WINICK, M., BRASEL, J. A., and ROSSO, P. (1972). Nutrition and cell growth. In *Current concepts in nutrition*, Vol. 1: Nutrition and development (ed. M. Winick). John Wiley, New York.

WINIKOFF, D. (1944). *Med. J. Aust.* **2**, 660. Calcium, magnesium and phosphorus in the milk of Australian women.

WINTER, G. B., RULE, D. C., MAILER, G. P., JAMES, P. M. C., and GORDON, P. H. (1971). *Brit. dent. J.* **130**, 271. The prevalence of dental caries in pre-school children aged 1–4 years.

WINTER, S. K. (1970). *Phychol. Today* **3**, 30. Fantasies at breast feeding time.

WINTER, S. T. (1972). *Clin. Pediat.* **11**, 127. Breast-feeding and the lying-in ward.

WOLSTENHOLME, G. E. W., and KNIGHT, J. (ed.) (1972). *Lactogenic Hormones: a Ciba Foundation Symposium*. Churchill Livingstone, Edinburgh and London.

WONG, H. B., PARAMATHYPATHY, K., and THAM NGIAP BOO (1963). *J. Singapore paediat. Soc.* **5**, 89. Breast-feeding among lower income mothers in Singapore.

—— (1971). *Breast feeding in Singapore*. Choon Kee Press, Singapore.

—— (1975a). *PAG Bulletin* **5**, 16. The role of the medical and health professions in promoting desirable policies and practices.

—— (1975b). Personal communication.

WONG, P. W. K., LAMBERT, A. M., and KOMROWER, G. M. (1967). *Develop. Med. Chld Neurol.* **9**, 551. Tyrosinaemia and tyrosluria in infancy.

WONG, Y. K. and WOOD, B. S. (1971). *Brit. med. J.* **iv**, 403. Breast milk jaundice and oral contraceptives.

WOOD, A. (1955). *J. Amer. diet. Ass.* **3**, 5. The history of artificial feeding.

WOODARD, B. T., FERGUSON, B. B., and WILSON, D. J. (1976). *Amer. J. Dis. Child.* **130**, 400. DDT levels in milk of rural indigent Blacks.

WOODBURY, R. M. (1922). *Amer. J. Hyg.* **2**, 668. The relation between breast and artificial feeding and infant mortality.

WOODRUFF, C. (1976). Cow's milk intolerance. (In press)

WOODY, N. C. and WOODY, H. B. (1966). *J. Pediat.* **68**, 344. Management of breast-feeding: how to be a grandmother.

World Health (1975). Aug.-Sep., p. 24. Guide for health.

WORLD HEALTH ORGANIZATION (1965). *The physiology of lactation*. Technical Report Series No. 305. WHO, Geneva.

—— (1968). *Pharmaceutical advertising: a survey of existing legislation*. WHO, Geneva.

—— (1972). *Nutritional anæmias*. Technical Report Series No. 503. WHO, Geneva.

WRAY, J. D. (1971). *Reports on population and family planning* **9**, 404. Population pressure on families: family size and child spacing.

—— and AGUIRRE, A. (1969). *J. trop. Pediat.* **15**, 76. Protein-calorie malnutrition in Colombia: prevalence, social and demographic causal factors.

—— (1975). *Pediatrics* **55**, 539 and 723. Child care in the People's Republic of China.

—— (1976*a*). Health maintaining behaviour in traditional, transitional and modern societies. Presented at the American Academy for the Advancement of Science, January, 1975. (In press)

—— (1976*b*). *Maternal and child health: the next twenty five years* (In press)

WYATT, R. G. and MATA, L. J. (1969). *J. trop. Pediat.* **15**, 159. Bacteria in colostrum and milk of Guatemalan Indian women.

WYNN, V. (1975). *Lancet* **i**, 561. Vitamins and oral contraceptive use.

XANTHOU, M., AGATHOPOULOS, A., SAKELLARIOU, A., ECONOMOU-MAVROU, C., TSINGOGLOU, S., and MATSANIOTIS, N. (1975). *Arch. Dis. Childh.* **50**, 304. Serum lysozyme in term and pre-term newborns.

YAMASHITA, F., SHIBUYA, S., TOWNLEY, R. R. W., DAVIDSON, G. P., BISHOP, R. F., HOLMES, I. H., and RUCK, B. J. (1975). *Lancet* **ii**, 1297. Duovirus in pseudocholera infantum.

YAO, A. C. and LIND, J. (1969). *Lancet* **ii**, 505. The effect of gravity on placental transfusion.

——, MOINIAN, M., and LIND, J. (1969). *Lancet* **ii**, 871. Distribution of blood between infant and placenta after birth.

YOON, J. J. and ID, K. M. (1970). *Korean Nutr. J.* **3**, 6. Study of weaning pattern and nutritional status of infants and toddlers in Korea.

YOUNG, H. B. and BUCKLEY, A. (1976). Milk and lactation: some social and developmental correlates. (In press)

YUNG-EN KAO (1948). *Acta Paediat.* **36**, 233. Breast-feeding in China.

ZAGREB GUIDELINES (1973). *Nutr. Abstr.* **43**, 1. Nutrition programs for pre-school children.

ZALTMAN, G., ALTWOOD, J., and CARRILLO, G. (1971). *Bull. Wld Hlth Org.* **45**, 827. Child feeding practices and the influence of educational level and mass media in Costa Rica.

ZAWAHRY, M. R., ABOU EL-ALLA, W. M., NESHAAT, O., ZAWAHRY, K., and EL-SOKKARY, S. A. (1974). *Proceedings of the XIV International Pediatric Congress*, Buenos Aires, Vol. 3, Sect. 4, p. 142. Studies on the seasonal variations in the composition of breast milk.

ZERFAS, F., SHORR, I., JELLIFFE, D. B., and JELLIFFE, E. F. P. (1977). *Disaster* (In press) Direct indicators.

ZIEGLER, F. E. and FOMAN, S. J. (1971). *J. Pediat.* **78**, 561. Fluid intake, renal solute load and water balance in infancy.

Additional Bibliography

Acta paediatrica, Stockholm (1977) **66**, 129. A Swedish code of ethics for marketing of infant foods.

ALLEN, J. R. and BARSOTTI, D. A. (1976). *Toxicology* **6**, 331. The effects of transplacental and mammary movement of PCBs on infant rhesus monkeys.

ALMROTH, S. G. (1977). Water requirements of breast-fed infants in a hot climate. Western Hemisphere Nutrition Congress, Quebec, August 1977.

American Academy of Pediatrics (1974). *Pediatrics* **53**, 115. Committee on Nutrition: Salt intake and eating patterns of infants and children in relation to blood pressure.

ANDERSON, G. H., BRYAN, H., JEEJEEBHOY, K. N., and COREY, P. (1977). *Am. J. clin. Nutr.* **30**, 1110. Dose-response relationship between amino-acid intake and blood levels in newborn infants.

ANDERSON, P. O. (1977). *Drug Intell. and Clin. Pharm.* **11**, April. Drugs and breast-feeding — a review.

ANDERSON, S. A. (1977). *Am. J. Mat. Chld. Nursing* August, 240. Childbirth as a pathological process: an American perspective.

ARNAND, S. B., STICKLER, G. B., and HOWARTH, J. C. (1976). *Pediatrics* **57**, 221. Serum 25-hydroxyvitamin D in infantile rickets.

ATKINSON, S. A., ANDERSON, G. H., and BRYAN, M. H. (1977) (in press). Human milk: differences in nitrogen content in milk from mothers of term and premature infants.

——, BRYAN, M. H., RADDE, I. C., CHANCE, G. W., and ANDERSON, G. H. (1977). Effect of premature birth on total N and mineral concentration in human milk. Western Hemisphere Nutrition Congress, Quebec, August 1977.

AYNSLEY-GREEN, A., BLOOM, S. R., WILLIAMSON, D. H., and TURNER, R. C. (1977). *Archs Dis. Childh.* **52**, 291. Endocrine and metabolic response in the human newborn after the first feed of human milk.

BADRAOUI, M. H. H., FAWZI, G., and HEFNAWI, F. (1977). *J. Biosoc. Sci.* Suppl. (in press). Effect of progestational contraception on lactation in Egyptian women. Proc. I.P.P.F./Ciba Foundation Workshop on *Regulation of fertility during lactation,* London, November 1976.

BARNESS, L. A. (1976). *Curr. Med. Res. and Opin.* **4**, suppl. 1, 28. The importance of fats and fatty acids in infant nutrition.

BANATVALA, J. E. (1976). Discussion, p. 233. In *Acute diarrhoea in childhood,* Ciba Foundation Symposium no. 42. Elsevier, Amsterdam.

BAUER, E. S. (1977). *Lancet* ii, 44. Marketing infant foods.

BEER, A. E. and BILLINGHAM, R. E. (1975). *Ann. Intern. Med.* **83**, 865. Immunologic benefits and hazards of milk in maternal-perinatal relationships.

BELAVADY, B. (1978) (in press). Quantity and composition of breast milk in malnourished mothers. In *The mother–child dyad: nutritional aspects,* Swedish Nutrition Foundation Symposium, Uppsala, June 1977.

BELTON, N. R., COCKBURN, F., FORFAR, J. O., GILES, M. M., KIRKWOOD, J., SMITH, J., THISTLETHWAITE, D., TURNER, T. L., and WILKINSON, E. M. (1977). *Archs Dis. Childh.* **52**, 167. Clinical and biochemical assessment of a modified evaporated milk for infant feeding.

BEN SHAUL, D. M. (1962). The composition of the milk of wild animals. In *The International Zoo Year Book,* vol. 4, eds. Carolyn Jarvis and Desmond Morris. Hutchinson, London.

BENTOVIM, A. (1976). Shame and other anxieties associated with breast-feeding: a systems theory and psychodynamic approach. In *Breast-feeding and the mother,* Ciba Foundation Symposium no. 45. Elsevier, Amsterdam.

BRADSHAW, J. S. (1976). *Br. med. J.* i, 1468. Bottle feeding.

BOLDUAN, N. W. (1976). *Science, N.Y.* **191**, 1267. Differentiation of differing concentrations of sucrose and glucose by human newborns.

BOURGES, H., MARTINEZ, C., and CHAVEZ, A. (1977). Effect of dietary supplementation on the nutrient content of milk from mothers in a rural Mexican town. Western Hemisphere Nutrition Congress, Quebec, August 1977.

BROWN, R. E. (1977). *Pediatrics* **60**, 116. Relactation: an overview.

British Medical Journal (1977) i, 189. Suppressing lactation.

——, (1977) ii, 1372. Heating human milk.

——, (1977) iii, 595. Helping mothers to have their babies.

BULLEN, C. L. (1977). The role of pH and buffering capacity of faeces in the control of the Gram-negative intestinal flora. In *Food and immunity,* p. 142. Swedish Nutrition Foundation Symposium XIII (eds. L. Hambraeus, L. A. Hanson, and H. McFarlane), Almquist and Wiksell, Stockholm.

BURGESS, A. P. (1978) (in press). *J. trop. Pediat. env. Chld. Hlth.* Breast-feeding: the knowledge and attitudes of some health personnel in Metropolitan Manila.

BUZINA, R. (1977) (in press). Country Case Study: Yugoslavia. Proc. I.P.P.F./ I.U.N.S. Workshop on *Lactation, fertility and the working woman,* Bellagio, Italy, July 1977.

CARLSSON, B., AHLSTEDT, S., HANSON, L. A., LIDIN-JANSON, G., LINDBLAD, B. S., and SULTANA, R. (1976). *Acta paediat. Stockh.* **65**, 47. *Esch. coli* antibody content in milk.

CARROLL, K. K. and ROBERTS, D. C. K. (1977). The fat and cholesterol content of infant formulae and human milk in relation to plasma cholesterol levels in infants during the suckling period. Western Hemisphere Nutrition Congress, Quebec, August 1977.

ČEVRESKA, S., KOVAČEV, V. P., STANKOVISKI, M., and KALAMARAS, E. (1975). *Gadisen na Medicinskiot Facult. Skopje* **21**, 30. The presence of immunologically reactive insulin in the milk of women.

CHEW, W. C. and SWANN, I. L. (1977). *Br. med. J.* i, 72. Influence of simultaneous low amniotomy and oxytocin infusion and other maternal factors on neonatal jaundice: a prospective study.

CHOWDRY, A. K. M. (1977) (in press). Effect of maternal nutrition on fertility in rural Bangladesh. Proc. Conf. on Nutrition and Reproduction, National Institute of Child Health and Human Development, February 1977.

CLEMENT, E., GUERIN, J., and ALAIS, C. (1976). *Biomedicine* **25**, 303. Study on the composition of casein from individual human milks.

COLE, J. P. (1977). *Clin. Pediat.* **16**, 352. Breast-feeding in the Boston suburbs in relation to personal social factors.

CONNERS, C. K., GOYETTE, C. H., SOUTHWICK, D. A., LEES, J. M., and ANDRULONIS, P. A. (1976). *Pediatrics* **58**, 154. Food additives and hyperkinesis: a controlled double-blind trial.

CONSUMER REPORTS (1977) March, p. 152. Is breast-feeding best for babies?

CRAWFORD, M. A. (1977). *Lancet* i, 1204. Polyunsaturated fatty acids and the brain.

CRUSE, P., YUDKIN, P., and BAUM, J. D. (1977 (in press). *Archs Dis. Childh.* Establishing demand feeding in hospital.

CUNNINGHAM, A. S. (1977). *Pediatrics* **59**, 467. Infant feeding and SIDS.

DAVIES, D. F. (1976). *Proc. Nutr. Soc.* **35**, 293. Immunological aspects of atherosclerosis.

DAVIES, D. P. (1976). *Curr. Med. Res. and Opin.* **4**, Suppl. 1, 73. The suitability of expressed breast-milk for pre-term infants.

——, and EVANS, T. I. (1976). *Lancet* ii, 1194. Failure to thrive at the breast.

——, ANSARI, B. M., and MANDAL, B. K. (1977). *Lancet* i, 252. Hypernatraemia and Gastroenteritis.

——, GRAY, O. P., ELWOOD, C., and SMITH, S. (1977). *Br. med. J.* ii, 7. Effect of solid foods on the growth of bottle-fed infants in the first three months of life.

DE CHATEAU, P. and WINBERG, B. (1977*a*). *Acta paediat., Stockh.* **66**, 137. Long-term effect on mother–infant behaviour of extra contact during the first hour post partum: I. First observations at 36 hours.

—— and —— (1977*b*) *Acta paediat., Stockh.* **66**, 145. Long-term effect on mother–infant behaviour of extra contact during the first hour post partum: II. A follow-up at three months.

DELITALA, G., MASALA, A., ALAGNA, S., DEVILLA, L., LODICO, G., and LOTTI, G. (1977). *Br. med. J.* i, 744. Metergoline in the inhibition of puerperal lactation.

DEPARTMENT OF HEALTH AND SOCIAL SECURITY (1977). The composition of mature human milk. Report no. 12. H.M. Stationery Office, London.

DE SWIET, M., FAYERS, P., and COOPER, L. (1977). *Lancet* i, 892. Effect of feeding habit on weight in infancy.

DOBBING, J. (1977). *Lancet* i, 1107. Polyunsaturated fatty acids and the brain.

DREJER, G. F. (1978) (in press). *J. trop. Pediat. env. Chld Hlth.* Bottle feeding in Douala, Cameroons.

DU BUSC, J. V. (1977). *Pediatrics* **59**, 714. Comments on breast-feeding and immunity.

ECKHERT, C. D., SLOAN, M. V., DUNCAN, J. R., and HURLEY, L. S. (1977). *Science, N.Y.* **195**, 789. Zinc binding: a difference between human and bovine milk.

ELIOT, N., DENIEL, M., and RUMEAU-ROUQUETTE, C. (1975). *Archs fr. Pédiat.* **32**, 681. Resultâts d'une enquête sur l'allaitement maternel dans les centres de P.M.I. du XIV arrondissement de Paris.

EMÖDI, G. and JUST, M. (1974). *Scand. J. Immunol.* **3**, 157. Interferon production by lymphocytes in human milk.

EUROPEAN SOCIETY OF PAEDIATRIC GASTROENTEROLOGY AND NUTRITION (ESPGAN) (1977). *Acta Paediat. Scand.* Suppl. 262. Guidelines on infant nutrition (I). Recommendations for the composition of an adapted formula.

EVANS, C. W. and JOHNSON, P. E. (1976). *Lancet* ii, 1310. Zinc-binding factor in acrodermatitis enteropathica.

—— and —— (1977). *Am. J. clin. Nutr.* **30**, 611. Prostaglandin E_2: the zinc-binding ligand in human breast-milk.

FILER, L. J., STEGINK, L. D., and CHANDRAMOULI, B. (1977). *Am. J. clin. nutr.* **30**, 1036. Effect of diet on plasma aminograms of low birth-weight babies.

FINBERG, L. (1977). *J. Pediat.* **30**, 511. PBBs: the ladies' milk is not for burning.

FLYNN, D. M., HOWARD, F. M., BRADLEY, J., and NOONE, P. (1977). *Lancet* i, 545. Necrotizing enterocolitis.

FOMON, S. J. (1977). *Amer. J. publ. Hlth* **67**, 361. Human milk in premature infant feeding: report of a second workshop.

——, and WEC, S. H. Y. (1977) (in press). Prevention of dental caries.

FOOD AND AGRICULTURE ORGANIZATION (1950). Calorie Requirements. FAO Nutritional Studies, No. 5. Food and Agriculture Organization, Washington, D.C.

—— (1972). Calorie Requirements. FAO Nutritional Studies, No. 15. Food and Agriculture Organization, Washington, D.C.

—— and WORLD HEALTH ORGANIZATION (1976). Codex Alimentarius Commission: Recommended International Standards for Foods for Infants and Children. Joint FAO/WHO Food Standards Programme, FAO, Rome.

FORD, J. E., LAW, B.A., MARSHALL, V. M. E., and REITER, B. (1977). *Pediatrics* **90**, 29. Influence of the heat treatment of human milk on some of its protective constituents.

—— and SCOTT, K. J. (1968). *J. Dairy Res.* **35**, 85. The folic acid activity of some milk foods for babies.

FORREST, J. M. (1976). *Med. J. Austral.* **2**, 138. Drugs in pregnancy and lactation.

FRISCH, R. and McARTHUR, J. W. (1974). *Science, N.Y.* **185**, 949. Menstrual cycles: fatness as a determinant of minimum weight for height for their maintenance or onset.

FUGELSANG, A. (1976). PAG (Protein–Calorie Advisory Group of the U.N.) *Bulletin.* **6**, 9. Vested interests and future perspectives in mass communication and media.

GAULL, G. E., RASSIN, D. K., RÄIHÄ, N. C. R., and HEIONEN, K. (1977). *J. Pediat.* **90**, 348. Milk protein quantity and quality in low-birth-weight infants: III. Effects on sulfur amino acids in plasma and urine.

GEISSLER, C., CALLOWAY, D. H., and MARGEN, S. (1977). *Am. J. clin. Nutr.,* in press. Lactation and pregnancy in Iran: II. Diet and nutritional status.

GELLEN, J. J. (1977). *J. Biosoc. Sci.* Suppl., in press. Side-effects of steroid contraception during breast-feeding. Proc. I.P.P.F./Ciba Foundation Workshop on *Regulation of fertility during lactation*, London, November 1976.

GERRARD, J. W. and TAN, L. (1978) (in press). Breast is still best.

GOTHEFORS, L., OLLING, S., and WINBERG, J. (1977). The effect of human milk on the intestinal flora. Relevance for host resistance. In *Food and immunity,* p. 154. Swedish Nutrition Foundation Symposium XIII (eds. L. Hambraeus, L. A. Hanson, and H. McFarlane), Almquist and Wiksell, Stockholm.

GRACA, I., FERNANDES, A. M. S. S., and MOURÃO, H. C. (1974). *Pestic. Monitor. J.* **8**, 148. Organochlorine insecticide residues in human milk in Portugal.

GREINER, T. (1977). Cornell International Nutrition Monograph Series no. 4. Regulation and education: strategies for solving the bottle-feeding problem.

GUERI, M., JUTSUM, P., MOHAMMED, I., and McDOWALL, M. F. (1977). *J. trop. Pediat. env. Chld Hlth,* in press. Breast-feeding campaigns and hospital practices as factors affecting age of weaning.

GUPTA, A. N., MATHUR, V. S., and GARG, S. K. (1977). *J. Biosoc. Sci.* Suppl., in press. Effect of oral contraceptives on quantity and quality of milk secretion in human beings. Proc. I.P.P.F./Ciba Foundation Workshop on *Regulation of fertility during lactation*, London, November 1976.

GUTHRIE, H. A. and KAN, E. J. (1978). *J. trop. Pediat. env. Chld Hlth*, **23**, 264. Infant feeding decisions — timing and rationale.

HADJIMARKOS, D. M. and SHEARER, T. R. (1973). *Am. J. clin. Nutr.* **26**, 583. Selenium in mature human milk.

HAILE, R. (1978). *J. trop. Pediat. env. Chld Hlth,* in press. Review of the epidemiology of breast-feeding and SIDS ('sudden infant death syndrome').

HAMBRIDGE, K. M. (1976). *Curr. Med. Res. and Opin.* **4**, Suppl. 1, 44. The importance of trace elements in infant nutrition.

HANSEL, W., HIXON, J., SHEMESH, M., and TOBEY, D. (1976). *J. Dairy Sci.* **59**, 1353. Symposium: Prostaglandins in bovine reproduction.

HANSON, L. A. (1976). *Archs Dis. Childh.* **51**, 737. *Esch. coli* infections in childhood: significance of bacterial virulence and immune defence.

HARFOUCHE, J. K. (1977). *J. Biosoc. Sci.* Suppl., in press. Side-effects of exogenous steroids during lactation: appearance in milk and effects on child. Proc. I.P.P.F./Ciba Foundation Workshop on *Regulation of fertility during lactation,* London, November 1976.

HARRIS, R. S. and BUNKER, J. W. (1939). *Am. J. publ. Hlth* **29**, 744. Vitamin D potency of human breast milk.

HARRIS, S. G. and HIGHLAND, J. H. (1977). *Birthright denied: the risks and benefits of breast feeding.* Environmental Defence Fund, Washington.

HARRISON, M., KILBY, A., WALKER-SMITH, J. A., FRANCE, N. E., and WOOD, C. B. S. (1976). *Br. med. J.* i, 1501. Cow's milk protein intolerance.

HELSING, E. (1976*a*). Lactation education: the learning of the 'obvious'. In *Breast feeding and the mother.* Ciba Foundation Symposium no. 45. Elsevier, Amsterdam.

—— (1976*b*). *Ecol. Food and Nutr.* **5**, 115. To the inevitable inevitable?

—— (1977) (in press). Women's liberation and breast-feeding. Proc. I.P.F./ I.U.N.S. Workshop on *Lactation, fertility and the working woman,* Bellagio, Italy, July 1977.

HENDRICKSE, R. G., WOOLRIDGE, M. A. W., and RUSSELL, A. (1977). *Br. med. J.* i, 1194. Lactulose in baby milks causing diarrhoea simulating lactose intolerance.

HENNERT, P. and VIS, H. L. (1977). *J. trop. Pediat. env. Chld Hlth,* in press. Breast-feeding and post-partum amenorrhoea in Central Africa: I. Milk production in rural areas.

HERNELL, O., GEBRE-MEHDIN, M., and OLIVECRONA, T. (1977). *Am. J. clin. Nutr.* **30**, 508. Breast-milk composition in Ethiopian and Swedish mothers. IV. Milk lipases.

HILPERT, H., GERBER, H., AMSTER, H., PAHUD, J. J., BALLABRIGA, A., ARCALIS, L., FARRIAUX, F., DE MEYER, E., and NUSSLE, D. (1977). Bovine milk immunoglobulins (Ig). Their possible utilization in industrially prepared infant's milk formulae. In *Food and immunity,* p. 182. Swedish Nutrition Foundation Symposium XIII (eds. L. Hambraeus, L. A. Hanson, and H. McFarlane). Almquist and Wiksell, Stockholm.

HOFVANDER, Y. (1978) (in press). Patterns of breast-feeding and weaning. In *The mother–child dyad: nutritional aspects.* Swedish Nutrition Foundation Symposium, Uppsala, June 1977.

HOLDRINET, M. V., BRAUN, H. E., FRANK, R., STOPPS, G. J., SMOUT, M. S., and McWALL, J. W. (1977). *Can. J. publ. Hlth* **68**, 74. Organochlorine residues in human adipose tissue and milk from Ontario residents, 1969–74.

HORNABROOK, R. W., DYMENT, P. G., GOMES, E. D., and WISEMAN, J. S. (1972).

Med. J. Austral. **1**, 1297. DDT residues in New Guinea natives.

HUMAN LACTATION CENTRE (1977). *Mothers in poverty.* Westport, Connecticut.

HULL, V. J. (1977 (in press). A study of birth interval dynamics in rural Java. Proc. Conf. on *Nutrition and reproduction,* National Institute of Child Health and Human Development, February 1977.

HYTTEN, F. E. (1976). *J. hum. Nutr.* **30**, 225. The physiology of lactation.

IKONEN, R. S. and MÄKI, K. (1977). *Br. med. J.* ii, 387. Heating human milk.

INDEPENDENT STATE OF PAPUA NEW GUINEA (1977). Baby Feed Supplies (Control) Bill, 1977.

ING, R., HO, J. H. C., and PETRAKIS, N. L. (1977). *Lancet* ii, 124. Unilateral breast-feeding and breast cancer.

JELLIFFE, D. B. (1977) (in press). Breast-feeding in the U.S.A. and the world. Proc. Conf. *Recent advances in breast feeding,* Washington, D.C., October 1976.

—— and JELLIFFE, E. F. P. (1975). *Pediatrics* **56**, 837. Comments on breast-feeding: second thoughts.

—— and —— (1976). *Assignment Children* **35**, 104. The dyadic nature of mother and child nutrition.

—— and —— (1977a). *Int. J. Health Serv.* **7**, 249. The infant-food industry and international child health.

—— and —— (1977b). *Lancet* i, 1053. Necrotizing enterocolitis.

—— and —— (1977c). *J. Mat. Chld Hlth* **2**, 214. The humanization of bottle feeding (a non-starting concept).

—— and —— (1977d). *Clin. Pediat.,* **6**, 1140. Alleged inadequacies of human milk.

—— and —— (1977e). *New Engl. J. Med.,* **297**, 912. 'Breast is best': modern meanings.

—— and —— (1977f). *Trans. R. Soc. trop. Med. Hyg.,* **71**, 331. The cultural *cul-de-sac* of western medicine (towards a curvilinear compromise?).

—— and —— (1978a). *Tropical Doctor,* in press. Breast-feeding: a necessity for child health in the tropics.

—— and —— (1978b) (in press). Cultural traditions and nutritional customs related to pregnancy and lactation. In *The mother–child dyad: nutritional aspects.* Swedish Nutrition Foundation, Uppsala, June 1977.

JELLIFFE, E. F. P. (1976). Maternal nutrition and lactation. In *Breast feeding and the mother.* Ciba Foundation Symposium No. 45. Elsevier, Amsterdam.

—— (1977a). *Pediat. Clins N. Am.* **24**, 1. Infant feeding practices: associated iatrogenic and commerciogenic diseases.

—— (1977b) (in press). Nutritional aspects of human lactation. Proc. Conf. *Recent advances in breast feeding,* Washington, D.C., October 1976.

—— (1977c) (in press). Breast-feeding and the working woman — bending the rules. Proc. I.P.P.F./I.U.N.S. Workshop on *Lactation, fertility and the working woman,* Bellagio, Italy, July 1977.

JENSEN, R. G., HAGERTY, M., and McMAHON, K. E. (1978). *Am. J. clin. Nutr.,* in press. Lipids of human milk and infant formulas: a review.

JONES, R. W. A., ROCHEFORT, M. J., and BAUM, J. D. (1976). *Br. med. J.* ii, 1347. Increased insensible water loss in newborn infants nursed under radiant heaters.

JONSSON, V., LIU, G. J. K., ARMBRUSTER, J., KETTELHUT, L. L., and DRUCKER, B. (1977). *Am. J. clin. Nutr.* **30**, 1106. Chlorhydrocarbon pesticide residues in human milk in Greater St. Louis, Missouri, 1977.

KAMAL, I. (1977) (in press). Country case study: Egypt. Proc. I.P.P.F./I.U.N.S. Workshop on *Lactation, fertility and the working woman,* Bellagio, Italy, July 1977.

KARLIN, R. (1967). *Int. Z. VitamForsch.* **37**, 334. Folic-acid levels in human and cow's milk.

KENNY, J. F. and ZEDD, A. J. (1977). *J. Pediat.* **91**, 158. Recurrent group B streptococcal disease associated with the ingestion of infected mother's milk.

KINDLEY, A. D., ROBERTS, P. J., and TULLOCH, W. H. (1977). *Lancet* i, 649. Neonatal necrotizing enterocolitis.

KLAAS, E. and BELISLE, A. A. (1977). *Pestic. Monitor. J.* **10**, 149. Residues in fish, wildlife and estuaries.

KLAUS, M. H., LEGER, T., and TRAUSE, M. A. (eds.) (1974) *Maternal attachment and mothering disorders: a round table.* Sausalito, California, October 1974. Johnson and Johnson.

—— and KENNELL, J. H. (1976). *Maternal–infant bonding: the impact of early separation or loss on family development.* Mosby, St. Louis.

KNEEBONE, G. M. (1976). *Curr. Med. Res. Opin.* **4**, suppl. 1, 105. Some reflections on infant nutrition — a world-wide problem.

KNODEL, J. (1977*a*). *Science, N.Y.,* in press. Breast-feeding and population growth.

—— (1977*b*) (in press). Breast-feeding and population growth. Proc. Seminar on *Natural fertility,* International Union for the Scientific Study of Population, Paris, March 1977.

—— and KINTNER, H. (1977). *Demography,* in press. The impact of breast-feeding patterns on the biometric analysis of infant mortality.

KNOWLES, J. A. (1974). *Clin. Toxicol.* **7**, 69. Breast-milk: a source of more than nutrition for the neonate.

KORCHOUNOVA, E. (1977) (in press). The International Labour Organization — legislation and working woman. Proc. I.P.P.F./I.U.N.S. Workshop on *Lactation, fertility and the working woman,* Bellagio, Italy, July 1977.

LADITAN, A. A. O. and REEDS, P. J. (1976). *Br. J. Nutr.* **36**, 411. A study of the age of onset, diet and importance of infection in the pattern of severe protein–energy malnutrition in Ibadan, Nigeria.

LAKDAWALA, D. R. and WIDDOWSON, E. M. (1977). *Lancet* i, 167. Vitamin D in human milk.

Lancet (1976) i, 412. Breast is best.

—— (1976) ii, 503. The infant-food industry.

—— (1977*a*) i, 339. Towards prevention of allergy.

—— (1977*b*) i, 459. Necrotizing enterocolitis.

—— (1977*c*) i, 1372. Heating human milk.

LANDMAN, J. P. and SHAW-LYON, V. (1976). *West Indian med. J.* **25**, 43. Breast-feeding in decline in Kingston, Jamaica, 1973.

LAWTON, J. W. M. and SHORTRIDGE, K. F. (1977). *Lancet* i, 253. Protective factors in human breast-milk and colostrum.

LE BOULCH, N., GULAT-MARNAY, C., and RAOUL, Y. (1974). *Int. J. Vitamin Nutr. Res.* **44**, 167. Derivés de la vitamine D₃ des laits de femme et de vache: ester sulfate de cholecalciferol et hydroxy-25-cholecalciferol.

LECHTIG, A., HABICHT, J. P., and YARBROUGH, C. (1975). *Nutrition* **2**, 44. Influence of food supplementation during pregnancy on birthweight in rural populations of Guatemala.

———, ———, WILSON, P., ARROYAVE, G., GUZMAN, G., DELGADO, H., MAR-TORELL, R., YARBOROUGH, C., and KLEIN, R. E. (1977). Maternal nutrition, human milk composition and infant nutrition in a rural population of Guatemala. Western Hemisphere Nutrition Congress, Quebec, August 1977.

LEWIS, C. T., DICKSON, J. A. S., and SWAIN, V. A. J. (1977). *Archs Dis. Chldh.* **52**, 68. Milk-bolus obstruction in the neonate.

Life and Health (1976). November, 28. Editorial: Don't hook your baby.

LILLINTON, A. W. (1975). *Lancet* ii, 512. Inflation hits the bottle.

LOZOFF, B., BRITTENHAM, G. M., TRAUSE, M. A., KENNELL, J., and KLAUSE, M. H. (1977). *J. Pediat.* **91**, 1. The mother–newborn relationship: limits of adaptability.

LUCAS, A., GIBBS, J., and BAUM, J. D. (1977). *Lancet* i, 1012. What's in breast-milk.

MANSKE, D. D. and JOHNSON, R. D. (1977). *Pestic. Monitor. J.* **10**, 134. Pesticide and other chemical residues in total diet samples.

MATA, L. J. and URRUTIA, J. J. (1977). Infections and infectious diseases in a malnourished community: a long-term prospective field study. In *Food and immunity*, p. 42. Swedish Nutrition Foundation Symposium XIII (eds. L. Hambraeus, L. A. Hanson, and H. McFarlane), Almquist and Wiksell, Stockholm.

MATTHEW, D. J., NORMAN, A. P., SOOTHILL, J. F., TAYLOR, B., and TURNER, M. W. (1977). *Lancet* i, 321. Prevention of eczema.

MATTHEWS, T. H. J., LAWRENCE, M. K., NAIR, C. D. G., and TYRRELL, D. A. J. (1976). *Lancet* ii, 1387. Antiviral activity of milk of possible clinical importance.

McLELLAND, D. B. L. (1977). *Lancet* i, 1600. Heating human milk.

———, McGRATH, J., and SAMSON, R. R. (1977). *Acta paediat., Stockh.,* in press. Antimicrobial factors in human milk: studies in concentration and transfer to the infant.

McMILLAN, J. A. and OSKI, F. A. (1977). *Keeping Abreast Journal* **2**, 33. Iron nutrition in the breast-fed infant.

McNEILLY, A. S. (1977). *J. Biosoc. Sci.* Suppl., in press. Physiology of human lactation. Proc. I.P.P.F./Ciba Foundation Workshop on *Regulation of fertility during lactation,* London, November 1976.

MILLAR, E. R. and SHEPPARD, A. D. (1972). *N.Z. Jl Sci.* **15**, 3. Alpha-tocopherol and selenium levels in human and cows' milk.

MILLER, D. L. (1977). *Birth Famil. J.* **4**, 65. Birth and long-term unsupplemented breast-feeding in 17 insulin-dependent diabetic mothers.

MILLER, R. W. (1977). *J. Pediat.* **90**, 510. Pollutants in breast-milk.

MODAK, M. J. and MARCUS, S. L. (1977). *Lancet* i, 431. Ribonuclease as antiviral agent in milk.

MOHR, J. A. (1973). *J. Pediat.* **82**, 1062. The possible induction and/or acquisition of cellular hypersensitivity associated with ingestion of colostrum.

MONK, E. L., ERB, R. E., and MOLLETT, T. A. (1975). *J. Dairy Sci.* **58**, 34. Relationships between immunoreactive estrone and estradiol in milk, blood and urine of dairy cows.

MOORE, A., ANSELL, C., and BARRIE, H. (1977). *Br. med. J.* i, 129. Metabolic acidosis and infant feeding.

MORATH, M. (1974). *Int. J. Chronobiol.* **2**, 39. The four-hour feeding rhythm of the baby as a free running endogenously regulated rhythm.

MORLEY, D. (1977*a*) (in press). A review of breast-feeding and birth spacing. Proc. I.P.P.F./I.U.N.S. Workshop on *Lactation, fertility and the working woman,* Bellagio, Italy, July 1977.

—— (1977). *J. Biosoc. Sci.* Suppl., in press. Biosocial advantages of an adequate birth interval. Proc. I.P.P.F./Ciba Foundation Workshop on *Regulation of fertility during lactation,* London, November 1976.

MOSLEY, W. H., OSTERIA, T., and HUFFMAN, S. (1977). *J. Biosoc. Sci.* Suppl., in press. Interactions of contraception and breast-feeding in developing countries. Proc. I.P.P.F./Ciba Foundation Workshop on *Regulation of fertility during lactation,* London, November 1976.

MROUEH, A. (1977) (in press). Country case studies: Lebanon. Proc. I.P.P.F./I.U.N.S. Workshop on *Lactation, fertility and the working woman,* Bellagio, Italy, July 1977.

MÜLLER, H. R. (1974/75). *Nestlé Res. News.* Infant nutrition today: a new rationale in infant feeding.

NATIONAL COUNCIL OF CHURCHES (1977). Newsletter 691.CCR5/20. Church group plans appeal in 'bottle baby law suit'.

NEWTON, N. (1977). Psychosocial aspects of the mother/father/child unit. In *The mother–child dyad: nutritional aspects.* Swedish Nutrition Foundation Symposium, Uppsala, June 1977.

Nutrition Action (1977). July, 18. Boycotts and baby bottles.

Nutrition Reviews (1976) **34**, 151. Special article: diet and hyperactivity: any connection?

—— (1977) **35**, 72. Insecticides in human milk.

OAKLEY. J. R. (1977). *Archs Dis. Chldh.* **52**, 79. Differences in subcutaneous fat in breast- and formula-fed infants.

O'CONNOR, P. (1977). *Clin. Pediat.* **16**, 361. Vitamin D-deficiency rickets in two breast-fed infants who were not receiving vitamin D supplementation.

OLSZYNA-MARZYS, A. E. (1977) (in preparation). Contaminants in human milk.

ORME, M. L., LEWIS, P. J., DE SWIET, M., SERLIN, M. J., SIBEON, R., BATY, J. D., and BRECKENBRIDGE, A. M. (1977). *Br. med. J.* ii, 1564. May mothers given warfarin breast-feed their infants?

ØRSKOV, F., ØRSKOV, I., JANN, B., and JANN, K. (1971). *Acta path. microbiol. scand.* Section B **79**, 142. Immunoelectrophoretic patterns of extracts from all *Escherichia coli* O and K antigen test strains correlation with pathogenicity.

OUNSTED, M. K. and SIMONS, C. D. (1976). *Curr. Med. Res. and Opin.* **4**, suppl. 1, 60. Infant feeding, growth and development.

PAPPOE, M. E. (1977 (in press). Country case study: Ghana. Proc. I.P.P.F./I.U.N.S. Workshop on *Lactation, fertility and the working woman,* Bellagio, Italy, July 1977.

PARMELY, M. J., BEER, A. E., and BILLINGHAM, R. E. (1976). *J. exp. Med.* **144**, 358. *In vitro* studies on the T-lymphocyte population in human milk.

PARTRIDGE, J., THOMPSON, G., and THOMPSON, J. (1977). *Archs Dis. Chldh.* **52**, 813. Breast or bottle? Antenatal survey of influences affecting this decision.

PATTERSON, B. (1976). Every life needs nutritional and emotional satisfaction: the midwife's opportunity. In *Breast-feeding and the mother,* Ciba Foundation Symposium no. 45. Elsevier, Amsterdam.

PEAKER, M. (1976). Lactation: some cardiovascular and metabolic consequences, and the mechanisms of lactose and ion secretion into milk. In *Breast-feeding and the mother,* Ciba Foundation Symposium no. 45. Elsevier, Amsterdam.

PELLETT, P. L. (1977). *Ecol. Food and Nutr.*, **6**, 53. Marasmus in a newly rich urbanized society.

People (1976) **3**, 1. Breast-feeding: a motive for family planning.

PETROS-BARVAZIAN, A. (1977) (in press). WHO perspectives. Proc. I.P.P.F./ I.U.N.S. Workshop on *Lactation, fertility and the working woman,* Bellagio, Italy, July 1977.

PHILLIPS, V. (1977). *J. trop. Pediat. env. Chld Hlth,* in press. Children in early Victorian England. (i) Infant feeding in literature and society, 1837–57.

PIPES, P. (1977). *J. Nutr. Educ.* **9**, 57. When should semisolids be fed to infants?

POLIN, R. A., POLLACK, P. F., BARLOW, B., SANTULLI, V. T., and HEID, C. W. (1974). *Pediat. Res.* **8**, 384. A fresh look at necrotizing enterocolitis.

POLISHUK, Z. W., RON, M., WASSERMANN, M., WASSERMANN, D. and LEMESCH, C. (1977). *Pestic. Monitor. J.* **10**, 121. Organochlorine compounds in human blood plasma and milk.

POPKIN, B. M. and SOLON, F. (1976). Economic determinants of breast-feeding behavior: the case of rural households in Laguna, Philippines. Paper No. 76–25, Institute of Economic Development and Research, School of Economics, University of the Philippines.

PORTER, P. (1976). *Proc. Nutr. Soc.* **35**, 273. Immunoglobulin mechanisms in health and nutrition from birth to weaning.

PULLAN, C. R., DELLAGRAMMATIKAS, A., and STEINER, H. (1977). *Br. med. J.* i, 619. Survey of gastroenteritis in children admitted to hospital in Newcastle upon Tyne in 1971–75.

RÄIHÄ, N. C. R. (1976). *Curr. Med. Res. and Opin.* **4**, Suppl. 1, 85. Milk protein, quality and quantity, in the feeding of low-birth-weight infants.

RAJU, T. N. K. (1977). *J. Pediat.* **91**, 347. The injured neonate of the seventies.

RASSIN, D. K., GAULL, G. E., HEINONEN, K., and RÄIHÄ, N. C. R. (1977). *Pediatrics* **59**, 407. Milk protein quantity and quality in low-birth-weight infants: II. Effects on selected aliphatic amino acids in plasma and urine.

——, STURMAN, J. A., and GAULL, G. E. (1977). *Early Human Development,* in press. Taurine and other free amino acids in milk of man and other mammals.

RATOPOULOU-GIGI, M., MARWICK, K., and MCLELLAND, D. B. L. (1977). *Br. med. J.* i, 12. Antimicrobial proteins in sterilized human milk.

REDDY, V., BHASKARAM, C., RAGHURAMULU, N., and JAGADEESAN, V. (1977). *Acta paediat., Stockh.* **66**, 229. Antimicrobial factors in human milk.

RESMAN, B. H., BLUMENTHAL, P., and JUSKO, W. J. (1977). *J. Pediat.* **91**, 477. Breast milk distribution of theobromine from chocolate.

ROBINSON, J. E. and SHORT, R. V. (1977). *Br. med. J.* ii, 1188. Changes in breast sensitivity at puberty, during the menstrual cycle and at parturition.

ROSE, G. (1977). Epidemiology of familial factors and salt intake in man. In *Paediatric implications in some adult disorders,* p. 139, ed. D. Barltrop. Fellowship of Postgraduate Medicine, London.

RUMEAU-ROUQUETTE, C. and CROST-DENIEL, M. (1977) (in press). Country case study: France. Proc. I.P.P.F./I.U.N.S. Workshop on *Lactation, fertility and the working woman,* Bellagio, Italy, July 1977.

RUTISHAUSER, I. H. E. (1974). *Ecol. Food and Nutr.* **3**, 213. Factors affecting the intake of energy and protein by Ugandan preschool children.

SAARINEN, U. M., SIIMES, M. A., and DALLMAN, P. R. (1977). *Pediatrics* **91**, 36. Iron absorption in infants.

SACK, J., AMADO, O., and LUNENFELD, B. (1977). *J. clin. Endocr. Metab.* **45**, 171. Thyroxine concentration in human milk.

SAHASHI, Y., SUZUKI, T., HIGAKI, M., and ASANO, T. (1967). *J. Vitam.* **13**, 33. Metabolism of vitamin D in animals. 5. Isolation of vitamin D sulphate from mammalian milk.

——, ——, ——, and —— (1969). *J. Vitam.* **15**, 78. Antirachitic potency of vitamin D sulphate in human milk.

SALK, L. (1960). *Scient. Am.* **201**, 26. The role of the heartbeat in the relations between mother and infant.

SANDERS, T. A. B., ELLIS, F. R., and DICKERSON, J. W. T. (1977). *Lancet* i, 1204. Polyunsaturated fatty acids and the brain.

SAS, M., VISKI, S., and GELLEN, J. (1969). *Arch. Gynäk.* **207**, 452. Der steroidgehalf der frauenmilch (Steroid content of human milk.)

SCHAMS, D. (1976). Hormonal control of lactation. In *Breast-feeding and the mother.* Ciba Foundation Symposium no. 45. Elsevier, Amsterdam.

SCHREINER, R. L., COATES, T., and SHACKLEFORD, P. G. (1977). *J. Pediat.* **91**, 159. Possible breast-milk transmission of group B streptococcal infection.

SCHUSTER-CORTES, A. (1977) (in press). Country case study: Chile. Proc. I.P.P.F./I.U.N.S. Workshop on *Lactation, fertility and the working woman,* Bellagio, Italy, July 1977.

SCHUTZ, Y., LECHTIG, A., and BRADFIELD, R. B. (1977). Energy intakes, energy expenditures and weight changes of chronically malnourished women in Guatemala. Western Hemisphere Nutrition Congress, Quebec, August 1977.

SCRIVER, C. R., PERRY, Jr., T., LASLEY, L., CLOW, C. L., COULTER, D., and LABERGE, C. (1977). *Pediat. Res.* **11**, 411. Neonatal tyrosinemia in the Eskimo. Result of protein polymorphism?

SEGALL, J. J. (1977). *Br. J. prev. soc. Med.* **31**, 81. Is milk a coronary health hazard?

SEGAR, W. E. and CHESNEY, R. W. (1977). *Am. J. Dis. Child.* **131**, 137. On certain physical-chemical properties of infant formula.

SHAH, P. M., KARNIK, D. J., SHAH, K. P., and SHAH, B. P. (1978). *J. trop. Pediat. env. Chld Hlth,* in press. Lactation failure in the urban and rural communities: a cohort study.

SHELDON, P. G., BERKOWITZ, R. J., and FORRESTER, D. J. (1977). *Pediatrics* **59**, 777. Nursing bottle syndrome.

SHORT, R. V. (1976). Lactation — the central control of reproduction. In *Breast-feeding and the mother.* Ciba Foundation Symposium no. 45. Elsevier, Amsterdam.

SIMPSON, J. W., LAWLESS, R. W., and MITCHELL, A. C. (1975). *Obstet. Gynec., N.Y.* **45**, 481. Responsibility of the obstetrician to the fetus. II. Influence of pregnancy weight and pregnancy weight gain on birthweight.

SIMS, D. G. (1976). *Br. med. J.* ii, 1070. Oxytocin and neonatal jaundice.

SJÖLIN, S. (1976). *Curr. Med. Res. and Opin.* **4**, Suppl. 1, 17. Present trends in breast-feeding.

—— (1977). Causes and consequences of early weaning. In *The mother–child dyad: nutritional aspects.* Swedish Nutrition Foundation Symposium, Uppsala, June 1977.

——, HOFVANDER, Y., and HILLERVIK, C. (1977). *Acta paediat. Stockh.* **66**, 505. Factors related to early termination of breast-feeding.

SLOPER, K. S., ELSDEN, E., and BAUM, J. D. (1977). *Archs Dis. Chldh.*, in press. A follow-up survey of infant-feeding practice in Oxford.

SMITH, C. A. (1976). *N.Z. med. J.* **82**, 370. Breast-feeding and the community.

SMOTHERMAN, W. P., WIENER, S. G., MENDOZA, S. P., and LEVINE, S. (1976). Pituitary–adrenal responsiveness of rat mothers to noxious stimuli and stimuli produced by their own pups. In *Breast-feeding and the mother*. Ciba Foundation Symposium no. 45. Elsevier, Amsterdam.

SOEMILAH, S. (1977) (in press). Breast-feeding and the working woman in Indonesia. Proc. I.P.P.F./I.U.N.S. Workshop on *Lactation, fertility and the working woman*, Bellagio, Italy, July 1977.

SOOTHILL, J. F. (1976). *Br. med. J.* i, 1467. Breast-feeding: the immunological argument.

——, STOKES, C. R., TURNER, M. W., NORMAN, A. P., and TAYLOR, B. (1976). *Clin. Allergy* **6**, 305. Predisposing factors and the development of reaginic allergy in infancy.

SOSA, R., KENNELL, J. H., KLAUS, M., and URRUTIA, J. J. (1976). The effect of early mother–infant contact on breast-feeding, infection and growth. In *Breast-feeding and the mother*. Ciba Foundation Symposium no. 45. Elsevier, Amsterdam.

SOUTHGATE, D. A. T. and DURNIN, J. V. G. A. (1970). *Br. J. Nutr.* **24**, 517. Calorie conversion factors. An experimental reassessment of the factors used in the calculation of the energy value of human diets.

STACEY, C. I. and THOMAS, B. W. (1975). *Pestic. Monitor. J.* **9**, 64. Organochlorine pesticide residues in human milk.

STRASSMAN, S. C. and KUTZ, F. W. (1977). *Pestic. Monitor J.* **10**, 131. Insecticide residues in human milk from Arkansas and Mississippi, 1973–74.

STRBAK, V., MACHO, L., KOVAC, R., SKULTETYOVA, M., and MICHALICKOVA, J. (1976). *Endocrinol. Exp.* **10**, 167. Thyroxine (by competitive protein binding analysis) in human and cow milk and in infant formulas.

STURMAN, J. A., RASSIN, D. K., and GAULL, G. E. (1977). *Life Sci.* **21**, 1. Minireview: taurine in development.

SVANBERG, U., GEBRE-MEHDIN, M., LJUNGQVIST, B., and OLSSON, M. (1977). *Am. J. clin. Nutr.* **30**, 499. Breast-milk composition in Ethiopian and Swedish mothers. III. Amino acids and other nitrogenous substances.

SWEDISH INTERNATIONAL DEVELOPMENT AGENCY (SIDA) (1977) (in press). Low birth-weight: a novel yardstick of development. Proc. SIDA/WHO Workshop, Sigatuna, Sweden, July 1977.

SYKES, P. A., QUARRIE, J., and ALEXANDER, F. W. (1976). *Br. med. J.* ii, 1299. Lithium carbonate and breast-feeding.

TENORE, A., PARKS, J. S., and BONGIOVANNI, A. M. (1977) (in press). Proc. Sympos. Recent Progress Pediatric Endocrinology. Academic Press. Relationship of breast-feeding to congenital hypothyroidism.

The Age, Melbourne (1977), July 20, 1. Baby milk danger sparks world alert.

TONKIN, S. (1975). *Pediatrics* **55**, 5. Sudden infant death syndrome: hypothesis of causation.

TRIPP, J. H., WILMERS, M. J., and WHARTON, B. A. (1977). *Lancet* ii, 233. Gastroenteritis: a continuing problem in child health in Britain.

TURNER, R. W. D. (1976). *Lancet* ii, 694. Breast is best for coronary protection.

TYSON, J. E. (1977). *J. Biosoc. Sci.* Suppl., in press. Neuroendocrine control of lactational infertility. Proc. I.P.P.F./Ciba Foundation Workshop on *Regulation of fertility during lactation,* London, November 1976.

——, FREEDMAN, R. S., PEREZ, A., ZACUR, H. A., and ZANARTU, J. (1976). Significance of the secretion of human prolactin and gonadotropin for puerperal lactational infertility. In *Breast-feeding and the mother.* Ciba Foundation Symposium no. 45. Elsevier, Amsterdam.

UDALL, J. N., WALSON, P. D., HANSEN, R., WILSON, S., and MORROW, G. (1977). Carrageenan toxicity in newborn guinea pigs.

U.S. DEPARTMENT OF HEALTH, EDUCATION AND WELFARE. (1974). In adequate lactation (insufficient milk secretion). In *A barefoot doctor's manual* (translation of a Chinese *Instruction to certain Chinese health personnel*). D.H.E.W. Publication no. (N.I.H.) 75–695. Public Health Service, National Institutes of Health, Bethesda, Maryland.

VAHLQUIST, B. (1977) (in press). Country case study: Scandinavia. Proc. I.P.P.F./I.U.N.S. Workshop on *Lactation, fertility and the working woman,* Bellagio, Italy, July 1977.

VAN GINNEKEN, J. K. (1977*a*). *J. Biosoc. Sci.* Suppl., in press. The chance of conception during lactation. Proc. I.P.P.F./Ciba Foundation Workshop on *Regulation of fertility during lactation,* London, November 1976.

—— (1977*b*) (in press). The impact of prolonged breast-feeding on birth intervals and postpartum amenorrhea. Proc. Conf. on *Nutrition and reproduction,* National Institute of Child Health and Human Development, Washington, D.C., February 1977.

VAUGHAN, L. A., WEBER, C. W., and KEMBERLING, S. R. (1977). Trace elements in human milk. Western Hemisphere Nutrition Congress, Quebec, August 1977.

VISAKORPI, J. K. (1977). Gluten intolerance and its nutritional implications. In *Food and immunity,* p. 92. Swedish Nutrition Foundation Symposium XIII (eds. L. Hambraeus, L. A. Hanson, and H. McFarlane), Almquist and Wiksell, Stockholm.

VOBECKY, J. S., VOBECKY, J., SHAPCOTT, D., DEMERS, P., BLANCHARD, R., and FISCH, C. (1977). An objective analysis of the benefit of breast feeding. Western Hemisphere Nutrition Congress, Quebec, August 1977.

WAKO, H., HATAKEYAMA, T., KAMIHARA, M., WADA, S., HONJO, S., FUJIWARA, T., and CHO, F. (1975). *Exp. Anim.* **4**, 161. Artificial nursing of new-born cynomolgus monkeys as a model of the human infant and development of abnormal behavior.

WALDSTRÖM, T. (1977). The relationship of *E. coli* and malnutrition. The effect on food production and human utilization. In *Food and immunity,* p. 164. Swedish Nutrition Foundation Symposium XIII (eds. L. Hambraeus, L. A. Hanson, and H. McFarlane), Almquist and Wiksell, Stockholm.

WALETZKY, L. R. and HERMAN, E. C. (1976). *Am. Family Physic.* **14**, 69. Relactation.

WEIL, W. B. (1977). *J. Pediat.* **91**, 175. Current controversies in childhood obesity.

WENNEN-VAN DER MEIJ, C. A. M. (1977). *Lancet* i, 143. The infant-food industry.

WHALEY, P. and WALKER-SMITH, J. A. (1977). *Lancet* i, 51. Hypernatraemia and gastroenteritis.

WHITE, M. (1977). La Leche League International publication. Breast-feeding and the drugs in human milk. Franklin Park, Illinois.

WHITEHEAD, R. G. (1977). *Lancet* **i**, 136. Infant feeding in the developing world.

WICKSTROM, B. (1978) (in press). Infant-food companies in Europe and the United

States and their policies for marketing in the Developing World. Suppl. Project to the WHO/C.I.E. Collaborative Study on Breast-Feeding.

WIDDOWSON, E. M. (1976a). Changes in the body and its organs during lactation: nutritional implications. In *Breast-feeding and the mother*. Ciba Foundation Symposium no. 45. Elsevier, Amsterdam.

—— (1976b). Pregnancy and lactation: the comparative point of view. In *Early nutrition and later development*, p.1, ed. A. W. Wilkinson. Pitman, London.

—— (1976c). Artificial milks and their effects on the composition of the infant. In *Early nutrition and later development*, p.71, ed. A. W. Wilkinson. Pitman, London.

—— (1977a). The first feed. In *Gastrointestinal development and neonatal nutrition*, p.14. Ross Laboratories, Columbus, Ohio.

—— (1977b) (in press). Nutritional needs of the foetus and the young child. In *The mother–child dyad: nutritional aspects*. Swedish Nutrition Foundation Symposium, Uppsala, June 1977.

WILSON, C. S. and PETRAKIS, N. L. (1977) (in press). Traditional diets and breast cancer.

WILSON, D. J., LOCKER, D. J., RITZEN, C. A., WATSON, J. T., and SCHAFFNER, W. (1973). *Am. J. Dis. Child.* **125**, 814. DDT concentrations in human milk.

WINBERG, J., GOTHEFORS, L., and JUTO, P. (1976). *Curr. Med. Res. and Opin.* **4**, Suppl. 1, 9. The case for breast feeding.

WOODRUFF, C. W., LATHAM, C., and McDAVID, S. (1976). *J. Pediat.* **90**, 36. Iron nutrition in the breast-fed infant.

WORLD HEALTH ORGANIZATION (1965). Nutrition in pregnancy and lactation. Technical Report Series no. 302. Geneva, Switzerland.

—— (1976). *Family formation patterns and health: International collaborative study in India, Iran, Lebanon, Philippines and Turkey.* Geneva, Switzerland.

WRAY, J. D. (1978). Maternal nutrition, breast feeding and infant survival. In *Nutrition in reproduction*, ed. W. H. Mosley. Plenum Press, New York.

WRIGHT, R. (1976). *Proc. Nutr. Soc.* **35**, 285. Immunology of food intolerance in adults.

YEH, C.-Y., KUO, P.-H., TSAI, S.-T., WANG, G.-Y., and WANG, Y.-T. (1976). *J. Formosan med. Ass.* **76**, 463. A study on pesticide residues in umbilical cord blood and maternal milk.

YURCHAK, A. M. and JUSKO, W. J. (1976). *Pediatrics* **57**, 518. Theophylline secretion into breast milk.

Index

490   *Index*